NIGHT WITHOUT END

NIGHT WITHOUT END

THE FATE OF JEWS IN
GERMAN-OCCUPIED POLAND

| THE INTERNATIONAL INSTITUTE
FOR HOLOCAUST RESEARCH

The Center for Research on the Holocaust in Poland

INDIANA UNIVERSITY PRESS

This book is a publication of

Indiana University Press
Office of Scholarly Publishing
Herman B Wells Library 350
1320 East 10th Street
Bloomington, Indiana 47405 USA

iupress.org

Yad Vashem—The World Holocaust Remembrance Center
P.O.B. 3447, Jerusalem, 9103401, Israel
www.yadvashem.org

© 2022 by Yad Vashem and Indiana University Press

All rights reserved
No part of this book may be reproduced or utilized in any form or by any means, electronic or mechanical, including photocopying and recording, or by any information storage and retrieval system, without permission in writing from the publisher. The paper used in this publication meets the minimum requirements of the American National Standard for Information Sciences—Permanence of Paper for Printed Library Materials, ANSI Z39.48–1992.

Manufactured in the United States of America

First printing 2022

Library of Congress Cataloging-in-Publication Data

Names: Engelking, Barbara, editor. | Grabowski, Jan, editor.
Title: Night without end : the fate of Jews in German-occupied Poland / edited by Jan
    Grabowski and Barbara Engelking ; translated from Polish by Anna Brzostowska, Jerzy
    Giebułtowski, Jan Grabowski, Elżbieta Olender-Dmowska, and Tomasz Frydel.
Other titles: Dalej jest noc. English.
Description: Bloomington, Indiana : Indiana University Press, [2022]
    | Includes bibliographical references and index.
Identifiers: LCCN 2022000114 (print) | LCCN 2022000115 (ebook) | ISBN 9780253062857
    (hardback) | ISBN 9780253062864 (paperback) | ISBN 9780253062871 (ebook)
Subjects: LCSH: Holocaust, Jewish (1939-1945)—Poland. | Poland—History—Occupation, 1939-
    1945. | Jews—Persecutions—Poland. | Poland—Ethnic relations. | Antisemitism—Poland. |
    World War, 1939-1945—Atrocities—Poland. | Poland—History—Occupation, 1939-1945.
Classification: LCC DS134.55 .D3513 2022 (print) | LCC DS134.55
    (ebook) | DDC 940.53/1809438—dc23/eng/20220406
LC record available at https://lccn.loc.gov/2022000114
LC ebook record available at https://lccn.loc.gov/2022000115

The research leading to the publication of this book has been funded by the Ministry of Science and Higher Education (Poland, grant 12H/13/0484/82); the Social Sciences and Humanities Research Council of Canada (Canada, grant 8945330-2012-0018); and the Conference on Jewish Material Claims Against Germany (grant SO42-14283).

Maps created by Zbigniew Gałęza.

Translated from Polish by Anna Brzostowska, Jerzy Giebułtowski, Jan Grabowski, Elżbieta Olender-Dmowska, and Tomasz Frydel. Language editing: Leah Goldstein.

Originally published by the Polish Center for the Holocaust Research at the Polish Academy of Science as Dalej jest noc: Losy Żydów w wybranych powiatach okupowanej Polski, Tom 1, 2 © 2018, Centrum Badan nad Zaglada Zydow

Preface vii

Acknowledgments xxxix

1. Jews in Bielsk Podlaski County, 1939–1945 · *Barbara Engelking* 2
2. Biłgoraj County Before and After 1939: Parallel Worlds · *Alina Skibińska* 54
3. Węgrów County · *Jan Grabowski* 109
4. Łuków County · *Jean-Charles Szurek* 173
5. Złoczów County · *Anna Zapalec* 234
6. Nowy Targ County · *Karolina Panz* 295
7. Dębica County · *Tomasz Frydel* 349
8. Bochnia County · *Dagmara Swałtek-Niewińska* 419

Index 473

INTRODUCTION

Historians of the Holocaust often refer to World War II as the "war against the Jews." This term is particularly true in the case of Polish Jews—the largest Jewish community in prewar Europe. Out of more than approximately three million Jewish citizens of the Second Polish Republic who found themselves under German rule (excluding those who survived in the Soviet Union), no more than 1.5–2 percent survived the war. Despite decades of work, we still do not know enough—and sometimes we know woefully little—about what happened during those horrifying years. This book is much less about interpretations; it is driven, most of all, by our desire to know more, to shed light on events that have been, and that should have never been, largely forgotten, pushed aside, belittled, or relativized.

This book is a result of the cooperation between a group of scholars affiliated with the Polish Center for Holocaust Research at the Institute of Philosophy and Sociology of the Polish Academy of Science in Warsaw. The studies presented here are the fruits of several years of research on the history of the Holocaust in the Polish provinces. We have examined this issue for quite some time, resulting in the publication of two books by the center devoted entirely to this subject: *Prowincja noc* (2007) and *Zarys krajobrazu* (2011). Our current studies summarize the next phase in our work, inspired directly by earlier research conducted on the history of Dąbrowa Tarnowska County.[1] Many questions that stemmed from this first "county study" demanded further in-depth investigation of German activities, Jewish reactions and behaviors, and Polish attitudes. In searching for meaningful answers, we elected to adopt a similar methodological approach. This time, however, we used this approach as a framework for a much broader investigation, and as a result, we are able to offer the reader a closer look at several selected counties of occupied Poland.

The volume contains eight studies, each one devoted to a different area of occupied Poland. Each study begins with an overview of the situation of the Jewish population prior to 1939 and its prewar relations with the rest of Polish society. These relations evolved along different trajectories, which usually were tied to the makeup of the local political scene. In the eastern part of the country, the overlapping Polish-Ukrainian conflict made Polish-Jewish relations even more complex. After the outbreak of World War II, two of the selected areas (Bielsk and Złoczów) found themselves under Soviet occupation, while the others were occupied by the Germans. After June 22, 1941, all counties described in the book fell under German rule, with all its consequences. It was the so-called first phase of the Holocaust, marked by branding regulations, terror, robbery, death through forced labor, and enslavement in the ghettos. The two eastern areas also went through a wave of pogroms and mass executions associated with the arrival of the Germans. Soon after, the second phase of the Holocaust—or the liquidations of the ghettos—began. At this point, the great majority of the Jews living in the studied areas were deported to one of the five extermination camps established by the Germans in Poland. During the liquidation actions, a part of the Jewish population was murdered in situ, in the liquidated ghettos, while some (according to our count, around 10 percent) managed to flee. The fate of these refugees is what we call the third phase of the Holocaust, and this is the part that finds itself at the core of our accounts: the strategies of survival of Jews fighting for their lives outside the ghettos, on the Aryan side, among the Christian population. Their struggle lasted until liberation by Soviet forces.

It was during this third phase (labeled by the Germans as the *Judenjagd*, or "hunt for the Jews") that the attitude of the Polish (or in the case of two counties, Ukrainian and Belorussian) population toward Jewish refugees became a factor that either greatly increased or substantially diminished their chances of survival. The beginning of the discussion of the scale of Polish participation in the events under discussion was marked by the publication of Jan Gross's book *Neighbors*[2] in 2000. In the two decades or so since then, the debate has continued among Polish scholars and the media, with recourse not only to pure historical reasoning but also invoking emotional and political arguments. This has made us acutely aware of the importance of in-depth research and analyses that might produce reliable data, both quantitative and qualitative. This book has been written with the hope of providing solid data, which would allow future discussions to be based on a firm factual foundation.

METHODOLOGICAL FRAMEWORK

Our county studies rely on a type of historical writing developed in the 1970s, known as microhistory.[3]

"Microhistory is essentially a historiographical practice,"[4] wrote one of the originators of this method, Giovanni Levi. "Microhistory tries not to sacrifice knowledge of individual elements to wider generalization, and in fact it accentuates individual lives and events. But, at the same time, it tries not to reject all forms of abstraction since minimal facts and individual cases can serve to reveal more general phenomena."[5]

German historiography that ties microhistory closely to the history of everyday life and the history of "small-life worlds" (*kleine Lebenswelten*) aims to explore, in detail, small communities, usually delimited to small areas. Microhistory—as conceived by both the historians who developed its theory and those who put it into practice—acknowledges its own fragmentary nature and makes no claims to comprehensiveness, but it still leads to general conclusions, provides a broader historical framework, and recognizes and explains links between the local and the global. This microscale approach opens a vantage point to understanding phenomena and mechanisms that transcend the locality, allowing historians to draw macroscale conclusions.

The framework of these studies is founded on our belief that microhistory, which delves into the level of individuals and their experiences, offers the best method for exploring and understanding the Holocaust. "This historiographical movement calls into question the certainties of earlier historiographies, notably the grand explanations based on economic or cultural determinations, by granting renewed importance to individual practices and experiences."[6] This methodological approach, along with the subsequent quantitative analysis of the data collected, has allowed us to trace the fates of entire communities and reconstruct the policies of the occupiers, as well as the attitudes and various types of behavior of the Polish people. It has also enabled us to present, in minute detail, the unprecedented level of terror instituted in the public and private spheres by the Germans throughout occupied Polish territory. The terror, it should be stressed, not only focused on the Jews but was also directed with extraordinary fury against mainstream Polish society. It is through a microhistorical approach that we can truly observe and recognize the effect of German law and lawlessness, which resulted in death sentences and summary executions leveled against all people, groups, and even entire communities that demonstrated even the slightest opposition to German designs.

In recent years, microhistorical studies of the war and the occupation have brought new knowledge and a deeper understanding of the Holocaust. It is no coincidence that this type of methodology was adopted for the first time for the purpose of investigating and analyzing the course of the Holocaust in France.[7] It is considerably easier to study the fate of numerous people in a country where the number of Holocaust victims is smaller, and reconstructing their stories is therefore not as challenging as in the eastern parts of Europe. Equally important is a large volume of documents from the period of World War II available in French archives. In France, from where approximately 75,000 Jews were deported to their deaths, historians have at their disposal extensive collections of records produced by local, municipal, and central governments of Vichy France, as well as the German-occupied zone. They can also access complete and exceptionally detailed police records, accompanied by hundreds of lists—sometimes updated on a monthly basis—containing the names of Jews subjected to arrest.

Around 25 percent of local Jews living in the territory of France were deported to extermination camps. In the meantime, in the Netherlands, a country known for centuries for its tolerance, as many as 75 percent of local Jews fell victim to the *Endlösung* (Final Solution). Prompted by this disparity and looking for new explanations, Dutch historians turned to the methods used in microhistory. The subsequent studies of selected Dutch regions have not only yielded a better understanding of the mechanisms of extermination but also revealed the role of "bystanders," that is, the attitudes of a broad range of Dutch people toward their persecuted fellow countrymen. The ensuing and still ongoing debate sparked by this approach has transcended the narrow limits of professional interests and garnered much attention in the Dutch media.[8]

As far as occupied Poland is concerned, the methodology of microhistory has been used, for example, by Christopher R. Browning as a framework for the investigation of the history of a forced labor camp in Starachowice. Facing a scarcity of archival material, Browning decided to reconstruct this history through the prism of the individual fates of 472 Jewish prisoners.[9] Michał Kalisz and Elżbieta Rączy adopted a similar approach in their research on the history of the Jews in Gorlice County.[10] We must stress here that microhistory should not be confused with local history, standing alone on the historical stage and disconnected from any larger context.[11] Regarding the counties selected for our studies, the stories we have told are linked not only to the history of the whole of Poland (and occupied Europe) through the fate of the deported and annihilated Jews but also through the moral choices made by their neighbors that appear especially dire when seen against the background of the Jewish struggle for survival.

PRIMARY SOURCES

The descriptions of the counties would not be possible without extensive and thorough archival research. We believe that the main strength of this book lies in the profusion and diversity of varied, and often unique, primary sources on which we based our studies. We made use of primary source material preserved in Polish, Israeli, American, German, Ukrainian, Belarussian, and Russian archives. Our research encompassed documents authored by the Polish Underground State and Government-in-Exile, Jewish self-help organizations, German-Polish and German authorities, the gendarmerie, and the Blue police. We have surveyed newspapers—both underground and "reptile" (the adjective used to describe local language newspapers serving as German propaganda channels)—and Jewish and Polish diaries and accounts. We have scrutinized vast collections of judicial documents and researched depositions and testimonies given during postwar investigations and trials in Polish courts of law and taken by prosecutors of the district commissions for the investigation of Nazi crimes in Poland. We have also analyzed case files of investigations and proceedings against perpetrators that were conducted in postwar Germany, mostly in the 1950s and 1960s. Moreover, we have combed through the files of municipal and district courts from the period of the occupation—primary sources that are being utilized in the literature on the subject for the first time. We have perused copious resources in Polish regional archives, looking for documents that were produced by lower, local-level government bodies of towns and municipalities; among them, we often discovered official correspondence produced by the heads of the local administration, known as voits (*wójt*) and village elders (*sołtys*), and minutes of meetings held by municipal authorities. Finally, we have also made a use of oral history resources, such as recorded accounts of survivors and interviews with Polish participants and witnesses of the pertinent events.[12] In addition, we conducted a number of interviews in the course of the research. Quite often, we managed to gain access to archival material from private collections—mostly letters, memoirs, and iconographic materials, which have never before entered academic circulation.

Nevertheless, even the most meticulous research cannot fully deliver satisfying answers to a number of questions regarding some aspects of the events described. Some problems have proved impossible to investigate fully due to the diversity of sources relating to each county and have therefore been left unresolved. Among the factors that inevitably have forced researchers to leave some questions unanswered were, for example, numerous documentation gaps, the fallibility of human memory, lies and misrepresentations incorporated into testimonies, and the sheer difficulty of imagining and estimating the number of victims. As we acknowledge the importance of caution when "filling in the blanks," the numbers and estimations this book contains have been calculated conservatively.

In our county studies, we have benefited greatly from the valuable research of many local historians, both professional and amateur.[13] In every region we studied, periodicals were published that constituted a vast trove of knowledge on local history.

GEOGRAPHIC AREAS OF INQUIRY

The history of Polish Jews during the Holocaust has generally been told through the prism of what happened in the larger cities and their ghettos (for example, Warsaw, Kraków, or Łódź), but in actuality, the majority of Polish Jews lived and died in the hundreds of small towns scattered throughout the entire territory of German-occupied Poland. As their history is far less known, we have attempted to narrow the gap by analyzing the Holocaust as it played out in the provinces.

This book comprises eight chapters, each devoted to a separate county located in the territory of occupied Poland.[14] These counties are, in alphabetical order: Bielsk Podlaski, Biłgoraj, Bochnia, Dębica, Łuków, Nowy Targ, Węgrów, and Złoczów. In total, 110,000 Jews resided within their territories in 1942, on the eve of Operation Reinhard, constituting between 5 and 10 percent of the population of each county. The objective of our work was to trace—in the greatest detail possible—the fate of the Jews living within each of these counties between 1939 and 1945. We paid particular attention to the period of the so-called liquidation actions, (referred to either as "Actions", or – using the German term – "*Aktionen*") carried out over the course of several months between mid-1942 and 1943, and the hiding period that lasted until liberation. Our research focused on towns with open ghettos and small or medium-sized Jewish populations (up to 12,000 people), and smaller, sometimes rural settlements of Jews who managed to avoid relocation to larger towns until the winter to spring of 1942. As the administrative divisions selected for our study were located in various regions of Poland, we were able to draw comparisons between the extermination policies of the occupiers and the survival strategies adopted by their Jewish victims. And because there were no larger urban centers within any of these counties, the opportunities for the Jews to escape during the "resettlement actions" (using the euphemistic code name for the mass murders and deportations to extermination camps) and measures they could take to stay alive on the Aryan side were typical of the countryside.

In five cases, the authors focused on prewar Polish counties and, more specifically, on all communes (*gminy*, the lowest level of local government) that made up the prewar counties. In three other cases, they selected as the research field for their studies the *Kreishauptmannschaften*,[15] or German counties. *Kreishauptmannschaften* were the administrative units formed after the GG was established on October 12, 1939, and subsequent reform implemented in early 1940. They replaced the prewar Polish counties (*poviats*); a typical German county encompassed areas of two or more former *poviats*. (A "poviat" is a phonetic rendition of the Polish word "powiat," or a county.) Initially, the GG was divided into four districts: Warsaw, Kraków, Radom, and Lublin. Starting in August 1941, the fifth district, Galicia, was set up on the territory incorporated into the GG territory after the German invasion of the Soviet Union. The capital city of each district was given the status of an "urban county" (*Stadthauptmannschaft*).[16] Apart from urban counties, districts comprised the aforementioned *Kreishauptmannschaften*. There were nine of them in the Warsaw district, and ten in the Lublin and Radom districts; the Kraków district consisted of twelve *Kreishauptmannschaften*, and the Galicia district consisted of eleven. The population of each German county generally numbered between 150,000 and 300,000, but there were certain exceptions to this rule.[17] In the summer of 1941, after the Galicia district had been incorporated, the GG extended over an area of 150,000 square kilometers and had a population of 17 million.[18] On July 22, 1941, the Germans formed the Białystok region (*Bezirk Bialystok*) from the recently invaded northeastern Polish territories, which were inhabited by approximately 1.13 million people.[19] This new administrative entity comprised the larger part of the prewar Białystok voivodeship (one of the sixteen administrative regions of Poland before the war), as well as parts of the Prużana and Brześć counties that had belonged to the former Polesie voivodeship. The region was not incorporated into the GG but was set up as an administratively separate regency (*Regierungsbezirk*). Its administrative organization was modeled on East Prussia; therefore, the region was subdivided into *Kreiskommissariaten* (the equivalent of counties), eight of them in total. Together with the *Bezirk Bialystok*, the population of the five districts of the GG amounted to over 18 million, including 2.2 million Jews.[20]

Seven of the eight counties studied were located in the territory of the GG, each within the boundaries of a different district. Węgrów County, incorporated into the larger *Sokolow–Wengrow Kreishauptmannschaft* during the occupation, was part of the Warsaw district; the counties of Łuków and Biłgoraj were included within the boundaries of the Lublin district (with the former being part of Radzyń Podlaski *Kreis*); the counties of Dębica, Bochnia, and Nowy Targ were subdivisions of the Kraków district; and Złoczów County was, from the summer of 1941, part of the Galicia district. Bielsk County was located outside the boundaries of the GG; it was included within the *Bezirk Bialystok*. Due to such a diverse selection of territories under investigation, we have been able to demonstrate a broad range of economic, geographic, and social conditions that could, and did, impact both the progression of the persecution of the Jews, and the options available to those who decided to go into hiding. But by the same token, it has allowed us to bring to the fore certain commonalities: In every county, we found examples of human determination and courage but also of fear and depravity.

GERMAN POLICY AND LOCAL VARIATIONS

Historians (beginning with Raul Hilberg) have had a tendency to speak of German policies and strategies regarding the extermination of the Jews as if they had been planned precisely and in detail. The findings of our research, however, call this theory into question. The scrutiny of the wartime history of the eight counties has provided evidence that the activities of, and measures taken by, the occupation authorities were routinely adapted to local conditions. The diverse and distinct local realities played a significant role in changing and shaping the behaviors of the victims, the perpetrators, and those to whom we usually refer as "bystanders." Despite these differences, and regardless of whether the subject of our scrutiny was the history of Biłgoraj, Bielsk Podlaski, or Węgrów, in each case, only a small number of Jews managed to survive until the end of the war. Out of approximately 110,000 Jewish residents who lived in the eight counties in 1942, only 2,387 (2.2 percent) survived—which in a way corroborates and confirms the overall statistics for the entire occupied country. This is the number of individuals about whom we have been able to find and verify information using all available sources. It is possible that future research will compel us to revise these figures.

In each county, Jews displayed a wide array of behaviors and survival strategies that they developed in response to specific local circumstances, as well as to the flexibility of the German bureaucracy, which allowed local police and civilian authorities some room for creative approaches to many aspects of their extermination policy. As Christopher Browning and Raul Hilberg[21] have already noted, the German bureaucratic system relied heavily on bottom-up creativity, that is, on the efficiency, adaptability, and improvisational skills of low-ranking officials who were able to anticipate their superiors' wishes, even those not expressed in writing. Such improvised measures, once introduced

Table 0.1 Holocaust survivors

County	Jewish population in 1942	Number of Jews in hiding (%)	Survival rate in relation to the number of Jews on the eve of the deportations (%)
Bielsk Podlaski	22,500*	1,300 (6%)	1.4
Biłgoraj	14,500	1,500 (10%)	1.9
Bochnia	11,157	1,100 (10%)	3.5
Dębica	18,000	1,257 (7%)	1.7
Łuków	15,988	986 (6%)	0.8
Nowy Targ†	4,445	651 (15%)	2.6
Węgrów	11,200	1,390 (12%)	1.8
Złoczów	10,359	1,356 (13%)	6.1
TOTAL	**108,149**	**9,543 (median = 10%)**	**2.5**

Source: Data obtained by the authors.
Notes:
*The data concerns the eastern part of the county, which was incorporated into Polish territory after the war.
†About 80 of those who survived in various labor camps, 26 people survived outside Nowy Targ County, and only 9 within its borders.

by the Germans, tended to trigger chains of subsequent impromptu responses undertaken by Jews as well as Poles.

German policies for dealing with the Jews evolved differently in each of the discussed counties. Moreover, the relationships between Jews and their neighbors exhibited local variations, which additionally modified the course of events in each area. Some factors were capable of fundamentally altering the progression of the "resettlement actions." Among them were, by way of example, the distance between liquidated Jewish settlements and a railroad line, or the availability and strength of "liquidation commandos," which were garrisoned in the vicinity, ready for action. During the liquidations of the ghettos in Biłgoraj County, which provide a particularly striking example, Jews were sometimes forced to march to very distant "gathering points," and hundreds of them died in the process. Much the same happened in Węgrów County. As for Biłgoraj County, it is worth noting that the extermination there was not carried out according to a single pattern; an alternative technique was employed to achieve the "Final Solution to the Jewish Question," namely killing on the spot. It can be considered as the most characteristic feature of the Holocaust in Biłgoraj County that both methods of killing Jews—transportation to extermination camps and instant execution by shooting—were applied to the same extent. A reasonable assumption would be that the latter was introduced due to the significant dispersion of the county's Jewish population. Prior to the war, Jews had been scattered across Biłgoraj County territory, living not only in towns but also in about eighty villages and hamlets (*kolonia*), some of which were fairly isolated. In certain areas, then, instead of relocating the Jewish inhabitants to nearby towns, firing squads were sent into the field. They moved from one village to the next, capturing and murdering Jews on the spot. A similar extermination method was adopted in the village of Baczki near Łochów (Węgrów County) and in the Podhale villages: Krościenko and Ochotnica (Nowy Targ County). In some cases, we see a combination of different schemes. To run them, the Germans usually relied—due to limitations of their own resources—on the Polish Blue police, local fire brigades, and units of *junaks* (members of the Construction Service, *Baudienst*). Our research uncovered similar "improvisations" in Węgrów and a number of small towns in Biłgoraj County, where Polish policemen, firefighters of the OSP (*Ochotnicza Straż Pożarna*, Volunteer Fire Brigades), and large groups of locals took part in the extermination operations, along with gendarmes. In the vicinity of the town of Łuków, the events took a different course: Two battalions of the German Reserve Police, which had been stationed there for a long time, carried out numerous mass murders of the local Jews almost on their own. A local variation of tactics was introduced in Bielsk County (as well as all of *Bezirk Bialystok*), where the liquidations of almost all of the ghettos took place on the same day: The Jews were then transported to the two largest ghettos in the area and, from there, to Treblinka.[22] A different tactic was used to liquidate closed ghettos (which were also usually the largest ones), and another one was employed to liquidate open or partially closed ghettos, from which the probability of escaping to the Aryan side was particularly high. The following chapters will provide the reader with a great many pertinent examples to illustrate the local variations summarized here.

The studies conducted on the microhistorical level show clearly that the oft-mentioned, alleged "inevitability of the Holocaust" consisted of many elements that were by no means inevitable.

LIQUIDATION ACTIONS: VICTIMS

Each of our regional studies provides an account of the *Liquidierungsaktionen*—the liquidation actions carried out during Operation Reinhardt—as one of the watershed events in the history of the extermination of the Jews. We have tried to reconstruct the course of these actions as accurately as possible and have sometimes found it useful to present them hour by hour. In most cases, however, the reader will learn only the most critical facts—whether it be a day or a few days, which we believe determined the fate of the victims. The liquidations were conducted with unspeakable brutality in full view of the neighbors and constituted grim spectacles of horror. What we discovered and described in our studies shows, beyond a shadow of a doubt, that this terror was aimed at suppressing any will of resistance the victims might have preserved. As far as the non-Jewish populations were concerned, the public mass executions served both as a warning and as a clear message that the life of a Jew no longer held any value.

The numerical data we have collected, and the figures we have calculated (or estimated), may help the reader understand the scale of this violence. In the town of Węgrów, at least one thousand Jews (10 percent of the ghetto's inhabitants) were murdered outright on the day of its liquidation, in situ, on September 22, 1942. Twenty percent of the local Jews were killed in the course of the actions in the county of Nowy Targ; 36–38 percent were murdered during the liquidation of the local secondary ghetto and labor camps in Złoczów County. Readers should keep in mind that behind the façade of these dry statistics lies the tragic fate of thousands of women, children, the elderly and infirmed, and men. The order in which they are listed here derives its meaning from the fact that the weakest—children, women, and the elderly—comprised the majority of those victims who were executed first, shot and killed by death squads and their local "helpers."

In none of the cases analyzed and described have we been able to determine precisely how many of the Jews selected for direct murder during the liquidation actions had tried to save themselves, how many were dragged out of ingeniously designed bunkers and previously prepared hiding places. We are ignorant of how many were killed despite the fact that they did not try to hide or put up any resistance. Nor do we know the exact number of fugitives from the ghettos who were caught shortly after the "actions," within a few hours or days. Therefore, the estimates we present and discuss later have been calculated as conservatively and meticulously as our detailed research allowed.

PERPETRATORS AND THEIR ACCOMPLICES

The careful analysis of the course of events during the liquidation actions has allowed us to increase and broaden the existing knowledge of the subject. Records of German and Polish postwar trials were particularly useful to this end, and they helped us establish fairly precisely the structure of the German forces engaged in the operations. While Polish and Jewish accounts tend to paint the Germans as homogeneous units of uniformed men and describe them in generic terms (such as "SS men," "Gestapo," "schutzmen," "Schupo-men," or "gendarmes"), a variety of police forces—local or sent from other regions—was actually assigned to participate in the liquidations of the ghettos. Among them were officers of the Security Police (Sipo); *Ordnungspolizei* (referred to in this book as the Order Police), which included the Gendarmerie and the Schupo (which operated, respectively, in rural and urban areas); the armed SS force; the Waffen SS; railroad police (*Bahnschutzpolizei*); Criminal Police (Kripo); reserve police battalions (Order Police, Orpo); and even functionaries of the civil administration. An important part was played by auxiliary units of the SS, which comprised former Soviet POWs (Poles and Jews called them *askari, hiwi*, or the "blacks") and other German units, such as security guards, factory security (*Werkschutz*), and sometimes members of the Hitler Youth (*Hitlerjugend*).

One of the goals we set forth several years ago, when we started this project, was to unearth the names of previously unknown perpetrators of the Holocaust, among them the German gendarmes and functionaries of the occupation administration who, in many cases, have never faced justice. There is, however, a voluminous and still-growing body of historical writings devoted to German perpetrators.[23] More uncommon, and for this reason more important, are findings in our research that relate to the question of the complicity of the Polish people—and Belarussians and Ukrainians as well—who in various ways and for various reasons joined in, or were conscripted to, the extermination of the Jews. That fact that we have been able to expand knowledge on this subject is, in our view, of the most original and valuable results of our work. What should be stressed regarding this question is the sinister role played in the GG by the Polish police. The so-called Blue police—named after the navy blue color of their uniforms—became a significant element in the German strategy for the extermination of the Jews. The activities of Polish policemen were by no means restricted to sealing off the provincial ghettos during the liquidation actions. The "Blues" entered Jewish districts alongside German gendarmes, participated in searches for Jews in hiding, escorted those captured to death trains, and often carried out executions by shooting. Later, when the liquidation of the ghettos had already been completed, they guarded the deserted closed quarters. When the German killing squads started to withdraw and the third phase of the Holocaust began, Polish policemen participated in hunts for escapees from the ghettos and executed those delivered to police posts. Often, though not always, they did so on orders of their German superiors. Furthermore—on their own initiative and without any orders—they searched for and murdered Jews hiding in small towns and rural areas that had a limited gendarmerie presence, or where there were no Germans at all.

A second Polish organization, members of which were visible during the liquidation actions in several counties, was the fire service. The participation of the Polish OSP in the extermination operations has, to date, been scarcely investigated by historians.[24] Some of the essays contained in this book reveal that Polish firefighters played a disgraceful role in the liquidation of the Jewish settlements, for example in Biłgoraj and Węgrów Counties. In the towns of Węgrów and Stoczek Węgrowski, the firefighters did not merely participate in the liquidation of the local ghettos but volunteered to do so, as was later reported by the Polish underground press.

Now we approach a separate question, the one that stirs the most intense emotions: the question concerning the role the Polish population played in the liquidation of ghettos, specifically the role of ordinary, small-town residents and peasants who swarmed in from nearby villages upon hearing about progressing deportations and who watched in horror as scenes of the massacre played out all around them. Some of them were prepared to help Jewish fugitives, while others hunted Jews and handed them over to the uniformed forces. Still others looted freshly deserted Jewish homes, often discovering there Jews in hiding. Many sat by idly as Jews were murdered before their eyes, their idleness indicating something more than just passivity and indifference. Images of neighbors and acquaintances peering from behind policemen's backs while the mass-scale killings were taking place in the ghetto streets have surfaced in our research with disturbing frequency.

ESTIMATES

The essays that comprise this volume compelled us to challenge many of the convictions that are deeply ingrained in Polish historical writing on the Holocaust and that have given rise to many controversies and misconceptions. First, we should attempt to estimate the number of Jews who tried to save themselves by going into hiding when the ghettos in their towns were liquidated. This is not an easy task, and the subject has usually been omitted from demographic studies of the period of the war and occupation. With regard to Wołyń, Shmuel Spector has estimated that 25 percent of Jews attempted to escape in the face of liquidations of the ghettos and labor camps.[25] Grzegorz Berendt has put forward a broader quantitative analysis of the phenomenon of escapes. On the basis of the data (often incomplete) collected in Yad Vashem's *Encyclopedia of the Ghettos During the Holocaust*,[26] he reached the conclusion that the scale of escapes was much larger in the Eastern Borderlands (*Kresy*) than in the GG, while there were almost no such attempts in the territories incorporated into the Reich. In addition, there were significant differences between various districts and counties, as well as between the large cities and the countryside.[27] Because it is extremely difficult to determine an unambiguous number of Jews who sought refuge during the third phase of the Holocaust, we must settle for estimates.

As noted above, before the deportations to extermination camps, the total population of the GG and *Bezirk Bialystok* amounted to just over 18 million, out of which 2.2 million were Jews.[28] Shmuel Krakowski estimated that the number of escapees from the ghettos and camps reached about 300,000.[29] Szymon Datner assessed that between 200,000 and 250,000 Jews sought refuge on the Aryan side.[30] Both historians were aware that their figures were unreliable to say the least and not grounded in any real statistical research. This motivated us to undertake painstaking inquiries to gather the widest possible range of sources as the basis for our estimations. Because these figures do matter, all the more so because the probability of the survival of the Jews who went into hiding after the ghettos had been liquidated suggests correlation with the attitude of the local population, or so one can speculate on the basis of the research design. At this stage of the Holocaust, it was the Poles (along with their other neighbors, Ukrainians and Belarussians) who had considerable influence over who among the Jews was able to survive and who died. Therefore, the number of those who tried to save themselves but still did not manage to survive has not just historical but also moral significance.

How many of those 200,000–300,000 Jews seeking refuge survived? Here, we have also to rely on estimates. The number of Jews who lived to see the end of the German occupation, including those who survived in labor and extermination camps, ranges—according to various historians—from 30,000 all the way to 120,000, with 40,000 being the most generally accepted reckoning.[31] This is an important estimation because it determines the number of Jewish fugitives who did not manage to survive, which in turn defines our research field and offers a point of departure for further research on the fate of Jewish outcasts and the attitudes of the local gentiles who crossed their path.

Our studies offer the reader a chance to understand better the scale of escapes and subsequent strategies and chances of survival in various and diverse areas of occupied Poland.

It must be pointed out that the sources provide us with an abundance of information on attempts to hide during the deportations—in various hideouts, either inside or outside of the ghettos. Most of these accounts, however, are far from precise: They mention "a few dozen," "a few hundred," or "hundreds" of

Table 0.2 Jews in hiding

County	Number of Jews in hiding for whom information is available	Number of Jews who survived the Holocaust	Number of Jews who were killed while in hiding
Bielsk Podlaski	974	322	608
Biłgoraj	1,092	274	712
Bochnia	629	395	297
Dębica	1,257	312	945
Łuków	986	140	846
Nowy Targ	651	115*	536
Węgrów	398	195	330
Złoczów	1,115	634	501
TOTAL	**7,102**	**2,387**	**4,775**

Source: Based on the authors' case studies.
Notes:
*See note 21.

Jews trying to avoid resettlement. For obvious reasons, people in hiding were not able to furnish more exact figures, but even the order of magnitude they suggest cannot be taken at face value. If, however, the data has been confirmed by several sources, we utilized the smallest (or most-often repeated) number of escapees to estimate the size of the group in hiding; these numbers were entered in the second column of the table. Here, as in all other cases, we calculated the estimates very conservatively. If a source mentioned "a few" Jews, we entered three; if it mentioned "a dozen or so," we entered eleven; "a few dozen" became twenty-one; and "a few hundred" became two hundred. This means that figures we have provided herein are most likely on the low side.

The median for Jews seeking shelter—which is less than the mean[32] affected by the regional differentiation of the numbers of escapees—for all the counties studied was 10 percent and does not diverge from the intuitive estimates of Krakowski and Datner.[33] The local differences, however, were huge. In the territory of Bielsk Podlaski County, by the way of example, about 20 percent of Jews escaped from Brańsk, 18 percent from Drohiczyn, 5 percent from Siemiatycze, and as far as we know, no one from Orla. Future research in other areas will probably once again verify the estimates, and subsequently the median and the mean, of the escapees.

It needs to be underscored that these estimates—like all others given in this book—are very conservative. It is usually impossible to offer a credible answer to the question of how many Jews attempted to hide inside of the ghettos either on the day when the liquidation took place or immediately thereafter. It is much easier to estimate the number of Jews who managed to flee from a ghetto and survive the first weeks and months on the Aryan side.

STRATEGIES OF SURVIVAL

Along with highlighting and revealing the policies of the occupiers and fate of the Jews in selected counties, an important goal of these studies was to paint a picture of the Jews' efforts and struggles for survival, and to reconstruct their survival strategies. The "strategies of survival" were selected as the main subject of, and pivotal term for, our research project. Therefore, a relevant question that needs to be answered now is, In what context can the word *strategy* be used meaningfully with regard to the Jews who sought refuge after the liquidation of ghettos? Strategy, as various dictionaries define it, is "a long-term action to achieve planned, long-range goals." It is based on an assumption that there exists an ability to influence events. In addition, it contains a psychological aspect of agency, related to a nonfatalistic vision of the future. For this reason, we are using this term in a metaphorical, rather than a literal, sense. Although the Jews who were escaping from ghettos had as their goal to save their own lives, taking truly strategic steps to achieve that goal was beyond their reach. Instead, they had to make their decisions on an ad hoc basis, and these separate decisions set in motion a chain of events that shaped their fates.

The repertoire of available options was quite small, the freedom to make decisions was extremely limited, and their results were uncertain. Practically, the only autonomous decision they could have made in the face of the deportations was to hide on the grounds of the ghetto, or to escape. Hiding inside a ghetto required a great deal of preparation: One had to amass stocks of food, build a hiding place, and devise a warning system. To escape, in turn, required contact with locals, as well as the possibility of obtaining their assistance. But in both scenarios, what would happen to Jews later depended more upon circumstances and external events than on the actual implementation of a plan.

With time, the number of available options shrank, the strategies had to be flexible and readily adaptable to perilous and difficult situations, and each decision was laced with the risk of failure and had to be made in a state of total unpredictability. The survival strategies—planned and intuitive—as well as spontaneous decisions depended on many factors. They were, of course, significantly impacted by the German extermination policies, but as it turned out, a key role in the survival of Jewish fugitives was played by Aryan surroundings and a series of often unforeseen circumstances.

The term "strategies for survival," as it is used in the context of our studies, covers all attempts made by Jews in their struggle to survive.

On the basis of data gathered from the nine counties, we are able to draw the conclusion that about 30 percent of the Jews in hiding survived, and more than 60 percent died. Unfortunately, the fate of the rest of the fugitives still remains unknown. Information on how the Jews survived, or how they died, in each of the counties can be found in their respective chapters.

In terms of percentages, out of those who had tried to hide inside and outside the territory of a county, the Jews from Złoczów County had the largest (47 percent) ratio of survivors. The smallest number (12 percent) was among the Jews from Łuków County. Several factors combined to affect the survival rate in Złoczów County, starting with the liquidation of the secondary ghetto that took place in the late spring of 1943. Because the occupation there lasted less time than in western areas, the Jews had to survive only one winter (1943–1944) before the occupation ended, and they mostly did so by hiding in shelters in the forest. The Soviet partisan movement operating in this area offered shelter to many Jewish fugitives, and in contrast to those in other parts of the country, Polish villagers there were more willing to help their Jewish neighbors in hiding. It is possible that local Polish people, being themselves threatened by the increasing Polish-Ukrainian conflict, had more compassion and understanding for others who were seeking refuge.[34] By contrast, the relatively high survival rate for Dębica County (25 percent) was helped by the existence of numerous, often porous labor camps within its territory, A significant part of this county's Jews who lived to see the end of the occupation survived working for the German aircraft factory, the *Flugzeugwerk Mielec.*

Jews would engage in various activities to escape death. Their strategies were determined by the diverse circumstances that prevailed in each of the counties. Among the factors involved were natural and demographic conditions, as well as a road network, local social and ethnic structures, the manpower and distribution of German occupation forces (police and civilian), and the presence and strength of partisan groups. These and other diverse factors affected their chances, and various strategies of survival are thoroughly discussed in each of the essays. Here, however, let us set all this diversity aside in order to make some comparisons and point out some similarities.

In all of the regions studied, there were groups of Jews in hiding that were living in one place for an extended period of time; in our premise, an extended period means staying with one host for no less than eighteen months (fifteen months in Złoczów County). In the first days and weeks after a deportation, most of the ghetto escapees had to look constantly for somewhere to spend a night, always moving from one place to another. However, some were fortunate enough to relatively quickly find a safe harbor in which they were able to stay throughout the German occupation.

Another commonly used strategy was to seek shelter in different hideouts, which meant living sequentially in several (sometimes a dozen or so) different homesteads. Most often, money or skills (e.g., tailoring) were offered in exchange for the opportunity to stay for a longer period on a farmer's property. These arrangements always hinged on the goodwill of the hosts, the resources of their "guests," and the curiosity of neighbors. There were also many other factors that could jeopardize these refugees, such as roundups to meet quotas of conscripts for forced labor in the Reich or frequent searches; all of these have been analyzed in detail in the present studies.[35] Those who were not able to find a safe hideout in a house, stable, or barn were destined to wander about, staying periodically in the forest or spending nights in the fields (in haystacks in summer, or in primitive dugouts in winter), only sometimes having an opportunity to stay for a short period on a farm. They were moving from place to place, constantly looking for a safe haven where they could stay longer.[36]

Another strategy employed in almost all of the counties presented here was to hide in a forest bunker. Forests, as natural shelters, became the first hiding place for most of the escapees from the ghettos. Hundreds of Jews found refuge there, but subsequently their numbers dwindled due to roundups and "hunts," as well as to generally difficult living conditions. It was extremely challenging to survive the autumn and winter months in the forest. The category "hiding in the forest" covers the Jews who survived until the end of the occupation in dugouts and holes in the forest but who had no links with partisans. They kept building bunkers in the forest and moving from place to place, while the neighboring villages served as a base, supplying them with sustenance they would buy or barter for and, if they did not have anything, steal or rob. Partisans and underground members posed a risk for them, as did forest guards and all locals who could stumble upon them accidentally. But the biggest threat was posed by organized roundups and local informants. Of course, the ability to use the strategy of remaining in the woods depended on the scale of afforestation in each of the counties[37] and, in turn, was affected by the presence of partisans. The latter could create a new option—an opportunity to join a partisan unit—but it would depend on the affiliation of the unit as well as the associated attitude toward Jews (the attitude of the partisans themselves, and especially their leaders, was also an important factor). Generally, only Soviet partisans and Communists took on Jews, although the latter were not entirely free of antisemitic prejudices. Other organizations posed a deadly threat to them, but sometimes Jews joined their units regardless, concealing their Jewish identity. Joining the partisan movement and participation in combat usually represented only an episode in the whole story of someone's survival, but it seemed appropriate to single it out as a separate category—the more so because this strategy is mentioned in survivors' testimonies.

Passing as an Aryan was a strategy adopted by Jews in all eight counties. Living on Aryan papers required changing one's identity, which almost always necessitated that Jews abandon their place of residence where people knew one another, and the risk of being recognized was high. Aryan papers could be acquired in parishes (via baptismal certificates), through contacts with local government clerks (who could provide blank identity cards or German identifications—*Kennkarten*), or with the Polish underground (from whom it was possible to buy "genuine" false papers). In a modified version of this strategy, one could attempt to live on Aryan papers outside the boundaries of a county, especially by signing up voluntarily for work in the Reich, which was an option suitable mainly for women. No doubt the strategy that demanded traveling and living in new places was easier to pursue for city dwellers than for residents of the small towns or villages we have studied.

Certain strategies could only have been used in some counties because of their geographical location or the policies introduced by local German authorities. Escapes across the border were only possible in Bochnia, Dębica, and Nowy Targ Counties. Labor camps could provide protection only if there were labor camps nearby, as there were in these three counties. A survival strategy that involved getting into one of the many labor camps for Jews (*Juden Arbeitslager, Julag*) that were scattered all over Poland has hardly been addressed by historians, but research conducted at the county level clearly reveals its significance.[38] However, this strategy (seeking refuge in a *Julag*) left the final result of the Jewish struggle for survival in the hands of German decision makers.

At this point, one of the most essential elements of any survival strategy must be mentioned: pure chance or a stroke of luck. This factor cannot be subjected to quantification or explained in a rational way, but without it, all decisions, efforts, and strategies would be doomed to failure without exception.

STRATEGIES THAT ENDED IN FAILURE

Despite the many and varied efforts to save themselves, most of the Jews who escaped from ghettos during the resettlements did not survive. In the counties studied, the ratio of those who tried to save their own lives to those who succeeded was depressingly consistent: between 60 and 80 percent of the fugitives died in Węgrów, Bielsk, Nowy Targ, Dębica, and Biłgoraj Counties. The smallest percentage of Jews died in the counties of Bochnia (30 percent) and Złoczów (37 percent). The median percentage for all the counties was 67 percent; in other words, two-thirds of the Jews who sought rescue died.

Escapees were at a grave risk of being exposed and murdered at all times. The German police posed an obvious threat to them: the gendarmerie in villages and the *Schupo* in towns. German policemen were proactive in hunting for Jews, more often than not executing those fugitives who were denounced and brought in to police stations by villagers. In many well-documented cases, the Germans were called to places where Jews were found in hiding; village elders were responsible for reporting such events. In response to such a call, the German police (often assisted by Polish policemen) arrived at the site to shoot the victims on the spot, sometimes along with the Poles who had been sheltering them. It should be reiterated here that oftentimes the Germans, who were not familiar with the regional topography, conducted liquidation operations in response to denunciations received by the authorities, typically accompanied by the Blue police (or the *Ukrainische Hilfspolizei* in Złoczów). The reader should also keep in mind that residents of Polish villages made denunciations to the local Polish police more often than to the Germans. In the cases in which the Blue police were summoned, they might kill the Jews right at or near the place where they had been found, or right next to the Polish police post. Sometimes Blue policemen murdered Jews on their own initiative, unbeknownst to the Germans.

At times, an encounter with members of the Polish underground exposed Jews to grave danger too. Many of those in hiding who did not survive were murdered by the local underground.

As for the Jews murdered by local civilians, their "neighbors," our estimates must come with a caveat: We are aware of a "dark number," a notion taken from criminology, referring to unknown and impossible-to-learn figures of unreported crimes. Apart from murders that are mentioned in sources, others were committed for which no records are available or ever existed. Knowledge of the killings perpetrated by the civilian population is (and most likely remains) incomplete because of the character of the primary sources pertaining to the subject. Jewish accounts tend to provide fragmentary information, as those in hiding had limited access to information, and court sources mostly concern crimes that were committed jointly by a few perpetrators or more because these kinds of murders were discovered more often, whereas the ones committed single-handedly and secretly rarely came to light.

Jews in hiding could also die of other causes: illness, exposure, starvation. Some were assaulted by robbers, and some committed suicide. In many cases, we have not been able to learn any details of how they died; just the fact that they did is briefly mentioned in the sources, and we had to put "no data" in the corresponding space on our data sheets.

Our research based on data from examined and verified cases clearly shows that in the territories in question (excluding Bielsk and Złoczów Counties[39]), a large majority of Jewish fugitives died at the hands of Poles or were murdered with their participation.

HELPING JEWS

It was extremely risky to shelter Jews permanently or to provide them with any other form of assistance. Those who did lived under the threat of punishment, even indiscriminate retribution, and faced hostility from their neighbors, who were not always motivated solely by fear but rather by clearly noticeable antisemitism. Polish Holocaust literature tends to approach the question of rescuing Jews as a subject in and of itself, isolated from the social context in which the help was given and received. Hence, an abundance of studies (of different value) has been published that present an extremely idealized picture of the occupation and either eliminate the subject of rescue-related threats or limit it to a discussion of threats posed by the Germans. In reality—as can be seen in our studies—serious danger facing those who helped Jews often came not from the Germans but rather from their own neighbors or from "Blue" or other non-German policemen, who were ready to denounce them and deliver them into the hands of the occupiers.

Aiding Jews amid the reality of war, and risking one's own life and the lives of one's family in the process, posed a challenge that was enormous and difficult to take on. According to popular belief, there were only two possible outcomes for helping Jews: Rescuers paid for it with their lives, or they were eventually recognized as Righteous Among the Nations (though these scenarios are not mutually exclusive, as the prestigious award, bestowed by Yad Vashem on behalf of the State of Israel, can be given posthumously). In reality, a few other possible outcomes of these wartime stories are to be found in between these extremes. Sometimes, it happened that only Jews were murdered, while Poles who had sheltered them suffered different forms of punishment: Their homes were burned down, and they were beaten, imprisoned, sent to concentration camps, and/or fined.

Finally, it needs to be noted that not every offer of help was of equal quality, though when one looks at the subject years after it took place, what matters most is survival, and mistreatment or exploitation by the hosts most often fade into oblivion. The case files that the Righteous Among the Nations Department at Yad Vashem has amassed rarely mention cases of abuse; they also seldom mention payment for shelter (as the medal and title are meant to be awarded to altruistic rescuers). In contrast, one must bear in mind that Yad Vashem has not collected these records for research purposes but rather to pay tribute to those non-Jews who risked their lives to save Jewish persons during the Holocaust.

There were wealthy persons among the rescuers, as well as poor ones, the town intelligentsia and illiterate villagers, members of the underground, *Volksdeutsche* (sometimes even Reich Germans), Catholics, Orthodox Christians, Jehovah's Witnesses, and atheists. Clearly, nationality, class, economic status, and religious affiliation cannot be singled out as a determining factor in the decision to help Jews. Undoubtedly, those who decided to aid the hunted and socially excluded Jews had to be brave and ready to break the rules imposed by the occupier. In addition, they had to be prepared to stand up to the social pressure of their community that was either overtly antisemitic, or at the very least unfriendly to the Jews. Our findings seem to confirm that their decision to help was motivated by their individual value system, personality, or other inner merits rather than their social or economic position.

Various reasons may have laid behind someone's decision to offer aid: a prewar relationship was a frequent motive, as was friendship, compassion, love, deeply internalized religious principles, or simply a conviction that any human being—no matter who they are—should be helped. Some acted on the desire to stand up to the Germans; some acted out of belief that it was the right and proper thing to do, despite the risk to their own lives. Those who offered help in exchange for money should be mentioned here as well. For some of them, it was simply a way to earn income that was facilitated by the reality of the occupation; for others, it was a method—no matter how unethical—to get rich, mercilessly taking advantage of people in extreme need.

As our studies demonstrate, the types of assistance the local people offered Jews during the period that began in 1942 with the liquidation actions and lasted until 1944 or 1945 (depending upon the region) most often consisted of providing them with food and sheltering them in farm buildings—a stable, cowshed, barn, and infrequently a house—or in specially prepared hideouts. It involved removing waste from the shelter, supplying means for personal hygiene, and safekeeping Jewish belongings (among them money and valuables, such as jewelry that could be sold if needed). Material help included providing fugitives with clothing, food, buying Aryan papers, or providing them with a train ticket. Nonmaterial assistance may have taken the form of information regarding possible dangers or the situation at the front. Acts of moral support, such as consolation, offering encouragement, showing compassion and understanding, and keeping hope alive should also be considered forms of nonmaterial assistance.

In each county, some of the rescuers were later recognized as Righteous Among the Nations.[40] According to the data we have gathered, statistically, an average Righteous helped two Jews. One should keep in mind, however, that the number of the Righteous recognized since the end of the war is smaller than the actual number of rescuers. The reason these numbers differ are complex: Some rescuers, who considered their behavior as absolutely normal, did not wish to be rewarded for it; others died, leaving no trace of their story; and still others lost contact with those they had saved. In each county, between a few and a few dozen people were subjected to repression for assisting Jews,[41] while the Jews they had helped were usually murdered. These rescuers are rarely awarded the title of Righteous, even though they paid the ultimate price for their deeds, because the testimony of a survivor is required as part of the award procedure, but none of the fugitives they had tried to save survived to testify and vouch for them. As mentioned earlier, the Germans murdered some rescuers on the spot, along with the Jews whom they had sheltered. They punished others by burning down their homesteads or incarcerating them in jail or even concentration camps, from which few returned.

CONCLUSIONS

Among the most important findings of these studies is an abundance of evidence of resourcefulness and ingenuity displayed by Jews in the face of the impending, and ongoing, Holocaust. The victims engaged in a struggle for survival, both their own and those close to them, with striking determination, courage, and mobility. These observations, when scaled up to the level of the entire occupied country, belies a portrait of the alleged passivity of the victims and the belief that Jews went to their deaths "like sheep to the slaughter." In the years preceding the extermination, Polish Jews succeeded in creating a system of social resistance, relying on formal (Jewish Social Self-Help, *Judenräte*, the Joint) as well as informal (neighborly and family help) structures to alleviate the draconian laws and terror introduced by the occupiers. Escapes from the territory occupied by the Germans continued (at various levels of intensity) during the period between the fall of 1939 and the German invasion of the Union of Soviet Socialist Republics in June 1941. With the beginning of the liquidation actions—at which point virtually no one could labor under any misapprehension regarding the ultimate goals of German policies towards the Jewish population—Jews intensified their desperate struggle for survival.

Our recent studies revealed the scope and range of these preparations. They show, on the one hand, that the ghettos became sites of large-scale "fortification" works: Hideouts and bunkers were constructed in and under buildings, and ingenious hiding places in double walls and attics were built. On the other hand, contacts were sought and made on the Aryan side to arrange for help and shelter. Wherever possible, networks—underground railroads of a sort—were arranged to move people abroad, mostly to Slovakia and Hungary.

Our research has uncovered an incredible range of survival strategies devised by the Jews who went into hiding among the non-Jewish population. But we have also analyzed the decisions made by those who did not believe that they could save themselves among the Polish people and so tried to survive in labor camps or deliberately decided to collaborate with German authorities (as did, for example, some members of the *Judenräte* or Jewish councils—both terms in this book will be used interchangeably—or the Jewish Order Police, henceforth referred to simply as the Jewish police). We found, however, that such collaboration did not ultimately make any difference with regard to their survival.

We have analyzed what happened to those who escaped into the forest and tried to survive either in bunkers or by joining partisan units. Sometimes Jewish partisans became protectors of Jewish children who were in hiding with peasants in nearby villages, and they took revenge on local murderers and informants, as happened in the vicinity of Łuków and Bielsk Podlaski. In Adamów (Łuków County), Jewish partisans first liberated several dozen Jews from a local prison and then took revenge together on those Poles who had denounced the Jews and helped the Germans during the deportations.

Equally impressive was the scale of mutual assistance—all of the networks of Jewish contacts and support that linked Jewish hideouts. The present studies reveal the extent to which Jews helped each other, challenging the common misconception that they were passive victims and that only the Poles were active in helping them.

What is equally important is that our microhistorical approach allowed us to restore the memory of the fate of individual human beings—that is, the fate of thousands of men, women, and children—the majority of whom are mentioned by name in the Holocaust literature for the first time. In all of the counties, Jews rarely sought refuge in towns; hence the number of fugitives who survived on Aryan papers is small. Rather, they looked for help in nearby villages, in the homes of their neighbors and acquaintances. Their chances of survival depended greatly on the latter's willingness to help and whether villagers were able to overcome their fear of the danger posed to any rural community that was exposed hiding a Jew.

The established group norms, ubiquitous antisemitism, and social mechanisms of conformity all worked against the rescuers, so one should admire all the more the resolve of those who were able to disobey not only the German laws but also the unwritten rules of group.

The numbers are staggering: Two out of every three Jewish fugitives died, and in most cases, their Christian neighbors contributed to their deaths in various degrees. As a whole, with some local variation, our studies offer evidence pointing to the fact that Poles (Ukrainians and Belorussians in the eastern areas) participated in the extermination of their Jewish fellow citizens on a significantly larger scale than previously assumed. Even though it may be difficult for many to accept, the historical evidence gathered in this book leaves no room for doubt: Sizable parts of Polish populations participated in liquidation actions and later, during the period between 1942 and 1945, contributed directly or indirectly to the death of thousands of Jews who were seeking refuge among them. The available historical sources make possible to determine these groups and sometimes identify individuals.

Close scrutiny of the progress of liquidation actions in each county has allowed us to show the role that local German authorities (civilian and police) played in the killing. We were able to reveal the adaptability of German tactics and place on historical record the names of those Germans who had operated at the level of county, town, or gendarmerie stations and who have never previously been held responsible for their participation, direct and indirect, in the murder of Jews.

Finally, it is necessary to emphasize that our research has shown the prevalence of antisemitic behavior and aggression against the Jews that did not diminish over time. On the contrary, at the very end of the war, when partisan activities increased, so did the number of murders of Jews. The retreat of the Germans sadly did not put an end to these crimes: In each of the eight counties, some Holocaust survivors were murdered.

NOTES

1. See Jan Grabowski, *Hunt for the Jews. Betrayal and Murder in German-Occupied Poland* (Bloomington: Indiana University Press, 2013).

2. Jan T. Gross, *Sąsiedzi: Historia zagłady żydowskiego miasteczk* (Pogranicze: Sejny, 2000). Published in English as *Neighbors: The Destruction of the*

Jewish Community in Jedwabne, Poland (Princeton, NJ: Princeton University Press, 2001).

3. On microhistory, see a seminal work by one of the originators of this approach: Carlo Ginzburg, "Microhistory: Two or Three Things That I Know about It," *Critical Inquiry* 20, no. 1 (Autumn 1993): 10–35.

4. Giovanni Levi, "On Microhistory," in *New Perspectives on Historical Writing*, ed. Peter Burke (University Park: Penn State Press, 2001), 99.

5. Ibid., 113.

6. Claire Zalc and Tal Bruttmann, eds., *Microhistories of the Holocaust* (New York: Berghahn, 2017), 2.

7. Nicolas Mariot and Claire Zalc, *Face à la persécution. 991 Juifs dans la guerre* (Paris: Odile Jacob i Fondation pour la Mémoire de la Shoah, 2010). Mariot and Zalc studied the history of the Jews of Lens. Alexandre Doulut and Sandrine Labeau focused on those of the Garonna department: *Les 473 Déportés juifs de LotetGaronne. Histoires individuelles et archives* (Marmande: Après l'oubli, Paris: les Fils et filles des déportés juifs de France, 2010). On the fate of Jews of Grenoble, see Tal Bruttmann, ed., *Commission d'enquête de la ville de Grenoble sur les spoliations des biens de juifs, Persécutions et spoliations des Juifs pendant la Seconde Guerre mondiale, Résistances* (Grenoble: Presses Universitaires de Grenoble, 2004).

8. See Pim Griffioen, ed., *The Persecution of the Jews in the Netherlands, 1940–1945. New Perspectives* (Amsterdam: Vossiuspers UvA, 2012); Christina Morina, "The 'Bystander' in Recent Dutch Historiography," in *German History* 32, no. 1 (2014): 101–111.

9. Christopher R. Browning, *Remembering Survival: Inside a Nazi Slave-Labor Camp* (New York: W. W. Norton, 2010). For another example of a microhistorical study, see Christopher R. Browning, *Ordinary Men: Reserve Police Battalion 101 and the Final Solution in Poland* (New York: Harper Collins, 1992).

10. See Michał Kalisz and Elżbieta Rączy, *Dzieje społeczności żydowskiej powiatu gorlickiego podczas okupacji niemieckiej 1939–1945*, 2nd ed. (Rzeszów: IPN, 2020).

11. See, for example, Tom Lawson and Thomas Kuhne, eds., *The Holocaust and Local History: Proceedings of the First International Graduate Students' Conference on Holocaust and Genocide Studies (Strassler Family Center for Holocaust and Genocide Studies, Clark University, 23–26 April 2009)* (London: Vallentine Mitchell, 2011), esp. "Introduction," 1–12.

12. Mainly from the collection of the USC Shoah Foundation, Visual History Archive, but also USHMM, Yad Vashem, the Oral History archive of the History Meeting House, Polish Righteous—Recalling Forgotten History, and others.

13. We are indebted to many researchers who have explored and described the history of individual regions or cities: Zbigniew Romaniuk, who has written about Brańsk; Krzysztof Czubaszek, who has researched the history of Łuków; the late Jan Ziobroń, a historian of Radomyśl Wielki; Andrzej Krempa and Stanisław Wanatowicz, of Mielec; Tomasz Czapla and Ireneusz Socha, of Dębica; and Regina Smoter Grzeszkiewicz, who for many years has studied the fate of the Jews of the town of Szczebrzeszyn, Radecznica County, and other towns of the Zamość region.

14. The original Polish edition of this book also contained a chapter devoted to Miechów County, an area in southern Poland, close to Kraków.

15. The studied prewar Polish counties include Bochnia, Węgrów, Łuków, Bielsk Podlaski, and Złoczów. The *Kreishauptmannschaften* include Dębica, Biłgoraj, and Nowy Targ. While discussing the German administrative units, the authors use the German spelling of the given location (for instance, Kreishauptmannschaft Sokolow-Wengrow and not Węgrów, and Zloczow, not Złoczów).

16. With the sole exception of the Radom district, in which there were three urban counties: Częstochowa, Kielce, and Radom.

17. See *Amtliches Gemeinde und Dorfverzeichnis für das Generalgouvernement* (Krakau: Burgverlag, 1943); Max Freiherr du Prel, *Das Generalgouvernement* (Würzburg: Triltsch, 1942), chap. 1.

18. According to German estimates, in 1941 the populations of the individual districts numbered 3.7 million in the Kraków district, 2.5 million in Lublin, 2.7 million in Radom, and 3.5 million in Warsaw. See Friedrich Gollert, *Zwei Jahre Aufbauarbeit im Distrikt Warschau* (Warschau: Deutscher Osten, 1941), 35. The Galicia district, incorporated in August 1941, was home to 4.7 million residents. See Josef Bühler, ed., *Das Generalgouvernement, seine Verwaltung und seine Wirtschaft* (Krakau: Burgverlag, 1943), 30. Czesław Madajczyk estimated the combined population of the GG and *Bezirk Bialystok* to be around 18,183,000; *Polityka III Rzeszy w okupowanej Polsce* (Warszawa: PWN, 1970), esp. the chapter "Zmiany ludnościowe w czasie wojny i okupacji," 1:234–284, as well as 1:533, 631, and 2:165–176, 247, 259, 328.

19. Estimates in *The United States Holocaust Memorial Museum Encyclopedia of Camps and Ghettos 1933–1945* (hereafter *Encyclopedia*), vol. 2, ed. Martin Dean, in cooperation with Mel Hecker, *Ghettos in German—Occupied Eastern Europe*, part A (Bloomington: Indiana University Press, 2012), 858.

20. Albert Stankowski and Piotr Weiser calculated the number of Jews in the GG at about 1,990,000; "Demograficzne skutki Holokaustu," in *Następstwa zagłady Żydów. Polska 1944–2010*, ed. Feliks Tych and Monika Adamczyk-Garbowska (Lublin: Wydawnictwo UMCS, Warszawa: ŻIH, 2011), 19. In addition, around 150,000 lived in *Bezirk Bialystok* (see *Encyclopedia*, 858), for a total

of around 2,140,000. These are merely estimates, as it is not possible to unambiguously calculate demographic data under the dynamic conditions that existed during a time in which resettlements of Jews between various parts of the occupied country were being carried out by the Germans, Jews were escaping from their towns (sometimes to the East), and most important they were dying of starvation, disease, and exhaustion in the ghettos and labor camps or were being executed. In March 1943, the Germans conducted a census that showed the population of the GG to be 14.9 million or 15.8 together with *Bezirk Bialystok*. A comparison with the earlier data (18.1 million) shows a decrease in population of 2.3 million. The number of Jews murdered and in hiding most likely lies between these two estimates; we estimated their number to be approximately 2.2 million.

21. See Browning, *Ordinary Men*; Raul Hilberg, *Perpetrators, Victims, Bystanders: The Jewish Catastrophe 1933–1945* (New York: Aaron Asher, 1992).

22. With the exception of Prużana, from where the Jews were deported to Auschwitz-Birkenau in January 1943.

23. It is not possible to list all of the publications on German perpetrators. Among the more recently published monographies are Wolfgang Curilla, *Der Judenmord in Polen und die deutsche Ordnungspolizei 1939–1945* (Paderborn: Schöningh, 2011); Stefan Klemp, *Vernichtung: Die deutsche Ordnungspolizei und der Judenmord im Warschauer Ghetto 1940–43* (Münster: Prospero, 2013); Frank Bajohr and Dieter Pohl, *Massenmord und schlechtes Gewissen: Die deutsche Bevölkerung, die NS Führung und der Holocaust (Die Zeit des Nationalsozialismus)* (Frankfurt am Main: S. Fischer Verlag, 2008); Thomas Sandkühler, *"Endlösung" in Galizien: Der Judenmord in Ostpolen und die Rettungsinitiativen von Berthold Beitz 1941–1944* (Bonn: J. H. W. Dietz Verlag, 1996); Rupert Butler, *The Gestapo: A History of Hitler's Secret Police,1933–45* (London: Amber, 2015); and Waitman Wade Beorn, *Marching into Darkness: The Wehrmacht and the Holocaust in Belarus* (Cambridge, MA: Harvard University Press, 2014).

24. The first book that dealt with this subject was the study by Tadeusz Markiel and Alina Skibińska, *"Jakie to ma znaczenie, czy zrobili to z chciwości?" Zagłada domu Trynczerów* (Warszawa: Stowarzyszenie Centrum Badań nad Zagładą Żydów, 2011). Jan Grabowski and Dariusz Libionka gave a preliminary account of the complicity of Polish firefighters in the murders of Jews in Subcarpathia, in the village of Markowa and its vicinity, in "Distorting and Rewriting the History of the Holocaust in Poland: The Case of the Ulma Family Museum of Poles Saving Jews During World War II in Markowa," *Yad Vashem Studies* 45, no. 1 (2017): 29–60. Jan Grabowski and Dariusz Libionka, "Bezdroża polityki historycznej. Wokół Markowej, czyli o czym nie mówi Muzeum Polaków Ratujących Żydów podczas II Wojny Światowej im. Rodziny Ulmów," *Zagłada Żydów. Studia i Materiały* no. 12: 617–641.

25. Shmuel Spector, "The Jews of Volhynia and their Reaction to Extermination," *Yad Vashem Studies* 15 (1983): 167.

26. See Guy Miron and Shlomit Shulhani, eds., *The Yad Vashem Encyclopedia of the Ghettos during the Holocaust* (Jerusalem: Yad Vashem, 2009).

27. See Grzegorz Berendt, "Żydzi zbiegli z gett i obozów śmierci", in Adam Sitarek, Michał Trębacz, and Ewa Wiatr, eds., *Zagłada Żydów na polskiej prowincji* (Łódź: IPN and Wydawnictwo Łódzkie, 2012), 121–158.

28. Not counting the Jews of the territories annexed to the Reich.

29. His estimate was based on a survey of Magistrates Courts, thousands of Jewish accounts, and books of remembrance [*Izkorbuch*]. See Shmuel Krakowski, "The Attitude of the Polish Underground to the Jewish Question During the Second World War," in *Contested Memories. Poles and Jews During Holocaust and Its Aftermath*, ed. Joshua D. Zimmerman (London: Rutgers University Press, 2002), 100. The IPN (Institute of National Remembrance) historians provided the same figure: "Only 300,000 of the 3 million Jewish population risked escape from the points designated by the Germans." "Polacy ratujący Żydów w latach II wojny światowej," in *Teki Edukacyjne IPN*, ed. Kamila Sachnowska et al. (Warszawa: IPN, 2008), 7.

30. Szymon Datner, "Zbrodnie hitlerowskie na Żydach zbiegłych z gett. Groźby i zarządzenia "prawne" w stosunku do Żydów oraz udzielających im pomocy Polaków," in: *Biuletyn ŻIH* 75, no. 3 (1970): 28–29; Interview with Szymon Datner, in Małgorzata Niezabitowska, *Ostatni współcześni Żydzi polscy* (Warszawa: Wydawnictwa Artystyczne i Filmowe, 1993), 150.

31. The estimated numbers of Jews who survived in occupied Poland (among Poles, in partisan units, or in the forests) are varied; some historians estimated their number at 80,000–120,000 (Stankowski and Weiser, *Demograficzne skutki Holokaustu*, 31); Shmuel Krakowski stated (after Lucjan Dobroszycki) that 30,000 Jews had survived in the Polish territories; Krakowski, *Attitude of the Polish Underground to the Jewish Question*, 104. According to Michał Borwicz, they numbered 40,000–50,000; Czesław Pilichowski, ed., *Eksterminacja Żydów w Polsce* in *Ekspertyzy i orzeczenia przed Najwyższym Trybunałem Narodowym* (Warszawa: Ministerstwo Sprawiedliwości, Główna Komisja Badania Zbrodni Hitlerowskich, 1981), 8:123. According to Czesław Łuczak, it was 100,000 Łuczak, *Polska i Polacy w drugiej wojnie światowej* (Poznań: Wydawnictwo UAM, 1993), 128. Borwicz's and Łuczak's estimates cited after Piotr Eberhardt, *Przemieszczenia ludności na terytorium Polski spowodowane II wojną światową* (Warszawa: Instytut Geografii i Przestrzennego Zagospodarowania PAN, 2000). Teresa Prekerowa estimated that 30,000–60,000 Jews had survived among Poles, 20,000–40,000 in the camps, 10,000–15,000 among partisans and in the forests; Prekerowa, "Wojna i okupacja," in *Najnowsze dzieje Żydów w Polsce w zarysie (do 1950 roku)*, ed. Jerzy Tomaszewski (Warszawa:

Wydawnictwo Naukowe PWN, 1993), 384. All these figures are estimated, based mainly on the survivor registers maintained by the CKŻP; however, many Jews did not register and others registered multiple times, so determining more accurate numbers, if it is possible at all, would require further research.

32. As table 2 shows, the mean (9 percent) diverges only slightly from the median.

33. Similar estimates have been produced for Dąbrowa Tarnowska County (which has been researched earlier), where some 11 percent of Jews went into hiding.

34. Shmuel Krakowski points out that the largest number of the Righteous Among the Nations lived in Galicia, and the people of Galicia helped Jews more willingly than those in central Poland: "We have to stress here that in the region of prewar southeastern Poland, the Polish population was confronted with the enmity of Ukrainian nationalists and it was much more difficult and dangerous for them to shelter Jews." Krakowski, *Attitude of the Polish Underground to the Jewish Question*, 102.

35. Data indicates 44.6 percent of the Jews who survived in Węgrów County used this strategy, 15.7 percent in Biłgoraj County, 8 percent in Bochnia, 5 percent in Łuków, 3.4 percent in Nowy Targ, and 2.2 percent in Złoczów.

36. In percentage terms, the survival rate among the Jews who followed this strategy was highest for the counties of Dębica (44 percent), Bielsk (25.4 percent), Węgrów (23 percent), and Łuków (25 percent), and the lowest percentages were Biłgoraj (6.1 percent) and Złoczów (1.1 percent) Counties.

37. The effectiveness of this survival strategy in the individual counties was as follows: It was most effective in the counties of Biłgoraj (31 percent of the survivors hid in the forest), Dębica (30%), Bielsk (16 percent), and Złoczów (24.6 percent). The strategy proved to be the least effective in the counties of Łuków (2.5 percent), Węgrów (3 percent), and Nowy Targ (4.3 percent).

38. Martin Dean conducted pioneering and noteworthy research on this topic. Dean, "Strategies for Jewish Survival in Ghettos and Forced Labor Camps," in *Holocaust Resistance in Europe and America*, ed. Victoria Khiterer (Newcastle upon Tyne: Cambridge Scholars, 2017), 38–50.

39. The population of *Kreishauptmannschaft* Bielsk Podlaski consisted partly of Belarusians, while part of Złoczów County's population consisted of Ukrainians. Even in cases when sources confirm that neighbors denounced Jews, we still might not know their nationality.

40. Yad Vashem awarded titles of Righteous Among the Nations to 18 families (51 persons) from Bielsk County, 13 families (26 persons) in Biłgoraj County, 61 persons (20 families and 8 single persons) in Bochnia County, 103 persons in Dębica County, 9 families (21 persons) in Nowy Targ County, 10

families and 4 persons in Łuków County, 51 persons in Węgrów County, and 40 persons in Złoczów County.

41. In Bielsk County, five persons were killed in retaliation for helping Jews; in Biłgoraj County, thirteen Poles were murdered, and another three were sent to camps and their possessions were confiscated; in Dębica County, five villages were raided, twenty-four Poles were executed, and two died in camps; fifteen person died in camps or were shot to death in Nowy Targ County, and at least twelve Poles were murdered in Węgrów County; in Złoczów County, at least nine Poles were shot for aiding Jews, while one Ukrainian and six families were probably arrested.

We are very grateful to Yad Vashem Publications and Indiana University Press for their firm commitment to this project. We also want to recognize the hard work of our translators and editors and all those who put countless hours into making this edition possible. Finally, we would like to express our gratitude to all people of goodwill who, along the way, offered us support and encouragement.

NIGHT WITHOUT END

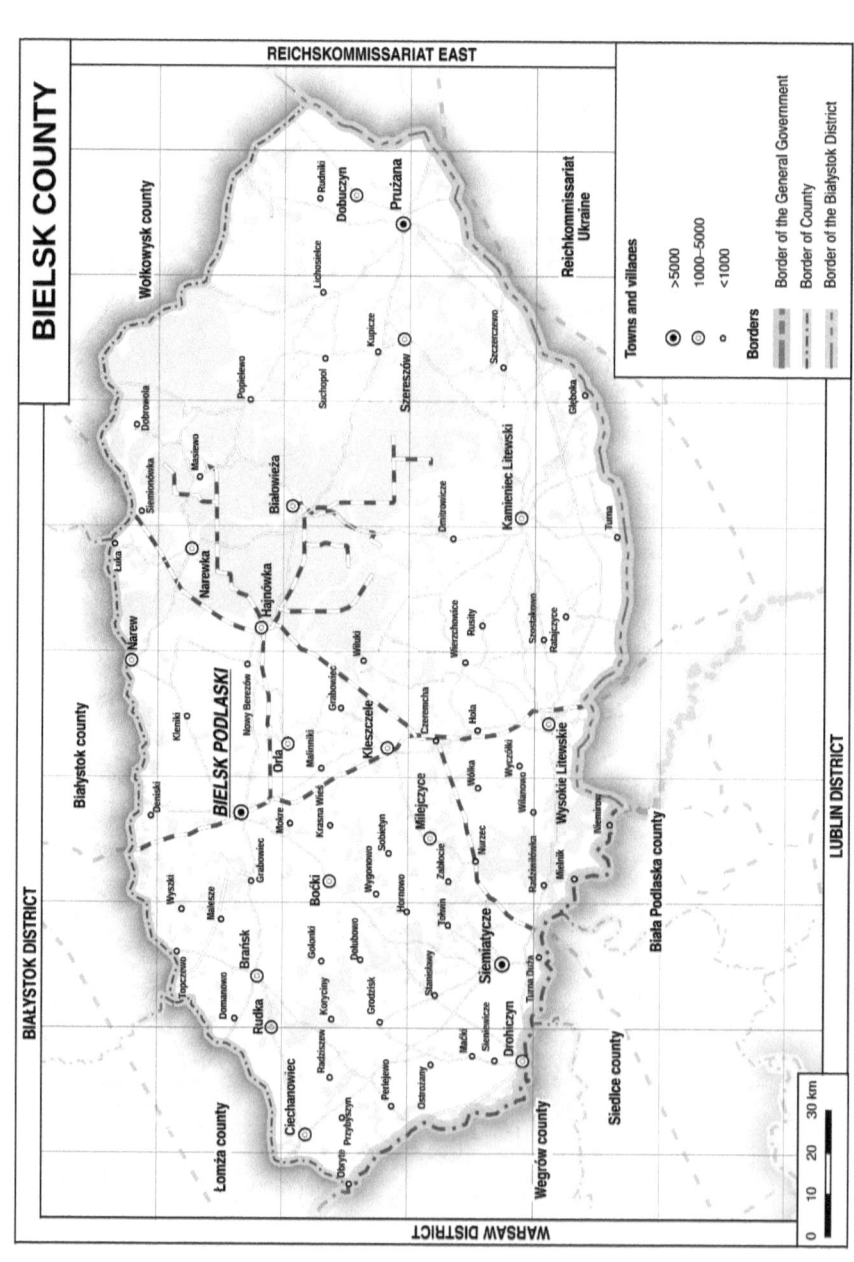

ONE

JEWS IN BIELSK PODLASKI COUNTY, 1939–1945

BARBARA ENGELKING

PREWAR

Over the centuries, Bielsk County was a melting pot of intermingled and competing Polish, Russian, and Lithuanian influences. In the late sixteenth century, the settlement of the *szlachta drobna* (petty nobility) began there, encouraged by Mazovia dukes seeking to colonize the East Mazovia and Podlasie regions. Before long, Lithuanian dukes began colonization of the land from the east, settling peasants of Russian origin there. These types of settlements, combined with invasions, wars, and the repeated redrawing of borders, shaped a unique social and national structure of the region: Polish, Roman Catholics, and impoverished nobility dwelled in *zaścianek* (petty-nobility villages) in the western part of the county while peasant villages of the Orthodox and Uniate rural population (Russian and Belorussian) occupied its eastern territory. In the interwar period, Jews, who had settled in the county towns since the fifteenth century, made up about 50 percent of the towns' population.

The private and social life of the Jews dwelling in shtetls of a few thousand inhabitants followed a rhythm determined by tradition; their economic survival relied on trade, crafts, and services. There were no large cities in Bielsk County, which remained scarcely urbanized and economically poor. Podlasie was an area of poverty, and Bielsk itself was called *zajdene torbes* (silk valises): "All the worries of the town, all its local activities were framed by poverty. It was a town without industry, without sources of income . . . it was normal in Bielsk that people were simultaneously poor and highly respected. There was poverty, but not grinding poverty. People did not feel they were poor. Although they did not have enough to buy even herring... Jews lived off each other. And off trade with local *goyim*."[1]

The processes of modernization and emancipation of the Jews accelerated after Poland had regained its independence in 1918. Despite the increase in discrimination over the years, Jewish social, political, and cultural life flourished. Thriving youth organizations and movements, together with political parties expressing all kinds of views, provided reinforcement for emancipation tendencies and spurred changes in the traditional structure and functions of the shtetl. Jewish schools operated in towns, as did theatrical groups, orchestras, choirs, sports clubs, libraries, and more.

Podlasie, like the rest of the country in the second half of the 1930s, witnessed the rise of antisemitic sentiments. In Bielsk County, however—unlike in the neighboring counties of Łomża and Wysokie Mazowieckie—the influence of the *Narodowa Demokracja, Endecja* (National Democrats) was limited. In fact, it was only noticeable in the western, predominantly Catholic part of the county.[2] The difficult economic situation, modernization, and secularization processes led to a mounting crisis for the Jewish community and a rising tension between generations. A shtetl that until then was insulated from changes by the system of norms became the stage for rapid transformation. The outbreak of World War II compelled the shtetl community—torn by internal processes and numerous crises—to face new challenges.

There were nine cities and nineteen communes in Bielsk County before World War II, with a total population about 200,000 inhabitants.[3] During the German occupation, twelve communes with some 50,000 dwellers were also incorporated into the county.[4] Considering the population growth, escapes, and resettlements, the estimated number of Jews residing in the territory of Bielsk County at that time reached 40,000.[5]

UNDER SOVIET OCCUPATION

In September 1939, the Germans entered the territory of Bielsk County for a short period of time, giving the Jews a foretaste of what was to come. "Fear reigned, Jewish houses were robbed."[6] When the Germans had withdrawn after a dozen or so days due to the border regulation agreement with the Union of Soviet Socialist Republics (USSR), they were replaced with the Soviet army. The change of the occupying power came as a relief for Jews. It was believed the threat of physical violence, persecution, and terror that the Nazi occupation would have brought was being replaced by a political system promising equality and the absence of antisemitism, even if only in theory.

Often, it happened that the contentment that accompanied a change in the occupying force manifested itself in an enthusiastic welcome of the entering Red Army. Mosze Kleinbaum, chairman of the Zionist Federation in Poland, who found himself as a soldier in Poland's *kresy* (eastern borderlands) in the fall of 1939, wrote in his report to the Executive Committee of the World Jewish Congress: "Ukrainian peasants... and young Jewish Communists... applauded and hailed the Army with friendly greetings. The number of Jewish enthusiasts was not very large, but they made more noise than all the others that day. This created the false impression that the Jews were the chief hosts at this festival."[7] Such behavior on the part of the Jewish community set the tone for Polish-Jewish relations during the war, provided fuel to the accusations of all the Jews of being enthusiastic toward the invader, and later transformed into a stereotype, a convenient pretext to hostility, and retaliation.

After the rigged election of November 2, 1939, the USSR's borders moved westward, swallowing more than half of the lands of the Second Polish Republic. Prewar Bielsk County, divided between Brest and Bialystok oblasts, became part of so-called Western Belorussia.[8] Between 100,000 and 150,000 escapees, predominantly Jews, fled the German occupation for Polish land under Soviet occupation.[9] Before the outbreak of the war, there had been about 4,000 Jews residing in Bielsk Podlaski alone; this number was probably increased by more than 1,000 refugees with the onset of the occupation.[10] Around 80,000 Jews were among the 320,000 Polish citizens transported into the interior of the USSR in four deportations. Lack of detailed data, however, makes it impossible to confirm these numbers and determine the number of Jews—both refugees and permanent residents of Bielsk County—who were deported or conscripted into the Red Army.[11]

The Jewish community (and Polish likewise) underwent disintegration: the elites had been decimated, and political leaders and activists were arrested or deported, along with local luminaries or those who were simply more affluent. Sometimes this occurred with the participation of resident supporters of the new order: "The local communists, like Lejbke Katz, Lejzer Doliński, Józef Wolfson, Józef Kupczyk... and other prominent members of the party, eagerly took up positions under the new rule. They knew everybody, and knew perfectly well whom to oppress and persecute."[12] Nonetheless, a very few local Jews found positions within the new system of power; the Soviets had more confidence in their own apparatchiks, and it was they who formed the core of the new regime.

Among the lasting miseries of the Soviet system were shortages of basic foodstuffs and clothing, together with forced lodging of Soviet officials, repressions, and a constant threat by the secret police—NKVD—of surveillance, denunciations, and arrests.[13] Saturday was no longer a day of rest, and Jewish communities suffered a deprivation of income that undermined the existence of all institution funded by them, such as synagogues, prayer houses, schools, orphanages, and nursing homes. Jewish and Hebrew schools changed their character, the teaching of Russian was mandatory, and almost all of the Jewish children joined (or were made to join) the Pioneers (the Communist Scout organization). All of this hit the Jews' traditional lifestyle hard, leading to its destruction. The disintegration of the social infrastructure was accompanied by widespread ownership transformation. Small-shop owners and merchants—members of "the owning class"—became numbered among "ideological enemies of the system." As part of the nationalization process—which did not spare any national groups—Jews were dispossessed of their factories, workshops, and stores, which were in turn transformed into cooperatives, following the Russian pattern. Those who displayed no desire to join the cooperatives were subjected to high taxes, and some of them were arrested.

Most Jews became quickly disillusioned with the Communist system; "the great disappointment had come in the first few days and weeks—80 percent of Jews think like this."[14] Nonetheless, there were others—especially young Jews and Belorussians—whom the new system attracted, for it opened up to all national minorities possibilities of advancement that had been closed to them. "Sovietization, for them, meant an escape from life on the margins [of society] and a chance to take advantage of various opportunities offered by the modern Soviet state."[15] Now, they were equal citizens and could find employment in earlier inaccessible professions, such as public administration.

While Jews might have had a partly ambivalent attitude toward the Soviet occupation, for Poles, the Soviet Union's attack on Poland on September 17, 1939, was disastrous. A dozen or so Polish partisan groups had sprung up in the Białystok region. They were made up mainly of military units that had been dispersed during the September campaign. These groups had managed to operate there until June 1940, when they were defeated by the NKVD (People's Commissariat for Internal Affairs). In May 1940, emissaries from Warsaw arrived in the region tasked with setting up the ZWZ (*Związek Walki Zbrojnej*, Union of Armed Struggle), the underground organization that was to consolidate the spontaneously emerging resistance groups. In late November 1940, Lieutenant Colonel Władysław "Mścisław" Liniarski assumed command of the ZWZ Białystok District (which he kept until January 1945). But despite many efforts, the attempt to organize a large-scale, cohesive underground structure had failed: "There were repeated arrests, [our] newly woven 'underground webs' snapped again and again," recollected his adjutant.[16] Next, three former commanders of the district and several dozen commanding officers of various ranks,

Figure 1.1. Destroyed monument of Lenin in Bielsk Podlaski.

as well as many ordinary members, were arrested by the NKVD. The range of activities of the Polish underground in the Białystok region remained limited—*primarily focused* on keeping communication channels open, propaganda, and intelligence operations.

―⁂―

Soviet rule ended as suddenly as it began, and after twenty-one months, Bielsk County returned to German rule for the next three years. A certain number of Jews (it is impossible to know exactly how many) decided to flee to the east along with the retreating Red Army, while others were evacuated, together with their factories and work places. The Soviet authorities left behind a land thrown into chaos, and its inhabitants were tired, insecure, and confused. They also abandoned some symbols of freedom and the new, happy days that had been brought to the inhabitants of the Bielsk region along with the new system: monuments to Lenin in the central spots of the towns of Brańsk, Bielsk Podlaski, Siemiatycze, and Ciechanowiec. As for the Jews—who had suffered many months of uncertainty and fear, threats of deportations and arrests, daily struggles, and aggressive propaganda—they faced the upcoming events divided, physically and spiritually exhausted, and devoid of leadership.

UNDER GERMAN OCCUPATION

Operation Barbarossa, the Third Reich's invasion of the Soviet Union, commenced on June 22, 1941. The German army swiftly moved east, and in six days the whole of Bielsk County found itself under German occupation. The German Army Group Centre (Heeresgruppe Mitte) was followed by *Einsatzgruppe* B, one of four squads of the special task forces of the Security Police and Security Service (SD)[17] formed shortly before the invasion for "tracking down and eliminating hostile intents towards the Third Reich."[18] Actually, *Einsatzkommandos* carried out killing *Aktionen* in the occupied territories. Persons "to eliminate" were selected from among the civilian population—Soviet soldiers who had not managed to escape, local officials, Communist activists, and also Jews (at the beginning, mainly men). At least 281 people were murdered in more than a dozen executions that took place in Bielsk County in June and July of 1941.[19]

In the summer of 1941, several antisemitic riots broke out in towns and villages in the western part of the county. They were not as bloody as those in neighboring Łomża County (there were no fatalities in Bielsk, Brańsk, or Ciechanowiec), but here Jews were also forced to remove the symbols of the recently defeated Soviet power—the monuments to Lenin. They were ordered to break the monuments apart "into small pieces, so everyone would get a piece. Then, [the Jews] were placed in rows and ordered to march with great 'pomp' around the whole town, singing and shouting out, for example: 'Down with Lenin!' 'Down with the Soviets!' and so on. Then they reached the river, into which all of the pieces of the shattered monument were thrown."[20] In Siemiatycze, however, the events took a bloody turn. On July 10, after a few days of mounting tension, "Poles, on their own initiative, gathered all Jews ... and ordered them to dismantle a monument of Lenin. The Jews had to wrap the dismantled pieces up in sheets and carry them to the cemetery, where they were forced to shout out loud. The road to the cemetery led past the river, and when the Jews were crossing the bridge, they were pushed off of it into water. In the process of throwing the Jews off the bridge, one Jew died when his head struck a pillar of the bridge."[21]

The causes and motives of the anti-Jewish riots in the southwestern part of Bielsk County were similar to those known in other places: prewar antisemitism, amplified by the stereotypes and experiences of the Soviet occupation, and resentments that surfaced during the chaotic period of the change of power that became reinforced by a sense of impunity and encouragement on the part of the Germans.[22]

The German Administration in Bezirk Białystok and Bielsk Podlaski

On June 22, 1941, the Germans established the Białystok District in the newly seized Polish land, thereby replacing military occupation forces with a civil administration. The administration was headed by Erich Koch, Gauleiter and *Oberpräsident* (higher president) of East Prussia, who reported directly to Adolf Hitler.[23] Waldemar Magunia became Koch's deputy, residing permanently in Białystok; he was succeeded by Dr. Friedrich Brix on February 1, 1942. Despite the union and shared security apparatus with East Prussia, the Białystok District was not incorporated into it but became a *Regierungsbezirk* (administrative district). The district, with its population in excess of 1.5 million, was divided into eight *Kreisskommissariat* (counties, *powiat*), and Bielsk Podlaski County (with a territory of about ten thousand square kilometers) was the largest of them. A few communes of Prużana County (together with the town of Prużana) and of Brześć County (prewar Polesie Voivodeship) were incorporated into it. The entire Białowieża Forestry (containing the communes of Białowieża, Suchpol, and Szereszów) passed into Third Reich ownership.[24] The Białowieża Forest obtained a special status: at the request of Hermann Göring, the Reich "Master of the Hunt," it was transformed into a state-owned game reserve and came under his direct care. The residents of nearby villages were relocated.[25]

Heinrich von Bünau was appointed Bielsk Podlaski, *Kreis Kommissar* (county commissar, *Landrat*) in August 1941; he was followed by Walter Tubenthal, who held this position from February 1942 until the end of the occupation.[26] In *Bezirk Białystok*, the county authorities—*Kreis* and *Amtskommissariats*—assumed responsibility for establishing ghettos, housing problems, provisions, employment, and the health of the Jewish population.[27]

The offices of the State Police in the city of Olsztyn and the Criminal Police in the city of Królewiec (Königsberg) established their branches in Białystok. In April 1942, an independent office of the *Kommandeur der Sicherheitspolizei und des SD für den Bezirk Białystok* (Commander of the Security Police and Security Service for the Białystrok District, KdS), was set up in Białystok; it also had a branch in Bielsk Podlaski. One of the departments of the KdS was in charge of Jewish affairs (Gestapo IV B *Judenangelegenheiten*). *Obersturmführer* SS Schröder became the head of the Bielsk branch of the Gestapo.[28]

The Order Police came under the civil administration and consisted of the gendarmerie and the Schupo (State protection police, *Schutzpolizeidienstabteilungen*) responsible for, among other things, guarding ghettos. In addition, various special agencies[29] were active in the territory of the district, among them detachments of the border and customs guards with the duty of safeguarding the General Government (GG) border.

In the GG, the Schupo was assigned to the cities, while the gendarmerie carried out its activity in the countryside. The Białystok District was different in this respect. First, the Polish (so-called Blue) police were never established there.[30] Second, the structure and objectives of the police forces were shaped to resemble those adopted in Królewiec and East Prussia, rather than those in Kraków and the GG. Third, the scope of responsibilities of both the police and gendarmerie was to a great extent the same; even their offices were often located in the same building. The authors of testimonies often tended to confuse gendarmes with *schutzmen*.[31] The name *Schutzpolizei* was applied inconsistently, while the words *Schupo* and *schutzmen* (*szucmani*) were in widespread use. The Schupo itself was frequently mixed up with the gendarmerie, and—adding further still to the confusion—the Schupo in *Bezirk Białystok* recruited locals, Catholics and Orthodox, to serve alongside the Germans.

The chief of the Schupo in Bielsk Podlaski was Franz Lampe; the chief of the gendarmerie was first Klein and then Ulrich Renner. Renner testified during his trial that "there were 420 gendarmes under his command between November 1942 and July 1944; among them were also Polish auxiliary policemen, who were allocated among 30 police stations."[32] From information on thirty-three police stations and several dozen Polish citizens who had served there, it seems that at least forty-six policemen from Bielsk County were sentenced to imprisonment

Figure 1.2. Officers of Schutzpolizei detachment standing in Siemiatycze in front of the police station located in the former house of Dawid Muzykant, Placowa Street. Antoni Nowicki.

after the war. Polish prosecutor's offices also investigated former German gendarmes and policemen and sought extradition of several dozen of them; nonetheless, none of them have ever been located (maybe all of them had already died), so none were brought to justice. Only their Polish subordinates have been punished. As they testified after the war, they had mostly joined the police under pressure[33] or out of poverty.[34] Their job was mainly to search villages for moonshiners,[35] to hunt partisans and escaped Soviet prisoners of war (POWs), and to make rounds in response to various tips[36]—very often concerning Jews in hiding. Policemen and gendarmes carried out these operations jointly with the Germans in command.

Polish and Soviet Partisans in Bielsk County

The Bielsk Podlaski district of the Home Army (AK) came under the Białystok. The AK was the largest underground organization in this area.[37] In June 1944, most of the other organizations, including their local chapters, decided to join forces and team up with the AK. The strategic goal of the AK operating in the region—as was the case in all of occupied Poland—was to prepare Operation

Tempest, a general uprising against the Germans that was supposed to be launched before the arrival of the Red Army. Toward this goal, the AK carried out various intelligence, propaganda, subversion, and sabotage actions. As a part of its subversion activities, the underground resistance liquidated Polish traitors, collaborators, henchmen of the Germans, informers of the Gestapo, and Communist agents.[38] The next wave of the Polish partisan movement began to form in the Białystok region in the second half of 1942.[39] There were more than "a dozen partisan groups (220 men in total) by the end of 1943, and by June of the following year, before Operation Tempest was launched in this territory, the units had already numbered about 2,000 partisans."[40] The AK was strong in the areas east and north of Bielsk Podlaski, mostly in the Wilno and Nowogródek regions; in the Białystok region, the partisan movement was particularly active near Łomża, Suwałki, Augustów, and Grajewo.

Early Soviet partisan groups in the Polish lands under German occupation comprised deserters, *okrużeńcy* (soldiers from defeated units of the Red Army) trapped behind enemy lines, and POWs[41] who had managed to flee German camps where the living conditions were inhumane.[42] The first spontaneously formed groups were driven by self-preservation and were unable to undertake regular partisan activities. Some of them turned into criminal bands that plagued the area. Only a few units made it through the first winter; most of them dissolved. The situation took a turn for the better in the second half of 1942, when the *Centralna Szkoła Przygotowania Kadr Partyzanckich* (Central Training School for the Partisan Cadres) was set up in the USSR to prepare commanders and chiefs of staff for partisan units, as well as instructors and special tasks operatives. As a result, the partisan movement was strengthened and provided with more arms. It became politicized, better trained, and more disciplined, and an effort was made to fight internal banditry and terrorism—all of which together helped the movement gain strength during 1943.

Jewish Life under German Occupation

The German authorities soon introduced the new rules of life under the occupation, among them special anti-Jewish regulations. One of the earliest of these regulations required Jews to wear identifying markings: At first, they were ordered to wear armbands like the Jews in the GG, and later the marking was changed. Order No. 14 of July 21, 1941, which can be found in the Ordinance Book of the Mayor of the Town of Brańsk and which came into force "with immediate effect," states, "All the Jews of the town Brańsk and its vicinity must replace [their] armbands with a patch of the Star of Zion, 10 cm in diameter, stitched to outerwear. . . . To be implemented by 5 a.m. on July 22, 1941."[43]

The Germans also imposed heavy "forced contributions" on the Jews, deciding amounts freely and demanding to be paid repeatedly—for example, twice in Bielsk Podlaski[44] and three times in Prużana.[45] Often they collected them under threat of mass murder. *Judenrate* (Jewish councils) were established in all communes of Bielsk County. They comprised twelve to twenty-four members and were subordinate to the civil administration (as well as to the police departments under its authority—the gendarmerie and the Schupo). In November 1942, however, when the resettlements started, the KdS assumed control of the *Judenrate*.[46] Until that time, the *Judenrate* administered the *gmin żydowskich* (day-to-day affairs of Jewish communities). At least, this was the case in theory: the *Judenrate* in Bielsk County—as with *Judenrate* everywhere—had to carry out German orders first and foremost. The Jews showed understanding for the thankless role the *Judenrate* had to play and appreciated their efforts. "The *Judenrat's* activity [in Pużana] was generally positive. They paid ransoms for the Jews who had been arrested by the Germans. They purchased products from local peasants and distributed them among Jews, who were confined to the ghetto."[47] The Jewish police was set up at the same time that the *Judenrate* were formed, but the attitude towards the police was not as positive. "Among their ranks were bastards—sons-of-bitches.... They only wanted to save their own skin, but not one of them survived."[48]

The Germans established fifteen ghettos in the territory of the county. Table 1.1 shows the summary data.

The ghetto usually comprised several streets designated for Jews; they were most often surrounded by a wooden or barbed-wire fence with a guarded entrance. The living conditions in the Jewish districts were harsh and continuously deteriorating: "Everyone struggled to survive by any means possible.... Most of the Jews lived in destitution and grinding poverty."[49] Small ghettos, however, did not experience mass starvation. Smuggling food into the ghetto was easier here than in big cities due to the less anonymous nature of social ties: Jewish artisans and shopkeepers knew neighboring villages well and, moreover, had many acquaintances and former customers among the local residents. Rubin Rosenthal recalls that he used to make the rounds of villages in the Ciechanów vicinity. He was equipped with a false certificate obtained from a Polish acquaintance, and he purchased food that he later smuggled into the ghetto.[50] Leaving the ghetto, however, required some courage: if caught outside, Jews faced punishment. It could and did happen that a hunt for food cost one one's life.[51]

From the very beginning, the Jews in Bielsk County, like Jews everywhere in occupied Poland, were rounded up on the streets and forced to perform various work, which usually also resulted in humiliation and beating. When

Table 1.1 Bielsk County: number of Jews, ghettos, and members of *Judenrate*.

Town	Number of Jews (estimated)	Ghetto	Judenrat	Fate of Jews
Bielsk Podlaski	5,000*	From July 1941; one ghetto, the first one in the county	Szlomo Epstein (chairman), Ajzensztat, Jakow Galant, Kalman Frejdkies, Chaim Abramowicz, Mendel Bekerman, Grajewer, Jakow Elberg, Jakow Sznajder, Lipa Słochowski, Mosze Sztern	200 working Jews sent to the Białystok ghetto (November 6, 1942), the rest (along with the deported) sent to Treblinka (November 2–15, 1942)
Boćki	600–750	From March to June 1942; two ghettos	Rabbi Szlomo Zimny	Sent to the Bielsk ghetto (November 2, 1942), and from there to Treblinka. A dozen or so (?) artisans returned to Boćki; then they were sent to the Białystok ghetto (December 1942) and finally to Auschwitz (January 1943)
Brańsk	2,400	From April 1942; two ghettos	Alter Jamsin, Mojsze Tykoćkin	Sent to the Bielsk ghetto (November 5 and 7, 1942) and from there to Treblinka
Ciechanowiec	4,000	From fall 1941	Efraim Wiener	About 240 Jews were murdered during the liquidation of the camp in Pobikry. The rest were taken to the railroad station in Czyżew, and from there to Treblinka

Drohiczyn	1,500	From April 1942; two ghettos	Łazarz Reznik, Abraham Reznik, Fiszel Gruda	Sent to the Siemiatycze ghetto (November 5, 1942) and from there to Treblinka
Grodzisk	40	From May 1942; all Jews on one property		Sent to the Siemiatycze ghetto (late October 1942) and from there to Treblinka (November 1942)
Kamieniec Litewski	approx. 5,000	From January 1942	Szlomo Mandelbrat	2,500 Jews were resettled to Prużana (August 1941), the rest sent to Wysokie Litewskie (November 2, 1942) to Treblinka
Kleszczele	750	From May 1942; partially enclosed ghetto	Bunim Weiner (Weiman?)	Sent to the Bielsk ghetto (November 5, 1942) and from there to Treblinka
Mielnik	400			Sent to the Siemiatycze ghetto (November 2, 1942) and from there to Treblinka
Milejczyce (where Jews of Nurzec were relocated)	1,000	From spring 1942		Sent to the Kleszczele ghetto (November 5, 1942), from there to the Bielsk ghetto and Treblinka (November 4 or 5, 1942)
Narew	300	For working men; the others were sent to Prużana in October 1941		Sent to the Bielsk ghetto (November 4, 1942)
Orla	1,450	From March 20 to April 1942; two ghettos		Sent to the Bielsk ghetto (November 2, 1942) and from there to Treblinka.

continued

Table 1.1 continued

Town	Number of Jews (estimated)	Ghetto	Judenrat	Fate of Jews
Prużana†	9,000 plus the resettled, in total 10,000	From August 1941; thousands Jews from the Białystok vicinity	24 *Judenrat* members, e.g., Janowicz, Goldberg, Breskin, Chajkin	The final liquidation and transportation to Auschwitz (January 28–February 2, 1943)
Siemiatycze	5,000–6,000	From August 1942‡	Izrael Rosencwajg	Sent to Treblinka (November 2–15, 1942)
Wysokie Litewskie	2,500	From August 1941, open; enclosed in the spring of 1942		Sent to Treblinka (November 2, 1942)

TOTAL: about 40,000; in the "Polish" part of county, 22,500§

Source: *Encyclopedia of Camps and Ghettos*; testimonies from AŻIH and YVA; memorial books.

Notes:

* As estimates of the Jewish population in Bielsk County range from 3,000 to 6,000, I have taken 5,000 (indicated most frequently). See Martin Dean and Mel Hecker, eds., *Encyclopedia of Camps and Ghettos 1933–1945* [hereafter *Encyclopedia*], vol. 2, *Ghettos in German-Occupied Eastern Europe*, parts A and B (Bloomington: Indiana University Press, 2012), 871.

† Most of the 2,000 Jews from Białystok who had been resettled in Prużana escaped back to the Białystok ghetto; many others died of disease or starvation. In November 1942, the Germans registered 9,976 persons in Prużana (*Encyclopedia*, 940).

‡ It was formed on the block between Górna, Wysoka, Słowiczyńska and Koszarowa Streets, and it was enclosed by a high barbwire fence. See Waldemar Monkiewicz, "Zbrodnie hitlerowskie w Siemiatyczach w okresie II wojny światowej, in "Studia i materiały do dziejów Siemiatycz," ed. Henryk Majecki (Warsaw, 1989), 164.

§ For my further calculations, I have taken into account the following data: a total of about 40,000 Jews in the entire Bielsk County, and 22,500 in the area that became part of the Polish territory after the war.

Figure 1.3. Siemiatycze Jews work under German supervision to remove the rubble form the site of the city hall. Antoni Nowicki.

compulsory labor was officially introduced for men aged eighteen to sixty, the Jews performed a variety of tasks: they were "cleaning streets or constructing barracks,"[52] working "at the train station seven kilometers outside the city, clearing [rubble] of the town hall destroyed during the air strike,"[53] dismantling *matzevahs* [tombstones] in the cemetery,[54] and working "at the aerodrome, on roads, and on farms appropriated by the Germans."[55] Nevertheless, the forced labor offered certain advantages too. Some "thanked God that they could go to work. Because [when leaving the ghetto] they could buy a bottle of milk, a piece of bread—otherwise one was not able to feed oneself. One met Christians, bartered some things, a pair of boots, a piece of cloth for a bottle of milk, a piece of bread. These were brought into the ghetto. In that way, one brought a little food for small babies, women, and men."[56] The Jews of Prużana, who performed forced labor in ex-Soviet armories, began to smuggle out guns and grandees and considered joining the partisan movement.[57] The most active resistance in Bielsk County operated in the Prużana ghetto beginning in 1942. Its leaders worked with young people and wanted to resist the liquidation of the ghetto. They came up with a plan to set fire to the ghetto, enabling as many Jews as possible to break out and retreat to the forest. Unfortunately, they were not able to put this plan into action.

EXTERMINATION ACTIONS AGAINST JEWS IN BIELSK COUNTY

The Course of Events

In November 1942, the office of the Chief of the Security Police in Białystok, headed by Dr. Wilhelm Altenloh, assumed control over all the ghettos in the district. It was the commencement of the ultimate extermination of the Jews in the *Bezirk Białystok*. The liquidation of the ghettos in Bielsk County—as well as in the entire district—began on November 2; "Everywhere on the same day and at the same time: between half past four and half past five in the morning."[58] By February 1943, about 110,000 Jews had been deported from the district to Treblinka and Auschwitz-Birkenau,[59] among them 40,000 Jews from Bielsk County.

In the early morning of November 2, the German gendarmerie and police surrounded all the ghettos in the county. The simultaneous operations that were launched not only in the vast territory of Bielsk County but also in the entire *Bezirk Białystok* required the use of considerable, well-coordinated forces. The deportations were carried out by joined forces of the gendarmerie and auxiliary police, as well as supplementary police forces: Reserve Police Battalions 11, 13, and 22, reinforced by a detachment of the KdS from Białystok,[60] "*Jagdzug* gendarmes (anti-partisan, search platoon), Wehrmacht soldiers, and even German civilian officials, post-office clerks, [and] railmen."[61] Polish guards (*Schutzmänner*) also participated in the liquidation of the ghettos in the county as part of their duties.[62]

Between November 2 and 15, the Jews from Bielsk County were gradually transported to Treblinka, with those from smaller localities concentrated first in the ghettos in Bielsk Podlaski and Siemiatycze. The Jews from Orla, Rudka, Narew, Brańsk, Boćki, and Kleszczele (where the Jews from Milejczyce had been relocated earlier) were herded into Bielsk Podlaski, which became a transit ghetto for eleven to fifteen thousand Jews. About one thousand persons per day were sent from there to the Treblinka extermination camp during the two-week-long "resettlement operation." In Siemiatycze, the Germans concentrated the Jews from Drohiczyn, Grodzisk, and Mielnik. In Ciechanowiec, the Jews had been kept in the ghetto for several days before they were taken to the railroad station in Czyżew, twenty kilometers away, and from there to Treblinka. Every day beginning on November 2, Jews were sent to Treblinka from Bielsk and Siemiatycze, as well as from the ghettos in the east of the county (among other

Figure 1.4. Jews before the deportation, Bielsk Podlaski (YVA, 5701/51).

places from Wysokie Litewskie, where the Jews from Kamieniec Litewski had been sent).

In Ciechanowiec, a labor camp for a few hundred[63] workers was formed two days before the deportation at the Pobikry estate, twelve kilometers away. It was probably set up to protect the "useful" Jews—the only such case in the county. On November 2, however, the Germans not only sealed the Ciechanowiec ghetto but also rounded up the inmates at Pobikry and executed them in the nearby grove. Many Jews managed to escape.[64] On November 6, some two hundred of those Jews concentrated in Bielsk Podlaski—shoemakers and tailors along with their families—were taken to the Białystok ghetto to work. Later, they were sent back to the already empty Bielsk ghetto, where they worked making boots for the Germans. In January 1943, they were transferred to the village of Pietrasze near Białystok, and from there, in February 1943, the women and children were transported to Treblinka, while the male craftsmen went to Majdanek and Auschwitz. Few of them survived.

Over the two weeks of the deportations, some Jews fled the towns while others sought to hide within ghettos. A large group of seventy to one hundred persons tried to hide in the Brańsk ghetto, but other Jews, under torture, revealed many of their hideouts. The rest of them set the ghetto on fire on November 15,[65] and some were subsequently caught by the Germans and shot to death. At least a dozen or so Jews remained in the ghetto until their bunkers were discovered on

November 20 and 21; at that time, the Germans executed ten or eleven people.[66] In Siemiatycze, an armed resistance was planned that was supposed to involve setting the ghetto ablaze.[67] It did not succeed, and all of the Jews in hiding were successively caught; the last transport from the Siemiatycze ghetto carried away all members of the *Judenrat* and the Jewish police. But in Bielsk, the *Judenrat's* members and policemen, along with the elderly and the hospital patients (a total of seventy-eight persons), were shot to death "at the garden between Wąska Street and today's 21 Puszkin [Street]."[68]

The deportation action was carried out hurriedly, accompanied by violence, shouts, beatings, and terror, which only aggravated widespread chaos and anxiety. Shots were fired at those who were too slow or who tried to resist, hide, or escape; many Jews were murdered on the spot. Based on sources, we can estimate that in the period from November 2 to 15, 1942, at least seven hundred persons were murdered on the grounds of the ghettos liquidated in the "Polish" part of Bielsk County.

The only ghetto that was not liquidated in November 1942 was Prużana—probably because of the transportation problems, as Himmler had halted transports until the end of 1942 due to the situation on the front.[69] At the beginning of 1943, the expulsions were resumed, and between January 28 and February 1, eighteen thousand Jews were sent from the Prużana ghetto to Auschwitz. Before the deportation, Icchak Janowicz, chairman of the *Judenrat*, allegedly committed suicide.[70] Many Jews managed to escape on the way from Prużana to the railroad station in Orańczyce. Some of them joined the partisan ranks.

Escapes at the Time of Deportations

Mass breakouts were characteristic for Bielsk County, which witnessed large groups of inmates escaping from just a few ghettos. Certainly, the proximity of forests, combined with awareness of what "resettlement" actually meant, made the decision to escape easier. Sometimes, encouragement came from the ghetto's authorities. The vice chairman of the *Judenrat* in Siemiatycze, Kruszewski, allegedly urged inmates to escape by saying: "Children, save yourselves, let the Lord deliver you,"[71] while in Ciechanów, "the *Judenrat* told the Jewish policemen to open the ghetto's gates if the Germans came."[72] According to various sources, the greatest number of escapees fled from Brańsk (seven hundred[73] or eight hundred,[74] that is, about 30 percent), and Drohiczyn (250,[75] 270,[76] or 300,[77] that is, 20 percent). Smaller numbers of Jews fled from Siemiatycze (150[78] to 300,[79] or 3–6 percent), and about 150 fled from Bielsk Podlaski (3 percent). On average, around 10 percent of Jews escaped from these four ghettos, on which the most extensive information is preserved, although differences in the percentage of escapees between the ghettos are huge. There is no such data concerning other localities, but many Jewish testimonies mention escapees. These sources examined for this paper mention some 1,300 fugitives from the ghettos in the "Polish" part of the county, which constitutes 5.7 percent of the total population of the ghettos. Although the scale of the phenomenon is smaller in comparison with other counties, it is difficult to ascertain whether the disparity results from a lack of data, or whether the number of Jewish escapees from Bielsk County ghettos was in fact smaller than in other regions of Poland. This issue requires further study, as does the huge disparity in the number of escapees from different ghettos. As has already been mentioned, almost 20 percent of inhabitants fled from the Drohiczyn ghetto, in reality 15 percent from Brańsk, while no one escaped from Orla, and just eight Jews escaped from Kleszczele. The disparity in number of escapees might have been caused by the fact that the Jews from there were first relocated to Bielsk, and the earlier resettlements within the region had not seemed particularly risky. Moreover, the Germans announced (in Orla) that this time the transportation would take them to the Black Sea region, or (in Kleszczele) to Ukraine. It is possible that the deception was effective to some extent, but both ghettos were also completely sealed on the day of the deportation. Those who at some point considered leaving the ghetto in Orla abandoned the idea upon hearing that the Germans threatened to execute the families of escapees.[80] Besides, when they arrived in Bielsk, the decision to escape became more difficult, if only because they found themselves in a new and unknown neighborhood. There were different reasons why many Jews did not even try to escape. Apart from various limitations such as age, illness, or lack of means or energy, there was a responsibility to others at play ("They were persuading me that a responsible man should not leave his family and run away"[81]), or yielding to a peculiar fatalism, but there was also a conviction that such an attempt would be fruitless: "Peasants will catch us anyway and hand us over to the Germans."[82]

Rarely were the escapes adequately prepared, and even if they were planned, in the end they were executed among the chaos and panic of deportation. Finally, many attempts ended in failure. Some escapees came back to the ghetto disheartened by the futile search of rescue; some returned to join their families. Chaim Marmur recollects that some sixty escapees from the Siemiatycze ghetto returned after just few days, as they had been unable to find any shelter; others, who had been hiding in the nearby forest for two weeks, gave up in the end and turned themselves over to the police, who murdered them in the Jewish cemetery.[83]

While the escapees were trying to size up the situation, identify opportunities, and work out some strategies, the abandoned ghettos were stripped of any valuables left there and combed in search of Jews in hiding. In Siemiatycze, "removing the remaining property from the ghetto's territory, the gendarmes discovered on the Fabryczna Street, in the destroyed buildings of the former factory . . . that there was a small group of Jews in hiding, among whom were women and children. The Jews coming out of the hideout carried out the bodies of infants in their arms. The gendarmes drove the whole group toward Polna Street and there, shot them dead."[84] Many Jews died within the first days and weeks of the "resettlement,"[85] but certainly at least 1,000 persons made an effort to save themselves using different survival strategies.

SURVIVAL STRATEGIES

The sources analyzed mention approximately 1,300–2,000 escapees from the ghettos in Bielsk County. More detailed information was discovered on 974[86] of them. As it is impossible to verify the number of escapees who fled in large groups—Jews of unknown names and surnames whose fate has not been confirmed; presumably they all died, but they remain nameless—they have not been included in my statistics. To give an example: From the estimated number of 700 Jews killed during the expulsions in the first half of November, biographical details could be found on 124 persons—so it is the latter number that was taken into account when calculating statistics. Thus, the statistical data covers 974 Jews seeking refuge after the deportations, which constitutes only 4.3 percent of the inhabitants of the ghettos in the "Polish" part of the county.[87] With all this in mind, one can examine the subject of Jewish survival strategies, as well as their failures.

Failures at Seeking Refuge

The ratio of failure to success in seeking refuge was two to one—62.4 percent (608) of the Jews died, 33 percent (322) survived—and we do not know what happened to 44 (4.5 percent). The absence of favorable outcomes at the time of deportations and within few weeks after were primarily the result of the German roundups. In these heated times, at least 124 of those who had been hiding in the nearby forests from November 15, 1942, were captured. The last large-scale roundup, conducted in mid-December 1942, captured Jews hiding in several barns in the settlement of Oleksin-Kolonia (near Brańsk): Sixteen escapees[88] were caught and locked in a pigsty, two of them fled,[89] and the rest were murdered.

The analyzed sources contain data on 265 Jews that were murdered by the Germans. It is impossible, however, to assert whether all of these deaths are proof of Germans' efficiency. The sources do not allow one to determine, for

Table 1.2 The Jews who died in the territory of Bielsk Podlaski County after November 15, 1942

Dead	Number of Jews	Percentage of dead
Murdered by the Germans (and/or Polish policemen); including those killed in roundups or soon after their escapes from a ghetto	265 124	43.5 20
Denounced or captured by neighbors and murdered by the Germans (and/or Polish policemen)	241	39.6
Died in partisan battles	40	6.5
Murdered by neighbors	32	5.2
Died of natural causes	5	0.8
Killed by the Polish underground	5	0.8
Cause of death unknown	20	3.2
TOTAL	**608**	**100**

Source: Author.

example, in how many cases the Germans not only murdered their victims but also had tracked them down, as these murders also could have resulted from denunciation.[90] In many cases (maybe most of them), the whereabouts of the escapees were disclosed by locals. For example, in the village of Zajęczniki-Kolonia near Drohiczyn, eight elderly members of the Gruda family hid—with the consent of the owner—in the abandoned house of Karol Zalewski. Their sons and nephews had decided to hide in the adjacent woods, from where they were able to watch their prewar acquaintances as they robbed the elderly Jews and brought the Germans, who took them to Drohiczyn and shot them dead at the foot of the hill of Zamkowa Góra (Castle Mountain).[91]

Factors that played a key role in denunciations of Jews were, on one hand, fear and the shrewd fear management on the part of the Germans, and on the other hand the concurrence of malice and coincidence. There was no shortage of malice, and by pure chance, Jews often found themselves in the wrong place at the wrong time, as happened to four Jews who were crossing the village of Romanówka during the day just when there was a meeting of the village elders. They were spotted and caught; an attempt to exchange shoes for life failed—and they were tied and transported to the gendarmerie post in Siemiatycze.[92]

Helping Jews required overcoming the fear of punishment that the occupier was skillfully fueling. The story of Icek Chajt can serve as an example. He was caught in the settlement of Śliwowo-Kolonia. The Germans led him from house to house "demanding from the Jew that he show them those who had given him food—testified Akulina Kalinowska in the court.—They were also in the front of [my] house . . . I saw through the window as a *szucman* [Schupo-man] of [the village of] Klejnik led Icek by a string . . . Upon entering, the gendarmes began to ask me if I had given Icek any food, which I refuted, so they took me to the hall and confronted me with Icek, who kept saying that he had been at my place . . . Seeing that Icek [repeated] the same over and over again, as he actually went partially crazy, the older of these gendarmes was ordered to shoot him."[93] Of course, inhabitants of Śliwowo—and Akulina Kalinowska was among them— had given Icek food and dreaded the consequences. The *szucmen*—who also were their neighbors—protected them: They concluded that Icek had lost his mind from fear of death (which, of course, could well have been true), so they executed him themselves; by doing this, they saved residents of Śliwowo from the repercussions they would have suffered at the hands of the Germans for helping a Jew.

At the beginning of 1943, when the chaos of the first days had ended, specific strategies for survival began to emerge—planned strategies, based on a better understanding of the options and resources. However, if effective strategies as those that can shape events, for the Jews who were seeking refuge, they proved ineffective because their resources, determination, or will to live could only influence the outcome of the venture called survival to a small degree. Malice—in the form of fear, hate, or the greed of others—was of larger importance here. Most attempts to survive ended in death.

In more than 240 cases, the death of the Jews resulted from denunciations by the locals. We usually do not know what motivated people to denounce Jews to the authorities. Most often, an account of the death of a Jew comes down to just one sentence: in the fall of 1943, in the village of Patoki (Brańsk commune), Paweł Tur captured Jankiel Olendzki and took him to the gendarmerie post in Brańsk;[94] two Jews caught in the village of Romanówka were taken to the post in Siemiatycze;[95] four Jewish children caught in the village of Czechy Zabłotne were taken to the post in Kleszczele;[96] three anonymous Jews caught in Biszewo were taken to the post in Grodzisk;[97] two unknown Jews caught in Skórce were taken to the post in Pobikry.[98]

At least thirty-two Jews died directly at the hands of the county's residents. The county was a scene of a few notorious murders that have been reported in accounts and, moreover, ended up in the courts after the war. First and foremost are the murders committed by the Hyć brothers and the gamekeeper, Koszak. Their story has already been covered in another article;[99] the final chapter of the gamekeeper's story involves the Jewish partisans and will be brought it up later. No fewer than forty Jews died in battles with the Germans. Five were murdered by the Polish underground; five others died of natural causes (illness or starvation); as to the twenty others, the cause of their death is impossible to determine.

Survival in Hiding

Out of the 947 Jews on whom information was gathered, 322 persons survived, which constitutes about 1.4 percent of the overall population of the ghettos in the "Polish" part of the county prior to the resettlement. The most effective method to endure in this territory turned out to be staying in the same place for an extended period. At least ninety-eight Jews—that is, one-third of the survivors—had found refuge (in forty-two places) in which they were able stay more than fifteen months (most of them stayed more than twenty months). The most significant number of permanent hideouts were situated near Siemiatycze (twelve), Brańsk (eleven), and Drohiczyn (ten); these three towns constituted islands of survival.

One of those who managed to survive in this way was Benjamin Feldman, owner of a mill in Siemiatycze. He escaped a ghetto on November 2, 1942, taking with him his wife, Liba, and his four children. Liba's brother-in-law, the *shochet* [ritual slaughterer] Beniamin Fuks, and his three-year-old daughter, Cipora, went with them. They spent the first night in the woods; the next day, they went to a veterinarian they knew, Bolesław Leszczyński. Leszczyński, his wife, and his three sons lived far from the village in the settlement of Kajanka-Kolonia.

Table 1.3 Jews who survived the occupation in Bielsk County

Means of survival	Number of Jews	Percentage of survived
In one place	98	30.5
Wandering	78	24.2
In forest bunkers	70	21.8
By joining partisan units	26	8
Using "Aryan" papers	11	3.1
Working in Prussia (outside the county)	3	0.9
Unknown	36	11.2
TOTAL	**322**	**100**

Source: Author.

At first, eight Jews hid in his farm, inside a potato clamp;[100] later, they moved to a dugout in the forest. The Leszczyńskis provided them with food—usually potato soup. Fuks, a devout man who would not eat anything nonkosher, died after some time. The remaining seven spent entire days in their bunker, "holding hands and praying, thanking God for the miracle—although hungry and sick, broken and frightened—that they were still alive."[101] They remained there for twenty-two months until liberation, surviving a hooligans' attack, a German search of the farm, and serious illnesses. When the Russians arrived, it came to light that there were five more Jews in hiding on Leszczyński's homestead, the Grodzicki family; the two groups had not known about each other. The Grodzickis had lived in the Siemiatycze ghetto until mid-December 1942. When food ran out, Szlomo Grodzicki, with his wife and daughter, decided to look for help while Grodzicki's two teenage children from his first marriage, Miriam and Mosze, and their three cousins settled upon building a bunker in the woods. Szlomo came to Leszczyński in Kajanka, and he agreed to shelter them in the barn. Meanwhile, the five teenagers barely subsisted: They were always cold and hungry and were being trailed. After a while, rumors about their death spread through the neighborhood and reached their father. He resolved to hang himself, as he felt responsible for their demise. One night, he removed his belt from trousers and hanged himself from a barn beam. "At the time when he was hanging himself," recounted Miriam Kuperhand, "my stepmother had a dream that my deceased mother was shaking her, saying: 'Rojzke, Szlomo is hanging himself. Tell him that the children are alive and will come to you soon.' She woke up and told her husband that the children were alive and would come soon."[102] And so it happened—Mosze and Miriam had found their father at the Leszczyńskis, and together they survived there until the end of the war.

Several dozen other Jews were able to survive in a similar way, staying almost the entire time in the same place. For instance, the Szapiro brothers, Lejbl and Fajwel together with their mother and sister; Lejbl's fiancée, Mina Waser; and Sonia Weinstein, hid with the Popławski family in Oleksin-Kolonia (Brańsk commune).[103] On the outskirts of Brańsk, the Finkelsztejns, a family of five, hid at the Puchalskis, who provided them with a bunker and food supplies.[104] Wolf Farber survived in hiding at the Kryńskis in the village of Bystre (Boćki commune),[105] while Ita and Wolf Ptaszek (and their sister Róża with her husband, Rubin Chazan, and three children) survived at the Złotkowskis in Złotki (Ciechanowiec commune). Szyja Żółtak, his parents, and his uncle found the shelter at the home of Mrs. Kryńska in Krynki-Sobole (Grodzisk commune);[106] Lejzor Gruda; his wife, Leja; and their son Chaim stayed at the home of Grzegorz and Konstancja Czapek in Drohiczyn-Kolonia.[107] From May 1943 until the end of the war, Symcha Bursztein and Zelman Waserman endured in the hideout arranged in the barn of Skarżyński in Saki (Kleszczele commune),[108] while in the town of Kleszczele itself, Józef Białostocki spent the entire time in hiding at the home of the Markiewicz family.[109] Eugenia Kotler, with her daughter Alina and son Borys, stayed until the end of the war with Helena Morza in Korzeniówka (Siemiatycze commune). Dwora and Szlomo Goldwasser, as well as Szlomo's brother Kalman and cousin Szmuel, found shelter at the Sołomachs in Siemiatycze.[110] Chaja Kagan, with her father and sister, survived in a dugout under the pigsty of an anonymous shoemaker from Zalesie (Siemiatycze commune).[111]

Wandering and Forest Bunkers

Wandering around [neighborhoods] and obtaining sporadic help or protection from a handful persons was the second most effective survival strategy—seventy-eight Jews survived in this way. As "wandering" involved staying with various farmers in turn, and sometimes in temporary in bunkers in the forests, the division into categories of "wandering" and "in the forests" is, to some extent, arbitrary. The distinction was introduced by survivors to describe a way of their survival.[112] Seventy Jews saved their lives by staying in bunkers and "in the forests" of Bielsk County; pursuing both strategies, 148 persons survived. The wandering followed a specific repetitive pattern (with some minor variations). At the beginning, there was the escape from the ghetto, disorientation, conferring with other escapees, and staying in the forest. This was followed by the division into smaller, often family-based groups and attempts to find an anchoring point, a base, if only temporary. Most often, they could find shelter for the night or provisions to carry them through a day, a few days, a week, or sometimes longer. The next leg of the journey comprised more wandering toward another place, interspersed with stopovers in the forests, encounters (often chance encounters) with other Jews, looking for the next point of anchor, and so on. Threats periodically disrupted this pattern: accidents, betrayals, robbery, a denunciation, or a lucky escape (as only those who survived are taken into account here). Over the course of time, the Jews gained experience, and their expertise at hiding grew. As one of the survivors said, hiding was "a skill that you learn."[113] With time, they knew better whom to approach for help and whom to avoid, how to build bunkers in the woods, how to sneak (unbeknownst to farmers) into barns and cowsheds, and how to keep company with farm animals. Essential support came from those who were willing to help, such as, for example, the Catholics in Brańsk—the Klinickis,[114] the Sobolewskis,[115] Nikodem Miśkiewicz,[116] and

Maria Klinicka[117]—or the Ortodox family of Kłos and Olga Paszkowska[118] in the village of Świrydy, who used to give the Jews in hiding food, bring them news, or leave the doors to their farm buildings open.

Estera Fiszgop, her aunt, and two cousins walked from one person who took their belongings and money and promised to help to another, but all of them, one by one, threw them out with no intention of giving back anything. The women spent six months in a dugout beneath Stefania Jurczuk's pigsty, but as Stefania's neighbors grew suspicious, they had to leave, part company, and seek rescue separately. Estera roamed through the neighborhood barefoot and in ragged clothes, stealing food from farm animals and spending nights in barns. From time to time, she would return to Mrs. Jurczak's for a few days. She learned to hide well and knew the area, and the dogs got used to her. Estera recalls that her instinct to live was so strong that she was unaware of the feelings of constant uncertainty, humiliation, and pain, because she was consumed by the thought of survival. She neither planned nor analyzed her circumstances; she acted instinctively so as to survive from one threat to another. She was forever alert, as at any time she could have run into danger. "Most of all, I was afraid of peasants; the Germans would not take me for a Jewess, but the peasants would." Estera's life became easier at the end of the occupation due to the protection extended by partisans: They gave her some clothes and, most importantly, "posted an announcement that if a Jew is killed on your land, you and your family be killed, and your farm will be burned."[119] Just before liberation. Estera met her aunt and cousins again—they had all survived.

Nineteen-year-old Icchak Grodziński, who survived in the forests, is an example of how Jews on the run learned and gained experience, and how they gradually became more and more versed in the art of survival. Grodziński had escaped from the ghetto in Brańsk together with an eight-year-old child, Jehoszua Goldberg, whom he had encountered accidentally. They wandered around the neighborhood for a month. "Several times, while they were asking for food or were caught at night in the barn, the farmers wanted to hand them over to the Germans, but they were able to plead with them for mercy."[120] Icchak was confused; he did not know whom he could trust. A shoemaker promised to help them but robbed them and threw them out nearly naked in the snow. A miller promised to help—he gave them a knife, told them to go back to the shoemaker and retrieve the things that were stolen from them, and then sheltered them through the worst winter months. Then Grodziński and Goldberg stopped being fearful and begging for food; they simply entered peasants' dwellings and demanded food, and Grodziński put something beneath his jacket that looked like a gun. Meir Studnik, a teenager and an escapee from a transport from the

Białystok ghetto, joined them in March 1943. Later on, they were joined by another three Jews from Brańsk who were known to them. "Icchak was the leader of the group. He instructed [us] on how to behave in the woods, [that they should] never stay in the same place; he secured food for them all." Their group numbered twelve escapees, and they "held out until the liberation, hiding in the Brańsk vicinity, taking food away from peasants with the threat of the weapon."[121] Icchak's people constituted a typical group of forest Jews fighting for survival.

Penalty for Assisting Jews

Providing aid to Jews in hiding was punishable by death, and at least five district inhabitants died for this, while several others suffered severe repercussions. The butchers from Brańsk, brothers Lejbka and Fiszka Doliński, were hiding at the place of an elderly couple, the Jakubowskis, in the village of Popławy-Kolonia (commune of Brańsk). On April 12, 1943, gendarmes killed the brothers and Walentyna Jakubowski; her husband was at church at the time.[122] Walentyna was shot on the spot alongside the Jews she had assisted, but the other county residents who were punished for helping Jews died in the camps. There were Olędzki of Szmurły;[123] the wife of Antoni Kazimieruk of Suchowolce;[124] and Konstanty Dobrogowski with his son, Stanisław, who both died in the Stutthof camp.[125] In this last case, additional punishment was meted out to the Dobrogowski family: Their homestead was dismantled, and the rest of the family had to move to another village.

There were other penalties the Germans imposed on those who aided the Jews in Bielsk County. Stanisław Popławski had sheltered a man called Josiel, his wife, and their two daughters on his farm in Oleksin (commune of Brańsk). The Jews were killed by gendarmes from Brańsk, and he was sentenced to three months in the penal camp in Bielsk Podlaski.[126] When he was released from the camp, Popławski gave shelter to the other Jews, for "he was not capable of refusing people help. He was a devout Catholic."[127] The Danilczuk family of Pace-Kolonia (commune of Brańsk) was punished with the burning down of their homestead.[128] In Poletely-Kolonia (commune of Brańsk), the Gołembieckis, a widow and her four children, sheltered four Jews and were punished with the dismantling of their house and farm buildings.[129]

Kosiński of Koczery-Kolonia was beaten by the Germans, but the Błaszczuks of the village Baciki Średnie did not suffer any consequences, nor did the Skrzypkowski brothers of Sienkiewicze-Kolonia, to whom many Jews had come asking for food. Maciej Skrzypkowski, a father of seven, gave shelter to a couple of

Jewish children for several months, but the Germans discovered them and murdered them. Zygmunt Skrzypkowski, Maciej's brother, who had five children, sheltered several Jews in a hideout under the floor. The Skrzypkowskis suffered no consequences for hiding the Jews. Neither did the Kurek family, who were hiding Estera Mężyńska, or the Turs, who, at the request of Father Zalewski, sheltered a Jewish physician, Dr. Julian Charin.[130] It is impossible to explain why the death penalty for giving shelter to Jews was not imposed in these cases, upon what conditions the type of the punishment inflicted depended, or why some avoided any punishment at all. Of course, those who decided to help could not know that they would evade punishment had they been exposed. On the contrary, they did it knowing that they risked their lives and the lives of their entire families. The repercussions against helpers served as a warning to all who thought of defying the German orders; their function was to intimidate. Both Jewish accounts and Polish testimonies are filled with a sense of fear, but it had no binding effect, and it was divisive. There was fear of the Germans but also fear of each other: The Jews in hiding feared the threat posed by local inhabitants; they, in turn, were on the one hand afraid of partisans and bands, and on the other hand afraid of helping Jews and risking German repercussions. Fear of punishment was one of the essential factors that interfered with the willingness to aid the Jews.

"Aryan Papers": Hiding in Plain Sight

Assuming an Aryan identity was the least-often employed strategy in Bielsk County. The Jewish population of the county consisted of small-town and village Jews, the majority of whom had no Aryan documents: They hid at neighbors or in the forests and did not even bother to get any proper papers. Nevertheless, eleven persons survived in the county using so-called Aryan papers, in a manner known to be typical of larger cities. This was how Cyla Kalecka survived. Before the war, she had married Roman Jastrzębski, a Pole who became involved in underground and partisan activities. Because he was a country teacher, the family lived for an extended period in the village of Żale. Their daughter, who was a teenager at the time, recollects they were arrested and kept at the police station in Pobikry, but it was due to her father's illegal work rather than suspicion about their Jewish origin. She and her mother were again detained in Siemiatycze, but a policeman, who had ties to the underground and knew her father, let them out.[131]

Eugenia Wiszrubski, wife of an attorney from Wysokie Litewskie, and her two young daughters, Regina and Adela, survived in a similar way. The father of the family had been shot by the Germans during deportation from Hajnowka to Prużana in 1942, but a casual friend helped them—the woman gave Emilia documents stating the Karaite identity of the Wiszrubskis—and, aided by some more acquaintances, they moved to the village of Narew, where they lived as Karaites until the end of the occupation.[132] "Sarenka," the owner of a bar in the Krzyże neighborhood, survived on an Aryan identity in Białowieża, as no one knew that she was Jewish; throughout the occupation, she worked as a housekeeper for a German from Kłajpeda, *Oberleutenant* Schultz.[133] In Bielsk Podlaski, the Sperlings, a family of three, survived by posing as Hungarians,[134] and a student from Warsaw, Adolf Jużelewski, survived assisted by the Sielicki family.[135] In May 1943, Anastazja and Walerian Sobolewski brought Inka Grynszpan from the Father Baudouin orphanage in Warsaw; she survived living with them until the end of the war.[136]

Three other Jews survived as "Aryans" in Prussia, where they were sent to work: Batszeba Szwarzberg of Siemiatycze, who, under the assumed name of Walentyna Zajcew, worked cleaning a post of the gendarmerie;[137] Szaja Wiprawnik, who passed himself off as the Soviet orphan Iwan Orłow and became a servant to an SS officer;[138] and Estera Drogicka, who worked as a help in the German family of Fittkau in Rastenburg (Kętrzyn).[139]

In the Ranks of Partisans

Of the 322 Jews who survived in the territory of Bielsk County, at least 26 fought in the ranks of partisans. There were more Jews of Bielsk County who had joined the partisans, but a number of them died in combat. In 1942, Himmler proclaimed the Białystok District a *Banden-Kampf-Gebiet* (bandit-combat-zone),[140] where partisans were "to be mercilessly eliminated in combat or [killed] attempting to escape,"[141] and where summary courts punished people swiftly and ruthlessly for helping them. To intimidate inhabitants of the occupied Polish territory and force them into submission, the Germans punished with violence any sign of resistance, underground activity, or aid to escaped POWs or partisans. The civilian population faced a no-win situation: Helping partisans could bring severe punishment, and not helping them was risky too, as the partisans were ready to take what they needed by force, and also to plunder and set fire to property.

At the end of 1942, Soviet partisan units operated in the county, and detachments of Polish partisans were formed—both movements relied on supplies from local peasants, and both fought the Germans. Jews, outlawed and in desperate need of help, were forced to compete with these two forces. Some Jewish partisans, especially in the area near Prużana, came from the Jewish resistance movement that, even before the liquidation actions, had tried to send young people to the forests and form ties with Soviet partisans already operating there. A plan to attack the Germans was devised by a group of Jews who were assigned to forced labor outside the ghetto in the former Soviet ammunition warehouses and who began to take weapons from there and stockpile them.[142] They planned both a defense within the ghetto and an escape for the forest. The first group that left the Prużana ghetto consisted of ten people.[143] The next group was getting ready to leave on January 28, 1943, but on the same day, the Germans began the liquidation of the ghetto. Reportedly, shots were fired,[144] and several dozen people[145] got out through the cut barbed wire and escaped to the forest. They built bunkers and obtained food by threatening to use weapons. This led to a denunciation and an attack by the Germans, during which a number of the Jews were killed. The next group was killed by the Russians,[146] and finally the last eighteen Jews found their way to the Kirow detachment.[147] This was where the Jews of Prużana became real partisans: As "fighters" they carried out "subversion work, such as cutting telegraph and telephone wires, laying road mines, setting up barricades, [road] blocks, and so on."[148]

The Jewish partisans from the vicinities of Drohiczyn, Brańsk, and Siemiatycze had at first belonged to "survival groups" of escapees from different ghettos before they gradually became partisans. Although at first not all Jewish attempts to establish contacts with the Russian partisan movement had been successful,[149] the first self-defense groups did emerge. The one formed by the Gruda brothers not only fought for its own survival but—being armed—also actively defended the Jews hiding nearby and punished those who handed them over to the Germans. Many of the future partisans lived through the first winter in villages. Hersz Szabes and Izrael Krawiec stayed throughout the winter together and, with the spring, set up a group of men together with Israel Morer, Hersz Smoluch, and Chaim Brzeziński. Their first goal was to obtain a weapon. Equipped with "sticks painted to look like firearms,"[150] the Jews reclaimed the money and other things they had left with some peasants for safekeeping. That allowed them to buy a gun, and then—using it to make threats with—they were able to get another. Having two guns, they obtained the next two. Now, "the group began to plan more intensive activity against the peasants who were informing on or killing Jews. A warning was issued to the district peasants that revenge would be taken for betraying a Jew to the Germans. And the Siemiatycze Jews soon proved that they would follow through. They learned that a peasant had caught Welwl Szoszkes, Izrael Krawiec's uncle, chained him to his cart, and taken him to the Gestapo where he was shot. Several days later, the peasant was killed by a Siemiatycze bullet."[151]

Figure 1.5. Group of Jewish partisans in a forest close to Brańsk (YVA, 47382).

Apart from acts of vengeance and actions that protected the Jews in hiding, the partisans also carried out sabotage operations.

The assistance Jews were able to find in the petty-nobility villages constituted a curious phenomenon against the backdrop of the premodern peasant mentality. Most of the families aiding and rescuing Jews were Catholics, and more precisely Catholics and residents of former petty-nobility villages.[152] There is, it seems, a certain pattern, a tendency that needs in-depth study but should not be overlooked—the dividing line between help and denunciation is clearly formed by the line between social classes. One of the possible interpretations of the phenomenon is to explain it by the sense of subjectivity that resulted in an attitude (active for nobility and passive for peasants) toward the world. While economic status barely distinguished the impoverished petty nobility from the peasantry, the former maintained a strong sense of their own class distinctiveness and aspiration, cultivated their noble heritage, upheld class division, and fostered a spiritual culture. What is essential is that this social group (unlike peasantry) has a sense of subjectivity, including political agency. No wonder members of the petty nobility were engaged in local political and social activities before the war, during the occupation, and in the early postwar years, when they fought against the new system. While analyzing the phenomenon of the assistance extended to Jews by some representatives of the petty nobility, one needs to take into account different factors such as the social distance between the Jews and those who helped them, prewar contacts, and friendships. Topography also seems to be of importance; the location of *kolonie* (settlements), which were somewhat remote and isolated from villages, together with the relative self-sufficiency of farms, could also facilitate aid. Not without significance was the attitude of various pillars of the community. Many cases of aid to Jewish people that took place in the vicinity of Brańsk may have been connected to efforts of the dean, Father Bolesław Czarkowski, who called for helping Jews, preaching "constantly, from the pulpit, to love one's neighbor, stressing that one should help those in hiding."[153] The Brańsk priest, Father Józef Chwalko,[154] and Father Józef Perkowski from the Hodyszew, twelve kilometers away from Brańsk,[155] also extended help to the Jews.

CONCLUSION: BIELSK PODLASKI COUNTY FROM 1944 TO 1945

The Red Army entered the region of Bielsk County in late July 1944, liberating its towns one after the other. As Operation Tempest required, AK forces engaged in battles with retreating German troops to demonstrate themselves to the Russians as the hosts of the territory. In Białystok, the regional government delegate Józef Przybyszewski[156] emerged into the open on July 29 and was arrested by the NKVD a few days later. On July 31, 1944, a plenipotentiary of the PKWN (*Polski Komitet Wyzwolenia Narodowego*, Polish Committee of National Liberation) assumed his responsibilities in Białystok under the agreement signed in Moscow a day earlier, and on August 23, 1944, the County National Council in Bielsk Podlaski was formed. The creation of the new, socialist system had begun. At first, the MO (*Milicja Obywatelska*, Citizen's Militia) set up in Bielsk County amounted to 250 ill-equipped, uneducated country youths. The county security forces looked similar: According to documentation, in January 1945, it comprised eighteen operatives, of whom only one had a college degree.[157] Nonetheless, according to other sources, before the end of 1944, there were already 487 inmates in the jail of the PUBP (*Powiatowy Urząd*

Bezpieczeństwa Publicznego, County Public Security Office) in Bielsk, among them more than 200 members of the AK.[158]

The PKWN Decree of August 22, 1944, restored the prewar administrative division on *województwo* (voivodeships), *powiat* (counties), *gmina* (commune), and *gromada* (community). The county of Bielsk Podlaski was the largest in Poland; 45 percent of its inhabitants were Orthodox Christian.[159] Facing an emerging postwar conflict, the new regime turned to the Ruthenians as its essential base. From among them, the authorities recruited a staff of the MO and UB (*Urząd Bezpieczeństwa*, Security Office), as for the young people born and raised in poor rural communities, it created an opportunity for quick social advancement. Apart from the social advance, Belorussians were at first also promised an increase in their national autonomy.[160]

In January 1945, the Red Army launched an offensive that took it farther west, leaving the newly established Bielsk County authorities (as well as those in the entire region) without protection. On January 19, 1945, General Leopold Okulicki issued an order under which the AK was dissolved, but the AK commandant of the Białystok District, Lt. Col. Liniarski, did not comply with it and, on February 15, formed a military organization, the AKO (*Armia Krajowa Obywatelska*, Citizen's Home Army). In the spring of 1945, the AKO was 27,000 strong; in May, it joined the WiN (*Zrzeszenie Wolność i Niezawisłość*, Freedom and Independence) underground organization, becoming a part of its territorial formation "Central Area." The Fifth AK Wilno Brigade, led by Zygmunt "Łupaszko" Szendzielarz, became one of its largest detachments (about 300 soldiers). The NOW (*Narodowa Organizacja Wojskowa*, National Military Organization) with its 5,000 soldiers, was another quite active group, but it did not join the AK despite some attempts being made. Instead, in the spring of 1945, it became a founding member of the NZW (*Narodowe Zjednoczenie Wojskowe*, National Military Union), which was also joined by the Third Wilno Brigade, headed by Romuald "Bury" Rajs. Apart from the organized underground movement, armed bands impersonating partisans were also active in the territory of the county, terrorizing its inhabitants by robbing them, imposing "contributions," and committing acts of rape.

What is important here is that the underground movement (all units except those that arrived from the Wilno region) came from among Polish inhabitants of *zaścianki*, petty-nobility villages in the western part of the county, while the Belorussian population of the eastern part of the county, who supported the new administration, became hostile toward it. That is to say that the framework of the conflict was not just political but also national. Bielsk County was actually divided into two mutually hostile parts—the western one that tried to fight the new system, and the eastern one that supported it. The underground units raided the Belorussian villages, murdering their population. At the turn of January 1946, a 200-strong unit led by "Bury"—which at the time was a part of the NSW, its Fourth Detachment, the so-called *Pogotowie Akcji Specjalnej* (Special-Action Emergency Team)—committed a mass slaughter having the character of genocide.[161] In the span of several days, they murdered thirty-two wagon drivers and Belorussians who had been forced to supply transportation, and then they massacred the Belorussian villages of Zaleszany, Wólka Wyganowska, Zanie, and Szpaki. "Seventy-nine random people were brutally murdered [there]; several dozen more were mutilated. The inhabitants of Zaleszczany were burned alive in a locked building."[162]

The anti-Communist underground put up military resistance to the new regime. "Communists" were its main enemies: NKVD operatives, soldiers of the Red Army, members of the PPR (*Polska Partia Robotnicza*, Polish Workers' Party). The underground detachments raided MO posts, disarmed their personnel, and murdered many of their militiamen and even their family members. Chaos and violence ruled Bielsk County throughout the first years following the war. The central administration's reach did not extend there, and local authorities were losing the battle with the armed underground and common banditry. The outcome of the terror in Bielsk County was as follows: In 1945, there were 248 robberies of municipal offices, cooperatives, state institutions, and privately owned farms;[163] from 1944 to 1946, 1,753 members of the resistance movement were arrested;[164] there are records of 65 assaults in total on MO posts in the county in 1945–1946;[165] between 1944 and 1947, 411 persons were murdered in these attacks, including 105 MO and UB men, 38 Soviet soldiers, 20 soldiers of the WP (*Wojsko Polskie*, Polish Army), and 219 civilians.[166] Thirteen among them were Jews.

There were 322 Jews (known by name) who survived in the Polish part of Bielsk Podlaski,[167] most of them in the vicinities of Brańsk (59), Drohiczyn (43), and Siemiatycze (35). Another thirty persons were hid in the nearby forests, being helped by local residents. These three towns constituted islands of survival, with the highest number of places in which the Jews were provided with ongoing aid for a prolonged time. Not all survivors registered themselves with the CKŻP (*Centralny Komitet Żydów w Polsce*, Central Committee of Polish Jews), as on its lists there are only 220 names of Jews who stated that the territory of Bielsk Podlaski County was their place of residence on September 1, 1939. These Jews who had survived in the county's territory, now being free, directed their first steps toward their hometowns but were by no means welcomed there. They now had to face new dangers. The sources of these dangers can be traced to three main roots: greed related to appropriated Jewish property, demoralization (that manifested itself in widespread banditry[168]), and antisemitism founded on stereotypes, both old and new.

At least twelve assaults on Jews who had survived occurred in Bielsk Podlaski County after the war. The first took place on December 13, 1944, when "the Jew Brukier of Siemiatycze, who is now in a hospital in Białystok, was injured."[169] The next, on the night of January 4–5, 1945, during which a robbery was carried out on the apartment of the miller Benia Lew,[170] who was killed. Arie Blustein died under similar circumstances."[171] In January 1945, in Drohiczyn, there was an assault on the house of Symcha Warszawski, who stayed there together with three his younger siblings; they had all survived in the territory of the county and miraculously found one another after the war. Symcha, the oldest brother, died when a grenade was thrown into the room; the three younger children were separated and sent to different children's homes.[172] Some murders were continuations of the wartime hostility, as happened in the case of Stefania Jurczuk, who turned over the Grudas to the Germans, and his act sparked a spiral of vengeance. Two of five Gruda brothers were killed.[173] After they died, the Grudas brought Jurczuk to justice after accusing him of murdering their parents.[174] The next assault on a Jew took place in Brańsk, on March 17, 1945: Zisl Topaczewska, the fiancée of Arie Prybut, went with her friend Rachela Wolson to the Polish dressmaker Mrs. Sztejman. "Two unknown individuals" came to her apartment and murdered all three women.[175] Also in March, one Jew was murdered in the village of Boćki, and two were murdered in a *kolonia* (settlement) in the forest.[176]

Jews were ready to defend themselves, all the more so because there were partisans among them who had weapons. A battle broke out on April 6, 1945, when an attack was launched on two buildings inhabited by Jews. A participant in those events remembered: "All Jews, some fifty persons, gathered in the attic [of the house] on Ciechanowiecka Street, and began to fire and throw grenades. ... The battle lasted for three hours. One woman was killed. By chance, several vehicles carrying Soviet soldiers arrived... We were saved by this accident. The next day after this incident, several military cars came and took us to Bielsk."[177] Perhaps at the same time, someone planted a bomb in the house of Szloma Kuperhand in Siemiatycze.[178] The last murder was committed on July 27, 1945: Chawcia and Meir, two of three siblings who survived the war, were murdered in Ciechanowiec.[179] Their sister, Rachela Kosower, escaped to Białystok.

Thirteen Jews (and a Polish woman) died in the twelve attacks described; four were injured. It is difficult to establish for certain what the reasons were behind each of these assaults. It seems that some were of a vengeful character, while others were acts of mere banditry and pillage. Still others were committed for more political reasons. They were part of the wave of antisemitic violence that spread throughout all of Poland,[180] drawing from the reserves of traditional antisemitism and feeding efficiently on the climate of fear, hatred, and vengeance prevailing after the war.

As the new Communist regime cemented itself in place, the situation in Bielsk County and throughout Poland gradually calmed down. On June 30, 1946, the authorities held a rigged referendum requesting approval to change the system in Poland (January 1947). The Communists then assumed ultimate power. By February, an amnesty was enacted for members of underground organizations—some of them emerged into the open, but a large number of their members remained underground. The battles and skirmishes with the new authorities lasted in Bielsk County until the end of the 1940s.

The number of Jews living in Bielsk County gradually decreased. Of the few hundred living there for a time in the 1940s, only forty Jews were left in 1948. The others gradually left. Of the Jews who had survived the war in the territory of the county, only Mojżesz (Mieczysław) Kamień and Kiwa Gruda continued living there to the end of their lives; after the war, they married Polish women and started families there.

NOTES

1. See Fania Grinberg, "*Bielsk* Niezwykły," in: *Księga pamięci Bielska Podlaskiego*, ed. Wojciech Konończuk and Doroteusz Fionik (Bielsk Podlaski: Stowarzyszenie Małej Ojczyzny w Studziwodach, 2017), 83.

2. Henryk Majecki, "Chrześcijańska Demokracja w województwie białostockim w latach 1918–1935," *Studia Podlaskie* 3 (1991): 150.

3. According to the census of 1931, Catholics numbered about ninety thousand, Orthodox Christians numbered ninety thousand, and Jews numbered twenty thousand. These numbers had probably changed by 1939.

4. Among them (accoding to 1931 data) about four thousand Catholics, thirty thousand Orthodox Christians, and eleven thousand Jews.

5. As there are access restrictions to documents posted in the Belorussian archives, I was not able to conduct the full preliminary research. Due to lack of sources relating to the eastern region of the county, which lies outside Poland's contemporary borders, most of my paper and the final conclusions are concerned only with the western part of the county. My calculations refer mostly to the 22,500 Jews confined to the ghettos that lay in the territory that remained within Poland's borders after the war.

6. YVA, M.11/50, Testimony of Rabin Halperin, "Opis martyrologii Żydów miasteczka Orla za czasów okupacji," translated from the Yiddish by Anna Szyba.

7. Moshe Kleinbaum, report in *Jews in Eastern Poland and the USSR 1939–1946*, ed. Norman Davies and Antony Polonsky (London: Palgrave Macmillan, 1991), http://catalog.nypl.org/search/025915273, cited in Alexandra Garbarini, *Jewish Responses to Persecution: 1938–1940* (AltaMira Press: Walnut Creek, 2011), 180.

8. Jerzy Hawryluk, "Kraje ruskie, Bielsk, Mielnik, Drohiczyn," in *Rusini-Ukraińcy na Podlasiu—fakty i kontrowersje* (Krakow: Fundacja Świętego Włodzimierza Chrzciciela Rusi Kijowskiej, 1999), 131.

9. According to a report of February 5, 1940, by Lavrentiy Tsanava, People's Commissar for State Security of the BSSR (Belorussian Soviet Republic), there were 72,896 refugees in the territory of the Belarussian SSR, among them 65,796 Jews. See Daniel Boćkowski, "Polscy uchodźcy wojenni na ziemiach wschodnich II RP zajętych przez ZSRR w latach 1939–1941 (próba oceny problemu)," *Prace Komisji Środkowoeuropejskiej PAU* 15 (2007): 88.

10. In November 1939, 2,384 refugees were registered in Bielsk, and they were "predominantly Jews." See Daniel Boćkowski, *Na zawsze razem. Białostocczyzna i Łomżyńskie w polityce radzieckiej w czasie II wojny światowej (IX 1939—VIII 1944)* (Warsaw: Neriton and IH PAN, 2005), 68.

11. The estimated number of Polish citizens deported from Poland's eastern borderlands is between 300,000 and 330,000, including some 80,000 Jews; Alina Skibińska, "Żydzi polscy ocaleni na wschodzie (1939–1946)," in *Narody i polityka. Studia ofiarowane profesorowi Jerzemu Tomaszewskiemu*, ed. August Grabski and Artur Markowski (Warsaw: ŻIH and Instytut Historyczny UW, 2010). The Index of the Repressed (https://indeksrepresjonowanych.pl) contains incomplete information on Jews deported from the individual county's localities. The Central Card File of the Jews Who Survived the Holocaust mentions as many as 113 persons who survived in the USSR territory out of 220 from Bielsk County registered by the Central Committee of the Jews in Poland.

12. Dora Galperin, "Tragedia i zniszczenie Kamieńca," in *Księga pamięci: Kamieniec Litewski, Zastawie i okolice*, http://www.jewishgen.org/yizkor/Kamenets/Kamenets.html.

13. "Class enemies" were arrested, among them Ruben Chazan of Ciechanowiec, who was sentenced to five years' imprisonment. USC Shoah Foundation, Visual History Archive (hereafter—USC, VHA), 25881, Testimony of Sheldon (Szaja) Chazen.

14. Ibid.

15. Ben Cion Pinchuk, "The Sovietization of the Jewish Community of Eastern Poland 1939–1941," *The Slavonic and East European Review* 56, no. 3 (July 1978): 387–410.

16. Stanisław Kossakowski, *Byłem adiutantem "Mścisława"* (Rajgród: Towarzystwo Miłośników Rajgrodu, 1999), 55.

17. The *Einsatzgruppen* were directly responsible to the *Reichsführer* SS and Chief of German Police Heinrich Himmler. Each unit was one thousand men strong and comprised small units, *Einsatzkommandos* and *Sonderkommandos*; their members were recruited from among officers of Waffen-SS and German police forces.

18. Edmund Dmitrów, "Oddziały operacyjne niemieckiej Policji Bezpieczeństwa i Służby Bezpieczeństwa a początek zagłady Żydów w Łomżyńskiem i na Białostocczyźnie latem 1941 roku," in *Wokół Jedwabnego*, vol. 1, *Studia*, ed. Paweł Machcewicz and Krzysztof Persak (Warsaw: IPN, 2002), 280.

19. Kazimierz Leszczyński, "Eksterminacja ludności na ziemiach polskich w latach 1939–1945. Opracowanie materiałów ankiety z 1945 roku," *Biuletyn Głównej Komisji Badania Zbrodni Hitlerowskich* [hereafter *Biuletyn GKBZH*] 8 (1956), 115–204.

20. AŻIH, 301/1829, Testimony of Symcha Burstein.

21. AŻIH, 301/1463, Testimony of Jehoszua Kajles.

22. The extensive literature attends to the pogroms that took place in the eastern territories of the Polish Commonwealth in the summer of 1941 and analyzes their causes. See Paweł Machcewicz and Krzysztof Persak, eds., *Wokół Jedwabnego*, vol. 1–2 (Warsaw: IPN, 2002); Andrzej Żbikowski, *U genezy Jedwabnego. Żydzi na Kresach Północno-Wschodnich II Rzeczypospolitej, wrzesień 1931–lipiec 1941* (Warsaw: ŻIH, 2006); Witold Mędykowski, *W cieniu gigantów. Pogromy 1941 roku w byłej sowieckiej strefie okupacyjnej. Kontekst historyczny, społeczny i kulturowy. Zarys teorii pogromów* (Warsaw: ISP PAN, 2012).

23. Hitler's decree of August 15, 1941, also vested him with the power to issue directives that had the force of law (AIPN, GK 318/748, Court records of the criminal case against Erich Koch, vol. 7, 26).

24. YVA, O53/10, Ludwigsburg USSR Collection, Amtsblatt des Oberpräsidenten der Provinz Ostpreussen, Zivilverwaltung für den Bezirk Bialystok.

25. The ressettlements of thirty-four villages took a bloody course: "After the evacuation was completed, most of villages were burnt to the ground" (AIPN Bi, 484/7. Displacement of the villages of Masiewo I and II, Hajnówka area, 224; fragments of the "Police Journal of the Police Battalion 322" in the case file).

26. Walter Tubenthal was the *starosta* in Oleck and the chief of the NSDAP in the region; from 1940, he was also the *starosta* in Suwałki. He died aged eighty-seven in Hamburg and was never brought to justice.

27. See Christian Gerlach, *Kalkulierte Morde. Die deutsche Wirtschafts- und Vernichtungspolitik in Weißrussland 1941 bis 1944* (Hamburg: Hamburger Edition, 2000), 656. No Joint or ŻSS operated in *Bezirk Bialystok*.

28. See Janusz Porycki, "Niemieckie policyjne organy terroru w Bielsku Podlaskim w latach 1941–1944, ze szczególnym uwzględnieniem karnego obozu pracy," *Bielski Almanach Historyczny* (Fundacja Ochrony Dziedzictwa Ziemi Bielskiej, Bielsk Podlaski, 2016), 86–114.

29. Among them were the forest service, motorized gendarmerie units, killing squads, and so forth.

30. Instead, two units (*Hubderteschaften*) of the so-called Belorussian police (*Weissruthenische Schutzmanschaft*) operated in *Bezirk Bialystok*. They were formed by the collaborationist Belorussian Committee (*Weissruthenische Vereinigun*), set up by the German administration in Warsaw in the winter of 1939–1940.

31. Especially because both forces wore very similar uniforms. Józef Nazarewicz testified during his interrogation on March 17, 1967, "First we wore green uniforms, but later they were changed to uniforms of the same color as the uniforms the Germans had" (AIPN Bi, 408/250, 35).

32. BAL, B 162/15216BAL, B 162/15966. It was impossible to find out whether the number 420 comprises both gendarmes and *schutzmen*, but because according to another source each post was ten to fourteen men strong, it would suggest that the number 420 covers the German and Polish policemen together.

33. Mikołaj Gonta, for example, testified, "I did not want to be in the police, but my father—the elder of the village of Miklasze—forced me to." His mother testified, "[My] son was to be taken to Prussia, and my husband asked the Germans to give him a job locally, so they gave him this job with the police" (AIPN Bi, 408/250, Court records of the criminal case against Mikołaj Gonta, 73).

34. Feliks Gałek, *schutzman* of the post in Hajnówka, testified, "I was forced to enlist to serve the gendarmerie as I was in very difficult circumstances ... I had no warm clothing, went unshod" (AIPN Bi, 404/274, Court records of the criminal case against Feliks Gałek, 48).

35. One of the accused *schutzmen*, Marian Żuchowski, stated that he alone was assigned to do it (AIPN Bi, 408/245, Court records of the criminal case against Marian Żuchowski).

36. For instance, "a resident of the village of Reduta informed the gendarmerie post in Orla that two partisans were sleeping in his apartment" (AIPN Bi, 408/250, Court records of the criminal case against Mikołaj Gonta). "Antoni Statkiewicz arrived at the post at dawn and reported that Jews were staying in his barn in Dziecinne-Kolonia" (AIPN Bi, 07/3, Court records of the criminal case against Kazimierz Kawiński).

37. At the end of the occupation, its strengh in the region was estimated at about thirty thousand men. The units of the NSZ supposedly numbered about seven thousand, the NOW three thousand, and the BCh one thousand members who had taken the oath.

38. Kossakowski, *Byłem adiutantem "Mścisława,"* 108.

39. "Taking into account that three classes of our youth have been enlisted for work in Prussia, some our soldiers and a considerable number of the youth had to leave their places of residence and hide in the forests. To prevent these forces from demoralization or joining Communist bands, partisan detachments started to be formed" (Gen. Komorowski do N[aczelnego] W[odza]: Biannual Report on Home Army Affairs and Location in the Country, August 31, 1943, *Armia Krajowa w dokumentach*, 3:120–121).

40. Jerzy Kułak, "Walka zbrojna na Białostocczyźnie," in Daniel Boćkowski, Jerzy Kułak, Wiesław L. Ząbek, and Stanisław Zybała, *Walka i martyrologia narodowa w latach 1939–1945. Materiały z sesji popularnonaukowej* (Nadarzyn: Vipart, 1997), 17. For more about the underground in that area, see Rafał Wnuk, *Za pierwszego Sowieta. Polska konspiracja na Kresach Wschodnich II Rzeczypospolitej (wrzesień 1939—czerwiec 1941)* (Warsaw: IPN, 2007).

41. The Germans captured about 5.7 million soldiers of the Red Army; 3.3 million of them died—most of them of the delibarately dreadful conditions created in German POW camps; Zdzisław Łukaszkiewicz, "Zagłada jeńców radzieckich w obozach na ziemiach polskich," *Biuletyn GKBZH* 5 (1949): 125–172.

42. There were several POW camps in *Bezirk Białystok*: in Bogusze near Grajewo, Białystok, Kiełbasin, Zambrów, Choroszcz, Hajnówka, and Augustów. None of them (except the one in Hajnówka) was located in Bielsk County; nevertheless the escapees could manage to get to them.

43. AP Białystok, Zespół Zarząd Miejski w Brańsku ([1941] 1946–1950), 566/1, Book of Regulations of the Mayor of Brańsk, 4.

44. "The contribution imposed on the Jewish population was 2.3 kilograms in gold, 5 kilograms in silver, and a large cash payment. All these were to be collected just in a few hours. In the event that these things were not delivered at the mandated time, a designated number of Jews was to be executed.... In early September of 1942, a subsequent contribution was imposed on the Jewish population, in the same amount as the first one.... [Only] a great effort on the part of every single person enabled the contribution to be paid." See AŻIH, 301/811, Testimony of Symcha Burstein.

45. "As had happened in Orla, the mayor ordered the Jews to dig three large graves not far from the synagogue. There was widespread panic. Terror and mortal fear struck the Jewish population. It took great effort to substitute this order with a contribution amounting to half a kilogram in gold, three kilograms in silver and 40,000 rubles" (YVA, M.11/50, Testimony of Rabin Halperin).

46. See Katrin Stoll, "Antyżydowska polityka w Białymstoku z perspektywy niemieckich sprawców," in *Stosunki etniczne podczas wojny i okupacji. Białystok i Wilno 1939–1941–1944/1945*, ed. Edmund Dymitrów and Joachim Tauber (Białystok: Wydawnictwo Uniwersytetu w Białymstoku, 2011), 158.

47. AŻIH, 301/6427, Testimony of Kadisz Goldberg.

48. Meir Peker, *W bielskim getcie i obozach*, in: *Księga pamięci Bielska Podlaskiego*, 524. In English: "In the Bielsk Ghetto & the Camps" in H. Rabin, ed., *Bielsk-Podliask: Book in the Holy Memory of the Bielsk-Podliask Jews* (Tel Aviv: Bielsk Societies in Israel and the US, 1975); accessed June 15, 2018, https://www.jewishgen.org/yizkor/Bielsk/Bie002.html#Ghetto.

49. Michel Dawidowicz, "Z getta Bielska przez Białystok do Auschwitz-Birkenau," *Księga pamięci Bielska Podlaskiego......*, 558.

50. USC, VHA, 10313, Testimony of Rubin Rosenthal.

51. "In the summer of 1942 . . . several youngsters went to a nearby village to trade some things for food. Just at that time, the Germans were terrorizing partisans. Finding the Jews in the village they, after brutally torturing them, shot them dead" (YVA, M.11/50, Testimony of Rabin Halperin).

52. Michel Dawidowicz, "Z getta Bielska przez Białystok do Auschwitz-Birkenau," *Księga pamięci Bielska Podlaskiego*, 558.

53. YVA, O.3/12628, Testimony of Cwi (Zvi) Prinz.

54. YVA, M.11/50, Testimony of Rabin Halperin.

55. AŻIH, 301/3521, Testimony of Fejga Rubin.

56. Lejzer Dawidowicz, "Skrawki z największej katastrofy ludzkiej," *in Księga pamięci Bielska Podlaskiego*, 542.

57. YVA, O.3/727, Testimony of Izaak Friedberg.

58. Szymon Datner, "Eksterminacja ludności żydowskiej w okręgu białostockim," *Biuletyn ŻIH* 4, no. 60 (1966): 24.

59. Yitzhak Arad, *Belzec, Sobibor, Treblinka: The Operation Reinhard Death Camps* (Bloomington: Indiana University Press, 1987), 135.

60. Franz Lampe testified that the police and the detachment of the KdS from Białystok, led by Schwede, carried out the liquidation of the Bielsk Podlaski ghetto jointly (see Stoll, *Herstellung der Wahrheit*, 263). He also testified that they executed between thirty and forty Jews "unfit for transport" (ibid., 264).

61. Waldemar Monkiewicz, "Zagłada skupisk żydowskich w regionie białostockim w latach 1939, 1941–1944," *Studia Podlaskie* 2 (1989): 348.

62. See e.g. AIPN Bi, 408/185, Court records of the criminal case against Włodzimierz Naumiuk; AIPN Bi, 408/288, Court records of the criminal case against Jan Charyton.

63. According to Ben Monsher (né Berko Monczar), two hundred boys and forty girls were there (USC, VHA, 05977). The commemorative plaque, which is now in Pobikry, states that it is a mass grave of 106 Jews from Ciechanowiec, executed by the German gendarmerie on December 2, 1942 (the date is incorrect). He himself found shelter in in a haystack.

64. Ben Monsher relates that when the Germans started to shoot the elderly, the young people dispersed. He himself found a shelter in a haystack and later

went to Brańsk, where the Jews were still awaiting transportation to Bielsk; USC, VHA, 05977, Testimony of Ben Monsher (Berko Monczar).

65. AŻIH, 301/1988, Testimony of Mosze Jęczmień; "Zagłada Żydów z Brańska oraz rozwój oddziału partyzanckiego Żydów z Brańska," translated from the Yiddish by Sara Arm.

66. Information provided by Zbigniew Romaniuk, *Brańsk i okolice w latach 1939–1953*, 9.

67. See http://cmentarze-zydowskie.pl/siemiatycze.htm.

68. AIPN Bi, 1/1716 Stanisław Janucki, "Powiat Bielsk Podlaski w latach 1918–1956. Dzieje polityczne, społeczne i gospodarcze," 20.

69. See Katrin Stoll, *Deportacje Żydów z Okręgu Białystok*, 128–129. The second ghetto that was not liquidated in the *Bezirk Bialystok* at that time was the one in Grodno (located outside the county of Bielsk Podlaski).

70. YVA, O.93/44194, Testimony of Lea Kirschner (née Lola Szpialter), translated from the Hebrew by Ela Linde. This information is unconfirmed.

71. AŻIH, 301/4086, Testimony of Kałmen Krawiec, "Przeżycia w Treblince."

72. USC, VHA, 25881, Testimony of Sheldon Chazen.

73. According to Lejb Trus's testimony (AŻIH, 301/2100).

74. According to testimony of Mojżesz Jęczmień (AŻIH, 301/1988). Both numbers seem overstated. Most of the escapees had returned to the ghetto "after few days," which most likely means before the final deportation to Bielsk Podlaski. Zbigniew Romaniuk reports that some 350 Jewish escapees were hiding in the Brańsk vicinity; Romaniuk, *Brańsk i okolice w latach 1939–1953*, 8).

75. AŻIH, 301/973, Testimony of Wolf Wiśnia, "Przeżycia Żydów drohiczyńskich."

76. AŻIH, 310/1257, Testimony of Symcha Burstein.

77. AŻIH, 301/2130, Testimony of Gerszon Lew.

78. Chaim Marmur, "From the Bunker in the Ghetto to the Life of a Member of the Resistance in the Woods," in *Kehilat Semiatycze*. Marmur writes that 150 persons were killed while attempting to escape, and 150 succeeded. Nevertheless, as far as large groups are concerned, any estimated numbers are highly uncertain.

79. AŻIH, 301/4086, Testimony of Kałmen Krawiec

80. *Encyclopedia*, 930.

81. AŻIH, 301/1853, Testimony of Symcha Burstein, translated from the Yiddish by Adam Bielecki.

82. AŻIH, 301/6640, Testimony of Hersz Gail.

83. Chaim Marmur , "From the Bunker in the Ghetto."

84. Monkiewicz, "Zbrodnie hitlerowskie w Siemiatyczach," 167.

85. Among others, the Jews who worked at the road construction in Klin-Połosy were shot after the resettlement; the German railroad worker, Albert

of Stuttgart, shot two Jews. In total, seventy persons were buried in the Jewish cemetery in Bielsk Podlaski; Monkiewicz, *Zbrodnie hitlerowskie w Siemiatyczach*, 170. In Trzeszczotka, the gendarmes from the Klejniki post killed seven Jews; AIPN Bi, 408/185, Court records of the criminal case against Włodzimierz Naumiuk.

86. In fact, there were 975, but one person, Golda Lew, is not included in my calculations, as some accounts mention her death, and at the same time, a person of that name is listed in the 1946 register of the Jews in Bielsk Podlaski. It is possible that two women in the Lew family (which had many branches) had the same first name and were of the same age. I was not able, however, to establish this conclusively.

87. As I have already mentioned, the ghetto in Prużana and the ghettos in the towns that are today located within the territory of Belorussia are not included in the final calculations.

88. They were, among others: Estera, Moszko, Sara Oskard; Liba, Rubin, and Leja Kozak; Joel Prybut; Pinie Szczygielski; Jankiel Rotensztejn; Naftali Chawal; Abram Dawidowicz; Sara Tabak; Pesza Rozen; Lejb Rosse; and Szymszon Brański (AIPN Bi, 404/130, Court records of the criminal case against Józef Adamiuk).

89. Moszko Oskard testified during the trial on February 17, 1948: "I was hiding with [Moszek] Klejnot near Oleksin. Once we had spent a night in a barn, early in the morning, we wanted to go to the house and ask for bread and matches. The guards walked by, and they surrounded us. Adamiuk grabbed me by the scruff of the neck. They herded us into the yard, where there were other Jews as well, and were about to lock us in a pigsty. When the elder went to bring keys, Klejnot and I started to run away together. People rushed after us with pitchforks. We managed to escape" (AIPN Bi, 404/171, Court records of the criminal case against Kazimierz Półtorak, Jan Ryczkowski, Jan Kindeusz, 127).

90. Often it is even difficult to establish what kind of "Germans" they were, as this general term is usually found in accounts. In Bielsk County, however, the prominent place among murderers of Jews was occupied by Polish *schutzmen*. They worked at the German police posts, where captured Jews were taken to be hand over to the "Germans."

91. AIPN Bi, 07/870, prosecutor's records of the criminal case against Antoni Jurczuk.

92. AIPN Bi, 404/293, Court records of the criminal case against Filip Sirocki.

93. AIPN Bi, 408/185, Court records of the criminal case against Włodzimierz Naumiuk, 95.

94. AIPN Bi, 404/299, Court records of the criminal case against Paweł Tur.

95. AIPN Bi, 404/416, Court records of the criminal case against Władysław Fionik and others.

96. AIPN Bi, 408/19, Court records of the criminal case against Piotr Tołoczko.

97. AIPN Bi, 404/331, Court records of the criminal case against Stanisław Kondraciuk.

98. AIPN Bi, 408/152, Court records of the criminal case against Józef Bandysiak and others.

99. Barbara Engelking, Such a Beautiful Sunny Day: Jews Seeking Refuge in the Polish Countryside 1942–1945 (Yad Vashem: Jerusalem, 2016), 202, 281–284.

100. An earth cellar; a large pit filled up with potatoes and covered with a thick layer of dirt.

101. USC, VHA, 01194, Testimony of Cipora Katz (née Fuchs). The story of hiding at the Leszczyńskis is also told by the Feldmans' daughters, Ester Amir Feldman (YVA, O.3/7531) and Szoszana Sapirstein (USC, VHA, 24839). The Leszczyński family was recognized as Righteous Among the Nations in 1987.

102. USC, VHA 50632, Testimony of Miriam Kuperhand; see also her memoirs: Miriam Kuperhand and Saul Kuperhand, *Shadows of Treblinka* (Urbana: University of Illinois Press, 1998), 48–49.

103. AIPN Bi, 1/1028, Case regarding the storage of four Jews: Herszko and Dora Rubinsztajn as well as Moszko and Mulko Klejno, Brańsk Kolonia), 120.

104. AŻIH, 301/2952, Testimony of Zofia Puchalska.

105. Israel Gutman, ed., Księga Sprawiedliwych wśród Narodów Świata. Ratujący Żydów w czasie Holocaustu. Polska (Krakow: Instytut Spraw Strategicznych, 2009), 879.

106. USC, VHA, 07427, Testimony of Sidney (Szyja) Żółtak.

107. AIPN Bi, 1/1032, Kolonia Popławy, commune Bransk. Help for Jews, 134.

108. AIPN Bi, 1/1349, Saki commune Kleszczele. Hiding of Jews by the Skarżyńskis.

109. Księga Sprawiedliwych, 678.

110. YVA, O.3/9891, Testimony of Chaja Kagan Sukman.

111. Ibid.

112. For example, on the 1946 list of the Jews of Bielsk (see *Bielski Hostinec* 2010, vol. 3, 81–84), the survivors, explaining how they survived on the "Aryan" side, filled in a questionnaire only with "in the forest" (two persons explained that they had "Aryan" documents).

113. USC, VHA, 41607, Testimony of Ester Fiszgop.

114. At the homestead of Zygmunt Klinicki, the Jews (among them the Finkelsztajns and Welwel Alperin) had three bunkers in the forest; they spent the nights in his barn, and he supplied them with food (AIPN Bi, 1/1757, Brańsk, losy Żydów, Bransk, fate of the Jews).

115. The family of Paweł Sobolewski at first sheltered Chaim Wróbel and Srul Brenner at home, then tended to them when the Jews moved to the bunker beneath the chapel (AIPN Bi, 1/1020, Brańsk—pomoc Żydom, Bransk—help to the Jews, Testimony of Chaim Wróbel).

116. He also looked after other Jews who, like Mulka Rechelzon, lived in the bunker beneath the chapel (AIPN Bi, 1/1757, Brańsk, losy Żydów, Bransk, fate of the Jews).

117. She fed those in hiding, including Jose Broide, Welwl Alperin (AIPN Bi, 1/1757, Brańsk, losy Żydów, Bransk, fate of the Jews).

118. "These Jews were supplied with food by the inhabitants of our village. They came to [our] homes at night and were given foodstuffs" (AIPN Bi, 1/1029, Swirydy: help to the Jews).

119. USC, VHA, 41607. Testimony of Ester Fiszgop.

120. YVA, SAPIR #7421797, Testimony of Icchak Grodziński.

121. Ibid.

122. The gendarmes took him to the post several days later, kept him for few days, and then released him (AIPN Bi, 1/1039, Popławy-Kolonia, pomoc Żydom, Popławy-Kolonia help to the Jews). There are different versions of the first names of the brothers—here they are mentioned as Mośko and Wełwko.

123. Four Jews of unknown names, who had been hiding at the Olendzkis' in Szmurły, were executed by the gendarmes of the post in Rudka (AIPN Bi, S31/70, Post in Rudka, Bielsk Podlaski County).

124. Majer Biały and Symcha Burstein were hidden for some time in the pigsty belonging to Kazimieruk. They were betrayed by the village elder; Burstein managed to escape, Biały was murdered. "After all that, the Germans arrested my wife, whom they shot three months later in the Bielsk Podlaski [camp], and I had to join the partisans, where I was until the Red Army's offensive in 1944" (AIPN Bi, 404/10, Court records of the criminal case against Włodzimierz Szklaruk, testimony by Kazimieruk).

125. Two anonymous Jews of Ciechanowiec were hiding in their barn, in the settlement of Łempice-Kolonia. On March 7, 1943, the gendarmes of Rudka found them and shot them dead behind the barn, while Konstanty Dobrogowski and his son were taken to the penalty camp in Bielsk Podlaski, and "from there, they went to Stutthof, where they both perished" (AIPN Bi, S31/70, Post in Rudka, Bielsk Podlaski County, 16).

126. In the fall of 1941, the German set up a penal camp (Straff-Lager) in Bielsk Podlaski in a former Jewish school building at 11 Zamkowa Street. The inmates of the camp were sentenced to hard labor, for example, digging up peat. The camp also served as a jail. It operated until July 16, 1944, with an average number of inmates between 100 and 150, and 1,500–2,000 in total; three persons died, and sixty-nine were shot (AIPN Bi, 1759, Waldemar Monkiewicz, "Obozy hitlerowskie w regionie białostockim").

127. AIPN Bi, 1/1028, Case regarding the storage of four Jews, 119. Those Jews, who were later sheltered, were Fajwel and Lejbko Szapiro, Mina Waser, and Sonia Weinstein; they survived there until the end of the occupation. The Popławskis had a large farm (twenty-five hectares of land), and as Popławski testified, "after the quotas were delivered, we still had some produce left." They also provided food for other Jews hiding in the area.

128. At the Danilczuks' (denounced by "one of the farmers of the village of Markowizna"), the Germans found and shot three Jewish women and a small child who were hiding there. They shot them immediately on the Danilczuks' property, dragged the bodies to a barn, set the homestead on fire, and left. This happened on May 10, 1944, when Apolonia Danilczuk and her two children were in her home village of Łazy, where a church *fair* was being held, and Antoni managed to escape into the forest (AIPN Bi, 1/1115, Chojewo—help to the Jews, 12, 30).

129. Someone had to inform on them, as Anna Glinka (née Gołąbecki) testified; Falkowski, a *schutzman* who was known to them, had visited them earlier. He said, "Denunciations have been made that you give Jews food. Tell your mom that if they find a Jew at your place, they will kill everybody on the spot together with Jews" (AIPN Bi, 1/1028, The Case of Keeping Four Jews, Brańsk-Kolonia, 113–114).

130. Dr. Charin's sister was hiding at the priest's, who assisted them and organized othere necessary help. Policemen from Topczewo came to the Turs, took Dr. Charin away, and brought the farmers and their son Wacław to the police station. Three days later, they released them (AIPN Bi, 1/1032, Kolonia Popławy, commune Brańsk. Pomoc Żydom).

131. USC, VHA, 22019, Testimony of Zuzanna Jastrzębska-Szydłowska. The NKVD arrested Colonel Szydłowski in 1944 and sent him to a camp. He came back to Poland several years later; his wife and daughter survived the war.

132. USC, VHA, 28361, Testimony of Regina Szymańska (née Wiszrubska); USC, VHA, 45233, Testimony of Adeli Boddy (née Wiszrubska).

133. http://www.jewish-bialowieza.pl/ocaleni/sarenka/.

134. Janusz Porycki, "Pomoc mieszkańców Bielska Podlaskiego ludności żydowskiej," *Bielski Almanach Historyczny*, 2017, 101–111.

135. Ibid.

136. https://sprawiedliwi.org.pl/pl/historie-pomocy/historia-pomocy-rodzina-sobolewskich.

137. YVA, O.3/7885, Testimony of Ariela (née Szwarzberg), Bat Szewa, translated from the Hebrew by Ela Linde.

138. USC, VHA, 5893, Testimony of Sheldon Wiprawnik.

139. AIPN Bi, 403/18, Court records of the criminal case against Edward Malinowski.

140. Szymon Datner, "Niemiecki okupacyjny aparat bezpieczeństwa w Okręgu Białostockim (1941–1944) w świetle materiałów niemieckich (opracowania Waldemara Macholla)," *Biuletyn GKBZH* 15 (1965): 9.

141. Geoffrey P. Megargee, *Front wschodni 1941. Wojna na wyniszczenie* (Warsaw: Świat Książki, 2009), 70.

142. "We came up with weaponry in the form of 20 rifles, 20 handguns, 2 handheld flamethrowers, machine guns, grenades—many boxes of, various explosives, flamethrowers—automatic ones" (AŻIH, 301/511, Testimony of Józef Elman).

143. "Josel Waterszulaza (with his wife Galia), Towi Brejtbard, Abraham Frydman, Beryl Segal (with his brother Lolek), Herszel Dinerman, Herszel Hanowski, Józik Frydman, and a Jew of Białystok whose name I do not remember, left the ghetto in early January [1943], armed with grenades, pistols, machine guns, carrying a Philips 6-vacuum-tube radio.... I, together with my brother Szmul, Misza Rawicki, Lejzer Izraelit with his wife, Abraham Rybnik, and others stayed in the ghetto to organize arms and urge people to come with us [to join] the partisans" (AŻIH, 301/511, Testimony of Józef Elman).

144. "The youth were put on alert. On Łajbel Majster's order, the combat organization began firing at the Germans from the roofs. Panic broke out, catching the Germans by surprise. The Jewish youth fired from all sides. The Germans responded with heavy fire. The exchange did not last long, however. The Germans ordered [the people] to seat [themselves] on the top of sleighs, and it was the beginning of the 'resettlement.' The Jews of Prużana were taken to the railway station in Orańczyce, where freight cars were already waiting" (AŻIH, 301/6427, Testimony of Kadisz Goldberg). The Jews of Prużana were transported to Auschwitz.

145. According to Goldberg, thirty-five persons escaped; according to Józef Elman, it was forty-five.

146. AŻIH, 301/511, Testimony of Józef Elman.

147. According to the diagram "Organizacja partyzantki radzieckiej w okręgu Białystok" (Michał Gnatowski, *Białostockie Zgrupowanie Partyzanckie* (Białystok: Uniwersytet Warszawski Filia w Białymstoku, 1994), sketch 3, 138), there was no Kirow Detachment within the Ponomarienko Brigade (or any other); the author might have had in mind a smaller formation, as the detachments were divided into companies, platoons, and squads. There were no more than ninety-seven Jews in the entire Ponomarienko Brigad (ibid., table on 142).

148. AŻIH, 301/511, Testimony of Józef Elman.

149. In November 1942, Hersz Szabes of Siemiatycze, *having previously been connected* with Russian partisans, brought to them a group of a dozen Jews who had escaped during the liquidation of the ghetto. "The first command issued by the partisan leader was to find out whether the Jews had gold and money and

if so—to return it immediately.... Several weeks later, new Russian partisans arrived in the district. A new leader, a Ukrainian, was elected. His first plan was to shoot all the Jews in his division. He confided this to Hershl Shabbes, to whom he had taken a liking, and told him to escape." *Semiatych: Its Growth and Destruction*, http://www.jewishgen.org/yizkor/siemiatycze1/sie500.html.

150. Ibid.

151. Ibid.

152. There is no data on two of eighteen families that provided long-term assistance; the remaining sixteen were inhabitants of the petty-nobility villages. At the beginning of the twentieth century, there were 182 villages in Bielsk County, of which 92 were petty-nobility villages, and the impoverished petty-nobility amounted to 20 percent of the inhabitants of the county.

153. AŻIH, 301/2100, Testimony of Alter Trus.

154. He helped, among others, the Szapiro brothers, initially hidden by the pharmacist Janina Woińska, for whom he found a place with the Popławski family in the Popławy-Kolonia (AIPN Bi, 1/1020, Brańsk—pomoc Żydom, 122).

155. He took care of the five-year-old daughter of Josel Tykocki (Waldemar Monkiewicz, *Pomoc dla Żydów w regionie białostockim*, 372) and helped the physician Dr Kamieniecka and her son (AIPN Bi, 1/1033, Koczery—pomoc Żydom).

156. Józef Przybyszewski (1906–1972), an activist of the national movement, was the regional government delegate for the Białystok Voivodeship and was arrested by the Soviets on August 7, 1944; he was held in prisons in the USSR until 1947. After returning to Poland, Przybyszewski was arrested, released after six months, and died in Warsaw in 1972.

157. For three of them, there was no data (AIPN, 0177/108, Provincial Headquarters of the MO in Białystok, Department C, "Organization of the people's authority and poviat public security office in the Bielsk Podlaski poviat in 1944–1945," Białystok, 1975, 5).

158. Tomasz Danilecki and Marcin Zwolski, *Urząd Bezpieczeństwa Publicznego w Bielsku Podlaskim (1944–1956)* (Białystok: IPN, 2008), 57, http://gminawyszki.pl/index.php?option=com_content&view=article&id=233&Itemid=428.

159. According to the census of Bielsk County (January 5, 1945), the total population was 191,353, and 105,195 were Polish, 85,945 were Belorussian, and 213 were "others" (Jews, Ukrainians, and Russians). AP Białystok, 354, 2, quote from Helena Koniuszek, "Społeczno-ekonomiczne położenie Białorusinów Białostocczyzny jako dominujący czynnik decyzji o przesiedleniu w latach 1944–1947,"*Acta Univeristatis Lodziensis Folia Historica* 91 (2013): 101.

160. For example, Belorussian schools were set up, activities of the Belorussian Theater and other organizations were allowed, and so on. It was short-lived,

however, and by the end of 1946, the Polish authorities suppressed all of the activities through which the Belorussian community of the Bialystok region had manifested its identity and independence.

161. See official IPN announcement after the investigation: http://ipn.gov.pl/pl/dla-mediow/komunikaty/9989,Informacja-o-ustaleniach-koncowych-sledztwa-S-2802Zi-w-sprawie-pozbawienia-zycia.html.

162. Eugeniusz Mironowicz, "Stosunki etniczne i główne linie polityki narodowościowej komunistów na Białostocczyźnie w pierwszych latach po wojnie," in *Stosunki etniczne podczas wojny i okupacji*, 376. Witnesses of the murders and former comrades-in-arms in Agnieszka Arnold Bohater talk about "Bury": https://www.youtube.com/watch?v=To8OWLnClbU.

163. I give the data for AIPN, 001834/98, Jan Pawluczuk, "Wkład organów bezpieczeństwa w walkę o utrwalanie władzy ludowej i likwidację reakcyjnego podziemia w powiecie Bielsk Podlaski w latach 1944–1947" (master's thesis, Instytut Nauk Społeczno-Politycznych Akademii Spraw Wewnętrznych, Warszawa, 1975), 124, 140.

164. Ibid., 141.

165. Ibid., 138. Every post was attacked more than once; the one in Siemiatycze was assaulted as many as six times.

166. Ibid., 150. In 1944, 22 people were murdered; in 1945, 242 people; in 1946, 66 people; in 1947, 35 people; and in the years 1947–1951, 26 people.

167. The postwar data refers to the part of the county that was in Poland's borders; I could not find any credible data on the eastern communes, which remained in the USSR.

168. On postwar banditry, see Marcin Zaremba, *Wielka trwoga. Polska 1944–1947. Ludowa reakcja na kryzys* (Krakow: Znak, 2012), especially the chapter "Banditry: Peasant War of Fallen Soldiers", 315–354.

169. AIPN Bi, 047/13, vol. 1, Report of the MO commandant in Drohiczyn on January 5, 1945, 2.

170. See report commandant MO in Bielsk Podlaski to MO Command in Białystok on January 13, 1945: "I report that Lew Benjamin, the owner of the 'Karpiniec' watermill near Siemiatycze, was murdered on January 5, 1945. The murder was committed by six armed bandits, who afterward utterly robbed his house" (AIPN Bi, 047/13, vol. 1, 4).

171. See http://cmentarze-zydowskie.pl/siemiatycze.htm. Most likely Arie Blustein is Icie. B., who was mentioned by Zbigniew Romaniuk, although Romaniuk provided different details of his death: "In the vicinity of Drohiczyn, peasants killed Icie B., who stole a cow" (Romaniuk "Brańsk i okolice w latach 1939–1953. Reminiscencje zdarzeń," *Ziemia Brańska* 6 (1995): 17).

172. YVA, O.3/12432, Testiomony of Jehoszua (Szaja) Warszawski. Szaja managed to return from Brześć on the Bug River to Poland. Later, he went to

Mandatory Palestine, where he tracked down his sister, who had been sent to Winnica. They were not been able to find their younger brother, Chaim Hirsz (Testimony from 2005, translated from the Hebrew by Ela Linde).

173. "On January 11, 1945, two members of the Communist party, Szloma Goldwaser and Szloma Gruda, were gunned down in Drohiczyn, probably by the detachment of the AK-WiN, [led] by Władysław 'Młot' Łukasiuk, That same month, in the nearby village of Smarklice, a detachment of NSZ most likely killed Szloma Gruda's brother, David." See Marek Chodakiewicz, *Po Zagładzie Stosunki polsko-żydowskie 1944–1947* (Warsaw: IPN, 2008), 156.

174. Gdal Gruda testified during the trial: "My brother Kiwa Gruda was a militiaman in Drohiczyn in 1945, and if he did not charge Jurczuk, it was only because it was a tumultuous time, and he even resigned from serving in the militia for that reason, as our two brothers had been murdered, and it had been related to this case" (AIPN Bi, 404/329, Court records of the criminal case against Antoni Jurczuk). In 1949, Jurczuk was sentenced to life imprisonment. He died in prison in 1950.

175. AIPN Bi, 047/1, vol. 1, A telephoneogram from the MO post in Brańsk, 10.

176. ABLG, 1/005974, Protocol written in the Group [?] CK, March 21, 1945, 8. These three murders were not confirmed by other sources.

177. See AŻIH, 301/1164, Testimony of Jankew Baszkes [Jankiel Blusztein]. The author gives the wrong date of the event: 15 III 1945.

178. Information on this is found in the testimony of Hersh Gail at the trial of the policeman Józef Fleks (AIPN Bi, 403/17/2, 125).

179. See: AŻIH, 301/2795, Testimony of Rachela Kosower. Arie Chazan also mentions this murder in an interview, (YVA, SAPIR #5247278).

180. According to Andrzej Żbikowski, about 650–750 Jews perished as a result of pogroms, underground activities, armed assaults, and assassinations in Poland after the war (*Żbikowski*., "Morderstwa popełniane na Żydach w pierwszych latach po wojnie," in *Następstwa zagłady Żydów. Polska 1944–2010*, Feliks Tych and Monika Adamczyk-Garbowska (Lublin and Warszawa, 2011), 93). For postwar murders of Jews in Poland, see (among others) David Engel, "Patterns of Anti-Jewish Violence in Poland 1944–1946," *Yad Vashem Studies* 26 (1998): 43–85; Aleksandra Bańkowska, Agnieszka Jarzębowska, and Magdalena Siek, "Morderstwa Żydów w latach 1944–1946 na terenie Polski na podstawie kwerendy w zbiorze 301 (relacje z Zagłady) w Archiwum Żydowskiego Instytutu Historycznego," *Kwartalnik Historii Żydów*, 3 (2009): 356–367.

BARBARA ENGELKING is a professor of social sciences, and for more than thirty years, she has worked on the Holocaust. She is the author or coauthor of ten books about the Holocaust as well as of several articles in Polish and international journals. She is head of the Polish Center for Holocaust Research in the Institute of Philosophy and Sociology, Polish Academy of Sciences, Warsaw. Her major publications include *"It Is Still Night..." The Fate of Jews in Selected Counties of Occupied Poland* (editor, with Jan Grabowski), *Getto warszawskie. Przewodnik po nieistniejącym mieście* [Warsaw Ghetto: The Guide to the Perished City] (with Jacek Leociak), and *"Jest taki piękny słoneczny dzień..." Losy Żydów szukających ratunku na wsi polskiej 1942–1945* ["Such a Beautiful and Sunny Day": Jews Seeking Refuge in the Polish Countryside, 1942–1945].

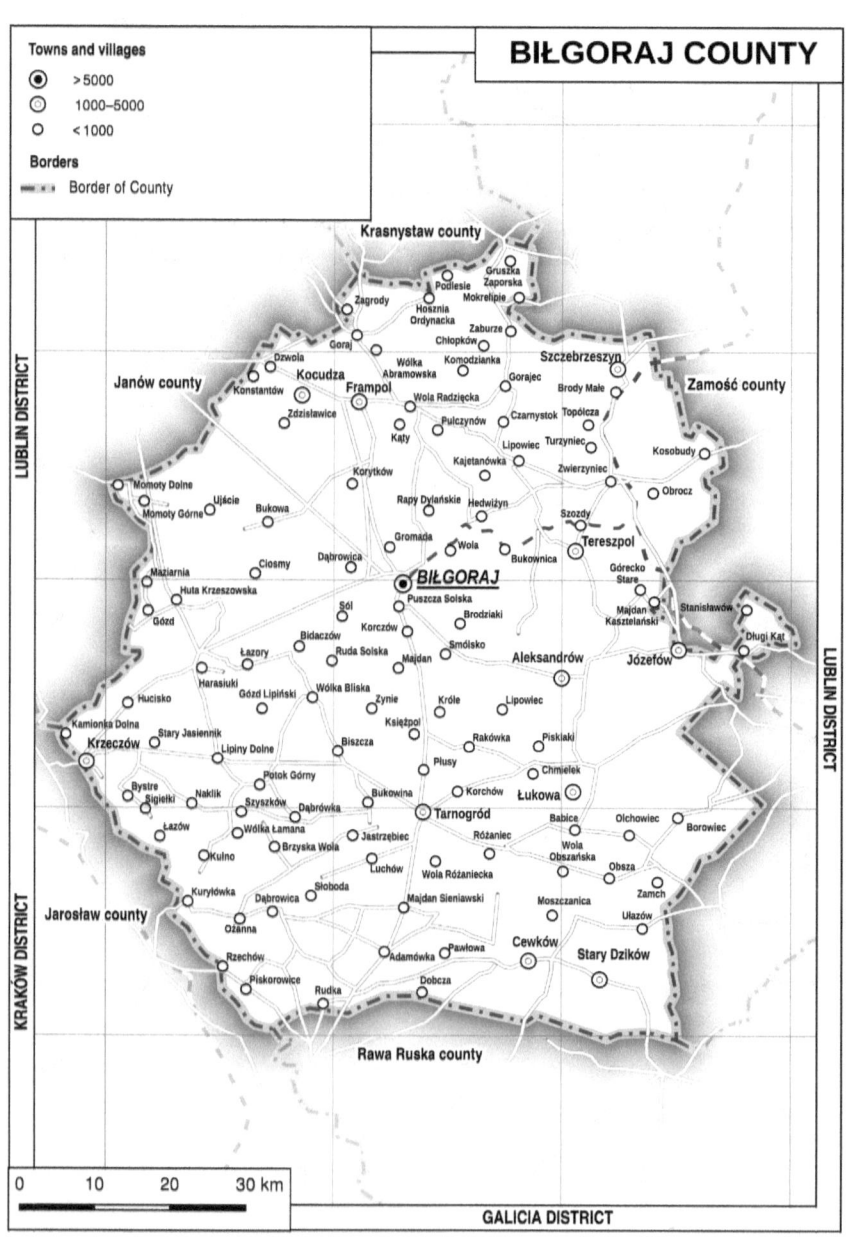

TWO

BIŁGORAJ COUNTY BEFORE AND AFTER 1939

Parallel Worlds

ALINA SKIBIŃSKA

THE COUNTY BEFORE THE WAR

Biłgoraj County (*powiat biłgorajski*) is located in today's Lublin Province, in southeastern Poland. In 1931, the county had a Jewish population of 12,938. When its borders changed to become *Kreishauptmannschaft* Biłgoraj in 1939, the population increased to around 16,000 Jews. Before the war, the county consisted of fifteen communes, but the number rose to twenty-three during the occupation. The following paper refers to its borders from the war, and thus describes the communities of Aleksandrów, Babice, Biszcza, Biłgoraj, Cieplice, Dzików Stary, Frampol, Goraj, Huta Krzeszowska, Kocudza, Krzeszów, Księżpol, Kuryłówka, Łukowa, Potok Górny, Puszcza Solska, Radecznica, Sól, Szczebrzeszyn, Tarnogród, Tereszpol, Wola Różaniecka, and Zwierzyniec. The terrain in the region is hilly, and almost half of its area consists of forests, mainly the Solska Forest (*Puszcza Solska*) and the Janów Forest (*Lasy Janowskie*).

Biłgoraj was a typically agricultural—rural, peasant, and economically backward—county. Its road infrastructure was poor and lacked not only broad-gauge railway but also surfaced roads (except for a section of forty kilometers); many villages were almost completely cut off from the outside world. There was no sewage system or electricity in the towns, but the county was rich in forests, providing resources for small industrial plants and craft workshops. The economic lives of most of the local Jewish residents revolved around small shops, workshops, door-to-door sales and hawking, leasing orchards, and cultivating small agricultural lots. Around 2,200 Jews lived in eighty farms as well as in villages.

The population of the county was rather conservative, which is visible in both its Polish and Jewish culture.[1] The society was half feudal, with a weak and small middle class and intelligentsia, and because of the dominant position of the Zamoyski family *(Ordynacja Zamojska)*, which was one of the largest private estates in Poland and Europe at that time, there were only a few other bigger estates in the county.

Brought there to lease estates, Jews appeared in the county in the first half of the seventeenth century. There were Jewish communities in several towns: Biłgoraj, Goraj, Frampol, Józefów, Krzeszów, and Tarnogród, as well as in Szczebrzeszyn and Zwierzyniec, which were annexed to the county during the occupation. There were two national and religious minorities living in the county: the Jews, and—according to a census taken in 1931—a group of 20,913 members of the Orthodox Church (around 17.9 percent).[2] In the interwar period, the Orthodox Church members (called "Ukrainians" in this paper for the purpose of simplification) had still only a vague sense of national consciousness and considered themselves to be "Ruthenians" or "locals." They spoke Ruthenian and Polish, and their families often included both Catholics and Orthodox affiliates at the same time. They lived in the villages both in south of the county and in Tarnogród. A strict policy of denationalization was adopted against them in the 1930s, with Orthodox churches being transformed into Catholic churches by force. As a result, the Polish-Ukrainian conflict intensified even before the outbreak of World War II.

The Jews living in Biłgoraj County were very religious. They attended orthodox or Hasidic synagogues, and they followed Hassids from Ger (Yiddish name for Góra Kalwaria), Aleksandrów, Warka, or Bełz. Although some assimilated to some extent into the Polish culture, the secularization process was much slower and less thorough there than in any other region of Poland. Jewish political life was dominated by all of Zionist parties, especially Agudath Israel and the Mizrachi party. Leftist parties were weak and never consisted of more than several dozen members, among whom were both non-Jews and Jews. It is notable that there were different political parties active in the Polish and in the Jewish circles. The only two exceptions were the Polish Socialist Party-Left *(PPS-Lewica)* and the Communist Party of Poland *(Komunistyczna Partia Polski)*, which gathered representatives of both nations but still organized them in two different fractions.

The separation of various institutions, sociocultural organizations, and political parties was complemented by the spatial division of small towns (shtetls) inhabited by both nations and creating one organism. Jews and Poles lived next to each other, but in clearly separated quarters. The former lived near the market square and in several adjacent streets, and they gathered around the commercial center and the most important religious buildings. If one were to find a keyword to most accurately describe Polish-Jewish relations in the interwar period, it would be a word like "beside," "apart," "separate," or "parallel." Cultural and religious life, tradition, customs, historical remembrance, and languages were separate. The local Jews, both adults and young people, used Yiddish in their circle even though their children attended regular Polish schools. The worlds of the Poles and the Jews were parallel to each other: The communities followed different customs, paths, and rhythms and came into closer contact mainly in the economic sphere. This was the only sphere that was common for the two national and religious groups, and it was precisely here that conflicts arose, especially the fierce fight against the "Jewish competitors," which intensified in the 1930s. But harsh antisemitic campaigns organized at that time by the Polish extreme right generally failed, and response was minimal in this region. There were no pogroms or major incidents, nor were there any casualties. Just as everywhere else, however, there were instances of boycotting and picketing Jewish shops, smashing windows and removing shop signs, starting fights, and distributing and posting antisemitic posters and leaflets.[3] The radicalization of opinions and attitudes was encouraged by the economic crisis of the 1930s and, as a result, the general lack of stabilization, increasing poverty, and overpopulation of the countryside, and yet antisemitic agitation was not spectacularly successful in the county, which was related to the weak influence of the National Democracy (*Narodowa Demokracja*) in the region. Among the local peasantry, who constituted the vast majority of the inhabitants of the county, the most popular were peasant parties. Their members maintained a rather neutral attitude toward the Jews and were never overtly antisemitic.[4]

The diary of Doctor Zygmunt Klukowski will be quoted often in this article, so herein are a few words of explanation about both the author and his unique journal.[5] It is the most detailed description of the Holocaust on the Polish province seen and systematically noted down by a Polish witness. The work is an incredibly important study of the atmosphere in a small town and nearby villages, and it is a reliable analysis of the occupier's crimes. It was precisely this journal that persuaded me to choose Biłgoraj County as the object of my research. I was interested in how Klukowski's observations and opinions compare to other eyewitness accounts and different sources, and to what extent the conclusions drawn from the facts he describes can be generalized. I was looking for the answer to a very important question raised by Dariusz Libionka: Was the scenario of the Holocaust in Szczebrzeszyn a common phenomenon?[6] As the director of the hospital in Szczebrzeszyn, Klukowski belonged to the elite of not only the town but also the whole Zamość Region. He lived on the ground floor of the hospital building, whose windows faced the market square and Zwierzyniecka Street. He did not look away or plug his ears, and he never avoided discussions or questions. He wrote several times that he was standing at the window and observing, sometimes even through binoculars. Klukowski was an extremely acute observer and chronicler of the fate of the Jews. At the same time, he was a consistent and careful legalist who never violated German resolutions, bans, or orders. He did not take risks for the Jews and treated them only after he had been given official permission. He was an ambivalent, far from black-and-white figure who was hard to judge. As to the questions of how many Jews he knew personally, what circle they belonged to, and whom he mentioned by (sur)name, it was a group of fourteen people, including mainly doctors, dentists, and pharmacists, as well as Lejzor Zero (a butcher employed by the hospital), who were part of his own professional circle. Other Jews were mostly anonymous for him; he was observing the tragedy of generally unknown people, of strangers. Regardless of how we perceive Klukowski himself, his diary should be greatly valued, as the author performs a true dissection and quotes many facts and details that are particularly important for us today in understanding human behavior.

1939–1941: SURVIVAL

The Outbreak of the War and the New Rule

The first days of September 1939 saw bombs falling on Biłgoraj, fires erupting around the whole city, and many injured and dead. Almost three hundred residential buildings, including a synagogue, a church, and a town hall, were burned to the ground. The fire swept through the center of the city and the streets inhabited mainly by Jews.[7] Frampol experienced a similar fate, where 80 percent of all buildings were destroyed. When the Germans entered the city on September 16, its inhabitants fell into despair. Acts of arson and violence were accompanied by flagrant acts of robbery in houses, shops, and workshops, as well as other acts of terror: Jews were forced to carry out various humiliating tasks. There were also mass executions of Jewish and non-Jewish hostages organized in public.

The Polish loss in the Battle of Tomaszów Lubelski meant the end of the September Campaign in the area. On September 26, the Polish side decided to capitulate. The Red Army had crossed the eastern border of Poland several days earlier, during the morning of September 17, but Soviet rule did not last very long. The Russians began to retreat on October 3, followed by thousands of civilians marching east. It is unclear how many Jews from Biłgoraj County got to the Eastern Borderlands at that time, but it is possible that there were as many as two, or even three, thousand. Whole families escaped to the east, especially young people and those who had nothing to lose: the homeless, the robbed, and the fire victims. For most of them, this desperate and hasty decision was also a lifesaver.

Jewish Communes during the Occupation

As in all of Poland, Wehrmacht soldiers and the German police destroyed thousands of Jewish sacred objects in Biłgoraj County, and the buildings that remained were turned into warehouses and stables; the soldiers also decimated religious books and Torah scrolls, and prohibited the practice of religion in public.[8] A decree proclaiming a new political and administrative entity, the General Government (GG), came into effect on October 12, 1939. The laws passed by its authorities would now control and regulate in detail every sphere of life of the inhabitants of the occupied lands and treat them as second-class citizens; the occupied territory as a colony would be exploited with impunity. There was a separate "law" concerning the Jews that put German racial policy in practice: They were ordered to wear armbands with the Star of David, their freedom of movement and right to use public means of transport were limited, and they were instructed to live in separate parts of towns that were isolated from the rest of the society (and that later turned into ghettos). The Jews were, in effect, deprived of all basic rights and liberties, as well as all of their property, and forced into slave labor. Their social degradation was seen also in everyday life. They were forbidden from visiting public parks and playgrounds and ordered to take off their hats for the Germans, bow to them, and move out of their way. The Jews were under a longer curfew than the "Aryans" and had to keep their homes "at all times open to the security authorities, Gendarmerie, and local authorities."[9]

The imposed Jewish councils (*Judenräte*) served as intermediaries between the Jews and the German authorities, and their members vouched with their lives for the execution of all of the German orders, the provision of the daily quota of forced laborers, and the payment of large "contributions" demanded from the Jews on the basis of perfidious pretexts. Regular Jewish communities ceased to exist, and all Jewish parties, organizations, and associations were banned and replaced with new self-help structures. All local community leaders, mayors, and *Judenräte* were ordered to prepare registers of all Jews living in the area; migration was closely monitored; and every Jew was charged with an absolute duty to register at their address. Jews' possessions served as the spoils of war for the Third Reich, so all of their personal and real property had to be registered (based on an ordinance of January 24, 1940) or risk its immediate confiscation.[10] The demands must have been treated very seriously, because the regulations by Biłgoraj *Kreishauptmann* (county governor), under which all community leaders and mayors had to register Jewish lands and buildings and put them into trust, were regularly repeated and constituted—together with forced labor—the most important topic in official correspondence about the Jews up until 1942. The Jews existed in the occupation sphere merely as a source of cheap labor, as well as a threat of diseases and epidemics. The aim was to degrade, objectify, exclude, and intimidate them. Subsequent restrictions, orders, and bans would push them further to the sidelines of the society, until they would finally find themselves totally outside of it.

Relocation

The decrease in population caused by many people escaping to the east was balanced out by resettlement from the western parts of Poland annexed to the Reich. More than 2,500 Jews altogether were relocated from Łódź, Włocławek, Kalisz, and the municipalities of Konin County to Biłgoraj County, especially Tarnogród, Szczebrzeszyn, Józefów, and Zwierzyniec. Moreover, almost 2,000 people were forced to migrate within the county, which additionally weakened the physical and mental condition of many of their inhabitants.

The borders of the GG were closed to migrants from the west in the spring of 1941. Moreover, starting from the fall of 1942, parts of the Lublin District, including especially the counties of Zamość, Hrubieszów, Biłgoraj, and Tomaszów (called the Zamość Region), were subjected to intense Germanization, which resulted in the deportation of around 30 percent of Poles and the relocation of some twelve thousand Germans to the region, mainly from Bessarabia. As a part of the General Plan for the East (*Generalplan Ost*), the German colonization was supposed to spread over huge areas of the countries of Eastern Europe, and it was initially implemented precisely in the Zamość Region.

German Administration and Police

As the capital of the county, Biłgoraj became the seat of all local civilian and military authorities. These included the most important office of the *Kreishauptmann*, as well as police units, the most significant one being the Order Police. It operated using a network of Gendarmerie, Polish Blue police, and Ukrainian police stations. Jewish policemen served in the Jewish quarter. There were only three Gendarmerie stations in Biłgoraj County: in Biłgoraj, Tarnogród, and Szczebrzeszyn. Polish Blue police stations were installed in the twelve places.

Table 2.1 Jews in Biłgoraj County in 1939, 1941, and 1942

Town and community	Late 1939	1941	1942
Aleksandrów (together with Józefów)	1,119 (1,700 before September 1939)	2,147	2,076
Babice	105	no data	142
Biłgoraj	5,010	1,900	2,200
Biszcza	205	96	180
Cieplice	25	no data	151
Dzików Stary	no data	no data	84
Frampol	1,537 (1,939 before September 1939)	538	500
Goraj	416 (498 before September 1939)	1,350	776
Huta Krzeszowska	17	no data	75
Kocudza	20	201	166
Krzeszów	348 (281 before September 1939)	432	446
Księżpol	83	no data	no data
Kuryłówka	no data	no data	223
Łukowa	263	no data	214
Potok Górny	243	no data	243
Puszcza Solska	37	no data	18
Radecznica	263	437	400
Sól	30	no data	no data
Szczebrzeszyn	2,748 (3,200 before September 1939)	2,810	2,912
Tarnogród	2,238 (2,515 before September 1939)	2,723	2,000
Tereszpol	39	no data	no data
Wola Różaniecka	83	no data	no data
Zwierzyniec	474 (520 before September 1939)	350	372
TOTAL	**15,303 (17,076) before September 1939**	**14,534** [Total of 12,984 plus 1,550 living in small towns not included in the above list]	**13,178**

Source: Data gathered on the basis of documents from Joint, the Jewish Social Self-Help (Żydowska *Samopomoc Społeczna*, ŻSS), the Central Welfare Council (*Rada Główna Opiekuńcza*, RGO), and local administration from the occupation period.

There were twenty-one policemen working in the county police headquarters in Biłgoraj, and the staff of local stations included usually eleven to thirteen policemen.[11]

The position of the *Kreishauptmann* in the GG was offered to German officials brought from the Reich. In Biłgoraj, the office was taken in turn by Dr. Werner Ansel from October 26, 1939, to March 31, 1942; Hans Augustin from April 1, 1942, to December 1, 1942; Dr. Karl Adam from December 1, 1942, to July 26, 1943; and Erich Löwner from July 1943 to June 1944.[12]

Everyday Life

From 1940, the Jews in the county were forbidden to leave the Jewish districts without a special pass. There were never any officially created and enclosed ghettos in the region, but Jews were ousted from houses adjacent to the street and from main streets. Their everyday life became a continuing struggle for the fulfillment of basic needs, especially finding something to eat. Deprived of their workshops and most of their legal sources of income (many Jewish shops and workshops were closed and put up for auction in 1940), they were doomed to existence in extremely difficult conditions. Just as everywhere else, displaced people were in the worst situation. There were large groups living in one room in burned villages, with no chance of permanent employment. Undernourishment and inability to maintain hygiene were commonplace, and it was impossible to avoid typhus epidemics in such conditions.[13] The number of people in need far exceeded the possibilities for help in every town and village, and "beggary reached staggering proportions."[14] People tried to manage, and some even ignored the German bans, engaging in illegal trade; working on farms grazing sheep, harvesting, and haymaking; and working seasonally in forests and sawmills.[15]

Forced Labor and Camps

Roundups for forced labor, for which the Jews did not receive any remuneration or even starvation wages, began with the first day of the occupation. It was initially short-term work: cleaning streets, removing snow, repairing war damage, and clearing forests, and later digging canals and irrigation channels, building the road from Biłgoraj to Krzeszów, and repairing the one from Lipiny Górne to Lipiny Dolne. The Jews were also sent to camps outside of the county and worked in quarries near Kraków, drained water meadows in Turkowice (Zamość County), and helped in Bełżec, where prisoners were hired to build border reinforcements in 1940. They were sent to camps in Werbkowice and Tyszowce, working in terrible conditions, wading waist-deep in water and mud, with "leeches crawling out of muddy water and sucking out the last drains of blood from the already exhausted people."[16] That same year, the Germans started to deport Jews from the county to five small labor camps. In Bukowa, near Biłgoraj (May 1940–November 1941 or 1942), there was a small camp where both Jewish and non-Jewish forced laborers drained and regulated the Bukowa River. When it was closed, the prisoners were sent to the camp in Dyle.[17] This camp consisted of several barracks located in the center of the village enclosed with a tall fence,[18] and its prisoners were forced to dig peat, work in the limestone quarry in Gliniska near Hedwiżyn, and construct roads. When Dyle was liquidated, the non-Jewish workers were dismissed, and the Jews were shot.[19] The camp in Bortatycze (near Zamość) was located in farm buildings, and its Jewish prisoners dug drainage ditches and worked on river regulation projects. The last camp was situated in Klemensów. Its prisoners built and repaired runways at the local military airfield. There was extreme hunger among them from the very beginning, and those unable to work were murdered. It was only in the spring of 1944 that the camp was liquidated.

In the face of all of the changes and events taking place in that time, the Polish-Jewish relations in 1939–1941 did not improve compared to the prewar times. Quite the opposite, they seem to have worsened, and even Klukowski "simply could not get rid of" the Jews. His words indicate irritation, fatigue, and emotional torpor. Toward the end of October 1942, the gendarmes offered him linens and all kinds of equipment for the hospital left by the murdered Jews, and he accepted the gift, although somewhat half-heartedly and not without reluctance, saying, "They could really be of use to us."

Relations between the two communities were very diverse already in the first period of the occupation, and as always with social phenomena, it is difficult to assess their scale and range. The Jews met with both negative and positive behaviors from Poles. The latter were much less common and may be reduced to several types of help only. This was usually offered for a fee, or was supposed to bring some benefits, and consisted in trade deals that were against the occupation regulations and thus risky and punishable by law. It also meant that such help was outside of the scope of regular behavior or trade exchange, and it was thus beneficial for the Jews and helped them survive in the difficult conditions. Aid offered in 1939–1941 falls into several categories closely connected to the situation of the Jews: helping with escapes to the east, providing the Jews in the ghettos and labor camps with food and medicines, and helping them get out of the camps. The attitudes of the non-Jewish Poles living in towns and villages and serving as appointed administrators of Jewish properties and companies were of crucial importance. It was their behavior that determined whether the Jews, the former owners, could continue receiving income from the seized property. What also mattered was help in hiding precious personal belongings and trade goods from confiscation, as well as continuing to conduct business together illegally, for example in shops, workshops, or slaughterhouses. Finally, there was the most explicit form of aid. It was very common and offered directly to those extremely poor people who resorted to the most desperate measure: begging in the streets. Hard living conditions drained the Jews of strength and reserves. They entered the most difficult period both physically and mentally exhausted and helpless.

1941–1942: CHANGES

A Harbinger of the Holocaust and the First Months of 1942

A ban on [Jews] leaving Jewish residential districts and a ban on providing Jews with any kind of aid—both punishable by death—were introduced on October 15, 1941, in the entire GG.[20] The terror was growing by the week. Public executions and acts of violence on the Jews for failure to wear armbands, illegal trade, hiding goods and furs, walking alongside footpaths, or any other made-up infraction became an element of daily life. The madness was driven by gendarmes and Gestapo members, including Stanisław Mrozik, Stanisław Majewski, Ryszard Barda, Roman Kolb, and Jan Siring, aiming to eliminate the elite and thus deprive the Jewish societies of their leaders. The following people were killed from June 1941 until May 1942: Krzeszów *Judenrat* chairman Mordka Furer[21] and Biłgoraj *Judenrat* chairmen Hillel Janower,[22] Szymon Bin, Szmuel Lejb Olender, and Efraim Waksszul.[23] Members of the *Judenräte* in Tarnogród and Zwierzyniec suffered a similar fate.[24] A series of mass shootings as part of the so-called *Kommunistenaktion*, an operation against the Jewish communists, was organized in May 1942. The first larger roundup ("sheer hell") took place suddenly on May 8, in Szczebrzeszyn:[25] People were "hunted" and shot "like game birds";[26] witnesses spoke of 100 or even 250 casualties in their testimonies. The murderers took the opportunity to bolster their finances when, after the operation, they "demanded three kilograms of coffee and 2,000 zlotys for the wasted bullets from the *Judenrat*."[27] The crime included one more aspect: outings of the local "tramps" (as Klukowski called robbers and thieves) to the Jewish district to rob the abandoned houses. Such a scenario, with local people cooperating in the activities aimed against the Jews and their property, would be repeated many times. The next massacre took place on May 11 in Józefów Biłgorajski. Three Gestapo members from Biłgoraj murdered 120 people in the town and a nearby quarry. Another large group of Jews died in Biłgoraj several days later, on May 14,[28] and the situation was repeated during an execution of forty-nine people in the cemetery in Tarnogród.[29] Next, more Jewish people were murdered in May and June on a road, in a square facing the town hall in Szczebrzeszyn, and out in a street of Radecznica and Gorajec. The repeating crimes created an atmosphere to which the locals were already becoming accustomed. "People ... ask themselves the following questions: How many Jews were shot? Who was assaulted? These are completely everyday events that are no longer a sensation."[30] The end of May brought another batch of information about Jews being "liquidated" in nearby towns: Krasnobród, Zamość, and Tomaszów Lubelski.[31]

The ghettos in Lublin and Lvov were the first in the GG from which freight trains filled with people left to a death camp. The first transport took place in March 1942. During the next few months, Jews from the Lublin and Cracow districts as well as from Galicia were sent to Bełżec and Sobibór; and from July 1942, Jews from Warsaw, Radom, and Bialystok were transported to gas chambers in Treblinka. Some 62,000 Jews died during the first three months in Bełżec, and around 66,000 in Sobibór. At the same time, thousands of people were killed in their dwelling places. Mass executions by firing squads as a method of extermination were still rather isolated events until mid-July, but it changed later.

The extermination of Jews in Zamość began on April 11, and the news soon reached Szczebrzeszyn and Zwierzyniec. Panic broke out: Some people ran into the streets looking for help, while others apparently sank into apathy and resignation. As Klukowski noted, "Old Jewish women spent last night in the cemetery ... Some take a risk and run away to the countryside. Many prepare hideaways here. Others put their children in the care of trusted 'Aryans' and send them to Warsaw."[32] Jews started making quick deals with Poles who promised to store their belongings. "People were carrying bundles, baskets, sewing machines, and the like all day long."[33] Someone denounced a group of Jews trying to enter Warsaw by train, and five of them were shot at the station in Zwierzyniec.

Tension and panic grew during the next months to finally be replaced by struggle with the torment of everyday life. April 1942 was marked by operations carried out in the next towns in the districts of Kraśnik, Lubartów, Izbica, and Lublin. Bełżec was a destination also for trains from the district of Galicia: Lvov, Stanisławów, and Kołomyja.[34] Everything was controlled by Globocnik's chief of staff, SS-*Hauptsturmführer* Hermann Höfle, and the genocidal orders were carried out by police special operations groups supported by local uniformed services. With the aim of intensifying conflicts and isolating Jews from the Aryan population as much as possible, the authorities escalated anti-Jewish propaganda in the province by distributing antisemitic materials; for example, local administration leaders put up posters saying "Avoid the Jew" on public buildings beginning in February 1942.[35]

Perpetrators and Their Helpers

From the middle of 1942, the police force in the Zamość region consisted of three reserve battalions (the 41st, 67th, and 101st) constituting the Twenty-Fifth Lublin Police Regiment. The extermination of the Jews in Biłgoraj County was managed by Battalion 67 (2)[36] with the help of local forces: the Gestapo, Gendarmerie, Polish and Ukrainian police, and *Sonderdienst* members,[37] as well as Jewish policemen used mostly to find people in hiding and those deluded with promises of survival. Neither the victims nor the eyewitnesses to the Holocaust knew who was committing the crimes; the only people they could recognize among the murderers were local gendarmes and police officers. Most of the perpetrators remained anonymous. No one knew where they had come from or who they were. Witnesses could describe only their behavior or the language they spoke, and sometimes they added some details about their uniforms or weaponry.

The next several weeks after the liquidation operations were a period of intensified roundups ("hunts" for the Jews); gendarmes and the German police caught Jews with the aid of the Blue police[38] and local fire brigades. This was the case, for example, in Łukowa, Józefów, Szczebrzeszyn, Radecznica, and Frampol. In addition, unspeakable crimes were committed even on children, and the number of victims was very high according to clandestine press: "There are Jewish refugees in forests near Szczebrzeszyn. The Germans prepare hunts with the help of the 'Blue' Police and Soviet prisoners-of-war.[39] Children are liquidated by smashing their heads against stones ... One 'blue' has already hunted down 69 Jews."[40] Those who got caught were put in local jails and once in a while led out in larger groups to execution sites organized sometimes outside of the town but most often in a Jewish cemetery.

Another matter that also needs attention is the active cooperation of the Polish civilians, who often entered campaigns against the Jews for profit and persecuted or caught them, took part in manhunts, denounced them, or even murdered them themselves. Thanks to Klukowski's invaluable notes and postwar witnesses' accounts and testimonies provided during criminal trials, we now know that a large part of local civilians joined the "anti-Jewish campaign." Referring to Szczebrzeszyn, Klukowski wrote about "civilians" and "quite a lot of Polish people, especially boys," and when he wrote about robberies, he had in mind many people who sought "loot." "People scramble for everything within their reach in opened Jewish houses; they are shamelessly carrying whole bundles with poor Jewish goods and chattels and commodities from small shops."[41] Tomasz Jamiński from Łukowa is a negative example of such an attitude. He filled in for his son in a fire brigade and took part in catching and robbing Jews.[42] From the files of a criminal case that ended with a death sentence and the actual execution, we learn also about Franciszek Kulesza from Biłgoraj. Employed as a worker at the municipal board during the occupation, he helped the Germans in deportation operations and hunts for Jews: "He searched for those hidden in cellars and bunkers and accompanied Germans officially during the day, hunting the Jewish people at every turn. I myself saw Kulesza hold a Jew by the scruff of his neck during the liquidation so that he could not escape from the Gestapo and mass executions. He was the only one in the whole of Biłgoraj, the biggest blackguard known to both the Poles and the Jews who had masses of lives on his conscience. After the operation, Kulesza was drinking with [the Gestapo men] and telling them about everything he had heard from others for around a month."[43] Witnesses saw him "raking through the pockets of Jewish bodies."[44]

1942: EXTERMINATION

The Course of "Liquidation Operations"

The execution of at least one thousand Jews in Józefów Biłgorajski on July 13, 1942 was the first operation aimed at murdering the entire Jewish population of a town, excluding a small group selected for forced labor. The murder operation was committed by Reserve Police Battalion 101, the "Death Commando."[45] German troops returned to Józefów twice more and, with their autumn manhunts, finally ended their extermination plan in the entire county, making sure not a single Jew remained legally in the town. It is a characteristic feature of Operation Reinhardt in Biłgoraj County and other counties of the Lublin district that the extermination was stretched over time, and that the operations were repeated every several weeks in almost each bigger village or town in order to catch those who escaped and those in hiding who sooner or later left their hideouts after an operation was finished and returned to the ghetto. It is clearly visible in Klukowski's diary, whose first entries about the murder of "every Jew met outside of the ghetto" appear in January 1942, and the last notes about the extermination of Jews from Szczebrzeszyn, the manhunt organized there, and the behavior of local people are from November of the same year. The "real" extermination in the county lasted six months—from July to December 1942—and ended in January 1943:

Józefów Biłgorajski (July 13–October 21, 1942)
Tarnogród, Biłgoraj, Szczebrzeszyn, and Zwierzyniec (August 8–9, 1942)
Szczebrzeszyn (August 8–9; October 21, 1942)
Łukowa (August/September 1942)
Zwierzyniec (October 21, 1942)
Goraj and Frampol (November 2, 1942)
Tarnogród (November 2–4, 1942)
Krzeszów (November 2–4, 1942)
Biłgoraj (November 2–4, 1942; January 1943)

―――※―――

What were the characteristic elements of the "Jewish operations" (*Judeneinsatz, Judenumsiedlung*) organized in the analyzed region from the perpetrators' point of view? We know that they were preceded by meetings led by representatives of the Operation Reinhardt staff and attended by commanders of local German police forces and SS as well as local civilian authorities, representatives of *Kreishauptmanns* and *Stadthauptmanns*, and a delegate of the Department for Population and Social Welfare (*Bevölkerungswesen und Fürsorge*), who was particularly interested in the population and economic effects of this massive operation.[46] I conclude from communal records that the dates of operations in a given village were known around three to four weeks in advance. Village administrators were then informed that they would have to "bury any bodies found" and report that to the Criminal Police.[47] On March 12, 1943, they were reprimanded and informed that the order required "burying Jewish corpses very carefully."[48] Furthermore, the summer of 1942 brought the beginning of rural night watches (*Wachdienst*), whose aim was, among others, to catch the Jews entering villages at night. The fact that the dates of extermination operations were set much earlier is also proven by deportations of Jews from smaller towns and villages to larger ghettos, from which they were supposed to be deported collectively to a death camp.

Murdering people on a mass scale required planning, coordination, and a way of dealing with thousands of people condemned to death in order to make sure relatively small units of police, Gendarmerie, and auxiliary services could control a crowd filled with fear and panic with as few losses on their side as possible. The course of a typical deportation operation was as follows: The Jews were gathered at a rallying point (*Sammelplatz*) and separated into groups of men, women, and children. It was a psychological maneuver meant to make resistance more difficult and force the victims to focus on their relatives—parents, spouses, and children—of whom they were losing sight. At the rallying point, the Jews were searched and robbed of money and all valuables. Those still fit for physical work were singled out and driven by cars to labor camps.

The rest of the victims, intended for "deportation" on the "Jewish train" (*Judenzug*), were sent to the deportation point; there was only one in all of Biłgoraj County: the station in Zwierzyniec. It was only fifty kilometers from there to the death camp in Bełżec via Długi Kąt, Susiec, and Maziły. The ride gave the Jews the last chance to escape, but only few of those who tried to escape from death trains survived the jump itself and the time in hiding until the end of the war.

A "perfectly" executed operation was supposed to start and end on the same day without any losses on the German side. The last operation, which was also organized in the whole county, lasted from November 2 to November 4. Larger towns of the county are located around twenty kilometers away from each other there, so it had to take more than a day to walk forty kilometers between Tarnogród and Zwierzyniec. Only children, old people, and luggage were transported by wagons provided by peasants. The columns were escorted by policemen on bikes, and during the night the road was lit by cars. The march was an incredibly difficult, and for some even impossible, effort. Its routes were strewn with hundreds of bodies. Mass graves are scattered along the routes between Tarnogród, Krzeszów, Frampol, and Biłgoraj, as well as between Biłgoraj and Zwierzyniec, although today most of these are unmarked and forgotten.

Extermination in Biłgoraj County was not carried out following one pattern only. Because the Jews lived in towns that were widely scattered around an area with a poor communication network, one more method of "solving the Jewish question" was adopted there. Instead of relocating people from the whole neighborhood to the closest larger settlement, the Germans sent a firing squad from village to village to catch and murder Jews on the spot.[49] Inquiries conducted by municipal courts right after the war and informing about executions and mass murders give us some idea of the huge number of Jews murdered in their hometowns.

All movable belongings of the murdered Jews that were neither looted nor destroyed during the operation itself were burned (this was the case for example in Józefów), while more valuable objects, clothes, and furniture were stored in warehouses and sent for further use in the Reich. Less valuable things were sold at auctions, first to Germans and *Volksdeutscher* (ethnic Germans living in Poland) and then, if not wanted by the former, to local Poles. Pots, plates, pieces of furniture, bed linen, lamps, clocks, window curtains, and clothes were among the spoils. They were all "ownerless objects" that did not belong to anyone, meaning "objects whose owners were shot by the Gendarmerie or deported."[50]

The above emotionless description of the deportation and extermination operations does not depict what really went on and the terrible and heartbreaking scenes that could be witnessed. The victims put up resistance, running and hiding across the whole county—it was only the scale of such behavior that differed, depending on the time and place. After the August deportations, when the news of "the deported to work in the East" were replaced by information about massacres committed against the Jews, there was almost no one left to believe in the German lies. During the autumn deportations, many people tried to escape, which was met with increasingly brutal reactions by the perpetrators. Above all, it is the unusual brutality and quick responses of policemen and gendarmes that need to be emphasized.[51] Everything happened at staggering speed: Dogs trained to hunt and attack people barked incessantly; people were kicked, beaten, and pushed with rifle butts; and orders were shouted all the time. There was no time to think. One's whole body and all one's senses were under constant attack. Each sign of resistance, each word of objection, or any gesture that showed contempt for the perpetrators was immediately punished, and the stubborn and disobedient ones were brutally killed in a show of deterrence. It has to be clearly mentioned that the phrase "being shot" during "liquidation operations" is just a matter of convention that distinguishes between dying on the spot and dying on the way to a rallying point, during the ride to the camp, or in a gas chamber in Bełżec. Dying on the spot often meant tortures inflicted with spades, sticks, rifle butts, or boots, or dying of suffocation in a mass grave. Some victims did not immediately die from bullets but were buried together with the dead and died clinging to lifeless, naked, blood-covered, and cold bodies, with sand clogging their eyes and mouth, fighting to the last moment of their lives and their last breath of air. Although covered with soil, the mass graves moved for a long time after the perpetrators had left.

Testimonies of people present at the liquidation operations leave no doubt that the blood of the victims literally flooded the streets. Everyone dragged out from a hideout or caught while escaping was either immediately killed or put in jail and afterward led in groups of several dozen people to a Jewish cemetery and executed by a mass grave that had been dug in advance. Bodies of people killed in the streets and squares were cleared away and buried in mass graves by local Poles, who also assisted during the executions and covered the bodies with lime and sand. The German perpetrators did not try to hide what they were doing from the locals; everything happened openly and publicly. Whoever wanted to know, knew; whoever wanted to hear, heard.

The days and weeks after the last operation in November 1942 were a period of intense "hunt for the Jews" (*Judenjagd*); the perpetrators knew they would not manage to catch and deport all the victims on one day. Despite the fact that the operations were repeated, hundreds of Jews were still in hiding in shelters and hideouts, forests, or houses of peasants they knew. This period up until the liberation is the last, third stage of the Holocaust. Almost the whole effort of hunting, denouncing, or even murdering the Jews at that time lay on the local people (*nichtdeutsche Bevölkerung*, non-German population, as German officials in the occupied lands called them), just like the effort of helping, hiding, and saving those condemned to death. Luck, both good and bad, depended largely on the Polish surroundings, but there was a large group of Jews in the county who fought for survival entirely alone. How some survived or did not manage to survive that period is described in the next parts of this paper.

The Number of Victims and Refugees—Estimates

The most probable number of Jews living in the county on the day before the extermination operation is 14,500 (based on ŻSS data and RGO files from 1942), including around 3,000 refugees and displaced people. It appears from all the facts about the operations and executions of 1942 that the number of people who died would exceed the number of those who lived in the county by 2,400–4,700, yet the overall balance should include also the people who hid or escaped. Unfortunately, most of the data comes from narrative sources, as well as two postwar questionnaires that were full of errors.[52] One should assume that the witnesses considerably overstated the number of victims by at least 25–35 percent. Having compared much numerical data and considered all kinds of reservations, the conclusion is that the number of victims of Operation Reinhardt in Biłgoraj County in 1942 did not exceed 13,000; at least a half of them were murdered on the spot and the rest in Bełżec.

It is also very hard to determine how numerous the groups of refugees were. The number of refugees from Szczebrzeszyn is estimated at 500, from Józefów at 300, from Biłgoraj at several hundred, and from Krzeszów at several dozen. Many people from Goraj and Frampol escaped to forests, fields, and closest villages, but the numbers are unknown. Based on the above information, around 1,500 people in the whole county attempted to hide in the towns or escape and hide, with the lower limit being 1,100 people. The estimate is inaccurate but based on all available sources, probable, proportionate, and correlating with the number of the Jews staying in a given village or town during the last operation.

1942–1944: SURVIVAL STRATEGIES

Resistance and Escape

It was relatively uncommon for the Jews to leave towns and villages before murder operations. Such decisions were taken by young people who were ready to do anything to survive, despite the great difficulty in leaving their family and community. Many Jews were restrained by fear of abandoning the sphere that was so close and familiar to them, and of entering the "Aryan," alien, and terrifying sphere in which refugees were condemned to loneliness and confrontation with a hostile, unfriendly, or at best indifferent environment.

Escaping during the operation itself, although most common, involved the risk of immediate death. The fear of dying paralyzed some and filled others with strength needed to mount resistance. Fear and repression caused some to put off the decision to escape until the very last moment, deluding themselves that they would avoid misfortune by being deemed "necessary" and thus safe if they keep working. The Germans fueled that conviction in the Jews, which is why many sought any job in the county, real or fake, when the deportation operations intensified. The return of a group of refugees to Krzeszów was an extreme example of despair and helplessness in the face of the Holocaust, accompanied by the apparent reasonableness of such thinking. They came to basket-maker shops and voluntarily, under no external compulsion, started to help at their workshops. They wanted to believe they would not be deported if they were perceived as being useful. It was no use: Within a short time, all of them had been executed outside of the town.

Many tried to escape at the very last moment: during a long march to the deportation site (the forests surrounding the shtetls in the region favored this option), or when they were already on the train to Bełżec. Last-moment escapes reduced the time spent outside of the Jewish districts and far from one's own community to the bare minimum, as well as the time spent on the threatening Aryan side. Israel Gajst was one of those who escaped from the train. He set off back for Biłgoraj to be among the Jews in the ghetto, in a place that was still much safer for him than the Aryan side. In the forest, Gajst met another refugee, Szloma Fajl, who had been shot in the leg. They both wandered around the forests for several days and nights, feeding on "various forest plants" and whatever they were offered by peasants. Eventually Gajst was determined to return to Biłgoraj and Fajl to Frampol, so their paths diverged. Gajst was lucky to receive an *Ausweis* (work permit) and stayed in a remnant ghetto[53] as a worker until January 1943. He was selected for labor in camps and miraculously survived the war in the HASAG camp in Częstochowa. He was one of the few Jews from the county to survive the liberation in a labor camp. His own influence on his survival was limited: From the moment he returned to the ghetto, fortune favored him—he was selected for labor groups at each stage and somehow managed to survive in the difficult labor conditions.

Jan Juryczkowski, from Szczebrzeszyn, wrote that the population under the occupation was highly divided. Apart from the Poles, who themselves were

Figure 2.1. Helena (Hencia) Wagner (*right*; after the war, Helen Abraham), with a group of Polish women, forced laborers in a munitions plant in Menden, Germany, where she arrived armed with Aryan papers (USHMM, 41420).

divided into those openly or quietly cooperating with the authorities, opportunists, and a group mounting resistance and operating in various underground structures, the region was inhabited by *Volksdeutscher*, Germans from the Reich, and many Ukrainians. Only those Jews who were highly assimilated could live "on the surface" (according the nomenclature proposed during the occupation by Emanuel Ringelblum), using Aryan papers. There were only several cases like that in Biłgoraj County. Estate owner Jan Zamoyski gave shelter and a job to Ignacy Fabrykant, an outstanding specialist in wood trade, and his wife;[54] composer Jerzy Wasowski[55] and his father, Józef Wasowski; and Doctor Dionizy Gelbart (who officially went under the name Edward Gadomski).[56] Henryk Rubanek and Ludwik Ehrlich, a renowned international law professor, worked in Huta Krzeszowska as officials at the local forest district office.[57] Krystyna Mazurkiewicz (her husband was Polish) and her father, Stanisław Kleiner, came to the village of Topólcza from Lvov and stayed with the Kołodziejczyk family, who did not know that the tenants were Jewish. Krystyna's brother-in-law was a priest in Topólcza. He betrayed them before the hosts, blackmailed them, and finally forced them to move out. "Fortunately, there was a single young girl in Topólcza ... who was willing to invite us to her only room and with whom we stayed with our father until August 1944."[58]

A small group of assimilated Jews from Biłgoraj County survived "on the surface," mainly outside of the county, where they could not be recognized by their former acquaintances. They bought fake documents with Polish names, obtaining blank *Kennkarte* (ID card) forms from, among others, Mieczysław (or Stanisław) Paczos, who worked in the Registration Department of the Municipal Office in Biłgoraj.[59] Another very risky method of surviving was to leave for the Reich to work, thanks to which several people survived, almost exclusively women.[60]

In the eyes of the Polish witnesses to the Holocaust, the Jews maintained a passive attitude: "It was a sad fact for the local people that the Jews went to their deaths with such calmness and resignation."[61] "Most Poles asked themselves the question why the Jews in Tarnogród did not defend themselves against the extermination."[62] The same author highlighted, however, that there were no favorable conditions for the Jews to start armed self-defense. They were convinced that subordinating to the German regulations would increase their chances of survival. Moreover, the Jews—mainly Hassidim—believed in succumbing to "God's will" in a kind of fatalism of history. Yet another author noticed the psychological basis of the Poles' opinion about the Jews: It served as a way to boost their self-esteem and console themselves. "The more insecure I felt, the more often I and the others recited with suspicious eagerness that the Germans wouldn't have it as easy with us they had it with the Jews. That's totally out of the question! The consolation was cheap and short-term."[63]

There was no Jewish resistance that would display the characteristics of an organized, armed rebellion in Biłgoraj County. In those conditions and circumstances, the oppressed, ruined, antagonized, and isolated from the rest of the society had no chance to organize themselves and start fighting, which would actually have made it possible to think about the survival of at least a larger group. It was also clear that each rebellion was doomed to failure, accompanied by bloodshed and the suffering of others. The author of a paper about the factors determining the attitudes of the Jews during the occupation often highlights that larger groups of Jews could not even consider hiding on the Aryan side because of the radically devastating German policy.[64] Many Jews, however, tried to save themselves individually or, if possible, together with their families. The decisions and attitudes of individual people were influenced by both material and psychological factors. Years after the events, Feliks Urman's daughter quoted her father, for whom fear and hunger were the biggest motivation for survival.[65] Some fought for their lives in order to give testimony about the crimes committed, while others were motivated by the innate survival instinct. But weak, exhausted, and poor people most often did not engage in any kind of resistance.

"[Tajwlowa and her family from Józefów] washed themselves, took the most valuable things only, no bundles, and said goodbye to us. She told me that it was over, that they were going to die. She asked me only to look after her son, who could survive because he grazed cows outside of the town. She did not try to hide, but went courageously with her children to the market square. She had nothing left to sell for food or any other necessities. Despite her composure, she was trembling from head to foot."[66]

Hideouts in the ghettos were planned for survival during the operations themselves and a short period afterward. Sooner or later, one had to leave and hide elsewhere. One of the major factors that broke the will to survive and made any long-term or reasonable planning impossible was the inability to forecast how much time one had to spend in hiding. Some Jews managed to prepare bunkers (in the town itself or outside of it) supplied with much food and water, but this did not happen often and—as we know—did not ensure survival. The majority escaped spontaneously wherever they could and hid in attics, cellars, concealed nooks, domestic equipment or furniture, and even cemetery tombs.

What they did in advance usually consisted of safeguarding their possessions, entrusting them with various friends for safekeeping (if possible more than one person), and arranging the methods to reach them if needed. These Jews often had problems with recovering their property and sometimes had to pay with their lives for it.[67] The topic of objects, money, jewelry, and gold that the Jews really or allegedly had is addressed in many statements. The Jews in hiding were a potential "source of income" and could be robbed at any moment without risking anything; they could be denounced, chased away, or even killed. "Peasants were hiding Jews in the countryside and taking gold, clothing, or other necessary things from them in exchange. It happened sometimes that after they had taken the things they wanted, they turned them in to the police or even secretly murdered [them]," Tema Wajnsztok wrote.[68] There were, however, also very honest people—for example, the Stańczyk family from Frampol, who stored the possessions of the Birk family and returned everything to Chana Birk after the war. They also helped her both during the occupation and afterward.[69]

Boruch Wermut, the owner of a mill in the district of Bojary, Biłgoraj, turned out to be particularly enterprising and farsighted. "I went to the forest together with [Herszek] Kahan and [Lejb] Kacenberg to work so that I could still live and get to know the terrain in case I had to hide during persecution."[70] Wermut prepared several bunkers in the forest, and later circulated between them and the mill. He returned to Biłgoraj to obtain food, entered the ghetto, and dug up previously hidden objects. The mini ghetto that existed there until the middle of January 1943 made it possible for several dozen people to hide inside in attics and cellars. This is where the refugees returned to spend some time with their friends and families, exchange information, or find the vital items and food. As long as there was at least one legal group of Jews in the ghetto, it served as a point of reference for those in hiding and a place to which they could return.

Pretending to be "Aryan," even without the right documents, was another desperate way of trying to survive during the extermination operations; however, this method required a cool head and was available to very few people. During the operation, when everything was happening chaotically and with lightning speed, gendarmes and policemen sometimes skipped checking people's documents and simply assessed their appearance, which saved some Jews.[71] There is even testimony of Germans helping Jews. Such a situation happened in Szczebrzeszyn, described by Wanda Kinrus, Doctor Bołotny's wife. There was some "very nice and kind *Volksdeutsche*" employed at the municipality, she wrote, who helped her and other people during the operations. One was Bołotny's patient, but Kinrus unfortunately did not remember his name.[72]

Help offered to the Jews during the operations or right afterward most often included one-time, spontaneous acts that were more or less risky but most of all saved somebody's life at a given moment.[73] It was not about satiating someone's appetite or quenching their thirst, but about helping immediately and acting decisively, thanks to which it was possible to escape the clutches of the perpetrators. People offered temporary shelter and useful information, or they misled policemen and their assistants. Whoever escaped the manhunts and survived the first two to three weeks after the deportation operation sought a more permanent shelter. Some of the Jews remained in forests and settled down in camps (described later in the paper); others wandered around villages and settlements.

Hiding in Villages

To survive, one had to satisfy one's hunger and defeat the cold, exhaustion, illnesses, fear, and lack of hope. One needed strength and the will to survive. Some found the obstacles on the Aryan side to be insurmountable, broke down, and turned themselves in to the police or the authorities.[74] Although he survived the massacre in Winiarczykowa Góra, shoemaker Flug from Józefów Biłgorajski committed suicide in his hideout several days later.[75] Among other tragic cases was a seventeen-year-old girl surnamed Merec from the village of Kusze, who starved to death while hiding in an attic.[76] It was also extremely painful for those fighting for survival when people callously chased them away, set dogs on them, or threatened, robbed, or even murdered them ("they threatened to kill me," "he beat me up and threatened to kill me if I didn't leave the house"[77]). Going from door to door; knocking at windows; and begging for mercy, a slice of bread, or permission to warm themselves up or to sleep in a barn, a cowshed, or in the attic for at least one night; running away from local guards and barking dogs—this is what every refugee from the ghettos experienced. The homeless often did not even ask for permission to sleep in farm buildings but rather burrowed into the hay under the cover of darkness and left back to the forest before dawn.

Finding food came only after the need for safety, and it was very risky. It ranged from picking up mushrooms and blueberries in the forest to begging to trying to buy something (unfortunately, testimonies lack information on prices and their possible inflation); stealing from orchards, fields, and cellars at night; or robbing and assaulting others. Foodstuffs obtained were absolutely basic: bread, milk, potatoes, swede, and sometimes soup or groats, rarely seasoned with some fat. Those who helped and rescued others were common, poor people; their houses were often thatched, wooden, single-room cottages. It was impossible to hide anyone in such conditions. The homeless Jews therefore searched for shelter in farm buildings, attics, haystacks and mounds, bunkers, pits, ditches, or burrows dug in the ground.

There were no underground organizations in the countryside that would financially support Jews in hiding or those who helped them. Everyone—both the refugees and their helpers—was left to his or her own resources. Their narrow inner circle included only closest family members and sometimes also several trusted friends or neighbors, and as such it constituted a small support group. Usually, the whole family that hid the Jews shared all the duties; the most important of these were providing them with food and disposing of waste.

People "roamed and wandered about"[78] within a radius of no more than ten to fifteen kilometers to make sure they did not come too close to the towns. They would most often go from door to door within one village and move forward under the cover of darkness only if they could not find any help there. Some villages and farmers were favored over others. The majority of the Jews hid alone or with one or two closest family members or friends. It was very rare to hide with people whom one had just met. After escaping together, Jewish families often had to split, but they were still determined to maintain contact and sent each other messages via their Polish friends. At night, if possible, they would leave their hideouts to relieve themselves, get some air, loosen up their stiff bodies, look at the sky, or set off in search of another hideout.

The survival conditions were largely dependent on the permanency of the hideout. Only a certain percentage of people survived the whole period from 1942 to 1944 in one to three safe places. They were exceptionally lucky to find Poles who offered them long-term help, or sometimes even treated them like family. These cases often involved children and girls, as it was easier to present them to the world as Polish cousins or even one's own children, and harder for strangers to unmask them. Even younger children knew they had to hide

Figure 2.2.
From the left: Chaim Rozenbaum, Perl Frajberg, Bencjon Rozenbaum, rescued by forest ranger Jan Mikulski from Wola Duża, close to Biłgoraj. Caption under the picture: "Wola, 1943. Lunch in the storeroom in the ranger's house. Glory to Chaim Rozenbaum who fell fighting for Berlin. J. Mikulski." Jan Mikulski, from the collection of Danuta Mikulska-Renk.

their true identity and could not speak Yiddish. They quickly learned Catholic customs and prayers, and as orphans they aroused others' sympathy. Examples include Rywka Dawidowicz, who stayed in one place (the village of Kąty near Frampol) throughout the period under the name of Stefa;[79] Dora Birk, who was saved by a Polish-German family in Zamość;[80] and Feliks Urman, who lived with the Siek family.[81] Children thrown out of trains almost always died, but miracles happened. A three-year-old girl was found near the tracks in Majdan Niepryski and adopted by the widow Aleksandra Knap.[82] Another person who survived in only one hideout was Henryk Fladell (Fledel) from Leżajsk, who was offered shelter by Walek (Walenty) Kaczyński from the village of Brzyska Wola. Kaczyński was a very poor man who supported his whole family working in a small farm and as a chimney sweep. Despite his own extremely difficult financial situation, he still gave shelter to Fladell and his friend Abraham Hamfing. They spent eighteen months in the hay of the attic in Kaczyński's house. They never left the attic, ate potatoes only, and never washed or changed clothes. Kaczyński

Figure 2.3. Małka Wakslicht (after the war, Rita Goldshmid), born in 1932 in Biłgoraj, daughter of Cudyk and Estera (née Gidbert), residing on Bagienna Street. Both parents were murdered. For some time, she hid alone in a forest, where Jan Mikulski brought her food. Later, she moved to his ranger's farm in Wola Duża, where she stayed together with other Jews in a hideout built under the shed where rabbits were kept. She survived. After the war, she found her way to an orphanage in Lublin and later immigrated to the United States. Photo by Jan Mikulski, from the collection of Danuta Mikulska-Renk.

Figure 2.4. Rywka Wajnberg (after the war, Lila Stern), born in 1932 in Biłgoraj, daughter of Mosze and Basia (née Goldberg), rescued by forest ranger Jan Mikulski. Rywka's father and Jan Mikulski knew each other from before the war. Photo by Jan Mikulski, from the collection of Danuta Mikulska-Renk.

saved them because he was an honest, compassionate, and decent man. People like him, capable of long-term, selfless help, are "autonomous altruists." They are fiercely independent, free from external pressure and unaffected by social control, and act in accordance with their internal moral imperative.[83] Stanisław Sobczak, a Righteous Among the Nations from Frampol and a good, kind, brave, religious, and truly unique man, was another example of such people.[84] He hid twelve people from the fall of 1942 until the end of the occupation in July 1944, and "when he learned from posters that helping and hiding Jews was punishable by death, he remarked that the punishment was the same for one Jew and for ten Jews, only it was harder to feed ten."[85] After liberation, partisans (or perhaps ordinary bandits) punished Sobczak by beating and robbing him "for his crimes": hiding Jews and communists. They took his pigs, horses, and anything else they could lay there hands on, and they beat him so severely that he could not move for several months. It is generally considered that many people's help was needed to save one person, but the example of Sobczak or the forester Jan Mikulski (who hid five people) illustrate that one person or one family could save many; this is also confirmed by Zuzanna Schnepf-Kołacz's research.[86]

Most of the Jews had to keep looking for new hideouts. Their lives were marked by fear, stress, and tension. Aron Kisłowicz wandered around the vicinity of Frampol, going from one farm to another and laying false trails. He finally came to Władek Paszkow, to whom he later owned his survival. Tema Wajnsztok from Frampol kept coming back to the same homes—of Aniela Chmiel and Janina Sitarz (Ducherka). They shared hunger, cold, fear, and everyday work at the farm. Wajnsztok was a typical rural girl. She was hardworking and dressed like other women in the village. She was "family." As she explained after the war, in spite of all that, her road was still thorny, just like a hungry, cold, frightened, and hunted dog that does not know what the next hour will bring. After the liquidation operation, when the peasants were particularly afraid to help the Jews, she spent three months in the forest and in the swamps with her two brothers, Mojsze and Izrael. She described how some people treated the "wandering" Jews: "They have to be chased away or shot like a dog. After all, why would you risk [your lives on their behalf] and suffer?" "I hung on tightly to life, I didn't want to die. I was brave and took risks entering the smallest dungeons to hide myself." Begging for a place to spend the night, she promised to repay whoever would agree, but she knew she was a "plague that disturbed their peace." [87]

Another issue worth attention is work in hiding. Those who were tailors or shoemakers provided clothing or shoes for the whole family with whom they stayed, and in this way they repaid them for the help and food. Then they moved on to another family, and another. Women helped on farms, and children grazed cattle. Work had a salutary effect, as it not only produced some income but also filled one's time, helped to overcome boredom and hopelessness, provided some sort of independence, and limited the effects of depression and despair, all of which afflicted people in hiding. After all, the financial resources the Jews had at their disposal were constantly shrinking, and as a result their chances of survival decreased by the day.

The distance the persecuted Jews had to cover was an area I call simply "between the village and the forest." Jews from the forest visited houses on the edge of villages as well as isolated farms in distant settlements, which, though like havens, were unfortunately also much more exposed to assaults and robberies and visits of Polish partisan forces. The forest, in contrast, was a temporary shelter for those Jews who had a permanent hideout at farmers' properties but had to run away due to danger.

It was very rare to build bunkers close to the villages,[88] and it was even rarer to build them in the fields. Yet this is how Icie Sztemer from Szczebrzeszyn survived almost the whole period after 1942. After many attempts at finding shelter with farmers, he erected a bunker for his whole family in the middle of a field belonging to a peasant from Żrebce near Sułów, and with the peasant's consent. If it had not been for the farmer's help, surviving in such a bunker would have been impossible. He brought the family some food at night every two weeks and sympathized with them: "He kept crying over our fate and saying that our suffering never left his mind."[89] Despite all that, they were forced to leave in the spring for fear of being noticed by other villagers during fieldwork. Because of the danger of being exposed, Sztemer had to move many times; by the end of 1943, he had built as many as five bunkers. When they were almost freezing to death in their damp pit in winter, the farmer suggested that they warm themselves with horse manure and let them come to the stable at night. Naked, they plunged their bodies into the dung and slowly recuperated. While these were surely extreme experiences, everyone survived.

In totally, several dozen people from fourteen families from Biłgoraj County saved at least thirty-nine people and were later recognized as Righteous Among the Nations:[90]

- Aniela and Janina Chmiel from Czarnystok saved Tema Wajnsztok.
- The Dudziak family from Kajetanówka saved Rózia Bejman (later Shoshana Golan).
- The Frelas family from Stara Wieś near Frampol saved Aba Becher.
- Jan and Katarzyna Grum from Potok Górny saved one person and helped three people: Szmul and Szloma Szprung, Wela (surname unclear), and an unknown Jew.

- Franciszek Łyda from Krzeszów saved Abraham Westrajch, Elza (Elżbieta) Westrajch, and Maria Westrajch.
- Felicja Mazurek from Bagno near Zwierzyniec saved Sonia Elbaum (later Irena Burstin).
- Jan Mikulski and his family from Wola Duża near Biłgoraj saved Rywka Wajnberg, Bencjon and Chaim Rozenbaum (Rozenbojm), Perla Frajberg, Pola Kening (aka Twerski), and Miriam (Małka, Maria) Wakslicht (later Lila Stern).
- Paweł and Edward Saj from Kąty near Frampol saved Natan, Leon, and Rywka Bryk.
- The Siek family from Lipiny Dolne saved Feliks Urman.
- Stanisław Sobczak and his family from Frampol hid twelve people: Nachman Kestenbaum; Mosze Cymerman; Szmul Honigman and his wife; Mosze Zalc and his sister; Szmul Mahler; Abram Sztajnberg, his wife, and two children; and Dina Huf.
- Jan and Stefania Sosnowy from Komodzianka saved Ela Ashenberg.
- Stanisław and Wiktoria Stańczyk from Frampol helped Chana Buksenbaum-Brik and Szmul Brik as well as several other people.
- Jan and Ewa Tadra from Potok near Józefów saved Sura Wiener, her daughter Ester (married Miller), her son Leon (Lonek), and Necha Wasserman.
- Stanisław Zaśko and Maria Zaśko (née Niespiał) from Józefów helped Godel Wargacz (who did not survive) and Eugenia Sieradzka.

Two other families from the immediate area (although outside of Biłgoraj County) saved Jews from the county in question and were also recognized as Righteous Among the Nations:

- The Małek family from Łada[91] near Goraj saved Bella Hot (née Nestelbaum).
- Jan and Rozalia Wołoszyn from Branew[92] helped Morris (Mordka) Shapiro and his sister Drejzl Zylbercweig (née Shapiro) from Goraj.

Sources, including most often testimonies and memoirs, describe ten cases of repression against people helping the Jews in Biłgoraj County, but they are very poorly documented. Polish people paid with their lives for such help, or at least with imprisonment and loss of property.

Help after the liquidation operations most often comprised providing the Jews with food, allowing them to find shelter and maintain personal hygiene, hiding money or valuables, or cashing them. Sometimes it was also about supplying goods other than food (clothes, shoes, matches, or papers) or occasionally medical assistance. Nonmaterial help consisted of conveying information; advising and instructing Jews; putting them in contact with other people; and allowing them to obtain Aryan documents and weapons. Finally, there were cases and approaches that can be labeled "spiritual and moral" help, which included staying with those in hiding from time to time, consoling them, raising their spirits, and convincing them to not to lose hope or give up.

My research confirms that "most of those who sought refuge did not survive the occupation," and "helping and trying did not automatically mean saving."[93] We do not know much about their experiences, but sources indicate that those hiding fell more often into the hands of the Polish "Blue" Police than into the hands of the Germans. For the Jews hidden in the countryside, it was always a critical and very difficult moment when other refugees were found nearby. If the latter discovery ended with repression against a Polish family, the whole area became seized with fear, and the Jews were forced to leave their hideouts. Their only hope lay in the forest.

Forest Groups

The Solska Forest and the Janów Forest surround the villages of the Roztocze region, and the beautiful lands between Szczebrzeszyn, Radecznica, and Goraj are a mosaic of fields, meadows, woods, and groves, as well as ravines and gorges, with poor, unpaved roads and paths leading to the villages and settlements located somewhere between the forests. Such a landscape was favorable for people escaping from the ghettos.

For the first several hours after an operation, the fugitives were in a state of fear, bewilderment, and confusion. They were devastated and did not know what had happened, how many had been murdered, who had survived, and where the survivors were, so they desperately sought information. In a letter to Natan Bryk, Edward Saj from Kąty near Frampol described the first evening after a massacre in the village:

> A large group gathered at our place after that day. There was Słomka with his son, daughters and wife, and you with your brother and sister, Rywka. Słomka was wounded in the leg; he had escaped a train transported to Bełżec. I don't remember how many people came. You were all cold, soaking wet, and hungry. You ate something, warmed yourselves, and stayed overnight in the barn. Father and I took turns in keeping guard so that no one unwelcome came and you could escape the barn in case of danger. Then we woke you up at dawn, gave you food, and you all went

to the forest. After several days, you came with your brother at night and told us there were only three left out the whole group: you, your brother, and sister Rywka. Others had been caught and shot by the Germans in the cemetery in Frampol. You slept in the barn and left at dawn with some food, I don't know where [to].[94]

Only in the beginning was it possible for the groups that escaped to the forest to be quite large, often consisting of even several hundred people. Without any preparations, equipment, or weaponry, they could camp out in the open air no longer than several days; it was already late autumn, freezing weather was on its way, and soon it started snowing. The chaotic and disorganized groups of fugitives quickly broke down into smaller ones, which helped them survive. The first period after the operations was particularly dangerous: The Germans' collaborators were combing the forests, catching the fugitives, and taking them to municipal jails, from which there was basically no escape. Groups hidden in the forests were denounced and hunted until the end of the occupation.

Only six families as well as individual fugitives survived from the group of Bluma (Holler) Kamerman, which initially included around two hundred people. According to her, it was only because they split into smaller groups that not everyone was killed. Bluma accused AK units of murdering Jews.[95] In the testimony of A.H., a women from Szczebrzeszyn who wanted to remain anonymous, we read that all (!) of the members of her group were murdered. They were hiding near Kawęczynek; she survived only because it was her turn to bring food from the village.[96] As a result she became suicidal but eventually decided to join a partisan group that included several dozen Russians, Poles, and Jews.

Hiding in the forest was unbearable for some, but it was salvation and a last resort for others—for example, Morris Shapiro and his sister Drejzl (later Zylbercweig).[97] When they had used up all their supplies, they entered the forest and found a group of similar unfortunates. They stayed there during the day and sneaked in to barns during the night. A young Pole they knew, Tekla Wołoszyn from Branew,[98] brought them food to the edge of the forest, consoling them and crying over their terrible fate. She was an exceptionally kind and warm-hearted person. Whoever went to the forest, just as they did, had to reach Jewish camps. Otherwise, they died. Women were safe if accompanied by men, so pairs were formed among forest groups.

According to the survivors, many people from Józefów itself sought shelter deep (seven to nine kilometers)[99] inside the Solska Forest.[100] They built bunkers and even made bonfires in smaller groups of several dozen people, but they had to keep moving and starting new camps every few weeks. It was optimal to build several well-camouflaged bunkers and move quickly from one place to another if needed. They lived from day to day, made no plans, never thought about the future, prayed, tried to maintain the Jewish customs and traditions, established romantic connections, and even got married and had children.[101] But forests were not necessarily safe and deserted: there were loggers, forest service, poachers, robbers, runaway Soviet prisoners of war, peasants escaping from deportations and trying to hide nonearmarked animals, and—with time—the partisan units of AK, Peasants' Battalions (*Bataliony Chłopskie*, BCh), People's Guard (*Gwardia Ludowa*, GL), and People's Army (*Armia Ludowa*, AL). Born in 1937, Irving Lumerman naturally remembers the time from the perspective of a child for whom a nomadic life in the backwoods was an exciting adventure. There were several children in his camp. Years later, he would describe their lighthearted play and even Hebrew and religion lessons they took. Israel Szlajcher, who was then fifteen years old and for whom it was all simply interesting, kept similar memoirs.[102] Many people in hiding were in poor health and suffered from lack of shoes and warm clothing, disease, frostbite, and ulcers and other skin conditions, yet dying of natural causes in hideaways was very rare. Breakdowns came later, after the war.

The ways in which the Jews survived in the forests may be divided into three categories: numerous groups (of several dozen people) included even old people and very young children (family camps); groups of several people, usually families hidden in forest bunkers located most often at the edge of the forest (i.e., married couples with children or siblings); and armed, usually mixed Polish-Russian-Jewish groups that consisted mainly of men who fought against the Germans and committed sabotage acts against them. Large armed groups knew about each other and maintained contact.

Hunger was the biggest problem. To alleviate it, people stole food and robbed nearby farms of anything to eat, although this was obviously not the only way to obtain sustenance. Forest groups covered the distance "between the village and the forest" much more often than the Jews hiding in villages. Coming for food at night, they risked much more and often never returned. Aleksander Piwowarek mentioned that finding food became increasingly difficult. Peasants themselves had less and less to eat and did not want to sell anything, much less give away anything for free. They were increasingly afraid of maintaining any contact with the Jews and the repression this could entail. In view of death from starvation, there was only one choice for those who hid in the forest: They were determined to find food, even if it meant using force. According to Piwowarek, a "gang of robbers" formed near Szczebrzeszyn, which—in addition to Jews—included several runaway Russian prisoners of war. The gang was particularly troublesome for the locals.[103] Klukowski also wrote that there were many Jews among "the bandits." "In fear of repression, peasants catch Jews in the countryside

Figure 2.5. Jan Kędra, aka "Błyskawica", "Jaskółka"; and a Jewish nurse, "Krysia" (real name unknown), Osuchy, 1943 (AZHRL, 8540).

and bring them to the town or sometimes kill them on the spot. Some kind of brutalization towards the Jews has started. People have been overcome by some psychosis. Just like the Germans, they often no longer see the Jews as human beings, but rather consider them to be some kind of vermin that had to be dealt with by all means possible, just like rabid dogs, rats."[104]

It is often impossible today to determine with which groups or organizations the Jews in the forests had contact, to which groups they belonged themselves, which groups supported and helped them, and which robbed and plundered them. The Jews adopted a tactic of avoiding everyone. But one thing is certain: They were not admitted to partisan units active in the area under the aegis of AK. In his postwar statement, Konrad Bartoszewski (aka Wir),[105] one of the commanders of Region V Józefów of ZWZ-AK [Związek Walki Zbrojnej – Armia Krajowa],wrote that both the Jews hiding individually and those taking refuge in the forest "used the organization's help."[106] Unfortunately, many Jewish survivors stated that the AK considered Jewish camps to be dangerous for the underground and wanted to get rid of them.[107]

There was a similarly negative opinion about the soldiers led by Lieutenant Tadeusz Kuncewicz (aka Podkowa), whose unit operated in the AK Zamość district near Zwierzyniec and Szczebrzeszyn. One of Podkowa's soldiers, Bolesław Polakowski (aka Wiarus), noted in his diary on January 10, 1944, "They will perform calls to each unit except the Jewish one tomorrow. There are 60 people in the unit. We don't know why they are still alive."[108] Suffice it to mention that it was Podkowa's unit that admitted Tadeusz Niedźwiecki (aka Sten), who in 1945 was sentenced to death and executed by the underground for numerous rapes, robberies, and assaults. If such people as Sten found themselves under Podkowa's command, it should not come as a surprise that the antisemitism present in the unit led to other cruel acts against the Jews as well.[109] In their book published in the 1980s, two Israeli historians mentioned around 120 cases of murder committed on the Jews by Polish underground members, some of which took place in Biłgoraj County.[110] Today we know that the list they compiled is incomplete.

AK units joined by BCh groups probably protected the Jews, namely the unit of Jan Kędra (alias Błyskawica) and Michał Myszka (alias Jawor). According to one of the partisans in the unit, Florian Wójtowicz (alias Listek), the unit helped a group led by "Jankiel Berko Josel,"[111] which was stationed in the forests near Nowy Lipowiec, Osuchy, and Łukowa.[112] One could take the information about Kędra's unit helping the Jews with satisfaction if it were not for the fact that his people created a criminal group incorporated into the AK structures; thanks to that, as observed by Rafał Wnuk, with time "the members of the band turned out to be valuable underground soldiers" (Wnuk, 432).

In practice, the Jewish groups and Polish AK and BCh partisan units could come into contact (or rather start avoiding each other) only from spring 1943, which is when the first of them started to form. Before, from the summer of 1942, runaway Soviet prisoners of war formed armed groups joined also by some of the Jewish fugitives. The first one was most probably the group of Captain Aleksy Rajewski,[113] stationed in the forest between Frampol, Gorajec, and Szczebrzeszyn, but already in August 1942, the group dispersed and Rajewski died.[114] It received food, weapons (buried already in September 1939), and support from the Met brothers and other Jews from Gorajec.[115] In November 1942, an unidentified group of Poles[116] attacked the refugees' camp at night. Fortunately, several armed Russians and Jews from the group were sleeping a bit farther away, which saved them. The Poles threw grenades into the bunker and killed around forty people.[117] Mendel Dym and Jankiel Met later went to the Józefów forest, where other Polish-Jewish-Russian groups were active.[118] The second murder of Jews who escaped from Gorajec and Szczebrzeszyn was committed in June 1943.[119] One of the witnesses attributed the crime to the partisans from Podkowa's unit. In his opinion, "it was an operation against spies, bandits, and thieves, and Jews were killed on the way." But the perpetrators were not identified, and the investigation was terminated.[120]

Biłgoraj County became a true "partisan country" only in 1944; according to Jerzy Markiewicz, there were twenty-three units from AK, BCh, NOW, and AL, as well as Soviet units stationed there in that time. This is when the First Ukrainian Partisan Division came to the county. It was named after Sydir Kovpak and led by the legendary Pyotr Vershigora, and it consisted of 2,500 partisans, commonly referred to as *kowpakowcy* [Kovpaks] after their patron.[121] Many Jews joined the division and moved to the Janów Forest and then to Belarus. The Soviet units were not free from antisemitism, and had Jewish victims on their conscience too; one of the witnesses wrote that the fighters from Czapajew's unit had been prisoners of war who had escaped from camps in Bełżec, Sobibór, and Treblinka,[122] where they had belonged to the camp staff, and "their attitude toward the Jews was terrible."[123] The last months of the occupation, marked by extensive German anti-partisan operations codenamed *Sturmwind* [Whirlwind] and the biggest battles fought by Polish partisan units in Porytowe Wzgórze and near Osuchy, had dramatic consequences for the Jews hiding in forests. Only a small group of several dozen people survived out of hundreds of refugees.

Immediately after the extermination of Jews, the Germans launched a pacification and deportation operation aimed at the Polish population (*Generalplan Ost*). In Biłgoraj County, it lasted from November 1942 until July 1943. The Germans wanted to make the Zamość Region the first area of settlement for the German population and "cleanse" it of the Poles. At the same time, they were resettling Ukrainians around the Solska Forest to create a protective cordon. This way, the Jews hiding in the forest had less and less food supplies. The Poles were taken from villages to transit camps, where they were screened, and children meant for "Germanization" were taken away from their parents. Some of the adults were sent to forced labor in the Reich; some were sent to concentration camps; some died; some were resettled on other, worse lands; and the rest could return to their original dwelling places. Although in the end the German plans were not fully implemented, the amount of suffering, material and nonmaterial losses, and human tragedy was huge. Suffice it to say that almost forty thousand people from eighty-nine villages were deported from Biłgoraj County itself,[124] some villages were pacified several times, others were completely destroyed, and local people were brutally murdered in retaliation for helping the partisans. This is what happened, for example, in Sochy[125] and Szarajówka. As established by the War Reparations Bureau during its research into nineteen communities of the county carried out in 1945, 12,886 Poles altogether died as a result of military activity, time spent in prisons and camps, forced labor, diseases, wounds, exhaustion, and hiding; 1,833 people suffered mental and physical losses such as disability, health problems, rape (the Bureau registered 244 acts of rape), and mental diseases; 20,827 people were transported to the Reich to forced labor; and 7,097 were imprisoned and put in camps. However, the information is incomplete, as there is no data on what happened to 5,000 other people.[126]

The climax of the pacification and anti-partisan activities came with *Grossaktion*, which started in June 1943 and aimed at intensifying the deportations as much as possible. It consisted of sweeping the forests and catching the refugees, and the victims of those manhunts were also the Jews. *Generalplan Ost* and operations directed against underground organizations and their armed units were only an element of a common whole connected in a chain of causation. Such strong development of the partisan movement in the Lublin District and especially in the Zamość Region was possible thanks to the natural conditions in the area (large forest complexes) and was caused by the response of the Polish underground to deportations, pacifications, or even extermination directed against the local Polish population. It was natural for civilians to escape; already on December 14, 1942, Klukowski wrote that there was a host of people in the forests,[127] and half a year later he used even harsher phrases: "In a word, we're more and more squeezed. For those who want or have to hide, there remains only one way. They have to go 'to the forest,' 'to the band.'"[128] The events of 1943 resulted in not only depopulation of some villages or even whole communities but also a farming crisis in the whole county. While there was a need to plough and sow, villages were being depopulated and pacified, and peasants were taken to forced labor. It should not come as a surprise that from 1943, food in the region was in desperately short supply, and the majority of the population lived on the brink of hunger and feared for their future.

This is why the question regarding how those events influenced the Jews in hiding seems obvious, and yet there is virtually no reference to all these tragic facts in the memoirs and testimonies of those Jews who survived, as if it never happened. It is difficult to say why the survivors do not refer to these events. We can find only isolated mentions about the fate and condition of the Poles in that time in Jewish testimonies. Perhaps the reasons for this are of psychological and existential nature. The Jews were, for example, cut off from sources of information and engrossed in their own difficult situation. One should also remember that the main topic of survivors' postwar testimonies were their own experiences. This is what they focused on and what they were asked about.

No more than several dozen Jews left the forests of Biłgoraj County in July 1944. The biggest group probably survived in the Solska Forest near the village of Borowiec (which is where the forest quarters of Michał Atamanow and—in the spring of 1944—Vershigora were located). The memory of the survivors has been preserved by the inhabitants of the small village to this day. In his diary, Polakowski wrote that in January 1944, the group consisted of sixty people, and according to Estera Fefer, twenty-six Jews died during the great German operation against partisan units (*Sturmwind*). According to a report taken after the war for GKBZHwP, forty-two Jews ultimately survived in the forest.[129]

1944–1946: JEWISH ABSENCE

The end of the war brought an opening of a new perspective and a time when lives had to be put together anew. The Jews who left their hideouts were frail, homeless, and robbed of everything they had had before. Their houses were either completely empty or occupied by someone else, and many of those to whom they had entrusted their belongings did not want to return them. Leaving the hideouts, bunkers, or forests turned out to be as difficult and dangerous as entering them in the first place.[130] This was due to the changing situation and political system transformation, as well as attitudes toward the Jews that seemed not to have changed at least since 1942, because social relations are characterized by the power of inertia and long duration. The postwar pogrom atmosphere and murders committed on the survivors were not an incomprehensible postwar outbreak or phenomenon but—among others—a continuation of what had happened before under the cover of the occupation.[131] It had simply suddenly become visible, exposed. Polish-Jewish antagonism was at the same time intensified by the changes taking place directly after the war. It took three years to cool down the intense antisemitic emotions, a process described as "the dead wave" in a collection of essays by postwar intellectuals worried about the vast scale of aggression and antisemitism,[132] and yet they have never completely disappeared. The numerous underground organizations active in the Lublin Region during the occupation metamorphosed into anti-communist ones, and among their victims were not only members of the new authorities (both Poles and Jews) but also Jewish civilians, who were commonly identified with the communist ideology or at least believed to support it. The situation was extremely complicated, tense, and dynamic, and there was no one who could guarantee the safety of the Jews who had somehow survived the Holocaust. Unable to count on the Polish administration and the emerging structures of the new authorities, they turned to Soviet soldiers for help and protection, at the same time confirming their alleged "pro-Soviet" attitude in the eyes of the Polish society. As noticed by Rafał Wnuk, the figure of the Jew in the underground anti-communist press in 1944–1946 had only extremely negative connotations: as a foreigner, a communist, and an enemy.[133] "The Soviets brought salvation to the Jews and enslavement to the Poles. The Jews could not and did not want to understand the anti-Sovietness of the pro-independence underground; and AK soldiers considered the Jews' pro-Sovietness an act of treason against the Polish State."[134] The consequences of the situation were disastrous: No fewer than fourteen Jews, including one child, were murdered in the county within just half a year after the liberation. Only mixed couples had any possibilities of staying in the region. There were several marriages like that in the county, and the Jewish spouses were probably the only Jews who remained there—with changed names, a new Catholic faith, and a new Polish identity.

Biłgoraj County was liberated by the Red Army in July 1944. When the front line moved, the Jews left their hideouts and forest bunkers and organized themselves into local Jewish committees. Individual repatriation from the Ukrainian, Belarussian, and Lithuanian Soviet Socialist Republics began in November that year, and in February 1946, repatriation from deep inside the USSR started. This is when larger groups of Jews who left the lands occupied by Wehrmacht with the Red Army in September 1939 returned, including Jews from Biłgoraj, Tarnogród, Szczebrzeszyn, and other towns of the county. They were also the biggest group of survivors percentagewise. They settled in the so-called regained territories. Figures indicate that at least eight hundred people who survived in the East came back to Poland.

Jewish committees were established in the fall of 1944 in Tarnogród, Biłgoraj, and Krzeszów. As far as other places are concerned, the Jews were just passing through. No one stopped them there, welcomed them, or encouraged them to stay. It was natural for them to return to their old home; it was a spiritual need of the survivors. But the places that had been vibrant with Jewish life several years before turned out to be "dead," strange, and alien, and the Polish environment seemed like a social vacuum. Everyone eventually left for the bigger cities (Zamość, Lublin) and from there out into the world.

Whoever had any chance to regain the property they had lost before their departure tried to do so. One could sell one's house and start a new life somewhere else. Regained machines and tools could be the beginning of new workshops and sources of income. It is clear from many cases between Poles and Jews brought immediately after the war to municipal courts what Jews had entrusted Poles for safekeeping and what the Poles did not wish to return. Lejzor Fruchtlender, a craftsman making shoe uppers from Biłgoraj, fought for his machine; Boruch Wermut wanted to recover a pair of scales and regain the possession of a mill; Estera Fefer demanded the return of real estate and a sewing machine; and Nusym and Lejba Bryk fought for their cow, chaff-cutter, mill belts, and eviction from land. Among the subjects of the disputes were millstones, various machines, cows, horses, bicycles, and most often real estate and the settlement of prewar debts. Disputes or even criminal cases into crimes committed during the war[135] were almost everything that connected the Jewish survivors with their old homelands and Polish neighbors.

―⚀―

I have reached many sources and gathered data about 1,092 people who tried to save themselves and survived the liquidation operations and the several days afterward. The number includes 106 people of whom there is no information regarding whether they managed to survive. According to the data, no fewer than 274 people survived the Holocaust, and no fewer than 712 people died between January 1943 and July 1944. I estimate the number of those who escaped liquidation operations in Biłgoraj County at around 1,500, which means that 400–450 people, that is, 30 percent of those who wished to save themselves, died during the first period of the *Judenjagd*, meaning during the first two to three weeks after the liquidation operations, especially after the final operation organized on November 2–4, 1942.

Escaping to forests and staying there for the entire period turned out to be as (in)effective as hiding in villages. It was undoubtedly long-term, and most often selfless, help from Poles that was the most effective way of saving one's life. This group includes also those who wandered about for some time looking for a safe haven and survived by staying for a longer time in one place protected by the Poles. Those who were doomed to wander and move from one place to another all the time were in the greatest danger. Their chances for survival turned out to be minimal. The data concerning the age and gender of the survivors is also worth attention. The average age of adults in 1942 was only thirty-two. As far as genders are concerned, men definitely predominated among adults, and the number of children who survived is also very high.

Table 2.2 Demographic data

	Number	Percentage
Number of Jews in the county before 1939	16,000	11%
Number of Jews in 1942 before the operations	14,500	
Jews who tried to save themselves out of the total number of Jews in 1942	1,092	7.53% (out of the total number of Jews in 1942)
Number of survivors (excluding the USSR)	274 (239 in the county) (25 outside the county)	1.71% (out of the total number of Jews in 1939) 1.88% (out of the total number of Jews in 1942) 25.09% (out of the total number of Jews who tried to save themselves)
No data if survived or died (of those who tried to save themselves)	106	
Female survivors	98	35.7%
Male survivors	117	42.7%
Survivors under 16 in 1942	59 (23 boys, 32 girls, 4 no data)	21.5%
Number of those deported during the operations	around 6,500	
Number of those murdered on the spot during the operations	around 6,500	
Number of those murdered on the spot soon after the operations	around 400	
Number of those murdered during the period of hiding	712	65.20% (out of the total number of Jews who tried to save themselves)

Source: Author's calculations based on all collected documentation.

Table 2.3 Place and ways of survival

Number of survivors (in and outside of the county)	274 (35)
Forests and bunkers (including partisans)	72 (27)
The villages—in one place	53
The countryside—in several places, including wandering about, forests, and villages	46
"Aryan" papers in the county	22
Labor camp in the county	—
Surviving outside of the county, including (escaping abroad) using "Aryan" papers, staying in camps, forced labor in the Reich	35 including: –14 (Aryan) –11 (Reich) –10 (camps)
No data about the way of survival	46

Source: Author's calculations based on all collected documentation.

Table 2.4 Murderers and causes of death

Number of victims	712
Murdered by the German gendarmerie and police (on their own initiative)	175
Murdered by the German gendarmerie and police (denounced by the locals)	265
Murdered by Blue policemen	26
Murdered by the local underground	46
Murdered by local civilians	130
Other causes of death (in hideouts, suicide)	13
No data about the circumstances of death	57

Source: Author's calculations based on all collected documentation.

—⚏—

The greatest number of people in hiding died at the hands of the German Gendarmerie and police, but this data demands some commentary. Most of the Jews were murdered by the Germans, but a large percentage of the victims were in fact caught and denounced by the Poles. The testimonies are full of phrases such as "exposed by Poles," "caught and handed over," "caught and turned in," "caught as ordered," "caught and handed over to the Germans," "caught and brought," "caught, beaten, and driven back," or "driven from the forest." A surprisingly large number of the Jews in hiding was murdered by Poles themselves: civilians, Blue policemen, or armed groups, including both regular bandits who robbed anyone they could as well as various armed units of the Polish underground. As to the question whether the scenario of the Holocaust from Szczebrzeszyn, which was so detailed and shockingly described in Zygmut Klukowski's diaries, was common and whether the conclusions can be generalized, the answer is unfortunately affirmative with reference to the region in question. Extremely brutal methods were used in all towns and villages of Biłgoraj County, and as a result many Jews were killed on the spot, in the presence of their Polish and Ukrainian neighbors. Local civilians and uniformed services across the entire county participated in the liquidation operations themselves first, and then in hunting and denouncing the refugees. Without their official and voluntary involvement, the efficiency of the *Judenjagd* would have been much lower and the chances of saving Jewish lives would have been adequately higher. Finally, there were Poles in the entire county who robbed Jews of their possessions.

There were different ways of surviving the Holocaust, but they all share similar patterns of behavior, reactions, and decisions. The survivors were characterized by their will to live, resistance, ability to adapt to extreme conditions, hope, and confidence in others, which they had not lost despite everything. Material resources were not a sine qua non of survival for everyone, but they were indeed very helpful. What was also important was that the people in hiding knew the area and its topography and whom they could ask for help. They were very familiar with the agricultural and definitely provincial county. Thanks to such a character of the region, the Jews who lived their everyday lives beside their non-Jewish neighbors were economically connected with them, and the difference between the Jews living in the countryside and those living in towns was practically irrelevant. Those ties and connections served a crucial role because it was only the support of their non-Jewish compatriots that guaranteed a chance of survival during the two years of hiding. Social capital turned out to be the most important element in survival, including prewar connections and contacts with the Polish neighborhood. In forests and bunkers, in contrast, it was cooperation and efficient organization of people fighting for survival that also necessary. Another resource that never depleted was the experience gained by the Jews. They learned to avoid danger, listen, recognize sounds, quickly build solid and invisible bunkers, heal using what nature provided, and obtain food and weapons in all circumstances. Intuition turned out to be extremely important as well. Whoever had it and knew how to rely on it often avoided danger that could not be foreseen in the process of rational analysis. Such people based their reactions on extreme sensitivity and acted immediately and without thinking, thus avoiding deadly threats. Their intuition told them whom to trust, and premonition influenced their behavior. Sometimes both failed, and sometimes complete strangers appeared in one's life in the most hopeless situations and offered selfless help and salvation. But no decision and no choice guaranteed success. It was coincidence, fate, a chain of unforeseen events, or spontaneous decisions that ultimately decided everything. Nothing could be neither foreseen nor planned for a longer future. Everything was temporary, uncertain, and fragile.

NOTES

1. Dorota Skakuj, *Zarys dziejów powiatu biłgorajskiego w latach 1867–1939* [An outline of the history of the Biłgoraj County in 1867–1939] (Biłgoraj: Muzeum Ziemi Biłgorajskiej, 2005), esp. "Specyfika kulturowa powiatu biłgorajskiego" [The cultural peculiarity of the Biłgoraj County], 196–215.

2. Data gathered by the Lublin Province Office for 1931. See Radosław Dąbrowski, *Mniejszości narodowe na Lubelszczyźnie w latach 1918–1939* [National Minorities in the Lublin Region in 1918–1939] (Kielce: Wszechnica Świętokrzyska, 2007), 22, table 7.

3. Zygmunt Klukowski. All of the information comes from reports of the Socio-Political Department of the Lublin Province Office, quoted in Dorota Skakuj, "Żydzi w powiecie biłgorajskim w okresie międzywojennym w świetle zachowanych dokumentów i wspomnień" [Jews in the Biłgoraj County in the interwar period in the light of preserved documents and memories], in *Biłgoraj, czyli raj. Rodzina Singerów i świat, którego już nie ma* [Biłgoraj, or the Paradise: The Singer Family and the Lost World], ed. Monika Adamczyk-Garbowska, Bogusław Wróblewski (Lublin: Wydawnictwo UMCS, 2005), 99. The antisemitic campaigns intensified across Poland especially in 1935–1937, which is when 1,289 people were hurt in the course of various events. See Tatiana Berenstein, "KPP w walce z pogromami antyżydowskimi w latach 1935–37" [The Communist Party of Poland fighting against anti-Jewish pogroms in 1935–1937], *Biuletyn ŻIH* 3–4, no. 15–16 (1955): 23. See also Jolanta Żyndul, *Zajścia antyżydowskie w Polsce w latach 1935–1937* [Anti-Jewish Incidents in Poland 1935–1937] (Warsaw, 1994); Jolanta Żyndul, *Kłamstwo krwi. Legenda mordu rytualnego na ziemiach polskich w XIX i XX wieku* [The Blood Lie: The Legend of the Ritual Killings on Polish Lands in the Nineteenth and Twentieth Centuries] (Warsaw, 2011).

4. See Sławomir Mańko, *Polski ruch ludowy wobec Żydów (1895–1939)* [Polish Peasant Movement Toward the Jews (1985–1939)] (Warsaw–Rzeszów: Muzeum Historii Polskiego Ruchu Ludowego, 2010).

5. Dr. Zygmunt Klukowski (b. January 23, 1885, Odessa; d. November 23, 1959, Szczebrzeszyn) served as the director of the hospital in Szczebrzeszyn

from 1919 to 1946. He was a physician, a historian specializing in medicine and the Zamość Region, a bibliophile, and a collector of bookplates and historical mementoes. Klukowski was a member of the Armed Combat Union (*Związek Walki Zbrojnej*, ZWZ), renamed Home Army (*Armia Krajowa*, AK), and served as a doctor in partisan units. After the war, he testified during the Nuremberg Trial and was sentenced to six years imprisonment, which he served in Wronki. He was vindicated in 1956. In 1959, the *Polityka* weekly named his *Dziennik z lat okupacji Zamojszczyzny 1939–1944* [A Diary from the Occupation Period in the Zamość Region 1939–1944] the most outstanding historical work: Zygmunt Mańkowski, "Biogram Zygmunta Klukowskiego" [Zygmunt Klukowski's biographical entry], in *Polski słownik biograficzny* [Polish Biographical Dictionary], vol. 13 (Wrocław: Zakład Narodowy im. Ossolińskich, 1967–1968). Fragments of Klukowski's diary have also been published in English. See *Diary from the Years of Occupation 1939–44* (Champaign: University of Illinois Press, 1993).

6. Dariusz Libionka, "Polska ludność chrześcijańska wobec eksterminacji Żydów—dystrykt lubelski" [Polish Christians toward the Holocaust—the Lublin District], in *Akcja Reinhardt. Zagłada Żydów w Generalnym Gubernatorstwie* [Operation Reinhardt. Extermination of the Jews in the General Government], ed. Dariusz Libionka (Warsaw: IPN, 2004), 306–333.

7. AP Kraśnik, 3/132, Starostwo Powiatowe w Biłgoraju [County Office in Biłgoraj], Wykaz szkód wojennych poniesionych na terenie powiatu biłgorajskiego sporządzony 30 V 1945 r. [A list of war damage suffered in the Biłgoraj County of 30 May 1945], 78–88.

8. Tatiana Berenstein and Adam Rutkowski, "Prześladowania ludności żydowskiej w okresie hitlerowskiej administracji wojskowej na okupowanych ziemiach polskich (1.IX.1939—25.X.1939 r.)" [Persecution of the Jewry during the Nazi war administration on occupied Polish lands (September 1, 1939–October 25, 1939)], *Biuletyn ŻIH* 2, no. 38 (1961): 3–87; Jochen Böchler, *Zbrodnie Wehrmachtu w Polsce. Wrzesień 1939. Wojna totalna* [Wehrmacht Crimes in Poland. September 1939. Total War], trans. by Patrycja Pieńkowska-Wiederkehr (Cracow: Znak, 2009); Alexander B. Rossino, *Hitler Strikes Poland: Blitzkrieg, Ideology, and Atrocity* (Lawrence: University Press of Kansas, 2003).

9. Klukowski, *Zamojszczyzna*, 165, entry of October 13, 1939.

10. See Jan Grabowski and Dariusz Libionka, eds., *Klucze i kasa. O mieniu żydowskim w Polsce pod okupacją niemiecką i we wczesnych latach powojennych 1939–1950* [Keys and Cash: About Jewish Possessions in Poland under the German Occupation and in the Early Postwar Years 1939–1950] (Warsaw: Stowarzyszenie Centrum Badań nad Zagładą Żydów, 2014).

11. AP Lublin, 1072/133, ZWZ-AK Okręg Lublin [ZWZ-AK Lublin Region], Wykaz polskich policjantów w powiecie biłgorajskim [List of Polish policemen in Biłgoraj County], no date. I have determined the names of 114 "Blue

policemen" from Biłgoraj County using various archival documents, but the list is most probably incomplete.

12. For more information on the topic, see Bogdan Musial, *Deutsche Zivilverwaltung und Judenverfolgung im Generalgouvernement. Eine Fallstudie zum Distrikt Lublin 1939–1944* (Wiesbaden: Harrasowitz), 379–380.

13. AŻIH, ŻSS, 211/223, Korespondencja Prezydium ŻSS z Powiatowym Komitetem ŻSS w Biłgoraju [Correspondence between the Presidium of ŻSS and the County Committee of ŻSS in Biłgoraj], January 4, 1942–March 2, 1942.

14. Ibid., 3.

15. An author of memoirs about Józefów wrote that a group of girls from Józefów were raped in a forest; see Zbigniew Jakubik, *Czapki na bakier* [Tilted Hats] (Warsaw: Pod Wiatr, 1997), 18–19; Edward Herc, "Czasy niezapomniane. Gehenna Żydów w Józefowie" [Unforgotten times: The Gehenna of the Jews in Józefów], *Aspekty. Biłgorajski rocznik społeczno-kulturalny* 3 (2006): 77. Edward Herc (born in 1914 in Józefów, died in 1997 in Tomaszów) owned a bakery in Józefów. During the war, he provided Home Army units with bread and took part in sabotage actions.

16. *Biłgoraj izker buch*, typewritten.

17. AŻIH, 301/5505, Testimony of Jan Strzęciwilk; AŻIH, 301/5506, Testimony of Jan Małyszek; Wojciech Malec, *Wspomnienia* [Memoirs] (Biłgoraj: Gminny Ośrodek Kultury w Biłgoraju, 2015), 29–33.

18. AŻIH, 301/5507, Testimony of Adam Kitaj and Kazimierz Mazurek.

19. See: GKBZHwP and Rada Ochrony Pomników Walki and Męczeństwa, eds., *Obozy hitlerowskie na ziemiach polskich 1939–1945. Informator encyklopedyczny* [The Nazi Camps on the Polish Lands: 1939–1945. Encyclopedic Guide] (Warsaw: PWN, 1979), 164.

20. Decree issued by Governor General Hans Frank on October 15, 1941, Tatiana Berenstein, Artur Eisenbach, Adam Rutkowski, eds., *Eksterminacja Żydów na ziemiach polskich w okresie okupacji hitlerowskiej. Zbiór dokumentów* [Extermination of the Jews on Polish Lands] (Warszawa: ŻIH, 1957), 122–123.

21. AŻIH, 301/5502, Testimony of Aleksander Falandysz, Wincenty Chałkiewicz and Mieczysław Śleboda.

22. YVA, M.1.Q.22, Testimony of Izrael Harman, Mosze Tajer and Abraham Tajman.

23. Isaiah Trunk, *Judenrat. The Jewish Councils in Eastern Europe under Nazi Occupation* (Lincoln: University of Nebraska Press, 1972), 440.

24. Klukowski, *Zamojszczyzna*, 301, entry of April 29, 1942.

25. Ibid., 302, entry of May 8, 1942.

26. Expressions such as these were used by many witnesses.

27. Klukowski, *Zamojszczyzna*, 304, entry of May 9, 1942.

28. Ibid., 304, entry of May 15, 1942.

29. AŻIH, 301/5504, Testimony of Franciszek Hułaś and Leon Rak.
30. Klukowski, *Zamojszczyzna*, 306, entry of May 22, 1942.
31. David Silberklang, *Gates of Tears. The Holocaust in the Lublin District* (Jerusalem: Yad Vashem, 2013), 318.
32. Klukowski, *Zamojszczyzna*, 300, entry of April 12, 1942.
33. Ibid., 301, entry of April 13, 1942.
34. Kuwałek, *Obóz zagłady w Bełżcu*, 235–238.
35. See: Jan Grabowski, "Propaganda antyżydowska w Generalnej Guberni, 1939–1945" [Anti-Jewish propaganda in the General Government, 1939–1945], *Zagłada Żydów. Studia i Materiały* 6 (2010), 130–141.
36. This battalion was formed at the beginning of the war in Essen (the Ruhr District), mainly from reserve police officers, and sent to the Polish lands on May 29, 1942. Its second platoon (*Zug*, which consisted of thirty to forty people) of the 1st Company was responsible for the area of Józefów, Susiec, and Biłgoraj only, while all of the three platoons of the 3rd Company operated in all Biłgoraj County communities. The battalion was withdrawn from the Lublin Region only in July 1944, when it was dismantled (see: Stefan Klemp, *"Nicht ermittelt." Polizeibataillone und die Nachkriegsjustiz. Ein Handbuch* (Essen: Klartext Verlag, 2005), 179–181; the investigation against policemen from Reserve Battalion 67 was conducted by the prosecution in Dortmund; file No. 45 Js I/64).
37. Sonderdienst units in the Lublin District took part in deportations of Jews from Hrubieszów, Biłgoraj, and Puławy (Musiał, *Deutsche Zivilverwaltung und Judenverfolgung im Generalgouvernement*, 250–251, 253, 259–260, 291, 309, 335; cf. Peter Black, "Sonderdienst w Generalnym Gubernatorstwie" [Sonderdienst in the General Government], *Zagłada Żydów. Studia i Materiały* 12 (2016), 91–118.
38. AŻIH 301/7010, Testimony of Bolesław Omiotek.
39. Soviet prisoners-of-war kept in terrible conditions in special camps established especially for them were enlisted in the service to the Third Reich, which for them was a way to survive while knowing what they would be used for. The enlisted were trained in special centers and assigned particularly ruthless and cruel tasks, including murdering the Jews. Their training camp in GG was localized in Trawniki (Lublin district), which is why they were often called *Trawnikimänner* (people from Trawniki; see: Peter Black, "Prosty żołnierz 'akcji Reinhardt'. Oddziały z Trawnik i eksterminacja polskich Żydów" [A simple soldier in Operation Reinhardt. Units from Trawniki and the extermination of the Polish Jews], in *Akcja Reinhardt*, 103–131.
40. *Przez Walkę do Zwycięstwa* [Through Fight to Victory] (a magazine of the People's Party [Stronnictwo Ludowe]), November 20, 1942, 28 (66).
41. Klukowski, *Zamojszczyzna*, 327–329, entries of October 26–30, 1942.
42. AIPN Lu, 326/60, Sprawa Tomasza Jamińskiego 1951–1954 [The case of Tomasz Jamiński 1951–1954]. The defendant was sentenced to six years'

imprisonment. The sentence was shortened to two-and-a-half years as a result of an amnesty declared in 1956, and in 1967 the conviction was expunged.

43. AIPN Lu, 327/31, Sprawa Franciszka Kuleszy, Władysława Bełżka i Jana Blicharza 1946–1954 [The case of Franciszek Kulesza, Władysław Bełżek, and Jan Blicharz 1946–1954], Testimony of Lejzor Fluchtlander, 40. Kulesza was sentenced to death and executed, Blicharz was sentenced to ten years' imprisonment, and Bełżek was acquitted.

44. Ibid., Testimony of Moszek Sztern, 48.

45. For mass murders committed by the unit, see the alarming book by Christopher R. Browning, *Ordinary Men: Reserve Police Battalion 101 and the Final Solution in Poland* (New York: HarperCollins Publishers, 1993).

46. David Silberklang, Żydzi i pierwsze deportacje z dystruktu lubelskiego, in *Akcja Reinhardt. Zagłada Żydów w Generalnym Gubernatorstwie*, ed. Dariusz Libionka (Warszawa: IPN, 2004), 54 [Jews and the First Deportations].

47. AP Kraśnik, 27/3, Akta gminy Puszcza Solska [Records of the Puszcza Solska commune], Protokoły sesji sołtysów 1940–1944 [Reports from Sessions of Village Elders 1940–1944], 67. The county governor's decree ("on burying human corpses found in fields and forests') was passed during a session of county governors in the commune of Potok Górny (AP Kraśnik, 26/790, Akta gminy Potok Górny [Records of the Potok Górny Commune], Pismo starosty z 5 X 1942 r. [Letter by the County Governor of October 5, 1942], 59; AP Kraśnik, 26/697, Akta gminy Potok Górny, Oryginał zarządzenia starosty [Original County Governor's Decree], 59; AP Kraśnik, 26/190, Akta gminy Potok Górny, Pismo starosty z 10 X 1942 r. [Letter by County Governor of October 10, 1942], 189.

48. AP Kraśnik, 27/3, Akta gminy Puszcza Solska, Zarządzenie gminy z 12 III 1942 r. [Communal Decree of 12 March 1942], 79.

49. AŻIH, 301/1474, Testimony of Estera Fefer; Testimony of Chaim Mordechaj Szlajcher in *Biłgoraj izker buch*, typewritten, 139.

50. AP Kraśnik, 28/484, Akta gminy Sól [Records of the Sól Commune], Protokoły sesji sołtysów 1942–1944, Sesja z 23 XII 1942 r. [Reports from Sessions of Village Elders 1942–1944. Session of December 23, 1942], 36.

51. See: Jacek Andrzej Młynarczyk, "Rola przemocy wobec ludności żydowskiej w Europie Środkowo-Wschodniej w procesie decyzyjnym Zagłady" [The role of violence toward the Jews in East Central Europe in the Holocaust decision-making process], *Kwartalnik Historii Żydów* 4, no. 260 (2016): 799–909.

52. The first questionnaire was conducted in 1945 and entitled "Kwestionariusze o egzekucjach masowych i grobach masowych" [Court inquiries about mass executions and mass graves], known as "Ankieta Sądów Grodzkich" [Municipal Courts Questionnaire]. The second one was devoted to a similar topic and prepared in 1968 by the Main Commission for the Investigation of Nazi

Crimes in Poland (*Główna Komisja Badania Zbrodni Hitlerowskich w Polsce*, GKBZHwP). The data from both questionnaires, complemented by information from other documents gathered in the archives of the Main Commission for the Prosecution of Crimes against the Polish Nation at the Institute of National Remembrance (*Główna Komisja* Ścigania *Zbrodni przeciwko Narodowi Polskiemu, Instytut Pamięci Narodowej*, GKŚZpNP IPN), was published in separate volumes devoted to particular provinces entitled *Rejestr miejsc i faktów zbrodni popełnionych przez okupanta hitlerowskiego na ziemiach polskich w latach 1939–1945 Województwo zamojskie* [Register of Places and Acts of Crime Committed by the Nazi Occupier on the Polish Lands in 1939–1945. The Zamość Province] (Warsaw: GKŚZpNP Instytut Pamięci Narodowej, 1994).

53. A "remnant ghetto" usually consisted of several houses still inhabited by Jews who survived deportations. The Germans employed these Jews to search abandoned houses or to demolish them; usually after a few months, the Jews from these remnant ghettos were murdered.

54. After the war, Fabrykant (aka Faberka) stayed in Poland, moved to Warsaw, and worked as a commercial director at the Paged foreign trade center.

55. The Wasowski family was assimilated and converted to Catholicism, although this did not guarantee protection from the German persecution.

56. AŻIH, 301/5624, Testimony of Helena Gadomska, née Hanerman.

57. YVA, O.3/994, Testimony of Henryk Rubanek. Ludwik Ehrlich was arrested in September 1943 and incarcerated in a prison run by the Biłgoraj Gestapo (Ehrlich was the director of the Office for Information and Propaganda of AK). Together with seventy-one other prisoners, Rubanek was freed during an operation conducted by AK in the prison on September 24.

58. AŻIH, List Stanisława Kołodziejczyka do ŻiH z 31 VII 1994 r. [Letter of Stanisław Kołodziejczyk to the ŻIH of 31 July 1994]; List Krystyny Mazurkiewicz do ŻIH z 22 VIII 1994 r. [Letter of Krystyna Mazurkiewicz to the ŻIH of 22 August 1944].

59. Państwowe Muzeum na Majdanku [The State Museum at Majdanek], VII/0-33, Testimony of Czesław Witkowski of 1970. According to Witkowski, for safety reasons, Paczos "kept this as a secret and revealed it to Witkowski only after the war." According to information received from Jan Grabowski, for which I am very grateful, "*Kennkarten* had local identification numbers. Although they provided each *Kennkarte* form with a serial number, the office issuing the documents had no central record of the issued documents. If a suspicious *Kennkarte* was found, an inquiry was sent to the issuing office and to the Central Registry of Convicts." See also USC, VHA, 16038, Wywiad z Fredą Dymbort z domu Guterman, ur. w 1927 r. w Woli k. Tarnogrodu [Interview with Freda Dymbort, née Guterman, b. 1927 in Wola, near Tarnogród].

60. The list may be incomplete, but they include: (1) Genia Dawidowicz, born in Lublin. (2) Rachela Mosze from Frampol, who died in Germany during

a bombing. She left for Germany aided by a Pole, Frelas. (3) Sierpińska or Ślepińska (first name unknown) from Tarnogród. (4) Rywka Adler, née Lustrin, from Tarnogród (she most probably left under the name of Aniela Sitarz). (5) Lea Lustrin, Rywka's sister. (6) Sara Lacher from Tarnogród. (7) Zelig Tripf from Tarnogród. (8–9) the Cwajman sisters (first names unknown). (10) Rubin Weistuch from Radecznica. (11) Hencia Wagner (later Helen Abraham) from Dąbrowica Mała.

61. Aleksander Przysada, *Zygmunt Klukowski, lekarz ze Szczebrzeszyna 1885–1959* [Zygmunt Klukowski, a Doctor from Szczebrzeszyn 1885–1959] (Szczebrzeszyn: Miejski Dom Kultury, 2000), 81.

62. Janusz Wrona, *Dzieje Tarnogrodu* (Tarnogród: Urząd Miasta i Gminy, 2006), 278.

63. Jakubik, *Czapki na bakier*, 19.

64. Grzegorz Kołacz, *Czasami trudno się bronić. Uwarunkowania postaw Żydów podczas okupacji hitlerowskiej w Polsce* [It Is Sometimes Difficult to Defend Oneself. Factors Determining the Attitudes of the Jews during the Nazi Occupation in Poland] (Warsaw: WAiP), 141.

65. USC, VHA, 44697, Wywiad z Feliksem (Efraimem) Urmanem [Interview with Feliks (Efraim) Urman].

66. Edward Herc, "Czasy niezapomniane. Gehenna Żydów w Józefowie" [Unforgettable times: Gehenna of Jews in Józefów], *Aspekty. Biłgorajski rocznik społeczno-kulturalny* 3 (2006): 78–79.

67. Barbara Engelking, "Czarna godzina. Rzeczy żydowskie oddane na przechowanie Polakom" [A rainy day: Jewish possessions given to Poles for safekeeping], in *Klucze i kasa*, op. cit., 387–437.

68. YVA, O.33/635, Testimony of Tema Wajnsztok.

69. The Stańczyk family were recognized by Yad Vashem as Righteous Among the Nations. They helped not only the Birks but also other Jews who hid in the forest and came to them for food.

70. AIPN Lu, 327/31, The case of Franciszek Kulesza, Władysław Bełżek and Jan Blicharz 1946–1954; Testimony of Boruch Wermut at the Main Court Session, 162.

71. There were opposite situations too when Poles were mistaken for Jews.

72. YVA, O.3/3510, Testimony of Wanda Kinrus, née Litwak.

73. Similar help was offered by Ukrainians to Poles fleeing the genocidal operations in Volhynia in 1943; cf. Romuald Niedziełko, ed., *Kresowa księga Sprawiedliwych 1939–1945. O Ukraińcach ratujących Polaków poddanych eksterminacji przez OUN i UPA* [The Borderland Book of the Righteous 1939–1945: On Ukrainians Saving Poles Subjected to Extermination by OUN and UPA] (Warsaw: IPN, 2007), 14.

74. Klukowski, *Zamojszczyzna*, 311, entry of November 18, 1942; 332, entry of November 20, 1942.

75. Herc, "Czasy niezapomniane," 80.
76. AŻIH, 301/5502, Testimony of Aleksander Falandysz, Wincenty Chałkiewicz and Mieczysław Śleboda.
77. YVA, O.33/635, Testimony of Tema Wajnsztok.
78. Cf. Barbara Engelking, *"Jest taki piękny słoneczny dzień..." Losy Żydów szukających ratunku na wsi polskiej 1942–1945* ["Such a Beautiful Sunny Day..." The Fate of the Jews Seeking Refuge in Polish Villages in 1942–1945] (Warsaw: Stowarzyszenie Centrum Badań nad Zagładą Żydów, 2011).
79. YVA, O.3/3078, Testimony of Rywka Dawidowicz.
80. YVA, O.3/3109, Testimony of Dora Kislowicz, née Birk.
81. USC, VHA, 44697, Interview with Feliks (Efraim) Urman.
82. Władysław Bartoszewski, Zofia Lewinówna, *Ten jest z ojczyzny mojej. Polacy z Pomocą Żydom 1939–1945* [He is from my Homeland. Poles Helping Jews 1939–1945], (Warsaw: Świat Książki, 2007), 511.
83. Nechama Tec, *When Light Pierced the Darkness. Christian Rescue of Jews in Nazi-Occupied Poland* (New York: Oxford University Press, 1986), 188–189.
84. YVA, M.31/589, Testimony of Szmuel Maler. Stanisław Sobczak was recognized as Righteous Among the Nations on November 11, 1969.
85. Ibid.
86. Zuzanna Schnepf-Kołacz, "Pomoc Polaków dla Żydów na wsi w czasie okupacji niemieckiej. Próba opisu na przykładzie Sprawiedliwych wśród Narodów Świata" [Poles helping the Jews in the countryside during the German occupation: The case of the Righteous Among the Nations], in *Zarys krajobrazu. Wieś polska wobec zagłady Żydów 1942–1945* [A Landscape Outline: Polish Countryside toward the Holocaust 1942–1945], ed. Barbara Engelking, Jan Grabowski (Warsaw: Stowarzyszenie Centrum Badań nad Zagładą Żydów, 2011), 220.
87. AŻIH, 301/7214, Testimony of Tema Wajnsztok, née Rottman.
88. YVA, O.3/3082, Testimony of Aharon Kislowicz.
89. Testimony of Icie Sztemer, *The Book of Memory to the Jewish Community of Szczebrzeszyn*, translated by J.S. Berger (New Jersey, 2006), 95.
90. The files with documents about each of those cases are available in the Yad Vashem Archives in Jerusalem.
91. The village of Łada, three kilometers away from Goraj, is administratively outside the Biłgoraj County, in the Chrzanów commune, Janów Lubelski County.
92. The village of Branew, ten kilometers away from Goraj, is in the Dzwola commune, Janów Lubelski County.
93. Marcin Urynowicz, "Zorganizowana i indywidualna pomoc Polaków dla ludności żydowskiej eksterminowanej przez okupanta niemieckiego w okresie drugiej wojny światowej" [Organized and individual help offered by Poles to the Jewish population exterminated by the German occupier during the

Second World War], in *Polacy i Żydzi pod okupacją niemiecką 1939–1945. Studia i materiały* [Poles and Jews under the German Occupation 1939–1945: Studies and Materials], ed. Andrzej Żbikowski (Warsaw: IPN, 2006), 246.

94. List Edwarda Saja do Natana Bryka z 5 V 1995 [Letter from Edward Saj to Natan Bryk of May 5, 1995]; YVA 7582, Teczka Sprawiedliwego Saja [Files of Righteous Saj].

95. USC, VHA, 10269, Wywiad z Blumą Holler Kamerman [Interview with Bluma Holler Kamerman]. A similar opinion was expressed by Szlajcher: "There were AK bandits scouring the area and attacking us regularly. This way, they murdered 300 people" (AŻIH, 301/105; Testimony of Israel Szlajcher).

96. *Book of Memory to the Jewish Community of Szczebrzeszyn*, translated by J. S. Berger (New Jersey, 2006), 123.

97. USC, VHA, 9679, Wywiad z Morrisem Shapiro [Interview with Morris Shapiro].

98. Tekla's parents, Jan and Rozalia Wołoszyn, had previously hidden the Shapiro siblings; in 1992, they were posthumously recognized as Righteous Among the Nations.

99. USC, VHA, 10269, Interview with Bluma Holler Kamerman.

100. Irving Lumerman claims that there were twenty-five families, Estera Fefer talks about three hundred people, and Israel Szlajcher mentions a group of four hundred.

101. Bluma Kamerman met her fiancé in the forest, where they got married and where Bluma became pregnant. She gave birth to her daughter after liberation. According to her testimony, many people formed relationships in the forest.

102. AŻIH, 301/105 Testimony of Israel Szlajcher.

103. https://www.szczebressyn.pl/wspomnienia/Aleksander_Piwowarek.pdf (accessed October 30, 2016).

104. Klukowski, *Zamojszczyzna*, 332, entry of October 26, 1942.

105. Bartoszewski was one of the first three commanders in the region, which was the most important one for the Jews hiding in the forests. The remaining two commanders were Hieronim Męc ("Korsarz") and Edward Błaszczak ("Grom").

106. "The problem of the Jewish population was another issue. After a mass murder committed by the occupier on 23 July 1942, the part of the population who survived hid in the forest on their own, and many found shelter in Polish homes. Both of these groups used the organization's help." Konrad Bartoszewski ("Wir"), ed., *Relacje, wspomnienia, opracowania* [Testimonies, Memoirs, Studies] (Lublin: Oficyna Wydawnicza Czas, 1996), 54.

107. On the very negative attitude of Polish underground units toward the Jews in hiding, see the testimony of Chaim Mordechaj Szlajcher, "Żydzi

biłgorajscy w oddziałach partyzanckich" [Jews from Biłgoraj in partisan units], in *Biłgoraj izker buch*, typewritten, 137–163.

108. Bolesław Polakowski "Wiarus," "Dziennik z lasu" [Diary from the forest], *Karta* 72 (2012): 26.

109. "The behavior of the AK soldiers from the unit led by Lieutenant Tadeusz Kuncewicz 'Podkowa' should be considered an act of extreme cruelty. In the spring of 1945 near Krasnystaw, they caught two Jews returning to the camp and ordered them to fight each other. They promised that the survivor would be released. When they started fighting, the AK soldiers shot them both." Rafał Wnuk, "Bandytyzm na Lubelszczyźnie w latach 1944–1953: propozycja typologii" [Banditry in the Lublin region in 1944–1953: Suggested typology], *Problemy bandytyzmu w okupowanej Polsce w latach 1939-1947* [The Problems of Banditry in Occupied Poland in 1939–1947], ed. Tomasz Strzembosz (Warsaw: ISP PAN, 2003), 89–90. See also Testimony of Eugeniusz Tchórzewski in Rafał Wnuk's collection; Klukowski, *Zamojszczyzna*, 432, entry of May 31, 1944.

110. Yisrael Gutman and Shmuel Krakowski, *Unequal Victims: Poles and Jews During World War II* (New York, 1986), 33, 211–215, 222, 233.

111. I have not managed to determine whom he meant.

112. AŻIH, 301/6825, Testimony of Florian Wójtowicz.

113. I quote after Shmuel Krakowski, *The War of the Doomed. Jewish Armed Resistance in Poland, 1942–1944* (New York: Holmes and Meier), 77–83. Krakowski in turn relies on the testimony of David Shtokfish quoted in *Sefer Frampol* [The Book of Frampol] (Tel Aviv, 1966), 59, 98–109.

114. Józef Bolesław Garas, *Oddziały Gwardii Ludowej i Armii Ludowej 1942–1945* [Units of the People's Guard and the People's Army] (Warsaw: Ministerstwo Obrony Narodowej, 1963), 94–95.

115. AIPN, GK 377/4, Śledztwo w sprawie przeciwko Michałowi Wolskiemu i Władysławowi Kowalczykowi [Investigation in the case against Michał Wolski and Władysław Kowalczyk]; Testimony of Michał (Mendel) Dym of September 24, 1949, 79.

116. According to Dawid Goldgraber, they were from Gorajec.

117. Among the murdered ones were Abram Met, Josef Met, Chaskiel Met, Abram Goldgraber, Dawid Kleiner, and Ita Kleiner (née Fink). The four survivors were Mendel Dym, Dawid Goldgraber, Icek Met, and Herszek Altman.

118. The most famous group organized in the region by former prisoners of war was led by Michał Atamanow (Umer Achmołła Atamanow), alias Miszka Tatar [Tartar Mihail] or Miszka Groźny [Mihail the Terrible], and consisted of seventy people. It broke up after Atamanow's death in the battle of Józefów on July 1, 1943; see AAN, Zbiór akt osobowych działaczy ruchu robotniczego 1918–1990 [Personal Files of Labor Movement Activists 1918–1990], file of Michał Atamanow No. 14691; Jerzy Markiewicz, *Partyzancki kraj* [Partisan Country] (Lublin: Wydawnictwo Lubelskie, 1985), 76.

119. AIPN, GK 377/4, Śledztwo w sprawie przeciwko Michałowi Wolskiemu i Władysławowi Kowalczykowi [Investigation in the case against Michał Wolski and Władysław Kowalczyk]; Testimony of Dawid Goldgraber of September 19, 1946, 6.

120. AIPN, GK 377/4, Wniosek o umorzenie śledztwa [Motion to Terminate the Investigation], 121.

121. Estera Fefer mentioned several more Soviet partisan groups: "*kołapkowcy, sitowcy, chruszczowcy, kowalowcy*, the group of grandpa Pietia" (AŻIH, 301/1474, Testimony of Estera Fefer).

122. The witness meant the so-called "people from Trawniki," Soviet prisoners of war who agreed to undergo a training in the SS training camp in Trawniki, where they were prepared for service in death camps and in support units for extermination and pacification operations. A part of them managed to escape and join, among others, a Soviet partisan unit named after Czapajew (Black, "Prosty żołnierz 'akcji Reinhard.' Oddziały z Trawnik," 103–131).

123. AŻIH, 301/5344, Testimony of Marian Szarach.

124. See: Dorota Skakuj, "Wysiedlenia w powiecie biłgorajskim w 1943 roku" [Deportations in Biłgoraj County in 1943], *Nad Tanwią i Ładą. Przyczynki do historii i kultury Ziemi Biłgorajskiej* [By the Tanew and Łada Rivers: On the History and Culture of the Biłgoraj Region] 5 (2010): 35–41; Jacek Wołoszyn, "Powiat biłgorajski w okresie okupacji niemieckiej" [The Biłgoraj County during the German occupation], *Nad Tanwią i Ładą. Przyczynki do historii i kultury Ziemi Biłgorajskiej* 1 (2006): 19–30; Agnieszka Jarczyńska, *Sonderlaboratorium SS. Zamojszczyzna Pierwszy obszar osiedleńczy w Generalnym Gubernatorstwie* [Zamość Region, the SS Sonderlaboratorium: The First Settlement Area in the General Government] (Lublin: IPN, 2012).

125. Anna Janko, *Mała Zagłada* [Small Holocaust] (Cracow: Wydawnictwo Literackie, 2015).

126. AAN, 291/54 and 55, Biuro Odszkodowań Wojennych przy Prezesie Rady Ministrów w Warszawie [War Reparations Bureau at the Prime Minister in Warsaw], Straty biologiczne poniesione w woj. lubelskim. Kwestionariusze powiatowe i gminne [Biological Losses in the Lublin Province: County and Commune Surveys], 1945.

127. Klukowski, *Zamojszczyzna*, 336.

128. Ibid., 363, entry of April 24, 1943.

129. AP in Zamość, 382/158, Prezydium Gromadzkiej Rady Narodowej w Łukowej [Presidium of Gromada People's Council in Łukowa (*Gromadzka Rada Naukowa*, GRN)], Dokumentacja zeznań ustnych i pisemnych mieszkańców GRN w Łukowej nt. zbrodni hitlerowskich popełnionych na terenie gminy 1968–1971 [Records of Oral and Written Testimonies of the Inhabitants of GRN in Łukowa on the Nazi Crimes Committed in the Commune in 1968–1971].

130. Cf. Adam Kopciowski, "Zajścia antyżydowskie na Lubelszczyźnie w pierwszych latach po drugiej wojnie światowej" [Anti-Jewish Incidents in the Lublin Region in the First Years after the Second World War], *Zagłada Żydów. Studia i Materiały* 3 (2007): 178–207.

131. See Jan Tomasz Gross, *Fear: Anti-Semitism in Poland after Auschwitz* (New York: Random House, 2007).

132. *Martwa fala. Zbiór artykułów o antysemityzmie* [The Dead Wave: A Collection of Papers on Antisemitism] (Warsaw: Spółdzielnia Wydawnicza Wiedza, 1947).

133. Rafał Wnuk, *Lubelski Okręg AK 1944–1947* [The AK Lublin Region 1944–1947] (Warsaw: Volumen, 2000), chap. 9, "AK-DSZ-WiN a Żydzi" [AK-DSZ-WiN and the Jews], 199–219).

134. Ibid., 202–203.

135. Twenty-four criminal cases were heard in postwar courts, two of which involved German defendants. In the remaining cases, Poles were accused on the basis of the August Decree on acting against Polish citizens of Jewish origin.

ALINA SKIBIŃSKA, a historian, graduated from the University of Warsaw. She works as the United States Holocaust Memorial Museum Poland Representative. Since 2003, she has been a scholar of the Polish Center for the Holocaust Research at the Polish Academy of Science, and she is a member of editorial board of the journal *Holocaust: Studies and Materials*. She is the author of publications on the fate of Polish Jews during and shortly after the war and the attitudes of Polish society toward the Holocaust. She has published, among others, *"Jakie to ma znaczenie, czy zrobili to z chciwości?" Zagłada domu Trynczerów* with Tadeusz Markiel (Warsaw, 2011) and "Problemy rewindykacji żydowskich nieruchomości w latach 1944–1950. Zagadnienia ogólne i szczegółowe (na przykładzie Szczebrzeszyna)," in *Klucze i kasa. O mieniu żydowskim w Polsce pod okupacją niemiecką i we wczesnych latach powojennych 1939–1950*, eds. J. Grabowski and D. Libionka (Warsaw, 2014).

THREE

WĘGROW COUNTY

JAN GRABOWSKI

INTRODUCTION

Węgrów County (which is the focus of this study) has one specific unique feature: Treblinka. This small hamlet, located in the northeastern corner of Węgrów county, has become in the eyes of the world synonymous with the Holocaust—a place where close to one million Jews were put to death[1]. This is why today, this area is the second largest (after Oświęcim [Auschwitz] County) Jewish graveyard in the world. There is no doubt that the proximity of Treblinka and the widespread awareness of the ongoing extermination had a significant impact on the attitudes of the local Jews at the time when the ghettos were being liquidated. It should be stressed that the toxic influence of Treblinka was felt not only by Jews; it reached beyond the barbed wire surrounding the camp, poisoning the souls and hearts of the Polish inhabitants of the area within a radius of dozens of miles. The proximity of Treblinka is further reflected in the hundreds of Jewish graves that litter the countryside. Many of these graves are located close to the railway tracks used by the so-called death trains heading to Małkinia and, further, to their final destination at Treblinka. On the way, thousands of victims made their last desperate stand and fled the transports. Only a few managed to survive.

Another characteristic feature of the studied area is the undeniable participation of parts of the local Polish population in the German genocidal project. This issue has already been identified and commented upon during the war by the Polish underground press and in the reports of the Polish resistance. The local participation in the destruction of the Jewish community of Węgrów involved not only the officers of the Polish Blue police (which was a norm all

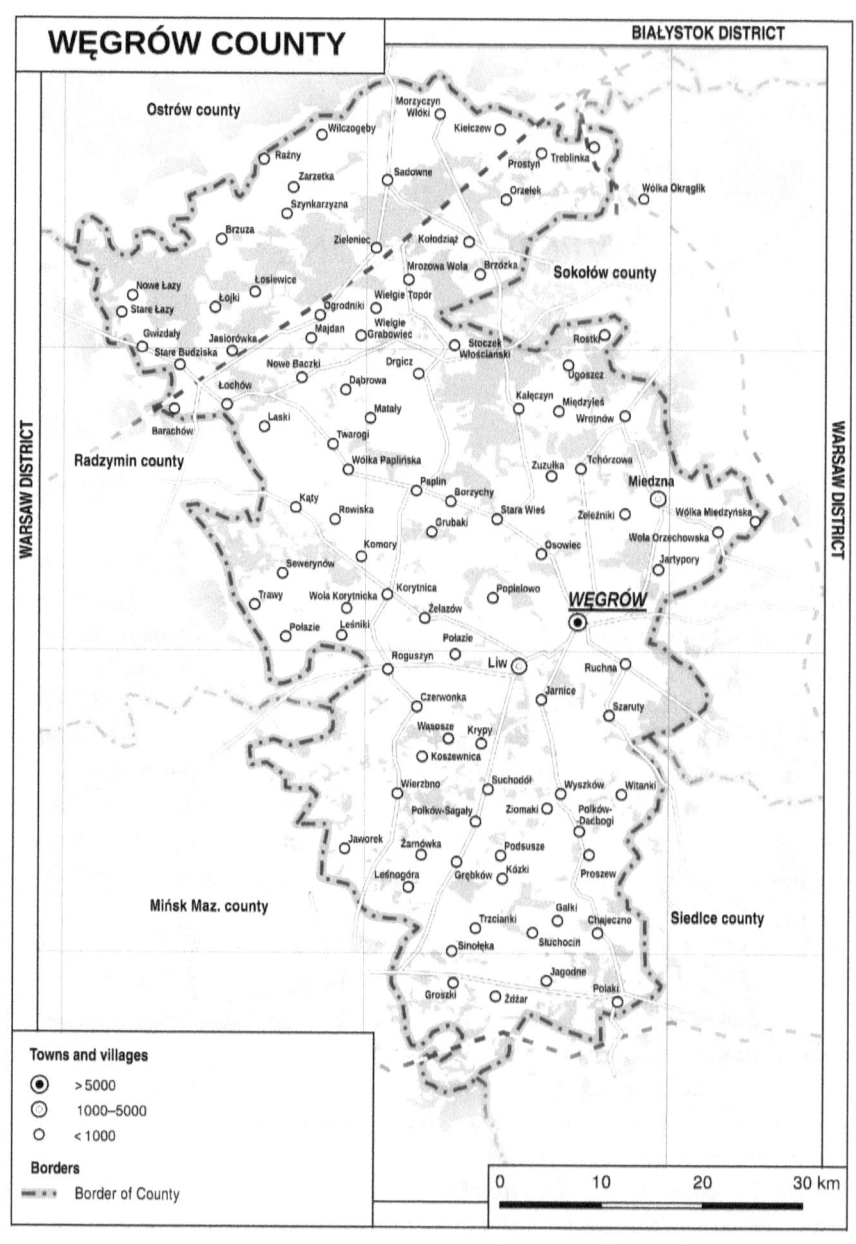

across the *Generalgouvernement,* GG) but also detachments of the voluntary firefighters and large numbers of so-called bystanders (i.e., local townspeople and peasants).

The County

Węgrów County straddles the Podlasie and Masovia regions of Poland. The city of Węgrów itself appeared for the first time in historical records at the beginning of the fifteenth century, when economic exchange with the Grand Duchy of Lithuania helped stimulate local demography and economic growth. The county was a typically rural area, with 90 percent of the population involved in agricultural pursuits as late as 1939.[2] Administratively, the area was subdivided into fourteen rural communes and the city of Węgrów. Today, Węgrów County has 68,000 inhabitants living on a territory of 1,222 square kilometers divided into seven rural and two urban communes: Węgrów and Łochów.

The Jews of Węgrów

The first information about the Jewish presence in Węgrów dates back to 1537.[3] A manuscript from Węgrów written in 1596 in Hebrew by "Uri, the son of Liezer" (also known as Leibman Ashkenazy) devoted to the art of healing and medicine testifies to the sophistication and knowledge of its author. The text makes reference to a drug that "healed a child from the holy community of Węgrów."[4] In 1765, the local Jewish community boasted 3,623 members, including 587 who lived inside the city limits. The most important demographic shift occurred in the nineteenth century, when the Jews became the largest ethnic community in Węgrów. In 1939, there were 5,900 Jewish inhabitants in the city, which equaled more than 60 percent of the total population. In the surrounding rural areas, the Jewish presence was much weaker compared to the city, but Jews lived in each and every commune of the county.

Jews in Węgrów Prior to World War II

During the 1930s, the deterioration of Polish-Jewish[5] relations, which went hand in hand with the growing power of *Endecja*[6] in the Węgrów area, began to undermine the economic foundations of the Jewish community.[7] Particularly disturbing was the *Endecja*-led and Church-supported boycott of Jewish stores and merchants. In June 1936, the boycott of Jewish commerce was endorsed even by the Polish prime minister, Felicjan Sławoj-Składkowski,[8] Acts of violence were present along with picket lines surrounding Jewish places of business.[9]

The brutality spilled into other spheres of everyday life and became a threat to Jewish students returning from school.[10] A local historian wrote about the deteriorating ethnic and racial relations during the latter prewar years: "Starting in 1937, the *Endecja* decided to adopt more radical measures against the Jews. On the days when people congregated in the public markets,[11] members of *Endecja* stood guard in front of the Jewish stores in order to scare away potential customers. In March 1937, the *Endecja* campaign gathered strength, and the authorities became concerned with the level of anti-Jewish violence (assaults, injuries, and confrontations with the police) reported from Węgrów and Sokołów. The following month, Poles beat up scores of Jews in Sokołów, while unknown hooligans smashed more than 600 windows in Jewish houses."[12] During the last years of peace, Jewish merchants in Węgrów came under heavy pressure from the members of right-wing militias. The police reports from the time provide ample evidence of this phenomenon. On June 15, 1937, for instance, the detectives reported from Węgrów: "The [anti-Jewish] boycott action involved some 130 men and 20 women from Sokołów and Węgrów counties. Czesław Grądzki [local Endecja activist – JG] strolled the market square, inspecting his subordinates who stood at attention and saluted him, raising their right arms. Men and women who took part in the boycott action wore dark blue headgear"[13]. The sight of "raised right arms" had become, as it seems, a familiar scene in the main square of Węgrów long before the Germans appeared in town.

The outbreak of war found the Jewish community in full retreat, and the violence against the Jews, so visible during the late 1930s, was to increase dramatically with the arrival of the Germans.

GERMAN OCCUPATION

The Germans entered Węgrów on September 7, 1939, just one week after the attack on Poland. The new masters quickly moved in to replace the Polish administration with their own structures of authority. In mid-October, they redrew and expanded the Polish counties, consolidating them into significantly larger administrative units known as *Kreishaptmannschaften*. Węgrów became part of the new *Kreishauptmannschaft Sokolow-Wengrow,* made up of two former Polish counties, and governed from Sokołów. The chief of the German civil administration (*Kreishauptmann*) wielded enormous powers, especially once the military presence in the area diminished. The tenures of the first two *Kraishaupmänner* (Friedrich Schulz and Ordensjunker Völker) were rather short. However, the third *Kreishauptmann*, Ernst Gramss, who received his appointment on June 10, 1940, was to hold his office until July 1944, fleeing in the face of the advancing

Red Army.[14] It was Gramss who therefore had a special role in shaping the German policies of terror in the studied area during the occupation. Despite three attempts on his life made by the Polish resistance, Gramss survived the war and, in 1945, was briefly interned in an Allied camp in Moosburg, Bavaria. He fled the camp in 1946 and disappeared without a trace; in 1956, he was legally declared dead.[15]

This study, unlike some of the other studies included in the present volume, focuses not on the whole *Kreishauptmannschaft Sokolow-Wengrow* but rather on the part that, before the war, had formed Węgrów County: fourteen rural communes (basic administrative units) that had belonged to Węgrów County until 1939, as well as the urban commune of Węgrów itself.

Early Measures

The war brought immediate and dramatic changes to the living conditions of all inhabitants of the area, but from the very first days of occupation, Jews were singled out for particularly harsh treatment. One of the first victims of terror was Ezechiel Szatensztajn, one of the wealthiest people in the town, whose property was stolen by the German officials immediately after his execution. A few days later, on Yom Kippur (the Day of Atonement, the holiest day of the Jewish calendar), which fell that year on September 23, 1939, German soldiers tortured and later murdered Jakub Mendel Morgenstern, the rabbi of Węgrów. The brutal and very public execution of Morgenstern was to serve—according to the Germans—as a "lesson to the Jews."[16] Acts of terror against the Jewish elites went together with brutal campaigns directed at the Jewish community as a whole, with all men regularly being forced to perform hard, unpaid, and often humiliating labor.[17] Some Jews decided to flee to the east under Soviet occupation and left Węgrów; many more were resettled in the county from the former Polish territories now incorporated directly into the Reich (*Eingegliederte Ostgebiete*). According to the Polish mayor, due to these migrations, the number of Jews living in the city soon reached eight thousand people.[18]

Three ghettos were created in the studied territory: in Węgrów, in Łochów, and in Stoczek. Jews living in outlying villages were gradually resettled into the three designated areas. The ghettos had their own *Judenräte* (Jewish councils), and Jewish police were responsible for maintaining order within the "Jewish Living Area."[19] The ghetto police force was small, most likely composed—in the case of Węgrów—of no more than a score of officers. A document signed by Mordechaj Zelman, chairman of the *Judenrat* and at the same time the head of the local section of the ZSS (*Żydowska Samopomoc Społeczna*, Jewish Self-Help),

Figure 3.1. A street in the Węgrów ghetto (GFH, 7109).

lists the names of four Jewish policemen detailed to escort Jewish forced laborers to the nearby Ostrów Mazowiecka.

The ghetto in Węgrów was rather unique because due to the large concentration of Jews, the entire city was initially designated as a "Jewish living quarter."[20] On September 13, 1940, Gramss officially restricted the right of residence for Jews to the indicated areas and, one month later, imposed a special curfew for the "non-Aryan" population.[21] In 1941, a string of new regulations made life for the Jews of *Kreishauptmannschaft Sokolow-Wegrow* even more difficult. Further restrictions on their freedom of movement brought about famine, followed by epidemics of typhus. The final separation of the Jewish population was ordered in March 1942, when the previously open ghettos (including the one in Węgrów) were closed.[22] In this manner, the stage was set for the implementation of the "Final Solution."

On the Eve of Extermination: Population Counts

During the first year of their rule, the Germans ordered two population censuses: The first, a rough one, was intended to reflect the counts as of September

Table 3.1 Population of the former Węgrów County during the war

Węgrów and Rural communes	September 1, 1939	July 1, 1940		March 1, 1943
		Total population	Jews	
Węgrów	10,000	12,821	7,364	5,182
Borze	4,430	5,968	47	4609
Grębków	5,523	5,900	142	5725
Jaczew	3,694	4,825	42	3726
Korytnica	4,994	5,417	86	5027
Łochów	11,821	14,015	1,200	12481
Miedzna	6,305	7,223	159	6827
Ossówno	4,180	5,579	73	4410
Prostyń	4,494	5,541	87	4576
Ruchna	5,580	6,727	150	6108
Sadowne	7,939	7,229	226	7124
Sinołęka	4,849	5,968	63	5269
Starawieś	6,236	6,486	56	5862
Stoczek	7,793	8,061	967	6670
Wyszków	4,382	4,554	63	4325
TOTAL	**92,220**	**106,314**	**10,725**	**87,921**

Source: Based on, for 1939 and 1940, "Regierung des Generalgouvernements. Abteilung Ernährung und Landwirtschaft. Statistische Amt. Die Ernährungs- u. Landwirschaft im Generalgouvernements Polen", series B: "Statistische Zusammenstellungen," dossier 6, Krakau 1940, 47; for 1943, *Amtliches Gemeinde- und Dorfverzeichnis für das Generalgouvernement auf Grund der Summarischen Bevölkerungsbestandsaufnahme am 1. März 1943* (Krakow 1943).

1, 1939; the second, conducted on July 1, 1940, was much more precise and separately took stock of the Jews. The censuses are of particular importance because they descend to the level of all communes (*gminy*), allowing a reconstruction of the population dynamics in the former Węgrów County.

A significant increase in the size of the Jewish population in the 1939–1942 period was largely related to a large number of people resettled to the area from western Poland, which had been annexed directly into the Reich. These deportees from the West more than compensated for the unknown number of local Jews who fled the German occupation and sought refuge under the Soviet rule. The demarcation line between the Germans and the Soviets was nearby, along the Bug River.

The Perpetrators

We do not know much about the policemen from the Węgrów area, but the little we do know needs to be described in some detail. The main detachment of *Schutzpolizei*[23] was based in Węgrów itself and, at least until the end of 1942, was placed under the command of Müller, a tall and strong man in his midforties. Sometime at the end of 1942 (or in early 1943), Müller was replaced by *Oberleutnant* Diestelhorst. Among his subordinates were Brenner and his colleagues, Giler and Langner.[24] In the area of interest, there were two other ORPO detachments: one in Sokołów (from which the officers were often dispatched to Węgrów) and another in nearby Budziska.[25]

In July 1940, the Budziska/Łochów police detachment received a new commander, Lieutenant Karl Tedsen.[26] In his new role, Tedsen also became the commanding officer of the Polish Blue police in Łochów. His own police force in Budziska included twelve gendarmes, among them Rudolf Pietsch (from Potsdam), the *Volksdeutscher* (ethnic German) Friedrich Hartmann, and officers Oprisnik, Schmidt, and Kögel. Tedsen's deputy, *Gendarmeriemeister* Wilhelm Pross, soon acquired notoriety as a murderer of Jews. According to Tedsen, he and his policemen were charged only with fighting common criminality; his gendarmes were never involved in any "illegal" activities. According to Kurnig, a gendarme from Sokołów, the forces responsible for the liquidations of the ghettos were recruited from among the unspecified "Finnish troops," SD officers, and members of the *Sonderdienst*[27] led by *Kreishauptmann* Gramss. In reality, however, the involvement of Tedsen and his people in the establishment of the German system of terror in Węgrów County was infinitely more important than one could judge on the basis of their self-serving testimonies. In the summer of 1942, for instance, Tedsen personally conducted the mass-shooting of more than seventy Jews in Budziska next to the police station,[28] and two of his officers, *Volksdeutsche* Hübscher and Hoppe, belonged to the so-called *Ghettokommando*, or gendarmes who were most often deployed in the Węgrów and Sokołów ghettos.

The second force involved in the implementation of the local *Judenpolitik* was the Security Police, most often referred to simply as the Gestapo. The External Detachment of the Warsaw Commander of SIPO (local security police) and SD in Sokołów (*Außenstelle des Kommandeurs der Sicherheitspolizei und des SD Warschau in Sokolow*) was led by SS-*Sturmscharführer und Kriminalsekretär* Friedrich Schröder. His subordinates included SS-*Scharführer* Uwe Karsten, SS-*Rottenführer* Gustav Friedrich, *Kriminalkommissar* Kurt Nicolaus, and SS-*Obersturmführer* Rudolf Weber, who replaced Schröder as commander in 1943. Other members of the Gestapo in Sokołów included Schweitzer, a driver, and

Hirsekorn, a *Volksdeutscher* and interpreter.[29] These were the people who were given the overall responsibility for coordinating the liquidations of the ghettos in the territory of *Kreishauptmannschaft Sokolow-Wengrow*.

In addition to the Gestapo, the SIPO also included the Polish Criminal Police (*Polnische Kriminalpolizei*, Kripo) with its headquarters located in Sokołów, headed by the previously mentioned Gestapo chief Schröder.[30] The German Order Police and the SIPO were further reinforced by the Polish Blue police (*Polnische Polizei*, PP), an essential element of the police presence in Węgrów County. The local Blue police had more than 130 officers on duty working out of eight stations located in Bojmie, Miedzna, Węgrów, Wyszków, Łochów, Sadowne, Stoczek, and Grębków. The names of most of the Polish officers are long forgotten, and most of the relevant police documentation was destroyed either during or after the war, but some of the Blue policemen shall later make an appearance in the pages of this study. Last but not least, the forces that were to be used in the destruction of the local ghettoes included the Ukrainian auxiliaries (the so-called *Trawniki-Männer*)[31] led by *SS-Sturmbannführer* Theodor van Eupen, commander of the notorious Treblinka I labor camp (*Arbeitserziehungslager*, AEL). Van Eupen was in charge of the liquidation *Aktion* in Sokołów Podlaski and, according to numerous witnesses, personally tortured and murdered Jews in the streets of the city.[32]

THE *AKTION* IN WĘGRÓW

The description of the liquidation of Węgrów and other nearby ghettos must be preceded by acknowledging the extent of ignorance about the topic. To start with, the evaluation of the number of Jews killed during the *Aktionen* is nothing more than a guess. Sometimes, as is the case of smaller locations, even the dates of deportations and liquidations cannot be firmly established. Finally, as has been shown above, precious little is known about the people involved in the destructions of the ghettos and about their tactics. Bearing all of this in mind, one can start to analyze the drama that culminated on September 22–24, 1942.

Shortly before the deportation, the German authorities decided to concentrate all the Jews living around Węgrów in the city. Nehama Rotbart and her family, for example, were forcibly removed from their home village of Bojmie, given just thirty minutes to pack up their possessions, and shipped off to Węgrów.[33] With the influx of deportees, the living conditions in the already overcrowded ghetto deteriorated further. In the same period, in the spring and early summer, terrifying news began circulating in the ghetto regarding the deportations from and liquidations of more and less distant ghettos. In July 1942, the Jews of Węgrów became aware of the gravity of their situation: Two main railway lines carrying "death trains" to Treblinka (the Warsaw-Tłuszcz-Małkinia and the Siedlce-Sokołów-Małkinia lines) crossed the borders of Węgrów County not far from the city. In July–August 1942, the "death trains" to Treblinka carried, for the most part, people taken from the liquidated Warsaw ghetto. In many cases, the desperate Jews tore away the wooden planks of the wagons or the barbed wires that covered the windows and fled. Some were shot by the guards stationed on the roofs of the wagons, some were killed during the jump, and some were later murdered by locals. There were some, however, who managed to reach one of the nearby ghettos, such as Węgrów, and gave accounts of the tragedy unfolding in Warsaw.[34]

"That Night We Could Not Sleep."[35] Węgrów-Sokołów: Monday, September 21, 1942, 11:00 p.m.

Rumors about the impending liquidation had been rampant in the Węgrów ghetto for quite some time, at least since the late spring of 1942. In the course of August and early September, these rumors were confirmed by the refugees fleeing the liquidated ghettos in Warsaw, Siedlce, and the nearby Mińsk Mazowiecki. With mounting panic, people started to prepare themselves for a siege. They built ingenious hideouts to survive the initial German fury. Many sought out contacts on the "Aryan side" of the city, looking for help among the Poles, including former neighbors, friends, and business partners. Leaving the ghetto was not really a problem, but avoiding capture and finding help on the other side of the fence was an altogether different matter. There is no doubt that for the Jews crossing to the "Aryan side," the greatest danger was associated not with the Germans but with the local Poles. Unlike the former, the latter could easily tell a Jew from a non-Jew by their accent, customs, or physical appearance.[36]

The first signs of the impending liquidation reached the office of the *Kreishauptmann* a day or two before the planned *Aktion*. This moment may be pinpointed precisely because that is when wives of German officials began in haste to recover shoes, dresses, and other items they had previously ordered from the Jewish shoemakers, tailors, and other artisans. The day before the *Liquidierungsaktion*, Polish Blue police were placed on alert, and local *voits* and village elders were ordered to prepare an adequate number of people, horses, and carts for the operation.[37] According to several testimonies, local Polish volunteer firefighters were also placed on alert. Finally, on September 21, 1942, the predominantly Ukrainian "Askars"[38] and the German *Liquidierungskommandos* from Warsaw and Treblinka arrived in Sokołów.

At the same time, on September 21, 1942, the Jews started to prepare for the observance of Yom Kippur, which was about to begin. While most of the Jews of Węgrów were praying in preparation for Yom Kippur, the cordon of German and Polish policemen and their Ukrainian helpers was rapidly closing around the city. On September 22, 1942, between 4:00 a.m. and 5:00 a.m., the ring finally closed. Węgrów, Sokołów, and Stoczek were cordoned off in such a way that the policemen taking part in the *Aktion* were spread apart at intervals of no more than one hundred meters. On September 22, the sun rose at 6:15 a.m., but the sky started to brighten around 5:00 a.m. so the members of the *Liquidierungkommando* could see each other. Importantly, the cordon closing around Węgrów was not impermeable; although no one could leave the city, people could gain access from outside. This was of particular importance for the local peasants who, that very day, had brought their products to the weekly market.

Węgrów-Sokołów-Stoczek: Tuesday, September 22, 6:00 a.m.–12:00 p.m.

Harry Miller (Hersz Meier), who had moved to Węgrów from Jarnice, a small village nearby, learned about the approaching soldiers from his neighbor just before 5:00 a.m. By that point, the ghetto had already been surrounded, and some armed men were strolling the streets.[39]

On September 22 at dawn, when the first shots were fired, Jews started to hide in previously prepared hideouts and bunkers. The members of the *Judenrat* made an attempt to convince people to report to the main market square "to go to work," but their appeals fell on deaf ears. The small Jewish police force was unable to herd Jews into the open, as few people doubted that the final destination was the death camp at Treblinka.[40] Hiding in cellars, attics, and bunkers was, in most cases, a short-term solution that ended in tragedy. It was at this stage that the Germans and the Ukrainians gained a powerful ally in the form of many Polish inhabitants of Węgrów, who joined the *Liquidierungskommando* in the search for hidden Jews. According to Efraim Przepiórka, Christian neighbors were additionally motivated by the Germans with the promise of a quarter kilo of sugar as a prize for every Jew delivered to the authorities.[41] Just after 6:00 a.m., the Germans reached a house where Szraga Fajwel Bielawski and his family were hiding in the attic. The Germans were not alone: "We heard the voice of our 'friend' Maniek Karbowski [a Polish neighbor of the Bielawski family] saying: 'I'll bring an axe and chop it down.' A moment later, an axe was hacking at the door. Maniek told the Germans, 'These bastard Jews are still sleeping.' When the door yielded, Maniek and the SS troops entered. The soldiers yelled *'Raus!'*

Figure 3.2. Sara Frajda Bielawska, Szraga Fajwel Bielawski, and Paula Bielawska in front of their clothing store, Węgrów, 1940. Bielawski Family Archive.

as they scoured the store and the cellar. They pounded at the floor boards but found no one."[42]

The searches were conducted with extreme brutality and violence, and the streets were soon filled with crowds of Jews being driven toward the market square, which the Germans had transformed into a holding pen for thousands of the ghetto inmates. "Jews, who woke up to the terrible news, ran like mad around the city, half-naked, looking for shelter," wrote Władysław Okulus, the mayor of Węgrów. Most of the people brought to the market square were those judged to be able to withstand the ordeals of further travel. Others—small children and the elderly, for the most part—were either murdered in the streets or executed in the nearby Jewish cemetery. The sixteen-year-old son of Müller, the chief of the Węgrów Schupo detachment, also took part in the *Aktion* and, dressed in his *Hitlerjugend* uniform, helped his father murder Jews.

Węgrów: Tuesday, September 22, 12:00 to 5:00 p.m.

Władysław Wójcik, an inhabitant of Liw (a village situated four miles south of Węgrów), later recognized as Righteous Among the Nations, observed the unfolding events from "the front row," as he wrote later. Having heard about the ongoing liquidation, Wójcik set off to Węgrów early in the morning. "Around noon, I finally reached the market square in the center of the city. I was able to see for myself that getting to the center was not a problem, and the sidewalks were filled with the [local Polish] population living on the 'Aryan side' of town. In order to gain a better view, I climbed the stairs of a building situated opposite the church. The place resonated constantly with rifle and revolver shots coming from the Jewish quarter, and I could hear the cries and moans of dying people. The market was right next to the ghetto, and the shootings and the moans drove us, spectators, to despair. As soon as I arrived at the market, I saw that the whole area had been surrounded by the gendarmes and their Ukrainian lackeys. In the middle of this ring, I could see a few thousand Jews, men, women, and youth, sitting on the stones or on their luggage. All the time more Poles of Semitic descent[43] were being marched into the circle from the ghetto."[44]

According to Wójcik, the children, the elderly, and pregnant women were murdered in the ghetto or in the Jewish cemetery. Henryka Grabowska, a young woman at the time, saw the masses of Jews being marched toward the market square. "I went out to fetch water from the well. Gendarme Gil [most likely officer Giler from the Schupo detachment in Węgrów] and two Ukrainians led a woman with a little child. With the mother watching, they took the baby by the legs, impaled it on a bayonet, and later shot the woman. I will never forget her horrible screams . . . Nearby, I saw another dead woman; she was lying in the street and next to her there were two children. One of them had its head smashed, and it cried: 'Mama!'"[45]

According to Mayor Okulus, during these tragic moments, the Polish population of the city splintered into three "nearly hostile" groups. "The first group, the most numerous one, not only sympathized with the Jews but offered shelter and provided [Jews] with food, even though it was a capital offense. The second group were the fascists who expressed their joy and satisfaction [with the German actions] but did not cooperate with the enemy." The third group of the Polish citizens of Węgrów, described Okulus, became directly involved in the extermination of the local Jewry. It must have been this third group of local citizenry whose role prompted Bielawski to note, "On the street, the cries of Jews mixed with the shouts of the Germans and with the laughter of the Poles. Throughout the day the *SS-Männer*, with the eager assistance of the Poles, loaded the Jews on open trucks, which left for Treblinka."[46] The search for hidden Jews was spearheaded by young teenage boys who scoured the city looking for new victims, whom they promptly delivered to the Germans. Twenty-year-old Renia Lipski was caught by a group of Polish boys. She was saved from the hands of the teenage hunters by the local teacher, who convinced the boys that the girl was actually a Pole.[47]

Some teenagers not only tracked the Jews but also murdered them. Seventeen-year-old Edward Witecki helped the gendarmes locate Jewish hideouts. Sometime around 2:0 p.m., a gendarme known as "Hans" shot a fleeing Jew in the groin and then handed his rifle to Witecki to finish off the wounded man lying in the street. One of the Polish witnesses recalled after the war, "Witecki wanted to shoot him through the head, from the front, but the 'Jew boy' couldn't stand it and kept writhing on the ground, so that finally Witecki grew bored of the dance and shot him through the head, from behind." "I saw all of this with my own eyes, because it happened right in my backyard," finished the witness.[48] Sevek Fishman, one of the Jewish survivors, also commented on the efficiency and brutality of "bystanders" who, with no warning, became associates in murder.[49] A few of them trapped his wife and, when she failed to take off her gold earrings as promptly as demanded, tried to cut off her ears together with the prized jewelry.

Early in the afternoon, shortly after 2:00 p.m., the majority of Jewish inhabitants of the ghetto had already been rounded up and delivered to the market square. While the roving squads of Germans, Ukrainians, and Poles continued to search the houses for bunkers and hideouts, some members of the *Liquidierungskommando* began mass executions of the elderly in the Jewish cemetery. The victims were delivered to the site on carts commandeered from the locals, and the shootings took place over shallow pits dug out earlier. Also in the early afternoon, Polish city officials were ordered to remove the bodies that littered the streets and the sidewalks of the ghetto, and to prepare additional carts for the evening. The Polish mayor set out with trepidation to follow up on the German orders, worried that it would be difficult at best to find anyone ready to do this terrible work. He was wrong. "Before I was able to leave my office in order to assess the situation and to issue orders, the removal of the bodies had already started. There were carriages, and people were ready—they volunteered for the job without any pressure. Our hyenas were after Jewish clothes, footwear, and the cash that could be found on the dead."[50] For the Jews, the liquidation, Okulus later wrote, was a "biological tragedy. For the Poles, it was a moral one. The extent of this moral tragedy was, of course, impossible to measure, but its consequences—were frightening."

The "hyenas" took their clues from their peers, most of all from the Polish Blue police and their neighbors, members of the firefighting brigades. The firefighters, led by Wincenty Ajchel, showed up in the liquidated ghetto, "and they threw themselves [on the Jews] like hunting dogs on their prey. Henceforth, they 'worked' hand in hand with the Germans and—as locals and firefighters— did it much better than the Germans." Chief Ajchel carried around a briefcase into which his men deposited precious objects taken from the Jews. Müller, the chief of the Węgrów Schupo, recognized the contribution made by the Polish firefighters and met with some of them in the evening in a local restaurant: "He pulled out from his case a wad of money, and gave it to them saying, 'Here, this is for your good work.'"[51]

Some bystanders who morphed into perpetrators volunteered to help with the removal of bodies from the streets, absconding with the clothes and shoes of the dead. "They even pulled out golden teeth with pliers. That's why people in Węgrów called them 'dentists.' The 'dentists' sold their merchandise through fences and go-betweens. When I mentioned to one of them (he was a court clerk) that this gold was soaked in human blood, he told me: 'Impossible, I personally washed this stuff,'" wrote Mayor Okulus.[52]

Very similar scenes played themselves out in Stoczek Węgrowski, a small town located to northeast of Węgrów. During the liquidation of the "Jewish area," "Germans, Ukrainians, and the 'Blue' police surrounded the city. Germans stood at the door, on the outside, while the Poles looked for the hideouts (they also gave the Germans all the names of the Jews) and—once found—they marched the victims out into the street."[53] Chaim Kwiatek, hiding in a barn of a Polish farmer, observed the actions of his neighbors up close. He knew his tormentors intimately: They were most likely his colleagues; some of them could have been his classmates. He listed the names of the murderers using diminutive forms. Instead of "John" he would write "Johnny," "Tom" was "Tommy," and Stanislaw became "Staszek."[54] The village elder, Łaszyński, moved around the assembly area in which the Jews awaited further deportation and struck the crying people with a stick.

> Tomek Figler and Czesław Grudziądz searched my apartment, and they talked to themselves: "We have caught the old Kwiatkowa (my mother) and her daughter, but we could not locate the old one and his sons." Sometime later, a small child ventured into the street; his name was David Sukiennik. Old Dzieciątek caught the child and gave him to Kazimierz Postek. Postek beat the child up to make him show where the others were hidden. Little David took him to a hideout where three Jewish families were hiding. Five Poles went there, armed with sticks and pitchforks; they beat them up in a savage way, and they made them join the other Jews waiting outside. Once all Jews were accounted for, the Germans placed them on carriages and delivered to the Sadowne station, from where they took them to Treblinka.

Later, the Germans left the city, leaving the Poles in charge: "Many firefighters kept searching the town and—whenever they found a Jew—they would rob and arrest him."[55]

Węgrów: September 22, evening

Jerzy Tchórzewski (who after the war became a well-known Polish painter) turned fifteen at the time when Węgrów ghetto was being liquidated. In his memoirs, he recalled the end of that fateful day: "The day slowly ended. Nothing moved in these horrible piles of rags under which one could see emerging heads, legs, and arms. Only the wind stirred, ever so slightly, this dead pile. Done. No, the horrors were not over, not everything was finished. A few minutes after the gendarmes had left, silhouettes started to emerge from behind the houses nearby. Having made sure that not a living soul was around, they approached (or rather crawled toward) the dead and then, rapidly, with circuslike ability, undressed the bodies. They took what? These rags? They took everything. The hyenas were most likely working as husband and wife. He, the male, lifted the body, threw it up in the air with the help of a mighty kick, and she, the female, at the same time, and in a heartbeat, took the shirt and the pants off the cadaver. After some time, the pile of rags changed into a heap of dead, naked bodies. Soon, the carts arrived with firefighters armed with pitchforks. . . . Boys in smart-looking uniforms—the defenders of human life—pierced the cadavers with pitchforks and threw them on the carts. The last, final movements of the rigid arms, legs, heads, and corpses, drawn toward the earth during this horrible last trip, from here to the grave." [56]

On September 22, 1942, late in the evening, Jewish Węgrów ceased to exist. After the mass shootings in the Jewish cemetery and the departure of the column of Jews forcibly marched to Sokołów, there were perhaps close to one thousand Jews remaining, hidden in various bunkers and hideouts. Nearly all of them were later discovered by the Blue police, the firefighters, and the locals and delivered into the hands of the Germans for execution. According to several testimonies, close to two thousand Jews (or around 20 percent of those marked for "deportation") were murdered in the city during the first day of liquidation alone.[57]

In the aftermath of the *Aktion*, surviving inmates of the ghetto were systematically plucked out, one after another, from their hideouts and murdered in the Jewish cemetery. Some who were able to slip out of the city and reach the dubious safety of the nearby woods would often flee to one of the restghettos (remnant, or secondary ghettos)[58] and *Julags* (*Judenlager*, or labor camps for Jews) located in the area. The camps were located in Karczew, Ostrów Mazowiecka, Mordy, and Mrozy, all within a radius of thirty miles from Węgrów. This option, for obvious reasons, was available only to strong men and women; others were turned away or shot on the spot by the guards.[59]

Resistance

It is not easy for a historian to establish how the Jewish inhabitants of Węgrów reacted to the liquidation of the ghetto. Although one cannot generalize, survivors recalled feeling widespread fear and horror, mixed with individual acts of desperate and hopeless defiance. The "hundreds of revolvers" in the possession of Jews mentioned in the Węgrów Memory Book can be dismissed as a fairy tale.[60] Nevertheless, as much as the cowed, defenseless, and disorganized people were no match for police and their civilian helpers, the struggle to survive, which had started well before the *Aktion*, lasted until the very end of Jewish Węgrów. The bunkers and hideouts were the first (and often the last) line of defense. In many cases, the hideouts allowed the Jews to weather the first few days, or even weeks, of the hunt and (later, taking advantage of the cover of night) leave the ghetto and slip away from the city.

At least one group of Jews decided to break out together and charged the police. Wrote Mayor Okulus, "On the way [to Sokołów], a group of young Jews and Jewesses, on a prearranged signal, scattered, and ran away. The Germans started shooting and killed quite a few, but many Jews reached the forests, and some of them even survived until the liberation."[61] There were also instances of hopeless and desperate resistance, always ending in a tragedy. Several such cases have been reported in the Węgrów Memory Book, although it is difficult to find corroborating evidence in other sources.[62] Michal Izbica and his wife are said to have barricaded themselves in their house and opened fire on the Germans. In response, the Germans set fire to the house and burned it down together with all of its occupants. Shmuel Halbersztat also resisted the Germans and was shot on the spot.

Some Jews were delivered to the station on horse-drawn carts, which were earlier requested by the Germans from the nearby villages. The carts started arriving in Węgrów in the afternoon, and the cart drivers, Polish peasants, were told to load young children first. One of these cart drivers testified after the war: "I drove them [to the Sokołów station] just once. They were crying the whole way; they knew they were going to their death."[63] The final acts of defiance were reported from the "death trains" headed for Treblinka. The Jews of Węgrów, after a few hours' march, reached Sokołów, where they were loaded into the cattle cars that had been waiting for them at the railway station. One of the survivors, twelve-year-old Dina Rubinstein, later wrote about the horrific scenes she witnessed while being loaded into the train and, later, inside the wagon, when people started to suffocate: "And the train stood, and stood, and stood. Only the next day, it started to move. We were all dying of thirst."[64] Once the train had left the station, some men began to tear away the wooden planks on the sides of the wagons and tried to escape, jumping onto the tracks.

The Beginning of the Hunt

The liquidation action lasted until the evening of September 23, although German forces started to leave the area during the day. After the two-day *Aktion*, the liquidation commando left Węgrów altogether, most likely moving on to nearby Kałuszyn and Mrozy.[65] From the German standpoint, the *Aktion* in Węgrów was a success: Within twenty-four hours, eight to nine thousand Jews were either deported to Treblinka or murdered on the spot. Now, a new, more tedious phase was to begin—the search for the Jews still hidden in the deserted ghetto, whose number was evaluated at close to one thousand people.

The overall supervision of the hunt for the remaining Jews was the responsibility of the local gendarmes and SIPO officers—in all, ten to fifteen people. Their task was to coordinate the actions of the Blue police, the voluntary firefighters, and the local "volunteers"—simple townsfolk who decided to join in "the suppression of the Jewish population," to use the contemporary expression. At this stage, the police were no longer interested in deporting the Jews. In the broadest terms, the Poles were tasked with searching for the hidden Jews and delivering them to the execution sites, and the Germans were responsible for the actual shooting. The search parties trawled the ghetto for several weeks, certainly until mid-October. That is when the last Jews who had managed to avoid the search parties slipped out of the robbed and ruined ghetto and sought refuge on the "Aryan side," most often in the nearby woods. It was during these days and weeks that the Polish officers and firefighters elaborated a technique of operations that on the one hand guaranteed success and on the other hand allowed them to maximize profits. There is no doubt that greed and the lure of the fabled "Jewish gold"—essential components of the old and toxic antisemitic clichés—were among the most powerful motives that moved and animated the local participants.

The system can be best seen through the lens of Moszek Góra's testimony. On the day the *Aktion* began, Góra was away from Węgrów, trying to find some food for his starving family. Having heard about the liquidation, Góra crossed police lines and entered the ghetto, but he arrived too late to save his wife and three children. Over the next few days, Góra hid together with eight other Jews. All of them were soon detected by Polish police and firefighters. The group was hauled to the surface and marched to a nearby shed. In this makeshift jail, Góra and his fellow captives found another group of seven Jews who had been caught earlier by the enterprising Poles. All along, the policemen conducted thorough searches, taking valuables and cash from their victims. Over the next twenty-four hours, Polish officers and firefighters delivered more and more Jews caught inside the ghetto to their primitive prison. After some time, when more than thirty Jews were crammed into the shed, the Poles formed their victims into a column and marched them straight to the execution area. Moszek Góra later recalled his ordeal: "They marched us through Kominiarska Street, to the cemetery. Once there, I saw trenches and people standing next to them with spades ready. The trenches were fifty meters long. They told us to sit on the edge of the trench with our feet hanging inside. At that point I saw that among the firefighters, there were also policemen and two gendarmes. I could only recognize the chief of the firefighters. Once they started shooting, I fell inside, together with the fellow next to me, whose blood splattered on my face. I fell inside the trench, face up. I have no idea how much time I spent lying down there; I could only sense someone approaching me and pulling off my shoes, sweater, jacket. Another one came up and struck me with the spade. Fearful of being buried alive, I opened my eyes to show that I was still alive. One of them, when he saw me moving, called: 'If you want to live, run!'"[66] Góra, half-naked, crawled from under the bodies of his dead comrades and fled to the forest nearby.

The events described above were part of the chain of horrors that played themselves out throughout the day in Węgrów and the surrounding areas. The Polish officers searched the ghetto; as locals, they were very familiar with the area, which made them particularly efficient and deadly. In one section of the former ghetto, the firefighters caught a group of Jews: "They took the cash off the 'Jew boys' and later brought back the gendarmes, knowing well where the hideout was located."[67] Once located, the Jews were searched for valuables and cash and robbed.[68] Finally, they were marched in larger groups toward the execution sites manned by the German Gendarmerie.[69] Some firefighters, such as Stanisław Elgas, offered to shelter Jews in their own houses, asking in return for outrageous amounts of money. "Once it became clear that the Jews had no more money left, he delivered them into the hands of the gendarmes," concluded the testimony of a neighbor of the enterprising firefighter Elgas.[70] Sometimes the cooperation with the Germans took a more murderous and direct turn. For instance, in these cases, the firefighters "threw the Jews, with their bare hands, from higher stories" straight into the courtyards below, where the Germans finished them off.[71] Cases like these occurred on the first and the second day of the "suppression of the Jewish nationality by the Germans," to use the officialese of postwar documents. That was when one Stanisław Dula saw firefighter Ajchel "leading two Jewesses and a 'Jew boy' in an unknown direction. The Jews kissed his hands and begged him to let them go. I, walking a few paces behind Ajchel, wanted to see what he would do with the Jews. He took them toward the market square, where he met a gendarme with two [Polish] policemen, who were coming back from the Jewish cemetery. Ajchel rendered these Jews to the gendarme, who shot them on the spot."[72]

Next to the market square, hidden in the attic of his house, Szraga Fajwel Bielawski observed the work of the hunters pulling the Jews out of their hideouts. A few days after the *Aktion*, he saw a group of Jews being led to an assembly point: "Clothing on many of the women was torn. They had fought, kicked, and scratched the Poles, who hauled them from their hiding places. 'Faster, faster!' the Poles hollered. A Christian wedding was to take place that afternoon, and they did not want to be late for the festivities. A child begged his mother, 'I want to live!' Another small child clung to her mother with a vise grip, as if she and the mother were one. Suddenly, the mother pried the child loose, snatched the shoes from her feet, and heaved them at the Pole as hard as she could . . . The woman throwing the shoes in the face of the Polish police showed true heroism. The biggest bombs in the world could not have made such an impression. She had resisted, doing everything she could."[73]

How can one explain, or understand, the participation of Poles in the destruction of the local Jewish community? Was the situation in this town much different from what was happening elsewhere? Was the liquidation *Aktion* in Węgrów following a different scenario?

It is known that in 1942 and 1943, Polish firefighters and Blue policemen not infrequently (and in many areas of occupied Poland) played an important role in deporting Jews to the extermination camps.[74] The degree of their involvement was tied to several local conditions, such as German strategy, the personal decisions of the leadership of the local police force and firefighters, and the attitudes of the local elites.

An appeal made by a local village elder, teacher, or priest could have—at least to a certain stage and to a certain degree—defused the growing tensions; it might have shaken peoples' consciences and cooled down murderous passions.[75] The level of Polish involvement in the killing and robbing of the Jews could not have been entirely unrelated to the attitudes of the local elites. The few dispersed documents and testimonies, however incomplete, suggest that the condemnation of participation in the liquidation *Aktion* was, unfortunately, not their priority. During the *Aktion*, Kazimierz Czarkowski, the canon of the local Roman Catholic parish in Węgrów, according to his own testimony, "tried not to leave the house." Reverend Czarkowski not only failed to stop the Polish firefighters from joining the German "liquidation commando" but also, several years after the war, lent his support to the murderous commander Ajchel.[76]

In the case of German strategy, much depended on the size of forces the occupier was prepared and able to commit to any given liquidation *Aktion*. The smaller the German (and Ukrainian) forces, and the larger the Jewish population, the more significant was the involvement of the Polish actors. No doubt members of the local elites always had some agency, and some were determined to make it matter. There were others—such as the priest in Węgrów—who decided to do nothing. Most important, however, was the leadership of the chiefs of the local police units and that of the leaders of the firefighter brigades. In Węgrów, they gave their people not only permission but also a direct order to take part in the plunder and the murder. Last but not least, the attitudes of the Jewish victims must be stressed again. Even in the midst of the horrors of the liquidation *Aktion*, large numbers of Jews decided to defy German orders and went into hiding. This, in turn, forced the Germans to make greater use of the local enablers and collaborators.[77]

The courage, determination, and resilience of Węgrów Jews can be, at least in part, tied to the proximity of the extermination camp at Treblinka. Unlike people living elsewhere, the Jews of *Kreishauptmannschaft Sokolow-Wegrow* could have no doubt as to the fate of people sent to the nearby Małkinia railway station. The ghetto was, after all, an open one, with no walls or fences, and the sizeable forests located nearby offered at least an illusion of safety.

One cannot say today with precision how many Jews were killed during the *Liquidierungsaktion* in Węgrów. According to the lowest counts, some two thousand people were executed in the Jewish cemetery during the *Aktion* and soon after. If one assumes that during the first and second day of the liquidation the Germans killed one thousand people on the streets and at the execution sites, then another one thousand Jews fell prey to the efforts of the Polish Blue police officers, their firefighting associates, and the unnumbered Poles, regular townspeople who took part in the communal genocide.

Secondary (Remnant) Ghetto in Węgrów: October 1942—April 30, 1943

After a few weeks of sweeping the ghetto for survivors, the German authorities declared Węgrów *judenrein* [Jew-free], or entirely cleansed of the Jews. This was not entirely true: Some survivors (such as the previously quoted Bielawski and his family) remained hidden in their hideouts. Nevertheless, in the second half of October 1942, the *Aktion* had officially ended, and the Jews still present in the Węgrów area received assurances that they could now safely return to the city.[78] One of the Polish witnesses described the situation in the following terms: "The operational unit of the SS had left the town; the gendarmes cooled down a bit. That's when they made an announcement that the Jewish artisans and workers were again needed. They wanted shoemakers, bootmakers, tailors, furriers, and so on."[79] The creation of the secondary ghetto was a ploy used by the Germans across the GG. It is quite likely that at the same time, the creation of the secondary ghetto in Węgrów was a purely local initiative, ordered by the *Kraishauptmannschaft* authorities, with the possible approval of the Warsaw district police officials. An official declaration issued by Ludwig Fischer, governor of Warsaw district (a higher administrative area of which *Kreishauptmannschaft Sokolow-Wegrow* was a part), provided for the creation of only six "Jewish living quarters" in Warsaw, Kałuszyn, Sobolew, Kosów Lacki, Rembertów, and Siedlce.[80]

For many Jews who had been hiding in the area for several weeks, whose financial resources were either running out, and who simply had nothing more left except for the clothes on their backs, the German offer was not to be easily dismissed. Jews understood very well the risks associated with moving back to Węgrów, but the approaching winter and the constant threat of exposure, denunciation, and death on the "Aryan side" made the German proposal akin to a temporary suspension of a death sentence. The Węgrów secondary ghetto was located in several buildings that, with time, become home to several hundred Jews.[81] The new "Jewish quarter" soon boasted a tailor's shop, a furrier's shop, a laundry (run by the Kreda family), and a couple of other smaller shops, all working for the Germans. The inhabitants of the secondary ghetto were either "legals," armed with special passes signed by the Germans, or "illegals," who spent most of their time in hiding. From time to time, the Germans and the Polish police conducted sweeps searching for undocumented Jews and executing them in the Jewish cemetery.[82]

At the same time, the theft of Jewish property continued unabated. According to the Polish mayor, as early as October 1942 the Germans ordered sales of buildings until recently owned by Jews. "There were many buyers—from the city and its environs. They demolished beautiful houses; they took apart—in order to acquire bricks—a wonderful synagogue. This is where one could get bricks to build large industrial and agricultural buildings. Hovels and huts that nobody wanted were torched."[83] Jewish movable property was also sold at auctions. The scale of the urban catastrophe that followed the genocide comes across strongly in the postwar records produced by the municipal authorities, which listed—house after house—the wartime losses of the city.[84]

Meanwhile, in the remnant ghetto of Węgrów, Romek Międzyrzecki, a local Jew, was hiding at the farm of Mr. Bielinski, halfway between Węgrów and Sokołów. In early December 1942, Ruwen Hersz, Międzyrzecki's brother-in-law, joined him in the hideout. Taking advantage of the momentary lack of vigilance of the Ukrainian guards guarding his work detail, Hersz had fled from Treblinka. In his diary, Międzyrzecki reported Hersz's story: "Running [away from Treblinka], he could hear shots being fired, but he never turned around; he just ran as fast as he could. He ran through the woods and fields until he could see that he was no longer in danger, and then he started walking. He walked for more than twenty kilometers. Soaking wet, cold, tired, hungry, and thirsty, he was barely able to reach his native Węgrów. When he arrived in the city, he walked (or rather crawled) from one house to the next, listening to whether people inside were speaking Yiddish or not. Finally, he stumbled upon one room that housed Jewish shoemakers working for the Germans. He listened at the window and felt relief washing over him. People were speaking Yiddish! Yiddish! He could not believe his ears—perhaps it was some kind of a mistake? No, they indeed spoke Yiddish!" Hersz's account is one of the very few testimonies from inside the remnant ghetto in Wegrów. He did not stay inside the Jewish quarter for long. Fearful of the inevitable, he fled once again to the "Aryan side" and soon managed to reach Międzyrzecki's hiding place.[85]

During the winter of 1942–1943, the situation of the Jews remaining in the Węgrów ghetto became increasingly desperate. According to the daughter of Judel Żywica, the inmates were dying of typhus and other diseases.[86] Israel Cymlich was one of the last Jews who managed to reach the quickly shrinking Restghetto and leave a record of his visit. Like Ruwen Hersz, he also fled his work detail in the Treblinka extermination camp, and in April 1943, upon having heard that some Jews were still alive in the city, he reached Węgrów and slipped into the ghetto. His initial observation concerned the ongoing destruction of houses—something that would confirm the previously discussed theft of "post-Jewish property,"[87] to use the term that was soon to enter the Polish everyday vocabulary. During his brief stay in Węgrów, Cymlich had a chance to talk to many of the ghetto inhabitants. They knew all about Treblinka, but even this knowledge was not enough to make them flee. Their answer was, "There is no way out." The vision of fighting for survival on the "Aryan side" was, quite clearly, more terrifying than swift death at the hands of the Germans.[88]

Cymlich left Węgrów on April 18, 1943. Two weeks later, the ghetto ceased to exist. And this is practically all that is known about the secondary ghetto in Węgrów. There is no information about its borders (located "next to the market square"); neither is it known whether there was any Jewish authority, or *Judenrat* left (although it seems that Kreda, the laundryman, was its informal leader), or how many inmates survived until the end. All of these questions shall most likely remain without an answer.

The Final Liquidation of the Ghetto: April 30, 1943

At the end of April 1943, the Jews remaining in Węgrów learned about the uprising in the Warsaw ghetto.[89] There was little concrete information available,

Figure 3.3. Jews killed during the liquidation in Wegrow ghetto (GFH, 7105).

but as Szraga Fajwel Bielawski wrote, the feeling of pride at the courage of the Warsaw Jews was mixed with a growing fear about possible German retribution directed at the Jews of Węgrów. These fears acquired new urgency when the secretary of the local German *landrat* (lower local administrator) Neumann asked the Jewish hatmaker to speed up the delivery of the ordered merchandise. Jews were thus aware of the looming liquidation, but for most of them, escape was still not an option.

The end of the "secondary ghetto" occurred on April 30, 1943. Just before dawn, the Germans, Polish police, and voluntary firefighters surrounded Kreda's place and other Jewish houses. This time, there was no pretense and subterfuge of "deportation"; the killing started right away, on the spot.[90]

The perpetrators moved from house to house, ticking off the names of the victims against earlier-drawn lists of legal inhabitants of the ghetto. A Polish woman described the fate of the *Restghetto* in the following words: "After some time, the Germans asked the Jews to come out of hiding, giving them assurances that they would kill them no more. Some people emerged, and they went to live in the [secondary] ghetto. It must have been late spring 1943 when they started to kill them again. They offered resistance. There was much shooting and burning of houses. In one building, the Jews had some hidden weapons, and they started firing at the Germans, so the Germans burned the whole house down. There were very many burned bodies strewn on the ground. We could not sleep

Figure 3.4. Jews pulled out of the hideouts in the Wegrow ghetto (GFH, 7110).

the whole night, because of the fire and the shooting. Later on, German planes flew overhead and took pictures of their murderous deeds."[91] It is hard to say anything more precise about the nature of Jewish resistance in the Węgrów ghetto. One can assume, however, that there is little truth in the accounts of armed resistance. Such a display of bravery and resilience would certainly have been reported by Bielawski, the only Jewish witness still inside the ghetto at the time and who left his account. Resistance, if any, was most likely limited to passive acts of defiance. Jews barricaded themselves in houses that have been previously cordoned off by police and firefighters and surrounded by curious gawkers and other civilians. A Polish citizen of Węgrów observed in his postwar testimony, "The Germans set the ghetto dwellings on fire, and [Polish] firefighters later pulled the soaked Jews with the help of grappling hooks from the burning houses, and they turned them over to the Germans, who killed those Jews."[92]

Menucha Bielawski worked in the ghetto, in Kreda's laundry shop. According to her testimony (as reported by her brother Fajwel Szraga), the liquidation was conducted with "real German precision." "The Germans and Poles came in with their machine guns and ordered everyone out. I slipped away, dived beneath a pile of old boards, and covered myself, lying still. I heard the others shouting and pleading for mercy, but they shot everyone, including the children, and counted the dead. Seventeen bodies. They went inside again and counted the nineteen names of the workers on Kreda's list. Two were missing. After searching all over, the Germans gave up and left. But one Polish policeman remained. He muttered that he had to find the 'dog Jews.' He began to remove boards from the pile and found me. He dragged me through the street to an open space, where he pointed his gun at me. 'Don't you know me?' I asked him. 'Let me go! No one is watching!' He refused. I was wearing a silk nightgown. I tore out of his grasp and ran. He ran after me and fired. I fell, bleeding, and he thought I was dead. He left. After a few minutes, I got up and ran toward the fields, bleeding profusely."[93]

There is no firm data available concerning the number of victims murdered during the April 30, 1943, liquidation action in *Restghetto Węgrów*. All we know is that anywhere between two and three hundred Jews were murdered, and their bodies were buried in the Jewish cemetery, next to the mass graves of the thousands of victims of the September 1942 *Aktion* and the later shootings.

Treblinka

In the late fall of 1941, the German authorities of the Warsaw District decided to build a forced labor camp near Treblinka, a small village in the northeastern corner of Węgrów County.[94] The camp (*Arbeitserziehungslager* [AEL] Treblinka I) was soon to become a place of misery and suffering for twenty thousand inmates, half of whom died while in custody. Both Jews and Poles were sent to AEL Treblinka I, but while the treatment of the latter was harsh in the extreme, the fate of the former was much worse.[95]

Between May and June 1942, the German overseers of the Warsaw ghetto concluded an agreement with the police and the SS that allowed for the transportation of hundreds of young Jews (mostly children and teenagers) caught on the "Aryan side" of Warsaw to AEL Treblinka I.[96] From what is known, none of them survived. At the same time, in the vicinity of AEL Treblinka I, the Germans started to build the extermination camp (known as Treblinka II), which would soon become the place of murder of close to nine hundred thousand Jews. The "death trains," which started to arrive on July 22–23, 1942, used the Warsaw-Małkinia and Lublin-Sokołów lines. Both railway lines crossed Węgrów County. Polish, German, and Jewish testimonies leave no doubt that the existence of Treblinka II cast a long shadow on Węgrów County. The presence of Treblinka II was felt, quite distinctly and without any metaphor, by all the local inhabitants. According to a historian of the camp, "The stench of the burning bodies could be smelled not only in the villages nearby, but even in places 20–30 km away."[97] If the witnesses can be trusted, whenever the wind was strong enough, the nauseating stench reached as far as Sokołów Podlaski and Miedzna. Further, beyond the radius of sensory perceptions, the tales of the fabled "Jewish gold" carried by Jews fleeing the "death trains" additionally fueled the imagination of the locals. The moral meltdown was primarily related to the lure of the riches taken away from the murdered Jews. Some of these possessions—pieces of jewelry and cash that were easy to conceal—trickled out of the camp, most often with the help of the Ukrainian guards, and found their way into the hands of the local Polish inhabitants. In other cases, the locals would barter food and water for gold and cash directly with the Jews working outside the camp in various work details.[98] From time to time, the death trains halted for long hours near the Małkinia station, waiting for their turn to enter the camp, giving the local bystanders a chance to conclude risky but very lucrative transactions with the Jewish victims who were willing to pay any price for a glass of water. Another highly valued prize was to be found in the wagons leaving Treblinka. Every day, trains left the camp carrying west masses of clothing belonging to the murdered Jews. The transports were robbed on a regular basis, and the whole process involved the railway workers and machinists who slowed down or stopped trains in appropriate places, giving the thieves a chance to get away with the loot.[99]

The rumors about "Jewish gold" were rampant: Eddie Weinstein, who fled Treblinka in September 1942, noted that in the eyes of the local peasants, the Jews on the run were nothing more than easy prey, with a promise of rich reward. With time, this conviction became deeply entrenched and universally accepted.

It is difficult to evaluate how many Jews tried to flee the "death trains." Unlike Polish Jews, foreign Jews most often had no inkling as to what awaited them at the end of their journey and consequently decided to escape only in exceptional cases. Chronology also had its impact: In the spring and summer of 1942, there were fewer escapes than half a year later. After the Warsaw ghetto uprising, no one could have any more doubts as to the true nature of the "Final Solution," and flights from "death trains" became commonplace. Even without hard data, one can—without any doubt—assume that thousands fled from the trains destined for Treblinka. Some survived and later left accounts of their ordeal. Others were shot by the train escorts, fell at the hands of the locals, or were later executed by the German or Polish police. Graves located close to the railway tracks are the only evidence of their fate.

Romek Międzyrzecki fled his native Węgrów with five other people on September 22, 1942, during the liquidation of the ghetto. After some time, all of them found refuge at the farm of Antoni Bieliński, a farmer and a good, decent man living in Księżopole-Budki, close to Sokołów. While in hiding, Międzyrzecki kept a diary. On Friday, December 18, 1942, he wrote, "In the morning Mr. Bieliński went to Węgrów. He came back late in the evening and told us about the liquidation of Sokołów, about people who jumped from the trains headed for

Treblinka. Masses of killed and wounded. There was a wounded woman lying next to the tracks. Christian hooligans cut off her fingers and ears because she had golden rings and earrings."[100]

Together with his wife and young daughter, Adam Starkopf lived in Sadowne, a village close to the Łochów railway station. Blessed with "good 'Aryan' looks," Starkopf remained "on the surface" and, using false identity papers, worked as a clerk in a local sawmill, pretending to be a Pole. In his memoirs, he recalled, "The Christmas season of 1942–1943 in Poland was not one of peace and goodwill. One cold night, early in January 1943 . . . Pela and I were already sound asleep when we were awakened by the rattle of a passing railroad train, followed by bursts of machine-gun fire. We could hear the train grind to a halt. I went to the window." Soon neighbors came knocking on Starkopf's door and shared the news: "'Didn't you hear the commotion outside? Some Jews just escaped from a train and the Germans started to shoot at them! They must have hit quite a few. Just think—all these Jews lying on the ground, ready for the taking! It's a windfall! We can go out, pick them up, and turn them over to the Gestapo. We'll take their clothes, clean out their pockets, and on top of that we'll get a reward from the Germans for bringing them in. Come on! Everybody else in the village is going, too, so we'd better hurry! Otherwise there'll be no Jews left for us to catch!' Minutes later, we could hear moans and screams outside as the wounded Jews were dragged through the snow to barns and stables. The chase went on all night long."[101]

Starkopf's testimony is just one of the many. Skupie, a small village, is located right at the border between Węgrów and Sokołów counties, next to the Siedlce-Małkinia railway line. The Skupie officers of the local detachment of the Polish Blue police soon acquired a reputation as vicious—and very efficient—killers of Jews. Jews fleeing the transports were at the center of their police work. According to one Jewish survivor, officers Kurabiak, Skanecki, Zimnacha, Wichalak, and several others from the Skupie detachment, "patrolled along the tracks, murdering all Jews who had jumped from the transports. To make it short, Kurabiak and his friends killed at least 100 Jews."[102] The victims were murdered just beyond the border of Węgrów County, so they are not counted in the statistics of this chapter, but one needs to remember the scope of the activities of the Polish Blue police as well as the extent of the own agency of the Polish officers. Prior to killings, the policemen in blue uniforms robbed their victims without any German involvement or presence. Most often, Jews were murdered indifferently, in a businesslike manner. With time, the executions became a common sight, something expected, even anticipated and obvious. The frequency of Jewish deaths has been corroborated by special lists of graves produced by the Polish municipal courts, right after the liberation, in 1945.

Uprising in Treblinka

On August 2, 1943, the Jewish inmates, members of the *Sonderkommandos* working in the Treblinka II extermination camp, struck out against their German and Ukrainian guards, torched the barracks and watchtowers, cut through the lines of barbed wires, crossed the outlaying minefields, and fled into the forests. According to very rough estimates, several hundred insurgents managed to flee the camp, and close to one hundred from among them survived the war.[103] The rest died in various circumstances while on the run. The focus in this section will be on Jews fleeing from the uprising who either lost their lives or went into hiding in the territory of Węgrów County.

The uprising in the camp triggered a general mobilization of German forces in the area. The detachments of Blue police and local brigades of the Polish voluntary firefighters were also placed on alert.[104] The fleeing insurgents were easy to spot: The area around the camp was sparsely populated and foreigners stood out. To make matters worse, the Jewish prisoners' heads were shaved, making them obvious targets. The local railway stations and other public spaces were also plastered with posters with information about "fifty Jewish bandits" on the loose. The massive search for the escaped Jews, conducted under the personal authority of *Kreishauptmann* Ernst Gramss, lasted for several days.

Złotki (Prostyń commune) is located right next to the camp. In fact, it is so close that one of the local women who was toiling in the fields "heard explosions, and learned from the children that the explosions had come from the camp and that many Jews had fled."[105] Later that day, the first refugee from Treblinka reached the village. One of the peasants agreed to hide the Jew, but a short time later his body was found in the fields nearby. Wrotnów and Międzyleś (Miedzna commune) are both small villages situated nine miles from Treblinka. The vegetation is dense, and the forests could offer a degree of protection to the Jewish insurgents fleeing the camp. Just north of Międzyleś, however, the forests and woods make way to fields and orchards. That was where the peasant "night guards," alerted earlier by the Germans, lay in the wait. For nine Jewish insurgents who, sometime on August 3 or 4, found themselves in this area, the encounter proved deadly. The guards first caught two Jews who, surrounded by the peasants, tried in vain to defend themselves with primitive bayonets of their own production. Before the end of the day, the members of the night guard caught seven more Jews, all insurgents from Treblinka. The prisoners were then taken to a makeshift holding pen (a hastily adapted cellar) and the next day were handed over to the Germans. Before calling the Germans, however, the peasants conducted a very thorough search of their victims. "All of them had their hands tied behind their backs," later reported one of the Polish witnesses.[106] A large group of gawkers and curious "bystanders" soon gathered around the doomed Jews. It was at this point that, according to another witness, *Kreishauptmann* Gramss himself arrived in the village.[107] The capture of nine insurgents must have been greeted in the offices of the *Kreishauptmann* as a major success. At one point, the gendarmes asked the peasants involved in the manhunt to identify themselves. "Many people raised arms in the air, and the Germans started to hand out bottles of vodka." Those "most deserving" received 1.5 liters of liquor each, and the others went away with half-liter bottles of alcohol. As soon as the gift-giving ceremony was over, the gendarmes herded the Jews toward the forest, in the direction of Wrotnów, to the execution site. After the execution, the peasants from Międzyleś buried the dead, and in return the gendarmes let them keep the clothes of the victims.[108] In the few available archival documents, the Jewish victims are an anonymous, nameless group of people. The only exception is Jarząbek, a Jew from Jadów (Radzymin area), who had been interrogated—and remembered—by Jan Bąk, the head of the peasants' night guard. Finally, at the end of the day, once the gendarmes left, the village elder and all the participants in the manhunt held a feast.

Brothers Zygmunt and Oskar Strawczynski had more luck then the nine Jews caught between Międzyleś and Wrotnów. Heading south from Treblinka through the forests, they encountered a group of Polish peasants who wanted to seize them and deliver them to the Germans. Oskar, armed with an axe, wounded one of the attackers and scared the rest of them away.[109] In this context, it is not altogether surprising that the Strawczyński brothers were so pessimistic about their chances of survival outside the camp. Actually, for a long time they preferred to stay inside Treblinka as members of the Jewish work detail and then try to flee while working outside the camp.[110] Samuel Rajzman, who also took part in the uprising, offered a more general statement about the attitudes of the locals: "Peasants around Treblinka were usually very hostile to Jews. They looked for Jewish children and delivered them, like calves on a string, to the Germans for execution. Sometimes they received a quarter kilogram of sugar, and sometimes they got nothing. In the villages around Treblinka, one can find today whole treasures taken away from the Jews."[111] Rajzman, one must add, survived because Edward Gołoś, a Polish farmer from the hamlet of Brzozów, halfway between Treblinka and Węgrów, decided to help him. Gołoś, who was later recognized as Righteous Among the Nations, went to school with Rajzman's sister and thus considered the Jewish refugee his friend. Rajzman spent nearly a year under Gołoś's roof and was eternally grateful to his Polish host.[112] He knew full well that betrayal, murder, courage, and rescue were all parts of the same horrible scenery. Today, to talk about the phenomenon of rescue without placing it within the historical context formed by betrayal and fear is not only pointless; it is also a fallacy and misrepresentation of history. It is also a mockery of the courage and resilience of Poles who decided to help the Jews despite the enormous dangers associated with such an act.

Betrayal and murder went alongside with acts of selfless generosity, courage, and rescue. While the peasants of Wrotnów and Międzyleś hunted down the Jewish insurgents and delivered them to the Germans, Stanisław Pogorzelski, a poor farmer from Orzeszówka (Miedzna commune), decided to open his door to the refugees. Despite constant threats, searches, and danger, he took in six Jews from Treblinka and kept them in a hideout until the end of the war.[113]

On the basis of (very incomplete) archival evidence, the movements and fates of seventeen Jews who took part in the uprising at Treblinka have been traced and documented. Having fled the extermination camp, these Jews later sought refuge in the territory of Węgrów County. Seven among them managed to survive. Samuel Rajzman and Arie Kucyk went into hiding close to Węgrów, while Gustaw Boraks and his comrades spent the rest of the war in Orzechówka. Ten other Jewish insurgents were either murdered by local Poles, or delivered by them into the hands of the Germans.

"Little Treblinka"

On May 1, 1943, after the liquidation of the "secondary ghetto," Węgrów indeed became *"Judenrein."* A small number of Jews who had managed to save themselves from the pogrom went into hiding in the forests or in the villages nearby. A September 1943 report filed by the AK (*Armia Krajowa*, Home Army) described the situation thus: "The 'Jewish question' in the area [Sokołów and Węgrów Counties] is no longer an issue. Rich Jews, who have the financial resources [to pay for shelter], hunkered down in hideouts and waited for the war to end. [At the same time] Jews hiding in the forests are hated by the population. They are the cause of the many problems and miseries of the Polish population."[114] The authors of the underground report were wrong. The "Jewish question" in Węgrów continued to exist; in the spring of 1944, it even triggered one more "liquidation *Aktion.*" This time, however, it was not about murdering the survivors but rather about covering up the traces of previous massacres and executions. Together with the Soviet advance, the Germans started, with growing haste, to remove the evidence of their crimes. These centrally planned operations had a code name: *Sonderaktion 1005* (Special Action 1005), or "exhumation action."[115] According to the confidential orders issued by Himmler, the goal of *Sonderaktion 1005* was to exhume and later burn the bodies of victims of mass executions in the East. In April and May 1944, *Sonderaktion 1005* visited Węgrów to unearth and to incinerate the bodies of the thousands of victims of the "liquidations" and executions from the 1942–1944 period.

In order to get the gruesome job done, the Germans brought to Węgrów a group of fifty Jews, who were placed in a small camp surrounded with barbed wire and watchtowers.[116] From the few surviving documents, one can gather that the Jewish slaves came from Łódź—from the last ghetto on Polish territory still in operation.[117] Jews were forced to unearth the cadavers and load them onto trucks. The trucks, with their horrible cargo, drove to a nearby location, where the Germans constructed primitive crematoria. Inhabitants of Węgrów soon started to call this place "Little Treblinka." Władysława Putkowska, back then a young girl, recalled Little Treblinka in the following terms: "They burned the bodies in May; I remember it well, because when we went to pray under the cross, we could see the fires burning, and when the wind blew our way, it stank to high heaven. It was about two kilometers from the cross to the crematorium. To burn the bodies, the Germans brought a group of Jews, who walked in wooden sandals, and who were chained one to another. We could hear from afar the sound of their sandals [on the pavement] and the rattle of iron chains."[118] According to one testimony, at one point the Jews rebelled, and all of them were shot. According to another witness, all Jewish slaves were simply executed in June 1944—right after their job has been completed—and their bodies were burned in the crematoria they had earlier helped to build. Two months later, the first units of the Soviet Red Army entered Węgrów.

SURVIVAL STRATEGIES, 1942–1944: ESTIMATES AND NUMBERS

Jew, you are not getting away this time!
They will make a good soap out of you![119]

Scholars involved in the study of the "third phase of the Holocaust" (the period between the liquidations of the ghettos in 1942 and the end of the war) tried to evaluate the number of Jews who made an attempt to avoid deportations to the death camps and sought shelter on the "Aryan side"—the streets of Polish cities, hideouts in the rural areas, bunkers in the forests, or partisan units. According to various estimates cited in the introduction to this book, anywhere between 200,000 and 300,000 Polish Jews (or around 10 percent of all Jews still alive in 1942) decided to flee or hide. More detailed studies conducted by the authors of the present volume corroborated and confirmed the educated guesses made earlier. The data reported by the Polish resistance, and contemporaneous to the described events, are also in line with the later estimates.[120]

One of the reasons for the current book is an attempt to reach beyond the qualitative analysis and to present a quantitative description of the personal trajectories of Jews who made an attempt to survive after the 1942 liquidations. Given the relative depth of the available historical sources, this is a difficult, but not impossible, task.

The mass flight of Jews of Węgrów County began with the liquidation of the ghettos in Węgrów and Stoczek. Many went into hiding inside the ghetto, and their fate has been described in the previous sections of this chapter. The time has come now to discuss the fate of those who decided to look for shelter among the Poles or in the forests. The 11,200 Jews of Węgrów County still alive on September 22, 1942, make up the initial point of this analysis. The point of arrival is the 195 Jewish survivors who reported to the Węgrów Jewish Committee shortly after the liberation, between August 1944 and June 1945.[121] These survivors include both the sixty-eight people included in the table below as well as others, about whose fate it was impossible to gather anything specific.

The counts indicate that 1.5–2.0 percent of Węgrów Jews managed to survive under the German occupation; this percentage is consistent with the data from

Table 3.2 Jewish survivors and nonsurvivors, Węgrów County, 1942–1944

Jews in Węgrów County, 1942, before the liquidations	11,200	100%
Jews deported to Treblinka, September 22–23, 1942	8,000	71%
Killed in the city during the *Aktion* (Węgrów and Stoczek)	1,200	11%
Jews in hiding, killed between 1942–1944 (including the 1,000 victims killed inside the ghetto after the liquidation)	1,330	12%
Jews who survived in the territory of the county in known circumstances	68	0.6%
Węgrów Jews who reported to the Jewish Committee after the liberation	195	

Source: AŻIH, Wojewódzki Komitet Żydowski w Warszawie [District Jewish Committee in Warsaw], 352/118, Incoming correspondence with the Jewish Committee in Węgrów. In this exchange, we read about 195 Jews who showed up in Węgrów after the liberation.
Note: This table does not include the 50 victims of "Little Treblinka" and the 250 victims of the final liquidation of the secondary ghetto, as well as the approximately 1,000 victims of flights from death trains. Estimate based on the grave registers from 1945. Firm data— people whose individual trajectories are known from the existing archival documentation (excluding 1,000 victims killed after the liquidation, while hiding inside the Węgrów ghetto).

Table 3.3 Circumstances of death of Jews in hiding, Węgrów County, 1942–1944

	Number of victims	Percentage
Victims of the gendarmerie (denounced to, or murdered with the participation of the "Blue" police)	168	42%
Victims of the Polish "Blue" police (own actions, no German presence)	89	22%
Killed by the local civilian Polish population	69	18%
Survived in Węgrów County	68	17%
Died of other causes	4	1%
TOTAL	**398**	**100%**

Note: The percentages have been rounded up to the nearest decimal point.

other areas of Poland. Contemporary evidence suggests that on the day of the liquidation, the Germans deported around 8,000 local Jews to Treblinka and simultaneously killed 1,200 others on the streets of Węgrów and Stoczek. The question, therefore, is what happened to the 1,398 Jews who went into hiding inside the ghetto or fled to the "Aryan side."

Information about the fates of 1,398 Jews who went into hiding in the studied area was gathered. There were at least 1,000 Jews who survived the initial part of the liquidation action, and who sought shelter inside the ghetto, in various hideouts, and in bunkers. Over the next days and weeks, these people were detected and executed. Sixty-eight Jewish refugees managed to survive until liberation, while 320 others died in various circumstances, which shall be described later. The list of survivors and of nonsurvivors are both incomplete. The majority of Jews who lost their battle for life shall remain anonymous; the only information about their final moments can be found in brief reports about the mass graves and exhumations. Nevertheless, the records allow the return and restoration to memory of at least some of the names of the victims of the *Judenjagd* (hunt for Jews) in Węgrów County. Summarizing the data above, one can say that 12 percent (1,398) of the local Jews decided to go into hiding, and 5 percent (68) of them managed to survive until liberation. If we look only at those who left the ghetto, the percentage of survivors increases to 17 percent. The Polish police and the German Gendarmerie were, no surprise here, the most deadly threats to the Jews hiding in Węgrów area. Both forces are responsible for 257 documented cases of Jewish deaths. Once again, the list is far from complete. The number of Jews murdered by the local civilians is no doubt underrepresented in the present study. Sixty-nine cases indicated in the table above represent only a portion of the total: These murders, usually committed far from public scrutiny, left few traces in any written documentation and therefore altogether escaped the scrutiny of historians.[122] The crimes that show up in official records were usually related to group violence. The larger the number of suspects and witnesses, the more likely it was that someone would later, after the war, report the crime to the authorities. The collective character of the murders that finally came to light has been earlier stressed and noted by historians.[123] In the case of murders committed without witnesses, or within a family setting, the chances of the deed coming to the ears of the police were slim.

Between the "Aryan Side" and the Secondary Ghetto

Between October 1942 and the end of April 1943—when the *Restghetto Wengrow* was liquidated—Jews on the run had an option to go back to the relative safety of the "Jewish quarter." Until late 1942, there were also a few isolated small labor camps in the area, where Jews still had the right to live.[124] The preserved testimonies indicate that between October 1942 and April 1943, no less than three hundred Jews returned to the city to stay, at least for some time, in the *Restghetto*. Usually they had no more financial means to compensate their Polish hosts for shelter, and consequently they could no longer survive on the "Aryan side." Only a handful, like Bielawski, remained in hiding and occasionally ventured back to the secondary ghetto to visit friends or family.

A careful analysis of several hundreds of cases of hiding in the area allows us to venture a hypothesis that looking for shelter and help in the city of Węgrów itself was the riskiest and the least promising of all the possible strategies of survival. Węgrów was densely populated and offered no anonymity typical of larger urban centers, with Polish and German police detachments close by, so it proved to be a deadly trap for Jewish refugees. Three-year-old Lusia Farbiarz, who was left behind by her mother on May 1, 1943, after the liquidation of the secondary ghetto, was one of the very few Jews to survive in the city. Farbiarz found refuge under the roof of Pelagia Vogelgesang, a teacher and the wife of the director of the Węgrów primary school. Mrs. Vogelgesang looked after the child as if she were her own until the end of the war.[125] The neighbors became aware of the child's presence in the Vogelgesang household. This in turn brought about several visits by the police looking for "hidden Jews." Despite the threats, the courageous and resourceful woman saved the child, taught her to speak Polish without an accent, and managed to legalize her official standing with the authorities. After the war, the members of the local Jewish Committee took interest in the Farbiarz, and sometime later, her uncle, her only surviving relative, took her away. Vogelgesang was heartbroken. "Lusia has been gone for two weeks," she wrote in September 1946. "It is so hard for us: Neither I nor my husband can eat anything; we cannot sleep. Lusia's place at the table remains empty, the house is empty, silence rings in my ears, there is no one to give me a hug, nobody sings, there is no one left to give lessons to, the days are long, without an end; I will never again see my child."[126] Gitl Przepiórka, another three-year-old Jewish girl, was the only other Jew who managed to stay alive in Węgrów.[127] Przepiórka found refuge in the house of Marianna Kowalczyk, who reported Gitl as a distant relative.

As mentioned earlier, hiding Jews in Węgrów was, without any doubt, the most dangerous kind of resistance, one that required more courage and determination than "ordinary" underground activity. While the struggle with the occupant enjoyed social approval, rescuing Jews did not. This lack of social solidarity resulted in denunciations and "confidential reports," which in practically all cases meant death for Jews and sometimes for their Polish hosts too. The sheer number of tragic cases from Węgrów makes it impossible to present even a fraction of them in this study, but the phenomenon of betrayal and death is well illustrated by the fate of Janina Rogińska.

Rogińska lived in Węgrów with her twelve-year-old daughter, Joanna. In the spring of 1943, most likely just after the liquidation of the secondary ghetto, Rogińska agreed to give shelter to ten Jews: Józef Frydman, Mosze Ptak, the Jęczmień couple, and the Rozenberg family.[128] The Jews dug out an ingenious hideout: a cavern under Rogińska's room, with the entry door carefully masked in the floor. A special tunnel linked the hideout to another escape hatch located in the barn, a few meters away. The fate of Jews (and that of Rogińska) was sealed on June 15, 1943, when the Germans, following up on a confidential tip, descended on the house. Many years after the war, Rogińska's daughter recalled the events: "The Nazis learned about the hidden Jews from Polish traitors who were working for them—Iwaszczuk, who was responsible for hundreds of other victims and a woman, a mistress of a Nazi, both of whom still live safely in Węgrów."[129] The Germans surrounded several houses, including that of Rogińska: "They came to my mother and me early in the afternoon. Two of them, both in steel-color uniforms, with sidearms, wearing saddlelike round hats, entered the room. They had dogs with them. First, they started to strike my mother and let the dog loose. The dog tore away her clothes and mauled her body; they wanted to force her to surrender the Jews. When she refused, they told her that they knew that she was lying." In the end, they found Jews in the barn and shot them dead. Rogińska fared no better: They killed her right behind the barn. "She begged them to spare her life; she cried terribly: 'Don't kill me, let me go to my child!'"[130] The Germans wanted to shoot the daughter too, but some neighbors intervened on her behalf, arguing that the child was innocent, that the guilt was the mother's alone. The same day, young Rogińska fled Węgrów, and the neighbors stole all her mother's possessions.[131] The death of Rogińska, Ptak, Frydman, the Rozenbergs, and the Jęczmiens is a clear indication of risks inherent in and associated with attempts to rescue Jews in small towns such as Węgrów. A dense network of informers; the proximity of curious, nosy, and unfriendly neighbors; and the presence of police forces and other authorities all conspired to create an atmosphere deadly to both Jews and their Polish hosts.

In Ziomaki, on Ratyński's Farm (Or: Once Again, about the Dangers of Rescue)

Wiktor Ratyński and his family owned a farm in the village of Ziomaki (Wyszków commune), where they sheltered Jews. On August 23, 1943, Czesław Kurkowski, the chief of the Polish Blue police detachment from Grębków, showed up at the farm in the company of another Polish officer. Commander Kurkowski's arrival in Ziomaki was not a coincidence: He came armed with a note from a police informer. According to Ratyński's testimony: "The commander held in his hand a note on which it stated clearly written how many people were hidden, and where."[132] Soon, the Germans also appeared on the farm. Eight Jews were led out of the barn. Finally, one of the policemen compared the names on the list and found out that one Jew listed on the sheet was still missing from the roundup. Indeed, another search of the premises helped locate the unaccounted Jew, who was promptly shot inside the barn. Later, the Jews were executed in the courtyard. After the execution, the Germans fined Ratyński five thousand zlotys for "having offered shelter to Jews" and left Ziomaki. Why did the Germans spare the Polish family? Possibly Kurkowski, the commander of Grębków detachment of the Blue police, intervened on their behalf. In any case, the sources offer no explanation.

The departure of the police, however, did not put an end to the killings on Ratyński's farm. The day was far from over. The police informer, whose report had earlier brought police to the village, did not know that on the other side of the barn, under the hay, several other Jews lay in hiding. There were, however, some neighbors who were painfully aware of this fact. A few hours after the police left, several unknown men started knocking on Ratyński's door. The posse that invaded the farm that night was made up of six neighbors, led by Franciszek Wrzosek. A fairly well-off farmer with a decent education, forty-year-old Wrzosek was also a soldier of the Polish underground.

After the war, on trial, Wrzosek gave his account of what transpired on the farm that night. Having learned from another neighbor that there were still some Jews left on Ratyński's farm, he gathered several men, and they moved into action: "One [of them] suggested that we kill the remaining Jews, and I accepted his plan. After a few minutes, I saw Czesław Nejman leaving his house, armed with two carbines and a rifle, and together we went to Wiktor Ratyński's place. On the way we met Ignacy K. and Kazimierz G. We explained to them what we wanted to do, and they joined us. Nejman gave one of them the rifle, while the other one carried a wooden bat."[133]

This quote is revealing on many different levels. First, it is a proof of the dangers associated with hiding Jews in a closely knit and well-informed village community. Second, it shows the presence of and easy access to firearms in the hands of the peasants. Third, one can see how easy it was to find people ready to join the murderous expedition in order to rob and to kill the Jews. Once at the farm, Wrzosek confronted Ratyński. Wrzosek and his comrades were right: There were still more Jews hidden at the farm. The Jews, terrorized by the earlier visit of the police and the mass murder that ensued, had prepared their own escape. They waited too long. In the course of a short struggle, two Jews managed to flee into the night, while three others were murdered. We do not have a complete list of the names of the victims. After the war, Ratyński could no longer recall their names he knew only that among them were Gutman and Jankiel Kuper, both from Węgrów and both known to him from older, better times. It seems that there was also Motek, a shoemaker from Węgrów who, from time to time, left the hideout and repaired the shoes of the local farmers.[134]

The bandits ordered Ratyński to bury the bodies in the field, behind the barn. During a thorough search of the hideout, Wrzosek and his men found thirty-five thousand zlotys—a huge amount of money at the time.[135] The same group, apparently hoping for new trophies, showed up at Ratyński's farm several months later, in February 1944, and started to "look for hidden Jews." This time, however, they beat up the farmer's daughter and left empty-handed, if one did not count half-liter bottle of vodka and one hundred cigarettes they stole from their neighbor. But even this was not the last invasion: News about "Jewish gold" in Ratyński's possession must have spread in the area. The two unknown men who showed up on the farm at the end of February 1944 also wanted to find Jews and, unable to locate any "citizens of Jewish nationality," attempted to extort ten thousand zlotys from Ratyński instead.

The two Jews who managed to get away from Wrzosek and his posse on the night of August 23, 1943, were most likely killed before the end of the war. Otherwise, they would have somehow reported their ordeal to the Jewish Historical Commission, or to the authorities, and Ratyński and his family would have no doubt been awarded the title of Righteous Among the Nations. Finally, one might add that Ratyński's farm, like so many other "farms of rescue," was situated at a distance from the village, on the edge of the woods.

A careful reading of the documents related to mass murder committed first by Germans and later by Poles against Jews hiding in Ziomaki on August 23, 1942, is revealing. First, one sees the crucial importance of the local network of informers: Without a "confidential report" from the local population, the police (and especially the German police) would have had little idea as to the whereabouts of the hidden Jews. In the case of this particular murder, one can also see the close cooperation of the Polish Blue police and the German Gendarmerie. Another striking feature is the extent of knowledge about the Jews in hiding among the local peasants. The members of the village community could learn about the hidden refugees, or they could quickly guess who would be the most likely candidate to break the German rules and give shelter to Jews. The tragedy on Ratyński's farm sheds even more light of the power of antisemitic prejudice and the role of the myth of "Jewish gold," so deeply entrenched in rural areas of Poland. The German regulations, native antisemitism, greed, and prevalence of everyday violence against the Jews—all these elements created an explosive and toxic mixture, which was deadly to the Jews on the run as well as to the rare Poles who decided to help them. The role and the attitudes of Polish underground to the plight of the Jews is another issue that begs further scrutiny. The fact that violence against Jews was not unconditionally and universally condemned by the Polish underground organizations is a key factor that helps one to understand why rescuing Jews became the most dangerous kind of resistance in occupied Poland.

The murders on Ratyński's farm were far from unique. Less than one month later, on September 17, 1943, German gendarmes, alerted by another informer, appeared on the farm of Stanisław Rostek in Stoczek (Stoczek commune). The informant was right; the gendarmes rounded up and immediately executed seventeen Jews. They also murdered Rostek's wife and sent the husband and their two sons to Auschwitz, where they died. According to some indications, the confidential report had been filed with the police by the local forest ranger, who was upset with the Jews who, driven by hunger, had ventured out from their hideout and into the fields and stolen his potatoes.[136]

Aryan Papers

Using Aryan (false) papers allowed hundreds, if not thousands, of Jews to survive in large cities. In smaller urban centers and in the rural areas, this option carried additional risks, which made survival highly unlikely. First of all, passing for "Aryans" was a viable option for Jews from assimilated families and for converts, who spoke excellent Polish and who knew a thing or two about Catholic rituals and liturgy. One also needed to have so-called good looks—in other words, no physical traits popularly associated with Jews. People using doctored identity papers were well advised to stay as far as possible from the areas in which they were known from prewar times. In Węgrów and the surrounding area, there was just a handful of Jews who survived the war passing as "Aryans." Quoted earlier, Adam Starkopf, a refugee from the Warsaw ghetto, worked after 1942 as a clerk in a Sadowne sawmill under an alias, Adam Bludowski. Together with his wife and a small child, they managed to avoid detection for eighteen months. During the time spent in Sadowne, Starkopf witnessed the fate of two other Jews passing for "Aryans" who were denounced to the authorities, arrested, and executed. There also were the sisters Nechama and Dina Abkowicz, originally also from the Warsaw ghetto, who for several months stayed under the roof of the Maliński family in the village of Gajówka (Stoczek commune) using assumed identities.[137] The Starkopfs also had to flee and spent the rest of the war hiding in the Siedlce area. The only Jews who survived in Węgrów area until the end of the war were the two small girls adopted by the Polish families, described earlier.

The Role of the Polish Blue Police in the "Final Solution of the Jewish Question" in Węgrów County

The involvement of the Polish police forces in the extermination of the Polish Jews was a process that evolved with time. From the early days of occupation, Polish officers were tasked with the enforcement of the many German regulations directed against the Jews. It started with the branding regulations, which obligated all Jews twelve years of age and older to wear armbands with a Star of David, to new laws that placed restrictions on Jewish property and their freedom of movement, to forced labor. In all these cases, the officers in blue had a significant—and sometimes crucial—role to play. In closed, walled-in ghettos such as Warsaw, the role of the Polish police from the German standpoint was important but not essential. In smaller ghettos (such as the one in Węgrów), which were essentially open and where Germans were few, their role acquired additional weight. In *Kreishauptmannschaft Sokolow-Wengrow*, there were no closed ghettos, and the borders to the Aryan side were only in the minds of the Jews, the gentiles around them, and the policemen enforcing the rules.

In the late fall of 1941, after the proclamation of the notorious III Regulation about the Right of Residence in the GG (the one that introduced the death penalty for Jews leaving the ghettos),[138] the execution squads formed of the officers of the Blue police were charged with shooting Jews found in violation of the new restrictions.[139]

The murder of innocent people was a logical progression in the accelerating wave of terror directed at the Jews. The persecutions of 1940 and 1941 were a springboard, through a steep learning curve, to the murders of 1942. The robberies, the exploitation, the assaults, the beatings, and the humiliation of the previous period paved the way to the next stage and made the Polish policemen an important—and often indispensable—element in the German machine of extermination.

There were eight stations of the Polish Blue police in Węgrów County,[140] with more than one hundred officers on duty. In addition to the Blue police, five or six Kripo officers were detached on a permanent basis from the Sokołów headquarters to the Węgrów station.

Constable Lucjan Matusiak served in the Łochów detachment, north of Węgrów. In late June 1943, Matusiak apprehended four Jews: two men, one woman, and a child.[141] In fact, he did not catch the Jews himself; they were delivered to him, with their hands tied with wire behind their backs, by local peasants. The event was rather unremarkable: After all, by mid-1943, Matusiak and his fellow officers had been hunting down, robbing, and murdering Jews on a regular basis for nearly a year. It can even be said that in 1942 and the first half of 1943, the officers in blue had acquired an extraordinary expertise in this particular area of police work. Their victims were either local Jews who went into hiding—until 1942, Łochów had had a sizeable Jewish population—or Jews who had escaped from the "death trains."

It is unknown whether the four Jews who found themselves at the mercy of the Polish constable in June 1943 were local Jews hiding in the area, or people who had escaped from the deportations. It was their number, however, and not their origin that forced Constable Matusiak to face some hard choices. He had to kill four Jews, and he had only one or two bullets left. Wacław Chomontowski, an eyewitness, who had to dig a grave, described the incident: "I saw with my own eyes how officer Matusiak executed four Jews using one bullet in the village of Łopianka. He stood these four 'Jew boys' in a row, one behind another, and shot the last one in the back. There was also a young 'Jew boy,' so he killed him with a separate bullet.... When we laid them into this ditch, one Jew, who had only been wounded, started begging: 'Mr. Officer please, have mercy, finish me off!' to which Constable Matusiak responded: 'You are not worth a bullet, you will croak anyhow!'"[142]

Chomontowski did not elaborate on why he had not thought—at that late stage—of saving the wounded Jew buried alive under his feet. This might be the first of the many troubling questions that come to mind in reading the archival records from the period immediately after the war: Did Chomontowski fear the return of the Blue policeman Matusiak? Or did he, like so many others across the occupied land, simply assume that for the Jews, death one way or another was inevitable? That digging the wounded man out of his grave would be pointless? The well-known historian of the Warsaw ghetto Emanuel Ringelblum noted while in hiding in Warsaw in 1944, shortly before he was betrayed and killed, "A Jew today is seen as 'the deceased on leave,' about to die sooner or later."[143]

There are several other troubling questions related to the execution in Łopianka. First, the killings of Jews in Łopianka occurred in the absence of any Germans and without any German knowledge or direct involvement. Indeed, Constable Matusiak acted on his own initiative; he solved the "Jewish question" in the town as well as he was able. There must have been no doubt in his mind that one way or another, it had to be solved. Furthermore, the Blue policeman was not acting alone; he could rely on at least some of the local inhabitants to assist him in his work. Third, Constable Matusiak was not, from what we know, a vicious killer whom the Germans had hired for his murderous skills. In fact, he was just an ordinary small-town cop with eleven years of prewar experience in the Polish police. As far as we can tell from the documents in his file, he was an ordinary man whom circumstances, antisemitism, greed, fear, and opportunity transformed into a killer.

Patriotic Policeman Królik

Grębków is a small village ten miles south of Węgrów, just north of the Warsaw-Siedlce highway, a few miles past Mińsk Mazowiecki. Before the war, Jews made up more than half of the population in the towns in this area, but they were also fairly numerous in smaller villages. In the spring of 1942, the 142 Jews of Grębków were seized by the local Blue policemen, placed in carts, and delivered to the nearby ghetto in Węgrów. On September 22, 1942, they were deported—together with most of Węgrów's Jews—to the extermination camp in Treblinka. Those Jews who remained in Grębków went into hiding. Unfortunately for them, the village was home to a detachment of the Polish Blue police under the command of Sergeant Bielecki and his deputy, Władysław Królik.[144]

Sometime in November 1943, a "confidential source" reported to the Blue police that Jews were hiding in the area. Indeed, a search of the house of Aleksandra Janusz in the village of Gałki, a few miles away, revealed the presence of nine Jews hidden in a primitive hideout—a crypt of sorts, dug out under the dirt floor of one of the rooms. Mrs. Janusz, the terrified rescuer, recalled that as soon as they showed up at her door, officers Iwanek and Królik began shouting: "Hey,

Figure 3.5. Władysław Królik, a photo from his dossier in the VI SS- u. Polizei Gericht Krakau (Bundesarchiv Berlin-Lichterfelde, NS 7, t. 1185, k. 4).

where are the poodles?" Mrs. Janusz pretended not to know who these "poodles" were, but the policemen kept saying one to another, visibly amused, "Oh, yes, yes, she has the poodles!" The levity of both policemen is lost in translation— *królik* is Polish for *rabbit*. The notion of a rabbit chasing poodles might have seemed hilarious to the arresting officers. Once the jokes were over, however, Królik took a pitchfork and—apparently well-informed about the location of the hideout—went looking for the trapdoor leading to the cellar. The door had been covered with manure and dirt. And under the manure-covered trapdoor were the Jews, or—as Królik jokingly referred to them—the poodles. Grochal descended into the hole and, not without trouble, hauled all of the offending "citizens of Jewish nationality," to quote the language of the documents, to the surface.[145] The Jews and the policemen, as immediately became obvious, were no strangers. The Rubins, their children, Mrs. Gurszyn, and Mrs. Kajzer all hailed from nearby Kałuszyn. When he saw them emerging from the pit, Królik started to laugh and said: "Ho ho, Mr. Rubin, I know you! You are from Kałuszyn, and you made shoes for me! Don't worry; we won't hurt you. We will just lead you toward the forest, we will shoot a few times in the air, and you will run for cover! I won't shoot you!"[146] After a while, four more policemen entered the Janusz home, and according to the rescuer's daughter, the still-smiling officer Królik grabbed a wad of banknotes from Rubin the shoemaker. Once Królik took the money from his victims, he and three other policemen marched the Jews toward the woods. Soon after, the peasants of Gałki heard numerous shots coming from the distance. After a while, the Blue policemen returned to the village, and Królik asked Mrs. Janusz to bring hot water because they needed to wash blood off their hands. After the officers had washed their hands, Constable Iwanek made an attempt to extort from Mrs. Janusz three thousand zlotys as a fine "for having sheltered Jews."[147]

Emanuel Ringelblum, mentioned earlier, spent the last months of his life hiding in a bunker in Warsaw. In the winter of 1943–1944, he wrote his last book: a somber analysis of Polish-Jewish relations during the war. It was a bitter text written by a Polish Jew who saw his entire nation being murdered in plain sight. Ringelblum also had a word to say about the murderers in dark blue uniforms. Referring to the Blue policemen, he wrote, "The blood of hundreds of thousands of Polish Jews, caught and driven to the 'death vans,' will be on their hands."[148] Referring to the blood on the hands of the Polish policemen, Ringelblum was using a figure of speech, a metaphor. He had not met Constable Królik, the Grębków policeman.

What initial insights can one gather from the fate of the Rubin family of Kałuszyn? First, we learn of the frequency of betrayal of hidden Jews by Poles through the sharing of "confidential" information with the Blue police. This betrayal, due to widespread hatred of the Jews, was combined with the seemingly universal conviction among Poles that "Jewish gold" was just waiting to be transferred to new owners. The myth of "Jewish gold" was so popular and so deeply rooted among Christian Poles that it sealed the fate of Rubin, the poor shoemaker from Kałuszyn, and the others hiding with him. Once again, it must be stressed that the prevailing atmosphere was one of fear and antisemitism. This was an atmosphere that proved devastating to Poles who dared to engage in rescue efforts, and it was all the more deadly for their Jewish charges.

A third observation concerns the surprisingly large margin for independent action, or agency, on the part of the Blue policemen in cases involving Jews. Very often, constables arrested, robbed, and murdered their victims without any German orders and without German knowledge. Last but not least, these Polish policemen were murdering people who were not strangers but rather neighbors they had known—as in the case of the Rubin family—since before the war. After the war, responding to charges of murder, the Blue policemen often argued that in fact, the killing of Jews was a patriotic act—one that saved the Polish villagers from the wrath of the Germans, who would have learned sooner or later about the Jews in hiding and who then would have burned down the entire village and perhaps shot a number of Polish hostages.

There was, however, more to Constable Królik than met the eye. In his personnel file, which by chance survived in what remains of the collection of the SS and Police Court of Krakow, we find several laudatory evaluations written by his German superiors. One of them reads, "Królik is an efficient, energetic, and brave police officer."[149] Not only the Germans looked favorably upon policeman Królik's actions; his wartime contributions were equally praised by his superiors in the Polish resistance. Królik, as we learned, was a patriot and a soldier of the II Department of the "Smoła" (Tar) District of the Home Army, which was responsible for gathering intelligence in the Węgrów area.[150] And the appreciation of Królik's wartime achievements survived the war and lasts until today. Both Królik and Grochal were recently described by a historian of the Węgrów area resistance as men "belonging to the most valuable human element among all the social strata."[151] It is not surprising, therefore, that Królik was widely respected by both his peers and his community. After the war, when facing trial for the less praiseworthy episodes of his wartime activity, his neighbors stood by him and sent letters in his defense to the Warsaw Court of Appeals.[152]

POLISH UNDERGROUND STATE AND JEWS IN WĘGRÓW COUNTY

In 1942, Węgrów County became part of Home Army "Smoła" (Tar) district. In terms of attitudes and relationships of AK units with local Jews, the historical accounts place particular stress on the "Treblinka Action." A historian of the local resistance writes, "An attempt to free Jewish prisoners from the extermination camp in Treblinka in August 1943 was the most important undertaking, an initiative with a national impact." Despite many difficulties, writes the author, "the thought of liberating the camp [had] germinated in the minds of Home Army [commanders] since the spring of 1943."[153] Sometime at the end of March 1943, the resistance headquarters in Sokołów Podlaski decided—according to the same author—to attack the extermination camp. Lieutenant Henryk Olesiak, alias Storm, and his platoon cut the telephone lines and went to ground in the local forests, waiting for the arranged signal to strike. Unfortunately, at the last possible moment, the high command called off the attack, but Storm's platoon nevertheless managed to open fire on Treblinka's watchtowers and "throw grenades on the main gate to the camp." The Germans responded with machine-gun fire, and the exchange allegedly lasted fifteen minutes. Finally, Storm's platoon withdrew, and its members went home. The story does not end there, however. "On August 2, 1943, all three partisan groups were ready and in position. Until 4:00 p.m., all was quiet. It was at that point that one heard explosions and shooting coming from the administration area of the camp. Kulesza's platoon opened fire, and some soldiers cut through the barbed wires with special cutters. The Germans were completely surprised."[154] Having opened an escape route for the fleeing Jewish insurgents, AK units, it is implied, shielded them and protected them from the pursuing enemy.

All these stories would have great meaning—if they were even partially true. Unfortunately, the stories of AK units supporting (or even planning together) the uprising in Treblinka are a complete fabrication and, from beginning to end, were based on falsified historical records. In the Sokołów AK headquarters, no decision was ever made to attack Treblinka, and there was never a Storm platoon[155] "opening fire on watchtowers" and "throwing grenades on the main gate of the camp." All of this is simply fiction.[156] Information about the Treblinka uprising is extensive, based both on German sources and on Jewish testimonies, and for the most part the accounts given by the surviving members of the Jewish resistance. Enough is known, therefore, to dismiss the alleged Home Army attack on the camp as one of the many "feel-good" stories and myths used today to whitewash the difficult history of Polish-Jewish relations during the war. The Węgrów AK had no plans to attack Treblinka; more important, not one of the "death trains" headed for the camp between July 1942 and August 1943 was derailed, and not one track leading to and from Małkinia was blown up.

However, all of the above does not mean that Treblinka II and the extermination of Jews was not of interest to the Polish underground. Quite to the contrary. The reports that reached Warsaw headquarters were generated by the local informers and produced by the members of the intelligence unit of the Polish resistance. Its most prominent members were the officers of the Blue police stationed in Sokołów and Węgrów, among them Kripo Chief Józef Dominiak, as well as the previously mentioned officers Piotr Grochal and Władysław Królik. According to a local historian, "They reported about military transports heading east [to the eastern front] and the Jewish transports going to the extermination camp at Treblinka."[157]

The time has come to take a closer look at the reports sent by the members of Węgrów AK to Warsaw, with particular stress on information pertaining to Jews residing and hiding in the area. Not all reports have been preserved, and not infrequently, it is impossible to say who "filtered" and censored the content of reports before they were cleared for final dispatch.[158] Nevertheless, the AK reports shed some light on the German policies of extermination, and most of all, they are revealing in terms of Węgrów area Home Army's perceptions of and attitudes toward the murdered Polish Jews. In the report dated November 1943 (mentioned before), the intelligence unit of the resistance from Węgrów stressed that while wealthy Jews hunkered down in their hideouts on Polish farms, praying for speedy liberation, Jews hiding in the forests were a threat to the local Polish population. "They attack the peasants, they steal, and they are often communist sympathizers. Once caught by the gendarmes, these "forest Jews" in nearly all cases denounce innocent local inhabitants. They are either vengeful for having received 'no help, or they follow the old adage: 'I will die, but so will you!' The cases of Jews denouncing the peasants are most frequent in the Sokołów, Węgrów, and Grójec area."[159] Authors of this report were quite likely unaware of the previous report, filed in August 1943, in which appears the following description of a search conducted on July 14, 1943, by the Blue police and the Gendarmerie in the Wyszków and Grębków area: "They herded the inhabitants into one place and then proceeded to search the houses. This time it was all about the failure [of the local peasants] to deliver the meat and egg quotas to the State. In the course of the search, the Germans seized 98 cows and 140 pigs. They found, at the same time, two Jews, who were later interrogated and asked about the Poles who had given them shelter. The Jews betrayed no one, and right after the interrogation they were executed."[160]

Summarizing "Jewish issues" in the Węgrów area, the intelligence unit reported that "from among the few Jews who are still hiding here, several were apprehended and shot in July."[161] Finally, the report went into detail discussing the Treblinka I forced labor camp while offering little insight into the situation at the Treblinka II death camp.[162] The paucity of the relevant information in the AK intelligence reports indicates how peripheral the "Jewish issue" was from the standpoint of the Polish resistance. It was clearly a distant concern for the local underground and, presumably, equally irrelevant for the central AK command in Warsaw. The question of the extermination of Jews was of secondary importance in 1942, and it became of no importance one year later. What really triggered the interest of the Polish underground were the acts of sabotage, attacks on German soldiers and police forces, and the occupant's reprisals against the Poles. On July 23, 1943, in nearby Mińsk Mazowiecki, someone shot dead Schmidt, the feared Kripo head; in Sokołów, members of resistance made an unsuccessful attempt on *Kreishauptmann* Gramss' life. These events, and the German reactions, were clearly the focus of AK reporting.[163] Whenever Jews were mentioned, it was rather as an obstacle that somehow needed to be solved.

One report reads, "Jews hide in the forests, congregating in small groups. Ninety percent of them are communists. They invade the local villages and they steal food."[164]

Were the "young commie Jews" hiding between Sokołów and Węgrów, mentioned in the AK report, insurgents on the run from Treblinka after the uprising? It is hard to say. At the same time, the AK intelligence warned about "young Jews who assault and rob the Polish population. During [house] invasions, they are brutal and sadistically torture the local gentile inhabitants."[165] In the fall of 1943, the Polish underground started reporting to Warsaw about Jewish prisoners who had escaped from Treblinka. Interestingly, the focus was clearly on the "Jewish gold" carried by the insurgents, and not on their plight or their cause: "Germans are constantly hunting down and killing Jews in our area. In the eastern parts of our district there are, on average, a few scores of Jews hiding in each county. In Sokołów County, in the Sterdyń forests, there are around 300 Jews who fled Treblinka. They have significant amounts of gold, which they took with them from the camp."[166] It is highly unlikely that a significant number of refugees from Treblinka would have survived in the forests into October. The AK intelligence report is less about the situation of the Jews in the area, however, than about the impact that the stories about "Jewish gold" had on the imagination of the local population. The November dispatches no longer mention "Treblinka gold" but makes reference to the "last Jewish survivors (*niedobitki*) who either wander in the forests or join the GL [a left-wing partisan organization] and quickly become communists."[167]

Although the "Jewish question" henceforth received no more attention in AK reports from Węgrów, the issue of Treblinka returned once again, in June 1944. This time, however, the information dealt only with the forced labor camp: "In Treblinka [I labor camp], Jews enjoy privileged positions as doctors, cooks, and laundrymen," reported the local section of underground intelligence. "They are well fed thanks to their dirty deals with Ukrainian guards. Poles [prisoners] find themselves in a much worse situation."[168] In fact, incarceration in Treblinka I for Jews meant death. If this report is set against the testimonies left by the very few Jewish prisoners who managed to survive the deadly conditions in Treblinka I, the tone and meaning of AK intelligence dispatch from Węgrów is obvious.

The Rescue

The theme of the rescue of Jews has appeared throughout this study. It is obvious that this issue is not a freestanding one, and it cannot and should not be discussed in the absence of other forms of Jewish-Polish interaction under the occupation. It so happens, however, that at least in Polish historiography, the issue of rescue provided by Poles to Jews has acquired its own life, one that has less to do with the historical methodology and all to do with requirements of the Polish "history policy."[169] The studies of rescue avoid, in most cases, all the more controversial and tragic aspects of everyday life under the German occupation.

There are two books that tackle the issue of help and rescue in the Węgrów area. There are also several minor contributions, such as articles and occasional papers, that for the most part are hagiographic in nature and have little academic value.[170] The existing feel-good literature about the Righteous Among the Nations would suggest that rescuing Jews under the occupation was a norm in Polish society. Nothing could be further from the truth. The experience of Jews seeking help and shelter was mostly one of betrayal and murder. It is striking that according to Bielawski and others, Jewish suffering was caused to a greater extent by Poles than by Germans. As far as the Germans were concerned, the Jews had no illusions: They were murderers who, true to their nature, murdered. For Bielawski, after the liquidation of the ghetto, the Germans were still a danger but a distant, remote one. The everyday threats were primarily associated with Polish neighbors who came in the form of police informers, greedy thieves, or murderers. To be betrayed by someone from whom one expected help (or at least indifference) must have been particularly painful. For Jews hiding in the forests and hunkered down in hideouts under barns or stables, their Polish neighbors were their possible saviors, but they were also their executioners, whose whims could decide who lived and who died. Seeking shelter, Bielawski met Korczak, a poor Polish peasant, whose generosity and hospitality shocked the author: "Was this all a dream? Was Korczak an angel in the guise of man? We couldn't understand it. Perhaps he knew that the war would soon end and figured it would be useful to be kind to us. Nevertheless, we had not been treated like this before, and it made little sense to us. Then the answer came. There were some Poles who cared and acted bravely, as kind, decent human beings."[171]

Bielawski's comment is not an isolated one: Reading the testimonies of Polish Jews, survivors of the Holocaust, one often comes across similar statements that testify to the bitterness caused by the widespread hostility of the Aryan society. The survivors from Węgrów, whose testimonies were collected decades later by the Visual History Foundation, have very similar recollections. First, they are endlessly grateful to those unique, extraordinary people who dared (usually against the wishes of their own neighbors and families) to offer help. Second, their testimonies are filled with deep disenchantment, bitterness, and even hate, directed at those Poles who contributed to the tragedy of the Jewish refugees. Looking at the issue of rescue from a more general perspective, one can see that to survive, Jews needed assistance, but what they needed most of all was simply a lack of bad will on the part of the Poles. Unfortunately, the often-invoked indifference, which allegedly characterized the attitude of Polish society to the dying Jews, was a desired state of mind rather than the social norm.[172]

This "lack of indifference" can be seen clearly in the case of three-month-old Tołpa Szemberg, abandoned by her mother on a Węgrów street during the liquidation of the ghetto. "It was in September 1942. I was laying in diapers and for three nights, and no one dared pick me up. People were afraid. Only a German gendarme brought me milk from time to time. He said that he knew that I was a Jewish child, but he could not kill me because he had a similar child back home." [173] On the fourth day, Marianna and Andrzej Ruszkowscy, citizens of Węgrów, picked up Szemberg and took her home. The decision was a difficult one because, in the eyes of the neighbors, such an act found little understanding and even less sympathy. "They said, 'You, Mrs. Ruszkowska, you should know what to say to the Germans, because they will come to Ruszkowska.'"[174] Ewelina and Andrzej Koniarscy from Popielów (a hamlet close to Węgrów) experienced a similar "lack of indifference." During the war the couple was most of the time engaged in smuggling food to Warsaw. [175] On November 18, 1943, Koniarskis learned about a baby abandoned at the edge of the village. The couple, who had lost a son several months before, took in the baby. They dismissed their neighbors' accusations that they had taken a Jewish child under their roof. According to a postwar testimony filed by Mrs. Koniarska with the Jewish Historical Institute, the baby boy was a newborn, and they knew nothing about the baby's parents other than "the mother's name was said to have been Mędel," which seems unlikely. The whole village knew that the baby boy adopted by the Koniarskis was Jewish. "We didn't care about the child's race," wrote Mrs. Koniarska later. "Wiesio [the name given to the baby boy] grew, and so did our love for him." The joy of having a baby did not last. Before too long, "the peasants from Todt organization, who worked for the Germans, informed upon us that we had a Jewish child." Despite the boy being baptized, the Koniarskis had to face threats from armed bandits who, on several occasions, blackmailed the terrorized couple.[176]

Our overview of individual trajectories of Jews hiding in the Węgrów area provides information regarding sixty-eight people who survived in the county, including forty-two who lived until liberation thanks to altruistic people who were later recognized as Righteous Among the Nations. This recognition was awarded to fifty-two people hiding Jews in eighteen separate locations.[177] If one were to include in this count the fifteen Jews who were sheltered by people but who died, one would see that one Pole saved, on average, one to two Jews. This is in line with an analysis done some time ago by Zuzanna Schnepf-Kołacz, who, having studied cases of 1,264 Polish Righteous Among the Nations, concluded, "In these cases, 1,571 Jews were saved, which means that, on average, ten Righteous [Among the Nations] saved twelve Jews."[178] According to the available data, the ratio between the rescuers and the rescued—at least in the rural areas—was relatively balanced. Unfortunately, the defenders of the Polish national myths continue to multiply the Righteous Among the Nations; recently, nationalist historians' evaluations of the number of Poles saving Jews surpassed an incredible one million. This kind of literature is abundant, and the number of titles more and more detached from historical reality continues to grow each year.

Can anything concrete be said about the people who saved Jews? Can one venture any general opinions? On the basis of the accumulated evidence, a hypothesis may be proposed that, at least in the rural areas, the socioeconomic position of the rescuers often situated them on the margins of the local community. More often than not, they were poor or very poor people who lived at the edge of the village. Physical distance reflected their social separation from the village mainstream. The phenomenon of the "hut at the edge of the forest," well-known from Jewish testimonies (and signaled earlier in this study), is corroborated by postwar court documents. The "hut at the edge of the forest" was thus the most natural place for the Jews to seek shelter. Unfortunately and tragically, it was also the first place where the police (and concerned neighbors) would start looking for hidden Jews. It is equally difficult to distinguish between those people who were motivated by greed and those who acted out of more noble causes. Most often we see a mixture of both; it often happened that a person sheltered Jews first for profit, but later, with the flow of time and the dwindling resources of the victims, altruistic motives took over. However, there were also opposite cases: when hospitality and safe asylum mutated into various forms of exploitation and violence.[179]

AFTER LIBERATION

Węgrów was liberated on August 9, 1944, by the units of the Twenty-Eighth Soviet Army of the Belorussian Front. Over the course of three days, the Germans were pushed out of the rest of the county. Although heavy fighting was reported south and west of the city, Węgrów itself was spared major damage.[180]

Slowly, the few Jews surviving in the area started to trickle back home. These were very difficult returns. Szraga Fajwel Bielawski was one of the first to show up in the town. He immediately noted the hostility and tension that accompanied the returning Jews. The balance sheet of wrongs and sins was long, and many Poles were unwilling to stand face-to-face with the people they either harmed during the war or taken advantage of their misfortune. But those who—until just beforehand—had provided Jews with shelter and assistance were also not eager to meet the returning refugees. Wrote Bielawski, "After breakfast, Moshe and I crossed the street to the market square. Again, we saw Poles standing off at a distance, staring in disbelief. They knew us well, but they did not have the decency to come over and ask how we were or if we needed anything. I saw Pierkowski, the one who had hidden Menucha in his small barn after she had been shot, and who stored some of our valuables. He stood there, tall and strong. I was so excited to see him that I ran over to him, grabbed his hand, and bent down to kiss it. Suddenly he shoved me away firmly, rejecting me. I looked up to see what had happened. I saw Poles standing and looking at us. I understood that Pierkowski had to push me away because he was ashamed to let them see a Jew getting so close to him."[181]

While the rescuers were fearful of the reactions of their neighbors, the murderers of Jews were initially afraid of legal reprisals and vigilante justice. Their fears were soon put to rest, however; the new Polish authorities were visibly uninterested in the active prosecution of wartime crimes committed by Poles against the Jews. At the same time, the Jews, fearful of the surrounding hostility and aware of murders of survivors at the hands of the locals, fled westward, abroad, or to larger urban centers, where they could hope for more security.

Jankiel Mendelson, a grain merchant from nearby Sterdyń, arrived in liberated Węgrów right after Bielawski. Mendelson wanted one thing: to confront Franciszek Suchodolski, the former Blue policeman and a murderer who, in July 1943 together with another man, had caught, raped, and killed his wife and murdered his eight-year-old son. At the time, Mendelson was the only one who had managed to flee their hideout. In the fall of 1943, having acquired a weapon, Mendelson encountered the man who had earlier helped Suchodolski murder his family. "I took out the revolver and asked him, 'What should I do with you?' The man admitted his guilt and said, 'Do with me whatever you want.' So I said to him, 'I don't want to have Polish blood on my hands; the time for justice shall come!' In 1944, soon after the liberation, I repaired to Węgrow in the company of Pinkas Lerman. We went to the house of Suchodolski's father-in-law. That's where we found Suchodolski himself. He also admitted his guilt and told us what had happened."[182] Jankiel Mendelson, who "didn't want to have Polish blood on his hands," hoped that Polish court would punish the killers of his wife and child. Indeed, both murderers stood trial and were found guilty. They were both sentenced to six years in prison, and both were soon set free.

Twelve-year-old Motel Cyranko spent nearly two years in hiding. Together with his sister, they managed to survive in a bunker in the forests close to their native Jasiorówka (Łochów County). They received help and food from Stanisława Roguszewska, a Polish woman who was later (1994) awarded the title of Righteous Among the Nations. Right after the war, Motel, his sister, and three members of their family returned home. In January 1945, armed men, Polish neighbors, surrounded the house and executed the Jewish survivors. Motel and one sister were the only members of the family who survived. They first fled to Łódź and later abroad.[183]

After liberation, Węgrów—like hundreds of other locations across Poland—became a scene of dramatic events involving the returning Jews. However, together with the fleeing Jews, the events soon disappeared from local peoples' memory. Sometime during the winter or 1944–1945, Isaac Kreda, the last surviving member of the wealthy and numerous Kreda family, was also murdered in an ambush. Young Kreda had survived his parents and siblings (murdered during the liquidation of the secondary ghetto) by barely eighteen months.

A historian could multiply examples of "difficult returns" (although the term "impossible returns" would be more adequate), but there is no doubt that even after liberation, Węgrów County continued to be a deadly trap for Jews. The problem was best described by members of the local Jewish Committee in a letter sent to the Central Jewish Committee in Warsaw: "Jewish Committee in Węgrów. Węgrów, June 6, 1945. To the District Jewish Committee in Warsaw. Due to several cases of Jews being killed in the territory of our county, and due to the extremely hostile attitude of the Polish population to Jews, only a few Jewish families remain in place. All the others have left for larger cities. Out of 195 Jewish souls in the territory of our county, no more than 20 are left. The majority went to Łódź and some went abroad. The Węgrów Committee has lost so many members that it can no longer assist the three Jewish children who still remain with Christian families, who are very poor and need help. Until we are able to co-opt new members of the Committee, please remain in touch with citizen F. Bielawski (coffee shop, in the market square), signed [Rajzman]."[184]

There is no complete list of survivors from the Węgrów area. Consequently, the letter of the Jewish Committee from June 1945 has particular importance and unique credibility. According to the information collected by the Węgrów Committee, 195 local Jews survived the war, although it remains to be seen whether they survived in the area of this study, in the camps, somewhere else under the German occupation, or in the Soviet Union.[185] There are two other lists of Węgrów County Jews surviving in the archives; both deal only with those Jews who chose to settle down after 1945 in Silesia, southwestern Poland.[186]

In October 1949, the Municipal National Council, a county-level office, informed the Jewish Historical Institute in Warsaw about the Jewish presence in the area. According to the municipal count, four years after the war, there were "three Jewish persons" living in Węgrów. And thus, the history of the once thriving Jewish community of Węgrów, a history spanning hundreds of years, came to an end.

NOTES

1. Village of Treblinka, until 1939, was located in Węgrów county. The labor and the extermination camps (Treblinka I and Treblinka II) built, respectively, in 1940 and 1942, have been located three miles away, on the territory of the adjacent Sokołów county.

2. Arkadiusz Kołodziejczyk, "Ludność, urzędy i władze powiatu węgrowskiego w latach 1918–1939," in *Węgrów. Dzieje miasta i okolic w latach 1444–1944*, ed. Arkadiusz Kołodziejczyk and Tadeusz Swat (Węgrów: Towarzystwo Miłośników Ziemi Węgrowskiej, 1991).

3. "Początki osadnictwa żydowskiego w Węgrowie i okolicach," in *Żydzi w Węgrowie*, ed. Wolfgang W. Ronge and Wiesław Theiss, vol. 2, Węgrowskie Listy series (Węgrów: Stacja Badawcza Wydziału Pedagogicznego UW, 1990); Nisan Słucki, "Dzieje osadnictwa żydowskiego w Węgrowie," in Mosze Tamari, *Kehilat Wengrow: Sefer zikaron* (Tel Aviv: Wengrow Immigrants in Israel, 1961).

4. http://www.textmanuscripts.com/manuscript_description.php?id=2812&%20cat=p3&# (accessed July 12, 2017).

5. I refer to Poles and Jews as two separate ethnic and national entities, with clear fault lines that were not bridged by the common Polish citizenship. The chasm between the two national communities grew deeper during the late 1930s.

6. National Democracy, a right-wing, nationalistic party founded by Roman Dmowski and fueled by his rabid antisemitism.

7. Archive of the Main Directorate of the Polish Peasant Movement (Archiwum Zarządu Głównego PSL), 171, Władysław Okulus, "50 lat życia, pracy i walki na terenie powiatu węgrowskiego" [50 Years of Life, Work and Struggle in Węgrow County].

8. In his parliamentary exposé, the Polish prime minister went on record: "No to violence, but yes to the economic boycott of Jews!"

9. USC Shoah Foundation, Visual History Archive (USC, VHA), 23573, Testimony of Sara Kaye (Nortman), born November 6, 1929 in Węgrów.

10. USC, VHA, 18608, Testimony of Sewek Fiszman [Sevek Fishman], b. 1928 in Kałuszyn; USC, VHA, 23137, Testimony of Nate Gruszka; USC, VHA, 24208, Testimony of Manny (Menachem Icchak) Orliński.

11. In small Polish towns, the so-called public markets were held usually once or twice a week and brought to the market squares peasants from the surrounding rural areas wishing to sell their products directly to their urban customers.

12. State Archive in Lublin (APL), Urząd Wojewódzki Lubelski 1918–1939, the Socio-Political Section, 35/403, 2145, 67–68, quoted from Katarzyna Markusz, "Tylu szlachetnych ludzi," unpublished manuscript in the possession of the author, 42.

13. APL, Urząd Wojewódzki Lubelski 1918-1939, Wydział Społeczno-Polityczny 35/403/0/2/2144, 85.

14. Markus Roth, *Herrenmenschen. Die deutschen Kreishauptleute im besetzten Polen—Kerrierwege, Herrschaftspraxis und Nachgeschichte* (Göttingen: Wallstein, 2009), 443. Initially Gramss had been groomed to rule the Sochaczew County, situated west of Sokołów and Węgrów.

15. Ibid., 477.

16. Shraga Feivel Bielawski, *The Last Jew from Wegrow. The Memoirs of a Survivor of the Step-by-Step Genocide in Poland* (Praeger: New York, 1991).

17. USC, VHA, Testimony of Najman Natan, 14739.

18. Archive of the Jewish Historical Institute in Warsaw (hereafter, AŻIH), collection 301/6043, Testimony of W. Okulus, 1. The German counts seem to confirm his estimate; see Regierung des Generalgouvernements. Abteilung Ernährung und Landwirtschaft. Statistiche Amt. Die Ernährungs- u. Landwirschaft im Generalgouvernement Polen. Reihe B. Statistische Zusammenstellungen, Heft 6, Krakau, 1940, 47. 1943: Dorfverzeichnis, (1939 I 1940).

19. Tadeusz Wangrat, *Polska i Powiat Węgrowski w Przededniu i w czasie II Wojny Swiatowej, Swiatowy Związek Żołnierzy AK Obwód "Smoła,"* (Węgrów, 2010), 100.

20. Public Library in Węgrów, access code 16 (6), Order no. 42, dated July 24, 1941.

21. Tomasz Szczechura, "Życie i zagłada społeczności żydowskiej w powiecie węgrowskim w latach 1939–1944," *Biuletyn ŻIH* 105, no. 1 (1978): 44.

22. Public Library in Węgrów, Bekanntmachung, Sokolow-Wengrow, March 3, 1942, access code 16 (4).

23. The *Schutzpolizei* operated in the cities, while the Gendarmerie detachments were located in rural areas. Both forces together were part of the Order Police.

24. The Christian Polish and Jewish witnesses made no distinction between the Schupo and the Gendarmerie; in their eyes, all of them were the feared "gendarmes" [żandarmi]. See Testimony of Cyla Rubenfeld from Węgrów, BAL, B 162/6843, 61–64.

25. A village situated two miles east of Łochów.

26. BAL, B 162/6843, Interrogation of Tedsen, March 7, 1968, 193–203.

27. *Sonderdienst* (Special Service) was a paramilitary organization created in 1940 in the GG and made up of ethnic Germans (*Volksdeutsche*) living in Poland.

28. BAL B 162/6846, Deposition of witness Stanisław Onisk, May 7, 1947.

29. BAL, B 162/6843, Interrogation of Rudolf Weber, June 26, 1967, 72.

30. Ibid., 75–76. Schoeder's Polish underlings included chief Józef Kosmala and two prewar undercover police agents, Marian Nowakowski and Jan Biługa. The Węgrów detachment of the Polish Kripo reported directly to the local chief

of the Gendarmerie and, indirectly, to the Gestapo in Sokołów. Józef Dominiak headed the Polish Kripo in Węgrów, and his men included Edward Podgórniak, Tadeusz Figiel, (Tolek?) Jarosz, Władysław Kuriański, Gorzoch, Ryszard Cymerman, and Stanisław Lange. Podgórniak, Dominiak, and Kuriański were stationed permanently in Węgrów, while other plainclothes officers were called into town whenever needed.

31. AEL Treblinka I, not to be confused with the extermination camp Treblinka II, was built in early 1942 and located in the vicinity.

32. BAL B 162/6843, 53–56. Witness Ruwen (Romek) Figowy, a Jewish policeman from Sokołów, describes the murders committed by van Eupen.

33. USC, VHA, 17292, Interview with Nellie Kaptsan.

34. [3] Dawid Nowodworski, one of the Jews deported from Warsaw, survived a day in the death camp itself and then smuggled himself out of Treblinka and returned to the Warsaw ghetto to inform the people about the real fate of the people "evacuated to the East." His testimony has been preserved in the Oneg Shabbat Archive as well as in the diary of Abraham Lewin.

35. Bielawski, *Last Jew from Wegrow*, 47.

36. USC, VHA, 35694, Testimony of Harry Miller from Jarnice.

37. AŻIH, 301/ 6043, Testimony of Władysław Okulus.

38. The term used to describe the members of the feared guard troops, also called "Trawniki-men" or "Hiwis." For the most part, they recruited from among the Soviet POWs and operated under the authority of SSPF Lublin.

39. AŻIH, 301/6043, Testimony of Władysław Okulus.

40. *Kehilat Wegrow: Sefer Zikaron* (Tel Aviv, 1961).

41. Ibid.

42. Bielawski, *Last Jew from Wegrow*, 58.

43. This awkward term was sometimes used in communist propaganda in the 1940s and 1950s.

44. YVA, O.33/1066, Testimony of W. Wójcik. After the war, Wójcik came into the possession of several parts of Chaim Kaplan's diary from the Warsaw ghetto. In the 1960s, he tried to sell the diary to the highest bidder.

45. *Listy Węgrowskie* vol. 2, 33, Testimony of Henryka Grabowska. Her other account can be found in the first volume of *Listy węgrowskie*, 29–34.

46. S.F. Bielawski, *The Last Jew From Wegrow*, 58.

47. USC, Visual History Archive, 13697, Testimony of Renia Lipska-Micznik.

48. IPN GK 317/144, Deposition of Stanisław Raczko, May 23, 1949, 26–27.

49. USC, VHA, 18608, Testimony of Sewek Fiszman.

50. AŻIH, 301/6043, Testimony of Mayor W. Okulus.

51. State Archive in Siedlce (APS), SOS, dossier 652, Deposition of Aleksander Ajchel, 5–6, April 2, 1947.

52. AŻIH, 301/6043, Testimony of Mayor W. Okulus.

53. AŻIH, series 301/668, Testimony of Chaim Kwiatek. Translated from the Yiddish by Monika Polit.

54. Among the murdering neighbors, firefighters, and Polish policemen, Chaim Kwiatek listed Czesław Grudziądz, his brother Lutek, Tomek Figler, Jasiński, Janek Kalinowski, Staszek, Kazimierz Postek, Staszek Pigul, and the "main murderer," village elder Łaszyński. There were also seventy other townspeople who took part—according to Kwiatek—in the Jew hunt.

55. AŻIH, series 301/668, Testimony of Chaim Kwiatek.

56. Jerzy Tchórzewski, Swiadectwo dojrzałości. Wspomnienia z lat 1928–1945, Wydawnictwo księgarnia św. (Katowice, 2007), 111–112.

57. BAL, B 162/6843, 61–64. AŻIH, 301/6043, Okulus. Cyla Rubenfeld put the number of dead as high as three thousand.

58. Two "remnant ghettos" were created in the area in November 1942, one in Kosów Lacki and another unofficial one in Węgrów. The ghetto in Kosów Lacki was liquidated in February 1943, and the unofficial one in Węgrów was liquidated on April 30, 1943.

59. For more information about the survival strategies related to camps, see Martin Dean, "Jewish Survival in Forced Labor Camps for Jews. The Agricultural Camps in Czortków County of Eastern Galicia, 1942–1944," in *Lessons and Legacies*, ed. Alexandra Garbarini and Paul B. Jaskot, vol. 13, *New Approaches to an Integrated History of the Holocaust. Social History, Representation, Theory* (Evanston, IL: Northwestern University Press, 2018), 112–140.

60. Kehilat Wegrow; sefer zikaron (Memorial book), ed. M. Tamari. Tel Aviv, former residents of Wegrow in Israel, 1961, Testimony of Rotsztajn (first name unknown), 108

61. AŻIH, 301/6043, W. Okulus, 8.

62. Kehilat Wengrow, the chapter entitled "Holocaust."

63. Stanisław Roguski, "Tę piłę, to ja rzeczywiście mam do dziś," *Listy Węgrowskie* no. 2.

64. YVA, M1E 2450.

65. Both ghettos were liquidated on September 25, 1942. See Wolfgang Curilla, *Der Judenmord in Polen und der deutsche Ordnungspolizei 1939–1945* (Paderborn–München–Wien–Zürich: Schöningh, 2011), 651.

66. AP Siedlce, SOS, vol. 652, Testimony of Moszek Góra, main proceedings, May 27, 1948.

67. AP Siedlce, SOS, vol. 652, Testimony of Roman Ajchel, April 19, 1947, 13–14.

68. AP Siedlce, SOS, vol. 652, Testimony of Władysław Ajchel, 18. Ajchel saw firefighters pulling Jews out of the hideouts and marching them in groups of twenty or more toward the Jewish cemetery.

69. AP Siedlce, SOS, vol. 652, Testimony of Władysław Ajchel, 18.

70. AP Siedlce, SOS, vol. 652, Testimony of Stanisław Zbrożek, 12.

71. AP Siedlce, SOS, vol. 652, Testimony of Franciszek Walecki 128.

72. State Archive in Siedlce (AP Siedlce), collection of SOS, v. 652, Deposition of Stanisław Dula, 17 May 1947, 42.

73. Bielawski, *Last Jew From Wegrow*, 62.

74. In order to comprehend the size of this widespread phenomenon, one can point to the contemporaneous testimonies from other comparable towns and locations, such as Opoczno, Biłgoraj, Szczebrzeszyn, Miechów, Dąbrowa Tarnowska, and Brzesko Nowe. The liquidation of the ghetto in Węgrów was not an exception, and the participation of Polish policemen and firefighters was a part of general strategy that can be observed throughout occupied Poland. In the areas incorporated into the Reich, where the Polish police had been abolished, the dynamics of extermination were different.

75. For more insights into the role of the local elites—in the context of the war in the Balkans—see Max Bergholz, *Violence as a Generative Force. Identity, Nationalism, and Memory in a Balkan Community* (London: Cornell University Press, 2016).

76. AP Siedlce, SOS, vol. 652, Deposition of witness Kazimierz Czarkowski and his declaration of support for the accused Ajchel, 64, 77–79.

77. See Friedrich Katzmann, *Rozwiazanie kwestii zydowskiej w dystrykcie Galicja/Lösung der Judenfrage im Distrikt Galizien*, ed. Andrzej Żbikowski (Warsaw, IPN, 2001).

78. YVA, O3.1585, Testimony of Mieczysław Supeł.

79. Zygmunt Klem, *"I wtedy przyszło najgorsze"* [And That's When the Worst Came], in *Węgrów: Stacja Badawcza Wydziału Pedagogicznego*, ed. Żydzi w Węgrowie, Wolfgang W. Ronge, and Wiesław Theiss, (UW, 1990), 42–44.

80. Ludwig Fischer's regulation of November 16, 1942.

81. It is impossible to establish precisely the number of Jews living in the secondary ghetto, especially with the high mobility of the inmates. Various testimonies mention anywhere between two and four hundred people.

82. One of the victims was Rachel Mandelbaum, Szraga Fajwel Bielawski's finacée, who was hidden in a hideout under Kreda's house.

83. Klem, *I wtedy przyszło najgorsze*, 42–44

84. AP in Warsaw (APW), Urzd Wojewódzki Warszawski, file 173, "Wykaz mienia opuszczonego" [Inventory of abandoned property], 1–25, December 15, 1944.

85. YVA, O.33/4905, The Diary of Romek Międzyrzecki, entry for December 27, 1942.

86. Bielawski, *Ostatni Żyd z Węgrowa*, 186.

87. In Polish, *"Mienie pożydowskie."*

88. Israel Cymlich and Oskar Strawczynski, *Escaping Hell in Treblinka* (Jerusalem: Yad Vashem, 2007), 54–55.

89. The Warsaw Ghetto Uprising broke out on April 19, 1943.

90. YVA, O.3/1585, Testimony of Mieczysław Supeł.

91. Grabowska, *Wojna nam zabrała dzieciństwo i młodość* [War Took Away Our Childhood and Youth], 33.

92. AP (State Archive in) Siedlce, Special District Court (SOS), dossier 653, Testimony of witness J. Sasim, 51–52, 167.

93. Bielawski, *Last Jew from Wegrow*, 114–115.

94. Regulation of Governor L. Fischer, dated November 11, 1941; "Amtsblatt für den Distrikt Warschau," December 16, 1941.

95. See Israel Cymlich and Oskar Strawczynski, *Escaping Hell in Treblinka* (Jerusalem: Yad Vashem, 2007).

96. YVA, TR/10/2861-1, Original documents in Zentrale Stelle der Landesverwaltungen zur Verfolgung nationalsozialistischer Verbrechen, Ludwigsburg, 211 AR-277/66, vol. 16–17, February 11, 1942.

97. Martyna Rusiniak, *Obóz zagłady Treblinka II w pamięci społecznej (1943–1989)* [The Extermination Camp Treblinka II in Social Memory, (1943–1989)] (Warsaw: Neriton, 2008), 19.

98. AIPN, GK 384/184, Interrogation of Czesław Sudak, 19.

99. Historians find the echoes of these robberies in the files of the Sondergericht and the *Deutsches Gericht*—German courts from Warsaw. Proceedings against Czesław L., one of the many enterprising peasants robbing "post-Jewish" clothes from the trains leaving Treblinka, offer insights into this phenomenon (AMSW, Sondergericht, file 1305, Czesław L.). He was sentenced by the Special Court (*Sondergericht*) to one month in prison (sentence of May 3, 1944).

100. YVA, O.33/4905, Diary of Romek Międzyrzecki.

101. Adam Starkopf, *Will to Live. One Family's Story of Surviving the Holocaust* (Albany: State University of New York Press, 1995), 158–160.

102. AŻIH, 301/4660.

103. Alina Skibinska's unpublished research results indicate that close to one hundred Jews survived the uprising and lived until liberation.

104. Witold Chrostowski, *Extermination Camp Treblinka* (London: Vallentine Mitchell, 2004), 92–93.

105. AIPN, GK 384/184, Testimony of Helena Sudak, March 18, 1950, 4.

106. AIPN, GK 318/27, Depositions of witnesses Stefan Gąsior, Hipolita Matusik, and Krystyna Panufnik, June 4–6, 1950, 239–246.

107. AIPN, GK 318/27, Testimony of Wacław Kosowski, June 9, 1950, 278.

108. AIPN, GK 318/27, Testimony of Jan Kosowski, June 10, 1950, 282.

109. Cymlich and Strawczynski, *Escaping Hell in Treblinka*, 187.

110. Howard Roiter, *Voices from the Holocaust* (New York: William Frederick, 1975), 124; Interview with Zygmunt Strawczyński: "I didn't run, because my brother was pessimistic about chances on the outside."

111. YVA, O.3/561, Testimony of Samuel Rajzman, 11.

112. Ibid.

113. YVA, Department of the Righteous Among the Nations, correspondence dealing with the award for Stanisław Pogorzelski. Five out of the six survived until the arrival of the Red Army in the summer of 1944.

114. AAN, AK, 203-X-68, Home Army intelligence report, September 1943, 31.

115. Yitzhak Arad, *Belzec, Sobibor, Treblinka: The Operation Reinhard Death Camps* (Bloomington: Indiana University Press, 1992).

116. Klem, *"I wtedy przyszło najgorsze,"* 47.

117. USHMM, RG-15.029, *Akta sądów grodzkich* [Dossiers of Municipal Courts], mf 45. In May 1944, the SS "together with Jews from Łódź ghetto exhumed and incinerated the bodies on wooden pyres in Węgrów."

118. Putkowska, "W naszym domu było bardzo zimno" [It Was Very Cold in Our House], in *Żydzi w Węgrowie*, Wolfgang W. Ronge, Wiesław Theiss (eds.), 12.

119. Bolesław Zalewski, addressing Uszer Szejnberg, whom he had caught in the village of Sulki, county Węgrów, on June 11, 1944 (AIPN, GK 317/106).

120. AAN, Delegatura Rządu na Kraj, 202-II-7, report filed by Jan Stanisław "Sobol" Jankowski with Władysław "Orkan" Banaczyk, August 31, 1943, 48.

121. AŻIH, Wojewódzki Komitet Żydowski w Warszawie, 352/118, Mail exchange with the Węgrów Jewish Committee. The committee informed Warsaw headquarters that 195 Jews reported locally. The documents from this file will be discussed later in this study.

122. It was only after the publication of the Polish edition of this book, in the spring of 2018, that the author became aware of the existence of mass grave of twelve Jews in the village of Warchoły, situated less than three kilometers north of Węgrów. The victims were two Węgrów shoemakers and their families, who were apprehended and murdered by locals while fleeing the liquidated ghetto in Węgrów.

123. Alina Skibińska and Jakub Petelewicz, "The Participation of Poles in Crimes against Jews in the Świętokrzyskie Region," *Yad Vashem Studies* 35, no. 1 (2007): 5–48. Originally published in Polish in *Zagłada Żydów. Studia i Materiały* 1 (2005): 131.

124. BAL, B 162/6843, Testimony of Simcha Polakiewicz, March 13, 1962, 27–28. Polakiewicz was one of the Jews who fled Treblinka. In his testimony, he draws upon the wartime memoirs of Stanisław Chomelańczuk, inhabitant of Kurczew, who was later deported as a forced laborer to Germany. Polakiewicz wrote a book entitled *In the Shadow of Treblinka* [*A tog in Treblinke: Kronik fun a jidisz lebn*] (Buenos Aires: Central-farband fun Pojlisze Jidn in Argentine cuzamen mit di Landslajt Farejnen fun Sokolow-Podlask in Argentine un Urugwaj, 1948).

125. AŻIH, 301/4875, Testimony of Pelagia Vogelgesang. Vogelgesang was later recognized as Righteous Among the Nations.

126. Ibid.

127. Letter exchange with Gloria Glantz (née Gitl Przepiórka), in the possession of the author. In 2013, Marianna Kowalczyk was recognized as Righteous Among the Nations.
128. AŻIH, 301/6810, Testimony of Barbara Suchodolska.
129. AŻIH, 301/6810, Letter of Barbara Suchodolska dated February 11, 1982, 2.
130. Ibid.
131. Sometime later, when Rogińska's daughter tried to recover the stolen objects, the neighbors threatened her with the Germans.
132. AIPN, GK 318/29, 227–231.
133. AIPN, GK 318/29, Interrogation of Franciszek Wrzosek, 203–207.
134. Interview with Mrs. Zofia Potocka, granddaughter of Wiktor Ratyński, Ziomaki, July 30, 2017.
135. AIPN, GK 318/29, Deposition of witness Wiktor Ratyński, April 19, 1948, 227–229.
136. 137. YVA, Department of the Righteous Among the Nations. The Malińskis were later recognized as Righteous Among the Nations for having rescued the Abkowicz sisters.
138. The full text of the Third Regulation, and other German regulations for the GG, can be found in *Verordnungsblatt für das Generalgouvernement*.
139. Barbara Engelking and Jacek Leociak, *Getto warszawskie: Przewodnik po nieistniejącym mieście* (Warsaw: Stowarzyszenie Centrum Badań nad Zagładą Żydów, 2013), 205. Twenty-four people were shot during the first execution.
140. Bojmie, Miedzna, Węgrów, Wyszków, Łochów, Sadowne, Stoczek, and Grębków.
141. For the details of this case, see numerous depositions of witnesses in IPN, GK 317/28, vol. 3.
142. Deposition of Wacław Chomontowski, November 4, 1948, IPN; GK, 317/28 v. 3, 27–28.
143. Emanuel Ringelblum, *Polish-Jewish Relations during the Second World War* (Evanston, IL: Northwestern University Press, 1992), 77.
144. Indictment (*Akt oskarżenia*), November 18, 1949, IPN, GK 317/133, 4–4v, 36–38. Officer Iwanek, who had served in the police since 1920, and who before the war was stationed in the Węgrów area, was deposed at length on the role of Królik.
145. Protokół rozprawy głównej [Minutes of trial proceedings], April 17, 1952, IPN, GK 318/460, vol. 1, 147–160. Piotr Grochal had served in the police since 1934.
146. Deposition of Aleksandra Janusz, May 22, 1949, IPN, GK 317/134, 5–6.
147. Ibid.
148. Ringelblum, *Polish-Jewish Relations*, 135.
149. "Bundesarchiv Berlin-Lichterfelde, SS- u. Polizei Gericht VI, Krakau," NS/7, vol. 1185, Personnel file of Władysław Królik from Grębków, 8.

150. Wangrat, *Polska i powiat węgrowski*, 56–57.

151. Wojciech Gozdawa-Gołębiowski, "Powiat węgrowski w latach okupacji niemieckiej," in *Węgrów – dzieje miasta i okolic w latach 1441–1944*, (eds.) Arkadiusz Kołodziejczyk, Tadeusz Swat, Węgrów 1991, 347.

152. Władysław Królik; found guilty of murdering Jews and Soviet POWs, was sentenced to death. His sentence was later commuted to life in prison. He was set free in 1959; AIPN, GK 318/126, 850–870.

153. Gozdawa-Gołębiowski, "Powiat węgrowski w latach okupacji niemieckiej," 366–368.

154. Ibid.

155. Interestingly, a Home Army report from 1943 describes Oleksiak, alias Storm, not as a member of the resistance but as a "bandit" (AAN, Delegatura Rządu na Kraj, 202-II-23, Situation report for November 1943, 80).

156. Similar fallacies can be found in Władysław Prażmowski, "Akcja Treblinka," *Dzieje Najnowsze*, no. 1 (1969): 167–182.

157. Wangrat, *Polska i powiat węgrowski*, 57.

158. See: Dariusz Libionka, "Polska konspiracja wobec eksterminacji Żydów w dystrykcie warszawskim," in *Prowincja noc. Życie i zagłada Żydów w dystrykcie warszawskim*, eds. Barbara Engelking, Jacek Leociak, and Dariusz Libionka (Warsaw: IFiS PAN, 2007), 466–470.

159. AAN, AK, 203-X-68, AK intelligence report from Sokołów-Węgrów, September 1943, 31.

160. AAN, Delegatura Rządu na Kraj, 202-II-23, AK report from Sokołów-Węgrów for August 1943, 5.

161. AAN, Folwark VII, Situational report, December 1–31, 1943, 2.

162. Ibid., 9.

163. Ibid., 24.

164. Ibid., 22.

165. Ibid., 16.

166. AAN, *Delegatura Rządu na Kraj* [Delegation of the Government in Exile], 202-II-23, Report for the period October 1–31, 1943, 56.

167. AAN, Delegatura Rządu na Kraj, 202-II-23, AK report for November 1943, 77, 93, "National Minorities" section.

168. AAN, Delegatura Rządu na Kraj, 202-II-41, June 1944 Home Army report, 28.

169. For a thoughtful study on the issue of rescue of Jews by Poles during the war, see Dariusz Libionka, "Polskie piśmiennictwo na temat zorganizowanej i indywidualnej pomocy Żydom (1945–2008)," *Zagłada Żydów. Studia i Materiały* 4 (2008): 17–79.

170. See Piórkowska, *Sprawiedliwi i ocaleni*; Edward Kopówka and Paweł Rytel-Andrianik, *Dam im imię na wieki. Polacy z okolic Treblinki ratujący Żydów* (Warsaw: Wydawnictwo Sióstr Loretanek, 2011).

171. Bielawski, *Last Jew from Węgrow*, 121.

172. See Elżbieta Janicka, "The Square of Polish Innocence: POLIN Museum of the History of Polish Jews in Warsaw and Its Symbolic Topography," *East European Jewish Affairs* 45, no. 2–3 (2015): 210.

173. Hanna Krall, Recollections of Zofia Ruszkowska-Żochowska, as noted during a meeting of Hidden Children, New York, May 25, 1991, quoted from Piórkowska, *Sprawiedliwi i ocaleni*, 58.

174. Ibid.

175. 301/5180, Testimony of Ewelina Koniarska.

176. Ibid.

177. Kopówka and Rytel-Andrianik, *Dam im imię na wieki*, 445.

178. Zuzanna Schnepf-Kołacz, "Pomoc Polaków dla Żydów na wsi w czasie okupacji niemieckiej. Próba opisu na przykładzie Sprawiedliwych wśród Narodów Świata," in *Zarys krajobrazu. Wieś polska wobec zagłady Żydów 1942–1945*, ed. Barbara Engelking and Jan Grabowski (Warsaw: Stowarzyszenie Centrum Badań nad Zagładą Żydów, 2011), 220.

179. For a recently published, and particularly pertinent, testimony, see *Buried Words: The Diary of Molly Applebaum* (Azrieli Foundation: Toronto, 2017). In Polish: Jan Grabowski, ed., *Szczęście posiadać dom pod ziemią... Losy kobiet ocalałych z Zagłady w okolicach DąbrowyTarnowskiej* (Warsaw: Stowarzyszenie Centrum Badań nad Zagładą Żydów, 2016).

180. Arkadiusz Kołodziejczyk, Tadeusz Swat, and Mariusz Szczupak, eds., *Węgrów. Dzieje miasta i okolic 1944–2005* (Węgrów: Towarzystwo Miłośników Ziemi Węgrowskiej, 2006), 12–13.

181. Bielawski, *Last Jew from Węgrow*, 147–148.

182. AIPN, GK 318/506, Jankiel Mendelson's letter to the court, undated, 9–11.

183. Interview with Motel Cyranko, Ottawa, April 8, 2018.

184. AŻIH, 352/118, Incoming Correspondence With the Jewish Committee in Węgrów.

185. Ibid., 1. Polish Jews started returning from the Soviet Union only later, at the end of 1945, so we can safely assume that the list deals most of all with Jews who survived on the "Aryan side," or in various labor and concentration camps.

186. AŻIH, CKŻP, Wydział Ewidencji i Statystyki, 303/V/377, Węgrów, Komitet Żydowski.

JAN GRABOWSKI is a professor of history at the University of Ottawa and a fellow of the Royal Society of Canada. His interests focus on the Holocaust in Poland and, more specifically, on the relations between Jews and Poles during the war. Professor Grabowski's book *Hunt for the Jews: Betrayal and Murder in German-Occupied Poland* was awarded the Yad Vashem International Book Prize for 2014. In 2020, Grabowski was appointed a distinguished fellow at the Institut für Zeitgeschichte in Munich, Germany. In 2018, he coedited and coauthored *Dalej jest noc*, a two-volume study of the fate of the Jews in selected counties of occupied Poland. His most recent book, *On Duty: The Role of the Polish Blue Police in the Holocaust* (Na Posterunku. Udział Polskiej Policji Granatowej i kryminalnej w Zagładzie Żydów, Czarne), was published in Poland in March 2020.

FOUR

ŁUKÓW COUNTY

JEAN-CHARLES SZUREK

SOURCES

This text is mostly based on video testimonies of survivors from Łuków and the surrounding area, including Kock and Stoczek Łukowski, recorded by the USC Shoah Foundation Visual History Archive, as well as testimonies, diaries, and recollections from the archives of Yad Vashem and the Jewish Historical Institute.[1] Also useful were other Jewish sources: lists of survivor names and documents of *Judenräte* (Jewish Councils), self-help organizations, and the Joint Distribution Committee (Joint, JDC), as well as various sources concerning the situation in Łuków County collected by Oneg Shabbat archivists. Another very important source was the memory book of the Jewish survivors from Łuków (*Le Livre de Lukow*[2]) and Krzysztof Czubaszek's monograph, *Żydzi Łukowa i okolic*.[3]

Also vital were the documents of the Main Commission of the Prosecution of the Nazi Crimes in Poland as well as trial files of people charged with collaboration after the war (based on the so-called August Decree).

Documents concerning the actions of the occupier's structures and files of German perpetrators tried by West German courts, mainly in the 1960s, were also used.

Łuków County, as understood here, covers its prewar area, notwithstanding the changes introduced by the Germans, who incorporated a part of the county to Kreis Radzyn.

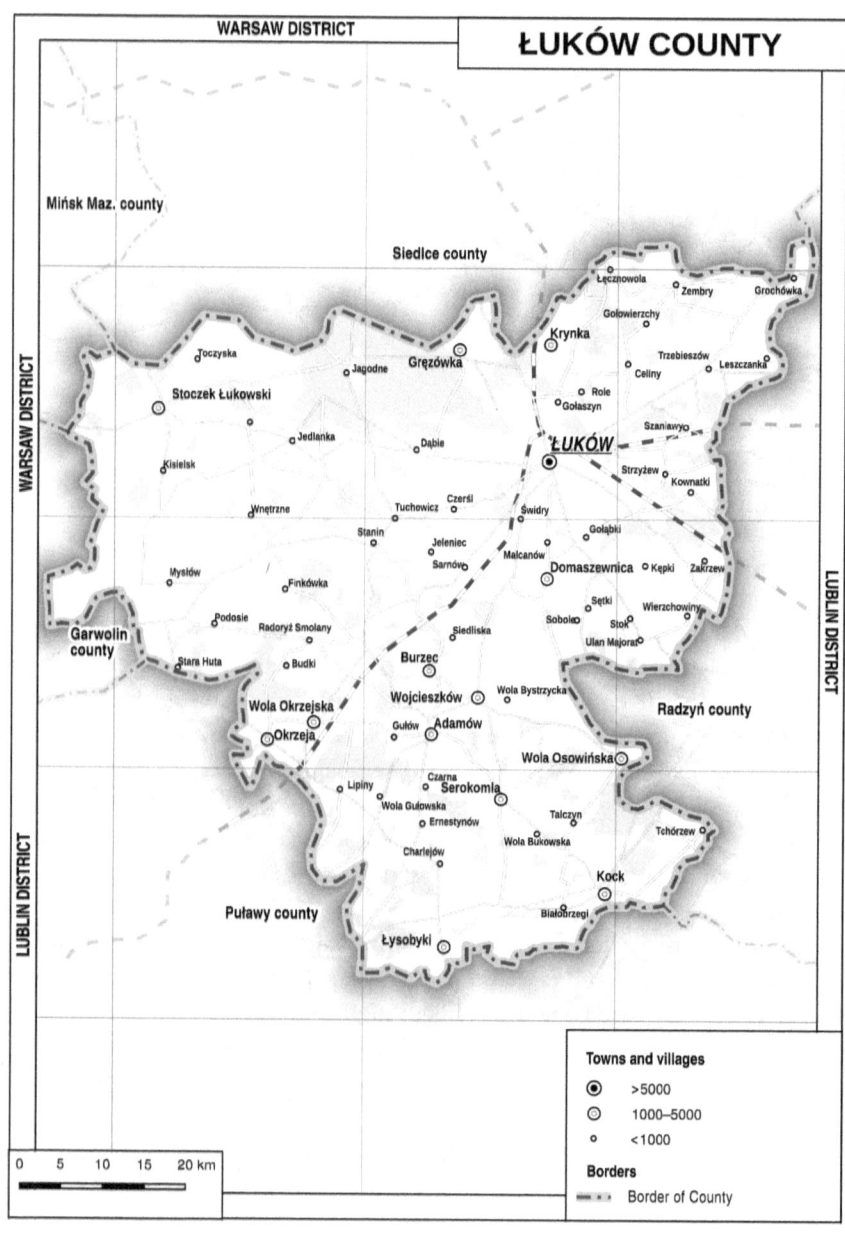

JEWS IN ŁUKÓW BEFORE 1939: A BRIEF INTRODUCTION

In Holocaust survivor testimonies, the picture of the relations between Polish and Jewish pupils was varied. Most recall instances of ruthless antisemitism (e.g., throwing rocks, splashing mud onto the coat of a *melamed* [Jewish religious studies teacher] on the way to a Polish school). Others speak of mutual understanding and even of some kind of solidarity of young Polish boys visiting Jews at Passover and young Jews visiting Polish families at Christmas, and also of Jewish children making up lessons they did not attend on Saturdays with the help of their Polish schoolmates.[4]

The Prengler brothers, who came from one of the most distinguished Jewish families in Łuków, recall good relations between Jews and Poles engendered around their mother's hardware store. Many peasants used to come to town especially on Thursdays, which was a market day. The Prenglers' mother spoke excellent Polish, knew everybody, and offered credit purchase, and this arrangement worked quite well. A number of Jews worked as farm laborers.[5] As David Brook (born in Dęblin) pointed out, "We were aware that we were second-class citizens, even though we had lived on this territory for a thousand years. Generally, we were tolerated. But were never considered equals."[6]

From the late 1930s, the relations between Jews and Poles become tenser due to intensifying antisemitism.

In 1937, many National Democracy sympathizers, with the help of Catholic activists, launched a boycott of Jewish merchants in Łuków. Supporters of the nationalist right (according to the newspaper *Przyjaciel Podlasia*, published in

Table 4.1 Łuków population, 1861–1945

Year	Total population	Jews	Percentage of Jews
1861	3311	2,255	68.1
1907	11,206	7,094	63.3
1897	8,781	4,799	54.6
1911	12,583	8,058	64
1921	12,571	6,145	48.8
1939	12,785*	c. 6,000	c. 48.8
1945	7,894†	60‡	<1*

* *Source:* Krzysztof Czubaszek, *Żydzi Łukowa i okolic* (Warsaw: Danmar, 2008).
† *Source:* Franciszek Gryciuk and Romuald Turkowski, eds., "Łuków w latach 1944–1975," in *Łuków i okolice w XIX i XX wieku* (Warsaw: Wydawnictwa Geologiczne, 1989), 301.
‡ *Source:* Ibid., 309.

Table 4.2 Łuków County population in 1921

Towns (urban communes)	Total population	Jews
Łuków	12,571	6,145
Kock	3,903	2,092
Stoczek	2,951	1,962
Communes	**Total population**	**Jews**
Białobrzegi	6,389	20
Celiny	2,811	126
Dąbie	3,575	75
Gołąbki	3,489	80
Gułów	7,454	916
Jakusze	2,382	163
Jarczew	3,421	220
Krasusy	2,263	88
Łuków—	4,767	46
Łysobyki	5,922	495
Prawda	8,206	47
Radoryż	4,117	136
Serokomla	5,573	239
Skrzyszew	2,288	166
Stanin	4,384	164
Trzebieszów	3,055	158
Turchowicz	6,208	146
Ulan	4,872	295
Wojcieszków	7,390	149
TOTAL	**107,991**	**13,928**

Source: *Skorowidz miejscowości Rzeczypospolitej Polskiej* opracowany na podstawie wyników pierwszego powszechnego spisu ludności z dn. 30 września 1921 r. i innych źródeł urzędowych, vol. 4: *Województwo lubelskie* (Warsaw: GUS RP, 1924).

Siedlce, some twenty kilometers from Łuków), fought openly to "cleanse Poland of Jews" and proclaimed, "Don't buy from the Jews" and "Boycott those parasites." The *Nowe Wieści* monthly, published in Kock, held the same positions in 1939. One of the editors wrote that the Jews already had a foretaste of what was to come, when "dejudification" gathers momentum.[7] Faced with the rampant antisemitism of the local cells of National Democracy and Catholic Action, left-wing parties (the Polish Socialist Party, *Polska Partia Socjalistyczna*, PPS, and elements of the peasant movement as well as communists) and the intelligentsia organized themselves against the boycott of Jewish stores in the name of antifascist action. Jewish milieus did not remain passive either and forbade the Jews from buying from "Christians" or to use Polish *droshkies* (carriages) and recommended the boycott of Polish theatrical performances. Eventually, the boycott and the accompanying atmosphere began to ease off but no doubt left its mark.

In the interwar period until the very eve of the war, the Jewish population stabilized at six thousand in Łuków, enriched by the activity of the Jewish library, drama club, and cinema; Yiddish newspapers (a daily and a weekly); schools and religious activities. This all ended, however, with the German invasion on September 1, 1939. "The moment the Germans appeared, the Poles changed," Sylvia Friedman summarizes.[8]

RESULTS OF NAZI POLICY IN THE LUBLIN DISTRICT

Following Operation Reinhardt, around 20,000 Jews in the Lublin district were left alive (out of over 260,000).[9] Those who survived were mostly workers needed in German factories. Only a few managed to escape the ghetto or one of the so-called death trains. It is estimated that by the end of 1942, 250,000 Jews all over Poland roamed woods and villages in search of help. No more than 40,000–50,000 of them survived the war.[10]

After the Lublin ghetto liquidation (on the night of March 16–17, 1942) under the command of SS-*Gruppenführer* Odilo Globocnik, Operation Reinhardt in the Lublin district began in places situated near railway lines and then spread all over the General Government (GG). In April 1942, the Jewish population of Lubartów (some forty kilometers from Łuków), Kraśnik, and mainly Zamość were deported to the Bełżec extermination camp. "One wonders why," writes Tatiana Berenstein, "that at that time the transport of Jews from abroad were not directed to the Bełżec death camp, but to depopulated ghettos. Probably the Germans wanted the deportees to leave some kind of a trace and correspond with their dear ones back home."[11] Eight hundred Lubartów Jews deported on April 9 and 10 were replaced by several hundred women and children from Slovakia. The men had been separated on the way and sent to build the death camp at Majdanek.[12] The Sobibór gas chambers (Lublin district) started operating in early May 1942, and those in Treblinka (Warsaw district) started in the second half of July that year. After a two-month interruption, deportations of Jews from the Lublin district were resumed. In August, Jews from Biłgoraj County were deported to Bełżec, and from Radzyń County to Treblinka. The largest towns in Radzyń County (apart from Radzyń itself) were Międzyrzec and Łuków. From Parczew and Międzyrzec, twenty thousand Jews were deported. In October 1942, Jews from other ghettos in Radzyń County were captured and deported to Treblinka on a regular basis, while Łuków and Międzyrzec became places of concentration for the Jewish populations from the entire Radzyń County.

Many Jews managed to escape from the ghettos in the fall of 1942 and hide. In order to gather again the scattered Jews, Friedrich Wilhelm Krüger, the Higher SS and Police Chief (*Höherer SS- und Polizeiführer*) in the GG issued on October 28, 1942, an order regarding the establishment of "new Jewish housing districts" (so-called secondary ghettos) in the Warsaw and Lublin districts. Accordingly, eight ghettos were reestablished in the Lublin district, including three in Radzyń County (which had the largest population): in Międzyrzec, Łuków, and Parczew. The Germans established new *Judenräte* there as well. The liquidation of the secondary ghettos in Międzyrzec and Łuków took place in early May 1943. Several thousand people were sent to the gas chambers, while some workers were deported to Majdanek.[13]

PERSECUTION OF ŁUKÓW JEWS, FORCED LABOR, SOCIAL HELP

Łuków and the surrounding area had strategic significance because of the railway hub and the crossing of two railway lines: Siedlce–Łuków–Lublin–Lwów and Brześć–Łuków–Dęblin–Radom.[14] In mid-September 1939, Łuków became the scene of heavy fighting. The last battle at Kock with the Polish forces under the command of General Franciszek Kleberg was fought from October 2 to 5.

The German invasion of Łuków was very bloody. In the bombings of September 4, 7, 260 people were killed.[15] The Jews soon realized that despite what one might expect, these events would have nothing in common with the course of World War I. On September 6, six Jews were murdered, and later another eight people, including six Jews, were murdered.

At that time, some witnesses saw a kind of rapprochement between Poles and Jews: "We were all in the same boat, with the threat looming over our heads the face of the German occupation."[16] On September 17, 1939, the Wehrmacht occupied Łuków. As part of retaliatory measures for an ambush on the Germans by Polish soldiers, seventy Jews were executed, and around one thousand Jews and Poles were sent to a penal camp near Ostrów Mazowiecka.

The secret additional protocol to the Molotov–Ribbentrop Pact provided, among other things, that Łuków would be annexed by the Soviet Union. However, due to subsequent modifications of the demarcation line, the town came again under German occupation. On October 4, the Soviets left Łuków, followed by five hundred Jews, who crossed the Bug River into the Soviet occupation zone. "Before pulling out," writes Shlomo Prengel, town councilor and one of the witnesses quoted in *Le Livre de Lukow*, "the Red Army made evacuation possible to all willing to leave."[17] His brother, Hershel Prengler, confirms: "The Russians offered to take all those willing to leave, and even entire families took advantage of the offer."[18]

On October 5, "the Germans returned to town."[19] Having seized Łuków again, the Nazis destroyed a synagogue, plundered Jewish stores, and humiliated local Jews. Leibish Barn testified: "I was on the street when the butcher Awigdor passed by. An SS officer approached me and said: 'I'll show you how to clean the streets.' He summoned Awigdor and told him to take off his hat and collect trash in it until the street was clean. Awigdor spent all day filling in his flat cap with trash and carrying it to a pile. Finally, the SS officer told him to lie on it and buried him in it by raking the trash with his foot."[20]

At the turn of November and December 1939, having returned from the country where she had been sent by her parents, Helen Biderman found the town full of shouting Germans, closed Jewish workshops and stores, children selling their last valuables, and German soldiers, Gestapo men, and members of the *Schutzpolizei* who set dogs on the kids until they bled.[21] An atmosphere of intensifying terror was also mentioned by Barbara Lipińska, a Polish witness, whose account was written down by Krzysztof Czubaszek: "The persecution of the Łuków Jews began. They were forced to wear Star of David armbands and had all kinds of duties and prohibitions. They had to obey them on pain of death. Sometimes, I saw groups of Jews driven by armed Germans to forced labor. They were ordered to sing. There was a very popular song at that time, with the refrain 'Our Śmigły-Rydz is worth nil / But the golden Hitler will teach us how to work.'"[22]

The new mayor of Łuków, Landrat Fischel, was a German; the German authorities established posts of German gendarmerie, railway police, and auxiliary police made up of *Volksdeutsche* (ethnic Germans) from the *Sonderdienst*.[23] Łuków was also a garrison for the 101st and 104th Order Police battalions and one of "SS-Totenkopf" battalions.

In December 1939, Fischel established a *Judenrat*, with twelve members and Mosze Aron Wajntraub as chairman. The *Judenrat*, in turn, created the Jewish police, headed by Salomon "Salk" Cukierman. In order to help the local needy, in November 1940 the *Judenrat* established an isolation hospital for twenty-five patients. Its director, Dr. Pikielny, had to deal with a typhus epidemic as well as several cases of tuberculosis. Pikielny took in far more patients than the hospital could hold.[24]

In November and December 1939, the first transports of deportees from the northeast (Suwałki) and towns north of Warsaw (Nasielsk, Serock) arrived in Łuków (a total of 3,550 Jews). Their final destination was not specified. First, they headed for Königsberg and toward Łuków and Międzyrzec. The Jews on the train had traveled for thirty-six hours without food or water; around 1,000 were sent to Kock. Łuków took in around 2,500 deportees, who could only rely on other Jews.[25] A committee to help the deportees was set up under the auspices of the Jewish community and Chairman Wajntraub, an important figure even before the war, who undertook to relocate most of the arrivals among Łuków families, with the others staying in prayer houses.[26] Most of the deportees' travel expenses were covered by the Joint, and the rest were covered by the Jewish community. The funds soon ran out due to many demands by the subsequent Jewish communities that took in deportees, as well as limits on help imposed by the Germans.[27] "The living conditions were very hard. So many people were dying that some bodies were buried after a three-day wait."[28]

From 1940, the Jews were sent to various labor camps. The most notorious was the camp at Łapiguz[29] near Łuków, but there were several in the area, big and small: Dminin,[30] Ulan, Stanin,[31] Adamów, and especially Rogoźnica. Jews from the Ulan camp (a village fifteen kilometers from Łuków), established in the fall of 1940 and liquidated on October 31, 1942, worked on a river-widening project.[32] This is how Leibish Barn, one of the chief witnesses whose testimony can be found in *Le Livre de Lukow*, describes this work:

> "In May 1940, an order was issued that summoned all Jews aged 16–60 to gather in the market square. From there we were sent to Rogosznice [Rogoźnica], Domnik [?] and Zarce [?], some 7 km from Mezritcch [Międzyrzec]. There were 500 of us, Łuków Jews. Our job was to widen the river that ran through the town to the width of 15 m. The camp commandant, named Lishko, a scumbag, proclaimed a roll call because two water resource management officials were visiting. During the presentation, Leibl, son of Józef the baker, fainted. Lishko lifted him up and shot him. This was the first death among us. A short while later, they also shot Leibl Karpikacz".[33]

In 1940, the Jews were forced to work on the Łuków railway station and at reconstructing the buildings of a German firm owned by Richard Reckman. Thanks to the testimony of Abram Chaim Sylbersztejn, deposited in 1947 at the Jewish Historical Institute, his experiences at that time were recorded:

> When the war broke out in 1939, I was living in Łuków. The Germans marched into Łuków on September 18 [actually 17] 1939. Richard Reckmann came to Łuków in 1940 and set up a construction company, which had its headquarters in the station building. Reckmann was the owner. The firm laid new railway tracks, running from Łuków station to the woods, where a car with weapons and ammunition was placed in order

to protect them in case of an air raid. All these jobs were done by Jews, forcibly assigned by the German *Arbeitsamt* [labor office] on Reckmann's demand.[34] Every Jew marked by the *Arbeitsamt* received an order from the labor office to report at Reckmann's firm for forced labor. On average, Reckmann employed 1,000 Jews. The Jews did only menial work. The foremen and supervisors were all Volksdeutsche. By 1942, Jewish professionals also did menial work.

Work started at 8 am and ended at 8 pm, with two hours for lunch. When a Jew was sick and failed to turn up for work for one day, Reckmann would immediately inform the Radzyń Gestapo and the Jew was taken away, never to return. There were also many cases of denunciation of Jewish workers by Reckmann to the Gestapo, which brought in Gestapo functionaries from Radzyń who executed the Jews on the spot in the town administration yard. That is how, after Reckmann's denunciation, the following people died in 1942, shot by the Gestapo: 1. Wolant Majer; 2. his son Wolant Izrael; 3. Slodzian Pinchas; 4. his son Slodzian Szachna; 5. another son of his—I don't recall his name; 6. Ochman Chaskiel; 7. Lichtenstein Szmuel.

At the same time, some 20 other people were shot—I don't recall their names. The *Volksdeutsche* supervisors would beat us when we worked, often until we bled. For our work, Reckmann paid us around two zlotys a day, which wouldn't buy a piece of bread. I also worked for Reckmann."[35]

Christopher Browning writes that after the war, one of the German policemen who guarded the Jewish workers confirmed that they "received practically nothing to eat," adding "even though they had to work for us."[36]

The Jews were also directed to the neighboring camps. Apart from work at Reckmann's firm, they also loaded and unloaded railway cars at the station and worked at the armaments depot and SS storeroom. The craftsmen did jobs for the SS, the gendarmerie, and the town's administration. The women, in contrast, were employed at Dieter Dietz's poultry farm that supplied the eastern front.[37] The two firms, Reckmann and Dietz, appear in a noticeable number of testimonies.[38]

—⁂—

On December 17, 1940, a transport of 957 Jews from Mława (situated some one hundred kilometers north of Warsaw) who had been expelled from the Wartheland, arrived in Łuków. The need to provide help to them became ever more pressing with the passing months of 1941. A branch of the ŻSS[39] opened in Łuków in early 1941; its aim was to support the deportees. The branch's establishment was approved by the *Kreishauptmann* (county governor) of Radzyń.

Three local notable individuals run this organization: Moszko Lejzerzon, Moszko Farel Fiszbajn, and Fiszel Rozenberg.[40]

Interestingly, at the same time, a competing organization was set up by the Łuków *Judenrat*, which was in turn approved by the Łuków *Landkommissar*. Its representatives were Mendel Zaremba, Szloma Rozenfeld, and Abram Prengler. Ultimately, the Kraków headquarters of the ŻSS decided that its representation was the latter organization. "It is hard to say," Czubaszek writes, "why this faction had won and not the other one. Perhaps it won the support of a distinguished Nazi official. All that hustle was a result of the clashes between different interest groups and the ordinary fight for survival. What was at stake was probably not only the desire to help the poor and the deportees, but also access to aid funds from ŻSS and the Joint."[41]

Naturally, in early 1941, when the fate of the Jews did not yet appear sealed, the chance to be employed by the ŻSS seemed very attractive. The new leadership was accused of nepotism and dismissed on October 31, 1941. Another branch of the ŻSS was appointed by the Germans on January 8, 1942. The chairman was Szachna Biderman, and the members were Mordko Morgensztern and Józef Żyto.

These institutions helped the neediest of the Jewish population. In 1941, they gave out two thousand meals. That May, a soup kitchen for children was opened, which provided meals for 145 boys under the age of fourteen.[42] Similar plans were possibly made for girls, but due to inadequate funds, the ŻSS branch had to reduce the number of meals to 470. That year, the ŻSS headquarters regularly allocated funds to the Łuków branch, quite aware that the local Jewish population had to care for some "2,000 refugees and an equal number of the local poor."[43]

From the beginning of 1942, the allocated subsidies became increasingly smaller, although the ŻSS branch was still able to distribute 1,700 meals a day. On April 1, 1942, a Women's Circle was established, which undertook to help all of the most needy who were unable to use the people's kitchen, a total of fifty families.[44] Funds for this came from contributions of Łuków's Jews, who paid between one and five zlotys a week. The arrival of over two thousand Jewish refugees from Slovakia on May 8 and 9, despite emergency help by the Kraków headquarters, made the matters considerably worse.

Individual refugees, such as Halina Bartosiak from the Warsaw ghetto, arrived in Łuków: "There were rumors that Łuków was a quiet place, that there was no closed ghetto, that the Jews could live there as long as they were working for the Germans (cleaning streets, or as tailors or cobblers)."[45] A similar account came from Lillian Fenster, who escaped from the Warsaw ghetto in the spring of 1941. Łuków was where her aunt lived: "We heard that there was no ghetto in Łuków."[46]

ŁUKÓW GHETTO AND THE JUDENRAT IN 1942

The "Jewish quarter" in Łuków, that is, the ghetto, was established in May 1941. Initially, it was an open area, roughly identical with the area inhabited by the Jews before the war. According to Joël Estrach's testimony,[47] some Jews lived quite well, earning good money smuggling and trading with the Warsaw ghetto. On the whole, the influential Jews, who had frequent contacts with the Poles, took advantage of them when the so-called open ghetto existed. Helen Biderman, whose family owned land near Łuków, recalls that one of her uncles supplied foodstuffs to the Germans and sent them to Warsaw as well. Because he worked for the SS, he enjoyed certain privileges. He could leave the labor camp, where they had landed. Even the less influential Jews who had good contacts with the Poles could take advantage of them at that time. When the Germans ordered Eta Wróbel's father to give over his bakery into receivership, the new baker whispered in his ear, "If you need assistance or food, please come to me, and I'll help you."[48]

"Until 1941," one surviving witness writes, "the Jews in town lived more or less normally. The calamity began when Germany invaded the Soviet Union."[49] From the summer of 1941 on, the Nazis prohibited the Jews from leaving the ghetto. Neither were they permitted to use public transport[50] or to own a dog; Eta Wrobel testifies that they had left their dog with a peasant, but the animal returned to them several times. Finally, they had to drown it.[51] The collaborative press, specifically *Nowy Głos Lubelski*, wrote about the benefits of isolating Jews. As Małgorzata Maria Opasiak-Piasecka testifies, "The author [from *Nowy Głos Lubelski*], who identified himself as '(sz)' lauded the Łuków authorities for their action, which was aimed at improving the appearance of shop displays[52]: 'So much has been done, and if work continues at this pace, let us hope that the Jew-ridden and messy Łuków will turn into a pretty and nice town.'"[53]

On November 4, 1941, the mayor of Łuków ordered announcements (*Bekanntmachung*) to be put up in German and in Polish, which upheld the governor general's decision: "'All Jews who leave their assigned district without authorization shall be punished by death. The same penalty shall be administered to those who give shelter to such Jews' ... I stress that this order concerns Łuków Jews as well."[54]

Although there are ample sources concerning Łuków, only a few focus on the first six months of 1942. Nevertheless, on the basis of several testimonies, during the early months of 1942, Nazi terror clearly intensified. "In early 1942, Mal Rozenblum and Szepsel Nasielski were murdered only because they wore flat caps during work. Several days later, some policemen raped twenty Jewish women. The cobbler Szmil Sztainberg tried to defend his wife. He was beaten to death on the spot with a hammer."[55] In his moving testimony, Stanisław Żemiński, a Polish teacher, recalls that in the spring of 1942, "the fur collection operation began. The Jews didn't give enough. As the deliveries arrived, in each town over a dozen Jews were murdered. In March of this year, 47 men, women, and children were murdered in Łuków. On April 31,[56] 49 people were murdered."[57]

In April 1942, there were 8,093 Jews, both local (from Łuków) and displaced persons. On May 8–9, 1942, 2,031 Slovak Jews arrived (many identified as Hungarian Jews). At the same time, Jewish property was put up for sale, and potential Christian buyers were given special training in trade. On this subject, Krzysztof Czubaszek recalls that the confinement of the Jews in the ghetto, then their physical liquidation, was a "blessing from heaven" for Polish craftsmen and shopkeepers.[58] The *Nowy Głos Lubelski* newspaper of April 15, 1942. reports that training for Polish traders had taken place on April 10, 1942. with high participation.[59] Another training was to take place in November. "Where does such a sudden interest for commercial training come from?" questions Czubaszek.[60]

JEWS IN KOCK AND STOCZEK ŁUKOWSKI

Apart from Łuków, the main towns in the county were Kock and Stoczek Łukowski. Kock was made famous by rabbi Menachem Mendel Morgenstern, a renowned nineteenth-century Talmudist, who brought there crowds of Hassidim. He, and later his descendants, lived in the "house with the tower" (now a local tourist attraction). This is where Józef Morgenstern, the last Kock rabbi, was killed in an air raid on September 9, 1939. The German army occupied the town in October; in November, the synagogue was burned down.

Radzyń *Kreishaptmann* Hennig von Winterfeld decided that some of the Jews would be resettled in Kock. Some 1,200–1,300 Jews were brought in from Lubartów, Nasielsk, Serock, Suwałki, and Chełm, among other places, and a *Judenrat* was established. By the end of the month, the Jewish population of Kock had risen from 2,000 to 8,000.[61] They were crammed in inhuman conditions. A typhus epidemic broke out, and many children died. One of the surviving witnesses recalls that the Jews had no choice but to go begging in the nearby villages, where they met with a warning: "'Don't let the Jews in, a Jew means typhus.' . . . The idea was to block the Jews from getting food by begging."[62]

A contribution of two kilograms of gold was imposed on the Jewish population—which they paid—and then Winterfeld permitted some to return home.[63] In April 1941, 3,191 Jews were living in Kock. Those who were to leave the ghetto were subject to the death penalty. The Jews were forced to do all kinds of jobs (e.g., drying swamps, felling trees, land irrigation).

Figure 4.1. Labor Camp for the Jews near Kock (GFH 7374).

That summer, the Kock gendarmerie arrested some Jewish inhabitants outside the town and executed them in the Jewish cemetery. On August 16–19, 1942, the Jewish Council earmarked one hundred families (four to five hundred people), mostly displaced persons, for immediate transfer to Parczew. They were then deported to Treblinka during the deportations of August 19–October 20. Reserve Police Battalion 101, stationed in Kock, supervised the deportation of a total of 1,700 Jews. One took place on September 10. In retaliation for the killing of one soldier near the village of Talczyn, Major Wilhelm Trapp, the battalion commander (who had the support of the authorities, including Globocnik himself), decided to execute all the inhabitants—two hundred people. Having killed eighty, he decided to complement the planned figure with Jews from a nearby town. In late September, over a hundred Jews were executed.[64]

From October 8 onward, hundreds of Jews were brought to the Łuków ghetto. In the Kock ghetto, now enclosed between several streets, no more than four to five hundred people were left. The successive deportations to Łuków and then to Treblinka took place on October 26–27 and on November 7–10. Fewer than thirty Kock Jews survived.

The Germans marched into Stoczek Łukowski on September 12, 1939, and began to set fire to buildings in the town center.[65] Eighty percent of the wooden houses, including the synagogue, were destroyed. Administratively, Stoczek Łukowski was part of Distrikt Warschau. Until April 1941, the *Kreishauptmann* was Dr. Hans Klein, later replaced by Dr. Carl Freudenthal, who terrorized the inhabitants with radical methods.[66] In 1939, there were 2,200 Jews in the town, while in late November 1940, this number had dropped to 1,956 in the wake of escapes to Soviet-occupied territories. In 1940, all kinds of contributions were imposed on the Stoczek Jews, but they still could trade with the local peasants. Two of them were sent to the labor camp at Chyżyny, some fourteen kilometers from Stoczek.

In 1941, the Jewish population rose to 2,450, and then to 2,950 the following April (according to other estimates, 3,330); that is, 15 percent of the entire Kreis Garwolin.[67]

In 1940, the Stoczek Jewish Council opened a soup kitchen that gave out six hundred meals to poor Jews, financed by the Joint. "The Jewish population of the town," wrote Aron Heller, the chairman, "is 1,956, of whom 1,200 need help."[68] He added that the Jewish quarter burned down completely and was not rebuilt.

The Stoczek ghetto was established in late 1941, but it was not fenced in. The total number of ghetto dwellers exceeded five thousand due to the influx of Jews from nearby ghettos, including the Warsaw ghetto. The town also absorbed many Poles expelled from the Poznań region (Wielkopolska). "From 1941 on," recalled a Stoczek survivor, Henry (Hersz) Rubinstein, "we were locked up in the town."[69]

LUKOW JEWS BEFORE DEPORTATION

When Operation Reinhardt began in March 1942, the ghettos were set to be liquidated one by one. On August 19, Jews were deported from Parczew; on August 25–26, from Międzyrzec; and on October 1, from Radzyń. As of June 1, 1942, the administration of the Łuków ghetto fell into the hands of SS officer Josef Bürger (Security Police). His deputy was Anton Neumann, a local *Volksdeutsch*.

The Jewish Council already had a new chairman, Hersz Lejzor Lender. The former chairman, Mosze Wajntraub, had been arrested by the Germans in October 1940 for unknown reasons. According to some, it was due to his involvement in the resistance movement; others claimed that it was embezzlement. But primarily the accusation was appropriating parcels with clothing that were to be sent to the front by the Joint.[70]

The Jews in the Łuków ghetto knew about the deportations. Lender tried to humor the Germans by bringing them gifts, especially to the head of Radzyń County. The German authorities ordered Lender to inform Łuków ghetto inhabitants that there would be no deportation, because 80 percent of the Jews worked for German firms. "Even before the first 'operation' aimed at extermination of Jews from our town," indicated an anonymous Łuków survivor, "incredible news started reaching us, ever more terrible. The news concerned Warsaw, Nowomińsk, Lublin, Lubartów, Chełm, etc. Those Jews who had fled from there, came to us. Among them, there were a few who had jumped out of a train heading for Treblinka. These people told us of the horrific suffering they experienced at the hands of the Nazi bandits. Stories of unbelievable acts of sadism toward women and the elderly were blood-curdling. Day by day, the atmosphere was becoming ever more hopeless. We were moving in circles like madmen. We couldn't sleep and kept thinking all the time how to find help. People would turn to the Jewish Council and to its chairman, asking what would happen. Why do we do nothing? Why do we keep quiet when we are in a tight spot? The reply was that we must work. Probably, the Germans won't harm those who work for them. And thus the race began. Everybody did all he could to find a job that could guarantee survival."[71]

The idea that work could guarantee survival was undoubtedly one of the primary survival strategies. Virtually everyone was convinced that one could avoid deportation through working. All the testimonies contain information about desperate searches for work, even unpaid or sorely underpaid. Being productive was considered a pass to extended life.[72] Susan Weiss says that in Kock, she risked her life "because I wasn't working."[73] Even children were sent to gather herbs—it was a kind of work, and by the same token also a kind of protection, relates Helen Biderman. Similarly, the testimony of Annette Smilovic, who was aged eleven or twelve then, is full of positive references to work. Even as an elderly lady, in the last months of her life, she still believed that those who had some kind of a job were protected, and when she recalled her own survival, she expressed her conviction that she survived thanks to working in the Dęblin labor camp, in the kitchen and looking after small children.[74]

At that time many Jews were also preparing hideouts, another survival strategy.[75]

> One had to prepare hideouts for family members—wives, children, and parents. One worked in the utmost secrecy, even from the neighbors, mainly at night, digging bunkers, where one could hide during an *Aktion*. Those who managed to escape from other towns told us that the Gestapo acted according to a preset plan—they were ordered to murder a given number of Jews... Chairman Lender did not waste any time. He often visited the German commandant and brought him valuable things, in order to postpone the deportation... Delegations traveled both to Radzyń and to the local chief. After accepting expensive gifts, this murderer assured that nothing bad would happen to the Łuków Jews, because 80 percent of them were employed by the German authorities.... All the beautiful declarations did not put people's minds at rest. They felt instinctively that

they were not to be believed, that they were made only to damp down our vigilance—the operation could begin any moment. That is why people kept watch in every house, and through the slits in the shutters monitored the streets. If we saw the Gestapo and the Ukrainians surround the town, we would have time to hide. For weeks we lived tormented, awaiting death that could come at any moment.[76]

Łuków Jews were perfectly aware of the noose that was tightening around their necks. Everybody also knew that *"Aktionen* were preceded by robbery."[77] After fur collection came stealing gold:

> The SS ordered the Jewish Council to deliver 10 kg of gold. Otherwise, they threatened to shoot half of Łuków's Jews. The Commission summoned people in the synagogue yard. The Council members took the floor and read out those verses of the Torah that concern the obligation to buy out one's life. The women were expected to set an example of faith, that God would help, and offer their wedding rings and jewelry. People started arguing about who was richer. People started throwing accusations at each other. The Council, assisted by Jewish police, detained the greediest. Through torment and starvation of Jews, success was achieved, and they were deprived of all gold jewelry. In the *Judenrat* building, the watchmaker Fiszel assessed and weighed all the delivered items and signed receipts. Four days later, the community chairman carried all the collected gold to the Gestapo, and received a guarantee of safety for the Jews in return. The Nazi murderers took the gold and at the same time lied that the town would be safe, that the Łuków Jews could work in peace.[78]

The Jewish police appears in a number of testimonies. In 1947, the few survivors associated with the Łuków Jewish Committee published the brochure *Lukower kdoszim un heldn*,[79] together with the Jewish Historical Commission. In it they described a group of Jewish policemen from Łuków who, together with their commander, "denounced the Jews, beat them up, and thus helped the Gestapo force them to surrender gold. Each new act of harassment was also a new source of income. Collaboration with the Germans brought them enormous wealth."[80]

In mid-September 1942, the Security Police ordered that the ghetto be surrounded with a barbed-wire fence. Stanisław Żemiński recalls that thanks to the contribution of the ten kilograms of gold and the fact that the ghetto was not closed in any way, the Łuków Jews, unlike the Jews in other nearby towns, were able to take advantage of postponed deportation. Krzysztof Czubaszek, referring to *Fahranordnung 586*, argues that the Jews were to be deported from Łuków as early as August 28. A train of twenty-five cars was to leave Łuków at

10:44 a.m. and arrive in Treblinka at 2:52 p.m., only to return to Łuków at 3:22 p.m.[81] The transport was temporarily halted because the Treblinka machinery of death was incapable of gassing and burning so many victims.[82]

LIQUIDATION OF GHETTOS IN STOCZEK ŁUKOWSKI AND ŁUKÓW

In the second half of September 1942 ("between Rosh Hashanah and Yom Kippur, around 5:00–6:00 a.m.," recalls Henry Rubinstein), most Jews from Stoczek Łukowski were deported to Treblinka via Parysów (some seventeen kilometers away), and probably via Sobolew, which became a transit point for different ghettos, including Stoczek. "It must have been Wednesday, because the day before was a market day, as every Tuesday," says Henry Rubinstein. "We did not expect that. We had to leave our things and go. Some were permitted to take something, some trolleys, everyone ran around, the elderly couldn't walk, others were murdered on the spot. One guy from the town carried his mother on his back for 23–25 km, and the Germans walked by him. We were heading for nearby Parysów."[83]

According to other sources, mostly Polish witnesses, the main deportation took place on September 12, the first day of Rosh Hashanah, the Jewish New Year.[84] The Germans surrounded the town, while Polish police and firemen drove people out of their homes and to the marketplace. Fireman Stanisław Sitkiewicz recalled when he was keeping watch at the fire station on the night of September 11–12, lest any Jew escape from Stoczek: "I didn't see anything special, but at dawn on September 12, some German appeared in the marketplace and through a metal bullhorn started to summon the Jews to gather round him. Several minutes later, he was surrounded by a group of lamenting Jews."[85] In the marketplace, some of the trolleys were taken by peasants, while the infirm, the elderly, and children were put on the remaining ones. The rest had to walk to Parysów—two thousand people, escorted by German soldiers with dogs. During the march, two hundred people were murdered.[86] The Stoczek Jews, together with those from the nearby ghettos (Łaskarzew, Żelechów, and particularly Maciejowice), waited in Parysów for ten days for transport to Treblinka, which was dispatched between September 27 and 30, 1942. The operation was carried out by the local gendarmerie and Polish police (aided by KdS[87] Warschau and the resettlement commando from Warsaw).[88] The Jews were murdered at Treblinka on October 2.

Several witnesses confirm that following the deportation of the Jews, robberies took place. Michalina Świątek, born in 1924, recalled, "I am ashamed to mention this, but that's how it was. Some plundered and stole Jewish property. I myself heard a German guard, probably from Poznań, because he spoke Polish, say loudly: 'Now, I wonder who'll be taking your things!'"[89] Local Poles were also involved in hunts for the Jews near Stoczek Łukowski, which were initiated by the Germans. During one such operation, the brothers Jojne, who lived in Toczyska (four kilometers from Stoczek), were murdered by a neighbor; others were denounced for a kilogram of sugar (Wola Kisielska).[90]

Some neighbors tried to rescue the Jews. One of them was Barbara Nowelska (1919–2012), who lived in a manor in Zgórznica, some two kilometers from Stoczek. The manor was an underground AK (*Armia Krajowa*, Home Army) cell, where, incidentally, many Germans use to stay. The young Chaim Lehrman arrived at the mansion in late October 1942. "We hid him above the cowshed," Nowelska recalls, "and for many weeks I brought him food. There were still Germans in the house. One evening, Chaimek came to them and asked them to shoot him. He could not go on like this. I did talk to him every day, but never realized he couldn't take it anymore. He was only sixteen. And I could have taken him home. The barn was large. Forgive me, Chaimek."[91]

Only several dozen Jews from Stoczek Łukowski survived, most of them in the Soviet Union. Aron Heller, the Chairman of the Jewish Council, immigrated to the United States after the war.

The deportation of Jews from Łuków and Łuków County to Treblinka was carried out in stages. Many were shot and buried in mass graves in a forest near Malcanów, some four kilometers from Łuków.

On the morning of October 5, 1942, the Łuków ghetto was surrounded by detachments of the Security Police from Radzyń, 101st Reserve Police Battalion, SS auxiliary formations (composed of Ukrainians, Lithuanians, and Latvians), gendarmes, ethnic Germans, and Polish policemen. The Jews were ordered to assemble in the marketplace on Międzyrzecka Street, and those who refused to leave the ghetto, as well as at the infirm and hospital staff, were shot. Men fit to work were separated from the women, children, and elderly. German employers read out the names of those who were exempt from deportation. Five hundred Jews and eleven *Judenrat* members, including Chairman Lender, were murdered on the spot. Around four thousand women and the elderly were marched toward the train station, from where they were deported to Treblinka.

On October 8, the Germans declared that all the remaining Jews, including those in hiding, were to report to the *Judenrat* to have their employment papers stamped anew. Two thousand people came and were immediately sent to Treblinka.[92] Bürger ordered the creation of a Jewish firefighting service to help the Polish police "clean" the apartments of deported Jews; he also ordered

Figure 4.2. Jews being humiliated by smiling Germans, Łuków, October 5, 1942 (YVA, 117FO3).

a "sanitary" group set up that would help the Jewish police and the *Hevra Kadisha*[93] bury the bodies of people murdered near Malcanów. The entire Łuków County was scrupulously combed by the Nazis. "In mid-October they brought to Łuków Jews from Adamów (1,724 people), Wojcieszków (213 people), the Stanin commune (460 people), the Ulan commune (446 people), as well as from Kock, Tuchowicz, and Trzebieszów."[94]

Another deportation of Jews from Łuków took place on October 27, 1942. Several hundred people were deported to Treblinka, and dozens were murdered on the spot. As was previously stated, the following day, October 28, Krüger permitted the reestablishment of the Łuków ghetto. In the hamlets and villages around Łuków, the Nazis hunted for those Jews who had managed to survive the *Aktion*. On November 6, 1942, Reserve Police Battalion 101 brought 600 Jews from Kock to Łuków.

Stanisław Żemiński describes the third deportation, which was carried out on November 7:

> Yesterday came the third deportation of Jews from Łuków. This time, I happened to witness this crime. I was planning to go to Trzebieszów, and had already left home. In the marketplace, I came across a crowd of Jews crammed tightly in one group, surrounded by Ukrainians. Individual shots showed that they guarded their victims well. A cold, windy, foggy day. They were kept in that square all day. At dusk, the crowd was escorted to the station. The road ran through our streets, right by our house. I was doing some digging in the garden when I heard thick gunfire; I came up to the street, where an enormous procession of 2,000–3,000 people crammed against each other marched on.[95]

Around three thousand Jews were deported to Treblinka, including those who were working and were taken to the train straight from their workplace. Browning writes, "During this final deportation, many Jews had apparently been hiding tenaciously. After the trains left, the Security Police employed a ruse to lure the surviving Jews from their concealment. It was announced throughout the ghetto that new identity cards would be issued. Anyone who reported for his card would be spared; anyone found without one would be shot immediately. Hoping at least for another brief respite between deportations, desperate Jews emerged from their hiding places and reported. After at least 200 Jews had been collected, they were marched outside Lukow and shot on November 11. Another group was collected and shot on November 14... In retaliation for the failure of the Jewish ghetto police to report hidden Jews, the Order Police carried out a shooting of 40 to 50 Jews."[96]

All those captured in Łuków were taken to Malcanów and shot there, mainly on November 11 and 14. That means that the "SS ghetto administrator, Josef Bürger, had 500 to 600 Jews shot in December to reduce the [Łuków] ghetto population."[97]

―――

In early 1943, in the Łuków ghetto, which was now reduced to three streets, there remained only workers of Dietz's poultry farm, Reckmann's firm, and SS storehouses. Already on October 28 of the previous year, the ghetto was granted the status of a "work ghetto."[98] The ghetto fence, dismantled during the *Aktion*, was put up again. Those born in Łuków accounted for 20–30 percent of the three to four thousand ghetto inhabitants.[99] There was also a sizeable group of Slovaks and Hungarians who had been deported to Łuków, as well as Jews from other places.

On May 2, 1943, the last of Łuków's Jews, some three to four thousand were deported to Treblinka. "The sound of gunfire was heard all day," Jakow Keselbrener recalls. "In the evening, through the hole which was our bunker's air inlet, we heard the shouts and shots die down. Then, the four of us, [me] with my brother Herszel, Aaron Erlich, and Abraham Wisznia, went out onto the street. It was empty and everything was swamped in darkness. There were many dead bodies lying around. One could see shadows sweeping by—those were Poles who ran to the deserted houses. The ghetto was guarded by the Polish police, which had been on alert after the ultimate Jewish sacrifice."[100]

WHAT WAS A GOOD SURVIVAL STRATEGY?

During the first years of the German occupation, the chief survival strategies were as follows.

- Persistent searching for work
- Searching for hideouts (in and outside the ghetto), out of fear of imminent events throughout the German occupation, especially preceding the ghetto liquidation (October 5, 1942) and during its final liquidation (May 3, 1943)
- Attempts (successful or not) to jump out of a train headed for Treblinka

To assess the survival strategies of Jews in Łuków County after the liquidation of the ghettos, it is necessary to summarize the figures—bearing in mind that the figures given are estimations.[101]

STATISTICS

Number of Jews

Table 4.3 Ghetto population on the eve of liquidations operations (county)

Murdered in Treblinka	13,000 out of 15,988	81.3%
Murdered during an *Aktion*	1,300 out of 15,988	8.1%
Hiding in the county	986 out of 15,988	6.16%
Murdered by Poles	356 out of 2,409	14.77%
Murdered by Poles among those hiding in the county	356 out of 986	36.1%

Table 4.4 Ghetto population on the eve of liquidation operations

Łuków ghetto	Kock ghetto	Stoczek Łukowski ghetto	Total
9,950 Jews in October 1942 (including Jews from Slovakia and other places)*	3,300 Jews in March 1942 (including other places)†; 3,138 Jews in July 1942‡	2,900 Jews in March 1942§	15,988

Source: Author's study based on collected documents.
* Documentation in Zentrale Stelle der Landesjustizverwaltungen in Ludwigsburg, currently Bundesarchiv Ludwigsburg (hereafter BAL), B 162/2184, Trial file of Fritz Fischer.
† Archiwum Akt Nowych (hereafter AAN), Rada Główna Opiekuńcza (RGO), March 1942.
‡ BAL, B 162/2184, Trial file of Fritz Fischer.
§ AAN, Rada Główna Opiekuńcza, March 1942.

Table 4.5 Jews murdered between April 1942 and late 1944 (Łuków County), except for organized actions

Circumstances	Number of Jews murdered	Percentage of Jews murdered
Murdered by the Germans without denunciation	1,435	59.57
Murdered by the Germans, circumstances unknown	342	14.2
Murdered by the Germans following denunciation	276	11.46
Murdered by Poles	356	14.77
—Murdered by peasants	250*	10.37
—Captured by neighbors and handed over to Polish police	75	3.11
—Murdered by Polish policemen without denunciation	13	0.54
—Murdered by the Home Army (AK)	18	0.75
TOTAL	**2,409**	**100**

Source: Author's study based on collected documents.
* Estimates of those murdered range from 224 to 291.

Table 4.6 Jews murdered from October 1942 (Łuków County), year by year, except organized operations

Period	Number of Jews murdered	Percentage of Jews murdered
October–November 1942	1,699	70.53
1943	544	22.58
1944	5	0.21
1945	2	0.08
no data	159	6.6
TOTAL	**2,409**	**100**

Source: Author's study based on collected documents.

WHAT DO THESE STATISTICS TELL US?

Obviously by the very nature of these statistics, it is impossible to present precise figures. Some of them are rounded up (for example, the number of Jews murdered in Treblinka, 13,000, or the number of Jews murdered in operations, 1,300). Other figures are more precise because they come from the bottom up, that is, all the available data concerning each person (mainly from testimonies, trials, etc.).

Naturally, they intersect but do not necessarily overlap, creating a certain margin of data discrepancy. The rounded-up figures come from diverse estimations, whereas the figures referring to precise field observation concern specifically identified persons.

Tables 5 and 6 are based on different sources, but chiefly on direct survivor accounts and trial documents. By their very nature, the data are fragmentary and rather indicative of certain tendencies.

1. To begin with, it should be emphasized that the Nazi death industry in Łuków County was extremely effective. If those Jews who fled to the Soviet Union and later returned to Poland (216 people) are left out, survivors account for 0.86 percent, that is, around 140 people of the total Jewish population of the county (as of 1939).[102] Among the 140 survivors from Łuków County, there are 63 men, 24 women, 28 children, and 17 survivors who had lived in Łuków County before the war, but we do not know where they survived the occupation (after the war they settled in the United States), and eight unidentified persons.

2. The Germans (SS, Order Police, Gestapo, gendarmerie, etc.) and the auxiliary formations (Ukrainians, etc.) were the chief perpetrators.
3. An overwhelming majority (13,000 Jews, i.e., 81 percent) were deported to Treblinka and murdered there. In addition, 1,300 Jews (8.1 percent) were murdered in the subsequent *Aktionen*.
4. The number of Jews murdered in Łuków County during 1942–1944 who sought refuge with the Poles (following escape from a transport or a ghetto), is 2,409 of 15,988, that is, 13 percent. Eighty-five percent of those deaths were by responsibility. Jews were murdered either as part of retaliatory measures (Serokomla, Kock) or in some other way.
5. What about the Polish side? If the number of all the Jews murdered is taken into consideration, Polish responsibility for Jewish deaths is marginal. But it ceases to be marginal if the essence of this discussion, the survival strategy of escaping Jews in the years 1942–1944, is referred to. Polish responsibility can be directly estimated at almost 15 percent of Jewish deaths among those seeking shelter (14.77 percent of 2,409 murdered).
6. This responsibility is even greater when the number of Jews seeking help and murdered by Poles in the years 1942–1944 is taken into consideration. This number is 356 murdered out of 986 hiding Jews, that is, 36.1 percent. It is impossible to determine the scale of responsibility of the Polish police or the AK, but murders of Jews by peasants account for a considerable figure—25.3 percent (i.e., 250 out of 986). If the cases of 75 Jews captured by peasants (7.6 percent out of 986 in hiding) and handed over to Polish police, which was tantamount to death, are included, the peasants are responsible for the death of 33.64 percent of Jewish victims. If Jews murdered by the Germans following denunciation (276) are added, Polish responsibility rises to 632 killed, that is, 64 percent of Jews seeking help.
7. This number is statistically irrelevant in comparison with the overall number of Jewish victims murdered by the Germans, but it is very significant if the chance of finding shelter in Polish countryside—or rather the lack of it—is taken into consideration. This shows that for the Jews, the Polish countryside was an open-air prison.
8. When the experiences of the survivors are analyzed, it is hard to draw any definite conclusions on the basis of such a small number of cases (140). Successful survival strategies are known of only with respect to 39 out of 140 survivors. One way or another, the following proportions emerge:

- 30 percent—hidden with peasants
- 25 percent—roaming
- 15 percent—in a partisan unit
- 9.17 percent—adopting an Aryan identity
- 8.33 percent—hiding in the woods (e.g., in a bunker)
- 5.83 percent—temporarily in a barn (sometimes unbeknownst to the farmers)

These strategies, often adopted spontaneously, were never exclusive and frequently cumulated. Tables 7 and 8 show certain tendencies in the adopted survival strategies, identified mainly on the basis of survivor testimonies.

Table 4.7 Survival strategies of Jews seeking help (survivors and victims)

Strategies	Number of Jews	Percentage
With peasants	136	47.72
In the woods	74	25.96
Roaming	40	14.04
In the woods and with peasants	11	3.86
In a partisan units	15	5.26
Adopting an Aryan identity	8	2.81
In a barn and adopting an Aryan identity	1	0.35
TOTAL	**285**	**100**

Source: Author's study based on collected documents.

Table 7 shows that out of 285 survival attempts (successful or not), nearly half (47.72 percent) were connected with seeking help from peasants, a quarter (25.96 percent) with hiding in the woods, and 14.04 percent with roaming. Other strategies accounted for less than 15 percent.

The survival strategies of the survivors and those murdered will now be compared, constantly bearing in mind that the calculations are relative because they are based on partial data. Table 7 contains all the strategies about which there is information (39 out of 140; there is no data concerning the survival strategies of 101 survivors).

Analysis of the data in Table 8 leads to several conclusions.

Table 4.8 Summary of survival strategies together with percentages

Strategies	All strategies for those murdered	Percentage of people murdered for a given strategy	All strategies for survivors	Percentage of survivors for a given strategy	Total
With peasants	120	88.2	16	11.8	136
In the woods	73	98.6	1	1.4	74
Roaming	30	75	10	25	40
In the woods and with peasants	10	90.9	1	9.1	11
In partisan units	7	46.7	8	53.3	15
Adopting an Aryan identity	5	50	5	50	10
In a barn and adopting an Aryan identity	1	100	0	0.0	1
TOTAL	246	86.3	39	13.7	285

Source: Author's study based on collected documents.

1. Out of 285 attempts made (Table 7), an overwhelming majority (246, i.e., 86.3 percent) are cases of those who lost their lives, and only 39 (13.7 percent), a definite minority, succeeded in surviving.
2. A great majority of the strategies most frequently adopted by those Jews who were ultimately murdered proved hopeless. Those include hiding in the woods (98.6 percent deaths), hiding with peasants (88.2 percent deaths), and combining hiding in the woods with hiding with a peasant (90.9 percent). Other strategies (partisan units, 46.7 percent; change of identity, 50 percent; roaming, 75 percent) turned out to be more effective, although at the same time, they were far less frequent (at least for identity change and partisan units).
3. The most successful strategies were partisan combat (53.3 percent), identity change (50 percent, although this calculation is based only on five cases), and roaming (25 percent). Combined strategies do not seem more effective.

Combined or not, on the whole, survival strategies do not seem effective. Joining a partisan unit was the only strategy that ended with death least frequently than all those discussed here, whereas seeking shelter with peasants was a solution that ended with death most often.

The survival strategies presented earlier on the basis of several survivors' stories will now be examined, in diminishing order of survival likelihood.

Partisan Unit, Armed Combat

Joining the partisans in the woods was the aim pursued by some young Jews, eventually survivors. Eta Wrobel (1918–2008) recalls how she left the Łuków ghetto and, with a group of several friends, joined a partisan unit. In the camp, where her friends took her, about sixty Jews from Lublin had already found shelter. It was located around "6 km from Łuków"—probably somewhat farther—in the heart of a forest. They had two bunkers, or, rather, two holes in the ground. The main problem was acquiring weapons. Eta Wrobel, who came from a wealthy Łuków family, knew many Poles and tried to utilize her contacts to that end. People did not necessarily realize that she was Jewish because she always wore a cross around her neck.

Wrobel's testimony raises the question regarding the behavior of the partisans during an armed operation. In her group, there was a rule that no gentile found in the vicinity could be left alive—the risk of denunciation was too high. The partisans also watched over Jews kept by Polish peasants. In case of denunciation of those hiding, they threatened to burn the farm. They watched over

Marianna Adameczek (1930–2017), among others, who upon her father's request was placed in a hideout at neighbors in their home village of Charlejów. She recalls that armed Jews would come regularly to check if she was safe there. The peasants who sheltered Marianna Adameczek experienced danger everywhere, first from their neighbors who were hunting for Jews, and then from members of the Jewish underground. Both would visit them, and it was not the partisans that were the worst. As for Wrobel's group, they stole chickens and robbed Poles who plundered Jewish homes.

Anshel Katz, who was hiding in a barn, recalls that the peasants "brought Home Army people," who wanted him to tell them where the "armed Jews" were. They beat him up, but he managed to get to a nearby forest: "There, I met a group of well-armed Łukowians [Jews]. They threatened the peasants with weapons to have them take us in. I was with Frida Ploug and Nisen Hirszberg. Three weeks later, our friends came to take us to a new hideout. There we stayed until liberation, miraculously saved!"[103]

These cases of survival thanks to armed resistance in the woods should not sideline the terrible scale of loses of the members of the Jewish resistance movement. One of the most poignant examples is the story of the Jews of Adamów, some twenty-two kilometers from Łuków. When the local Jews realized that deportation was imminent, they decided to defend themselves. Around fifty Jews hid in an enormous hideout in the woods, equipped with weapons and stored food. Some members of the Jewish police joined the group as well. They hoped that contacts with Polish policemen would help them find out when a liquidation *Aktion* was scheduled.

When the Adamów Jews heard about the Łuków deportation, they expected an assault any time, especially since in the nearby village of Krzywda, some eight kilometers away, the Germans and the Ukrainians carried out an exceptionally bloody *Aktion* against Jewish families. In late October 1942, the *Judenrat* found out that the Adamów Jews would be deported to Łuków and placed in the homes of Jews who had been deported from the town. The Polish voit of Adamów, who, as Grinbaum[104] stresses, gladly collaborated with the Germans, set the deportation date for October 30. The Jews were ordered to be ready. However, it turned out that a purposely "later date" had been given. Adamów was surrounded by a cordon of German gendarmerie, Ukrainians, and Polish policemen as early as October 26. The Jews were resettled to Łuków and then deported. Around three hundred of them (the elderly, women, and those who could not get on a truck) were shot on the outskirts and buried five hundred meters from the execution site.[105] Following this event, partisans freed several dozen Jews from the Adamów prison and murdered the Poles who helped with the deportation.

Soon afterward, a German detachment arrived in the area, organized a roundup in the woods, and shot seventy Jews hiding near Wojcieszków.

Irving Lumerman, who immigrated to the United States after the war, recalls that as a small child, he roamed the woods for two years. He came across several groups of Jews, including one made up of young people, who "walked barefoot or with one's feet covered with rags"[106] and were particularly aggressive and vengeful. Vindictive violence is something that another survivor, Many Orlinski, also mentions. He recalls that his "forest group" had weapons "bought for a pig." Having found out that some peasants had denounced Jews to the Germans, they poured gasoline on their farm buildings. "Only the farmers' son managed to get out of the fire, but he was shot. There is nothing to hide: It was the right move."[107] Indeed, armed combat taken up by the Jews as a survival strategy was ultimately the best choice in the light of (limited) statistics. This confirms what Claude Lanzmann used to call the "rediscovery of violence by the Jews."

Adopting an Aryan Identity, Change of Surname

Changing one's identity was difficult; actually, one should rather speak of individual cases of changing identity in Łuków County, perhaps even of mechanisms rather than strategies. There are five known cases of adopting an Aryan identity, including three of surname change.[108] Interestingly, these examples concern females: two young girls, Lilian Fenster[109] (b. 1926) and Ryszka Huberman-Iwan[110] (date of birth unknown); and three little girls, Marianna Adameczek[111] (b. 1930), Estera Borensztejn[112] (b. 1932), and Irena Krawczyk (b. 1932). It was mostly peasant women who looked after these girls and young women. All were orphaned in 1942. Only Adameczek came from Łuków County; the others found themselves in the town for diverse reasons, either because they had relatives in the area, because their families believed that their stay in the Łuków ghetto would be less harsh than the existence in their own ghetto, or simply because they found themselves in Lukow after jumping off a train to Treblinka. All remained in the vicinity between 1942 and late 1944. Also, all of them worked—for a shorter or longer period of time—with a peasant, frequently changing their employer. All of them grazed cows. Three changed their surnames at some point. Krawczyk was the daughter of Frajda and Pinkus, born in Warsaw, but the testimony collected on September 21, 1948, says nothing about her Jewish roots. Adameczek's original name was Blima Kurchant, while Fenster obtained "Catholic papers."

The process of identity change connected with at least two forms of violence: initial violence resulting from the change itself, and long-term violence related to "deculturization." Perhaps Krawczyk was motivated to abandon her Jewish identity and reach for Catholicism, the religion of her rescuers? From the moment she became an orphan at the age eleven or twelve, she was receiving regular help from local Poles. She must have had a "good appearance," because nobody suspected anything. A Polish woman in Siedlce, whom she knew, took her to a church organist, who wrote her out a birth certificate with the name Irena Jakubiak without suspecting anything, Krawczyk relates. With this document, she roamed from village to village. "I met a peasant in the field and told him that I wanted to work as a servant," she recalls in her testimony. "He took me to a farm owner, and they had me do the grazing. I grazed two cows. The farmer and his family had no idea that I was Jewish. I went to church, and to confession as well. Because the work conditions were bad, I left and moved on to another farm. There was also a lot of work there, and the money was scarce. I was there for two years, also after the Soviets came. I never wondered if there were any Jews there or not. They didn't know that I was Jewish, either. I had no unpleasant experiences."[113] During the occupation, Krawczyk converted to Catholicism. After the war, "Mr. Birger from the children's home in Łódź came to collect me, but I didn't want to get back to the Jews, because I had converted. And also because I didn't like the Jews. When a Jewish acquaintance from Serokomla wanted to approach me, I ran away, because I was ashamed to talk to Jews."[114]

Irena Krawczyk's testimony reflects an effective survival strategy, applied independently and successfully. The price she paid is obvious: She dropped her identity and her name, began to hate the world she came from (a kind of *Jüdische Selbsthass*[115]), and found a home in a new one, which provided her rescue. Finally, uprooted from her new milieu by a Jewish organization against her will, for some time she continued to say her Catholic prayers in the children's home, and she went to church at least once. What happened to her after 1948 is unknown to this author.

Pain caused by a new identity can also be found in the story of Marianna Adameczek, born Blima Kurchant.[116] Her father was the only cobbler in the village of Charlejów; her mother sold fruit at the marketplace. Kurchant had four sisters and two brothers. They went on foot to a Polish school in Krzówka, two kilometers away from Charlejów. She finished two grades there, which makes her fate similar to Irena Krawczyk: Both received only very basic education, and both spoke the local dialect, like their neighbors. There were no other Jews in their respective classes, but there were two more Jewish families in Charlejów. At home, Yiddish was spoken. Their father put on a tallit (prayer shawl) and prayed; their parents walked to the synagogue, some three kilometers from the village. On Saturdays, a Polish neighbor would come to milk the cow and light the stove.

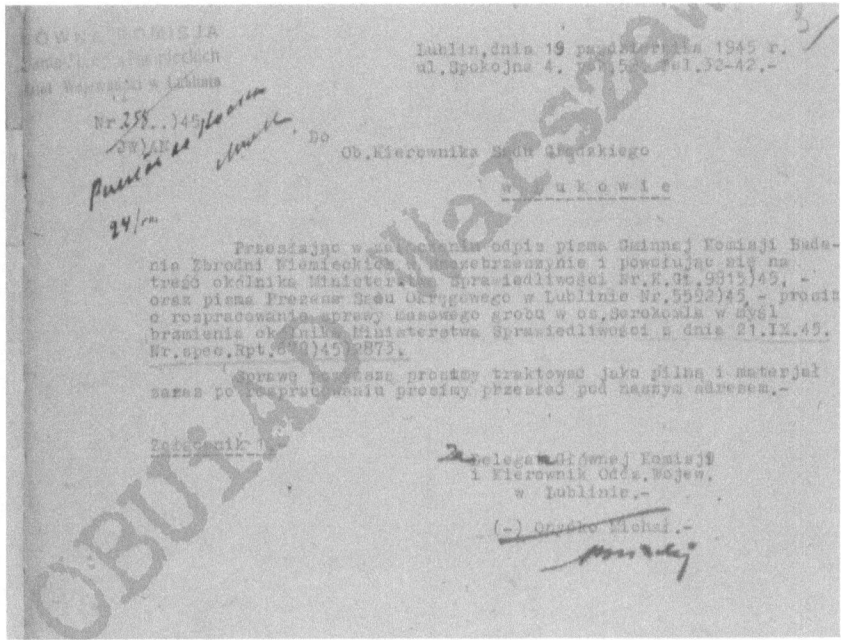

Above and following pages, Figure 4.3–Figure 4.21. Location of mass graves at Serokomla in 1945, the Main Commission for the Investigation of German Crimes in Poland.

"In the winter of 1940, life in the village was still tolerable," Kurchant recalls. Later, the situation became worse, mainly due to the changing of their neighbors. "A gang [of thugs] started to run rampant" and attacked the sisters. The family decided to move to Serokomla, seven kilometers away. Kurchant's mother, three sisters, and brother were murdered on September 22, 1942, when, in retaliation for the murder of two Germans, the occupiers massacred the Jewish population of Serokomla.[117] After this, she, her father, her brother, and her sister found a hideout with a peasant named Adameczek, who lived in Charlejów. All the family members except for Blima were murdered in different circumstances. She stayed in the hideout, together with another girl from Serokomla, Dora Ajzenberg, for two years, until the arrival of the Red Army in September 1944. The two little girls hidden together were very close but lost contact after the war.

When this region was liberated, Kurchant had no idea where to go because she did not know anybody. The Jews from her village were dead, and she was only fourteen. Although there was a Jewish committee in Łuków, she was not

Sąd Grodzki w Kocku
Nr.Ko: 24/45.

Kock, dnia 5.XI.1945 r.
B.pilne.

Do
Wydziału Śledczego
Komendy Powiatowej Milicji Ob[yw].
w Łukowie

W związku z pismem Głównej Komisji Badania Zbrodni Niemieckich Oddział Wojewódzki w Lublinie z dnia 19.X.1945 r.Gr.258/45 -JW/AK. Sąd tutejszy zleca przeprowadzić dochodzenie w sprawie masowego grobu w os. Serokomla, w którym pochowanych jest około 200-tu Żydów w celu ustalenia sprawców zbrodni dokonanego morderstwa, nazwisk osób biorących udział w morderstwie, nazwisk, wieku i ilości pomordowanych oraz dokładnego opisania grobu masowego.

Sprawę powyższą należy traktować jako bardzo pilną i dochodzenie nadesłać do Sądu w najkrótszym czasie.

Kierownik Sądu:
/ Wł.Chojnowski /

Łuków, dnia 30 listopada 1945.r.

Do
Sądu Grodzkiego   1 GRUD. 1945
w K o c k u.

Stosownie do powyższego polecenia w załączeniu przedkładam dochodzenie w sprawie omawianej w poleceniu.

Zał.7

Protokół

oględzin grobu zbiorowego zamordowanych
żydów w dniu 29/V 1944 roku.

Ja Stefan Budkiewicz, z Sekcji Śledczej przy
Pow. Kom. M.O. w Łukowie, w obecności funkcjo-
nariuszy M.O. w Serokomli Parzycha Eugeniusza
i Budkiewskiego Józefa, udaliśmy się na miejsce
masowego grobu zamordowanych żydów, gdzie
stwierdziłem, iż grób ten znajduje się przy szosie
idącej z Serokomli do Kocka, naprzeciwko
strzelnicy znajdującej się po przeciwnej stronie
drogi na placu Streleckim, który jest miejscem
egzekucji żydów. Jest odległość około 280 m.
od Serokomli. Grób ten jest długi na 12 m.
a szeroki 1 m 50 cm. Obok grobu ze strony północnej
znajdują się 3 groby mniejsze, i z zachodniej
jeden. Rozmiary ich są: (1 m × 2 m.) Groby są
mało znaczne bez naszych porośnięte murawą
poznać ich można po powierzchni lekko zapadłej
ziemi. Według zeznania miejscowych świadków
żydzi mieli być zamordowani przez niemców
oraz rozstrzelani za rabicz z niemcami w Budziskach gm. Serokomla. Po naocznym stwierdzeniu
w dniu dzisiejszym i sporządzeniu planu powyższego grobu oraz sporządzeniu i odczytaniu
protokółu oględzin podpisujemy.

Świadkowie:

Parzych

Budkiewski

Serokomla, dnia 16 listopada 1944 r.

Plan zbiorowego grobu zamordowanych żydów przez Niemców dnia 22/IX 1942 r. w m. Serokomla

- grunta parafialne
- ul. Cmentarna
- stary cmentarz | nowy cmentarz
- Pole kol. Serokomla
- grunta gr. Serokomla
- ul. Warszawska
- droga do Kocka
- zach.
- ul. Stodolna
- ul. poza Stodolna
- Plac szkolny
- grunta gr. Serokomla
- Płd.

Protokuł przesłuchania świadka.

Dnia ....1945 r. o godz. .... ja ....
.... z Sekcji Śledczej przy Pow. Kom. M.O.
w .... działający na mocy:

1/ polecenia Pana Wiceprokuratora .... Rejonu Prokuratury
w .... z dnia ....194.. r. L. ....
wydanego na podstawie art. 20 przep. wpr. K.P.K.

2/ art. 257 K.P.K. z powodu nieobecności Sędziego na miej
wobec tego, że zwłoka groziłyby zanikiem śladów lub do
przestępstwa, które do przyoycia Sędzie.o nie.łyby zat...

zachowując formalności wymienione w art. 235, 240, 258 i 259 K.P.K.

3/ przy udziale protokulanta, 4/ w obecności świadka ....
.... z Sekcji Śledczej przy Pow. Kom. M.O. w ....
5/ których uprzedziłem o obowiązku stwierdzenia swemi podpi-
dności protokułu z przebiegiem czynności, przesłuchałem niżej wym...
/a/ w charakterze świadka.
Świadek po uprzedzeniu o:
6/ ważności przysięgi, złożył przepisaną przysięgę,
7/ prawie odmowy zeznań z przyczyn wymienionych w art. 104 ".
8/ odpowiedzialności za fałszywe zeznanie w myśl art. 107 P.
odwiadczył:

Nazywam się: ....

Imiona rodziców: ....

Wiek: .... Urodz. w ....

Wyznanie: .... z zawodu ....

Narodowość .... Przynależność państwowa ....

Zam. w ....

W stosunku do stron ....

W sprawie niniejszej wiadomo mi co następuje: ....
....
....
....
....
....
....
....

z ukrycia i wyśli sić do pochowania zabitych żydów a następnie Polaków tych wywieźli do obozu „Majdanek" między nimi byli: Zagocki Sylwester, Sępoch Witold, Rachlcerowicz Bolesław, Zichwski Apoliwary, Biesak Tadeusz, Gurkowski Zygmunt, Gąsecki Henryk i Skwarek Wacław, którzy w Majdanku zamordowani. Powodem zamordowania żydów i wyżej wymienionych Polaków była zdwst za zabicie dwóch niemców w Brodziskach gm. Serokomla. Ile żydów zostało zamordowanych i pochowanych w spólnym grobie tego stwierdzić nie mogę gdyż w tym czasie udało mi się zbiec do Kałuszowa, jako Rotmistrz. Nadmieniam że dalszych danych o tym wypadku mogliby udzielić żydowie mieszkający obecnie w Łaskowie, a byli mieszkańcy Serokomli obecni przy wypadku, którym udało się zbiec: jak np. Abram Korcenwarm i Syncha Gunkiel.
Wszystko zeznałem, a po odczytaniu mi zeznania zgodnego z moim tekstem podpisuję.

Badał: Protokulant: Zeznał.

Protokuł przesłuchania świadka.

Dnia .... 194 .. r. o godz. ..... ja ....
.... z .... przy ....
w .... działający na mocy:

1/ polecenia Pana Wiceprokuratora ..... Rejonu Prokuratury
   w .... z dnia .... 194.. r. L. ..
   wydanego na podstawie art. 20 przep. wprow. K.P.K

2/ art. 257 K.P.K. z powodu nieobecności Sędziego na mie
   wobec tego, że zwłoka groziłaby zanikiem śladów lub d
   przestępstwa, które do przybycia Sędziego uległyby za
   zachowując formalności wymienione w art. 235-240,258 i 259 K.P.

3/ przy udziale protokulanta, 4/ w obecności świadków ....
....
5/ których uprzedziłem o obowiązku stwierdzenia swemi podpi
dności protokułu z przebiegiem czynności, przesłuchałem niżej wym
/ą/ w charakterze świadka.
Świadek po uprzedzeniu o:
6/ ważności przysięgi, złożył przepisaną przysięgę,
7/ prawie odmowy zeznań z przyczyn wymienionych w art. 104
8/ odpowiedzialności za fałszywe zeznanie w myśl art. 107
oświadczył:

Nazywam się: ....

Imiona rodziców: ....

Wiek: .... Urodz. w ....

Wyznanie: .... z zawodu ....

Narodowość: .... Przynależność państwowa ....

Zam. w ....

W stosunku do stron ....

W sprawie niniejszej wiadomo mi co następuje: ....

i Hersza Rozenmana, mieszkańców osady Serokomla. Więcej osób nie rozpoznaken i A nadmieniam iż rejestry mieszkańców w tutejszej gminie zostały zniszczone przez partyzantki i wykazu zamieszkałych żydów w Serokomli gmnmsk ich ustalić nie można Więcej w tej sprawie nic nie wiem i zeznać nie mogę Po odczytaniu mi go zeznania zgodnego z moim tekstem podpisuję:

Badał: Protokolant: Zeznał:

Protokuł przesłuchania świadka.

Dnia .12 listopada. 1945. r. o godz .9-tej... ja st. ser...
..Dankiewicz Stefan... z Sekcji Śledczej przy Pow. Kom. M.O.
w .Łukowie.......................... działający na mocy:

1/ polecenia Pana Wiceprokuratora......Rejonu Prokuratury
   w .... z dnia ....194...m L..........
   wydanego na podstawie art. 20 przep. wprow. K.P.K.

2/ art. 257 K.P.K. z powodu nieobecności Sędziego na miejscu,
   wobec tego, że zwłoka groziłaby zanikiem dowodów lub do
   przestępstwa, które do przybycia Sędziego uległyby zatarciu.

zachowując formalności wymienione w art. 235,240,259 i 259 K.P.K.

3/ przy udziale protokulanta, 4/ w obecności świadka .Kpr..........
....Rudaka Lecwa...................
5/ których uprzedziłem o obowiązku stwierdzenia swemi podpisami
dności protokułu z przebiegiem czynności, przesłuchałem niżej wymie
/6/ w charakterze świadka.
Świadek po uprzedzeniu o:
   6/ ważności przysięgi, złożył przepisaną przysięgę..........\
   7/ prawie odmowy zeznań z przyczyn wymienionych w art. 104 "
   8/ odpowiedzialności za fałszywe zeznanie w myśl art. 107 K.
oświadczył:

Nazywam się ....Szmuhr Lemkiel..................................

Imiona rodziców: .Pinches v. Nacha.. ze Smików...........

Wiek .35... Urodz. w .Serocku, gminie Serokomla, pow. Łuków.

Wyznanie: .Mojżeszowe............z zawodu...krawiec...........

Narodowość .Żyd.................Przynależność państwowa..Polska.

Zam. w .Łukowie, ul. Kolja N-3...........................

Stosunek do stron. ...obcy...................

W sprawie niniejszej wiadomo mi co następuje: Było to we
wrześniu 1942 roku, we wtorek, jak nie mylę, zjechali
do wsi Serokomla samochodami w liczbie około
100. w. zebrali wszystkich żydów i wybili na Serokomli
na szkolnym placu i pochowali przy szkole nieopodal
strzelnicy. Zabitych żydów łącznie z dziećmi było 200.
Ja sam odjechałem w szoferce na drugi dzień
rano bo wyjazmy która ocalała w ukryciu z czynił
do mnie do Adamowa, gdyż ja pieszo w ponjeniedziałek
uciekłem do Adamowa, przewyższając niebezpieczeń..
Ponieważ w poniedziałek w Budziskach, gm. Sero..

komba, odległych o 8 km od Serokomli, zabito dwóch niemców, którzy jeździli za kontygentem. Sprawcami tego mieli być sowieccy ludzie kryjący się w lasach. Znając niemców doskonale przewidywałem kary co się zemszczą na bezbronnym narodzie żydowskim i dlatego wcześniej zbiegłem i ocalałem jeszcze do dnia dzisiejszego. Towarzysze umieli też zamordowanie w Serokomli, ale niemoga uniknąć obozu i tam zginą. Wiadomo mi tylko że mordu dokonali niemcy, a zamordowanych żydów Serokomskich są następujące nazwiska:

Wojciech Tabacznik ze swoją żoną
Haim Rozenblum ze swoją żoną Libą i dziećmi
Josef Lustman z żoną i dziećmi i ojcem jego
Srluna Lustmann, Hell Rocenman, Hann Ofrenberg

Więcej nazwisk nie wiem, gdyż obecny przy mordzie nie byłem nadmieniam że ożydów było ostatnio w Serokomli z Warszawy, którzy zbiegli z Getta, a znać ich nieznałem, a niektórym żydom serokomskim też się w owczas udało schronić czy też żucić. To było mi wiadome w sprawie, co po odczytaniu mi mego zeznania zgodnego z moim tekstem podpisuję.

Badał: Protokolant: Zeznał:

Protokuł przesłuchania świadka.

Dnia .12 listopada 1945. r. o godz. 11-tej. ja St.sier...
Pankiewicz Stefan ...... z Sekcji Śledczej przy Pow.Kom. M.O.
w .Łukowie................., działający na mocy:

1/ polecenia Pana Wiceprokuratora......Rejonu Prokuratury
   w.................z dnia.........194..r. L..........
   wydanego na podstawie art. 20 przep. wprow. K.P.K.

2/ art. 257 K.P.K. z powodu nieobecności Sędziego na miejscu
   wobec tego, że zwłoka groziłaby zanikiem śladów lub dow...
   przestępstwa, które do przybycia Sędziego uległyby zata...
   zachowując formalności wymienione w art. 235-240, 258 i 259 K.P.K

3/ przy udziale protokulanta, 4/ w obecności świadków. Kpr. Kulaka
   Leona z Sekcji Śledczej M.O. w Łukowie
   5/ których uprzedziłem o obowiązku stwierdzenia swym podpisem
   dności protokułu z przebiegiem czynności, przesłuchałem niżej wymie
   /a/ w charakterze świadka.
Świadek po uprzedzeniu o:
   6/ ważności przysięgi, złożył przepisaną przysięgę,
   7/ prawie odmowy zeznań z przyczyn wymienionych w art. 104 K.
   8/ odpowiedzialności za fałszywe zeznanie w myśl art. 107 K.P
oświadczył:

Nazywam się: ...Dora Apcenberg.............................

Imiona rodziców: ...Majlech........... Ruchla z Apcenberg...

Wiek .14 lat. Urodz. w Wólce, gminie Serokomla, pow. Łuków...

Wyznanie: ...mojżeszowe.... bez zawodu............

Narodowość .żydowska.... Przynależność państwowa .Polska...

Zam. w ..Łukowie.. ul. Solna N.3.

W stosunku do stron ..obca........

W sprawie niniejszej wiadomo mi co następuje: Było to we wrześniu
1942 roku, kiedy jeszcze mieszkałam w Serokomli, o tak godziny
12-tej. Do Serokomli zajechali niemcy samochodami, trzema
ciężarowemi, autami. Ja wówczas znajdowałam się na ulicy.
Skoro ujrzałam jak niemcy wyciągają żydów z mieszkań i
prowadzą, zgłosiłam, schroniłam się do tegoż za niemcy...
wójta Józefa Pankrukowego, wójta gminy Serokomla, który
widząc to mi wydał moje. Siedziałam u niego w oborze
wraz ze swą siostrą Edka Apcenberg około trzech godzin aż
żona wójta, oznajmiła nam, że niemcy są obecnie na obiedzie
a Serokomla nie jest już obstawiona. Na czas obie z siostrą

uciekłyśmy do Adamowa. Do Serokomli już nigdy
nie wróciłam, a o mordzie domyśliłam się jeszcze
w czasie ucieczki, ponieważ słyszałam w stronie
Serokomli gęste strzały a reszty dowiedziałam się
na drugi dzień od tych, którzy uciekli i więcej widzieli.
Dowiedziałam się również, że żydzi z Serokomli zostali
zamordowani za zabicie dwóch niemców w Budziskach.
W akcji tej zginęła moja mamusia, Ruchla Ajzenberg,
i 3 siostry: Chana Rywka, Chaja Ajzenberg, Chuma
Rozenbaum, i siostra mieszka. Prócz tego zginęli rodzice mach
Szmul z żoną i ma dzieciakami i dobrze sobie więcej
przypomnieć niemogę gdyż byłam wówczas jeszcze
niedużą dziewczynką. Zeznałam wszystko, a po
odczytaniu mi mego zeznania zgodnego z moim
tekstem podpisuję:

Badał: Protokulant: Zeznała:
Ster Stankiewicz   Musiał   Dora Ajzenberg

Protokuł przesłuchania świadka.
=============================

Dnia 22 listopada 1945 r. o godz. 13:00 ja dow. Stefan
Klaukiewicz .... z Wydziału Śledczego P.G. w Łukowie, działający na mocy:
polecenia Pana Wiceprokuratora IV Rej. S.O. w Siedlcach, z dnia........
........1945 r. L. .... wydane na podstawie art. 20 przep. przech.
K.P.K.

zachowując formalności wymienione w art. 235-240 i 259 K.P.K.
przy udziale protokulanta kpr. Kutaka Leona ....

których uprzedziłem o obowiązku swymi podpisami zgodność protokułu z
przebiegiem czynności niżej wymienionego/a/ w charakterze świadka przesłuchałem.
Świadek po uprzedzeniu o:
    ważności przysięgi, złożył przepisaną przysięgę,
    prawie odmowy zeznań przyczyny wymienionych w art. 104 K.P.K.
    świadka pouczono o prawie przewidzianym w art. 106 K.P.K.
    odpowiedzialność za fałszywe zeznania myśl art. 107 K.P.K.
oświadczył:

Nazywam się ... Abram Rozenman ....
Imiona rodziców ... Moszek .... i Małka z domu Bronkach ....
Wiek .. 42 lata .. Urodz. w Serokomli pow. Łuków ....
Wyznanie: ... mojżeszowe ..... Narodowość: ... żydowska ....
Przynależność państwowa: ... Polska .... z zawodu ... handlarz .....
Zam. w Łukowie, ul. Solna N: 3 ....
W stosunku do stron: ... obcy ....

W sprawie niniejszej wiadomo mi co następuje: Dnia 22/IX
1942 r. w czasie gdy byłem w kontyngentowce w Serokomli pod
nadzorem polaka Matury Juljana z Serokomli, razem
ze mną pracował też Mordka Adamski. Było to
drugiego dnia po zabiciu dwóch niemców w Budziskach
Gospodzkie ósmej przyjechali niemcy gestapo z Radzynia
i okrążyli całą Serokomlę by nikt nie mógł uciec. Ludność
ośmiu niemców opuszczała do wsi i wyciągała żydów
z mieszkań i ukrycia prowadząc pod gminę, a
następnie wywieźli samochodami na strzelnicę i
wystrzelili bronią maszynową. Ja pracowałem wówczas
przy żniwie w Remizie. Skoro usłyszeliśmy tą tragedję
Matura Julian kazał nam schronić się na strych, co
też uczyniliśmy. Ale chłopiec sąsiedni Łagocki z Serokomli
umyślnie niewiem wskazał nas i niemcy przyszli
zabrali nas prowadząc na miejsce stracenia.

Gdy dochodziliśmy do miejsca śmierci ja szarpnąłem się obwom niemcom który mnie prowadzili, wyrwałem się z uciekłem, zaś Adamski i Morelka został zaraz zabity. Mimo że mówcy żołdaci za mną szereg licznych strzałów jednak nie zostałem trafiony. Uciekłem do Adamowa i mieszkałem do chwili wysiedlenia żydów. W akcji tej zostali zamordowani moi rodzice Moszek i Matla i bracia Wili i Ikaczek Rozenmanowie, żona Haja, dziecko trzyletni Gitla brata żona, Maśia Rozenmann Hegos syn Syfa Rozenmann i bratowa Sura Rozenmann i jej dzieci Dawid, Hana i Szyfka Rozenmann. Prawdopodobnie niemcy zamordowali żydków z zemsty za zabicie niemców w Budziskach. Więcej w tej sprawie nie wiem, a po odczytaniu mi protokułu zeznania zgodnego z moim tekstem podpisuję:

Badał. Protokulant; Zernst;
Kaudrus Milosz
Rozenmann
Adam

Protokół przesłuchania świadka.

Dnia 22/XI 1945 r. o godz. 10-tej ja Ober. Stefan Dankiewicz z Sekcji Śledczej przy pow. Kom. M.O. w Łukowie .... działający na mocy:

1/ polecenia Pana Wiceprokuratora ...... Rejonu Prokuratury ..O. w .... z dnia ......194... r. L. wydanego na podstawie art. 20 przep. wprow. K.P.K.

2/ art. 257 K.P.K. z powodu nieobecności Sędziego na miejscu, wobec tego, że zwłoka groziłaby zanikiem śladów lub dowodów przestępstwa, które do przybycia Sędziego mogłyby zatrzeć się.

zachowując formalności wymienione w art. 235-240,253 i 259 K.P.K.

3/ przy udziale protokulanta, 4/ w obecności świadka Kpr. Rutaka Leona z Sekcji Śledczej M.O. w Łukowie

5/ których uprzedziłem o obowiązku stwierdzenia swemi podpisami zgodności protokułu z przebiegiem czynności, przesłuchałem niżej wymienionego /ą/ w charakterze świadka.

Świadek po uprzedzeniu o:
6/ ważności przysięgi, złożył przepisaną przysięgę,
7/ prawie odmowy zeznań w wypadkach wymienionych w art. 104 K.P.K.
8/ odpowiedzialności za fałszywe zeznanie w myśl art. 107 K.P.K.,
oświadczył:

Nazywam się: Nosal Josek
Imiona rodziców: Judel i Rojza Romelberger
Wiek 35 lat, Urodz. w Serokomli, gminie Serokomla, pow. Łuków
Wyznanie: Mojżeszowe, z zawodu kamasznik
Narodowość: żydowska, Przynależność państwowa: Polska.
Zam. w Łukowie, ul. Piłsudskiego Nr. 31 m 19
W stosunku do stron: obcy

W sprawie niniejszej wiadomo mi co następuje: Dnia 22/XI 1942 roku ... [tekst nieczytelny] ... w Buczkiskach ... do Adamowa ... dowiedziałem się od swojej narzeczonej ... o strasznym wymordowaniu żydów. Moja żona Rachela Romelberger uciekła z Serokomli w dniu wypadku, jako polka, gdyż wyglądem ... była osobna. W dniu tym zastrzelona została moja matka Rojza Nosal, brat Abram, siostra Sura, bratowa Laja Nosal z dzieckiem Icek Nosal, Chana Goldfinger ... Abram-Meżek Goldfinger

i córka Tajga Kaszermacher, jej mąż
Szmul Kaszermacher i 2-je dzieci
Dwora i Fresza Kaszermacher.
Więcej w tej sprawie zeznać nie mogę, gdyż
albo niebyłem przytym obecny, albo
niepamiętam. Po odczytaniu mi mego
zeznania zgodnego z moim tekstem podpisuję:
Badał: Protokulant   Zeznał
Stankiewicz.   Mutas   Josek Noral

Sąd Grodzki w Kocku
Nr.Kps.24/45.

Kock, dnia 13 XII. 1945 roku.

Do
Głównej Komisji Badania Zbrodni Niemieckich
Oddział Grodzki
w Lublinie

Załączone przy niniejszym akta w sprawie Nr.Kps.24/45 o przesłuchanie sprawy masowego grobu w os.Serokomla, pow.Łukowskiem, Sąd Grodzki zwraca po wykonaniu.-

Sędzia:
/ Wł.Chojnowski /

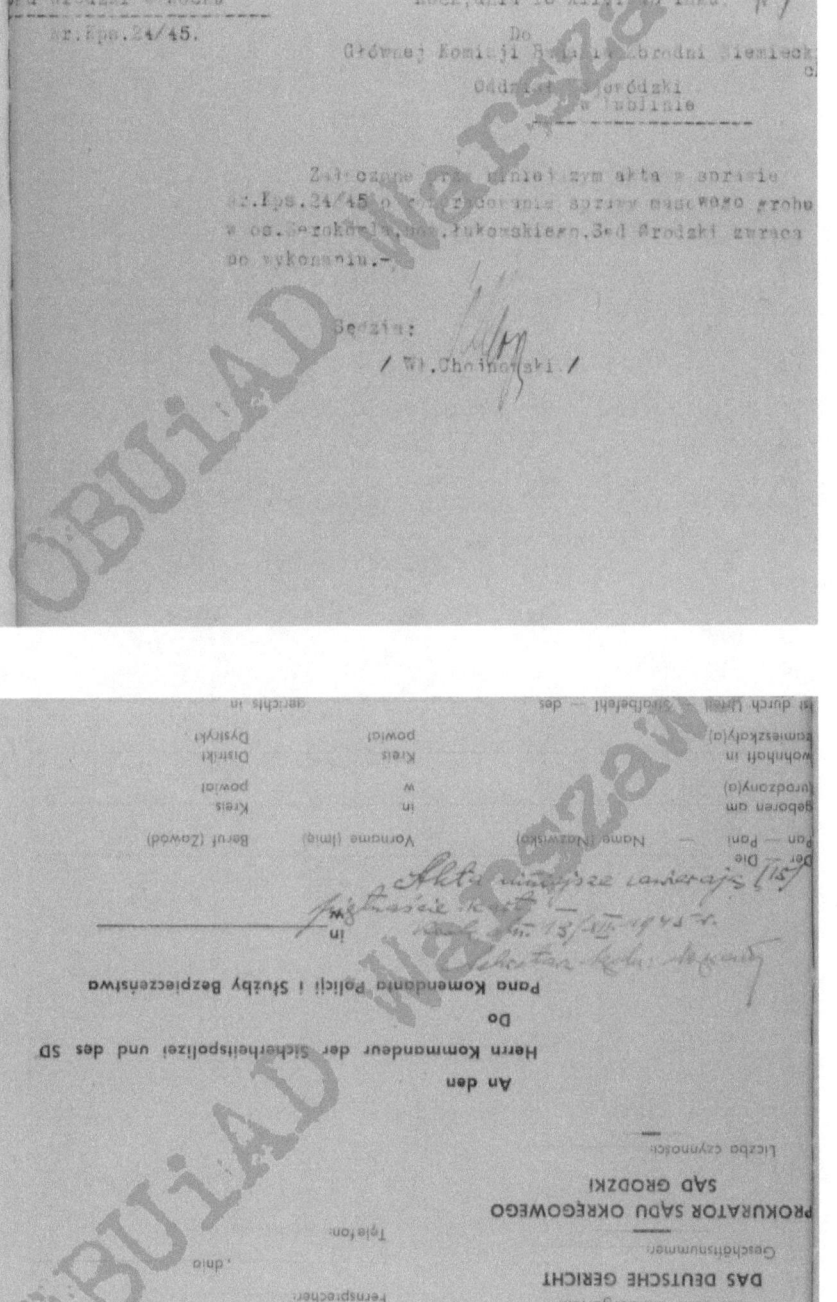

Lublin, dnia 8 stycznia 1946r.-
al. Spokojna 4, pok.58, Tel.32-42.-

Do

Ob. Kierownika Sądu Grodzkiego

w Kocku

Przesyłając w załączeniu akta Kps.24)45 w sprawie masowego grobu w os. Serokomla pow. Łukowskie, - uprzejmie prosimy o urzędowe potwierdzenie przez sąd protokółów przesłuchania świadków:

1) Eugeniusza Parzysza
2) Jana Mazura
3) Symchy Dunkiela
4) Dory Ajzenberg
5) Abrama Rozenmana
6) Joska Nork..

oraz protokółu oględzin grobu zbiorowego, poczym zaopatrzyć je w okrągłą pieczęć sądową a następnie całość nam zwrócić.

Nadmieniamy, że akta te wraz z protokółami prześlemy do Ministerstwa Sprawiedliwości (Główna Komisja Badania Zbrodni Niemieckich w Polsce) która żąda aby wszystkie protokóły były potwierdzone przez Sąd.

O ile załatwienie w ten sposób sprawy byłoby sprzeczne z przepisami, - prosimy o wezwanie wszystkich w/w. świadków do sądu, - sporządzenia ew. nowych protokółów, - które następnie należałoby zaopatrzyć cechami żądanymi przez Główną Komisję.

Delegat Głównej Komisji
i Kierownik Oddziału Wojewódzkiego
w Lublinie

zał.15.

Figure 4.22. Dora Ajzenberg (living in Israel) meets Marianna Adameczek (*right*) at her the home of her daughter, Barbara Adameczek, near Lublin, October 2015, after 71 years. Jean-Charles Szurek.

found until 1946. By that time, Kurchant had converted, changed her first name (to Marianna), and decided to prematurely marry the son of the landlady who had taken her in (coincidentally, the woman's name was also Adameczek, same as the peasant who hid Kurchant). She became a Polish peasant. The couple had six children. When the Łuków Jewish Committee came to bring her back to the Jewish community, she was already living a different life and blamed them for coming too late.

Marianna's story was rediscovered in the 1990s by the Polish Children of the Holocaust Association. Her testimony was taken down for the first time, albeit in brief.[118] She talks about her need to have a family: "The son of my landlady, who looked after me, decided to take care of me and proposed to me. I agreed because roaming was too hard for me and—having no family—I needed a friendly soul."[119] In the numerous interviews she subsequently gave, what transpired—apart from the sense of fulfillment, and despite the harshness of her experiences—was great bitterness. She was aware that had she kept her Jewish identity, her life would have been different.

Strategies of identity change were based on cooperation with the Poles, who often inspired such a step. The Polish women mentioned above had high moral standards. Identity change, despite all the criticism, was an effective strategy. All the stories about it are quite moving.

Roaming, Hiding with Peasants

It would be an illusion to believe that seeking shelter with peasants was a better survival strategy for the roaming Jews. It is true that the twelve Righteous Among the Nations recognized by Yad Vashem from Łuków County were peasants, but statistics show that staying with the peasants or, generally speaking, contact with them often ended fatally.

The countryside was ruled by German law and the German administrative structure, which was also based on certain formations: Polish Blue police, the fire department, and the village head. The village communities, characterized by strong local bonds and mutual acquaintances, formed a thick network, and every encountered Jew had to be reported or brought to the village head, who had the obligation to hand the person over to the police. From that moment on, there were several possible scenarios, which often made the actors face difficult choices. Following are a few examples that show the extent to which the impenetrable peasant world was dangerous for the Jews.

The 1949 trial of Jan Wereszczyński, village head of Poważe (three kilometers from Łuków), and Stefan Markowski, a peasant,[120] demonstrates the extent of possible interpretations of a given situation. In the summer of 1943, two Jews, a Jewish woman by the name Furman, who was known to the peasants, and an unknown Jew, were hiding in the nearby gravel pit. They were spotted, the village head was notified, and they were quickly arrested and taken to the police in Łuków, aided by Markowski and Domański, another peasant, who were forced to do so. Furman begged them to let them go (everybody knew that no one got out of the police station alive). Wereszczyński admitted that he contemplated letting them go, but—as he testified at the trial—Domański was afraid. Markowski testified, "We took those 'kikes' to the police station in Łuków. I advised the village head to let them go, but he said no, because too many people had seen them."[121]

On April 27, 1949, the Siedlce District Court acquitted the accused because it decided that they had acted in a "state of necessity" as they tried to protect the village from German repression. The judge presiding, in a dissenting opinion, questioned the existence of the "state of necessity." He assessed that the accused had not been in a state of imminent danger and could have facilitated the escape of the arrested Jews, and by escorting them to the Blue police station, which "was at the service of the Germans," they had committed a crime. On appeal, his opinion was admitted as decisive, and Wereszczyński was sentenced to six years, Markowski to five and a half.

This decision of the Siedlce District Court is so rare that it merits recognition. One's conclusions from reading the trial files might be construed as ambiguous. In a village situated so close to Łuków, the danger was quite real: The Germans visited frequently, and there was a local resistance movement (the village head himself sympathized with AK, his son was active in its structures; the village head was once detained for fifteen days by the Gestapo). The arrested Jewish woman was no stranger; they wanted to help her. But the moment the whole village found out about the Jews, collective responsibility became the order of the day. The village head, who was the chief accused, claimed that he had had no choice—if he wanted to protect the village, he had to take the Jews to the police station. He had fallen into a tragic trap against his will.

Berl Ryczywół, who roamed the countryside, recalls his encounter with another village head:

> I found myself in the village of Celiny, near Łuków. I thought only of a place to sleep, because it was freezing. I started to speak, and, stuttering, I crossed myself, but the village head did not like the way I did it. I didn't know yet how to do it properly—if you finish the sign on the left side or on the right—and I finished on the left. He saw it and said: "You are a Jew!" He told me to cross myself again. I replied: "Lord Jesus Christ doesn't want me to cross myself twice." The village head, without further deliberation, summoned the firemen so that they delivered me to the village center. There were no Jews anymore; the firemen were helping locate and capture them ... The firemen wore very wide stripes on their jackets; that was their sign. A *shegetz*[122] had already gone to fetch the firemen. With the Germans, there would have been no discussion; they would have shot me, plain and simple. I started begging the village head: "I'll tell you the truth. I'm a Jew, but baptized. I have a Polish wife, who was killed with our children. Now I will always be a gentile, I want to be buried on a gentile cemetery, I hate Jews and I can't stand the look of them. Bear in mind that if they kill me on your account, your brother will be killed, and there'll be no way for you to excuse yourself before the Lord Jesus Christ." He turned a bit softer, looked at me, [and then] looked at his wife. She said: "Let him go." He came out with me and ordered: "Run, before the firemen come!" He showed me the way to the village of Lipniak, 2 km away. It was already dark, but I headed off gladly, because, after all, my life was spared.[123]

The documentation of the numerous trials initiated by the August 31, 1944, decree of the Polish Committee of National Liberation shows that such behavior of the village heads was not frequent. They were often quite ruthless in implementing the occupiers' regulations. For example, Eugeniusz Świder, the village head of Siedliska (Wojcieszków commune), was involved in a roundup of Jews hiding in the local woods, organized at the initiative of the gamekeeper, a *Volksdeutsche*.[124] Initially the peasants were supposed to only gather wood, but later they jointly hunted for the Jews. Some of those captured were murdered on the spot; others were taken to jail in Wojcieszków. The same village head ordered a Jewish family, who were seeking help in the village, to be handed over to the Jewish police.

Cases of peasants' disobedience are rare. One example would be the trial of peasants Bolesław Przeździak; Jan Markowski, deputy village head; Antoni Walczak; Feliks Walczak; and Stanisław Kamecki[125] from the village of Krynka, Celiny commune. Two of the peasants opposed denouncing Jews and hunting for them. In the fall of 1942, the group was charged with capturing Jews who had jumped off trains and handing them over to the Germans. Some peasants, including deputy village head Markowski, followed German orders to arrest Jews and also robbed them, but two of them—Stanisław Czubaszek and Stanisław Wilczek—opposed it, taking the risk to let the Jews go free.

It should be pointed out that certain behaviors of the Righteous Among the Nations were possible, but for most of the time, the peasants were hostile, whether acting jointly or individually. An example of such joint action is described by a certain Finkelstein, who managed to get out of a train to Treblinka:

"A gang of thirty peasants aged twenty to forty, armed with clubs and metal rods, started a hunt for the escapees. They beat them, often to death, in order to take their bloodstained clothes and shoes. Hundreds of Jews fell victim. From me, they only stole my jacket and boots. After they finished the massacre, they called the police to collect those who were still alive. On the way, those who were most gravely wounded were finished off."[126]

Anshel Katz, a nine-year-old whom the Jews helped jump of a train, recalls, "The shouts of those who were planning to jump took me out my numbness. I heard 'Run, run!' Although I was wounded, I ran across the fields. Around me, I saw wounded and killed [shot] people. Apart from that, Poles armed with clubs tried to capture us."[127]

On the one hand, Polish peasants were dangerous when acting together; on the other hand, they were equally dangerous individually, when Jews turned directly to them for help. Most cases of individual seeking help with the peasants ended tragically, something all the analyzed sources confirm. One example is the story of three Jews (Gierszon Handelsman, Jankel Borensztajn, and Wolf Nosel) who were sent for food by the group hiding in the woods near Serokomla. They reached the village of Bielany and asked two peasants, Grabowski and Sławiński, for help. The peasants offered to put them up for the night in Grabowski's barn; they subsequently murdered them and notified German gendarmes. When the gendarmes arrived, they told the peasants to bury the bodies.[128]

Sylvia Friedman's mother did not want to go to the partisans. Her and her daughter's main survival strategy was roaming. Neither was she prepared to stay with a peasant, "fearing that they would be exchanged for a kilogram of sugar."[129] However, roaming forced them to stay with peasants from time to time. By some miracle, they managed to find refuge with a friendly peasant for eighteen months. When they first arrived, they were scared of peasants in general and of the "harsh gaze" of the farmer. Sylvia's mother recognized the farmer as a man who denounced Jews to the Germans. But he did spare these women: he wanted both to murder Jews and to prove that he was a good man.

Sylvia and her mother lived in permanent uncertainty: They spent the days in a bunker under the barn together with their aunt and uncle (who had arrived there earlier), leaving only at night. The Polish landlady was very scared that they would be spotted by her brother, who lived on the adjacent farm. The Jewish women did the laundry and sewed for the landlady. When she could let them in the house, they would scrub the floor on their knees while the landlady watched through the window for her brother. Apart from work, the farmer and his wife demanded money for hiding them. One night, Sylvia's mother set off for Łuków to reclaim money from some Polish debtors. She was supposed to return the following night but never came back. After the war, Sylvia returned to Łuków to find out what had happened to her. A Polish woman told her, "I'll show you where she is buried. The owners are not home; I'll show you the place." She had been murdered and buried in the yard. Sylvia made efforts to have the perpetrators prosecuted and convicted. As she put it, she "had her way."[130]

The story of Sylvia Friedman demonstrates well the complexity of private encounters of Jews with peasants: the difficult community and close existence, fear, dependence, the role of money, but at the same time the fear of the owners are all elements of these situations.

SUMMARY

This text presents merely one dimension of a complex issue, namely the survival strategies both of the survivors and of the victims. It is not an exhaustive monograph of the fate of the Jews of Łuków County. That is why certain topics that would appear obvious were not touched upon: the cruelty of the Germans, murderous practices marked for humiliating Jews (well-known from the pictures of Łuków Jews being humiliated), robberies, and violence. There is no doubt: The Jews were murdered by the Germans.

The Poles became an object of a closer analysis because they seem necessary partners in Jewish survival strategies. They were partners whom the Germans often put in difficult situations, sometimes in proverbial cul-de-sacs, but they were at best indifferent. This is confirmed, among others, by publications that reconstruct the story of the AK in Łuków County. The study by local historian Zygmunt Cichosz[131] is a good example. The author of this otherwise serious book describes in detail the establishment and successive AK operations, village after village. He describes battle intelligence and propaganda sabotage activity.

Figure 4.23. Malcanów (woods near Łuków where the Germans shot several thousand Jews). Three Łuków survivors, late 1940s (GFH, 43547).

In a word, it is an exhaustive monograph of the local AK, with a marked emotional engagement. At the same time, there is only one very general page (out of 277) on the extermination of the Jews. Such an attitude, and the way the story is narrated quite well, reflects the perception of the Jews in the AK structure during the war.[132]

No wonder the number of Jewish survivors, even those who adopted the pitifully "good" strategies, is so scant.

NOTES

1. Some testimonies and recollections were published; see, for example, Wiktoria Śliwowska, ed., *Dzieci Holocaustu mówią* (Warsaw: Stowarzyszenie Dzieci Holocaustu w Polsce, 1993); Régine Frydman, *J'avais huit ans dans le ghetto de Varsovie* (Paris: Taillandier, 2011); Michał Grynberg and Maria Kotowska, *Życie i zagłada Żydów polskich 1939–1945. Relacje* świadków (Warsaw: Oficyna Naukowa, 2003); Sonia Hurman, Abram Hurman, and Halina Birenbaum, eds., *Pod osłoną nocy. Wspomnienia z lat 1939–1945* (Kraków: Fundacja Instytut Studiów Strategicznych, Oświęcim: Państwowe Muzeum Auschwitz-Birkenau); Marian Turski, ed., *Losy* żydowskie. Świadectwo żywych (Warsaw: Stowarzyszenie Żydów Kombatantów i Poszkodowanych w II Wojnie Światowej), vol. 1 (1996), vol. 2 (1999).

2. Maurice Dab, ed., *Le Livre de Lukow 1200–1945: récits et témoignages. Pages de l'Histoire sorties de l'ombre*, translated from the Yiddish by Alain Zilbering (Paris: Associations des Originaires de Lukow d'Israël et des Etats-Unis, 1987). There is also a memory book in Hebrew and Yiddish: B. Heler, ed., *Sejfer Lukow. Gehajlikt chorew-geworener kehile* [Łuków Book. In Memory of a Destroyed Community] (Tel Aviv: Irgun Jocej Lukow be-Israel i Lukower Landsmanszaft in di Farajnikte Sztatn, 1968).

3. Krzysztof Czubaszek, *Żydzi Łukowa i okolic* (Warsaw: Danmar, 2008).
4. USC, VHA, 26955, Sylvia Friedman's testimony.
5. USC, VHA, 11663, Hershel Prengler's testimony.
6. USC, VHA, 50327, David Brook's testimony, 1999.
7. "Jesteśmy na dobrej drodze," *Nowe Wieści*, 1939, no 1.
8. USC, VHA, 26955, Sylvia Friedman's testimony.
9. See Dariusz Libionka, "Introduction," in *Akcja Reinhardt. Zagłada Żydów w Generalnym Gubernatorstwie*, ed. Dariusz Libionka (Warsaw: IPN, 2004), 7.
10. "Of the 3.3 million Jews who had lived in Poland in 1939, some 300,000 survived the war; among these, some 40,000 at most survived in hiding on Polish territory." Saul Friedländer, *The Years of Extermination. Nazi Germany and the Jews 1939–1945* (New York: Harper and Collins, 2007), 704.
11. Tatiana Berenstein, "Martyrologia, opór i zagłada ludności żydowskiej w dystrykcie lubelskim," *Biuletyn ŻIH* 21, no. 1 (1957): 39. Berenstein's work is still highly esteemed. "It is Tatiana Berenstein," points out the German historian Dieter Pohl, "to whom we owe the first detailed description of the persecution of Jews in the Lublin district. For decades, researchers in the West did not know about her achievements. Polish historians had used them, but had long ceased to develop them." Dieter Pohl, "La position du district de Lublin dans 'La solution finale de la question juive,'" *Revue d'histoire de la Shoah*. "Aktion Reinhardt. La destruction des Juifs de Pologne 1942–1943," July–December 2012, no. 197.
12. See Berenstein, *Martyrologia, opór i zagłada ludności żydowskiej w dystrykcie lubelskim*, 39.
13. Ibid., 44.
14. Janusz Odziemkowski, "Ziemia łukowska w wojnie obronnej 1939 roku," in Franciszek Gryciuk and Romuald Turkowski, eds., *Łuków i okolice*, 221.
15. Zbigniew Zaporowski, "Tajne nauczanie w powiecie łukowskim w latach okupacji hitlerowskiej (1939–1944)," in *Łuków i okolice*, 265.
16. USC, VHA, 32152, Robert Berg's testimony, 1997.
17. Shlomo Prengler, "La disparition du Lukow juif," in *Le Livre de Lukow*, 93.
18. USC, VHA, 11663, Hershel Prengler's testimony.
19. Ibid.
20. Leibish Barn, "Mes souvenirs du ghetto de Lukow," in *Le livre de Lukow*, 20.
21. USC, VHA, 10911, Helen Biderman's testimony.

22. Czubaszek, *Żydzi Łukowa i okolic*, 150. Edward Smigly-Rydz was Commander-in-Chief of the Polish armies when the Germans invaded Poland. In September 1939, he took refuge in Romania. The Germans forced the Jews to sing this song. Personal testimony of Barbara Lipinska, a Lukow inhabitant during the war, collected by Krzysztof Czubaszek.

23. Martin Dean, ed., *Encyclopedia of Camps and Ghettos 1933–1945*, vol. 2, *Ghettos in German-Occupied Eastern Europe*, part A (Bloomington: Indiana University Press in cooperation with USHMM, 2012), 678.

24. Czubaszek, *Żydzi Łukowa i okolic*, 143.

25. Czubaszek, *Żydzi Łukowa i okolic*, 139; Emanuel Ringelblum, *Kronika getta warszawskiego. Wrzesień 1939–styczeń 1943*, trans. Adam Rutkowski, ed. Artur Eisenbach (Warszawa: Czytelnik, 1983), 38, 40.

26. In her testimony, Helen Biderman (née Prengler) talks about the arrival of the deportees from Suwałki (USC, VHA, 10911); Mira Feldman recalls an exhausting roam from Suwałki to Łuków and her surprise at the sight of orthodox Jews speaking Yiddish (USC, VHA, 23342, Mira Feldman's testimony, 1996).

27. Czubaszek, *Żydzi Łukowa i okolic*, 141.

28. Prengler, *La disparition du Lukow juif*, 95.

29. Jews from Poland, Czechoslovakia, and Hungary worked here.

30. Labor camp at Dminin, located in a barn. It operated from the spring to fall of 1941. On average, there were two hundred Jews employed to dig pits near the village of Dminin. During its liquidation, the Germans took the last Jews to station, from where they were deported in an unknown direction (see *Obozy hitlerowskie na ziemiach polskich. Informator encyklopedyczny* (Warsaw: PWN, 1979), 155).

31. The Stanin camp was located in a parish building, and 150 Jews performed irrigation work there. They were deported in an unknown direction (probably to Treblinka).

32. *Obozy hitlerowskie na ziemiach polskich*, 534.

33. Barn, *Mes souvenirs du ghetto de Lukow*, 22.

34. In her testimony for the USC Shoah Foundation, Eta Wrobel recalls that she worked in the Jewish department of the *Arbeitsamt*, which enabled her hide some of the personal files and thus prevent some Jews from going to forced labor (USC, VHA, 13813).

35. Archive of the Jewish Historical Institute (subsequently AŻIH), Relacje Żydów Ocalałych z Zagłady [Jewish Survivor's Testimonies], 301/3880, Testimony of Abram Chaim Sylberszten, November 24, 1947.

36. Christopher R. Browning, *Ordinary Men. Reserve Police Battalion 101 and the Final Solution in Poland* (London: Penguin, 2001), 153.

37. *Encyclopedia of Camps and Ghettos*, 679.

38. For example, Eta Wrobel worked for Dietz (USC, VHA, 13813, Eta Wrobel's testimony), and Max Biderman worked for Reckmann (; USC, VHA, 10912, Max Biderman's testimony).

39. ŻSS (Żydowska Samopomoc Społeczna, Jewish Social Self-Help) was a Jewish humanitarian organization with headquarters in Kraków, established with German approval.

40. Czubaszek, Żydzi Łukowa i okolic, 143.

41. Ibid., 144.

42. Ibid., 145.

43. AŻIH, Korespondencja ŻSS [JSS correspondence] 1939–1941, 24, quoted in Czubaszek, Żydzi Łukowa i okolic, 145.

44. AŻIH, Korespondencja ŻSS [JSS correspondence] of 1942, 22, quoted in Czubaszek, Żydzi Łukowa i okolic, 146.

45. USC, VHA, 31545, Halina Bartosiak's testimony, 1997.

46. USC, VHA, 42816, Lilian Fenster's testimony, 1998.

47. USC, VHA, 9775, Joël Estrakh's testimony, 1995.

48. Eta Wrobel, *My Life*.

49. Moshe Graicer, "La lutte pour la vie," in *Le livre de Lukow*, 14.

50. "Żydom nie wolno używać publicznych środków lokomocji," *Nowy Głos Lubelski*, September 25, 1941, no. 224, quoted after Małgorzata Maria Opasiak-Piasecka, *Propaganda antysemicka w prasie gadzinowej na podstawie "Nowego Głosu Lubelskiego" 1940–1944* (master's thesis, Catholic University of Lublin, 2009), 53.

51. USC, VHA, 13813, Eta Wrobel's testimony.

52. Opasiak-Piasecka, "Propaganda antysemicka w prasie gadzinowej na podstawie 'Nowego Głosu Lubelskiego.'"

53. Ibid.

54. Czubaszek, Żydzi Łukowa i okolic, 153.

55. Barn, *Mes souvenirs du ghetto de Lukow*, 24.

56. April has only thirty days, so this must be a failure of memory.

57. AŻIH, Pamiętniki Żydów Ocalałych z Zagłady, 302/30, Stanisław Żemiński, Dziennik [diary], entry of November 27, 1942. Żemiński's notes were published in *Biuletyn ŻIH* in 1958 (no 3 [27]) under the title "Kartki dziennika nauczyciela w Łukowie z okresu okupacji hitlerowskiej" [Pages from a Łuków Teacher's Diary Written during the Nazi Occupation]. Translated into French, some excerpts were published in *Le Livre de Lukow*. Krzysztof Czubaszek discovered recently the real identity of Stanislaw Żemiński: he was Stanislaw Żemis, and he survived after the war. See Krzyszof Czubaszek, "Stanisław Żemis, Świadek Zagłady Żydów w Łukowie," *Zagłada Żydów*, no. 14 (2018): 279–307.

58. Czubaszek, *Żydzi Łukowa i okolic*, 186.
59. *Nowy Głos Lubelski*, April 15, 1942, no. 85.
60. Czubaszek, *Żydzi Łukowa i okolic*, 186.
61. Laura Crago, "Kock," in *Encyclopedia of Camps and Ghettos*, 647–649.
62. AŻIH, 301/2013, Testimony of Mojżesz Apfelbaum, 1946.
63. Crago, "Kock," 648.
64. Archive of the Institute of National Remembrance (subsequenty AIPN), GK 284/41, Trial files of Wilhelm Trapp. See also AIPN, GK 284/43, Gustav Drewes's files; *W 70. rocznicę tragedii Talczyna* (Kock: Dom Kultury, 2012).
65. Adam Budzyński and Józef Filipczuk, *Żydzi w Stoczku Łukowskim* (Stoczek Łukowski–Warsaw: Towarzystwo Przyjaciół Stoczka, 2010).
66. Stephan Lehnstaedt, "Stoczek Lukowski," in *Encyclopedia of Camps and Ghettos*, 448–449.
67. Ibid.
68. Budzyński and Filipczuk, *Żydzi w Stoczku Łukowskim*, 82.
69. USC, VHA, 35378, Henry Rubinstein's testimony, 1997.
70. Czubaszek, *Żydzi Łukowa i okolic*, 141–142, 156.
71. Anonymous testimony, *La première action d'extermination des Juifs de Lukow selon le témoignage d'un rescapé* in, *Le Livre de Lukow*, 36–37.
72. USC, VHA, 50327, David Brook's testimony.
73. USC, VHA, 48207, Susan Weiss's testimony, 1998.
74. USC, VHA, 3071, Annette Smilovic's testimony, 1995.
75. Preparation of hideouts was facilitated by the fact that "in Łuków, houses adhered to each other, and the attics were connected and formed one corridor" (USC, VHA, 5897, Hank Rosenbaum's testimony, 1995).
76. Anonymous testimony, *La première action d'extermination des Juifs de Lukow*, 36–37.
77. Ibid., 36.
78. Ibid., 38–39.
79. Mojsze Tirman, ed., *Lukower kdoszim un heldn* [Łuków Martyrs and Heroes] (Łódź: Algemajne Komitet fun Lukower Jidn baj der Central Jidiszer Historiszer Komisje in Pojlin, 1947).
80. Isaiah Trunk mentions this in his book on Jewish Councils, *Judenrat: The Jewish Councils in Eastern Europe* (New York: Macmillan, 1972). The quotation from the brochure is on page 134.
81. Czubaszek, *Żydzi Łukowa i okolic*, 159. The author based his study on *The Holocaust Chronicle* (Lincolnwood, 2000), 15. The time table order (*Fahrplanan-ordnung*) 565 gives a different time of return from Treblinka, 17:22.
82. Browning, *Ordinary Men*, 95.
83. Ibid.
84. Budzyński, Filipczuk, *Żydzi w Stoczku Łukowskim*, 87–88.

85. Ibid., 89.

86. See Jakob F's testimony, quoted to Jacek Andrzej Młynarczyk, "'Akcja Reinhard' w gettach prowincjonalnych getta warszawskiego 1942–1943," *Prowincja noc. Życie i zagłada Żydów w dystrykcie warszawskim*, ed. Barbara Engelking, Jacek Leociak, and Dariusz Libionka (Warsaw: Wydawnictwo IFiS PAN, 2007), 60.

87. Kommandeur der Sicherheitspolizei, the Office of the Commander of Security Police.

88. Ibid.

89. Budzyński and Filipczuk, *Żydzi w Stoczku Łukowskim*, 90.

90. Ibid., 91. The Germans gave one or more kilograms of sugar, or sometimes vodka, to those who denounced a Jew or brought him or her to the gendarmerie.

91. Ibid., 95. See Dorota Stefańska, *Barbara Nowelska (1919–2012)*, "Biuletyn Szadkowski" 2016, t. 16, 159–175.

92. Berenstein, *Martyrologia, opór i zagłada ludności żydowskiej w dystrykcie lubelskim*, 180. The number is repeated by Browning, *Ordinary Men*, 143.

93. A religious fellowship that prepares a corpse for burial.

94. Czubaszek, *Żydzi Łukowa i okolic*, 164.

95. AŻIH, 302/30, Stanisław Żemiński, Dziennik.

96. Browning, *Ordinary Men*, 111.

97. Ibid., 134.

98. Ibid., 148.

99. *Encyclopedia of Camps and Ghettos*, 680.

100. Yakov Kesselbrenner's testimony, in *Le Livre de Lukow*, 130.

101. These statistics appear in the original Polish version. Additional research show that the number of Jews killed by Poles in 1944 is larger than the five indicated for year 1944 and that they should amount to twenty-five. The data has not been changed because this difference does not significantly change the message.

102. According to preliminary postwar estimates of the Łuków Jewish Committee, as of May 4, 1945, there were 154 Jewish survivors, including 15 children (AŻIH, Centralny Central Jewish Committee in Poland, Statistics and Registry Department, 303/106). According to Adam Kopciowski, who analyzed the statistics of Jewish Committees of the survivors in the main of Lublin province, the number of child survivors in Łuków County rates among the lowest. Adam Kopciowski, *Żydzi w Lublinie w latach 1944–1949* (master's thesis, UMCS Lublin, 1998).

103. Anshel Katz, *La lutte pour la vie*, 109.

104. Yad Vashem Archives, O.3/1845, Icchak Grinbaum's testimony (in Polish), 1961.

105. Czubaszek, *Żydzi Łukowa i okolic*, 174.

106. USC, VHA, 15411, Irving Lumerman's testimony, 1996.

107. USC, VHA, 24208, Manny Orlinsky's testimony (born in Łuków on August 10, 1919 as Menachem Icchak Orliński), 1996.

108. The consequences of changing identity during the war in Poland was comprehensively dealt with by Małgorzata Melchior, *Zaglada a tozsamosc. Polscy Żydzi ocaleni na 'aryjskich papierach.' Analiza doświadczenia biograficznego* (Warsaw: Wydawnictwo IFiS PAN, 2004).

109. USC, VHA, 42816, Testimony of Lilian Fenster (born Luba Skorka), 1998.

110. Testimony of Rushkie Huberman-Ivan, "Dispersés et opprimés," in *Le Livre de Lukow*, 53–71. Summary of this testimony can be found in Krzysztof Czubaszek, *Żydzi Łukowa i okolic*, 246–251.

111. Marianna Adameczek, "Ludzie ludziom," in *Czarny rok..., czarne lata...*, ed. Wiktoria Śliwowska (Warsaw: Stowarzyszenie Dzieci Holocaustu w Polsce, 1996), 131–137.

112. AŻIH, 301/2989, Estera Borensztejn's testimony.

113. AŻIH, 301/3998, Irena Krawczyk's testimony.

114. Ibid.

115. The *Jüdische Selbsthass* concept was developed by the German Jewish philosopher Theodor Lessing (1872–1933). Through a certain number of cases, he described the rejection and hate of their Jewish identity by Jews who wanted so badly to integrate the German identity that they were able to adopt antisemitic behaviors.

116. USC, VHA, 49044, Marianna Adameczek's, 1998.

117. "At eight, the Germans arrived, Radzyń Gestapo," recalls Abram Rozenman, one of the massacre survivors, "and they surrounded the entire Serokomla, lest anyone escape. Some Germans barged into the village and started pulling Jews out from their homes and hideouts, and then drove in cars to the shooting range and shot [them] with machine guns." The Lublin Branch of the Main Commission to Prosecute German Crimes opened an investigation on October 19, 1945. As a result, the course of the massacre was reconstructed, and two mass graves were located (AIPN, GK 180/22).

118. Adameczek, *Ludzie ludziom*.

119. Ibid., 135.

120. AIPN Lu, Sąd Apelacyjny w Lublinie [Lublin Court of Appeals], Trial of Stefan Markowski and Jan Wereszczyński, village head [1949].

121. AIPN Lu, Sąd Apelacyjny w Lublinie [Lublin Court of Appeals], Stefan Markowski's testimony.

122. A punk.

123. AŻIH, 302/43, Pamiętnik Berla Ryczywoła [diary of Berl Ryczywoł], translated from the Yiddish by Monika Polit.

124. AIPN Lu, 326/23, Trial of Eugeniusz Świder, Władysław Kopyść, and Bolesław Kołodziejak, testimony of Władysław Kopyść.
125. AIPN Lu, 326/11, Trial of Proces Bolesław Przeździak, Jan Markowski, Antoni Walczak, Feliks Walczak, and Stanisław Kamecki, testimony of Bolesław Przeździak.
126. Testimony of the Finkelstein sisters, who summarized their brother's story in *Le Livre de Lukow*, 138.
127. Anshel Katz's testimony, in *Le Livre de Lukow*, 106.
128. Sąd Okręgowy w Siedlcach [District Court in Siedlce], zespół [collection] 1569, 709. Reserve Police Battalion 709 and the Final Solution in Poland.
129. USC, VHA, 26955, Sylvia Friedman's testimony.
130. Sylvia Friedman interviewed by the author, September 2014.
131. Zygmunt Cichosz, *Obwód Armii Krajowej Łuków "Łoś" "Wielkie Łuki" "Maciek" 1939–1945* (Biała Podlaska: Arte, 2009).
132. This is also confirmed by recollections of Polish underground activists. See, for example, Stanisław Wieczorek, *Partyzanckie wspomnienia. Relacje oraz dokumenty żołnierzy Armii Krajowej ze Stoczka Łukowskiego i okolic* (Warsaw: Światowy Związek Żołnierzy Armii Krajowej, 1996).

JEAN-CHARLES SZUREK is emeritus research director in the CNRS. He directed the Institut des Sciences sociales du Politique (CNRS-Université Paris Ouest-ENS Cachan) from 2003 to 2010 and taught in several universities (Paris Ouest, Paris Est, Paris V). His major publications include *Aux origines paysannes de la crise polonaise* (The Rural Roots of the Polish Crisis) (Actes Sud, 1982); *A l'Est, la mémoire retrouvée* (Recovered Memory in Eastern Europe), co-ed., préface de Jacques Le Goff, La Découverte, 1990; *Ecriture de l'Histoire et identité Juive, l'Europe aschkénaze, XIXème-Xxème siècle* (co-ed), Les Belles Lettres, 2003, 310; *Juifs et Polonais 1939–2008*, (co-ed. with Annette Wieviorka), "Shoah: From the Jewish Question to the Polish Question," in Stuart Liebman (ed.), *Claude Lanzmann's Shoah: Key Essays*, Oxford University Press, 2007, 149–169; Paris, Albin Michel, 2009, 527 pages; *La Pologne, les Juifs et le communisme*, éd. Michel Houdiard, 2012, 264 pages; "The Lukow county," in *Dalej jest Noc. Los Zydow w wybranych powiatach okupowanej Polski* [Barbara Engelking and Jan Grabowski, eds.], 2018, 547–620. English version to be published by Yad Vashem/Indiana University Press; *Les Polonais et la Shoah. Une nouvelle école historique* [co-ed. with Audrey Kichelewski, Judith Lyon-Caen, Annette Wieviorka], CNRS Editions, 2019.

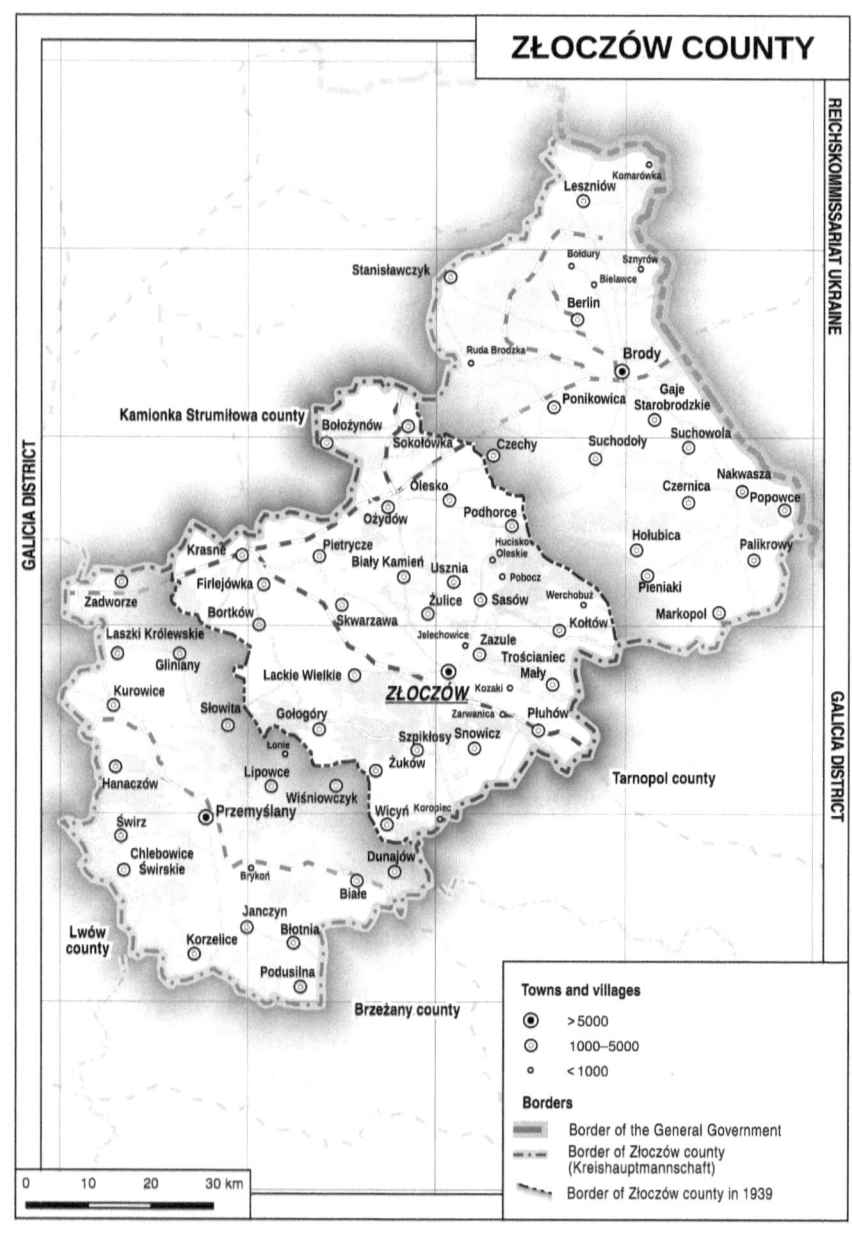

FIVE

ZŁOCZÓW COUNTY

ANNA ZAPALEC

AREA AND POPULATION

In the early 1920s, Złoczów (today Zolochiv in Ukraine) was a small town in Eastern Galicia. The area was a cultural and ethnic frontier, which gave the town a specific character with a culturally, religiously, and ethnically diverse population, and with different customs as well.[1]

From September 1, 1921, the town was a center of a poor and densely populated county in the Tarnopol Voivodship (Poland).[2] It was a typical farming area, with small village farms and little industry.[3] According to the census of December 9, 1931, Złoczów had 13,265 inhabitants (army personnel not included), while the two larger towns of the county, Olesko and Sasów, had 3,824 and 3,112 inhabitants, respectively.[4] The communities of Złoczów County were relatively small, and the residents all knew each other. In the early 1930s, the population totaled 118,609, with the majority residing in rural areas and living off the land. The territory was the home of many ethnic groups, where, next to Poles and Ukrainians, there lived 10,236 Jews (according to religion), that is, 8.6 percent of all inhabitants.[5]

The Jews were an urban group, as 72.3 percent lived in towns, with the majority in Złoczów. From 1934, the county (1,195 square kilometers) was made up of twelve rural communes, Biały Kamień, Folwarki, Gołogóry, Kołtów, Krasne, Ożydów, Płuhów, Podhorce, Remizowce, Skwarzawa, Sokołówka, and Złoczów (without the town of Złoczów), and three urban communes, Złoczów, Sasów, and Olesko.[6]

Figure 5.1. Złoczów, Sobieski Street, one of the most important streets in the city, 1914. Author's collection.

The Jewish elite in Złoczów were the well-educated intelligentsia who had been interns or students of the best European universities. Złoczów's claim to fame was the Zukerkandl booksellers, which had been in operation from 1870 and were renowned for beautiful editions of literary works.[7]

Various Jewish political parties were active in the county. The Zionist movement had a substantial following; the large Orthodox group was represented by the religious and cultural union Agudath Yisrael. It should be stressed that the structures of the Communist Party were weak, with rather few members, and its activity was carefully watched by the Investigation Department of the County State Police Command in Złoczów.[8]

The ethnic and cultural diversity of Złoczów County is reflected in Polish and Jewish recollections. The everyday life of the individual nationalities was shaped by their holidays. For example, in Sasów, its multicultural community made itself visible by the "enormous synagogue, and the nearby St. Nicolas's Orthodox church, with the Catholic St. John's across the Market Square."[9]

The national situation and relations in the county were fairly complicated during the interwar period. Polish–Ukrainian relations in particular flared up in the summer of 1930, when the Organization of Ukrainian Nationalists (*Orhanizatsyia Ukrainskykh Natsionalistiv*, OUN) launched a sabotage campaign,

Figure 5.2. Złoczów—general view of the city, 1920s or 1930s (NAC, 1-U-8205).

attacking Polish estates, farms of Polish colonists, and communal and state property—all in order to disorganize the local power structures and intimidate the Polish population. Złoczów County saw seven acts of sabotage, which was not much in comparison with the rest of the province, but it did alarm the local authorities and the Polish population. In response to the OUN operations, the Polish authorities sent troops and police to Eastern Galicia, where they launched a brutal repressive operation against a local Ukrainian village. This further exacerbated the relations between ethnic groups in the area.[10]

In the second half of the 1930s, the attitude of the other ethnic groups toward the Jews became more hostile. Although at that time county authorities recorded only two cases of antisemitic action,[11] witness testimonies mention business rivalry, the shouting of anti-Jewish slogans, and clashes between young people due to interethnic prejudice between Poles and Jews or Ukrainians and Jews. Most Jews could not find employment in Polish state or local government institutions, nor could they move up politically or socially, which contributed to a feeling of resentment.[12]

Figure 5.3. Złoczów, Sokoła street, 1918. Author's collection.

In 1939, the local population closely followed the developments in Europe and commented upon them vigorously, although each national group had different fears and expectations.[13]

THE SITUATION OF THE JEWISH POPULATION DURING THE SOVIET OCCUPATION, 1939–1941

Right before September 1, 1939, there were around 7,800 Jews living in Złoczów, with homes in different parts of the town, most of them near the synagogue on Bożnicza Street.[14] The outbreak of World War II brought an influx of Polish refugees into eastern Poland, among them many Jews from central and western parts of the country. Their exact number in Złoczów County is not known, but one could estimate that there were some 8,100–8,800 Jews, out of a total of 15,000–15,500 inhabitants, meaning that around 1,000 Jewish refugees found shelter in the town.[15]

The Soviet invasion of Poland of September 17, 1939, came as a surprise and shocked the Polish authorities. When the news hit Złoczów in the morning, Polish troops began to leave the city.[16] In contrast, Polish policemen remained, and on September 18, when the first Soviet tanks appeared, they were swiftly disarmed and taken prisoner. Several days later, ten (or twelve) officials, policemen, and prison guards were shot on prison grounds.[17]

The period of Soviet occupation in the Złoczów region and in the entire occupied zone was characterized by the Sovietization of all areas of life: political, social, economic, and cultural. First of all, Polish territory occupied by the Red Army was incorporated into the Ukrainian and Belorussian Soviet republics, and all Polish citizens—regardless of ethnic background—became Soviet citizens as of November 29, 1939. From that moment on, they were subject to Soviet law.[18] Furthermore, the administrative division was adjusted to the Soviet system, and the offices and institutions were staffed with arrivals from eastern Ukraine.[19] The lower levels of administration hired local people, mainly Ukrainians and Jews.[20] The local activists of the prewar Communist Party of Western Ukraine joined the administrative and political work, and promises of political and economic privileges attracted a part of the Jewish population, especially the poorest. However, they soon found out what the true Soviet intentions were, chiefly during nationalization, when small stores and Jewish workshops were seized by the state and their owners became employees of a cooperative. Some Złoczów Jews, particularly the large orthodox group, were rather disinclined to embrace Soviet rule and felt adversely affected by the changes, because they undermined the existing principles of Jewish social and religious life.[21]

Soviet repressions spared no nationality. Thousands of families, most of them Polish, and then Jewish and other ethnic groups, were deported to the Soviet heartland, including Kazakhstan and Siberia, while others were deprived of their homes and property. Social and economic organizations were attacked, schools were Sovietized, and young people were inducted into the Red Army. Even though in the early months national minorities were favored, once the Soviet regime consolidated, it began to arrest Ukrainian political and social activists, and repressions targeted not only Polish but also Ukrainian intelligentsia. The Ridna School (Ukr. *Ridna Shkola*) was closed, and Ukrainian cooperatives were dissolved. Ukrainian and nationalist organizations were targeted. The Jewish communities suffered as well. Although some of the Jews gained access to various posts and offices, the changes introduced by the Soviet authorities undermined the foundations of Jewish economic, social, and religious life. Jewish religious communities were dissolved, and Bund activists were arrested. A number of Jews were deported into the Soviet heartland, especially during the June 1940 deportation.[22]

Despite the various migrations and similar phenomena, the Jewish population of Złoczów still oscillated around 8,100–8,800; in Sasów it was 950, and in Olesko it was 600. In contrast, before the German invasion of the Soviet Union in June 1941, around 2,100 Jews lived in the rural communities (including Gołogóry, Sokołówka, and Biały Kamień).[23] To conclude, at the turn of June and July 1941, there could have been between 11,750 and 12,450 Jews in Złoczów County.

REPRESSIONS IN THE EARLY MONTHS OF THE GERMAN OCCUPATION

German troops seized Złoczów on Tuesday, July 1, 1941. Right before they marched in, peasants from the nearby villages started to plunder stores and houses in the town. The first to enter Złoczów were Wehrmacht units, followed by *Einsatzkommando* 4b from *Einsatzgruppe* B (renamed *Einsatzgruppe* C after July 11). It is not this unit that is regarded as the chief source of inspiration behind anti-Jewish incidents in Złoczów right after the German troops marched in, although it cannot be ruled out completely.[24] Probably in early July, SS-*Hauptsturmführer* Edmund Schöne's special operational group rode through Złoczów; initially it was twenty strong, but it grew substantially later.[25]

The Pogrom of Jews in Złoczów, July 1941

When German troops marched into Złoczów, the local population found near the town's prison, located in the old castle (citadel), mass graves of prisoners murdered several days before by the local Directorate of the People's Commissariat of State Security (*Narodny komissariat gosudarstvennoy bezopasnosti*, NKGB) that was pulling out of town. The victims included a great many local Ukrainians, a large group of Poles, and a certain (unknown) number of Jews, with about ten wealthy Złoczów merchants among them.[26] The Germans blamed the "Jewish–Bolshevik criminals" for the massacre, omitting to mention the Jewish victims.[27] This line of argument found sympathetic ears and was directed at the local Jews. Already on July 2, the Germans began shooting some of the captured Jews, and posters were put up on the streets informing that the Jews were to report for work the following morning in the main square on pain of execution.[28]

Recruitment was carried out by the local Ukrainian Committee, which was established soon after the Germans took the city, and it played an important role during the pogrom, while others saw its role as that of one of the main instigators. The committee was headed by Eliasz (Ilya) Antoniak; his deputy was his son-in-law Dr. Gilewicz.[29] The committee was probably connected to, or at least accepted by, the local OUN structures, although there is no direct evidence to support this.[30] Witness recollections ascribe the key role in the pogrom to the so-called Thirty, which should be identified with the Ukrainian militia, subordinated to the Ukrainian Committee.[31]

Figure 5.4. German bombing of a road close to Złoczów in July 1941 (NAC, 2–1796).

On the morning of July 3, 1941, some of Złoczów Jews reported for work. Those who failed to report were hunted in their homes and hideouts by the SS and the Ukrainian militia. The streets of Złoczów saw brutal scenes of violence and murder of Jews.[32] Most were marched to prison to exhume the bodies of the murdered prisoners.[33]

Elements of Waffen-SS "Viking" that marched through Złoczów took part in the pogrom, and some units spent the night outside of the town.[34]

The pogrom was not halted even when Major Eitel Friedrich Patzwahl intervened on the order of Colonel Otto Korfes, the commander of the 518th Infantry

Figure 5.5. Złoczów, exhumation of bodies of prisoners executed by the NKGB in Złoczów prison, July 1941. The mass grave was located in an orchard, next to the prison walls. Local Jews were forced to dig up the bodies (YVA, 65387).

Regiment of the 295th Infantry Division, to restore order in the town. The only result of this intervention was the release of Jewish women from the prison yard, where the SS was carrying out executions.[35]

Apart from the SS and some members of the Ukrainian militia and Ukrainian inhabitants of the town,[36] a substantial number of local villagers (who came en masse to Złoczów) joined the anti-Jewish actions. The peasants also joined the tormenting and murder of the Jews by means of hoes, spades, clubs, and stones. Plunder of Jewish property accompanied the murder. Some witnesses also mentioned cases where Poles were involved in various incidents during the pogrom. Helena Kitaj recalls two young Polish students of Złoczów schools who came to take her father.[37]

At the end of the day, the Germans guarding the exhumation began shooting Jews into the pits from which they had taken the bodies of murdered prisoners. According to witnesses, this took place both in the prison yard and outside the prison wall, in an orchard.[38] Because of a raging storm, the mass graves were not immediately covered with earth, and about thirty to forty wounded crawled out and escaped.[39]

In 1944, when the Germans were pushed out from the area, a Soviet Expert Forensic and Medical Commission carried out a partial exhumation of bodies from one of the graves outside the prison wall, where murdered Jews had been buried.[40] The commission established that over 3,200 people had been murdered.[41] These estimates should be deemed too high; the number of Jewish victims during the pogrom was more likely between 1,400 and 2,100.[42]

The Murder of Jews during the Military Occupation

On July 6, 1941, in the square in front of the Złoczów Orthodox Church, a Ukrainian rally was held and Ukrainian independence was declared. At the rally, the Act of Renewal of the Ukrainian State was proclaimed, which was signed by Yaroslaw Stetsko on June 30, 1941. The Złoczów County governor was Stepan Turkevych, and the town mayor was Mykolai Alyskevych. Similar rallies were held in other places in the county. However, the Ukrainian hopes did not materialize, and the independent Ukrainian administration did not survive beyond August 1941, when a German administration with a German county governor was put in place.[43]

But before that happened, under the military administration, many crimes against the Jews were committed, with the involvement of local Ukrainians, soldiers of the Wehrmacht, and SS-men.[44] In Złoczów, by July 7, thirty to forty Jews died every day.[45] On July 10, the Germans murdered around three hundred members of the local Jewish intelligentsia. Local Ukrainians pulled Jews straight from their homes.[46]

Thus one should estimate that during the days of the military administration, 420–460 Jews were murdered in Złoczów, 70 in Sasów, probably 120 in Olesko, and in the villages near Zarwanica possibly 30 Jews.[47]

The First Repressions against the Jews after the Establishment of a Civilian Administration

When District Galicia (*Distrikt Galizien*) was established and incorporated into the General Government (GG) as of August 1, 1941, a German civilian administration replaced the military administration. In mid-September, a new territorial division was introduced.[48]

Złoczów became the *Kreishauptmannschaft* (center of the county) that stretched across the area of three prewar counties: Złoczów, Brody, and Przemyślany. *Kreis* Złoczów (Zloczow County) was divided into *Bezirke* (quarters) and was now a much larger territorial unit than the prewar [Polish] Złoczów County.⁴⁹ Złoczów had a command of the Criminal Police *(Kriminalpolizei, Kripo)*, with Kripo stations in Brody and Przemyślany. Similarly, German gendarmerie was placed in Złoczów, Brody, and Przemyślany, and the nearest Protective Police *(Schutzpolizei, Schupo)* station was in Tarnopol.⁵⁰

Initially, the *Kreishauptmann* was *Regierungsassessor* Hans Mann,⁵¹ and from January 6, 1943, it was Dr. Otto Wendt; Wendt's deputy was Dr. Gerhard von Jordan, who had held this post since 1942 and at the same time headed of the Office for Internal Affairs.⁵² The warden of Złoczów prison and the chief of the local Kripo (probably from December 1941 to 1943) was SS-*Sturmscharführer* Otto Zikmund from Vienna.⁵³ His deputy was Hans (or Franz) Drexler of the Berlin Criminal Police headquarters. The Kripo station and the jail was located at Wały St. 7 and had twenty functionaries (some of them had signed the *Deutsche Volksliste*, the German National List, DVL), primarily Poles, but also Ukrainians and Germans. The Gestapo station was headed by SS officer N. Ludwig, who reported to the Tarnopol Gestapo, which from October 1941 was headed by Hermann Müller.⁵⁴ The commander of the German gendarmerie was Captain Schwartz, and his deputy was Captain Fueg-Lobenstein.⁵⁵ There were nine gendarmes. An eighteen-man auxiliary Ukrainian police formation was established, which had its command in Złoczów and local posts in the towns and villages.⁵⁶ There was also a local Wehrmacht command there.⁵⁷

During the German occupation, *Bezirk* Zloczow, which was part of *Kreis* Zloczow, in principle covered the same area as the prewar Złoczów County of 1939. However, certain changes were made to the administrative division. In the commune of Przemyślany, the villages of Lipowce and Łonie were moved to the Gołogóry commune. Certain prewar communes were integrated with others.⁵⁸ It should be stressed here that in this text on the fate of Złoczów's Jews, all the statistics and analyses concern the area of the prewar Złoczów County. According to German data in November 1941, this area had 121,449 inhabitants, including 9,660 Jews.⁵⁹ At that time, the Jewish population of Złoczów was 6,228, in Sasów it was 877, and in Olesko it was 480.⁶⁰

Kreis Zloczow was governed by German law. In August 1941, *Judenräte* (Jewish Councils) were set up all over the district of Galicia, and in September the Jews were formally ordered to wear special armbands and movement restrictions were introduced.⁶¹ However, the Złoczów *Judenrat* had been established earlier, even before the governor general's regulation was issued. It was made up of twelve people, with most being members of the influential Jewish intelligentsia—lawyers, physicians, and well-known social activists. The chairman was the famous Zionist lawyer Dr. Zygmunt Majblum from Złoczów,⁶² and his

Table 5.1 The number and strength of the Ukrainian auxiliary police in *Kreis* Zloczow (July 1942)

Kreis Zloczow total		Including *Bezirk* Zloczow
Police commands	Złoczów Brody Przemyślany	Złoczów
Number of stations	35	14
Number of commissioned officers	4	2
Number of policemen and NCOs	190	78

Source: Author's study. GARF, f. 7021, op. 148, d. 321, Anlage 1 zur Verfügung des Kommandeurs der Ordnungspolizei im Distrikt Galizien vom 27.7.1942—Abt. IIIb 27 01/12. Sollstärke der Ukrainischen Polizei im Distrikt Galizien für das Rechnungsjahr 1942/1943 [Attachment 1 for the Commandant of the Order Police in District Galicia of July 27, 1942, Department IIIb 27 01/12. Employment figures of the Ukrainian Police in District Galicia for the fiscal year 1942–1943], July 1, 1942, 1a; Güederung und Stellenplan des Kreiskommandos der Ukrainian Polizei in Zloczow (Bereich der Kreishauptmannschaft Zloczow) [Guidelines and employment plan of the County Ukrainian Police in Zloczow (area of the Zloczow *Kreishauptmannschaft*)], 16; Anlage 3 zur Verfügung des Kommandeurs der Ordnungspolizei im Distrikt Galizien vom 27.7.1942—Abt. III b 27 01/12. Waffenverteilungsplan betr: Ausrüstung der ukrainischen Polizeidienststellen im Distrikt Galizien mit Mannlihergewehren und Faustfeuerwaffen [Attachment 1 for the commandant of the Order Police in District Galicia of July 27, 1942, Department IIIb 27 01/12. Plan of Weapons Assignment: Equipment of the Ukrainian Police in District Galicia in rifles and pistols], 19.

deputy was the physician Dr. Abraham Hreczanik.[63] Recollections of Złoczów Jews reflect rather good opinions about the activity of the *Judenrat*, similar to what Helena Kitaj-Drobnerowa said: "The Złoczów *Judenrat* was famous in the region because it took great care of its people. Less respect was for the *Ordnunsgdienst*."[64] The Jewish Police (Ger. *Jüdischer Ordnungsdienst*) was headed by OD-man Dziuniek Landsberg, and his deputy was Henek Steinwurzel.[65] *Judenräte* were also established in Olesko and Sasów.[66]

Initially, the Złoczów ghetto was not fenced off as a closed area. According to one testimony in August 1941, the ghetto covered half of the following streets: Ormiańska, Sokoła, and part of Mickiewicza. Most of the Jews were already concentrated near the synagogue and behind it. In the fall of 1941, resettlement of Jewish homeowners began from the main streets: Legionów, Kolejowa, and Wały. Restricted freedom of movement for Jews was imposed: a curfew and prohibited shopping on the market square before 10:00 a.m., and there was total

Figure 5.6. A scene from the Złoczów ghetto (GFH, 6700).

prohibition from leaving Złoczów.[67] From the first days of the occupation, Jews were removed from the better homes and moved to those of lower standards; other families were moved to new apartments as well. They were allowed to take only a small amount of luggage. At the same time, the Jews were robbed of their money and valuables.[68]

In August 1941, *Judenrat* posters appeared all over town, calling on the Jews to help pay the Germans an enormous "contribution," set at 1,500,000 zlotys, payable in foreign currency, gold, or valuables. The *Judenrat* managed to pay the amount.[69]

When SS-*Obersturmführer* Friedrich Warzok arrived in Złoczów, he appeared in the *Judenrat* building. During the very first visit, he demanded a chauffeur, a fully furnished apartment, and other items to be delivered by the Jewish community. Allegedly, during a conversation with the chairman, attorney Zygmunt Majblum, Warzok hit Majblum with a bullwhip across the face.[70] It was the first of many such visits; during the occupation, Warzok was a veritable scourge of the town and the vicinity. From October 1941, Warzok was the commandant of the forced labor camp (Ger. *Zwangsarbeitslager*, ZAL) in Lackie Wielkie and of all the labor camps in *Kreis* Zloczow; at the same time, he was the *Judenreferent* (officer responsible for Jewish affairs) on the staff of Friedrich Katzmann (the SS and Police Leader in the district of Galicia).[71] Similar demands and attitudes were displayed by other SS men. Naturally, the failure to comply with these

Figure 5.7. SS officers Friedrich Warzok and Gustav Willhaus, Złoczów, 1943 (YVA, 1584/185).

wishes led to various negative consequences.[72] In order to meet these demands, the *Judenrat* collected valuables and money from Jewish families. In principle, every matter the *Judenrat* wanted to resolve involved paying off or bribing various German functionaries or officials, and there was no way around it.[73]

In December 1941, in Złoczów as in the rest of the GG, the so-called fur operation was conducted. The Jews were obligated to hand in furs. Those who failed to do so risked being shot. There were several such cases in Złoczów.[74]

FORCED LABOR: LABOR CAMPS

The Germans began to use Jews to do all kinds of work.[75] Among the chief forms of forced labor that should be mentioned were those in the vicinity of the Jews' place of residence (work details) and sending Jews to closed forced labor camps. The *Judenräte* were responsible for delivering the appropriate number of workers. In the early months of the German occupation, some Jews worked on granges in Kalinka and Pobocz and on large peasant farms, in German enterprises, and for the German administration and other institutions.[76]

After October 15, 1941, labor camps were established along the *Durchgansstraße* IV transit road (from Przemyśl trough Lvov, Złoczów, Tarnopol, Podwołoczyska, and farther toward Odessa); the prisoners were detained to work at road construction, at railway track repair, and in quarries. The construction work was conducted by the Radebeule firm, among others.[77]

There were several labor camps in Złoczów County: in Lackie Wielkie, Płuhów, Kozaki (October 1941), Sasów-Chomiec (May 1942), Złoczów (second half of 1942), Sasów (December 1942; a small camp in the town itself), and Olesko (spring 1943).[78] Essentially, in these camps people were subjected to physical exhaustion: They were constantly undernourished, performed hard labor, and suffered a lack of basic hygiene that led to emaciation, exhaustion, and disease. In 1941, the Lackie Wielkie camp had around four hundred Jewish prisoners, but the number could have increased in the years to follow. There were also Polish and Ukrainian prisoners. The number of Jewish prisoners in the other camps in the Złoczów County probably reached an average of three to four hundred.[79]

JEWISH SURVIVAL STRATEGIES BEFORE THE FIRST DEPORTATION OPERATION

Help and Care Institutions

One form of protection of the Jewish community were all kinds of aid for the most needy. The Złoczów *Judenrat* soon began organizing social help. In January 1942, a communal kitchen was organized in the ghetto, with 25 percent of meals offered for free. But due to the lack of adequate income, already in April 1942, meals were no longer distributed regularly, and sometimes the kitchen was closed all week. In Złoczów, there was also a general hospital with an autonomous contagious diseases ward and a dispensary. It was financed half from patients' contributions; another half came from *Judenrat* funds. A public bath was opened and operated once a week, with 150–200 clients.[80]

On March 25, 1942, the County Care Committee of the Jewish Self-Help was established, headed by Dr. Mojżesz Schwager, with committee branches set up in Sasów, Olesko, and Sokołówka, among others, but ultimately they were not approved by the German authorities. From day one of its operations, one of the committee's important help activities was sending parcels to Jews in forced labor camps.[81] In the following months, the committee organized a sewing workshop, a kitchen (financed with Jewish money), an embroidery workshop, and a laundry. It also collected linen for camp dwellers and the destitute, and oy tried to find employment for those without work, which was also an attempt to protect them from German repressions. There was a general shortage of foodstuffs and medicines, which the county administration did not distribute. Złoczów's Jews themselves tried to organize social help, and in this context one should consider these efforts one of the collective survival strategies, because their purpose was to help the poorest. Naturally, functioning in the committee also was a form of protection from deportation to a forced labor camp.[82]

At the turn of 1941–1942, a typhus epidemic broke out, and as a result, as well as due to the harsh living conditions, 369 people died in the ghetto.[83]

Bribes and Foes for Survival; Identity Change

From the first days of the occupation, the Jews living in Złoczów County had been making all kinds of efforts to forestall the threats the occupier had brought along. Initially, the local *Judenräte* tried their modest best to save Jews or to reduce the consequences of German repressions.

Many recollections and testimonies of Złoczów Jews mention bribery and payoffs as one of the survival strategies, both at the beginning of the occupation and in its later stages. This strategy could alter a decision, bail someone out from prison or a camp, or, during deportation operations, buy a place in a labor camp or in a German factory. The status of laborers working for the German economy or for the Wehrmacht gave them some temporary protection. In the long run, bribes and survival payoffs turned out to be rather ineffective because the growing pauperization of many Jews made it impossible to use this strategy constantly and thus achieve a minimum amount of safety.[84]

Already at that time, few Jews decided to leave and hide in the country or a small town under a false identity. Survivor testimonies show that one had to be truly determined and very courageous to pretend to be Ukrainian or Polish and live among them. Furthermore, the absolute prerequisite for success was the command of language and a good orientation in the culture of a given ethnic group. One had to be vigilant as well. When in danger, the refugees moved to another location.[85] This type of hiding, also used in the later stages of the occupation, required a lot of determination and adaptation to living in culturally different communities.[86]

GERMAN LIQUIDATION OPERATIONS IN ZŁOCZÓW COUNTY

In the district of Galicia, the first deportation operations of Jews to Bełżec began in mid-March 1942. Before, Jews had only been resettled from the country to the nearby hamlets and towns, as, for example, in the following counties: Brzeżany, Kołomyja, and Czortków. But in Złoczów County, no such resettlement took place, apart from sending a certain number of Jews to labor camps. The early days of the occupation were marked by "contributions," repressions against the Jewish intelligentsia, and executions in the ghettos, especially of people deemed to be an "unproductive element".[87]

Deportation Operations

As of April 1, 1942, Złoczów had 5,833 Jewish inhabitants.[88] The summer brought information about deportations from other areas, but not much credence was given to these reports.[89] The first deportation from Złoczów took place on August 28–29, 1942, and was carried out by the Tarnopol Gestapo. According to Jewish testimonies, in mid-August 1942, Zuckerkandel, appointed by the *Judenrat* to liaise with the office of Gestapo chief in Tarnopol, received an order from the Gestapo for the Złoczów *Judenrat* to deliver a quota of "unproductive" people. Failure to do so would mean a "wild deportation operation." On the night of August 27–28, Müller come to the Gestapo station in Złoczów and demanded from the *Judenrat* a list of those to be deported. He did not receive it, on the pretext that it was not ready. The operation began early in the morning. Müller then demanded that 2,500 people report at the assembly area, but no one volunteered. So a brutal operation began: breaking the doors of apartments and houses and pulling out individual people from shelters and hideouts. The Tarnopol Gestapo chief, together with his men, assisted by Schupo and the gendarmerie, combed the houses and all the possible hideouts. Kripo and the Ukrainian Police joined in; young Poles were seen pointing to places where Jews lived. The terrorized *Judenrat* members, together with the Jewish police in groups, as well as SS men and gendarmes, would go from house to house, searching for people. All those captured were driven into cattle trucks. A small group of young Jews were detached to be sent to the labor camp in Lackie. The others were deported to the Bełżec death camp. Only a handful managed to jump off the train and survive the fall.[90]

During the first deportation operation, around 1,650 Jews were deported from Złoczów alone, with another 100 from Sasów and probably most of the Jews from Olesko. The transport had about 2,000 people.[91] During the *Aktion*, a certain number of Jews were shot on the spot in Złoczów and in other towns.[92]

It was after those events that whatever hopes had been pinned to the *Judenrat* that it could protect the Jews vanished. Social work also substantially declined.[93]

The day after the deportation, Złoczów was the scene of the so-called furniture operation, during which the Germans, the Ukrainian Police, and the Jewish Police took all the furniture from the homes of the deported Jews and transferred it to storerooms for sorting. Jewish homes were marked with the Star of David in red paint.[94] The Złoczów *Judenrat* summoned all holders of labor cards to have them stamped by the Tarnopol Gestapo, which meant that another sizeable bribe was to be handed to Müller.[95]

This first deportation crushed the Złoczów Jewish population both mentally and physically. People feared another operation any moment. On the night of November 1, 1942, information came from the Jewish hospital about a column of military trucks waiting outside the town. This news stirred panic in town, and people started hiding in previously prepared shelters and hideouts.[96]

Another deportation of Złoczów Jews began on November 2, 1942. At that point, the Jewish population of Złoczów was 4,172 people. This time, the operation was carried out by Lvov Gestapo, under the command of SS-*Oberscharführer* Karl Wöbke, who had conducted several such operations all over the district.[97] Now there were no negotiations with the Złoczów *Judenrat*.[98] The operation was conducted by the following formations: a group of SS men and police, the Ukrainian Auxiliary Police, and a detachments of Latvians. They started to comb houses, search for hideouts, and destroy shelters. Those captured were directed to the assembly point, suffering torments along the way. Many were shot on the spot: the elderly, the infirm, and children. Some Jewish policemen were put on the train as well. The operation lasted two days. The victims were sent in groups to the Złoczów railway station and loaded onto cattle trucks. At the station, around fifty people were detached and sent to the Lackie labor camp.[99] During the operation, trucks ware also sent to Sasów, but according to one of the surviving inhabitants, no one was taken because the Jews had fled to the forest when they heard about the operation.[100]

It appears that during the second deportation *Aktion*, around two thousand people were deported to the Bełżec death camp.[101]

After the second deportation from Złoczów, Jewish laborers working for various German firms were put in barracks, whereas young men were placed in the camp on Jabłonowskich Street. The Jews worked repairing the Złoczów–Tarnopol road, within the camp itself, or in town as men of a given trade. This camp, as all the other forced labor camps in *Kreis* Zloczow, was subordinated to Warzok.[102]

The "Secondary Ghetto" in Złoczów and Its Liquidation

In November 1942, in accordance with the order of the Higher SS and Police Chief in the GG on the establishment of so-called secondary ghettos, the streets of Złoczów saw announcements ordering all Jews to be resettled (from

December 1) from their homes to the area near Zielony Rynek, which was walled off from the rest of the town. In order to separate the ghetto even more, the fence was fortified with barbed wire, guarded by Ukrainian policemen.[103] Along with Złoczów's Jews, all the Jews from villages and towns in the county were resettled there, except those who were detained in the following forced labor camps: Kozaki, Lackie Wielkie, Olesko, Płuhów, Sasów-Chomiec, and a small camp in Sasów itself.[104] Some 2,376 Jews were resettled to the Złoczów ghetto from the entire county; among them were also some people from outside the county who had been sent to work there.[105]

The ghetto was located on a few streets, where 4,548 Jews were concentrated.[106] The entrance was on the corner of Mickiewicza and Pocztowa Streets, and another on Sokola Street. It was guarded by Ukrainian policemen, and inside by the Jewish Police.[107]

In the overcrowded ghetto, there were shortages of food, water, soap, and cleaning supplies. As a result, there were many cases of typhus, and there were no facilities to treat the ill. The *Judenrat* set a makeshift hospital in Scharer's house on Chodkiewicza Street, but it did not have any funds to help the sick.[108]

The liquidation of the Złoczów secondary ghetto began on April 2, 1943, at dawn. People were woken by the sounds of gunfire from machine guns and rifles. According to witnesses, a detachment of local forces (German gendarmerie, Złoczów Criminal Police, the Ukrainian Auxiliary Police, and *Sonderdienst*), SS and *Schutzpolizei* from Lvov, plus a detachment of Latvians marched into the ghetto.[109] The attorney Salomon Altman recounted that on that day, SS-*Hauptsturmführer* Erich Engels[110] demanded the *Judentat* chairman sign a document on the ghetto liquidation in light of the typhus epidemic. Dr. Majblum refused, and Engels beat him to death on the spot. Councilors Schotz and Jakier also refused to sign this document and were murdered, and the entire *Judenrat* were lined up against the wall and shot.[111]

For three days, people were brutally pulled out from homes and hideouts and robbed of jewelry and money.[112] The Jews were transported in groups of fifty to one hundred, escorted by Ukrainian policemen, along the road to Brody toward the village of Jelechowice, five kilometers from Złoczów, and onward to the village of Zazule. There, three-quarters of a kilometer from the road in a young pine forest, about ten meters from a forest route, eight large pits were dug, where the victims were executed. Available sources mention not only the circumstances of the massacre but also the names of the murderers.[113]

In 1944, after the Germans were pushed out of the district of Złoczów, the Soviet Expert Investigative Commission drafted an opinion, estimating that around 3,500 Jews were shot during the ghetto liquidation.[114] Several people managed to escape right before the execution.[115]

METHODS OF RESCUE DURING GERMAN DEPORTATION OPERATIONS

Złoczów Jews tried to devise all kinds of ways to hide or avoid deportation. News of deportations and shootings were coming from various places, so people were aware of danger, especially soon after the first deportation, when blood-curdling scenes had taken place on the streets of the town.

During the deportation operations, people took shelter in all kinds of hideouts, including basements, walls, and roofs of houses, or in shelters in places that were hard to access.[116] In other towns of Złoczów County, many similar hideouts were also set up, both before the first deportation and after it, in case of another *Aktion*. But most of them offered poor protection.

Some people captured during a deportation operation made dramatic attempts to escape from the transports.[117] It is not possible to give the number of Jews from Złoczów County who decided to escape from the train during the deportation to Bełżec. Only a few are known to have survived the jump.[118]

Another method of rescue was attempts to seek help in the villages among Polish and Ukrainian neighbors. But in 1942, only a few Jews found that kind of help. Hiding Jews was punishable by death, and it was very likely that someone would denounce the helper to the Ukrainian Police.[119]

Far more people tried escaping to the nearby woods. Rarely, however, did they decide to build bunkers with a view to prolonged hiding. As a rule, after a German *Aktion* the Jews would return to their homes. Among possible reasons for this were the extremely harsh conditions of hiding in the woods, particularly in the fall and winter, when it was difficult to get any food, and smoke from fires that could easily give away the shelters. Some sources contain information that this method of hiding was used by some Jews from Gołogóry, who in the summer or fall of 1942 had built shelters in the nearby forest in case of a German threat. The Jews in Sasów made similar preparations, and indeed during the deportation operations, most Sasów Jews fled the town and subsequently returned. In contrast, in Złoczów, there were not so many such escapes. Only a few of those who had escaped to the woods in the second half of 1942 decided to stay there for good and carry on hiding.[120]

The Jews also tried to save themselves from German repressions, opening *Städtische Lagerwerstätte* (craftsmen workshops), because during a deportation operation, being employed in a crucial branch of the German economy or Jewish craft could protect one from deportation.[121]

The idea to set up craftsman workshops was taken up by Złoczów's Jews in August 1942. Probably they were not established until the first deportation operation. They employed furriers, goldsmiths, tailors, seamstresses, and embroidery experts. Apart from these, the workshops hired the elite of the town's Jewish community: physicians, lawyers, and *Judenrat* members and their families. According to one witness, in order to be employed there, a sizeable bribe had to be paid: seven to eight hundred dollars.[122] The workshops survived until July 23, 1943, when they were liquidated together with the labor camp, and these who worked there were shot. Probably some of them, with a group of selected Jews, were taken to the Janów concentration camp.

To sum up, the sources reflect around 112 cases of Jews in hiding in 1942, that is, at the time of the deportation operations and the establishment of the secondary ghetto in Złoczów. An overwhelming majority of those people sought hideouts within the county; only eleven Jews tried to escape beyond the boundaries of Złoczów County. The largest group survived only thanks to the help of friendly farmers. The fates of those survivors varied enormously, but of those who decided to flee, more than half survived until the end of the war. Other saw salvation in work in ghetto enterprises and in craftsman workshops because they believed that this would put off deportation, and for that reason they did not escape from the ghetto.[123]

THE HUNT FOR THE JEWS AFTER THE GHETTO LIQUIDATION

The hunt for Jews hiding in the ghetto and in other parts of the city lasted about two months. Such operations were also carried out all over the county because a sizeable number of Jews had fled from Złoczów to the woods and nearby villages. The roundups were organized by various police formations: German gendarmerie, Criminal Police, Ukrainian Police and the SS. In the county and in Złoczów itself, some local inhabitants joined in to point out Jewish hideouts. After the war, Zikmund, the chief of Złoczów Kripo, testified before the court that the effective hunt for Złoczów Jews was made possible by denunciations by the local population.[124]

In the sources, there is information that points to an estimate that during the liquidation of the ghetto, in Złoczów itself around 296 Jews managed to hide from capture and deportation, including 51 in three large bunkers, 10 with two Polish families, and probably 235 (men and women) found shelter in various temporary hideouts. Eighty Jewish women from this group left because they did not believe that they could survive in hiding. Eventually, they reported to Warzok themselves, asking him to take them to the labor camp in Złoczów. Forty were immediately taken to be executed, while the others probably died no later than during the camp's liquidation. Neither did the bunkers in town offer effective protection, because they were found and the Jews were pulled out and murdered. The estimate is that between April and July 1943, at least 199 people died, and there are a few dozen about whom there is no information. Sources confirm that out of those who had tried to hide in town or in the suburbs, only four people survived the war, including two Jewish boys hidden by a Pole, and another two who probably had left Złoczów in the fall of 1943.[125] According to the sources, on the eve of ghetto liquidation or soon after, many Jews fled the ghetto, and at least 180 were hiding in the county. Of them, 66 found shelter on peasants' farms, while 77 hid in forest or field bunkers, occasionally in abandoned houses. Some of the other Jews hid on different farms, changing their hideouts, and an even smaller group chose other survival strategies (e.g., the escaped from the county); the fate of fewer than twenty Jews remain unknown. The effectiveness of a survival strategy based on hiding outside Złoczów was nevertheless much higher than in the town, because among those who did the former, only twenty-six were killed, which is definitely fever than in Złoczów itself.[126]

Apart from Jews hiding in Złoczów after the ghetto liquidation, there still were four hundred Jews in the town itself, detained in the labor camp, performing all kinds of jobs for the Germans. In April 1943, this group were still alive because the camp had not been subject to liquidation.

LIQUIDATION OF THE LABOR CAMPS: SURVIVAL STRATEGIES OF CAMP INMATES

After the liquidation of the ghetto, the Germans left a certain number of Jews in labor camps and in German enterprises. Nevertheless, everybody sensed what would happen to them. Thus in nearly all the camps, small underground groups were formed (from a few persons to over ten strong), with a view to preparing for escape and building shelters in the nearby woods. But as a rule, the plans of the Jewish camp underground failed, and escape attempts, even if successful, ended tragically. The possibilities of any action were very limited due to the lack of funds and contacts with the outside world, and denunciation was a serious threat in the camp. The aim of these efforts was not resistance but self-defense.

Attempts to Organize an Underground in the Camps

In the Lackie Wielkie ZAL and in the Płuhów labor camp, small groups of prisoners organized an underground, which did not develop their plans on any great scale.[127] The underground in the Złoczów camp repair shop was better organized. After the liquidation of the ghetto, two groups of Jews that were planning to escape were formed. The first one was at least a dozen strong, but had very few weapons and fled to the forest near the village of Zazule, where they were spotted by a local boy. Someone notified the Germans, and some of them were killed in a bunker. The only Jews to avoid this fate were those who were outside the bunker when the Germans arrived.[128] Another group probably keeping in touch with Polish underground—among them the engineer Hillel Safran, a mechanic from Lvov, a betrothed couple from Rzeszów, and two Jews from Złoczów repair shops—was betrayed (in May 1943), probably by a prisoner, and subsequently arrested by the Criminal Police and murdered.[129] The largest number of Jews escaped from the camp at Chomiec near Sasów, where in early June 1943, two groups of prisoners formed and prepared shelters in the forest. One of the two groups did in fact escape. Other prisoners were planning a collective escape but did not manage to carry out the plan. When the German and the Ukrainian Police surrounded the camp and began its liquidation, the prisoners started fleeing. Many were killed, but over half managed to break out. Around 150 people are estimated to have fled and sought shelter primarily in the woods. The fate of a mere few of them may be traced precisely.[130]

The liquidation of labor camps in Złoczów County took place in the summer of 1943, which marked one of the last stages of the destruction of Złoczów Jewry. Probably as early as June, the Olesko labor camp was liquidated, and on the night of July 22–23, 1943, other camps were liquidated, including the Złoczów camp. Many Jews were killed on the spot, while others were transferred to the Jaktorów camp (where they were shot), or to the Janów camp. Preliminary estimates show that on the eve of the liquidation, there could have been 2,450 Jews from different areas of District Galicia, including Złoczów Jews. In the liquidation operations, some 1,650 Jewish prisoners were murdered, whereas others were deported from the county to other labor camps. Only a few managed to flee the camp or survive the liquidation. The fate or many of them remains unknown. Only a handful survived the war.[131]

Several Feet under the Ground: Bunkers and Shelters

Złoczów Jews built all kinds of shelters and bunkers through the entire German occupation, but in most of them, one could only stay temporarily because they contained not enough water, air, or food. Between April and July 1943, two groups of Jews still working in Złoczów built bunkers. They could hold ten or even several dozens of people. They were tunnels dug under the ground with living quarters, with access to water and air.

One was built in Brodzka Street on the promises of a construction company owned by F. Knell and E. Wyklick, where a large group of Jewish laborers worked. According to one testimony, thirty-five people hid there, while according to another source, it was thirty. In August 1943, the Aryan workers noticed one of the Jews in the square and informed the German gendarmerie. He was captured and forced to show where the others were hiding. The bunker was liquidated by German gendarmes, Ukrainian policemen, and the farm's employees, who dug out the earth and opened the entrance. Between eleven and fifteen people were murdered on the spot, and the others were murdered at the Jewish cemetery in Złoczów. Only two survived.[132]

The only undiscovered Złoczów bunker—despite vigorous German attempts—was built by the Strassler family. Before the war, Izaak Strassler owned a two-story house at Rynek (Market) 26, with a small candy and marmalade factory. During the occupation, it was taken over by the security apparatus (SS and police). The owners were permitted to stay in order to continue production. Therefore, they were not subject to deportation and thus survived the liquidation of the ghetto. In 1943, they already knew that the Germans would kill them, so they started to build a bunker for all the house dwellers. It was built several meters under the ground, and its construction was extremely difficult because all the bunkers previously built in Złoczów had been discovered by the Germans, or people had been forced to leave due to the lack of water, air, and food. Apparently, the Strasslers came up with the best solution. The shelter utilized old cellars built in the nineteenth century, located beneath the house's foundations. The largest of these was connected to a corridor leading to living quarters built several meters under the ground. In order to complete the task, it was necessary to perform lengthy underground work, carry out soil, gather food, and plan access to water and air. The Strasslers managed to meet all these conditions. First of all, they found a professional carpenter able to make a framework, and they dug over 120 meters to a well, made in its wall. Then several holes were made in storm sewers to let air into the underground corridor and the living quarters, a stockpile of food was amassed (meager, but sufficient to survive a few months), a small kitchen was built, as well as a room to store kerosene; and bunks were put in.[133]

The bunker looked like an shaft in a mine, and the living chamber, 3 meters wide and 2.2 meters high, was covered with planks. The Strasslers went into the bunker in July 1943, when the liquidation of Złoczów labor camp began. On July 23, at the sound of gunfire, the Strasslers with others (twenty-three people in total) climbed down the underground corridor several meters under the ground and blocked the entrance behind them. From that moment on, one could leave

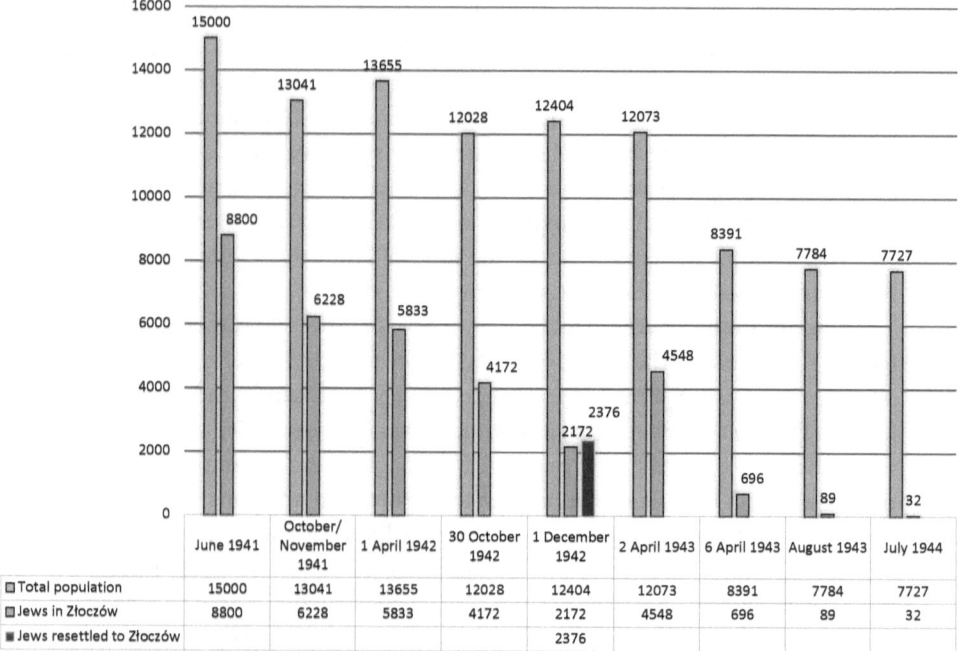

Graph 1. Estimates of Jewish population in Złoczów, 1941-1944

Source: Author's study based on collected documents

Note: The number of Jews hiding in Złoczów in July 1944 (thirty-two) presented in the graph pertains only to people hiding within the town itself. The total population is based on documents and other sources that contain such information, but it was not always possible to establish precise numbers. The number of Złoczów inhabitants in June 1941, August 1943, and July 1944 is only estimated and should be revised in the future. Similarly, the number of Jews resettled to the secondary ghetto in Złoczów after December 1, 1942, and in April 1943 (comprising inmates of the labor camp and those who were hiding in the town after the ghetto liquidation) have been estimated on the basis of available sources.

the bunker only through one of the storm sewers, but one had to negotiate a length of around one thousand meters. Most of those who had hidden in the underground bunker survived until the Red Army arrived in Złoczów.[134]

With regard to the methods of hiding, bunkers built in towns rated among the most expensive and at the same time among the least effective survival strategies, with the Strasslers' bunker being an exception. All the others who built such structures died or had to abandon them.

Table 5.2 Estimates of Jewish survival strategies in Złoczów County, 1941–1944

Survival strategy	Number of survivors (%)
Woods/bunkers	179* (28.2%)
Village, one place†	140‡ (22.1%)
Village, several places	14 (2.2%)
Wandering from village to village	7 (1.1%)
Partisan unit	128§ (20.2%)
"Aryan" papers	‖ 2 (0.3%)
Labor camp#	6** (0.9%)
Escape from the county	56†† (8.8%)
Labor in the Reich	3 (0.5%)
Survived, no information how	99‡‡ (15.6%)
TOTAL	**634 (100.0%)**

Source: Author's study based on collected documents.

Notes:

* Including the 23 people who survived in a Złoczów bunker. We did not manage to identify the names of all those who were hiding in the woods.

† Included here are also those who were hiding with Polish families in Złoczów.

‡ The estimate comprises the two people who survived in Złoczów, thanks to a Polish family who hid them.

§ This figure should be treated as an estimate to be revised for precision in the future. In a number of cases, it was impossible to establish precise biographical information

‖ Including those who survived within the county.

I assumed that the labor camp could have been a survival strategy only when someone chose this form of hiding and had some kind of action plan, i.e., when they deliberately chose the form rescue by entering a camp. Such situations were the case after the liquidation of the Złoczów ghetto, and later people would decide to enter the camp. Most of them were murdered (soon after their presence in the camp was discovered), or we know nothing about their fate; therefore, they were not included in the survival table. Other camp inmates who fled during the liquidation operation (July 1943) went into hiding in the territory of the county or in their home town, and they were included in figures concerning other survival strategies.

** We have included those Jews who mentioned the camp as a survival strategy in their statement submitted to the Central Committee of Polish Jews. Probably four of them found themselves outside the county.

†† Escapes from the county. I did not find cases of crossing the border and fleeing to a different country.

‡‡ These people survived, but it was impossible to determine whether they were hiding in the county or outside it.

JEWISH SURVIVAL STRATEGIES DURING THE "JEWHUNT" (JUDENJAGD) PERIOD

After the liquidation of Złoczów ghetto, and three and a half months later, following the liquidation of the labor camps in Złoczów County, Germans "clearing operations" began. These were roundups organized in the woods against the partisans and Jews in hiding. A rumor circulated among the local population to the effect that compensation for denouncing or capturing a Jew was five kilograms of sugar, one thousand marks, and some items of clothing.[135] The testimonies of Jewish survivors often mention the motif of denunciation or greed-motivated robbery.[136] The Ukrainian police's claim to infamy was its collaboration and involvement in the murder of Jews in the county. It took part in liquidation operations and in hunts for the Jews hiding in the area.[137]

During the German liquidation operations in Złoczów County in 1942 and 1943, many Jews took shelter in prepared hideouts. Unfortunately, most of them were captured. Out of the total number of people trying to hide during the German occupation, a decisive majority made such an attempt in 1943, mostly during and after the liquidation of the ghetto and the labor camps. However, their fates were very different. Most sought refuge in Złoczów County, and several dozen left the area, viewing it as a chance to survive. Only some of them survived. The fate of a few of them was never known.

Hiding Opportunities in Partisan Units

Złoczów County was an operational area of Polish, Soviet, and Ukrainian partisan formations. In the second half of 1943, OUN partisan units launched anti-Polish operations in this county as well as in other parts of Eastern Galicia. Initially, these were only isolated assaults of individual persons who enjoyed substantial authority in local communities, and on foresters who knew the way around the woods.[138] The first assault in Złoczów County regarded as collective murder took place in Kruhów on Christmas Eve, 1943: fifteen Poles and their two Ukrainian neighbors, who were celebrating with them.[139] The Ukrainian Insurgent Army (UIA; Ukr. *Ukrainska povstanska armiia*, UPA) had a quite hostile attitude toward the Jews, but an exception was made for Jewish doctors, who were welcome in the ranks because their services were in demand.[140] The doctors' subsequent fate is not known, not even whether they survived at all.[141] However, sources contain information about UIA assaults on Jewish groups hiding in the woods.[142]

In Złoczów County, no large group of Jews was ever admitted to a Polish partisan unit. But there is information that in October 1943, several Jews found themselves in the ranks of Mikołaj Mazurek's twenty-to-fifty-man-strong Polish partisan[143] detachment operating in the woods near Gołogóry.[144] Apart from sporadic individual cases, the Polish underground in this area did not exhibit any activity to help the Jews but rather only gathered information about the situation in the ghetto and liquidation operations. However, the scant archive records do not allow any determination of how often and what kind of information from the Złoczów Home Army (AK) district was passed to the AK Regional Command in Tarnopol.[145] Today, it is hard to explain certain incidents, such as the circumstances of the massacre of forty-eight or forty-nine Jews in the woods near Wicyń (now Smerekiwka) that took place in November 1943. They were members of a group of seventy to eight Jews who were trying to survive in the area. After the war, the suspect was found to be a member of the local Polish underground structures.[146] In the second half of 1943, large Soviet partisan groups (with some Jewish members, as OUN intelligence sources confirm) were stationed or marched through Złoczów County.[147]

It is impossible to determine the number of Jews in partisan detachments. On the basis of sources, one can only make a preliminary estimate that from the summer of 1943 in Złoczów County, some 128 Jews could have been hiding in partisan formations. Some of them joined Soviet partisans and thus probably survived the war.

Forest Bunkers

Most Jews from Złoczów County tried to hide in the woods, but the conditions of hiding were very hard due to food shortage. People were forced to ask for food in the villages or seize it from a farm or from a field, which meant being exposed to denunciation or otherwise risking one's life.[148]

During the German occupation, some 483 Jews were trying to hide on their own in the woods or in field bunkers in Złoczów County; only a few made such an attempt in 1942, and most did not flee to the woods until 1943. The largest number of Jewish refugees hid in the woods, even though this strategy was extremely difficult and not very effective. Only approximate figures may be given, namely that around 156 Jews (32 percent) survived in this way, 177 were killed (37 percent), and we have no information about the others hiding in the woods.[149]

Hiding on Peasant Farms and among Non-Jewish Town Dwellers

According to the sources, a total of some two hundred Jews (including those who had tried this method in 1942) sought shelter with farmers. Also in Złoczów itself, ten people were probably hidden by two Polish families, while another

Table 5.3 Families/people hiding Jews at home or on their farm in Złoczów County during the German occupation

Categories of helpers hiding Jews	Total number of families	Total number of people involved in hiding	Among them the number of people recognized as Righteous among the Nations	
			Families	People
Village dwellers	42 (3 Ukrainian, 31 Polish; no precise information about 8 families)	70	12 (including 1 Ukrainian)	26
Złoczów inhabitants	3 (Polish)	11	2	6
Helped hide or find people who gave shelter to Jews	2 (1 German and 1 Polish)	8	2	8
Total	**47**	**89**	**16**	**40**

Source: Author's compilation, based on collected documents.

two people received significant help that allowed them to survive outside. By the time the Red Army arrived in July 1944, a total of 154 Jews (73 percent) had survived thanks to their helpers, with only a few in Złoczów itself. Unfortunately, eight people had to escape from their hideouts; only two of them survived the war for certain, and there is no information about the others. In Złoczów County, five people were thrown out or had to abandon their hideouts for various reasons: for example, one in Sokołówka, during an assault by Ukrainian nationalists. During the German occupation, forty-eight Jews (24 percent) who sought shelter with the farmers in the villages lost their lives. The causes of death included arrest by Germans, denunciation by a local detention by the Ukrainian Police, and sometimes murder by people who offered the Jews shelter.[150]

The sources found so far show that in Złoczów County, most Jews hiding among the gentiles, found shelter with Polish families.[151] What is worth emphasizing is the behavior of a German official, Josef Meyer, who as the head of the Department of Supplies and Agriculture in Złoczów during the occupation used his position to help the Jewish population. For example, he increased food supplies for the Jewish hospital and helped Salomon Altman's family hide outside the ghetto, thus saving their lives.[152] Polish inhabitants of Huta Werchobuzka and Huta Pieniacka helped Fajwel Auerbach and his companion, who were hiding in the woods.[153] In April 1943, Majer (Martin) Perlmutter and his companion received help for some time in the woods near Pobocz from Ukrainian peasants.[154]

Hiding with non-Jewish neighbors proved the most effective survival strategy for Złoczów's Jews. However, it involved enormous risk because providing help to the Jews was punishable by death. Only isolated mentions of repressions for helping Jews survived in the sources, and they are not helpful in painting a broader picture of the rescuers' fates. Nevertheless, they should be mentioned. Allegedly, the following arrests were made for hiding Jews: in 1943 in Hucisko Oleskie, the Jaworski family; in the fall of 1943 in Złoczów, Karolina Hajek's family; in May 1944 in Zazule, an undetermined number of Poles. Unfortunately, there is only brief information to the effect that the following were murdered for helping Jews: in the second half of 1942 in Gołogóry, the Smoliński family; in late August or early September in Usznia, four Polish families, who were shot by Ukrainian policemen for hiding Jews and engagement in AK activity; in the second half of 1944 in the Zazule woods, a Ukrainian peasant was hanged.[155]

Wandering

Hiding sometimes meant wandering, changing one's place of stay to avoid being recognized, fleeing from blackmailers, or obtaining food and a place to sleep for the night. This always meant the need to be adaptable in a given terrain and making quick decisions to escape or stay put. This strategy was chosen by those Jews who could not hide permanently with the farmers and those who, instead of hiding in the woods, decided to seek shelter in the villages until they were driven away. Their fate was often determined by accident or bad luck, when they did not come across any heroic Polish or Ukrainian neighbors who could take them in more permanently.[156]

This survival strategy was the most difficult and was the method of hiding least often used by Złoczów's Jews.

Other Strategies: Using Aryan Papers, Forced Labor, Escape Outside the County

One Jewish survival strategy was obtaining false documents, which required adequate funds. Złoczów's Jews applied this strategy, but it did not always succeed.[157] There were very few Jews who had false documents in the county.

More Jews tried to save themselves by leaving their homes and the county. But it cannot be determined precisely how many took such a decision and survived. Such attempts were made at different times, and people would go in different directions. The sources contain information on sixty-nine cases (including forced labor and camps); most of these survived the war (see tables 2 and 5).[158]

Being qualified for forced labor in the Reich was easier for Jewish women. For the men the risk was much greater because those applying for labor in the Reich or taken by compulsion had to appear before a medical board that could easily see their circumcision. Still, some tried to hide in that way.[159]

Some sought rescue by denunciation or treason, which is sometimes reflected in the sources. There were cases when Jews who were trying to save their own lives or the lives of their close ones would resort to this meanest and illusory survival strategy.[160] It is often difficult to pass an unequivocal judgment on such an action because the analyzed events were taking place in a world full of terror, violence, hunger, disease, and death, and these constituted the reality in which Złoczów Jews had to live.

THE ATTITUDE OF POLES AND UKRAINIANS TO THE HOLOCAUST IN ZŁOCZÓW

The German occupation brought the Złoczów County population terror, violence, and repressions, including arrests, deportations to labor camps, and confiscations and appropriation of private property. The villages were heavily burdened with compulsory quotas of food commanded by the occupier. Another heavy burden was the deportations to forced labor in Germany.[161] In this context, the situation of the Jews was particularly dramatic. Not only were they being murdered by the Germans, but they also had to face the ambivalent attitudes of their neighbors. In the reality of the German occupation, there were people hunting for Jews, touts, *szmalcownik* (blackmailers), and thieves of Jewish property on the one hand, and on the other were the few who helped the Jews and hid them. There were also bystanders, who had different attitudes toward Jews. In this category, there were also antisemites who felt no sympathy for the Jews but did not take part in their destruction. Conversely, some bystanders who feared for their own safety refused to hide the Jews but took pity on them and from time to time would give them soup or bread, while others would chase them away and refuse to give them anything.[162]

Helena Kitaj-Drobner gave a generally positive opinion on the attitude of the Polish intelligentsia in Złoczów toward the Jews during the war.[163] One place that provided help for the Jews was the town's hospital.[164] Nevertheless, despite such favorable opinions about some of Złoczów's inhabitants, an overall assessment of the attitudes of the town's non-Jewish (particularly Ukrainian) inhabitants to the Jews and to helping them must be negative. This assessment is also based on such facts as the hideous massacres and plunder during the pogrom of July 1941, followed by hostile attitudes during the occupation and the liquidation operations, including denouncing Jews, whereas only a few Złoczów inhabitants offered help to their persecuted compatriots.

The attitudes of the peasants in the Złoczów region were generally unfavorable, and often even hostile, toward the Jews. Survivors recall that if they could count on any help, it came from the Poles rather than the Ukrainians.[165]

Particularly notorious was the Złoczów Ukrainian Police, which collaborated with the Germans and took part in anti-Jewish operations.[166] Afterward, it eagerly hunted for Jews in hiding. An especially negative role was that of Złoczów Criminal Police functionaries, some of whom had probably signed the *Volksliste*.[167]

It is hard to grasp, on the basis of available sources, the attitude of the local churches (Roman Catholic and Greek Catholic) to the massacre of the Jews. Among the Złoczów County survivors who had given testimonies on their wartime experiences, there was not one who had been saved by clergymen of either denomination. There are only mentions of two Jews from Złoczów County hiding in monasteries, but hardly anything more is known.[168] This thread—that is, the fate of Złoczów Jews and the attitude of the clergy of the local churches toward the Holocaust—should be dealt with at length in the future. It requires painstaking and lengthy research in church and monastic archives, which largely are closed to researchers.[169]

In conclusion, it should be repeated that apart from sporadic and individual cases, there is no evidence of local Ukrainian or Polish underground structures being engaged in broad activity and initiatives on behalf of the Jews, let alone any largescale operation to help the Jews escape and hide from the Germans. It is still an open question as to how Polish partisan detachments responded to the presence of Jewish groups hiding in the local forest, and what the attitude to those groups was. An AK report of mid-1942, which characterized the attitude of Polish society to the Jews in the Lvov area, reads:

> An overwhelming majority of Polish society is hostile toward the Jews or negative, to say the least. Only a few Poles sincerely sympathize with the fate of the Jews as individuals, with whom they are acquainted as good Polish citizens and do not hesitate to help them in need. Most ardent antisemites openly express their satisfaction with the large number of Jews liquidated by the Germans... The majority, however, condemn the brutal

methods of the Germans, but define their attitude to the Jews in the following words: It's good that the Germans and the Ukrainians are doing it, because then we won't need to do it ourselves.[170]

The Ukrainian population also displayed negative attitudes toward the Jews in hiding. One of the AK weekly reports of June 30, 1944, pointed at the Ukrainian population to the roundups of Jews hiding in the counties of Eastern Galicia: "All over the area, hardly a day goes by that the German authorities in collaboration with the Ukrainians don't capture some Jews.'"[171]

STATISTICS AND CONCLUSIONS

Based on recollections of Jewish survivors from Złoczów County and information from various databases, the estimation is that in this county (prewar borders), there could have been some 13,500–14,200 Jews under German occupation, including those who had not lived there previously but were brought there to labor camps, as well as war refugees.

A decisive majority of these Jews were murdered in German deportation and liquidation operations. Although many Złoczów Jews tried to escape arrest, as a result of different circumstances and local conditions—among which the most crucial were no support by the local population and the failure to hide the Jews—only 1,356 Jews in Złoczów County tried to save themselves by choosing one or more survival strategies. On the basis of the sources, it has been established that 634 Jews (46.8 percent) hiding in all kinds of ways survived, mostly thanks to the help of the local population, in the bunkers in the woods, and by applying other strategies (including leaving the county). It may be estimated that 472 survived in Złoczów County, and 63 escaped from the county and found rescue there. As for the others, it is not known where and how they survived. It has been estimated that of all those hiding, around 501 Jews died (including six outside the county), that is, 36.9 percent of those trying to survive. Most lost their lives in the county—around 495 Jews. Nearly half these murders, 243 (48.5 percent) of the deaths, involved certain inhabitants of Złoczów County. Most of them were the local Ukrainian policemen turned German helpers (they hunted and gave the Jews away, collaborated with the Germans during the deportation operations, and sometimes murdered them); there were also town dwellers and peasants, whose nationality is often hard to establish on the basis of the sources, but among them both Ukrainians and Poles denounced the Jews or murdered them themselves (ninety-six deaths are reported to have taken place directly at the hands of the local civilian population). These figures could be even higher if the responsibility and the participation of Ukrainian policemen, as well as a part of the local civilian population, is taken into consideration in the roundups

Table 5.4 Estimated number of Jews in Złoczów County and cases of Jews in hiding, 1941–1944

Number of Jews before 1939	1931: 10,236*
Number of Jews in 1941: 11,750–12,450†	
Number of Jews in 1942 to before the deportation operations	10,359‡
Number of Jews trying to save themselves (those hiding) by means of various survival strategies	1356
Percentage of those trying to save themselves in relation to the Jewish population in 1942	13.1
Estimated number of Jews trying to survive by escaping from the ghetto during the deportation operations in 1942 and who returned to the ghetto after the operations	800§

Source: Author's study.

Notes:

* See *Drugi powszechny spis ludności*, book 78, *Województwo tarnopolskie*, 32.

† The estimates are based on the figures regarding the Jewish population of Złoczów County cited in documents of October–November 1941, which give the figure of 9,660 Jews. We added the estimated number of deaths during the German military occupation, i.e., 2,080–2,780 (the Złoczów pogrom and murders in various places), and after rounding up, we came up with a figure of 11,750–12,450 Jewish inhabitants of the county in June 1941 before the German invasion of the USSR.

‡ Estimate obtained by adding the number of Jews in Złoczów in April 1942: 5,833 (AŻIH, 211/1160, Pismo Komitetu Powiatowego ŻSS do Prezydium ŻSS w Krakowie—Wydział Spraw Ogólnych i Organizacyjnych [Letter of the ŻSS County Committee to ŻSS Presidium in Kraków Department for General and Organizational Affairs], July 17, 1942, 12) to the number of Jews from other towns in Złoczów County and the estimated number brought in from outside the county to labor camps (AAN, Rada Główna Opiekuńcza. Biuro Centrali w Krakowie 1939–1945 [Main Care Council Cracow Headquarters, 1939-1945], 125, seria 2.4, vol. 703, Sprawozdanie I referenta organizacyjno-inspekcyjnego Polskiego Komitetu Opiekuńczego w Złoczowie za miesiąc lipiec 1942 r. [Report of the 1st Organization and Inspection Clerk of the Polish Care Committee in Złoczów], July 1942, 112. AŻIH, 211/1159, Pismo Komitetu Powiatowego ŻSS do Prezydium ŻSS w Krakowie [Letter of the ŻSS County Committee to ŻSS Presidium in Kraków] of April 15, 1942, 10; AAN, 125, seria 2.4, vol. 703, Sprawozdanie I referenta organizacyjno-inspekcyjnego Polskiego Komitetu Opiekuńczego w Złoczowie za miesiąc czerwiec 1942 r. [Report of the 1st Organization and Inspection Clerk of the Polish Care Committee in Złoczów for June 1942], 97; AAN, 125, seria 2.4, vol. 703, Sprawozdanie I referenta organizacyjno-inspekcyjnego Polskiego Komitetu Opiekuńczego w Złoczowie za miesiąc czerwiec 1942 r. [Report of the 1st Organization and Inspection Clerk of the Polish Care Committee in Złoczów for June 1942], 95–96, 98, 101). When there were no data for the individual towns and villages for 1942, we based our estimates on the statistics for the Złoczów court district for the period of October–November 1941 (DALO, f. R-370, op. 1, spr. 22, Anzahl der Bewohner in den Räumen der einzelnen Gemeinden Zloczower Bezirkes [Number of Inhabitants in the Communes of Zloczow County], 1; Gemeinden der Zloczow Bezirkes [Communes of the Zloczow District], 10–13). We assumed that in mid-1942, there were around 1,000 labor camp prisoners who had been brought in from outside Złoczów County.

§ It is now impossible to determine the precise number of people who attempted escape during the deportation operations of 1942 in order to hide. For example, during both deportation operations, the Jewish population of Sasów used escape to the nearby woods as a way of avoiding prison, whereas escapes from the Złoczów ghetto in 1942 seem far less frequent than those in Sasów, and the people usually hid in the ghetto, while others hid in other parts of the town.

Table 5.5 Causes of death and the estimated number of Złoczów County Jews murdered while hiding, 1941–1944*

Cause of death	Number of people killed (%)
Murder by German gendarmerie/police (own initiative)	232 (46.3%)
Murder by German gendarmerie/police (denounced by the locals, captured by the Ukrainian police or with their help)	122 (24.4%)
Murder by Ukrainian policemen (own initiative)	6 (1.2%)
Murder by Ukrainian policemen (denounced by the locals)	2 (0.4%)
Murder by the local underground	17† (3.4%)
Murder by local civilians	96 (19.2%)
Death by other causes (in a hideout, suicide)	7 (1.4%)
Murdered outside the county	6 (1.2%)
Circumstances of death unknown/no data/other	13 (2.1%)
Number of victims during hiding	**501 (100%)**

Source: Author's study, based on collected documents

* In certain cases, the number of deaths is approximate. It was often impossible to establish the identity of the victims.

† In fifteen cases, the witnesses said that the perpetrators were Bandera followers; two people were shot in the forest, probably by Ukrainian partisans.

of the Jews. The responsibility for capturing Jews after a liquidation operation in the ghetto lay among others in the hands of the Criminal Police, along with some local Polish functionaries that served on the force. In this context, one should not fail to mention the involvement of some locals in the pogrom of July 1941. All this made it easy for the Germans to carry out liquidation operations and hunt for the hiding Jews.[172] The fate of at least 221 people who tried to save themselves remains unknown.

It should be stressed here that the statistics of the causes of death of those Jews who tried to save themselves could not comprise unidentified people who fled from deportation transports. Many died in the attempt, but the size of this group is unknown. They were counted as Bełżec victims. It should also be assumed that sources do not contain information about all the Jews who were in hiding and who were murdered where there no witnesses; their deaths were not recorded, and no information survived.

In conclusion, during the war, around 130–145 Jews who were living in Złoczów County in September 1939 found themselves in the Soviet heartland (among them persecuted persons, war refugees, and people evacuated in June

1941).[173] In contrast, only some of those hiding survived the German occupation, which accounted for a small fraction of the total number of Jews who found themselves in Złoczów County during the war. These statistics should be regarded as estimates and approximations, but they do reflect certain trends in the area in question.

Studies show that the largest group of Jewish survivors in Złoczów County survived thanks to the help of their neighbors. However, these were quite few in comparison with the total non-Jewish population of the county. The sources indicate that only eighty-one locals offered shelter to the Jews for a longer period of time. In contrast, the woods were plagued with robbery and assault. Of those hiding in the woods, only a small percentage survived.

The Jews in Złoczów County adopted various survival strategies during the Holocaust. Everyone tried to save themselves by whatever means available: Some could buy false documents, pay for a room, and hide on the Aryan side; others would build a bunker in the woods, which had to be dug out and masked, and then get food every day; still others would ask their Polish or Ukrainian friends to help them hide. Therefore, different people had different chances of survived. The success of each of the adopted survival strategies most of all depended on other people's support, primarily the non-Jewish population of Złoczów and Złoczów County.[174]

NOTES

1. Tomasz Kunzek, *Przewodnik po województwie tarnopolskiem. Monografia krajoznawcza z 82 ilustracjami w tekście i 2 mapkami* (Tarnopol: Podolskie Towarzystwo Turystyczno-Krajoznawcze, 1928), 98–104.

2. *Rozporządzenie Rady Ministrów z dnia 17 maja 1921 r. w przedmiocie wykonania art. 3 ustawy z dnia 3 grudnia 1920 r. o tymczasowej organizacji władz administracyjnych II instancji (województw) na obszarze b. Królestwa Galicji i Lodomerji z W. Ks. Krakowskiem oraz na wchodzących w skład Rzeczypospolitej Polskiej obszarach Spisza i Orawy* [The Decree of the Council of Ministers of May 17, 1921 regarding the imoplementation of article 3 of the law of December 3, 1920 concerning the temporary establishment of the administrative authorities of II level (Voivodships) in the area of the former Galicia and Lodomeria and on the areas of Spisz and Orawa which now are included in the territory of the Polish Republic], Dz.U. RP 1921, nr 46, poz. 282; Kazimierz Żmigrodzki, *Powiat złoczowski* (Złoczów: Powiatowe Towarzystwo Turystyczno-Krajoznawcze, 1927), 7, 48–50.

3. *Drugi powszechny spis ludności z dnia 9 grudnia 1931 r. Mieszkania i gospodarstwa domowe. Ludność. Stosunki zawodowe*, "Statystyka Polski" [Second General Census of December 9, 1931. Apartments and family dwellings. Population.

Professional relations. "Statistics of Poland"], series C, book 78, *Województwo tarnopolskie* [Tarnopol Voivodship] (Warsaw: GUS RP, 1938), 72, 73, 89.

4. The population in the towns is based on the provisional results of the 1931 census because there is no detailed data for them. *Skorowidz gmin Rzeczypospolitej Polskiej. Ludność i budynki na podstawie tymczasowych wyników Drugiego Powszechnego Spisu Ludności z dn. 9 grudnia 1931 r. oraz powierzchnia ogólna i użytki rolne*, part. 3: *Województwa południowe*, "Statystyka Polski" [Index of the Communes of the Polish Republic: The Population and Dwellings Based Upon the Results of the Second General Census of December 9, 1931 as well as the general Surface and Agricultural Areas, Part 3, Southern Voievodsips, series B, book 8c, (Warsaw: GUS RP, 1933), 78.

5. There were 36,937 people who declared Roman Catholicism; for Greek Catholic, there were as many as 70,596 inhabitants in Złoczów County. Second General Census, book 78, *Województwo tarnopolskie*, 32, 35.

6. *Rozporządzenie ministra spraw wewnętrznych z 14 VII 1934 r. o podziale powiatu złoczowskiego w województwie tarnopolskiem na gminy wiejskie* [Decree of the Minister of Interior Dividing Złoczów County into Rural Communes of July 14, 1934], Dz.U. 1934, nr 64, poz. 572, 1139–1140; *Skorowidz gmin Rzeczypospolitej Polskiej. Ludność i budynki na podstawie tymczasowych wyników Drugiego Powszechnego Spisu Ludności . . .*, part. 3, series B, book 8c, 5.

7. Łucja Charewiczowa, *Dzieje miasta Złoczowa* (Złoczów: Powiatowe Towarzystwo Turystyczno-Krajoznawcze, 1929), 68; State Archive of the Lviv Oblast (Derzhavnyi Arkhiv Lvivskoy Oblasti, subsequently DALO), Urząd Gubernatora Dystryktu Galicja we Lwowie 1941–1944 [The Office of the Governor of District Galicia in Lvov 1941–1944], f. R-35, op. 9, spr. 358, Jüdisches Krankenhaus in Zloczow [Jewish Hospital in Zloczow], no date, 10; Curriculum Vitae of Dr, Abraham Hreczanik [November 20, 1941], 11; Curriculum vitae Dr, Chaja Zwerdling [November 19, 1941], 14; Curriculum Vitae Dr, Salomon Jollek, 16.

8. State Archive of the Tarnopol Oblast in Tarnopol (Derzhavnyi Arkhiv Tarnopolskoy Oblasti, subsequently DATO), Urząd Wojewódzki w Tarnopolu [Voievodship Office in Tarnopol] 1921–1939, f. 231, op. 1, spr. 3202, Pismo Starostwa Powiatowego w Złoczowie z 5 XII 1936 r. do Wydziału Społeczno-Politycznego Urzędu Wojewódzkiego w Tarnopolu w sprawie Rejonowego Komitetu KPZU [Letter of the County Governor's Office to the Sociopolitical Department of the Provincial Office in Tarnopol, regarding the Regional Committee of the Communist Party of Western Ukraine], 114. For political life, see DATO, f. 231, op. 1, spr. 1216, Żydowska partia "Aguda" [The Jewish Party "Aguda"] [data as of September 1, 1929], 48; Organizacja syjonistyczna "Allgemeine" [the Zionist organization "Allgemeine"] [data as of September 1, 1929], 47; spr. 3362, List do Jego Ekscelencji Pana Premiera gen. Felicjana Sławoja Składkowskiego od przedstawicieli żydowskich "Agudas Izrael" w sprawie rabina Sperbera, maj/czerwiec 1937 r. [Letter to His Excellency Prime Minister

Gen. Felicjan Sławoj Składkowski from Jewish Representatives of "Agudas Izrael" regarding Rabbi Sperber, May/June 1937], 2.

9. Ośrodek KARTA [The KARTA Center], Archiwum Wschodnie [Eastern Archive], Wspomnienia [Recollections], II/1420/2KW, Franciszek Sikorski, *Najpiękniejsze wzgórza i doliny* [The Most Beautiful Hills and Valleys] (recollections), 1.

10. Robert Potocki, *Polityka państwa polskiego wobec zagadnienia ukraińskiego w latach 1930-1939* (Lublin: Instytut Europy Środkowo-Wschodniej, 2003), 76–78; Karol Grünberg and Bolesław Sprengel, *Trudne sąsiedztwo. Stosunki polsko-ukraińskie w X–XX wieku* (Warsaw: Książka i Wiedza, 2005), 390, 424–426.

11. In February 1937, a Przewołoczna store was assaulted and anti-Jewish leaflets were thrown, an act of which young Ukrainians were suspected; in Ożydów in December, a liquor store was attacked. DATO, f. 231, op. 1, spr. 3062, 7, 8, 12.

12. USC Shoah Foundation, Visual History Archive (subsequently USC, VHA), 32492, Testimony of Maurycy Altstock; USC, VHA, 1518, Testimony of Jackob Gang; USC, VHA, 36932, Testimony of Pepe Chouak; Ośrodek KARTA, Archiwum Wschodnie, II/1420/2KW, Sikorski, *Najpiękniejsze wzgórza i doliny*, 2.

13. Russian State Military Archive (Rossijskij gosudarstwiennyj wojennyj archiw, subsequently RGWA), Korpus Ochrony Pogranicza Ministerstwa Spraw Wewnętrznych Rzeczypospolitej Polskiej (Warsaw) 1918–1939 [The Border Protection Corps], f. 354k, op. 1, d. 451, Biuletyn w sprawie ukraińskiej nr 7, Złoczów, March 27, 1939, 7–8; Grzegorz Hryciuk, *Przemiany narodowościowe i ludnościowe w Galicji Wschodniej i na Wołyniu 1931–1948* (Toruń: Wydawnictwo Adam Marszałek, 2005), 162.

14. Tatiana Berenstein, "Eksterminacja ludności żydowskiej w dystrykcie Galicja (1941–1943)", *Biuletyn ŻIH* 61, no. 1 (1967), table 12, "*Powiat Złoczów*" [Złoczów County].

15. The phenomenon of migration is reflected in testimonies and recollections: Archiwum Żydowskiego Instytutu Historycznego (Jewish Historical Institute Archive, subsequently AŻIH), Relacje Żydów Ocalałych z Zagłady [Testimonies of Jewish Survivors], 301/3285, Testimony of Anna Ulreich, typewritten, 1; USC, VHA, 38456, Testimony of Ruvim Rubin; USC, VHA, 36181, Testimony of Aleksander Safier; USC, VHA, 7345, Testimony of Szymon Borkowski.

16. Anna Zapalec, *Ziemia tarnopolska w okresie pierwszej okupacji sowieckiej 1939–1941* (Kraków: Księgarnia Akademicka, 2006), 65; Czesław K. Grzelak, *Kresy w czerwieni. Agresja Związku Sowieckiego na Polskę w 1939 roku* (Warsaw: Oficyna Wydawnicza Rytm, 2001), 218, 307, 309, 311; Ośrodek KARTA, Archiwum Wschodnie, II/1388/2K, Władysław Olesiński, Zapiski [Notes], 6.

17. Zapalec, *Ziemia tarnopolska*, 74; Archiwum Instytutu Pamięci Narodowej Oddział w Krakowie (Archive of the Institute of National Remembrance in Kraków, subsequently AIPN Kr), Collection of Adam Macedoński, 719/38. For more on the shooting of Poles, see Grzelak, *Kresy w czerwieni*, 497–498, 500.

18. For more on political and administrative action on territories occupied by the Red Army, see for example Michał Gnatowski, ed., *Radziecka agresja 17 września 1939 i jej skutki dla mieszkańców ziem północno-wschodnich II Rzeczypospolitej. Studia i materiały* (Białystok: IH UwB, 2000), 76–77; Albin Głowacki, *Sowieci wobec Polaków na ziemiach wschodnich II Rzeczypospolitej 1939–1941* (Łódź: Wydawnictwo Uniwersytetu Łódzkiego, 1998), 25, 54–61, 63.

19. For example, in the Tarnopol Oblast, in the Bureau of the Oblast Committee of the Communist Party (Bolsheviks) of Ukraine, all its members had been sent from eastern Ukraine; in the Tarnopol Oblast Executive Committee, only one person came from the area. Central State Archive of Social Organizations of Ukraine in Kiev (Centralnyj derzhavnyi archiv hromadśkykh obyednan Ukrayiny, subsequently CDAHOU), Komitet Centralny Komunistycznej Partii Ukrainy [Central Committee of the Communist Party of Ukraine], 1917–1991, f. 1, op. 6, spr. 513, 235; Central State Archives of Supreme Bodies of Power and Government of Ukraine in Kiev (Centralnyj derzhavnyi archiw wyszczych orhaniw włady i uprawlinnia Ukrayiny, subsequently CDAWOWUU), Rada Najwyższa Ukrainy 1917–1991 [Supreme Council of Ukraine, 1917–1991], f. 1, op. 16, spr. 7, 75.

20. Siergiej G. Filippow, "Diejatiel'nost' organow WKP(b) w zapadnych obłastiach Ukrainy i Biełorussii w 1939–1941 gg.", in *Riepressii protiw polakow i polskich grażdan*, ed. Aleksandr Gurjanow, book 1, Istoriczeskije sborniki "Memoriała" series (Moscow: Izdatiełstwo "Zwienja," 1997), 46.

21. Ośrodek KARTA, Archiwum Wschodnie, II/1420/2KW, Franciszek Sikorski, *Najpiękniejsze wzgórza i doliny*, 13; USC, VHA, 36932, Testimony of Pepe Chouak; USC, VHA, 32492, Testimony of Maurycy Altstock.

22. USC, VHA, 32492, Testimony of Leonid Vugman; USC, VHA, 36932, Testimony of Pepe Chouak; USC, VHA, 21772, Testimony of Fani Fulero; Centrum Dokumentacji Czynu Niepodległościowego w Krakowie (Krakow Independence Movement Documentation Centre, subsequently CDCN), Archiwum złoczowskie Romana Maćkówki [Roman Maćkówka's Złoczów archive], 2628, Wróbel [name unknown], "Dziennik złoczowski z lat 1939–1941: wydarzenia ze Złoczowa, kraju i ze świata" [The Złoczów Daily, 1939–1941: News from Złoczów, from the Country and from the World], part 1, 3. For more on the situation under the Soviet occupation in the Tarnopol Voivodship, see also Jan Tomasz Gross and Irena Grudzińska-Gross, eds., *"W czterdziestym nas matko na Sibir zesłali." Polska a Rosja 1939–1942* (Warsaw: Res Publica), 157–175, 439.

23. Calculations based on DALO, Sąd Okręgowy w Złoczowie [Złoczów District Court] 1941–1944, f. R-370, op. 1, spr. 22, *Gemeinden der Zloczow Bezirkes* [Communes in the Zloczow *Bezirk*], November 1941, 10–13; DALO, f. R-35, op. 9, spr. 37, *Kreis* Zloczow. Die Nachweisung der Stadt und Landgemeinden mit eingegliederter Ortschaften [*Kreis* Zloczow. List of rural and urban communes, together with incorporated towns and villages], November 1941, 9–13, 15–18. To these figures were added the estimated numbers of Jews murdered in Złoczów County between July and October 1941.

24. RGWA, Secret State Police Office in Berlinie (Gestapo) 1933–1945, f. 500k, op. 2, d. 229, Ereignismeldung UdSSR no 14 (July 6, 1941) [mf], 5–6; Ereignismeldung UdSSR no 24 (July 16, 1941) [mf], 73; Zakład Narodowy im. Ossolińskich we Wrocławiu (Ossoliński National Institute in Wrocław; subsequently Ossolineum), manuscript 16264/I (microfilm 27569), Walery Maryański, *Dziennik z lat 1919–1920, 1941–1946* [Diary 1919–1920, 1941–1946], notebook 5, 146–147; Dieter Pohl, *Nationalsozialistische Judenverfolgung in Ostgalizien 1941–1944. Organisation und Durchführung eines staatlichen Massenverbrechens* (München: Oldenbourg Verlag, 1997), 59, 62–63; Marko Carynnyk, "Złoczów milczy", in *OUN, UPA i zagłada Żydów*, ed. Andrzej Ziemba (Kraków: Księgarnia Akademicka, 2016), 344–345.

25. The first lineup of Edmund Schöne's operational group included mainly Sipo functionaries seconded from Warsaw, which is where reports were sent; RGWA, Police offices, and administrative offices in Germany and temporarily occupied territories 1806–1945, f. 1323, op. 1, d. 59, *Der Kommandeur der Sicherheitspolizei und des SD für den Distrikt Warschau an den Befehlshaber der Sicherheitspolizei und des SD im Generalgouvernement z. Hd. des Herrn Befehlshabers in Krakau* (Beglaubigte Abschrift) [Security Police and SD Commander in the Warsaw District to the Commander of the Security Police and SD in the General Government, by hand, Kraków (certified copy)], June 30, 1941, 237; *Pol. Insp. Anw. Mietzner an den Der Kommandeur der Sicherheitspolizei und des SD für den Distrikt Warschau* [Police Inspector Mietzner to Security Police and SD Commander in the Warsaw District], September 21, 1941, 258.

26. Zapalec, *Ziemia tarnopolska*, 265.

27. Gabriele Lesser, "Pogromy w Galicji Wschodniej w 1941 r.", in *Tematy polsko-ukraińskie. Historia, literatura, edukacja*, ed. Robert Traba (Olsztyn, 2001), 112; Witold Mędykowski, *W cieniu gigantów. Pogromy 1941 r. w byłej sowieckiej strefie okupacyjnej. Kontekst historyczny, społeczny i kulturowy* (Warsaw: ISP PAN, 2012), 263.

28. USC, VHA, 17071, Testimony of Shlomo Wolkowicz; CDCN, Roman Maćkówka's Złoczów archive, 2628: Wróbel, "Dziennik złoczowski z lat 1939–1941: wydarzenia ze Złoczowa, kraju i ze świata", part 1, 22.

29. Carynnyk, *Złoczów milczy*, 345; Aleksiej Bakanow, *"Ni kacapa, ni żyda, ni lacha". Nacjonalnyj wopros w idieołogii Organizacii ukrainskich nacjonalistow, 1921–1945*, (Moscow: Ałgoritm, 2014), 188-189; State Archive of the Russian Federation (Gosudarstvennyy Arkhiv Rossiyskoy Federatsii, subsequently GARF), Extraordinary State Commission for Establishing and Analysis of the German-Fascist Invaders and their Henchmen and the Harm Done to Private Persons, Collective Farms (*kolkhozes*), Social Organizations, State-Owned Enterprises and Institutions of the USSR (NKP) 1942–1951, f. 7021, op. 67, d. 134, A list of German-fascist criminals and their collaborators committing crimes on temporarily occupied territory of the Lvov oblast USRR; GARF, f. 7021, op. 67, d. 80, Witness interrogation report of Abram Rozen of September 16, 1944, 4; Witness interrogation report of Alte Bomze of September 16, 1944, 9. In Poland, in April 1945, Eliasz Antoniak was arrested based on an accusation of, among others, Menachim Fenster, of being actively involved in a pogrom of Jews in Złoczów. But he was acquitted in a trial before a Polish court. At that time, the public prosecutor's office did not have the investigation documents of the Extraordinary State Commission to Investigate the German-Fascist Crimes of the Committee for Soviet Territories. It did not find any Jewish survivors of the pogrom, not did it interrogate them; AIPN Kr, Specjalny Sąd Karny w Krakowie [Special Criminal Court in Kraków] 1945–1946, 502/609, Trial files of Eliasz Antoniak, OUN member, accused of taking part in pogroms of the Jewish population, in collaboration with the Nazi authorities, and by his actions caused the death of a man of Jewish nationality in the town of Złoczów in 1941, that is an act defined in Art. 1 of the Decree of August 31, 1944 (1945–1946);Report of the interrogation of the accused suspect Eliasz Antoniak of August 2, 1945, 35–36v.

30. A German report of July 1941 mentions the strong influence of Stepan Bandera's followers in Złoczów, while the Ukrainian administration that emerged in the town greeted the Germans as allies; RGWA, f. 500k, op. 2, d. 229, Ereignismeldung UdSRR nr 24, 74. Dieter Pohl estblished that some influence was gained by the *pochidna hrupa* (unit) of Ivan Klymiv (Lehenda). In Pohl's opinion, it could have "initiated or at least sympathized with the idea of joining the operation of *Einsatzkommando* 4b"; Pohl, *Nationalsozialistische Judenverfolgung in Ostgalizien*, 62). See also Ossolineum, manuscript 16264/I (microfilm 27569), Walery Maryański, *Dziennik...*, notebook 5, 150.

31. Bakanow, *"Ni kacapa, ni żyda, ni lacha,"* 188–189; GARF, f. 7021, op. 67, d. 80, Report of the interrogation of the witness Samuel Rozen of September 15, 1944, 2; Report of the interrogation of the witness Alte Bomze of September 16, 1944, 9; Report of the interrogation of the witness Jakov Taykhman of September 16, 1944, 12.

32. Salomon Altman, "Haunting Memories", in *Yizkor Books* [Memory Books]: *Zolochiv*, 38–39, translated into English, https://digitalcollections.

nypl.org/items/28c6dfd0-232c-0133-3191-58d385a7b928 (accessed July 19, 2016); AŻIH, 301/87, Testimony of Mendel Ruder, typewritten, 1; IPN OK Kr, S 47/13/Zn, vol. 3, translation from German into Polish of a copy of files of the American Military Tribunal II, case IV, Nuremberg Germany, testimony of Arnold Sauer of August 20, 1947 (6505–6506), 389–390, translated by A. Romanek. Transcript of Case IV, including the testimony of A. Sauer, is available in English: NMT Case 4, USA v. Pohl et al. (6572–6573), Harvard Law School Library's Nuremberg Trials Project, http://nuremberg.law.harvard.edu/transcripts/5-transcript-for-nmt-4-pohl-case?seq=6597&q=Arnold+Sauer (accessed July 11, 2018).

33. CDCN, Roman Maćkówka's Złoczów archive, 2628: Wróbel, "Dziennik złoczowski z lat 1939–1941: wydarzenia ze Złoczowa, kraju i ze świata", part 1, 24; "Protokoł doprosow żytielej g. Zołoczewa A. W. Roziena i J. W. Roziena o pogromach i uniczłożenii mirnych żytielej niemieckimi formirowanijami i sotrudniczawszymi s Niemcami priedstawitielami Ukrainskogo komitieta w 1941–1943 gg. (16 sientiabrija 1944 r.)", in *Ukrainskije nacjonalisticzeskije organizacii w gody wtoroj mirowoj wojny. Dokumienty*, vol. 2: *1944–1945*, ed. Andriey N. Artizov (Moscow: Rossyiskaja politiczeskaya enciklopediya [ROSSPEN], 2012), 320–322; USC, VHA, 17071, Testimony of Shlomo Wolkowicz.

34. According to the current historical findings, that is how some soldiers tried to avenge the death of the commander of one the regiments of "Viking" division, who died near the village of Slovita, some twenty-five kilometers west of Złoczów, shot by a Soviet soldier. However, blame was placed on the Jews. For more on this topic, see Kai Struve, "Wstrząsy w strefie starcia imperiów. Galicja Wschodnia latem 1941 r.", in *OUN, UPA i zagłada Żydów*, 163–164; Carynnyk, *Złoczów milczy*, 345–347.

35. Bernd Boll, "Zloczow, Juli 1941: Die Wehrmacht und der Beginn des Holocaust in Galizien", *Zeitschrift für Geschichtswissenschaft*, no 10 (2002): 906–907; Carynnyk, *Złoczów milczy*, 348.

36. Sources contain several names of local inhabitants who were to witness all kinds of incidents during the pogrom (they identified Jewish homes, carried out arrests, or tormented Jews). Among those there were not only the town's poor but also members of the local elite. See Bakanow, *"Ni kacapa, ni żyda, ni lacha,"* 189–191; YVA, Collection of testimonies from the Central Historical Committee of Liberated Jews in Munich, 1946–1948, M.1.E/668, Ilena Baum, 1; AIPN, Sąd Okręgowy [District Court] in Brzeg, GK 623/33, Case files: Michał Pawliszczyn; GARF, f. 7021, op. 67, d. 80, Report of the interrogation of the witness Samuel Rozen of September 16, 1944, 2–2v; Report of the interrogation of the witness Alte Bomze of September 16, 1944, 9; Report of the interrogation of the witness Jakov Taykhman of September 16, 1944, 12–13.

37. YVA, Collection of Testimonies of the Jewish Historical Institute, M.49.E/1524, Testimony of Helena Kitaj-Drobnerowa, 1–4; YVA, M.1.E/668,

Testimony of Ilena Baum, 1; IPN OK Kr, S 47/13/Zn, vol. 7, Report of the interrogation of the witness Roman M. of September 20, 2008, 1297; USC, VHA, 21772, Testimony of Fani Fulero; USC, VHA, 12624, Testimony of Marek Goldenberg; AŻIH, 301/801, Testimony of Bolesław Kapelman, 1; AŻIH, Pamiętniki Żydów Ocalałych z Zagłady [Memoirs of Jewish Survivors], 302/227, Pamiętnik [Diary of] Fani Laufer, 3; YVA, O.3/3302: M. Dul, "Z otchłani", 12–13; Altman, *Haunting Memories*, 42.

38. USC, VHA, 17071, Testimony of Shlomo Wolkowicz; *Protokoł doprosow żytielej g. Zołoczewa A.W. Roziena i J.W. Roziena o pogromach*, 320–321.

39. AIPN,GK 623/33, Main hearing transcript of July 15, 1947, Witness testimony of Hana Kandel-Kac, 160; IPN OK Kr, S 47/13/Zn, vol. 3, Interrogation of Salomon Jollek of September 3, 1947, translated by A. Romanek, 549–550; USC, VHA, 44638, Testimony of Sheiva Fradkina; USC, VHA, 17071, Testimony of Shlomo Wolkowicz; AŻIH, 301/531, Testimony of Chaim Wittelsohn, typewritten, 1.

40. GARF, f. 7021, op. 67, d. 80, Reports of the Forensic and Medical Expert Commission for the Location of Burial Sites and Corpse Examination in the town of Złoczów [certified copy], no date,1944–1945, 59–61.

41. Ibid., 77.

42. If we take into consideration the statistical data of November 1941 regarding the number of Jews still living in Złoczów, then the number of people killed in the pogrom could not have been higher than 3,200. At the turn of October and November 1941, the Jewish population of the town was 6,228 (statistical data for 1941 from DALO, f. R-370, op. 1, spr. 22, Anzahl der Bewohner in den Räumen der einzelnen Gemeinden Zloczower Bezirkes [Number of inhabitants of the individual communes in *Bezirk* Zloczow; document of late October/early November 1941], 1). During the military occupation, from July 3 to 10, around 420–460 more Jews were shot.

43. "Akt progłoszennja widnowlennja Ukrajinśkoj Derżawy u Zołoczewi" [Act of Proclamation of Renewal of the Ukrainian State in Złoczew], in *Zołoczіwszczyna: iji mynule i suczasne*, ed. Wolodymyr Bolubashm (New York: Kanadśkie Naukowe Towarystwo im. Szewczenka, 1982), 539–540; Petro Oryszkiewycz, "Szkilnictwo u Zołoczewi w rokach 1939–1941" [Schooling at Zolochiv in 1939–1941], in *Zołoczіwszczyna*, 549; O. Ilkiw, "Sieło Bużok za swaje nacionalnoje oblicza" [Village Bużok for its national identity], in *Zołoczіwszczyna*, 307; Ossolineum, manuscript 16264/I (microfilm 27569), Walery Maryański, *Dziennik...*, notebook 5, 163, 168–169.

44. Berenstein, *Eksterminacja ludności żydowskiej*, 4, 6; Józef Anczarski, *Kronikarskie zapisy z lat cierpień i grozy w Małopolsce Wschodniej 1939–1946*, Kazimierz Załuski, ed. (Kraków: Wydawnictwo bł. Jakuba Strzemię Archidiecezji Lwowskiej, 1996), 195.

45. GARF, f. 7021, op. 67, d. 80, Act of the Extraordinary Municipal Commission for Establishing and Analysis of German-Fascist Crimes in the Town of Złoczów, September 24, 1944, 77.

46. AŻIH, 301/4991, Testimony of Chaim Schöps, 1; Ephraim Sten, *1111 Days in My Life Plus Four* (Maryland: Dryad, 2006), 11, 13.

47. GARF, f. 7021, op. 67, d. 80, Act of the Extraordinary Municipal Commission for Establishing and Analysis of German-Fascist in the Town of Złoczów, September 24, 1944, 77; AŻIH, 301/4991, Testimony of Chaim Schöps', 1; AŻIH, 301/4670, Testimony of Majer Perlmutter, 1; YVA, M.49.E/3701, Testimony of Herman Weigler, 2–4; AŻIH, 301/7006, Testimony of Michał Kutny, 1; GARF, f. 7021, op. 67, d. 84, Act of November 18, 1944, from the village of Zarwanica [population losses during the German occupation], 26.

48. Berenstein, *Eksterminacja ludności żydowskiej*, 9.

49. DALO, Sąd Specjalny przy Sądzie Niemieckim we Lwowie dystryktu Galicja [Special Court at the German Court in Lvov, District of Galicia], 1941–1944, f. R-77, op. 1, spr. 225, Verteiler 4–7, 5–8.

50. DALO, f. R-77, op. 1, spr. 712, Data regarding the structure of Lvov organizations and other prosecution organs (1943), 1; Thomas Sandkühler, *"Endlösung" in Galizien. Der Judenmord in Ostpolen und die Rettungsinitiativen von Berthold Beitz 1941–1944* (Bonn: Dietz, 1996), 439.

51. Hans Mann, born 1908, from 1932 a NSDAP member, and *Kreishauptmann* of *Kreis* Zloczow until January 1943, subsequently inducted into the Wehrmacht; Pohl, *Nationalsozialistische Judenverfolgung in Ostgalizien*, 418.

52. After the invasion of the Soviet Union by Germany in 1941, Dr. Otto Wendt was appointed deputy county governor in Stryj and Kałusz and later, from January 6, 1943, Zloczow County governor. In the 1960s, the Public Prosecutor's Office of the *Landgericht* in Göttingen conducted proceedings in his case, but the conclusion was that "a life sentence cannot be passed, rather only imprisonment from 3 to 15 years." Proceedings were discontinued due to the statute of limitations; IPN OK Kr, S 47/13/Zn, vol. 7, Decision to Discontinue Proceedings against Dr. Wendt Issued by the Public Prosecutor's Office in Göttingen, 1406–1413, translated from the German by A. Romanek; Sandkühler, *"Endlösung" in Galizien*, 452; Martin Dean, ed., *Encyclopedia of Camps and Ghettos, 1933–1945*, vol. 2: *Ghettos in German-Occupied Eastern Europe*, part. A (Bloomington: Indiana University Press, 2012), 850.

53. AIPN Oddział w Lublinie (AIPN in Lublin, subsequently AIPN Lu), Prokuratura Sądu Okręgowego w Lublinie [Public Prosecutor's Office of the Lublin District Court 1944–1950], 319/1145, Akta prokuratora Sądu Okręgowego w Lublinie w sprawie Ottona Zickmunda (Zikmunda)] [Files of the Public Prosecutor of the Lublin District Court in Otto Zickmund's (Zikmund's) case], Pismo z Internationales Komitee für Jüd. KZ-ler und Flüchtlinee

Poln. Jüd. Hilfskomitee do kierownika Ekstradycyjnego Nadzoru Prokuratorskiego Ministerstwa Sprawiedliwości w Warszawie [Letter from Internationales Komitee für Jüd. KZ-ler und Flüchtlinee Poln. Jüd. Hilfeekomitee to the Head of the Extraordinary Prosecutorial Supervision of the Ministry of Justice in Warsaw], May 29, 1947 [copy in Polish], 2; Pohl, *Nationalsozialistische Judenverfolgung in Ostgalizien*, 423.

54. Altman, *Haunting Memories*, 54, 90; AIPN Lu, 319/1145, Copy of the testimony of Hermann Grünseid of May 2, 1947 (Vienna), 5; YVA, O.5/61, Otto Zikmund, Interrogation of Otto Zikmund of May 13, 1947, 6; Interrogation of Otto Zikmund of May 14, 1947, 5; Interrogation of Otto Zikmund of May 12, 1947, 8; Pohl, *Nationalsozialistische Judenverfolgung in Ostgalizien*, 255; IPN OK Kr, S 47/13/Zn, vol. 1, Report of the interrogation of Julian W. of May 9, 2001, 26.

55. The names of the gendarmes have not been established. Quoted from Altman, *Haunting Memories*, 54; IPN OK Kr, S 47/13/Zn, vol. 7, Decision to discontinue proceedings against Dr. Wendt issued by the Public Prosecutor's Office in Göttingen, 1408.

56. AIPN Lu, Specjalny Sąd Karny w Lublinie [Special Criminal Court in Lublin], 1944–1946, 315/76, Report of the interrogation of the suspect Henryk Lenc, April 15, 1945, 14; Gabriel N. Finder and Alexander V. Prusin, "Collaboration in Eastern Galicia: The Ukrainian Police and the Holocaust," *East European Jewish Affairs* 34, no. 2 (2004): 106.

57. IPN OK Kr, S 47/13/Zn, vol. 7, Decision to discontinue proceedings against Dr. Wendt issued by the Public Prosecutor's Office in Göttingen, 1411.

58. DALO, f. R-35, op. 9, spr. 37, An alle Kreishauptleute. Betrifft: Bildung der Sammelgemeinden [To all *Kreishauptmannschaften* regarding the creation of collective communes], October 16, 1941, 3; An den Herrn Kreishauptmann in Zloczow. Betrifft Bildung der Landgemeinden [To the *Kreishauptmann* in Zloczow Regarding the Creation of Rural Communes], 6. In the early days of the German occupation, heads of rural communes were almost exclusively Ukrainians. Only in Ożydów was there a German commune head. DALO, f. R-35, op. 9, spr. 37, *Sammelgemeinde* [Collective communes], no date, 43–44; Listenmässige Aufstellung der zur Kreishauptmannschaft Zloczow gehörenden 6 Städte und 29 Sammelgemeinden sowie namentliches Verzeichnis der Bürgermeister [List of 6 towns and 29 Rural Communes in Zloczow *Kreishauptmannschaft*, Including the Names of Mayors], no date, no pagination. Minute shifts of villages between communes were made (DALO, f. R-370, op. 1, spr. 22, Anzahl der Bewohner in den Räumen der einzelnen Gemeinden Zloczower Bezirkes, 1; Gemeinden der Zloczow Bezirkes, 10–13).

59. The figures reflect the Jewish population of the county only several months after the German invasion. Thus, they do not reflect the size of the Jewish population at the beginning of the German occupation because many Jews

were killed in pogroms and executions in July 1941, and in the following months they died under civilian administration.

60. DALO, f. R-370, op. 1, spr. 22, *Anzahl der Bewohner in den Räumen der einzelnen Gemeinden Zloczower Bezirkes*, 1; *Gemeinden der Zloczow Bezirkes*, November 1941, 10–13; DALO, R-35, op. 9, spr. 37, *Kreis Zloczow. Die Nachweisung der Stadt und Landgemeinden mit eingegliederter Ortschaften*, 15.

61. Berenstein, *Eksterminacja ludności żydowskiej*, 14–15.

62. DATO, f. 231, op. 1, spr. 1216, Organizacja syjonistyczna "Allgemeine" w Złoczowie [The Zionist Organization "Allgemeine" in Złoczów], 47.

63. Altman, *Haunting Memories*, 50; AŻIH, 301/3550, Testimony of Anna Szolder-Ulreich, typewritten, 2; AŻIH, 301/1524, Testimony of Helena Kitaj-Drobnerowa, typewritten, 5; USC, VHA, 12624, Testimony of Marek Goldenberg; USC, VHA, 06089, Testimony of Aron Frankel.

64. Quoted from YVA, M.49.E/1524, Testimony of Helena Kitaj-Drobnerowa, 7; AŻIH, 301/87, Testimony of Mendel Ruder, manuscript, 3; AIPN Lu, 319/1145, Copy of the testimony of Izak Wischnitzer of May 13, 1947 (Vienna), 4. The role of the *Judenrat* is hard and complex to assess because it operated under German terror. It seems that the Złoczów *Judenrat* did try to maneuver in Jewish affairs in its dealings with the German occupation apparatus. This caused much controversy, and some people were more critical than the opinion quoted in the text, cf. YVA, O.33/253, Wspomnienia Szymona Strasslera [Recollections of Szymon Strassler], 50; YV, O.33/1579: Testimony of Samuel Tennenbaum, 232, 235.

65. *Encyclopedia of Camps and Ghettos*, 2:850; Altman, *Haunting Memories*, 50. These people have not been identified.

66. AŻIH, Żydowska Samopomoc Społeczna [Jewish Social Self-Help]. Centrala Pomocy dla Żydów w Generalnym Gubernatorstwie [Help for Jews Headquarters in the General Government] 1939–1942 (subsequently ŻSS), 211/751, Pismo z Judenratu w Olesku do Prezydium ŻSS w Krakowie [Letter of Olesko Judenrat to ŻSS Presidium in Kraków] of May 16, 1942, 5–6; AŻIH, ŻSS, 211/943, Pismo Judenratu w Sasowie do Prezydium ŻSS w Krakowie [Letter of Sasów Judenrat to ŻSS Presidium in Kraków] of June 11, 1942, 18.

67. AŻIH, 301/3550, Testimony of Anna Szolder-Ulreich, 3; YVA, O.33/6659, Szlojme Mayer, *The Destruction of Zloczow*, 24; IPN OK Kr, S47/13/Zn, vol. 4, Testimony of Samuel Holender, translated from the Yiddish by A. Bielecki, 599.

68. YVA, M.49.E/1524, Testimony of Helena Kitaj-Drobnerowa, 6.

69. AŻIH, 301/3550, Testimony of Anna Szolder-Ulreich, 3; YVA, M.49.E/1524, Testimony of Helena Kitaj-Drobnerowa, 6.

70. YVA, O.33/253, Recollections of Szymon Strassler, 10; Pohl, *Nationalsozialistische Judenverfolgung in Ostgalizien*, 422; Sandkühler, *"Endlösung" in Galizien*, 437.

71. After the war, Friedrich Warzok was prosecuted by the Polish authorities. The investigation yielded no results, and he was never tried. AIPN, Główna Komisja Badania Zbrodni przeciwko Narodowi Polskiemu—Instytut Pamięci Narodowej 1991–1999 [Main Commission for the Prosecution of Crimes against the Polish Nation, Institute of National Remembrance], 3058/87, Egipt. Zbrodniarze hitlerowscy. Kartoteka [Egypt, Nazi criminals, Files], Warzok Friedrich, no pagination.

72. AIPN Lu, 319/1145, Report of the interrogation of the witness Juliusz Gutfreund of May 13, 1948 (Bielsko), 35v; YVA, O.5/61, Testimony of Benjamin Hochberg of May 23, 1947 (Vienna), 57.

73. YVA, O.33/253, Recollections of Szymon Strassler, 9–11; AŻIH, 301/3550, Testimony of Anna Szolder-Urleich, 6.

74. YVA, M.49.E/1524, Testimony of Helena Kitaj-Drobnerowa, 6; Ossolineum, manuscript 16264/I (microfilm 27570), Walery Maryański, *Dziennik...*, notebook 6, 18.

75. Already under the German military administration, Jews were made to do forced labor: cleaning streets, reconstruction, washing cars, and cleaning military barracks and buildings. They also had to do all kinds of jobs for German soldiers, SS men, and other German functionaries. For more, see Berenstein, "Praca przymusowa ludności żydowskiej w tzw. Dystrykcie Galicja (1941–1944)", *Biuletyn ŻIH* 69, no. 1 (1969): 3, 10.

76. Berenstein, *Praca przymusowa ludności żydowskiej*, 6–8, 13–14, 16; Altman, *Haunting Memories*, 50.

77. Friedrich Katzmann, *Rozwiązanie kwestii żydowskiej w dystrykcie Galicja*, translated by Jolanta Pawłowska (Warsaw: IPN, 2001), 19.

78. Berenstein, *Praca przymusowa ludności żydowskiej*, 20–21;Tabela: Obozy pracy przymusowej w dystrykcie Galicja, brak paginacji [Table: Forced Labor Camps in the District of Galicia, no pagination]; AŻIH, 301/4719, Testimony of Jakub Chamaides, manuscript, 1–6; AŻIH, 301/4025, Testimony of Mojżesz Teichman, manuscript, 1; AŻIH, 302/227, Pamiętnik Fani Laufer, 6; Altman, *Haunting Memories*, 61; AŻIH, 301/3777, Testimony of Chaim Wander, 1–6; AŻIH, 301/1403, Testimony of Samuel Wander, 3–4.

79. Information about labor camps can be found in a number of sources. Among others: USC, VHA, 32492, Testimony of Maurycy Altstock; YVA, O.3/434, Testimony of Bernard Gaeber, typescript, 1–4; YVA, O.3/2373, Testimony of Efraim Halpern, 10–14; AŻIH, 301/4024, Testimony of Herman Weigler, typescript, 1–2; AŻIH, 301/3777, Testimony of Chaim Wander, 1–6. The size of the camps can only be estimated on the basis of testimonies and recollections. The numbers given should be verified in the future.

80. AŻIH, ŻSS, 211/1159, Pismo Prezydium ŻSS w Krakowie do Komitetu Powiatowego ŻSS w Złoczowie [Letter of the ŻSS Presidium in Kraków to

the County Committee in Złoczów] of April 7, 1942, 6; Pismo Komitetu Powiatowego ŻSS do Prezydium ŻSS w Krakowie [Letter of the County Committee in Złoczów to the ŻSS Presidium in Kraków] of April 15, 1942, 10–13; DALO, f. R-35, op. 9, spr. 358, Pismo Chai Zwerdling do starosty powiatowego w Złoczowie [Letter of Chaja Zwerdling to the County Governor] of March 4, 1942, and other documents, 1–23.

81. AŻIH, 211/1159, Pismo Prezydium ŻSS w Krakowie do Komitetu Powiatowego ŻSS w Złoczowie [Letter of the ŻSS Presidium in Kraków to the County Committee in Złoczów] of April 7, 1942, 6; Pismo Komitetu Powiatowego ŻSS do Prezydium ŻSS w Krakowie [Letter of the County Committee in Złoczów to the ŻSS Presidium in Kraków] of June 17, 1942, 58.

82. Ibid., Pismo Komitetu Powiatowego ŻSS do Prezydium ŻSS w Krakowie [Letter of the County Committee in Złoczów to the ŻSS Presidium in Kraków] of June 17, 1942, 57–59; AŻIH, 301/4718, Testimony of Meier Heller, 3.

83. Archiwum Państwowe w Przemyślu (State Archive in Przemyśl, later: AP Przemyśl), Akta stanu cywilnego Izraelickiej Gminy Wyznaniowej w Złoczowie [Civil Registry of the Jewish Religious Community in Złoczów] 1829–1877; 1896–1942, 2257, vol. 5, Indeks do księgi zmarłych [Index of the Book of the Deceased] 1938–1942. The index does not include the victims of the Złoczów pogrom in July 1941 and those murdered during the deportation operation of August 28–29, 1942. Figures for 1940 and 1941 (during the Soviet occupation) are also incomplete because the files were taken over by the Soviet authorities. But in comparison with the prewar mortality rate, figures among the Jews in 1942 were several times higher.

84. AŻIH, 301/87, Testimony of Mendel Ruder, manuscript, 3; AIPN Lu, 319/1145, Copy of the testimony of Izak Wischnitzer of May 13, 1947 (Vienna), 4.

85. AŻIH, 301/531, Testimony of Chaim Wittelsohn, 1; AŻIH, 301/801, Testimony of Bolesław Kopelman, 1; YVA, O.3/1640, Testimony of Henryk Frankel, 22; USC, VHA, 17071, Testimony of Shlomo Wolkowicz.

86. USC, VHA, 32492, Testimony of Maurycy Altstock; YVA, Collection of Michał Borowicz, O.62/53, Testimony of Leokadia Bachner, 1.

87. Berenstein, *Eksterminacja ludności żydowskiej*, 4, 15–16.

88. I give the figures from AŻIH, ŻSS, 211/1160, Pismo Komitetu Powiatowego ŻSS do Prezydium ŻSS—Wydział Spraw Ogólnych i Organizacyjnych [the ŻSS County Committee to ŻSS Presidium in Kraków—Department for General and Organizational Affairs] of July 17, 1942, 11;Formularz A z danymi dla Prezydium ŻSS w Krakowie [Form A with data for the ŻSS Presidium in Kraków], no date, 12.

89. AŻIH, 301/3784, Testimony of Anna Szolder-Ulreich, typewrtitten, 1; YVA, O.33/253, Recollections of Szymon Strassler, 9.

90. Aleksander Kruglow, "Deportacje ludności żydowskiej z dystryktu Galicja do obozu zagłady w Bełżcu w 1942 r." [The 1942 Deportation of the Jewish Population from District Galicia to the Belzec Extermination Camp], Biuletyn ŻIH 151, no. 3 (1989): 103; USC, VHA, 32492, Testimony of Maurycy Altstock; *Encyclopedia of Camps and Ghettos*, 2:850; Altman, *Haunting Memories*, 99.

91. AŻIH, 301/3776, Testimony of Herman Weigler, typewritten, 1–2. The estimated number of Złoczów Jews deported to Bełżec during the first operation is based on documents of the County Committee of the Jewish Social Self-Help, which contains the number of Jews in April 1942 (5,833) and in October 1942 (4,172). The difference is 1,661. One should assume that some were murdered on the spot during the operation, a fact confirmed by eyewitnesses, so the number of Jews actually deported by train was around 1,650. To their group were added Jews taken from Sasów and Olesko. AŻIH, 211/1160, Pismo Komitetu Powiatowego ŻSS do Prezydium ŻSS—Wydział Spraw Ogólnych i Organizacyjnych of July 17, 1942, 11; Formularz A z danymi dla Prezydium ŻSS w Krakowie, no date, 12; Pismo Komitetu Powiatowego ŻSS do Prezydium ŻSS w Krakowie [Letter of the County Committee in Złoczów to the ŻSS Presidium in Kraków] of October 30, 1942, 48.

92. AŻIH, 301/3776, Testimony of Herman Weigler, 1–2.

93. YVA, M.49.E/1524, Testimony of Helena Kitaj-Drobnerowa, 8.

94. AŻIH, 301/3784, Testimony of Anna Szolder-Ulreich, 5; Sten, *1111 Days*, 29.

95. Altman, *Haunting Memories*, 100–101.

96. Ibid., 103.

97. In August 1942, the first deportation operation was carried out by the Tarnopol Gestapo. Only the subsequent anti-Jewish operations were carried out by the Lvov Gestapo. The head of the Tarnopol Gestapo testified that the Złoczów Gestapo reported to the Tarnopol Gestapo, but the operations against Złoczów's Jews were carried out by the Lvov Gestapo, because it was easier for them to get to Złoczów. This matter was regulated by an agreement between the two Sipo stations. AIPN, Zbiór akt z postępowań karnych dotyczących zbrodni nazistowskich [Files of Criminal Proceedings Regarding Nazi Crimes], BU 2586/115, Odpis wyroku Sądu Krajowego w Stuttgarcie z 15 VII 1966 w sprawie karnej przeciwko [Copy of the Decision of the Stuttgart Landgericht in a Criminal Case of July 15, 1966 against]: Paul Raebel, Hermann Müller, Walter Lambor, Paul Mellar, Thomas Hassenberg, Julius Aust, Hubert Schwach, Horst Winkler, Willi Herrmann, Erwin Czerwony—SS members, Security Police functionaries—of the external station in Tarnopol (Sicherheitspolizei—Aussendienststelle Tarnopol), accused of crimes against people of Jewish

nationality in the Tarnopol region in the years 1941–1943, vol. 1 (facsimile), 1967–1967, 93, 195.

98. *Encyclopedia of Camps and Ghettos*, 2:850.

99. Krugłow, *Deportacje ludności żydowskiej*, 116; *Encyclopedia of Camps and Ghettos*, 2:850; Altman, *Haunting Memories*, 104; AŻIH, 301/3752, Testimony of Leon Torczyner, 2.

100. AŻIH, 301/3776, Testimony of Herman Weigler, 2.

101. Encyclopedic studies estimate the number of Złoczów deportees during the second operation at 2,500 Jews; *Encyclopedia of Camps and Ghettos*, 2:850; Guy Miron, ed., *Encyclopedia of the Ghettos during the Holocaust* (Jerusalem: Yad Vashem, 2009), 1:987. If we take into consideration the number of Jews who subsequently landed in the secondary ghetto (4,548), then the number of people deported by train was rather smaller. Quoted from Grzegorz Hryciuk, *Przemiany narodowościowe i ludnościowe w Galicji Wschodniej i na Wołyniu 1931–1948* (Toruń: Wydawnictwo Adam Marszałek, 2005), 234. The author made his calculations on the basis of the German census of March 1, 1943. (Hryciuk, *Przemiany narodowościowe i ludnościowe w Galicji Wschodniej i na Wołyniu*, 225, table 35, "Ludność województwa tarnopolskiego w 1943 r." [Tarnopol Voivodship population in 1943]).

102. YVA, O.3/2373, Testimony of Efraim Halpern, 22; USC, VHA, 32492, Testimony of Maurycy Altstock; USC, VHA, 8443, Testimony of Herman Lewinter; USC, VHA, 51184, Testimony of Leonid Vugman.

103. Rozporządzenie policyjne o tworzeniu żydowskich dzielnic mieszkaniowych w Okręgach Radom, Krakau, Galizien (Galicja) [Police order regarding the creation of housing districts in the districts: Radom, Kraków, Galizien (Galicia)] of November 10, 1942, *Dziennik Rozporządzeń dla Generalnego Gubernatorstwa*, November 14, 1942, no. 98, 684; AŻIH, 301/87, Testimony of Mendel Ruder, 3; Altman, *Haunting Memories*, 105.

104. Berenstein, *Praca przymusowa ludności* żydowskiej, table "Obozy pracy przymusowej w Dystrykcie Galicja" [Forced Labor Camps in the Galicia District]; AŻIH, 301/87, Testimony of Mendel Ruder, 3–4.

105. The figure is an estimate. Grzegorz Hryciuk writes that in early March 1943, there were 4,548 people in the ghetto. One should estimate, therefore, that this figure comprises no more than 2,172 Jewish inhabitants of Złoczów. The others were probably deportees; Hryciuk, *Przemiany narodowościowe i ludnościowe w Galicji Wschodniej i na Wołyniu*, 225, table 35, "Ludność województwa tarnopolskiego w 1943 r." [Tarnopol Voivodship Population in 1943].

106. Figures as of March 1, 1943, ibid., 234.

107. Altman, *Haunting Memories*, 106; USC, VHA, 27766, Testimony of Joe Teitelbaum.

108. Ibid.; USC, VHA, 24249, Testimony of Clara Hoffmann.

109. AŻIH, 301/87, Testimony of Mendel Ruder, 4; YVA, O.5/61, Testimony of Emil Silber of May 3, 1947 (typewritten, original), 47; Testimony of Dr Spindel of May 2, 1947, 51; Altman, *Haunting Memories*, 123; AŻIH, 301/5879, Jan Kulpa, Juliusz i Hugon Gutfreund, manuscript, 3–4.

110. From the second half of 1941 to mid-1944, SS-*Hauptsturmführer* Erich Engels was the head of the Jewish Affairs desk of the Lvov Gestapo (Desk IV 5), where he had been transferred from the Warsaw Gestapo. He was responsible for anti-Jewish operations in Lvov, in the district of Galicia, and in Złoczów as well. After the war, he was tried and sentenced to death. Pohl, *Nationalsozialistische Judenverfolgung in Ostgalizien*, 255.

111. Altman, *Haunting Memories*, 123–124; YVA, O.33/253, Recollections of Szymon Strassler, 16, 18–21; GARF, f. 7021, op. 67, d. 80, Report of the interrogation of the witness Efren Rozen, September 16, 1944, 8; IPN OK Kr, S 47/13/Zn, vol. 7, Decision to discontinue proceedings against Dr. Wendt issued by the Public Prosecutor's Office in Göttingen, 1408–1410.

112. The incident was witnessed Leon Torczyner, who managed to slip out of the ghetto. For more on this topic, see: AIPN, GK 227/84, vol. 2, Report of the interrogation of the witness Leon Torczyner of April 12, 1949, 134–135.

113. GARF, f. 7021, op. 67, d. 80, Act of the Extraordinary Municipal Commission for Establishing and Analysis of the German-Fascist in the Town of Złoczów, September 24, 1944, 78–79; Protokół Eksperckiej Komisji Sądowo-Lekarskiej z oględzin miejsc pochówku i badania ciał zabitych osób w mieście Złoczowie i jego okolicach [Report of the Forensic and Medical Expert Commission for the Location of Burial Sites and Corpse Examination in the Town of Złoczów and its Vicinity], 68–69; AIPN Lu, 319/1145, Copy of the testimony of Emil Silber of May 3, 1947, 3; Copy of the testimony of Hermann Grünseid of May 2, 1947 (Vienna), 5; Sten, *1111 Days*, 63; Il'ja A. Altman, ed., *Chołokost na territorii SSSR. Encykłopiedia* (Moscow: Nauczno-proswietitielnyj Centr "Chołokost," 2011), 335; Sandkühler, *"Endlösung" in Galizien*, 258; AŻIH, 301/5879, Jan Kulpa, Juliusz i Hugon Gutfreund, manuscript, 3–4.

114. GARF, f. 7021, op. 67, d. 80, Report of on-site inspection of the mass burial sites of victims of the German-fascist terror near Jelechowice, in the village of Zazule near the town of Złoczów, 68–71; Report of exhumation of bodies of people shot by Germans and exhumed from a grave in the forest near the village of Jelechowice, 75.

115. Altman, *Haunting Memories*, 125; YVA, M.49.E/2541, Testimony of Zehawa Rothowa, 4.

116. AŻIH, 301/3784, Anna Szolder-Ulreich's testimony, 1–3; YVA, O.33/253, Recollections of Szymon Strassler, 10; YV, M.49.E/1524, Testimony of Helena Kitaj-Drobnerowa, 7–8; YVA, O33/1579, Testimony of Samuel Tennenbaum, 230.

117. Altman, *Haunting Memories*, 98–99; USC, VHA, 32492, Testimony of Maurycy Altstock; AŻIH, 301/1793/7, Testimony of H. Fromer, 2; YVA, O.62/53, Testimony of Leokadia Bachner, 2.

118. Wiesława Michałek, *Zapiski 1939–1944*, ed. Grzegorz Bębnik (Katowice: IPN, 2012), 130.

119. Ośrodek KARTA, Archiwum Wschodnie, II/1420/2KW, Franciszek Sikorski, *Najpiękniejsze wzgórza i doliny*, 29–30; Henryk Komański and Szczepan Siekierka, *Ludobójstwo dokonane przez nacjonalistów ukraińskich na Polakach w województwie tarnopolskim 1939–1946*, (Wrocław: Nortom, 2004), 978, "Wspomnienia Ignacego Pawlika" [Memoirs of Ignacy Pawlik]; YVA, O33/1579, Testimony of Samuel Tennenbaum, 230, 241, 257–258; Altman, *Haunting Memories*, 114–115.

120. AIPN, Zbiór dotyczący relacji osób, które przetrwały Holocaust na terenie III Rzeszy i okupowanej Europy, pozysknych z Muzeum Holocaustu w Waszyngtonie [Collection of Testimonies of People who Survived the War on the Territory of the Third Reich, obtained from USHMM], BU 2646/1/D, Wspomnienia Marii Davidson dotyczące życia we Lwowie, Gołogórze [Gołogórach] i w Warszawie w czasie II wojny światowej [Maria Davidson's Recollections Concerning Life in Lvov, Gologory and Warsaw during World War II], 5; AŻIH, 301/3776, Testimony of Herman Weigler, 2; Komański and Siekierka, *Ludobójstwo dokonane przez nacjonalistów ukraińskich na Polakach*, 986, "Wspomnienia Jana Zelka" [Recollections of Jan Zelek]; AŻIH, 301/1793/7, Testimony of H. Fromer, 2–3; YVA, O.33/4249, Pamiętniki Sali (Peczenik) Felzen [Diary of Sala (Peczenik) Felzen], 1–2.

121. Berenstein, *Praca przymusowa ludności żydowskiej*, 12–13.

122. YVA, O.3/2373, Testimony of Efraim Halpern, 22; USC, VHA, 32492, Testimony of Maurycy Altstock; AŻIH, 211/1160, Pismo Wydziału Pomocy Pracy ŻSS w Krakowie do Powiatowego Komitetu ŻSS w Złoczowie w sprawie warsztatów zbiorowych [Letter of the Help Department of the ŻSS in Cracow to the ŻSS County Committee in Złoczów Regarding Collective Workshops], August 27, 1942, 27.

123. Figures based on collected sources and existing data bases.

124. YVA, O.5/61, Testimony of Otto Zikmund of May 13, 1947, 6; YVA, O.5/61, Testimony of Benjamin Hochberg of May 23, 1947 (Vienna), 57; YVA, O.5/61A, Testimony of Hermann Grünseid of May 2, 1947 (Vienna), 18; AŻIH, 301/2541, Testimony of Zehawa Rothowa, typewritten, 4; AIPN Lu, 319/1145, Copy of the testimony of Emil Silber of May 3, 1947, 3; USC, VHA, 32492, Testimony of Maurycy Altstock; Altman, *Haunting Memories*, 126; GARF, f. 7021, op. 67, d. 80, Protokół przesłuchania świadka Abrama Czortkowera z 17 IX 1944 r. [Report of the interrogation of the witness Abram Czortkower, September 17, 1944], 33; Protokół przesłuchania świadka Rozy Falii z 21 IX 1944 r. [Report of

the interrogation of the witness Roza Falia, September 21, 1944], 48v; Altman, *Haunting Memories*, 126.

125. Chances of survival of hiding in the county for Jews can be assessed on the basis of a number of sources, including YVA, Rodzina Lewickich, http://db.yadvashem.org/righteous/family.html?language=en&itemId=4039722 (accessed November 21, 2016); Mayer, *Destruction of Zloczów*, 33; AŻIH, 301/3777, Testimony of Chaim Wander; USC, VHA, 32492, Testimony of Maurycy Altstock; AŻIH, 301/1200, testimony of Fajwl Auerbach, 2–3; AŻIH, 301/4025, Testimony of Mojżesz Teichman, manuscript, 2; AŻIH, 301/1779, Testimony of Jan Falsberg, 1.

126. The conditions of hiding are described in a number of sources, including YVA, Meyer Family, http://db.yadvashem.org/righteous/family.html?language=en&itemId=4044507 (accessed November 23, 2017); AŻIH, 301/3752, Testimony of Leon Torczyner, 4; YVA, M.49.E/ E/2541, Testimony of Zehawa Rothowa, 4; YVA, O.3/6973, Testimony of Gisha Weis, 23–25; YVA, M.1.E/668, Testimony of Ilena Baum, 2–3; AŻIH, 301/87, Testimony of Mendel Ruder, 5; AŻIH, 301/4670, Testimony of Majer Perlmutter, 2–4.

127. AŻIH, 301/4719, Testimony of Jakub Chamaides, 6–7; YVA, O.3/2373, Testimony of Efraim Halpern, 19–20.

128. YVA, O.33/253, Recollections of Szymon Strassler, 27–29; AŻIH, 301/4670, Testimony of Majer Permutter, 2–5; Altman, *Haunting Memories*, 131–132. Szlojme Mayer claimed that the bunker was detected by a local peasant. He also described the roundup in detail; see YVA, O.33/6659, Szlojme Mayer, *The Destruction of Zloczow . . .*, 35.

129. AŻIH, 301/4719, Testimony of Jakub Chamaides, 7; AIPN Lu, 319/1145, Odpis zeznania Hermanna Grünseida [Copy of the testimony of Hermann Grünseid], May 2, 1947 (Vienna), 5; YVA, O.33/253, Recollections of Szymon Strassler, 29–30; USC, VHA, 24249, Testimony of Clara Hoffmann; *Roald Hoffmann—Biographical*, https://www.nobelprize.org/nobel_prizes/chemistry/laureates/1981/hoffmann-bio.html (accessed July 22, 2017). Information on arrests and executions can also be found in YVA, O.5/61, Protokół przesłuchania Ernsta Stella [Interrogation Report of Ernst Stell], May 23, 1947, 17; Odpis zeznań Adama Imbera i Dory Marder [Copy of the testimonies of Adam Imber and Dora Marder], June 2, 1947, 28; Odpis zeznania Benjamina Hochberga [Copy of the testimony of Benjamin Hochberg], May 23, 1947, 56.

130. AŻIH, 301/3777, Testimony of Chaim Wander, 8; AŻIH, 301/4991, Testimony of Chaim Schöps, 2; AŻIH, 301/1403, Testimony of Samuel Wander, 5–6; AŻIH, 301/1200, Testimony of Fajwel Auerbach, 3–4. In our estimates, we assumed a smaller figure than in the sources.

131. The figures of camp inmates are only estimates. Information on the number of camp inmates can be found in all kinds of sources, including the

recollections of Jewish survivors. Archiwum Instytutu Pamięci Narodowej Oddział w Katowicach (Archive of the Institute of National Remembrance in Katowice, subsequently AIPN Ka), the collection of Prof. Andrzej Szefer, 315/1/J, Protokół przesłuchania oskarżonego Josefa Grzimka [Report of the interrogation of Josef Grzimek], February 9, 1948, 144; YVA, O.33/253, Recollections of Szymon Strassler, 45–49, 51–60, 70; AŻIH, 301/4027, Testimony of Herman Berman [Bergman], 2–3; AIPN Lublin, 315/76, Protokół przesłuchania świadka Andrzeja Pankiewicza [Report of the interrogation of Andrzej Pankiewicz], April 12, 1945, 9; Protokół przesłuchania podejrzanego Henryka Lenca [Report of the interrogation of Henryk Lenc], April 15, 1945, 14; AŻIH, 301/3752, Testimony of Leon Torczyner, 4; AŻIH, 301/4670, Testimony of Majer Perlmutter, 5; AŻIH, 301/87, Testimony of Mendel Ruder, 4; AŻIH, 301/1403, Testimony of Samuel Wander, 5–7; YVA, O.3/2373, Testimony of Efraim Halpern, 20, 24–25; YVA, O.3/1818, Testimony of Marian Ryszard Szadkowski, 12–13; Altman, *Haunting Memories*, 137–139; Berenstein, *Praca przymusowa ludności żydowskiej*, 35–36; YVA, Dokumenty z archiwów regionalnych na Ukrainie [Documents from the Regional Archives in Ukraine], M.52/246, Oficjalna dokumentacja Radzieckiej Państwowej Komisji Specjalnej dotycząca nazistowskich zbrodni wojennych we Lwowskiem [Documents of the Special Soviet State Commission for Nazi War Crimes in the Lvov Region], September 8, 1944–August 11, 1945, Akt z 29 października 1944 r., Olesko [Act of October 29, 1944, Olesko], 65 [incorrect date of camp liquidation given]. Chaim Schöps, who was a prisoner of the Sasów-Chomiec labor camp, provided much higher numbers of prisoners in the individual camps. In the light of available sources, these estimates should be considered definitely too high; AŻIH, 301/4991, Testimony of Chaim Schöps, 1.

132. AIPN Lu, 315/76, Protokół przesłuchania świadka Andrzeja Pankiewicza, April 12, 1945, 9; Protokół przesłuchania podejrzanego Henryka Lenca, April 15, 1945, 14; Protokół rozprawy głównej [Minutes of the main hearing], July 10, 1945, Zeznanie Andrzeja Pankiewicza [Testimony of Andrzej Pankiewicz'], 43; YVA, O.33/253, Recollections of Szymon Strassler, 54–55.

133. YVA, O.33/253, Recollections of Szymon Strassler, 32–36, 39–43.

134. Ibid., 40, 43–44, 46, 51–61, 64–65, 68, 70, 72.

135. A similar rate of one thousand zlotys for each captured Jew was also paid by the Polish Criminal Police in Lvov at the turn of 1943 and 1944; Jan Grabowski, "Hunting down Emanuel Ringelblum: The Participation of the Polish Kriminalpolizei in the 'Final Solution of the Jewish Question", *Holocaust. Studies and Materials* 1, no. 10 (2017): 54.

136. AIPN Lu, 315/76, Protokół przesłuchania Henryka Lenca [Report of the interrogation of Henryk Lenc], April 12, 1945, 10; AŻIH, 301/1403, Testimony of Samuel Wander, 6–7; AŻIH, 301/4991, Testimony of Chaim Schöps, 2; YVA,

M.49.E/2541, Testimony of Zehawa Rothowa, 3–4; GARF, f. 7021, op. 67, d. 80, Protokół przesłuchania świadka Dory Kremnicer (Kremnitzer) [Report of the interrogation of the witness Dora Kremnicer (Kremnitzer) of September 16, 1944], 30v; Protokół przesłuchania świadka Michała Genisa [Report of the interrogation of the witness Michał Genis], September 23, 1944, 54–54v; Altman, *Haunting Memories*, 114, 116–118; AAN, 203/XV/28, Meldunek tygodniowy z 30 czerwca 1944 r., powiaty [Weekly county report of June 30, 1944]: Kamionka Strumiłowa, Sokal, Radziechów, Złoczów, Zborów, Brody, Przemyślany, Brzeżany, Podhajce, Buczacz, Bóbrka, 138; Ossolineum, 14115/II: Leon Ciemniewski, *Poprzez skiby mazowieckie, podolskie i śląskie: wspomnienia z lat 1900–1964*, vol. 5 (microfilm: 4117), 177.

137. YVA, O.62/53, Testimony of Bachner Leokadia, 1; AŻIH, 301/4670, Testimony of Majer Perlmutter, 3; AŻIH, 301/1779, Testimony of Jan Falsberg, 1.

138. In 1943 in Eastern Galicia, individual liquidation operations against the Poles were carried out, but from late 1943 collective massacres began. The number of assaults on Polish villages began to rise considerably from February 1944; Grzegorz Motyka, *Ukraińska partyzantka 1942–1960. Działalność Organizacji Ukraińskich Nacjonalistów i Ukraińskiej Powstańczej Armii* (Warsaw: ISP PAN and Rytm, 2006), 376–377, 381.

139. It is estimated that throughout the war in the Złoczów County, several dozen assaults on Polish villages took place; during all kinds of anti-Polish operations in the years 1943–1945, 786 Poles were killed at the hands of the OUN-UIA and Ukrainian Police. See Ewa Siemaszko, "Straty ludności polskiej w wyniku zbrodni ludobójstwa dokonanych w latach czterdziestych XX wieku przez nacjonalistów ukraińskich. Aktualny stan badań" [The Losses of Polish Population Resulting drom the Genocide Perpetrated by the Ukrainian Nationalists in the 1940s. The Present State of Research], in *Wołyń 1943—rozliczenie. Materiały przeglądowej konferencji naukowej "W 65. rocznicę eksterminacji ludności polskiej na Kresach Wschodnich dokonanej przez nacjonalistów ukraińskich," Warszawa 10 lipca 2008*, ed. Romuald Niedzielko (Warsaw: IPN, 2010), 92. We do not know how many Ukrainians were killed in retaliation operations, but according to Grzegorz Motyka, in Eastern Galicia there were definitely fewer Ukrainian victims than Polish ones. For more, see Motyka, *Ukraińska partyzantka*, 411–412.

140. Bakanow, "*Ni kacapa, ni żyda, ni lacha*," 217–221; YVA, O.33/253, Recollections of Szymon Strassler, 38–39.

141. The only testimony of a Jewish doctor who found himself in the Złoczów labor camp, and subsequently became involved in the Ukrainian partisan movement, is that of Efraim Halpern, who together with his wife stayed with a detachment of "Bulba" followers and accompanied them all the way to Volhynia (*Wołyń*). YVA, O.3/2373, Testimony of Efraim Halpern, 23–25.

142. AŻIH, 301/1403, Testimony of Samuel Wander, 6–7; Altman, *Haunting Memories*, 117.

143. Mikołaj Mazurek's [pseudonym Dąb] partisan unit operated near Mitulin and close to the main road between Nowosiółki and Lackie, ten to twenty kilometers west of Złoczów. Probably in 1944, the unit relocated near the area of the village of Wicyń. For more on this topic, see Jerzy Węgierski, *Armia Krajowa w okręgach Stanisławów i Tarnopol* (Kraków: Platan, 1996), 181; Ośrodek KARTA, Archiwum Wschodnie, II/690, Edward Kisielewski, 8.

144. "Witiag iz wistok pro politicznu situaciju na tierienach Zołocziws'koji okruhi OUN u druhij połowini żowtnja 1943 r. [nie ran'sze 30 żowtnija]," in *Litopys UPA. Nowa seria*, vol. 24: *Zołocziws'ka okruha OUN. Orhanizacijni dokumenty: 1941–1952*, ed. Mychajło Romaniuk (Kiev: Litopys UPA), 2014, 61; "Wyciąg z 'Wisnyka Informacijnoj Służby OUN' z 1942," in *Polacy i Ukraińcy pomiędzy dwoma systemami totalitarnymi 1942–1945*, vol. 4, part 1: *1942–1945*, ed. Grzegorz Motyka and Jurij Szapował (Warsaw: IPN, 2005), 111; AAN, 1326/203/XV/41, Z terenu, translated from the Ukrainian, [second half of 1942], 47.

145. Some information on German operations against Jews in the district of Galicia can be found in *Biuletynie Informacyjny Ziemi Czerwieńskiej* for 1942–1944. This periodical was published by Biuro Informacji i Propagandy Obszaru 3 Związku Walki Zbrojnej-Armii Krajowej [Information and Propaganda Bureau of the Armed Combat Union-Home Army Area 3]. There is very little information about the situation of the Jews in Złoczów County. Most testimonies of Złoczów's Jews never mention either the threat or help from the local Polish underground. If any Jews did survive, it was by other means than thanks to the involvement of the Polish underground. As for sources regarding Złoczów County, I have found only single pieces of information about individual cases of help or hiding Jews by members of the Polish underground. In light of the scarcity of sources, it was difficult to establish any details or verify the information. See Jan Goniowski, *Armia Krajowa w Wicyniu—tarnopolskiej wsi* (Kraków: Platan, 1998), 64. In contrast, in neighboring Przemyślany County, near Hanaczów, there existed a Jewish detachment that reported to the local AK structures, but such a situation should rather be regarded as exceptional in this area. In this case, both sides cooperated for reasons of self-defence against OUN-UIA attacks. Cf. Adam Puławski, "Postrzeganie żydowskich oddziałów partyzanckich przez Armię Krajową i Delegaturę Rządu RP na Kraj", *Pamięć i Sprawiedliwość*, no. 2 (2003): 287, 297.

146. AIPN, Zbiór Głównej Komisji Badania Zbrodni Hitlerowskich w Polsce. Akta badawczo-dochodzeniowe, GK 164/2496, List Mosesa Reissa do Michała Ż. [Letter of Moses Reiss to Michał Ż.], June 16, 1947, 21–23; Protokół przesłuchania Michała Ż. [Report of the interrogation of Michał Ż.], June 5,

1947, 31; "Application," February 18, 1947, 33; Zeznanie Pepy Altman [Testimony of Pepa Altman], September 1946, 50; Oświadczenie Etki Preiss [Statement of Etka Preiss], September 26, 1946, 52–53; Identification of Prisoner, April 15, 1947, 59. In contrast, remarks on the hostile attitude of the National Armed Forces can be found in Altman, *Haunting Memories*, 117.

147. "Witiag iz wistiej pro suspilno-politycznie ta wijs'kowie stanowiszczie na tierienach Zołocziws'koji okruhi OUN w sierpni–wieriesni 1943 r.," in *Litopys UPA*, 24:52–53; "Nadzwyczajnij zwit pro diji czierwonich partizaniw na tierienach Zołocziws'koji okruhi OUN, 25 kwitnia 1944 r.," in *Litopys UPA*, 24:71–72.

148. YVA, O.3/1818, Testimony of Marian Ryszard Szatkowski, 14; AŻIH, 301/3777, Testimony of Chaim Wander, 5–6; AŻIH, 301/801, Testimony of Bolesław Kopelman, 1; AŻIH, 301/1403, Testimony of Samuel Wander, 6; AŻIH, 301/4991, Testimony of Chaim Schöps, 2.

149. Data based on collected source material and object literature.

150. For example, Marek Goldenberg's family had been hiding from 1942, first in a village on a peasant's farm, and when they were told to leave the hideout, they went into hiding in Złoczów from April to May 1943, where they luckily lived to see the end of the war; USC, VHA, 12624, Testimony of Marek Goldenberg. Three other people were arrested by the Germans and murdered in the woods, when they had to leave their hideout on a farm. At least three people (no exact figures are available) were killed in an attack of Ukrainian nationalists on one of the peasant's farms; the cause of death of one person remains unknown. The fate of those hiding is characterized, among others, by documents YVA, Department of the Righteous Among the Nations, https://righteous.yadvashem.org/?search=Z%C5%82ocz%C3%B3w&searchType=righteous_only&language=en (accessed September 21, 2016); AŻIH, 301/87, Testimony of Mendel Ruder, 5; YVA, M.1.E/668, Testimony of Ilena Baum, 3; and other sources found during research.

151. YV, The Righteous Among the Nations Database and other collected sources.

152. Meyer Family, http://db.yadvashem.org/righteous/family.html?language=en&itemId=4044507 (accessed 21 September 2016).

153. AŻIH, 301/1200, Testimony of Fajwl Auerbach, 4.

154. AŻIH, 301/4670, Testimony of Majer Perlmutter, 4.

155. I found relevant information, among others, in AAN, 203/XV/28, Meldunek tygodniowy [Weekly report], June 30, 1944, counties: Kamionka Strumiłowa, Sokal, Radziechów, Złoczów, Zborów, Brody, Przemyślany, Brzeżany, Podhajce, Buczacz, Bóbrka, 138; AIPN, 392/999, List Floriana Szpyta do Okręgowej Komisji Badania Zbrodni Hitlerowskich w Polsce [Florian Szpyt's letter to the District Commission to Investigate Nazi Crimes in Poland], November 21, 1988, no pagination; Protokół przesłuchania świadka

Bronisławy Stachuń z domu Hajek [Report of the interrogation of the witness Bronisława Stachuń née Hajek], January 31, 1989, 3–6; Ośrodek KARTA, Archiwum Wschodnie, II/1420/2KW, Franciszek Sikorski, *Najpiękniejsze wzgórza i doliny*, 29–30; *Politicznij zwit iz Zołocziwszczyny bid 30 kwitnja do 15 trawnja 1944 roku [nie ran'sze 15 trawnja 1944 r.]*, in *Litopys UPA*, 24:81; Komański and Siekierka, *Ludobójstwo dokonane przez nacjonalistów ukraińskich na Polakach*, 978, "Wspomnienia Ignacego Pawlika" [Memoirs of Ignacy Pawlik]; Węgierski, *Armia Krajowa*, 174.

156. USC, VHA, 32492, Testimony of Maurycy Altstock; AŻIH, 301/87, Testimony of Mendel Ruder, 1–5; AŻIH, 301/801, Testimony of Bolesław Kapelan, 1; AŻIH, 301/531, Testimony of Chaim Wittelsohn, 1–2.

157. Information about this type of hiding can be found in the testimonies of Zehawa Rothowa (YVA, M.49.E/2541), Helena Kitaj-Drobnerowa (YVA, M.49.E/1524), Mendel Ruder (AŻIH, 301/87), Rózia Kohn (AŻIH, 301/5329), Salomon Liberman (AŻIH, 301/2752).

158. Among those who survived in this manner were Helena Kitaj-Drobnerowa and Dr. Bernard Gaerber with his wife and son. On November 5, 1942, they were taken by three Poles (most likely AK members) to Warsaw and were furnished with false documents and quartered. YVA, M.49.E/1524, Testimony of Helena Kitaj-Drobnerowa, 10–11.

159. AŻIH, 301/811, Testimony of Marek Josch.

160. AŻIH, 301/4670, Testimony of Majer Perlmutter, 5; ŻIH, 301/4719, Testimony of Jakub Chamaides, YVA, O.5/61, Protokół przesłuchania Ernsta Stella 23 maja 1947 r. [Report of the interrogation of Ernst Stell of May 23, 1947], 17.

161. For more on population changes among the different nationalities in Eastern Galicia under the German occupation, see Hryciuk, *Przemiany narodowościowe i ludnościowe w Galicji Wschodniej i na Wołyniu*, 208-216, 234-257.

162. Raul Hilberg deals with "bystanders" in *Perpetrators, Victims, Bystanders* (New York: Harper Perennial, 1993), 195-268. In 2018, Omer Bartov published a book about Buczacz, a town which until 1939 was located in the Tarnopol Voivodship. The author undertook an analysis of relations between Poles, Ukrainians, and Jews in Buczacz and the immediate area, including during the period of war. To learn more about the dramatic situation of Jews hiding during the Holocaust in the Buczacz area and the attitudes of Poles and Ukrainians, see chapter 6, "The Daily Life of Genocide," in Omer Bartov, *Anatomy of a Genocide: The Life and Death of a Town Called Buczacz* (New York, Simon and Schuster, 2018).

163. YVA, M.49.E/1524, Testimony of Helena Kitaj-Drobnerowa, 8.

164. AŻIH, 301/2520, Testimony of Maria Cukier, 2. See also: YVA, O.3/434, Testimony of Dr. Bernard Gaerber, 2.

165. Apart from the above cited examples, let me add the testimony of Maurycy Altstock, who experienced a Ukrainian roundup in one of the villages, where a crowd of locals chased and searched for him in order to capture him (USC, VHA, 32492, Maurycy Altstock). In contrast, in Usznia, a German soldier, together with several Ukrainians and one Pole (supposedly who tried to pass off as a Ukrainian), attacked Abraham Cajzel's family, murdered his wife, and massacred his two sons. Quoted after AIPN Sz, Sąd Apelacyjny w Szczecinie 1945–1950 [Szczecin Court of Appeals, 1944–1950], 447/6, Protokół przesłuchania świadka Władysława Baśladyńskiego [Report of the interrogation of the witness Władysław Baśladyński], December 5, 1949, 71; Protokół rozprawy głównej w Sądzie Apelacyjnym w Szczecinie w sprawie Władysława Ś. [Minutes of main hearing before the Szczecin Court of Appeals in the case of Władysław Ś. born in 1912], October 20, 1950, 300–302, 308, 311; Sentencja wyroku w imieniu Rzeczypospolitej Polskiej Sądu Wojewódzkiego w Szczecinie [Sentence in the Name of the People's Republic of Poland in Szczecin], April 5, 1951, in the case of Władysław Ś., born in 1912, 437, 439; Protokół przesłuchania świadka Wiktora Górskiego [Report of the interrogation of the witness Wiktor Górski] in Brzeg of May 29, 1949, 153–154.

166. The role of the Ukrainian Police was analyzed by Gabriel Finder and Alexander Prusin, who underlined that it "played an integral part in the German destruction of the Jews in Eastern Galicia"; Finder and Prusin, "Collaboration in Eastern Galicia," 106–108.

167. See AIPN Ka, Wojewódzki Urząd Spraw Wewnętrznych w Bielsku Białej (1975) 1983–1990 [Provincial Office of Internal Affairs in Bielsko-Biała (1975) 1983–1990], 047/363, Sprawa operacyjna dot.: [Operational case of] G. Stefan, imię ojca [father's name] Wojciech, ur. [born] August 4, 1908. Kontrola operacyjna byłego funkcjonariusza Policji Państwowej II RP oraz policji granatowej w Złoczowie w czasie II wojny światowej (1946–1959) [Operational control of former functionary of the Polish Police before the war and of the "Blue police" during World War II (1946–1959)]. Unfortunately, no official documents of Złoczów Kripo were found.

168. Ośrodek KARTA, Archiwum Wschodnie, II/1420/2KW, Franciszek Sikorski, *Najpiękniejsze wzgórza i doliny*, 3

169. Let me add that surviving documents of the Lvov metropolis of the Latin rite deposed in the Archive of Archbishop Baziak in Cracow (consistory books and fragments of the surviving Złoczów parish files) contain no information on the Jewish population and possible help offered to the Jews. What we do know, however, is that at Uniów near Przemyślany (before the war, Przemyślany County), Jewish children were hidden in the Greek Catholic Studite monastery. Adam Daniel Rotfeld, "Tyle pamiętam," *Polityka*, no. 7 (2007): 71.

170. AAN, 203/XV/40, Raport [brak dokładnego tytułu] z "Orzecha" [kryptonim Obszaru Południowo-Wschodniego AK], Report (no exact title given) to "Orzech" (codename for the South-Eastern AK Area] by July 1, 1942, part II: Sytuacja polityczna [political situation], pkt. [item]: Żydzi [Jews], 29. The document discusses Jewish affairs in Eastern Galicia, among others. This harmonizes with the opinions of Efraim Sten of Złoczów, who survived thanks to the help of Grzegorz Tyż, Maria Koreniuk, and Helena Skrzeszewska; Sten, *1111 Days*, 33. For the actual conditions of Jews in hiding in the Złoczów countryside, see also USC, VHA, 46008, Testimony of Grzegorz Tyż.

171. On the basis of available sources concerning Złoczów County, we are not always able to determine the nationality of those who denounced the hiding Jews or helped capture them. But we do know of instances of the involvement of local Ukrainians or Ukrainian Police engaged to carry out roundups: among others, AAN, 203/XV/28, Meldunek tygodniowy [Weekly report], June 30, 1944), counties: Kamionka Strumiłowa, Sokal, Radziechów, Złoczów, Zborów, Brody, Przemyślany, Brzeżany, Podhajce, Buczacz, Bóbrka, 138; AŻIH, 301/4670, Testimony of Majer Perlmutter, typewritten, 3; YVA, O.62/53, Testimony of Bachner Leokadia, 1–2; USC, VHA, 51184, Testimony of Leonid Vugman; USC, VHA, 32492, Testimony of Maurycy Altstock; AIPN Lu, 315/76, Protokół przesłuchania podejrzanego Henryka Lenca, April 15, 1945, 14.

172. The data for statistical calculations were taken from Polish, Ukrainian, and Jewish recollections and accounts kept in archives as well as printed ones; trial documents of German war criminals; various databases, among them that of the Central Committee of Polish Jews; the census of Jews living in Złoczów County and those who were registered in Złoczów with the regional plenipotentiary of the Polish government for the evacuation of the Polish population from the Ukrainian Soviet Republic to Poland; postwar lists of compatriot associations; Yad Vashem Righteous Among the Nations Database; documents of the Soviet Extraordinary Municipal Commission for Establishing and Analysis of German-Fascist Crimes in the Town of Złoczów and Its Vicinity and Their Helpers; the collection of USC Shoah Foundation (twenty-two interviews with Złoczów Jews were analyzed); reports of the military underground ZWZ-AK, Tarnopol region, Złoczów, and Złoczów region Inspectorate; published reports of the Złoczów OUN District; and object literature.

173. The number of Jews in the Soviet Union was estimated (among others) on the basis of the database of the Central Committee of Polish Jews, the list of individual compatriot associations, and other documents collected during research.

174. I am very grateful to Ela Linde, Alex Zengin, and Witold Mędykowski of Yad Vashem for their help in archive-based research, and to Roman Maćkówka for his permission to publish some items from his private archive.

ANNA ZAPALEC is an associate professor in the Department of Contemporary History of the Institute of History and Archival Studies of the Pedagogical University of Cracow. Her scientific interests are the problems of Second World War, especially in the context of Polish history. Her publications focus, among other things, on crimes committed in Poland during the Second World War by the occupying forces. Major publications include "Powiat Złoczów" [Złoczów County], in *Dalej jest noc: losy Żydów w wybranych powiatach okupowanej Polski* [Night without end: The fate of Jews in selected counties of occupied Poland], vol. 1, eds. Barbara Engelking and Jan Grabowski (Warsaw: Polish Center for Holocaust Research, 2018), 623–760; *Druga strona sojuszu. Żołnierze brytyjscy w Polsce w czasie II wojny światowej* [The Other Side of Alliance: British Soldiers in Poland during the Second World War] (Gdańsk: Museum of the Second World War, (2014); and *Ziemia tarnopolska w okresie pierwszej okupacji sowieckiej (1939–1941)* [The Province of Tarnopol during the First Soviet Occupation (1939–1941)] (Kraków: Księgarnia Akademicka, 2006).

SIX

NOWY TARG COUNTY

KAROLINA PANZ

TWO AND A HALF YEARS OF WAR: A DESCRIPTION
OF THE COUNTY OF NOWY TARG

In a report submitted to the head of the Main Department of *Internal Affairs* of the *General Government (GG)'s administration* covering his twenty months' work as the Nowy Targ *starosta* (county executive), Victor von Dewitz, a young lawyer, clearly outlined the source of his frustration. When the posts of *starosta* had been handed out, the smallest and least-populated *powiat* (county) in the entire Kraków District (about 190,000 square kilometers,[1] population 170,000) had been relegated to his jurisdiction. Adding to his frustration were "the distinctive mountain character of the county" and its "entirely forestry and agricultural economy," with industry consisting only of "few sawmills, a brickyard, and some quarries."[2]

The county contained four *gminy miejskie* (urban communes)—Nowy Targ, Zakopane, Maków Podhalański, and Jordanów—and 22 rural communes containing 96 villages in total. Before the war, some 7,400 Jews lived in the communities incorporated into *Kreis* Neumarkt (Nowy Targ County), constituting 4.3 percent of the county's population. In none of the towns and villages where they lived did the Jews exceed 21 percent of the population. In a dozen or so villages in the Podhale region, just one Jewish family resided.

Nowhere in Podhale, the mountainous region where the town of Nowy Targ functioned as capital, was a district or even a street inhabited exclusively by Jews. On the contrary, the archival registers of residents show that Polish and Jewish inhabitants usually lived side by side. In the Podhale region, Poles and

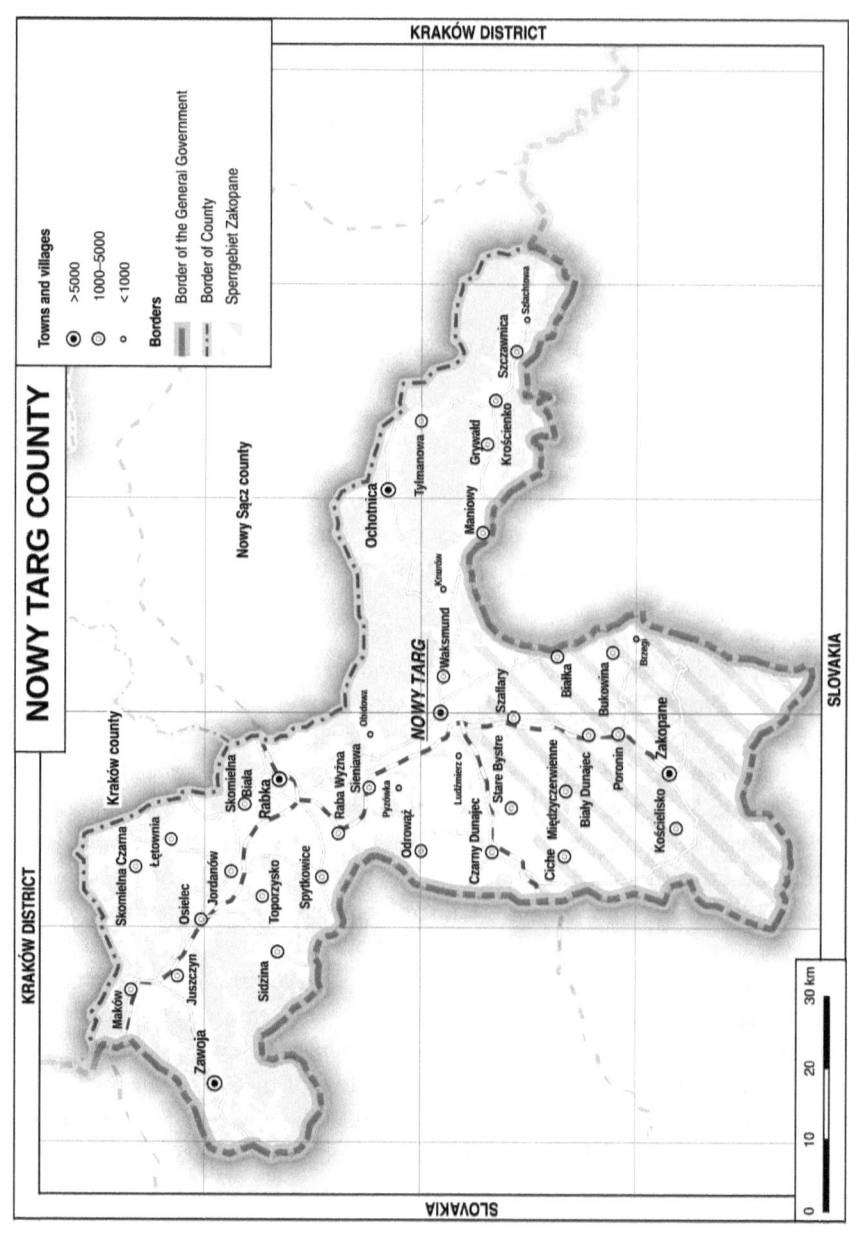

Jews almost always lived next to each other, separated only by a fence and often sharing backyards, corridors, and stairwells.

The *Górale* (highlanders, the *indigenous* people of Podhale) maintained ties with Jewish communities. Gentile men worked in Jewish workshops and stores, gentile women were hired by Jewish families as domestic help and nannies, and gentile children would deliver milk and dairy products to Jewish households. No separate Jewish school was established in Podhale, so Polish children sat at the same desks as their Jewish counterparts.[3] Moreover, Polish was spoken in the Nowy Targ synagogue, the largest in the county.[4] No one was anonymous, although sharing a common space and activities was not tantamount to constituting a Polish-Jewish community. And although there were no pogroms in the Podhale region before the war, in the second half of the 1930s, nationalists organized a boycott—posting pickets in front of Jewish shops and eateries,[5] smashing the windows of Jewish houses,[6] painting anti-Jewish slogans on walls,[7] and beating Jewish neighbors and fellow citizens.[8] In December 1937, at a staff meeting of the First Elementary School in Nowy Targ, a unanimous decision was reached to separate Jewish students from their Polish peers.[9] In June 1938, the largest local newspaper, *Gazeta Podhala*, announced to the residents of the region that government authorities considered "the Jews, in the present state of affairs, an element that weakens the normal development of national and state strength,"[10] and "the settling of the Jewish Question in Poland could, firstly, be achieved by a radical decrease in the number of jews [*sic*] in the Polish state."[11] As elsewhere in the country, in Nowy Targ County Poles and Jews were sharing space, but commonality of space was definitely not tantamount to commonality of citizenship.

On September 1, 1939, the German army entered Podhale from Slovakia at lightning speed.[12] Earlier that day, at dawn, the mass exodus of the Podhalanians had started. They were escaping to the east, into the nearby mountains, and to Hungary,[13] and almost all of the local Jews were among them. Only a very few had stayed, for example the Goldfingers of Jordanów, whose daughter Chana was preparing for her wedding. In her diary, written toward the end of the war, Chana Goldfinger recalled, "I had had a bad feeling, so I had put everything into our cellars: my beautiful trousseau, my bed linens, and other things. Only a handful of people had remained, and we were among them . . . Everything was on fire . . . Daddy shouted 'run!' because our neighbors' house was burning and ours was ablaze . . . we all ran out. All our possessions . . . went up in flames."[14] Hers was the town in the area that suffered the most severe damage in September 1939: 60 percent of the buildings in Jordanów were burned down.[15] While most of other towns in the county remained almost untouched, by September 12, the German civil authorities had already started functioning.

Figure 6.1. Jakub Schneider—Jewish inhabitant of Nowy Targ in folk costume from Podhale, Nowy Targ, late 1930s. Private archive of Joel Schneider.

The vast majority of the Jews who had escaped the day the war had broken out returned to their homes and shops, which had already been plundered by the German army and the Polish population.[16] The image that became most deeply engrained in the memory of those who returned to Nowy Targ was that of the synagogue, which had been converted into a stable.[17]

They found themselves in a new reality, molded by decisions of the German authorities, including one von Dewitz, who took over the position of the New Targ *starosta* on September 17, 1939.[18] Since the outbreak of the war, tourism, the main source of income in the region, had virtually ceased to exist, and the local resorts of Rabka, Szczawnica, and Zakopane were sustaining losses.[19] Furthermore, the newly drawn border with the fascist Slovak Republic contributed to "the severing of many long-established economic links."[20] Von Dewitz and his officials could not rely on seizing large Jewish factories and fortunes because there were none to be had in Podhale. To improve the difficult financial situation, the German civil authorities implemented further measures that provided for the confiscation of Jewish property.

To ensure the efficient "carrying out of tasks,"[21] von Dewitz had at his disposal the *Sonderdienst* (Special Service) unit of twenty-three officers stationed in Nowy Targ. "Ownerless" shops of the Jews who had fled on September 1 were appropriated right away. German, Ukrainian, and Polish trustees also took over the real estate and "valuable movables" of the Jewish escapees. At the turn of 1939, a ban was placed on Jewish-owned retail and wholesale companies in the entire county;[22] they were subsequently liquidated or handed over to the *Treuhanders* (commissar managers).

In October 1939, the Jews from *Kreis* Neumarkt were also deprived of their savings as their deposits, securities, and safe-deposit boxes were liquidated and their savings accounts were seized; Jews were allowed only to make a one-time withdrawal of 250 zlotys, and a Jewish household was permitted to have at its disposal no more than 2,000 zlotys.[23] A daily struggle to survive in this new reality had begun. Chana Goldfinger, who due to the turmoil of war had not married Izaak Windstrauch until the fall of 1940 (it was the only Jewish wedding in the wartime Jordanów), remembered, "They took our livestock, they took the farmland right away too, and Jews were prohibited from owning anything. Nothing but 'pleasures,' a new misery. They began to register Jews for forced labor."[24]

Most likely, the registration process took place at the beginning of 1940. The local *Judenräte* (Jewish Councils), formed at the end of 1939,[25] were obliged to carry it out. Apart from registering, supplying, and equipping forced laborers, the *Judenräte* had to resist the ever-increasing pauperization. The latter was accomplished in close cooperation with the local ŻSS (*Żydowska Samopomoc Społeczna*, Jewish Social Self-Help committees).[26] In all of the *Kreis* Neumarkt towns, the *Judenräte* enjoyed a good reputation among the Jewish population.[27]

A *Sperrgebiet* (closed zone) was to be set up around Zakopane, extending up to the area up to the southern border of Nowy Targ. *Kreis* Neumarkt was earmarked to become a resort center for German soldiers and elites,[28] and the *Sperrgebiet* was to be "cleared of any dubious Polish element and Jews."[29] Therefore, under threat of punishment, all Jews were to vacate Zakopane by June 1941 with the exception of the 40 designated *Judenrat*[30] members plus their families.[31] A similar fate befell all of the Jews living south of Nowy Targ who—deprived of almost everything that could have secured their livelihood—joined a group of displaced people searching for refuge in *Kreis* Neumarkt.

The number of refugees who arrived from outside the county amounted to several hundred. Most of them were Jews from the Warthegau,[32] who were resettled into towns in March 1941 as far from the closed zone as possible. The burden of providing for the people deprived of all belongings was laid upon the shoulders of local, impoverished Jews. The head of the Jordanów *Judenrat*, Erwin Kögel, kept sending impassioned letters to the Kraków office of the American

Joint Committee: "98 Jews resettled from Warthegau arrived on the 14th of this month... we cannot cope with our duties, and the displaced people are literally starving."[33]

It is puzzling that the process of ghettoization was not fully accomplished anywhere in the territory of the county. Nowy Targ was the only place where an open ghetto was created. Before the war, 306 Jews had lived within the three streets where, starting in May 1941, the Jewish quarter was created. Later, the number of Jews increased to 1,951,[34] but the ghetto lasted for only a few months.[35] The records of the Nowy Targ Municipal Board contain many different lists of residents compiled in the fall of 1941, among them a list of farmers who "were allowed to return to their previous place of residence for economic reasons."[36] It is unlikely, however, that "economic reasons" alone were the decisive factor in this instance. According to the memoirs of Captain Józef Wraubek, chief of the Blue police in *Kreis* Neumarkt, Lieutenant Sebastian Mehltreter, commander of the gendarmerie platoon in Nowy Targ, made the decision allowing Jews and Poles who had been resettled when the Nowy Targ ghetto had been created[37] to return home.[38] He "was a decent man, level-headed, who could not stand violence and extermination, a man with perfectly clean hands";[39] "he defended the Jews as often as he could."[40]

As no Jewish district was established in *Kreis* Neumarkt, nor was there any Jewish police formed, Poles and Jews shared a common space as they had done before the war. It greatly facilitated illigal bartering during the first stage of the Holocaust,[41] as well as allowing Jews to make some money working for Poles.[42] The Podhale Jews also took advantage of the border location of *Kreis* Neumarkt, as well as their contacts dating back to the prewar years, to carry contraband.[43] "On winter days, I used to go with my Polish friends on skis through the mountains to the Slovak villages at the foot of Babia Góra and bring spices, pepper, [and] bay leaves from there," reminisced Emanuel Warenhaupt, a member of the *Judenrat* in Maków Podhalański. The Nowy Targ farmer Dawid Grassgrün,[44] who knew every inch of ground in the immediate—and not so immediate—vicinity, was also involved in smuggling goods. In addition, he made use of his expertise and experience to smuggle people over the border.[45] Grassgrün collaborated with some Nowy Targ Jews, escapees to Slovakia, who set up a people-smuggling ring in Kieżmark. Józef Engländer escaped with his family in the fall of 1939. After a German officer had put a gun to his back, demanding that he hand over products from his soda water factory, Engländer concluded that a safer place for his wife and children would be abroad.[46] He and Benzion Kalb, another orthodox Jew from Nowy Targ, set up a smuggling operation, bringing goods from Kieżmark to Podhale and Kraków. Later, they used their contacts and experience to rescue people.[47] Surprisingly, although there was a well-organized network of Jewish-Polish smugglers, the Engländers, Kalb, and their friend Salomon Grünspan seem to be the only Jewish residents of *Kreis* Neumarkt[48] who took advantage of this opportunity and escaped to Slovakia, and from there to Hungary. Salomon Süsskind, who had lived in Krościenko, explained this phenomenon in the following way: "At the beginning of the war, I stayed in Krościenko; we were doing very well there, and that was our undoing. We did not even think of escaping, although I had many opportunities to save myself by escaping to Slovakia. Jews came to us from the entire Małopolska region as . . . it was all quiet here."[49] Peacefulness, even the "idyll" of the first two years of the war, was recalled by many Jews from *Kreis* Neumarkt. The outbreak of the German-Soviet war, however, resulted in a radical reversal of the situation as far as the range of influence of the police apparatus and security services and their relations with the civil administration of the county were concerned.

A Gestapo office that, due to the border location of the county, took over the functions of the border police was established in Zakopane as early as in September 1939,[50] with its headquarters in a modern building of Villa Palace. Gestapo posts were set up in Maków Podhalański and in the villages of Szczawnica and Czarny Dunajec.[51] The posts were manned by two or three men, who rotated every few weeks.[52] The staff of the Zakopane office totaled thirty-two officers and thirteen translators[53] and, from October 1939 to July 1943, was led by Robert Philipp Weissmann.[54] He had the reputation of being "a very tough man . . . even the Gestapo officers were afraid of him."[55] The Zakopane Gestapo cooperated closely with a training academy for leaders of the Security Police (Sipo) and the Security Service (SD) located in Rabka, in Villa Tereska. The academy was run by Wilhelm Rosenbaum,[56] "a sadist and an executioner."[57] It was the only such institution in the entire *GG. It* trained Ukrainian Sipo officers,[58] as well as Polish Kripo officers, who came there to take a six-week-long training course (there were about one hundred trainees per course).[59] The school employed Jewish forced laborers; initially there were about sixty, and later their number reached two hundred.[60]

Officers of the Zakopane Gestapo and the staff of the Rabka training school were sent to Lwów with the outbreak of the German-Soviet war.[61] At that time, when the SS men from *Kreis* Neumarkt were gaining expertise and experience in carrying extermination operations in the East, Lt. Sebastian Mehltreter, the head of the gendarmerie, who had been lenient toward the Jews, was transferred to Calais in France.[62] Allegedly, this change in position of the county gendarmerie commander was made at Weissmann's request: Mehltreter, as stated, had been regarded as of no use since the harsher policy toward Poles and Jews had begun to be implemented. Mehltreter's place was taken by his rival Erhardt Zimmermann, former head of the gendarmerie in Zakopane.[63] In July 1941, Hans

Malsfey, a good friend of Weissmann and a staunch member of the NSDAP (National Socialist German Workers' Party),[64] replaced Victor von Dewitz[65] in the position of *starosta* of *Kreis* Neumarkt.

Now working hand-in-hand with the *starosta*'s office, the Gestapo considerably extended its influence over the lives of the residents, especially the Nowy Targ County Jews. After the replacement of the position of the head of the gendarmerie, Weissmann could count on the absolute obedience of the commander and his twelve subordinates.[66] The gendarmerie had direct oversight of the Polish Blue Police, which held nineteen posts in the territory of the county.[67] The head of the Blue Police had also been replaced. In early February 1942, after commander Captain. Wraubek had escaped and was later arrested for his resistance activities,[68] Lt. Józef Andrzejewski[69] took his place as commander of the Blue police.

Robert Weissmann was in the habit of visiting the gendarmerie and Blue police station in Nowy Targ once a week. With the same regularity, he inspected the Nowy Targ Kripo office staffed with ten men.[70] Josef Kandzia was their commander;[71] Andrzej Szafraniec became his deputy responsible for Polish affairs. The latter had been a middle-rank policeman of the criminal police in Nowy Targ before the war. According to Józef Wraubek, Szafraniec was an exceptional "pest."[72] Weissmann also regularly inspected the *Zollgrenschutz* (Customs Border Guard Service).[73] It was the most important of the German uniformed services that had remained outside of the military and police structures for most of the war. Most often, about four hundred *Zollgrenschutz* functionaries were stationed in the territory of *Kreis* Neumarkt.[74]

Listing places inspected by his boss, the personal driver of the Zakopane Gestapo chief, Franciszek Gold, testified, "Equally often, Weissmann visited so-called *gminy żydowskie* [Jewish communes], but these visits, in my opinion, were of rather a private nature. On those occasions, various packages from members of a Jewish commune were handed to him, brought to the car. These packages had never been sent to the station but were stored at the place of the Weissmann's lady friend, Aleksandra Keller."[75] Wilhelm Rosenbaum paid similar visits in Rabka. Alicja Kleinberg, who had worked in the *Judenrat* in Rabka, testified many years later: "At the request of Rosenbaum, the *Judenrat* collected from among the Jews a considerable amount of money ... and jewelry. I handed over a diamond ring at that time, a pin with a pearl, and a silver cigarette case. Rosenbaum threatened that if we did not pay the ransom, he would take all of [our] men. Rosenbaum also burdened the *Judenrat* with quite specific demands. I recall that, as per one such demand, I handed over a coffee set for twelve and a tennis racket."[76] Jews were forced to pander to the endless whims of the Gestapo men (and their wives and lovers) everywhere in the territory of the county, suffering a further loss of their material resources, which had already been heavily depleted because they had to buy provisions on the black market.

No mass executions of Jews was carried out in *Kreis* Neumarkt until the spring of 1942. The position of the German Prosecutor's Office, which issued an indictment against Weissmann in 1964, was that the lack of mass execution could be counted in his favor: "At that time, isolated murders of persons of Jewish descent occurred in Nowy Targ County. These murders were not committed on order [of superiors]; they were arbitrary, and [as such] were cases of insubordination of individual [Gestapo] staff members. Generally, the results of the investigations allow us to establish that the Jewish Question did not play the same role in Nowy Targ County as it did in other counties of the district and in other districts."[77]

In the winter of 1941–1942, however, Jews from *Kreis* Neumarkt most likely heard about the mass murders of their fellow believers, as well as about pogroms and the terror spread by the *Einsatzgruppen* in the Galicia District, as Jewish refugees coming back from the East might have told them. It is impossible to establish the scope of the legal Jewish migration in the entire county. As for Nowy Targ, thirty-one persons came back there from the Galicia District between mid-December 1941 and mid-February 1942.[78] What remains unknown is how residents of the county without ghettos, where isolated instances of killing were considered to be cases of "insubordination of individual staff members," responded to their stories.

THE ONSET OF THE DIRECT EXTERMINATION

On April 28, 1942, "actions against communists" were carried out in every larger town of the county (similar actions were carried out in many places in the GG on that day).[79] A total of sixty people died; with a few exceptions, the victims had nothing to do with communism.[80] Apparently, officers of the Zakopane Gestapo wanted to prove themselves useful to their superiors, and the necessary fight against communists in the county constituted a sufficient reason for not sending them to the front. This operation opened the period of direct extermination of the Jews in *Kreis* Neumarkt. Soon after, Wilhelm Rosenbaum also decided to prove his "usefulness." Alicja Kleinberg remembered that the *Judenrat* was ordered in early May to prepare a detailed list of all Jews—inhabitants of Rabka.

> When the list had been delivered, Rosenbaum ordered all the Jews to gather in the yard of the SS school... One after the other, we had to approach a table... Rosenbaum examined the approaching [Jews] and marked an *X* next to the names of those whom he was condemning to death. Such *X*s were by the names of my mother and my mother-in-law...

Figure 6.2. Wilhelm Kleinberg, Krakow, late 1930s. Private archive of Anna Janowska-Ciońćka.

On May 20, 1942, those Jews whose names Rosenbaum had marked with Xs, notified by the *Judenrat*, had to turn up in the schoolyard at 3 p.m. I saw my mother Laura Paster and my mother-in-law Antonina Kleinberg off... I watched as all those gathered were forced into a garage; I waited for some time, and then I came back home... About 9 p.m., I heard loud single shots.[81]

Complete registers of Jews from *Kreis* Neumarkt have survived and are kept in the National Archives in Kraków. One of them is a list of Jewish residents of Rabka. Names of some residents are crossed out; there are check marks in pencil by them in the left margin; the date of death is recorded on the right. The annotation "20/5/42 *verstorben* [dead]" appears thirty-three times next to the names of people who were elderly and sick. Apparently, Rosenbaum had already known during this first execution who would die within in a few weeks—the Jews who had arrived at Rabka from Kraków and other towns. The name of

Figure 6.3. Alicja Kleinberg with her daughters, Rabka, 1942. Private archive of Anna Janowska-Giońćka.

seventy-seven-year-old Wilhelm Kleinberg from Kraków, Alicja Kleinberg's father-in-law, had also been marked. Letters sent by Alicja Kleinberg to her sister-in-law offer a glimpse into her fight to save his live, as well as her desperation and helplessness: "I am still taking care of him ... What I could do—i.e., to put him in a place which was, I believed, free from danger—I did. We live day by day here ... I muster all the strength possible to survive."[82] Meanwhile, Wilhelm Kleinberg, hidden in the apartment of the Rabka glazier Gustaw Netzer,[83] was unable to shake off his despair. Ten days after his wife's death, he wrote to his children, "I am alone, without her, not one child at my side! And so much misery around ... Do not be angry at me that I am only capable of this heartrending cry ... Thank you for so much love and I kiss you. Dad."[84] He died on June 25, 1942, shot along with eighty-four others in a grove just behind Villa Tereska. Alicja Kleinberg wrote to Wilhelm's daughter after the execution: "What had happened to Mama repeated itself. We are powerless and none of our efforts helped. Be strong, Zosia! I beg you! All four of us are healthy, but what does it matter."[85] Most likely it was about that time that Kleinberg started arranging an escape for herself and her two small daughters, Ewa and Hania.[86] She was only able to execute her plan in August.

There were others who also decided to escape from Rabka. Not all the checked names on the list are marked with the word *verstorben*. Instead, the date June 29, 1942, is written next to some of them, with the annotation *"verzogen ohne Abmeldung"* [delayed without registration]. This annotation about departure without notification and unknown whereabouts is written next to twenty-three names (3.3 percent of the Jews registered in Rabka at that time). The number of escapees was probably greater, as the list contains information about the absence only of those who had been required to turn up at the execution site and failed to do so.

Rabka is not the only place in *Kreis* Neumarkt where mass executions of Jews had been carried out before the *Endlösung der Judenfrage* [Final Solution to the Jewish Question] was implemented. On June 3, 1942, Hans Frank issued an executive order giving "the security police responsibility for Jewish affairs."[87] Five days later, on Monday morning, officers of the Zakopane Gestapo arrived in Nowy Targ. They had a list of the most affluent local Jewish families selected for deportation. It came as a surprise; ninety-eight people were deported to Bełżec that day. Thirty-nine elderly people—mostly Orthodox Jews whom the Gestapo men found, on entering their workplace, to be holding morning prayers—were shot in the cemetery; the local gendarmerie participated in the execution.[88] Yet despite these events, only seven persons—according to existing documents— had escaped from Nowy Targ by August 1942. Four of them were members of the Singer family,[89] who in this way had avoided the June deportation during which their relatives had been taken away.

The stories of those who decided to escape at the time of the first extermination operations raise the issue of their mental state, which was very important to those who attempted to save themselves. They needed to make crucial decisions and act swiftly, despite being in despair and feeling powerless while their loved ones had been slaughtered. In such a moment, one's decision to seek salvation must have been profoundly affected by the belief that there was someone willing to help. In Alicja Kleinberg's case, she received help from relatives of the Polish wife of her brother-in-law;[90] who was using Aryan papers. The Singer family had not been able to find any Poles willing to shelter them for a longer time, and their journey reached its end in the town of Wieliczka at the time of the selection.[91] Why did people not try to run away after the first *aktion*? Frania Tiger from Rabka, the daughter of Gustaw Netzer in whose apartment Wilhelm Kleinberg had been hiding just before his death, answered this question in the

1960s: "People did not run away because they had nowhere to run. The Poles did not want to hide anyone. You could not go to the forest, and you could not get out of the town, because everyone had an armband; besides, there was no place to hide. The Jews had nowhere to run." [92] In total, 434 Jewish inhabitants of the county lost their lives in the murder operations carried out before August 1942.

ENDLÖSUNG DER JUDENFRAGE IN NOWY TARG COUNTY

"On one day—it is not possible to establish which one—of the month of July or in early August of 1942, the head of the SS and police [in Kraków, Julian] Scherner paid a visit to the accused [Robert] Weissmann in Zakopane. The whole campaign was ordered and discussed there, and all the details were worked out."[93] Apart from Weissmann, his deputy Herbert Böttcher also participated in this conference. Perhaps then they decided to make the local forces of the Security Police responsible for the *Endlösung der Judenfrage* in *Kreis* Neumarkt.[94]

It is certain that Weissmann received an order from Scherner to shoot the Jews who were being kept in the Nowy Targ jail during a phone conversation they held in early August. The Jews had been relocated from Szczawnica to Nowy Targ at the end of July on the pretext that "allegedly, there were to be acts of sabotage."[95] This mass execution initiated the "Final Solution" in *Kreis* Neumarkt. It remained etched in the memories of Nowy Targ residents as the "Szczawnica *aktion*." That night, in Nowy Targ, the Jews from Szczawnica were murdered at the Jewish cemetery, on the streets, and in private yards and apartments. The tragedy unfolded for all to see.[96] Aside from about 100 Jews from Szczawnica, nine residents of Nowy Targ were killed as well.[97] After the operation, Weissmann called Scherner to report that the order had been executed.

Some 3,800 Jews were still dwelling in *Kreis* Neumarkt in mid-August 1942. The *Judenaktion*[98] was planned for August 30, 1942.[99] Deportees were to be loaded onto the train to Bełżec in Nowy Targ, Rabka, and Maków; therefore, all of the Jews from the county were to be gathered in these places. The entire Gestapo and Kripo forces of Zakopane, as well as the gendarmerie and Polish police units from the whole county, would participate in the closing stage of the "Final Solution." The physical extermination of all the Jewish communities in Podhale took place during a dozen or so days in August. In every area from where Jews were deported, the deportations followed a similar pattern. Weissmann, known for his commitment to order and discipline, also forbade any arbitrary deviations from the plan at this time.[100]

In the western part of Nowy Targ County, the deportation actions started on August 22 in Zawoja, one of the longest villages in Poland located in the western part of Nowy Targ County. Four Gestapo officers forced a Pole, Bronisław Kuś,[101] to point out houses occupied by Jews. The Blue police of Zawoja received an order to bring those Jews who lived in the center of Zawoja to house number 906. The Dukler and Sauerstrom families dwelled there. Local people remembered the Glücksmans and the Silberrings, with their hands raised, being escorted there by Polish policemen.[102] Polish policemen accompanied by a local gendarme surrounded the building[103] while Kuś and the Gestapo officers drove up to one house after another that had been indicated by the Pole, murdering their Jewish occupants[104] on the spot.

The building in the center of the village, where the Blue policemen were ordered to gather the Jews, was the last one to which the car pulled up. There were twenty-two people inside. Their Polish neighbors suspected what was going to happen. Marian Wojciechowski, who was in Zawoja on business at that time, was awakened by the noise. Someone shouted, "Get up and see how the Gestapo shoots the Jews!"[105] Wojciechowski approached a picket fence. The closest neighbor of the Duklers heard crying and commotion. She went outside to check what had happened and to whom. While on the street, she heard a woman locked in the neighbor's house calling her by name: "Pola! Help us and pray for us!"[106] Shouts of "Help us!" and crying were heard throughout the entire neighborhood. All this lasted about two hours.[107] Seventeen people were killed on the spot. Two men managed to escape: Leon Dukler and Adolf Sauerstrom. Both were killed later.[108] Those murdered that day were all adults;[109] children were sent to Maków Podhalański.[110] A letter in the archive of the Maków committee of the ŻSS, dated August 28, 1942, contains information about the arrival of Jewish orphans from Zawoja. Their condition was extremely dire; they had no clothing or money.[111] Among them were five-year-old Marta Fischer and thirteen-year-old Saul Glücskman with his siblings: seven-year-old Eda, four-year-old Georg, and one-year-old Lusia. None of the Jews living in Zawoja during the occupation survived.

It is unknown how quickly word spread about what had happened at the western end of the county, or whether in three days it had reached the Jews living in the then utterly peaceful village of Naprawa, about thirty kilometers away.[112] On August 25, 1942, however, six members of the Rabka training school's staff arrived in the village; Wilhelm Rosenbaum himself was most likely among them.[113] More than a dozen people were murdered on the spot, and over 110 Jewish inhabitants of Naprawa were ordered to report to Villa Tereska the following day.[114] Their belongings and children were loaded on a horse-drawn cart. According to a cart driver, some Jews wandered off along the way. The Pole unloaded the cart and left the passengers in front of Rosenbaum's school.[115] Soon after, news spread that the Jews from Naprawa, mostly women and children, had been murdered by Sipo and the SD commander recruits of the school during target practice on the range.[116]

On August 27, the "deportation action" in *Kreis* Neumarkt entered its next phase. It took place in the eastern part of the county,[117] as well as in its western section, in towns and villages around Maków Podhalański,[118] and it was carried out by the Zakopane Gestapo with the support of the local Blue police and border guards.[119] The people there were shot in their homes and gardens. The elders died on the spot. Those who tried to escape were caught and killed in mass executions.[120] As with had happened in Zawoja and other small towns, all of the adults were murdered on the spot in villages with a Jewish population of thirty persons or fewer; children and teenagers were left alive, along with one or two adults to chaperone them.[121] Those who were spared had to march to Nowy Targ, even though distances were sometimes long (the distance from Krościenko to Nowy Targ exceeded 30 kilometers).[122] Despite being escorted by Blue policemen, some people managed to escape to the forest.[123] The Jews who arrived from the eastern part of the county were lodged with the Jewish residents of Nowy Targ, and they talked about what they had experienced.[124] A few days earlier, an additional forced contribution was levied on the Nowy Targ Jews.[125] Probably during the evening of August 28, Weissmann briefed his subordinates on what was to happen in the near future and assigned tasks.[126]

The next morning, Saturday, August 29, a train arrived at the station in Nowy Targ, made up of covered freight carriages. Edward Marfiak, the cashier at the station, remembered that there were about twenty such carriages. The train was planned to be loaded with the Jews from Nowy Targ and dispatched to Bełżec, and on its way, it was to be loaded with even more Jews at the Chabówka and Maków stations. The same morning, another train arrived in Nowy Targ; this one came from Kraków and carried Gestapo officers. Shortly after their arrival, they brought a group of Jews to the station and ordered them to clean the train cars,[127] as the next stage of the operation, deportation of Jews from Jordanów, was taking place simultaneously.

The Gestapo and other German uniformed forces arrived in Jordanów in two trucks and a few taxicabs. Among them were the Gestapo men from Zakopane and the staff of the Sipo and SD commander training school.[128] They secured the perimeter of the entire town.[129] While the Blue policemen and some German servicemen were busy rounding up Jewish residents, others spent time drinking in a tavern in the market square.[130] One of the Gestapo officers informed the Jews that they should go, escorted, to Maków, fourteen kilometers away. Those who felt they were not fit to walk such a distance were to be grouped to be transported by in horse-drawn carts. These carts stopped just a few hundred meters farther on by a meadow at the foot of a hill.

"First, all of the Jews were gathered in one spot, and each of the officers removed one person from the group and took her aside. He would take her to the edge of the meadow, before the bushes. There these persons were shot from behind with a handgun. Each shooter selected one Jew from the group, led him by the hand or by the arm to the mentioned spot, and killed him or her while the Jew was still walking. The execution lasted about an hour . . . everything was thoroughly arranged. We left the bodies in the meadow. Escape from there was impossible because, as I have just remembered, the meadow was fenced."[131]

Mayor of Jordanów Michał Hołda had been obliged to take care of the bodies. The same day at 10:00 p.m., fifty men began to dig a grave. Among them was Franciszek Tyrpa, who earlier, from the safety of his home, had heard and counted the sounds of gunfire—sixty-seven shots had been fired. When the noise of the execution had died away, a municipal policeman showed up at his house and ordered to go with him and bring a pickaxe and a shovel. They worked guarded by Blue policemen while the Gestapo men "drove away to drink in Neubler's restaurant." [132]

At 4:30 a.m. the next day (Sunday), a messenger from Nowy Targ, the county instructor of the volunteer fire brigade, arrived at Jordanów on a motorbike. He brought Stanisław Karaś, secretary of the Jordanów Municipal Board, some posters to put up. They were printed on red paper and contained a new decree issued by the *starosta*:

> To carry out the resettlement of Jews from Neumarkt/Dun[ajec] *Starostwo* [county], by order of the SS und *Polizeiführer* [Police Leader] in the Krakau [Kraków] District, the following is announced:
> On August 30, 1942, the resettlement from the Neumarkt/Dunajec Starostwo is [sic] carried out.
> Every pole [sic] who hinders or weighs the resettlement down in whatever way, or who supports a jew [sic] in his action shall be shot dead.
> Every pole, who during and after the resettlement, takes in or hides a jew [sic], shall be shot dead.
> Every pole who enters the flat of a deported jew without permission shall be shot dead as a plunderer.
> Standing on a street is forbidden on the day of the resettlement, windows shall be kept shut as well.[133]

The deportation action was to be carried as follows: first, Jews were to gather on a given day at a fixed hour; then they would be transported to the railroad station and loaded into the freight cars provided. At the station, a *Transportkommando des Zuges* (railroad transportation commando) was to take responsibility for the Jews. Those unfit for work or transportation were to be executed, while those fit for work would be selected. Scherner instructed that the Jews should be executed naked "as their clothing is needed to harvest yarn." Another directive specified that all valuables—such as rings, jewelry, and money—should be taken from the Jews before transportation. "In accordance with these directives, Weissmann ... ordered that the Jews should gather at the sports stadium in Nowy Targ on Sunday, August 30, at 6 a.m. The decree was passed to the Jews through the *Judenrat*. The Jews were told that they would be resettled further toward the eastern territory, where a separate state would be established for them."[134] At the gathering point, people had to stand in rows, ten persons in a row. Under threat of death, everyone had to hand over all valuables.[135] Then, Leopold Stanner, member of the *Judenrat*, began to read the names of workers assigned to labor camps in the Hobag sawmills[136] in Zakopane, Nowy Targ, and Czarny Dunajec; several dozen young men were sent to each camp. Then, other names were read out—of thirty-five men, all of them Jewish artisans, and thirty women. Of the last group, Weissmann selected only ten women; the rest had to join the largest group of some 1,500 people. Members of the *Judenrat*, who had been ordered to stand separately, had to join a previously selected group of the elderly, disabled, and sick. Finally, amid screams and beatings, those marked for deportation were led out from the field.[137] The train departed the station in Nowy Targ at approximately 2:00 p.m. The trucks carrying the workers had left a little earlier. The artisans were escorted to a barrack near the station. When the field had been emptied, the members of the *Judenrat*, the elderly and the sick, about two hundred persons in total, were ordered to get onto three large trucks with trailers and were taken to the Nowy Targ cemetery. The train to Bełżec made a stop at the railroad station in Chabówka, where Jews from Rabka were already waiting. Only two hundred men had been left in Rabka—the Jews who worked in Rosenbaum's school.[138] None of the Jews rounded up near the railroad station in Maków Podhalański survived.[139]

That day, thirty young workers, members of a *Baudienst* (construction service)[140] labor battalion, had worked in the Jewish cemetery in Nowy Targ since the morning. They had been brought from Harklowa, where they worked in the trout farm. They had breakfast in the building of the Jewish prayer house on Nadwodna Street: black coffee and sandwiches. One of the men, Tadeusz Czubernat of Nowy Targ, remembered that they got half-liter mugs half filled with coffee, which were later topped up with vodka. Then they were taken to the cemetery, where they were ordered to dig three pits.[141] After some time, the trucks carrying those unfit for transportation arrived.[142] Another member of the same group, a resident of Ochotnica,[143] admitted years later that the workers had been allowed to decide either to stay in the cemetery or go outside to guard the fence. He had stayed. "Those Jews came off the cars, they went out one after the other and wham, wham, the Germans were killing. When one killed, another

Figure 6.4. Jewish cemetery in Nowy Targ, 1978. Photo courtesy of David Applefield.

was given a weapon and that other one fired, and a kick in the back, and in the hole, and in the hole a Jew... Then, as they already wiped [them] out, we [took] up spades to coat those Jews thick with earth, and [we were] done."[144]

Poles who lived in the vicinity of the cemetery watched the execution hidden in the attics of their houses and sheds,[145] following everything through knotholes[146] and binoculars.[147] In Nowy Targ, as in all towns and villages of *Kreis Neumarkt*, the tragedy of the Jewish inhabitants took place in full view of their Polish neighbors. In each and every one of these places, Poles watched Jews they knew being murdered, heard their screams, touched corpses, and breathed the air filled with the overpowering smell of their dead bodies. No one could have remained indifferent to this; to no one had the victims been distant or anonymous. And during the next phase of the Holocaust, the attitude of those Polish witnesses became critical for the Jews who tried to save themselves.

The Podhale Jews and Their Efforts to Survive

Did the Podhale Jews realize in August 1942 what was about to happen over the next few weeks, and if so, what were the sources of this information, and what did they do with this knowledge? They could have figured out that the operation was approaching by watching the Germans. Sabina Oberländer decided to move out of the county and take her mother and sister with her when Wilhelm Rosenbaum, whose mistress highly valued Sabina's skills as a dressmaker, hinted that she should move to their villa. He suggested that his word might soon not be enough to guarantee her safety. She made it just in time.[148]

Just before the operation, the Jews who worked in Villa Tereska were prohibited from going home for the night. Some of them managed to sneak out of the camp and warn their families and friends.[149] Others became alarmed when the Germans demanded a contribution. "I had experienced it in Lwów ... so I warned others not to pay the contribution, that this was *schitegeld* [money poured down the drain] and that the money should rather be spent on building hideouts and escaping the town. I did not trust the Germans, so I hid my entire family in the forest: my father, sister, sister-in-law, and two children."[150]

Poles also told Jews about upcoming deportations. Abraham Furman, a twenty-seven-year-old member of the *Judenrat* in Ochotnica, was warned by the commander of the local Blue police.[151] Frania Tiger (née Netzer), who had lived in Rabka and had been advised by her neighbor, Eleonora Wagner, suggested that Poles knew more than Jews did. Also, because "we Jews could not believe that we would meet such an end." Mrs. Wagener repeated to Frania what some railroad men she knew had said: "That they [the Germans] are taking us to the East and are burning us there. We could not believe it, but ..."[152] What could be done then? In the opinion of Nioniek Beck from Nowy Targ, many could only hope for survival, but in fact the upcoming deportation "was known but not spoken of."[153] In Nowy Targ in the last days of August 1942, it was hard not to know where those resettled from the eastern part of the county were being taken. The same can be said about Jordanów, the village neighboring Naprawa or Maków, where the Jews from Zawoja and Jordanów were brought. One can be sure therefore that everywhere in the Podhale region (with the exception of small communities in which the entire adult population had been murdered during sudden raids), Jews had tried to rescue themselves before the final extermination campaign began.

A few hours after a mass execution in Jordanów had been carried out, a public announcement was made in the local market square that one hundred persons had not appeared at the designated gathering site; the number constituted nearly 35 percent of Jews residing in Jordanów in mid-August 1942.[154]

Supposedly, the Jews of Maków fled the town in groups[155] to get to the woods before the operation. As stated in accounts given by local Polish residents, they all died later on the grounds of Villa Marysin, the Gestapo office in Maków Podhalański.[156] As was already mentioned, no selection was carried out in this

Figure 6.5. Villa Marysin, a postcard from 1965. Author's collection.

town on August 30, 1942, and none of those gathered at the train station had been left alive. Yet some Polish witnesses retained the memory of Jews working in the Gestapo office in Maków throughout the fall of 1942. They also remembered that for a dozen or so weeks after the operation, local Jews who had managed to survive hiding in the close vicinity were being brought into Villa Marysin. They stayed there as a labor force and were then murdered in group executions. There were several such executions at least.[157] The priest of the Maków parish, Stanisław Czartoryski, heard about them from an eyewitness, Jan Polak, a gravedigger who had buried the victims.[158] According to Father Czartoryski, no less than two hundred people had been murdered in Villa Marysin and the Maków Catholic cemetery (where smaller groups had been executed), but he believed that the number of victims could have been as high as several hundred.[159] He estimated the number by assessing the amount of food the Maków parish had supplied for the Jewish prisoners.[160]

One of these graves was exhumed in February 1964. It contained 92 skulls although, as the report on the on-site inspection states, the grave was supposed to hold the remains of 39 bodies. Any attempts to locate other graves have been unsuccessful.[161] It is certain, however, that at least 150 victims died in Villa Marysin alone (most likely the number was higher).[162] If the lowest estimate of Jews killed in Villa Marysin is compared with the total number of the Jews residing in Maków and its vicinity in the summer of 1942,[163] the rate of attempted escapes amounts to some 18 percent. No such estimation, even as rough as this is, can be made for other towns, including Nowy Targ.

The Jews from Nowy Targ had seen the freight cars at the train station.[164] They had already experienced the first deportation and the mass executions, so there is no doubt that they tried to save themselves. However, how many of them had not turned up at the assembly site remains unknown, because none of the Jews attempting to hide in the town and its vicinity survived. The testimonies of the men serving in the unit assigned to grave digging and the accounts of Poles living in the neighborhood of the Jewish cemetery provide the only evidence of the fate of the Jews who were hiding in the town during and right after the operation.

On the same day, August 30, 1942, when the mass execution was already over, the members of the *Baudienst* had dinner in the *Deutschehaus* and were locked in the synagogue for the night.[165] They worked on burying Jews who were caught after the operation for about three weeks.[166] Sometimes they were summoned by phone in the morning, and as the Jews had been killed before they arrived, they had to dig a hole and bury them. Sometimes they were summoned to dig a grave before an execution.[167] Few executions were carried out in their presence during these three weeks. The victims—young people and children—were always brought in groups of about thirty-five.[168] "What pretty lasses they were, beautiful Jewish girls, how they begged [the Germans] not to shoot, how they grasped one another's hands, how they pleaded terribly not to shoot [them]. And there was a boy, three years old, he was asking, loving [hugging] to leave this mother alive, probably this Jewess. They killed him, lifted him up by his arm, zap, they put a bullet in his head, and in the grave this child already was . . . it was awful to watch this."[169] At the end of October, the Central *Cashier's Office* of the GG paid the *Baudienst* 8,919 zlotys for the work done during the "Neumarkt *Judenaktion*."[170] Probably at least two hundred people lost their lives during these three weeks, which would amount to 11 percent of Jews living in Nowy Targ in the second half of August of 1942.

Equally little is known about those tracking Jewish hiding places and how they did it. A few terse remarks, accounts, and documents establish that the officers of the Nowy Targ Kripo played a crucial role in the process.[171] The Blue police from Nowy Targ also participated by securing the site of the execution[172] and delivering victims.[173] Except for the commander of the Kripo, Józef Kandzia, none of the perpetrators were ever brought to justice.

Tracking down and capturing the Rabka Jews also took some two or three weeks. According to accounts of Jewish witnesses, inmates of the forced labor camp run by the police school in Villa Tereska, between fifty and sixty people who had tried to take cover from the action were murdered there in the fall of 1942.[174] The victims were gathered in a bunker located next to the villa and then shot to death in a neighboring grove. According to witnesses, local civilian residents were responsible for capturing the Jews. Both the Rabka Jews working in Villa Tereska and the Poles employed there remembered very well the death of eighteen-year-old Helena Peller, who had left her hideout to get some food for herself and her mother. She was captured by a Rabka *Góral* [highlander] of unknown name and killed by a Ukrainian, Hwozdulowicz. "While we were cleaning upstairs, someone came to me and said that they brought Nyśka [Helena]. She was one of the Jewesses who had previously worked with us. A peasant brought her from the village of Rdzawka. They are asking him how he did it, so he said: 'She was [hiding] in [the field of] potatoes and walked down the road, asked me "where to Nowy Targ," so I ask—"Have papers?"—"Eh, no." So, I zap her.' He got two hundred cheap cigarettes and two liters of vodka for betraying her."[175] Rubin Traum, who had witnessed these events, testified in 1945 that relatively many Jews had found shelter with local peasants just before the operation: "Peasants turned them all in, except for one mother with her daughter who survived [hiding] with local residents, and who are in Kraków now."[176] They were Frania Netzer and her mother, Jetti, hiding under the roof of Villa Truskawka in Rabka.

The betrayal of Podhale Jews by local peasants is a constantly recurring motif in accounts given by survivors. As for Polish witnesses, this subject surfaced almost exclusively in their testimonies given at trials held at the end of the 1940s. Such valuable sources as the files of the prosecutor's later investigation of the crimes committed by the Zakopane Gestapo mentions only that Jews were "caught," "denounced," and "taken to" police stations, without any specificity in identifying who played a direct role in their deaths. Perhaps Prosecutor Maria Gacek did not pursue certain leads because it exceeded the scope of her investigation.[177] Or maybe she deliberately omitted names mentioned by witnesses. It is also possible that the perpetrators became a subject of deliberate, collective anonymization: Insiders knew them; outsiders did not need to know. The same happened to the victims. With the passage of time, they became more and more anonymous in the memory of their Polish neighbors and dissolved into a nameless, faceless mass of Jews and "israelites [*sic*]."

There is no known evidence suggesting that German uniformed forces combed the woods to track down Jews hiding there. The sources available show clearly that a crucial role in the systematic capturing of victims in the mountain forests was played by village guards organized in dozen-strong groups, or ad hoc gangs of youngsters who pretended to be village guards. Chana Windstrauch and her relatives, who were hiding in the forest separating Jordanów from the village of Łętownia, fell victim to both kinds of assailants. They were attacked several times, beaten with clubs, and robbed; in a group of twelve assailants armed with forks and clubs, they could recognize acquaintances pretending to be regular village guards.[178] They were lucky to have survived these attacks but heard about others whom peasants had turned in to the Jordanów Blue police and who were murdered by them next to their hideouts.[179]

Organized roundups and individual denunciations were not the only reasons for the deaths of Jews during the first weeks after the deportation. Oftentimes, lack of help from the frightened or indifferent Polish population was enough to cause someone's death from cold and starvation. The Germans would immediately seal houses of deported Jews, but it was often not enough to stop Polish looters.[180] Henryk Grüngras of Jordanów, who, after the deportation action, had been hiding close to his home, suffered cold and hunger for several months: "I could not return to my apartment as the Gestapo men would seal all Jewish apartments right away and my entire furnishing and everything I had had was taken away."[181] He survived finding shelter in barns of Jordanów farmers. There were others, however, who, due to the absence of any help and a lack of their own resources, turned themselves in to the police.[182] All of them—those caught and those denounced by peasants, as well as those who turned themselves in—were murdered in Jewish cemeteries or in their own homes at the hands of the Zakopane Gestapo and the staff of the Rabka training school, or—in Jordanów—at the hands of the Blue police. Apart from Villa Tereska in Rabka and Villa Marysin in Maków Podhalański, Villa Palace in Zakopane was another place where mass murders of Jews took place.[183]

Mountain forests could give shelter to Jewish families for only so long, as cold, hunger, and constant fear of roundups diminished their chances of survival. Some Podhale Jews[184] withstood several months in forest hideouts only to decide to flee the territory of the county later; some of them even moved into the Kraków ghetto or the ghetto in Bochnia.[185] Those who had stayed in the forests could survive only with the help of Polish people, especially in the face of approaching winter.[186] Jan Mirek of Łętownia took into his care Chana Windstrauch and her family. With his assistance, they completed their "winter flat" by the end of October: "The flat is situated on the slope next to the stream. This kindhearted man is helping us. So, we are covering the roof with sticks, then with forest litter, that is with moss and needles, which we are collecting with our fingers, with soil on top. We are masking it with spruce [branches] to imitate a growing forest. At night, we stock up on potatoes, which we put in clamps as they are to be our winter supply. Then, when everything is already done, we are buying a small pot-bellied stove, setting it up, and making two beds from four wooden planks. We do feel very happy to have this place of our own and a roof over our heads—and, most importantly—the stove where we can warm ourselves up and dry off, which has become a forgotten pleasure. To be sure, we do it only at night, as days have ceased to exist for us."[187]

Not many fugitives could have hoped for such living conditions, and meanwhile, the first snow fell in Podhale at the end of November 1942, which made hiding even harder. "The Gestapo offered a reward—1,000 zlotys for every Jew. He who delivered [a Jew], got this reward. So, when the first snow fell on some forgotten day in November 1942,[188] villagers set off through the woods, forests, clearings, and gorges, looking for tracks; at that time, our sisters and brothers were dragged from all corners of villages to the Gestapo [stations]; and in that way they were putting an end to us."[189]

It remains unknown how many of the Podhale Jews died during this first winter. Lists of prisoners of the Nowy Targ jail can offer some insight into their tragic fate. They contain names of 115 Jews who were held there between mid-September 1942 and mid-February 1944. On the first Friday of each month, the Jewish detainees were transported to the local cemetery and executed.[190] The names of thirty detainees held there in winter 1942–43[191] appear also in the registers of the Jews living in the *Kreis* Neumarkt territory.

Spring 1943 brought new hope to those who had managed to survive the first winter after the deportation action. "And in 1943, when the spring sun started to shine, I met a man who first brought me the news, that so-called forest bands were being formed."[192] It is not possible to establish how many local Jews attempted to rescue themselves by joining partisans, but they viewed it as one of the ways to survive. Abraham Furman, who was hiding in the Gorce Mountains, sought shelter among partisans for himself and his wife but also sought an opportunity to avenge his murdered sons. Mojżesz Eisenmann of Naprawa decided to join the "Harnasie" unit,[193] encouraged by the brother of a farmer who was sheltering him. He knew the commander of the unit, Wilhelm Winiarski,[194] from before the war.[195] Eisenmann escaped the unit two months later, after he heard that the commander had given an order to strangle him. After staying a few weeks with a unit of the Home Army stationed in the Gorce Mountains, Abraham Furman, already weary of their chaotic life and their "great hatred of Jews," was advised by a sympathetic partisan "to try to escape, as he could not take responsibility for our lives. Soon after, I legged it."[196]

Of 3,800 Jews registered as residents of *Kreis* Neumarkt in the second half of August, 1942, at least 600 people tried to save themselves in the territory of the county. Only nine of them lived until the end of the war, which means that only 1.5 percent of Podhale Jews who looked for help found effective shelter in their neighborhood.

The fate of those Podhale Jews who decided to leave the territory of *Kreis* Neumarkt should be considered a separate subject. There is no doubt that some of them made their way to the ghettos in Kraków and Bochnia in the fall of 1942. Others decided to move away and live under an assumed identity. Fellow townsmen and villagers posed a significant threat for the Podhale Jews living on Aryan papers.[197] A Kripo man from Nowy Targ grabbed Rita Felczer on the street in Kraków: "He said: 'You rotten Jewess! I know you.'"[198] Also in Kraków, *Volksdeutschers* from his hometown, Nowy Targ, caught a merchant, Emanuel Singer, and turned him over to the Zakopane Gestapo.[199] A Polish policeman from Maków Podhalański captured Emanuel Warenhaupt's brother, Chaim, in Wolbrom.[200] Despite the odds, however, thirty Podhale Jews who had escaped from the territory of *Kreis* Neumarkt shortly before or soon after the deportation action managed to survive the Holocaust.[201] It remains unknown how many Jews tried to save themselves in this way, but the number of those who succeeded is three times larger than those who tried to find a hiding place close to home. Paradoxically, the largest number of survivors was among those who, facing "the Final Solution," had not decided to escape or seek a hideout but rather, following the directives, had gone to the Nowy Targ stadium or to work (as was required of them in Rabka) and subsequently landed in local labor camps.

Jewish Inmates of the Podhale Labor Camps

The artisans (twenty-five men and ten women) selected to organize and repair the property of the deported Jews stayed in a barrack behind the railroad station in Nowy Targ.[202] The all-male group of 196 laborers from the training school in Rabka survived the deportation, and four additional men were selected to join them.[203] The Hobag company from Breslau that owned several sawmills in Podhale also needed only male workers; those selected to work in the sawmills were all young, and some were just teenagers. Some of them had already worked for Hobag before, when the company had made barracks for the Luftwaffe. Later, when the *Zwangsarbeitslager für Juden* (forced labor camps for Jews) were formed in the sawmills, the prisoners fell under the jurisdiction of the SS, and were "rented" to Hobag. A Polish worker of the sawmill in Czarny Dunajec, where ninety prisoners had been employed, wrote in his memoirs, "They used to examine those Jews' teeth [to check their health] and take them [Jews]."[204] Forty-eight men ended up in the sawmill in Nowy Targ, and ninety men in Zakopane.[205] They did not have numbers assigned to them and were allowed to wear their own clothing. Despite having two forty-five-minute meal breaks during the eleven-and-a-half-hour workday, prisoners of the Podhale labor camps suffered from hunger. In Czarny Dunajec, the prisoners were provided with nothing but a place to sleep on the floor of the barrack they had built a few weeks earlier.

The only way for prisoners to improve their living conditions was through contacts with Poles. The Germans were very well aware of this and took drastic measures to terrorize the Polish population. Andrzej Mazgaj of Nowy Targ paid the highest price for helping prisoners: "He brought a loaf of bread and a horse sausage. He was captured with these goods and taken to the office of Marbach [the sawmill manager]. The latter called the Gestapo, who took Mazgaj; he did not return again."[206] Mazgaj was taken to the Nowy Targ jail on November 26, 1942.[207] Two days later, he was sent to Auschwitz, where he died in mid-March 1943 at the age of forty-four.[208] Mrs. Kwaśniowska, a resident of Chabówka, also met her death for delivering bread to prisoners in Rabka. A Ukrainian guard arrested her; the Jewish workers were punished by flogging, and she was hanged in front of them in the ground of Villa Tereska.[209]

Despite the risk, Poles supplied prisoners with food—most often coworkers at the sawmill, as shared meal breaks provided them a window of opportunity.[210] The assistance was selfless, usually offered to prewar friends and acquaintances. Mrs. Downiłowicz, the owner of a pharmacy in Zakopane and a prewar client of Jeno Riegelhaupt's parents (they produced paper bags), sent Jeno weekly food packages, paying a guard from the Zakopane sawmill for delivering them.[211] Stanisław Rzadkoś assisted many Zakopane prisoners; he would travel to their hometowns and villages and ask their former neighbors for food,[212] and he also delivered them clothes and letters.[213]

Bartering with Poles was an option for survival for those who could not count on altruistic help. Chana Hornung, one of ten women working in Nowy Targ, remembered, "We managed. Sometimes, Poles brought us something to the wire fence in exchange for Jewish rags. So, our living conditions were not the worst ones."[214] A prisoner from Rabka, Jehuda Kestenbaum, also referred to "coping." He and his cellmates used to bribe Ukrainian guards to let them go to town to buy bread.[215] Both the artisans from Nowy Targ and the laborers from Villa Tereska had easy access to Jewish belongings that could be swapped for food. Prisoners who worked in the sawmills used to steal potatoes to avoid death by starvation. The inmates from Czarny Dunajec were able to stock up their "storage room" between joists of the ceiling with several hundred kilos of potatoes. They operated in two-man "teams" at night[216] and nicknamed these mortally dangerous trips outside the camp to find some food *chodzeniem na organizację* (going organizing).[217] Some attempted to recover material possessions they had left hidden somewhere or had entrusted to acquaintances. Natan Knobler from Nowy Targ, a prisoner of the Czarny Dunajec camp, slipped away from the camp in November 1942 to dig up hidden valuables. He was caught in his hometown and shot to death at the local jail.[218] As the Germans decided to apply the rule of collective responsibility, they also murdered eight of Knobler's cellmates, among them his brother.[219] When prisoners from Nowy Targ and Czarny Dunajec were relocated to Płaszów on May 25, 1943, the conditions in the new camp struck them, by comparison, as being almost luxurious.[220]

In all the cases that could be verified, attempts at fleeing a camp ended in failure. Two weeks after his arrival at the Hobag's sawmill in Czarny Dunajec, an underaged boy, Salomon Süsskind, unable to endure the backbreaking work and hunger any longer, decided to escape. "I wandered through the mountains and forests, not knowing the area, and I was so naive that I admitted to peasants that I was a Jew. I was just seventeen years old, I trusted people and could not imagine that it is possible to sell a man for a pound of sugar. They turned me in to the *Grenzschutz* [border guards] in Maniowy, near Czorsztyn."[221]

Only a few prisoners who attempted to escape during the liquidation of the camps in Rabka and Zakopane in the summer and fall of 1943 lived through the Holocaust. Six men escaped from Rabka at that time; two of them survived. Of the ten women selected to work at the Nowy Targ stadium, six managed to escape death. Out of several hundred of those who, on August 30, 1942, deliberately decided not to turn up at the gathering sites designated by the Germans, only five survived.

POLISH INHABITANTS OF NOWY TARG COUNTY AND THEIR ATTITUDE TOWARD THE HOLOCAUST

Why was it that the local Jews—despite being utterly familiar with the area and its inhabitants, and knowing very well who could come to their aid and who posed a threat to them—had virtually no chance of surviving unless they were imprisoned in forced labor camps? The fate of the Jews who ended up in the Podhale labor camps shows that at least some Polish residents were willing to offer assistance to, or risk bartering with, the prisoners, even though it was a capital crime. As was already mentioned, in this ghettoless county, the extermination was, at its every stage, carried out under Poles' very eyes. Their testimonies related to deportations are often filled with empathy; they contain names of particular victims and give a rough idea of their fate. But the picture of the third stage of the extermination, which emerges from Polish sources, looks different. It is vague and full of anonymous victims and unknown perpetrators.

The stance of Poles toward the Holocaust could have been heavily influenced by their approach to Jewish "immovables" and "movables," especially in a situation when the death of someone's neighbors or acquaintances translated into someone else's profit.²²² There was a clear connection between the assets of the Jews in hiding (and the Polish attitude toward Jewish possession) and the willingness of Poles to help them (or turn them in) in other counties as well. Therefore, there must have been another factor that resulted in catching and murdering nearly all Jews in this area. Indeed, there was something unique in comparison to the GG that was specific to *Kreis* Neumarkt—the movement of the *Goralenvolk* (*Góral* nation).

As early as the fall of 1939, the Germans began to advance the idea of *Goralenvolk*, a separate nation of the Podhale highlanders, which allegedly originated from Germanic peoples. They quickly enlisted the cooperation of well-known and respected activists from a prewar organization—*Związek Górali* (*Górale* Alliance)²²³—promising that representatives of *Goralenvolk*, "with support of the Authorities," would fill "various positions such as on the Municipal Board, education, trade and industry, as well as the cooperative movement."²²⁴ They were also to give performances upon the demand of the Germans, to propagate *Góral* culture, and above all to "provide financial help to its members." The "memorandum" written in the name of the *Góral* people also mentioned Jews, who had "weighed down the economic growth of the *Góral* population like a heavy stone."²²⁵

Though to be of *Goralenvolk* nationality created an opportunity to become richer, not many people identified themselves as such by the end of September 1941, and *Związek Górali* counted scarcely 2,158 members in the entire *Kreis* Neumarkt.²²⁶ The turning point came in February 1942, when the *Komitet Góralski* (Górale Committee) was set up in Zakopane. Its chairman, Wacław Krzeptowski, was directly accountable to the German *starosta*. The committee formed twelve branches in the territory of the county,²²⁷ and its members strongly advocated the idea of *Góral* nationality and advocated for *Goralenvolk* cards: IDs stamped with the letter G.²²⁸ Anti-Jewish demonstrations²²⁹ provided them with an excellent platform for pushing their agenda. Several rallies were organized for the *Góral* people in the summer of 1942.²³⁰ One was held in Rabka on August 30, the exact day when Jews were being deported from Nowy Targ County (and thus also from Rabka). Between 1,000 and 1,200 people attended the rally.²³¹ Speakers addressed the crowd from the stage, which was decorated with a *portrait of Hitler*. Wacław Krzeptowski said, "You are not Poles, but [rather] *Górale*," and added that he was grateful to Malsfey and Weissmann, who "liberated Podhale from the biggest enemy: the Jew."²³² In addition, Krzeptowski decided to reward "the Podhale liberators." For the resettlement of the Jews from Rabka, the *Górale* Committee awarded Rosenbaum and the staff of his school with a bonus in the form of five thousand Egyptian cigarettes and twenty-five liters of vodka.²³³

Speaking in Rabka, the leader of the *Goralenvolk* threatened that whoever refused to accept the *G* ID card, would have to "leave from Podhale with just twenty kilos on his shoulders."[234] His threats brought the desired effect. The day after the rally, six hundred people came forward to collect *Góral* cards.[235] A similar result was achieved throughout the entire Podhale district, and by January 1943, 25,390 people had already assumed the *Góral* nationality.[236]

However, the pressure applied by the *Górale* Committee activists and the fear of forced resettlements were hardly the only reasons for accepting the identity card stamped with the letter *G*. For many, the decision was a purely opportunistic one. There were people in almost every place who accepted the propaganda of the *Górale* Committee. They believed in the uniqueness of the highlanders and threatened their opponents with deportation. They also grew overtly wealthy by plundering Jewish possessions and applauded the murder of the Jews. Their presence must have had a considerable influence on the attitude that entire communities adopted toward those who, being on the brink of extermination, sought refuge in the Nowy Targ County territory. Throughout the entire GG, people denounced Jews in hiding and the Poles who took a risk to help them. It happened in *Kreis* Neumarkt as well, but with one difference: here, collaboration was on a mass scale and official in character.

The Fate of the Podhale Converts

The activities of the *Górale* Committee was closely intertwined with the almost unknown and unexplored fate of converts in Podhale. It is impossible to discover on what grounds lists of converts and their families were compiled during the occupation, or how many of those who had been put on those lists fell victim to repressions. Supposedly, the Germans demanded that the Metropolitan Curia of Kraków hand over "the register of the Jews baptized in recent years, but the curia categorically refused to do so."[237] According to the testimonies given by witnesses from *Kreis* Neumarkt, Polish police stations were responsible for collecting names and compiling those lists.[238] It is possible that local *voits* (community leaders) participated in the process too, as already in August 1940, they had obtained guidelines that might "considerably facilitate their work." The guidelines were to "outline the definition of a 'Jew' clearly and unequivocally."[239]

The names of prewar converts are not included in those registers of the Nowy Targ County Jews, which still exist today. It is known, however, that the converts, as well as their children, had to wear armbands like the other Jews.[240] In almost all cases, female converts who had been baptized and married to Poles appear in the sources.[241] Stanisława "Kucikowa" Szwab of the village of Witów

Figure 6.6. Stanisława Szwab with her son Bolek on the day of his first communion, Witów, Poland, 1941. Photo courtesy of the private archive of Ester Roynik.

was born in 1907 as Perel Langer. In 1931, she converted to Christianity and married Jacek Szwab, a highlander, who played music for patrons in her father's tavern. Their son was born soon after. Stanisława lost touch with the Langers in the aftermath of her conversion. Her husband's family rejected her as well. She lived alone and ran a shop in a house across the road from her in-laws' farm, where her husband and son lived. The boy received his First Communion in 1941. At that time, as a resident of Witów remembered, "This Staśka, the convert, she already had to report and got a band with the Jewish swastika [sic, star]."²⁴² A dozen or so months later, uniformed Germans took her to the Nowy Targ jail. The Szwabs' relatives sheltered her son.²⁴³

Descendants of two other elderly converted women, Antonina Stoch and Bronisława Dzioboń, were also forced to hide. Their rescue came from a most unexpected source: Wacław Krzeptowski, nicknamed the Górale Prince, and his lieutenant, Józef Cukier. When the latter was put on trial in 1946, the members of the Stoch, Król, Chyc, and Dzioboń families of the village of Ząb stated the following:

We are of Jewish descent. Somewhere around the year 1942, the parish priest warned us that all Jews and converts up to the third generation were to be deported; and, at the time, the occupiers took our two grandmothers, that is Antonina Stoch, who was eighty years old and Bronisława Dzioboń, a seventy-five-year-old, and shot them. Then, the twenty-four members of this family that were left all had to sign up to the Jewish denominational commune [probably the list prepared by the Blue police]; moreover, we were ordered to put up a list of our possessions, as the occupiers were to take them away. On the priest's advice, we came to Józef Cukier for help, who, at our request, agreed to rescue us and save us from the deportation and execution... On his own, he issued identification cards to us and told us to hide in various villages; in this way, he saved us all from the transport and death.[244]

This was not an isolated case because we know of other leaders of the *Goralenvolk* who acted in a similar way. Wojciech Szaflarski of the Szaflary branch of the *Górale* Committee rescued the children of Helena Kalata: Józef, Marianna, and Zofia.[245]

The names of all the converted women mentioned above appeared in the register of prisoners of the Nowy Targ jail. According to this list, they were imprisoned in the last week of October of 1942 and kept in the jail until December 4, 1942. That day, eleven prisoners were taken to the Nowy Targ cemetery.[246] We know for sure that one more, much larger-scale execution of converts and their families also took place in the Jewish cemetery in Nowy Targ. Chana Hornung, who had been held in Nowy Targ in the camp for Jewish artisans, reported years later that a group of men were once taken to the local cemetery: "And those people faced [saw] an open grave, a huge, mass grave. That group of people, which was taken to this cemetery, was to dismantle Jewish tombstones in the cemetery. As it turned out later, converts had been shot over this mass grave, the people [converts] who had never even known anything about being Jews. The descendants of the Jewish families, highlanders, who had never known that they were Jews."[247] Sources enabling an estimation of the number of converts and their relatives killed in Podhale in the second half of 1942 remain unknown. Certainly, it was at least fifty people.

What is intriguing about the *Górale* Committee leadership is that it was a factor that was able to bring such a radical change in attitude toward people subjected to religious persecution. For them, the Jews who practiced Judaism were enemies and, as such, should leave Podhale. In addition, Krzeptowski and his cronies were not influential enough, nor were they willing to rescue those who had converted even decades before. They revealed a determination and willingness only to help the converts' children, although they were not able to save them all anyway. Moreover, it seems there was not any top-down endorsement of saving highlander families of Jewish origin. Every case required a separate appeal for help and a separate determination by members of the *Górale* Committee. Witnesses in a postwar trial of the leaders of the *Goralenvolk* quoted several other cases, but this time the recipients of assistance remained unnamed.

The Righteous from Kreis Neumarkt

Just as it was impossible to establish the precise number of Podhale Jews in hiding, it was equally impossible to determine the number of Polish inhabitants who provided food for the Jews or allowed them spend the night in a barn, when they would knock on a window. It is certain, however, that they steadily decreased in number due to the ceaseless hunt for Jews and the risk associated with helping them. Those willing to offer assistance to Jews were usually met with hostility from their neighbors, who feared indiscriminate punishment. Ozjasz Szachner from Jordanów testified immediately after the war, "The peasant Sałachna had been helping me and my family selflessly, but local peasants betrayed him; and then, Mrs. Rychlik was sheltering us in her brickyard (for a lot of money), but as peasants began to threaten her, I said that she could not keep putting herself at risk anymore, and our relatives sent a car for us from Kraków. We managed to get to the Kraków ghetto."[248]

Fear of retaliation was justified, as punishment for helping Jews in *Kreis Neumarkt* was imposed swiftly and without mercy. In addition to the two Poles who met their death for giving bread to a Jewish prisoner, another fifteen Polish residents of the county died in the camps or were shot to death for assisting Jews.[249] It is hard to answer whether the number of murdered Poles was so great due to the exceptional ruthlessness of local authorities, or rather because of an unusually large scale of denunciations. After all, supporters of the *Goralenvolk* ideology lived in almost every village.[250]

At the time when their Jewish neighbors were being depicted by the propaganda and regarded by many as "parasites," there were still individuals who were able to see a Jew as a person in need of help, and who attempted to rescue him or her despite the hostile environment and the deadly risk. Poles saving the Podhale Jews throughout the whole third stage of the Holocaust occupy a special place in this story. There were just two such persons in the Nowy Targ County: Eleonora Wagner of Rabka, and Jan Mirek of Łętownia.

Facing, Figure 6.7. Villa Truskawka. Author's collection.

Wagner was helping her neighbor, Frania Netzer, in utter secrecy. Her husband, a local barber, was an antisemite, a supporter of the *Goralenvolk* ideology, and a "drunkard and card gambler."[251] Besides, Wagner did not have any friends in Rabka because people were afraid of her.[252] She had come to Netzer's aid before, when Jews were allowed to do shopping for just an hour daily: Netzer used to give Wagner money, and she ran errands for the entire family. It was Wagner who convinced thirty-one-year-old Netzer and her mother not go to the gathering point on the day of the deportation, and she promised them help. The Wagners lived in a large and very long home, named Villa Truskawka. Frania Netzer; her mother, Jetti Netzer; and her cousin Salomon Pistreich took shelter in an attic above a veranda and stayed there for two and a half years. Netzer never disclosed to Wagner the exact location of their hideout, although the latter delivered them food to the villa once a week for thirty months.[253]

Jan Mirek supplied food for Chana and Izaak Windstrauch, Chana's parents, and two other men hiding together in the forest. After they had been betrayed, their hideout was discovered, and all but the Windstrauchs were either killed or deported to Auschwitz,[254] Mirek decided to hide the couple in the attic of his house. The next day, on Sunday, the Mireks—parents of four and devout Catholics—went to church, where the priest announced from the pulpit that

> two Jews had escaped and [measures] are being toughened up now; there will be door-to-door inspections, and wherever [they] will be found, the whole village will be burned down and people killed. They returned from the church half dead and trembling... [and Mirek said] that may the Lord save us, but we had to leave, as he was afraid, and his wife in particular, and it was about [his] children, so I began to weep [and beg]: 'Kill us, as we have nothing to live for.' He [Mirek] approached me and, weeping with us, said that he would do what [was] in his power to help us. He came in the evening and said... that he owned a very old forest... and no human foot could reach there, but there was still snow, so one could not go there, [as] tracks could lead to us, so he would take us there in a sleigh, and he did.[255]

The Windstrauchs lived in the forest under Jan Mirek's care, as described earlier, until the end of the war.[256]

Chana Hornung of Nowy Targ, who had survived the war—first in her hometown working in the labor camp for Jewish artisans, then in Płaszow and Lipsk—and returned to Nowy Targ just as the war ended, said in her account given in the 1960s, "[Of] the Jews who had lived in the area, in the whole of Podhale, almost none survived the war except those who had migrated to Russia, because highlanders had not sheltered Jews."[257] Such an opinion is fully justified, as there was no collective entity that was involved in rescuing the Jews.

In every case, collectiveness translated into danger and death. The Righteous Podhalanians[258] who were able to perceive persecuted, denunciated, and murdered Jews as people in need of help acted totally alone and in the constant fear of their neighbors.

EPILOGUE

The people hidden in the attic of Villa Truskawka in Rabka did not see the entry of the Red Army into Nowy Targ. The Germans had placed antiaircraft guns next to the villa, and a Russian shell hit the roof and destroyed the gable. Two days later, when everything was quiet, Frania Netzer went down to Mrs. Wagner's apartment: "Her husband was struck dumb. He did not understand what was happening—where did I come from? I was black, incredibly dirty. Mrs. Wagner let me wash myself, gave me food, and let me take a nap. When Rabka was liberated, we were the only ones there. There were no more Jews."[259] Jan Mirek came to the Windstrauchs, hidden in the forested wilderness, and announced, "You are free, you have survived."[260] Józef Engländer and Dawid Grassgrün, who had survived in Slovakia, were the first Jews to return to Nowy Targ after the war. Grassgrün was the only one who had escaped the mass execution carried out in the Nowy Targ cemetery on August 30, 1942. He had managed to make his way to the Slovak town of Kieżmark. Engländer found Dawid Grassgrün a shelter, and he worked as a stable man in the nearby Slovak Red Monastery cloister.[261]

Those who had been taken to labor camps began arriving at Podhale in the spring of 1945. About 110 inmates from the camps had survived the war—24 percent of those selected on August 30, 1942.[262] Only in two towns of the former *Kreis* Neumarkt—Nowy Targ and Jordanów—were registers of Jews compiled just after the war. Five Jews were registered in Jordanów, and forty more in the capital of the county (six among them had survived the occupation in the territory of the USSR).[263]

Not all returnees had enough time to register; some were murdered just after the arrival. Wilhelm Reich, from the village of Maniowy, and Leon Kraus, Baruch Feit, and Chaim Blauder, from the village of Czarny Dunajec, died at the hands of partisans of the anti-communist group led by Józef "Ogień" Kuraś. That murder marked the beginning of the wave of anti-Jewish terror,[264] which included assaults on Jewish children in the orphanages in Rabka and Zakopane, the murder of Jews trying to cross the Slovak border illegally, and the deaths of those who had lived in Podhale before war. David Grassgrün, who wished to reactivate the Nowy Targ Jewish community, was murdered, as well as two young men from Nowy Targ, Gordonia activists Lonek Lindenberger and Ludwik

Herz, who had been saved by Oskar Schindler. Also murdered were Józef Oppenheimer, a prominent figure in Zakopane society who ran the Tatra Mountain Volunteer Search and Rescue organization during the entire interwar period, and twelve-year-old Józef Galler, the son of a veterinarian from Nowy Targ.

All in all, thirty-three Jews were murdered in Podhale after the war. The perpetrators of this violence wished to "chase away Jewish colonies"[265] and aimed at "the expulsion of all Jews" from the terrritory.[266] Their goal was achieved.[267]

NOTES

1. Archiwum Instytutu Pamięci Narodowej [Archive of the Institute of National Remembrance, hereafter AIPN], 196/177, Statistik der Bevölkerungsdichte im Generalgouvernement [Data about the Population Density in the Generalgouvernement], February 1, 1940, 26.

2. AIPN, 196/281, Tätigkeitsbericht der Kreishauptmannschaft Neumarkt (Dunajec) vom 17. September 1939 bis 31. Mai 1941 [Report About the Activities of the Neumarkt County Administration from September 17, 1939, until May 31, 1941], June 7, 1941, 117.

3. United States Holocaust Memorial Museum (hereafter USHMM), 1998.A.0300.287, Interview with Kazimierz Pajerski, Nowy Targ, 2009.

4. Icchak Neri (Licht), "Narodowy ruch religijny w Nowym Targu [National Religious Movement in Nowy Targ]," in *Remembrance Book Nowy-Targ and Vicinity: Zakopane, Charni Dunajec, Rabka, Yordanov, Shchavnitza, Kroshchenko, Yablonka, Makov-Podhalanski*, ed. Michael Walzer-Fass (Tel Aviv: Townspeople Association of Nowy-Targ and Vicinity, 1979), 22.

5. AN Kr, 29/206/556, Sprawozdanie sytuacyjne nr 1 za czas od 1 do 31 stycznia 1936 [Situational report no. 1 for January 1–31, 1936], 23.

6. AN Kr, 29/206/560, Wywrotowa działalność polskich organizacji politycznych, 14 IV 1938 [Subversive activities of Polish political parties, April 14, 1938], 48.

7. AN Kr, 29/206/558, Wywrotowa działalność polskich organizacji politycznych, 14 X 1937 [Subversive activities of Polish political parties, October 14, 1937], 515.

8. AN Kr, 29/206/560, Wywrotowa działalność polskich organizacji politycznych, 14 IV 1938 [Subversive activities of Polish political parties, April 14, 1938], 48.

9. AN Kr ONS 32/564/2, Protokół z konferencji grona nauczycielskiego, 15–16 XII 1937 [Minutes of the staff meeting, December 15–16, 1937], n.p.

10. *Gazeta Podhala*, June 5, 1938, vol. 22, 3.

11. Ibid.

12. Dawid Golik, *Partyzanci "Lamparta." Historia IV batalionu 1.pułku strzelców podhalańskich AK* (Kraków: IPN i Attyka, 2014), 29.

13. Nachum Beck, Interview, July 20, 2015, in Azor. Karolina Panz Private Collection.

14. Yad Vashem Archive (hereafter YVA), Collection of various testimonies, diaries, and memoirs, O.33/7327, Notes of Chana Windstrauch, c. 1944, 13.

15. Instytut Pamięci Narodowej Oddziałowa Komisja Ścigania Zbrodni przeciwko Narodowi Polskiemu w Krakowie [Institute of National Remembrance, District Commission for the Prosecution of Crimes against the Polish Nation, hereafter IPN OK Kr], Ds. 6/70/22, Zeznania w sprawie zbrodni Gestapo i niemieckich służb mundurowych na Podhalu, Zeznanie Franciszka Tyrpy, 7 VIII 1973. [Testimonies on the crimes committed by the Gestapo and German uniformed forces in the Podhale area. Testimony of Franciszek Tyrpa, August 7, 1973], 45.

16. AN Kr ONS, 30/603/497, Protokół z 10 XII 1940 [Minutes, December 10, 1940], 55; AN Kr ONS , 30/603/343, Wykaz towarów zarekwirowanych przez wojska niemieckie, 29 XII 1939 [List of goods confiscated by the German Army], 1058.

17. USC, VHA, 23852, Albert Neuwirt Testimony, Whitestone, December 2, 1996. It was converted into a cinema for the Polish population in September; AN Kr, Izba Przemysłowo-Handlowa [Chamber of Industry and Commerce, hereafter IPH]), Kr II/57, Industry Charter, January 1, 1943, n.p.

18. Golik, *Partyzanci "Lamparta,"* 32.

19. Ibid., 149.

20. Ibid., 118.

21. Indictment in the case against Robert Weissmann and Richard Arno Sehmisch issued by the State Prosecutor's Office at the National Court in Freiburg, translated into Polish, January 24, 1964, 86, in Michał Rapta Private Collection. I wish to thank Michał Rapta for making the document available to me.

22. Ibid., 148.

23. AN Kr ONS, ZMNT, 31/603/166, Rozporządzenie szefa Zarządu Cywilnego przy AOK [Directive of the Chief of the Civil Administration at the AOK 9 Armeeoberkommando, Army General Staff, dotyczące spraw płatniczych i wymiany pieniędzy [on the subjects of payments and currency exchange], October 14, 1939, 97–98.

24. YVA, O.33/7327, Notes of Chana Windstrauch, c. 1944, 20.

25. AN Kr ONS, ZMNT, 31/603/310, Pismo burmistrza Nowego Targu Jana Stanka do dyrektora Szpitala Powszechnego w Nowym Targu, 27 XII 1939 [Letter of Jan Stanek, Mayor of Nowy Targ, to the Director of the General Hospital in Nowy Targ, December 27, 1939], 1767.

26. AŻIH, ŻSS, 211/742–747, Zbiór korespondencji Prezydium ŻSS z Radą Żydowską i osobami prywatnymi w Nowym Targu [Correspondence of the Presidium of the ŻSS with the Jewish Council and private persons in Nowy Targ].

27. USC, VHA, 23852, Albert Neuwirt Testimony; USC, VHA, 1419, Testimony of Stanley Goodrich, March 20, 1995, in Studio City; YVA O.3/2975, Collection of various testimonies, diaries and memoirs, Chana Hornung Testimony, October 1966, 8; YVA, O.3/2974, Izaak Goldman Testimony, December 1966, 10.

28. A similar area had been designated in the borderland part of Nowy Sącz County. The relocation of residents of the towns of Krynica, Piwniczna, and Tylicz took place in the spring of 1940.

29. AIPN, 196/281, Tätigkeitsbericht der Kreishauptmannschaft Neumarkt (Dunajec) vom 17. September 1939 bis 31. Mai 1941, 7 VI 1941 [Report about the Activities of the Neumarkt County Administration from September 17, 1939, until May 31, 1941], 121.

30. List of the members of the *Judenrat* and craftsmen and the number of their family members, January 17, 1941, 60. This is a copy of the list in Piotr Jassem Collection; the original, kept in the archive of the Tatra Mountain Museum in Zakopane, has been lost. A copy of the document is in the collection of Piotr Jassem; I wish to thank Piotr Jassem for making it available to me.

31. Archiwum Muzeum Tatrzańskiego [Archive of the Tatra Mountain Museum, hereafter AMT], AR/NO/161, Formularz dotyczący wysiedlenia, 25 I 1940 [Resettlement form, January 25, 1940], 6.

32. The Warta Country (*Warthegau*) was the largest administrative unit in the territory incorporated into the Reich by a decree issued by Hitler on October 8, 1939. The incorporated territories underwent rapid Germanization, the first stage of which consisted of compulsory resettlements, arrests, and the murdering of the Polish elites, and was followed by the forced relocation of the entire Jewish population (435,000 in September 1939) and a part of the Polish one to make way for *Volksdeutschers*. See Michael Alberti, "Nikczemna perfidia, niska bezmierna chciwość oraz zimne, wyrachowane okrucieństwo—ostateczne rozwiązanie kwestii żydowskiej w Kraju Warty" [Awful Perfidy, Despicable Greed and Cold, Calculated Cruelty—the Final Solution of the Jewish Question in Warthegau], in *Zagłada Żydów na polskich terenach wcielonych do Rzeszy*, ed. Aleksandra Namysło (Warsaw: IPN, 2008), 73–76.

33. AŻIH, AJDC, 210/388, Letter of the chairman of the *Judenrat* in Jordanów to the AJDC in Kraków, March 16, 1941, 9.

34. AN Kr ONS, 31/603/338, Register of the Jewish residents, April 28, 1941, 537.

35. AŻIH, ŻSS, 211/745, Notice, n.d. 5.

36. AN Kr ONS, 31/603/338, Farmer's Register, n.d., 699.

37. Reportedly, the convincing argument was that "no one will be able to keep eye on them there, so better let them come to their own apartments." See Józef Wraubek, *Na Podhalu (od grudnia. 1939 do lutego. 1942). Dywizja Podhalańska w Konspiracji*, typescript, the 1960s, 289. I wish to thank Michał Chlipała for making this material available to me.

38. Dawid Golik's book describes organization and functioning of the gendarmerie and the Blue police in *Kreis* Neumarkt. See Golik, *Partyzanci "Lamparta,"* 63–78.

39. Józef Wraubek, *Na Podhalu*, 289.

40. Ibid., 295.

41. AŻIH, AJDC, 210/575, Notice of Mr. Braunfeld on behalf of the Jewish Council in Rabka, July 19, 1940, 15.

42. In exchange for bread, potatoes, and butter, Jehuda Stein, who had been resettled to Nowy Targ from Kraków, tutored farmers' daughters in their homes in accounting and Polish. See *Die Steins. Jüdische Familiengeschichte aus Krakau 1830–1999*, ed. Jehuda L. Stein and Erhard Roy Wiehn (Konstanz: Hartung-Gorre Verlag, 1999), 63.

43. YVA, O.3/1818, Marian Szatkowski Testimony, June 24, 1961, 4.

44. Stein, *Die Steins*, 50.

45. YVA, O.3/2975, Chana Hornung Testimony. Annotations, October 1966, 28.

46. USC, VHA, 21371, Rosalie Gelernter Testimony, November 2, 1996, in Stockton; Lydia Hughes, interview with the author in Boston, December 14, 2014, Karolina Panz Private Collection.

47. More on this subject will be written in my paper "Rescue and Smuggling Networks in the Polish-Slovak Borderland during the Holocaust" published in 2022 by Yad Vashem in the book *Jewish Networks in the Holocaust*, ed. Eliyana Adler and Natalia Aleksiun.

48. Unfortunately, I did not find any sources allowing me to conclude whether and at what scale the Jews, who had been relocated from *Sperrgebiet*, tried to escape across the Tatra Mountains.

49. AŻIH, 301/4707, Salomon Süsskind Testimony, c. 1945, 9.

50. Its full name was Der Kommandeur der Sicherheitspolizei und des SD im Distrikt Krakau Grenzpolizeikommissariat Zakopane; AN Kr, 30/603/365, Letter of Robert Weissmann to Landrat in Nowym Targu, December 9, 1939, 1299.

51. AIPN Kr, 075/1/9, Gestapo Structure, Zakopane—Nowy Targ, July 27, 1949, 403.

52. Golik, *Partyzanci "Lamparta,"* 60; AIPN Kr, 502/4085, Case files of Franz Victorin, Testimony of Genowefa Kaszycka, January 27 1951, 299.

53. AIPN Kr, 075/1/9, Gestapo Structure, n.d., 405.

54. His successor, Richard Arno Sehmisch, had held the position of the chief of the office for as long as it had existed.

55. IPN OK Kr, Ds. 6/70/32, Testimony of Irena Golik, May 18, 1961, 103.

56. First, it was located in Zakopane (from January 1940), in Villa Stamary, and was run by Hans Krüger. Due to the disgraceful behavior of course participants, which spoiled the atmosphere of the exclusive resort, the school was relocated to Rabka, and Krüger was replaced by Rosenbaum; AŻIH, 301/3272, Roman Dattner Testimony, July 2, 1947, 10.

57. AŻIH, 301/241, Stefan Blassberg Testimony, June 3, 1945, 1.

58. After the German-Soviet war had begun, Rosenbaum brought twenty "*wachmen* [guards] he himself had trained there" (ibid., 11). He later made them responsible for Ukrainian recruits who were being trained in the school. After the training, they were to carry out sabotage operations or join the Ukrainian Auxiliary Police. See Michał Rapta, Wojciech Tupta, and Grzegorz Moskal, *Mroczne sekrety willi "Tereska" 1939–1945* (Wadowice–Rabka-Zdrój: Grafikon i Fundacja Rozwoju Regionu Rabka, 2009), 111.

59. AIPN Kr, 075/1/4, "Policja Państwowa," edited by Adam Latawiec, November 22, 1950, 33.

60. IPN OK Kr, Ds. 6/70//26, Testimony of Abraham Schiffeldrin, February 22, 1968, 177–183; YVA O.33/3232, Jehuda Kestenbaum Testimony, October 1966, 12.

61. As a part of a group formed in Kraków by the SS-Brigadeführer Eberhard Schöngarth, see Rapta, Tupta, smf Moskal, *Mroczne sekrety willi "Tereska,"* 123.

62. Golik, *Partyzanci "Lamparta,"* 64.

63. Wraubek, *Na Podhalu*, 296. Zimmermann served in the position until 1943 and was later replaced by Peter Eichmann. See Golik, *Partyzanci "Lamparta,"* 64.

64. BAL, B 162/3897, Testimony of Victor von Dewitz, May 7, 1963, 2370.

65. He became *starosta* in Stryj; see USHMM, RG-31.003/1/1952/14, Letter of the Stryj railroad manager to the *starosta* Victor von Dewitz, October 10, 1941, 11.

66. AIPN Kr, 010/2448, Case Files of Henryk Kiss, Testimony of Henryk Kiss, May 12, 1949, 117. Additional, less powerful stations were in Zakopane, Rabka, Szczawnica, and Jordanów. There was also a gendarmerie academy in Zakopane, run by Col. Hoppe; Golik, *Partyzanci "Lamparta,"* 65.

67. There were 142 uniformed staff until 1942; later, the number increased to 157; Golik, *Partyzanci "Lamparta,"* 78.

68. Wraubek, *Na Podhalu*, 314.

69. AN Kr ONS, 30/603/338, Podanie o żydowskie mieszkania i meble dla polskich policjantów, 8 IX 1942 [Application for Jewish apartments and furniture for Polish policemen, September 8, 1942], 39.

70. Nine Poles (including an office clerk) and two Germans. See AIPN Kr, 075/1/15, t.47, Criminal Police in the Kraków District, February 1, 1941, n.p.

71. Replaced by Walter Männich in November 1943. See Golik, *Partyzanci "Lamparta,"* 61.

72. AIPN Kr, 075/131/4, Report of Andrzej Latawiec, November 22, 1950, 27; Wraubek, *Na Podhalu*, 290. Both the branch of the Criminal Police in Zakopane (*Nebenstelle* Zakopane, with five employees) and the post in Rabka (*Aussenposten* Rabka with two employees) were subordinate to the Kripo station in Nowy Targ (*pracownicy*); International Tracing Service (hereafter ITS) Bad Arolsen, 1.2.7.11/0005/0167, Das Generalgouvernement Sicherheitspolizei Gruppe IV Kripo [The Generalgouvernement, Security Police, Group IV, Criminal Police], n.d., 1; AIPN Kr, 075/131/4, Report of Andrzej Latawiec, November 22, 1950, 27.

73. The headquarters were in Zakopane; local customs station were located in Nowy Targ, Maków, Czarny Dunajec, and Zakopane. As Dawid Golik points out, Germans and Poles alike used the shortened name "Grenschutz." See Golik, *Partyzanci "Lamparta,"* 82.

74. Ibid., 86.

75. IPN OK Kr, Ds. 6/70/4, Testimony of Franciszek Gold, April 18, 1946, 3.

76. IPN OK Kr, Ds. 6/70/26, Testimony of Alicja Nogala, January 12, 1968, 108.

77. Indictment in the case against Robert Weissmann and Richard Arno Sehmisch issued by the State Prosecutor's Office at the National Court in Freiburg, January 24, 1964, 84.

78. The process of the legal immigration is to some extent explained by information I have found in the ŻSS's documents and in *Gazeta Żydowska*: To obtain a return permit, one had to send an application through the Jewish Council, who was to confirm the prewar address and whether his family would give him material support; AŻIH, *Gazeta Żydowska*, October 8, 1941, vol. 95, 3. In Nowy Targ, the Municipal Board was responsible for issuing such certificates, and it started to issue them as soon as August 1941; AN Kr ONS, 30/603/334, Certificate of the Nowy Targ Mayor to Józef Singer, August 5, 1941, 2799. Next, a travel permit had to be secured from a *starosta* office in the Galicia District, as well as permission from Malsfey. After all these formalities were completed, an applicant was allowed to register in his prewar place of residence; see AN Kr, 29/208/0/4/34, Registration card of Maria Singer, January 1942, n.p.

79. For example, in Radom, Ostrowiec Świętokrzyski, Biłgoraj, Warsaw, and Dąbrowa Tarnowska.

80. In Krościenko, for example, members of wealthy families were murdered (YVA, O.33/2974, Izaak Goldman Testimony, December 1966, 9) in Maków Podhalański—hostages who had been selected beforehand or members of

their families. See Artur Kunreich, "Holocaust Memories 1939–1945," in Rapta, Tupta, and Moskal, *Mroczne sekrety willi "Tereska,"* 260).

81. IPN OK, Ds. 6/70/26, Testimony of Alicja Nogala, January 12, 1968, 108.

82. Alicja Kleinberg's letter to Zofia Minder, June 1, 1942, n.p., private collection. Here and hereafter, unspecified ownership means that an owner wishes to remain anonymous.

83. YVA, O.33/3226, Testimony of Frania Tiger (née Netzer), November 1966, 11.

84. Wilhelm Kleinberg's letter to Zofia Minder and Edward Kleinberg, May 30, 1942, n.p., private collection.

85. Alicja Kleinberg's letter to Zofia Minder, June 1942, n.d., n.p., private collection.

86. Rapta, Tupta, and Moskal, *Mroczne sekrety willi "Tereska,"* 283.

87. Indictment in the case against Robert Weissmann and Richard Arno Sehmisch issued by the State Prosecutor's Office at the National Court in Freiburg, January 24, 1964, 36.

88. USC, VHA, 51497, Simon Katz Testimony, Miami Beach, March 18, 2001; IPN OK Kr, Ds. 6/70/30, Marian Drelich's letter to the Ministry of Justice and *Main Commission for the Investigation* of Nazi *Crimes in Poland*, April 20, 1965, 93.

89. I wrote about this family in "Singerowie mieli sklep... Historia pewnej rodziny i jej mienia" [The Singers Owned a Store: A Story of a Family and Its Property], in *Klucze i kasa. O mieniu żydowskim w Polsce pod okupacją niemiecką i we wczesnych latach powojennych 1939–1950*, ed. Jan Grabowski and Dariusz Libionka (Warsaw: Stowarzyszenie Centrum Badań nad Zagładą Żydów, 2014), 299–336.

90. Alicja Janowska-Ciońćka, "*Mój Sprawiedliwy*" [My Righteous], in *Dzieci Holocaustu mówią...*, vol. 5, ed. Anna Kołacinska-Gałązka (Warsaw: Stowarzyszenie Dzieci Holocaustu w Polsce, 2013), 236.

91. Alojzy Singer, "Memoirs", manuscript in Private Archive of Janet Singer Applefield.

92. YVA, O.33/3226, Frania Tiger Testimony, November 1966, 12.

93. Indictment in the case against Robert Weissmann and Richard Arno Sehmisch issued by the State Prosecutor's Office at the National Court in Freiburg, January 24, 1964, 102.

94. Ibid., 70. In many cities of the Kraków District (Tarnów, Rzeszów, Jasło, Przemyśl and Miechów), the operations were supervised by commanders of the SSPF headquarters in Kraków.

95. Ibid., 102. See also YVA, O.3/2975, Chana Hornung Testimony, October 1966, 13, "The Gestapo said that Szczawnica [Jews] committed an act of

sabotage, that they threw things in privies, that they destroyed their property, that the Jews hid their things and did not hand all of them over to the Germans."

96. OK, AHM, Maria Klocek, Interview, July 28, 2008, in Nowy Targ.

97. ZNO, 13528/II, Wiktor Ignacy Gutowski, "W ogniu swastyki."

98. Archiwum Akt Nowych [hereafter AAN], Rząd Generalnego Gubernatorstwa [hereafter RGG], 536, t. 7, Aufstellung am November 5, 1942, auf die Hauptkasse des GG übergiessen Entgelte [Payments to Be Charged on the Main Account of GG on November 5, 1942] 6. A codename for the final extermination operation in Nowy Targ County used to annotate payment made to the *Baudienst* for participation in it.

99. Indictment in the case against Robert Weissmann and Richard Arno Sehmisch issued by the State Prosecutor's Office at the National Court in Freiburg, January 24, 1964, 105.

100. Ibid., 107.

101. IPN OK Kr, Ds. 6/70/22, Testimony of Klemens Szczurek, March 13, 1975, 70.

102. Ibid.

103. IPN OK Kr, Ds. 6/70/22, Testimony of Józef Zawojski, September 28, 1973, 54.

104. IPN OK Kr, Ds. 6/70/22, Testimony of Klemens Szczurek, March 13, 1975, 70.

105. IPN OK Kr, Ds. 6/70/22, Testimony of Marian Wojciechowski, April 22, 1974, 100.

106. IPN OK Kr, Ds. 6/70/22, Testimony of Apolonia Kozina, May 22, 1975, 115.

107. IPN OK Kr, Ds. 6/70/22, Testimony of Otylia Kozina, May 22, 1975, 119.

108. IPN OK Kr, Ds. 6/70/22, Testimony of Józef Zawojski, September 28, 1973, 55; IPN OK Kr, Ds. 6/70/21, Testimony of Emil Czarny, May 20, 1975, 250.

109. IPN OK Kr, Ds. 6/70/22, Questionnaire on mass executions and mass graves in Zawoja, September 28, 1945, 20.

110. IPN OK Kr, Ds. 6/70/22, Testimony of Franciszka Mazur, May 22, 1975, 122. A similar action was carried in Czorsztyn and neighboring localities in the eastern part of the county (Grywałd, Maniowy, Dębno, and Szlembark). On August 13, thirty-three adults were killed there, while children were commanded to go to Nowy Targ. See AN Kr, 29/208/4/23, Register of the Jewish population in Nowy Targ County, 1941; AMT, AR/NO/627, Anna Drohojowska Testimony, September 6, 1970, 4; USC, VHA, 20889, Edgar Wildfeuer Testimony.

111. AŻIH, ŻSS, 211/682, Letter from the Branch Office in Maków Podhalański to the Presidium of the ŻSS in Kraków, August 28, 1942, 73. The

list contains the names of twelve persons; the names of orphans and half-orphans are marked. It indicates that it was already known that Dukler and Sauerstrom had escaped. The list includes the name of three children from Białka, where the Jews were executed on August 27.

112. Berta Liebermann and her family were resettled from Prokocim in late May 1942. They had landed in Naprawa. As she wrote in her memoir, "Life in Naprawa was very nice for wartime conditions. Every day, I gathered mushrooms and blueberries." AŻIH, Memoirs of Jews, 1939–1945, 302/334, Wartime memoir of Berta Liebermann-Józefowicz, 1.

113. Ibid.

114. IPN OK Kr, Ds. 6/70/22, Testimony of Jan Kłącz, May 10, 1974, 112.

115. IPN OK Kr, Ds. 6/70/22, Testimony of Stanisława Rzeźnik, March 15, 1975, 151.

116. Letter of Mark Goldfinger, March 8, 2007, in Rapta, Tupta, and Moskal, *Mroczne sekrety willi "Tereska,"* 252.

117. In Krościenko, Krośnica, Ochotnica, Tylmanowa, Grywałd, Maniowy, and Czorsztyn, and probably in Dębno, Szlembark, and Waksmund.

118. IPN OK Kr, Ds. 6/70/22, Testimony of Stanisław Wciślak, May 16, 1979, 149.

119. AŻIH, 301/4707, Salomon Süsskind Testimony, n.d., 9; AŻIH, 301/4716, Abraham Furman Testimony, n.d., 2.

120. IPN OK Kr, Ds. 6/70/32, Testimony of Zbigniew Kluz, April 20, 1961, 77.

121. AN Kr, 29/208/4/23, Register of the Jewish population in Nowy Targ County, 1941.

122. AŻIH, 301/4707, Salomon Süsskind Testimony, n.d., 9.

123. AŻIH, 301/4716, Abraham Furman Testimony, n.d., 2.

124. IPN OK Kr, Ds. 6/70/30, Marian Drelich's letter to the Ministry of Justice and *Main Commission for the Investigation* of Nazi *Crimes in Poland*, April 20, 1965, 85.

125. YVA, O.3/2975, Chana Hornung Testimony, October 1966, 15.

126. Indictment in the case against Robert Weissmann and Richard Arno Sehmisch issued by the State Prosecutor's Office at the National Court in Freiburg, January 24, 1964, 106.

127. IPN OK Kr, Ds. 6/70/32, Testimony of Edward Marfiak, May 5, 1961, 8.

128. IPN OK Kr, Ds. 6/70/23, Testimony of Jan Gringras [Henryk Grüngras], April 30, 1973, 59.

129. YVA, O.33/7327, Notes of Chana Windstrauch, c. 1944, 21.

130. IPN OK Kr, Ds. 6/70/22, Testimony of Władysław Ludwik Łazarski, June 4, 1974, 130.

131. BAL, B 162/3905, Testimony of Heinrich Karhoff, July 16, 1963, 4009.

132. BAL, B 162/3905, Testimony of Franciszek Tyrpa, August 7, 1973, 43.

133. IPN OK Kr, Ds. 4/75, Announcement, August 29, 1942, 136.

134. Indictment in the case against Robert Weissmann and Richard Arno Sehmisch issued by the State Prosecutor's Office at the National Court in Freiburg, January 24, 1964, 102.

135. YVA, O.3/2975, Chana Hornung Testimony, October 1966, 21.

136. Its full name was "Hobag" Holzbau Aktiengesellschaft Breslau. The Hobag industrial sawmills started to operate in Podhale in January 1940.

137. BAL, B 162/3890, Testimony of Moshe Natowicz, December 25, 1961, 417; YVA, O.3/2975, Chana Hornung Testimony, October 1966, 15; USC, VHA, 22889, Robert Mendler Testimony; USC, VHA, 1840, Joseph Linden Testimony, Forest Hills, April 6, 1995; USC, VHA, 51497, Simon Katz Testimony.

138. YVA, O.3/3232, Jehuda Kestenbaum Testimony, October 1966, 12.

139. IPN OK Kr, Ds. 6/70/22, Testimony of Stanisław Wciślak, May 16, 1979, 149.

140. IPN OK Kr, Ds. 4/75, Testimony of Stanisław Stołowski, September 20, 1973, 170.

141. IPN OK Kr, Ds. 4/75, Testimony of Tadeusz Czubernat, June 30, 1981, 536.

142. Ibid.

143. Ibid.

144. Stanisław B., Interview, August 10, 2013, in Ochotnica Dolna, private collection.

145. IPN OK Kr, Ds. 4/75, Testimony of Franciszka Węglarczyk, December 12, 1978, 341.

146. IPN OK Kr, Ds. 4/75, Testimony of Zofia Chowaniec née Ścisłowicz, October 26, 1978, 368.

147. IPN OK Kr, Ds. 4/75, Testimony of Eugenia Kubiak, October 27, 1978, 364.

148. IPN OK Kr, Ds. 6/70/25, Testimony of Maria Sobczak, December 18, 1965, 77.

149. AŻIH, 301/3269, Maria Żak (Grünberg) Testimony, June 30, 1947, 13.

150. AŻIH, 301/3453, Ozjasz Szachner Account, n.d., 7.

151. BAL, B 162/3910, Testimony of Abraham Furman, May 19, 1965, 4802. Abraham Furman born in Tylmanowa in 1915. He survived in Ochotnica thanks to help of the local farmer, Franciszek Ptaszek. Another man bearing the same name (Abraham Furman, b. 1898), who was also hiding near Ochotnica, survived as well.

152. YVA, O.3/3226, Frania Tiger Testimony, November 1966, 14.

153. Nachum Beck, interview.

154. YVA, O.33/7327, Notes of Chana Windstrauch, 27.

155. IPN OK Kr, Ds. 6/70/22, Testimony of Stanisław Wciślak, May 16, 1979, 149.

156. My preliminary research revealed only two survivors from this area—siblings from Osielec, Eleonora and Leopold Zollman. Their parents were

murdered after the action, and the siblings were helped, among others, by Mieczysław Wójcik and the Zawada family from Osielec. See YVA, M.31/8840, Material collected in support of the application to award the Zawada family and Mieczysław Wójcik the title *"Righteous Among the Nations."*

157. AIPN Kr, 502/4085, Testimony of Teofil Drobny, April 16, 1949, 196; IPN OK Kr, Ds. 6/70/20, Testimony of Jan Polak, May 27, 1968, 43.

158. IPN OK Kr, Ds. 6/70/20, Testimony of Jan Polak, May 27, 1968, 43.

159. The testimonies of other witnesses mention 150–180 victims.

160. IPN OK Kr, Ds. 6/70/21, Testimony of Fr. Stanisław Czartoryski, April 9, 1974, 144.

161. IPN OK Kr, Ds. 6/70/21, Letter [sent] from the MO station in Maków Podhalański to the OKBZH in Krakow, December 4, 1967, 9. The remains were transported in thirteen coffins to the Jewish cemetery in Wadowice. See IPN OK Kr, Ds. 6/70/21, Letter of the Congregation of the Jewish Faith in Krakow to the Presidium of the *National Council*, Municipal Utilities and Housing Company in Maków Podhalański, February 28, 1964, 15.

162. AIPN Kr, 502/4085, Questionnaire on camps, September 26, 1945, 138; IPN OK Kr, Ds. 6/70/21, Testimony of Jan Polak, March 21, 1974, 118; IPN OK Kr, Ds. 6/70/20, Letter [sent] from the MO station in Maków Podhalański to the OKBZH in Krakow, December 4, 1967, 9.

163. As we know, there were localities in which most of inhabitants were killed on the spot, such as Zawoja. Thus in this case, the ratio of self-rescue attempts is different. Because the number of those murdered in each town or village during the operations is unknown, the result I have obtained represents the average for this part of *Kreis* Neumarkt.

164. YVA, O.3/2975, Chana Hornung Testimony, October 1966, 4.

165. YVA, O.3/2975, Testimony of Tadeusz Czubernat, June 30, 1981, 536.

166. Ibid..

167. Stanisław B., interview, August 10, 2013, in Ochotnica Dolna, private collection.

168. Jan A., interview, July 20, 2016, in Ochotnica Górna, private collection.

169. Ibid.

170. AAN, RGG, 536, t. 7, Aufstellung am November 5, 1942, auf die Hauptkasse des GG überwiessen Entgelte [Payments to be Charged on the Main Account of GG on November 5, 1942] 6.

171. AIPN Kr, 502/1837, Files of the case of Józef Kandza, Testimony of Michał Thomas, November 24, 1947, 122.

172. IPN OK Kr, Ds. 4/75, Official note from the conversation with Franciszka Węglarczyk, May 24, 1977, 203.

173. BAL, B 162/3895, Testimony of Wenzel Jandl, September 20, 1962, 1565.

174. IPN OK Kr, Ds. 6/70/25, Testimony of Abraham Schiffeldrin, February 22, 1968, 187.

175. Zofia Pitek, Interview, May 11, 2005, in Rabka, quoted in Rapta, Tupta, and Moskal, *Mroczne sekrety willi "Tereska,"* 220. Just after it happened, an owner of one of the villas spotted the girl's mother, Maria, who was hiding on his property after she had searched in vain for her daughter. He reported her to Hwozdulowicz, who murdered the woman in the grove next to Villa Tereska.

176. AŻIH, 301/614, Rubin Traum Testimony, 1945, 6.

177. Maria Gacek, on request of the German prosecutor's office, assumed responsibility for the Polish part of the proceedings in the case of crimes committed by the Zakopane Gestapo in the territory of the wartime Nowy Targ county, as well as the proceedings in the case of the Gestapo crimes committed against the Polish and Jewish population in Nowy Targ. She did not, therefore, need to inform her German counterparts about crimes committed by Poles against Jews in hiding. The files of the both proceedings are kept in the archive of the branch office of the Commission for the Prosecution of Crimes against the Polish Nation in Kraków.

178. YVA, O.33/7327, Notes of Chana Windstrauch, 32.

179. Berta Liebermann had been hiding in the same area for a short period. After being assaulted by peasants several times—beaten, robbed, and blackmailed—and after her parents and brother had lost their lives, she decided to leave Nowy Targ County. See AŻIH, 302/334, Wartime diary of Berta Liebermann-Józefowicz, c. 1945.

180. The Windstrauchs broke into their own flat in Jordanów: "Iziek... surprised as the entire flat had already been plundered by neighbors, packed what he could into a bag—just some remains such as a pillow, a feather quilt, and some dishes—and lowered it all down using [a piece of] string, and Daddy caught it and bolted away. Thus, we had to steal our own belongings." YVA, O.33/7327, Notes of Chana Windstrauch, 30.

181. IPN OK Kr, Ds. 6/70/23, Testimony of Jan Gringras [Henryk Grüngras], April 30, 1973, 59.

182. AŻIH, 301/3453, Ozjasz Szachner Testimony, n.d., 8.

183. The Storchs—forty-two-year-old Wiktor, thirty-five-year-old Rachela, six-year-old Eugeniusz, and three-year-old Rozalia—were murdered there in fall 1942. During the war, they lived in Stare Bystre (after being expelled from Dzianisz, located in the *Sperrgebiet*), and then they were allegedly hiding in Ratułów but were denounced and ended up in Villa Palace. Throughout the night, they were kept in a corridor leading to inmates' cells and, at the dawn, were taken one by one to the yard and murdered. AN Kr, 29/208/4/23, Register of the Jewish population in Nowy Targ County, 1941, n.p.; IPN OK Kr, Ds.

6/70/34, Application of Stanisław Dzianiński, October 6, 1951, 115; IPN OK Kr, Ds. 6/70/32, Testimony of Czesław Trybowski, April 21, 1961, 78.

184. Unfortunately, extant sources do not permit a determination of their number.

185. AŻIH, 302/334, Wartime diary of Berta Liebermann-Józefowicz, 1; AŻIH, 301/3453, Ozjasz Szachner Account, n.d., 7; Note from the conversation with Ayala Lazar, 2016, in the author's collection.

186. In the winter of 1942–1943, the temperature sometimes dropped to -33°C [almost -27°F]. AN Kr, 31/912/1, Andrzej Florek Skupień—Memoir. Chronicle of Events September 1, 1942–August 2, 1945, note from December 29, 1942, 10.

187. YVA, O.33/7327, Notes of Chana Windstrauch, 33.

188. Chana Windstrauch wrote in her notes, "All of a sudden on November 25 snow falls that shuts us off completely due to the tracks." YVA, O.33/7327, Notes of Chana Windstrauch, c. 1944, 34.

189. AŻIH, 301/4716, Abraham Furman Account, n.d., 17.

190. IPN OK Kr, Ds. 4/75, Testimony of Franciszka Węglarczyk, October 12, 1978, 342; Testimony of Marian Kubiak, October 16, 1973, 78.

191. The largest group of Jews kept in the Nowy Targ jail.

192. AŻIH, 301/4716, Abraham Furman Testimony, n.d., 18.

193. The "Harnasie" unit was a part of the Third Podhale Rifles Regiment and operated in the Jordanów and Maków region.

194. Wilhelm Winiarski, also known as "Czarny Kruk," was to form dispatches in the territory of Naprawa and Jordanów; AIPN Kr, 010/6754/1, Files of Jan Tomana, Testimony of Jan Druzgała, July (day indecipherable) 1951, 159.

195. AIPN Kr, 010/6754/1, Testimony of Marian Karol [Mojżesz] Eisenmann, June 30, 1950, 165.

196. AŻIH, 301/4716, Abraham Furman Testimony, n.d., 18.

197. The fate of nonnative Jews in hiding in the Podhale territory under assumed (Aryan) identities constitutes a separate issue, which I do not pursue here due to constraints on the size of this paper (the Polish version of my chapter covers their story). My preliminary research revealed 138 such persons; however, there must have been many more. None of them, but for several small children taken in by Polish families, stayed in Podhale longer than a few months. My research shows that 62 of those 138 were murdered, 5 were caught and probably lost their lives, and 71 survived the Holocaust.

198. AŻIH, 301/4631, Rita Felczer Testimony, February 27, 1946, 22.

199. IPN OK Kr, Ds. 4/75, Testimony of Stanisław Olański, May 17, 1978, 313.

200. YVA, O.3/1818, Marian Szatkowski Account, January 24, 1961.

201. In seventeen cases, such attempts failed. The fate of ten other persons, whom I know to have made such an attempt, is unknown.

202. IPN OK Kr, Ds. 6/70/30, Marian Drelich's letter to the Ministry of Justice and *Main Commission for the Investigation of Nazi Crimes in Poland*, April 20, 1965, 94.

203. AŻIH, 301/614, Rubin Traum Testimony, 1945, 7.

204. Józef Nyka, "A potem zapadła cisza. Niemieckie obozy pracy dla Żydów pod Tatrami" [And Then the Silence Fell: German Labor Camps for Jews at the Foothills of the Tatra Mountains], in *Górska Biblioteczka Historyczna* 14, no. 34 (2012): 4.

205. ITS Bad Arolsen, 1.2.7.7/82186261, Bekleidung der Juden [Clothes of the Jews], January 7, 1943, 220; AN Kr ONS, 30/603/335, Population census, March 23, 1943, 1807.

206. IPN OK Kr, S 30/12/Zn, Testimony of Józef Budzyk, July 31, 1973, 49.

207. AN Kr ONS, 30/603/364, List of consumed food rations for the month of November, December 16, 1942, 136.

208. https://www.straty.pl (accessed in September 2016).

209. IPN OK Kr, Ds. 6/70/26, Testimony of Izaak Selinger, January 29, 1948, 24. Perhaps it was the event to which one of the inmates there, Juliusz Hochman, had alluded in his conversation with employees of the ŻSS Kraków headquarters on October 8, 1942: "As to food, it is worse. At the beginning, items of clothing were used to barter for foodstuff, but when the local population was scared away, all contacts with them ceased completely and so did foodstuff delivery." AŻIH, ŻSS, 211/850, Note from the conversation with Juliusz Hochman of Rabka, October 8, 1942, 62.

210. Jan A., interview, July 20, 2016, in Ochotnica Górna. Private collection.

211. Mrs. Korzeniowska, owner of a grocery store, had also supported him; John Radowski, "I Survived Prisons and Nazi Concentration Camps (Memoirs)," typescript, n.d., 7. I wish to thank Gisela Radowski for making the typescript available to me.

212. Ibid., 7.

213. In Rabka, similar help was provided by young men: Bala and Filipiak. Letter of Mr. Trześniower to the Rabka branch of ZBoWiD, 1978, in Rapta, Tupta, and Moskal, *Mroczne sekrety willi "Tereska,"* 227.

214. YVA, O.3/2975, Chana Hornung Testimony, October 1966, 19.

215. YVA, O.33/3232, Jehuda Kestenbaum Testimony, October 1966, 13.

216. Joel Schneider, interview, July 15, 2015, in Haifa, Karolina Panz Private Collection.

217. AŻIH, 301/4707, Salomon Süsskind Testimony, n.d., 13.

218. Mentioned in the list of prisoners—he was in the jail on November 14, 1942. AN Kr ONS, 30/603/364, List of consumed food rations for the month of November, December 16, 1942, 134.

219. Nyka, "A potem zapadła cisza. Niemieckie obozy pracy," 7.

220. IPN OK Kr, Ds. 6/70, t. 26, Testimony of Ada Rawicz, February 16, 1948, 37. Joel Schneider, interview, July 15, 2015, in Haifa, Karolina Panz Private Collection; Nachum Beck, interview, July 20, 2015, in Azor, Karolina Panz Private Collection.

221. AŻIH, 301/4707, Salomon Süsskind Testimony, n.d., 12.

222. Miriam Wildfeuer of Krośnica was murdered because she demanded her headscarf from a farmer who had leased land from her before the war. AN Kr, 29/439/1340, Files of the case of Jan Krężel and others. Minutes of the main proceedings, July 28, 1958, 329.

223. Wacław Krzeptowski—who as a member of the five-man delegation of the most distinguished *Góral* families paid homage to Hans Frank in the Wawel Castle on November 7, 1939—had been chairman of the County Board of the People's Party and, during the interwar period, used to represent the Podhalanians at the most important national ceremonies. Wojciech Szatkowski, *Goralenvolk. Historia zdrady* (Kraków: Kanon, 2012), 37, 178.

224. AMT, AR/NO/123, Account of the Górale Alliance in Zakopane, September 22, 1941, n.p.

225. *Memorial of Henryk Szatkowski*, cited in Szatkowski, *Goralenvolk*, 200.

226. AMT, AR/NO/123, Account of the Górale Alliance in Zakopane, September 22, 1941, n.p.

227. AIPN Kr, 502/788, Testimony of Władysława Faronówna, September 25, 1945, 74.

228. AIPN Kr, 502/868, Letter of Wacław Krzeptowski to the county office in Krościenko, August 25, 1942, 149.

229. IPN OK Kr, Ds. 6/70/32, Testimony of Czesław Trybowski, April 21, 1961, 79.

230. In Czarny Dunajec, Krościenko, Nowy Targ, Jordanów, and Rabka.

231. AIPN Kr, 502/867, Minutes of the main proceedings, November 16, 1946, 318.

232. Ibid., Minutes of the main proceedings, November 8, 1946, 12.

233. IPN OK Kr, Ds. 6/70/25, Testimony of Roman Dattner, January 29, 1948, 6.

234. AIPN Kr, 502/867, Minutes of the main proceedings, November 5, 1946, 154.

235. Ibid.

236. AN Kr ONS, St NT II/15, Einwohnerzahl in der Kreishauptmannschaft Neumarkt, styczeń 1943 [Population Census of Neumarkt County, January 1943].

237. AIPN, GK, 196/301, Fr. Dr. Jan Piwowarczyk, Prześladowanie Kościoła Katolickiego w Polsce przez tzw. Rząd GG [Persecution of the Catholic Church in Poland by the so-called GG Administration], October 25, 1946, 40.

238. AN Kr, 29/439/1243, Minutes of the main proceedings, November 4, 1949, 156.
239. AN Kr, 29/3094/3, Służba informacyjna dla wójtów [Voit's Information Service], no. 4, August 15, 1940, 22.
240. One of Czorsztyn's residents remembered the armband worn by Jakub Kurpiel. AMT, AR/NO/627, Anna DrohojowskaTestimony, September 6, 1970, 5.
241. Antoni Kroh, *Sklep potrzeb kulturalnych. Po remoncie* (Warsaw: Wydawnictwo MG, 2013), 207.
242. Stanisława Trebunia-Staszel, Małgorzata Maj, ed., *"Wywołane z pamięci." Wojna i niemieckie badania rasowe w relacjach mieszkańców Podhala* [w:] *Antropologia i etnologia w czasie wojny. Działalność Sektion Rassen und Volkstumsforschung Institut für Deutsche Ostarbeit, Krakau 1940–1944, w świetle nowych materiałów źródłowych*, (Kraków: Wydawnictwo UJ, 2015), 203.
243. I wish to thank Anna Staszel for recounting to me her great-grandmother's story.
244. AIPN Kr, 502/866, Statement, 1946, 97.
245. AIPN Kr, 502/864, Letter of Michał Syper to the Special Penal Court in Kraków, January 23, 1946, 120.
246. IPN OK Kr, Ds. 6/70/34, Testimony of Ludwik Sowiński, January 23, 1948.
247. YVA, O.3/2975, Chana Hornung Testimony, October 1966, 19.
248. AŻIH, 301/3453, Ozjasz Szachner Testimony, n.d., 7.
249. Those who lost their lives because they were helping Jews: Katarzyna Filipek, and Maria and Stefan Barglik were murdered in the spring 1944 for helping the six-person Sterlicht family from Tokarnia (IPN OK Kr, Ds. 6/70/16, Letter of "Kommendeur der Sichertspolizei und des SD im Distrikt Krakau Grenzpolizeikommisariat Zakopane" to *voits* of Szaflary and Łętownia municipalities, March 9, 1944, 25/1); Jan Ufir, shot to death near to his house in the Robów estate in Nowy Targ on October 15, 1943, about a month after a young Jewish woman from Nowy Targ had been arrested next to his property (IPN OK Kr, Ds. 4/75, Testimony of Jan Ufir, November 22, 1978, 397); N.N., a woman and a highlander, shot to death on May 5, 1944, in the Poronin cemetery along with three women she had sheltered (IPN OK Kr, Ds. 6/70/34, Testimony of Józef Matyga, January 22, 1976, 194); Władysław Długopolski and Cyryl Brynkus, farmers from Spytkowice, arrested on November 15, 1943 on the charge of helping a Jew, [Mr.] Beck of Podwilk, and both were shot in a mass execution in Płaszów on May 28, 1944 (IPN OK Kr, Ds. 6/70/8, Testimony of Stefania Możdżeń, June 15, 1971, 86); Wojciech Siedlarczyk of Krośnica, arrested on the basis of a denunciation that he delivered food to the Wildfeuers who were hiding in the forest; he probably died in Auschwitz (AN Kr, 29/439/1340, Files of

the case of Jan Krężel and others, Testimony of Anna Bandyk, July 5, 1949, 11); Stefan Kozak of Jordanów, arrested in February 1943 shortly after he had set up an ambush in which four Jews were caught whom he had earlier supplied with food, and he died in Auschwitz (AIPN Kr, 502/1826, Testimony of Józefa Wicher, April 19, 1950, 92); Stanisław Para and Stanisław Lichaj of Biały Dunajec, arrested in 1944 and charged with smuggling Jews to Slovakia, and they died in mass executions (IPN OK Kr, Ds. 6/70/15, Testimony of Helena Cachro, January 24, 1986, 130); Regina and Piotr Wiecheć; Tekla and Karol Chowaniak; and Karolina Marek, all from Zawoja, arrested for sheltering a couple of about thirty-year-old Jews from Kraków; Regina and Piotr Wiecheć, shot to death in the Villa Marysin (IPN OK Kr, Ds. 6/70/22, Testimony of Klemens Wiecheć, March 14, 1975, 189), and the Chowaniaks along with Karolina Marek died in Auschwitz (IPN OK Kr, Ds. 6/70/22, Testimony of Stanisław Chowaniak, March 14, 1975, 78).

250. Stanisława Trebunia-Staszel and Małgorzata Maj, eds., *"Wywołane z pamięci." Wojna i niemieckie badania rasowe w relacjach mieszkańców Podhala* [w:] *Antropologia i etnologia w czasie wojny. Działalność Sektion Rassen und Volkstumsforschung Institut für Deutsche Ostarbeit, Krakau 1940–1944, w świetle nowych materiałów źródłowych*, (Kraków: Wydawnictwo UJ, 2015), 202.

251. YVA, O.3/3226, Frania Tiger Testimony, November 1966, 20.

252. Ibid., 24.

253. Eleonora Wagner has not been awarded with the title of Righteous Among the Nations. Nor does any proof remain that any attempts were made to this end. Still, Frania Netzer recognized how extraordinary it was what Wagner had done. She mentioned her in *Remembrance Book Nowy-Targ and Vicinity*. See Frania Tiger (Netzer), "Memories from the Days of the Holocaust," in *Remembrance Book Nowy-Targ and Vicinity*, 80.

254. YVA, O.33/8570, Chaim Reichert Testimony, 1979.

255. YVA, M.31/1190, Letter of Chana Windstrauch to Yad Vashem, June 23, 1969, 13.

256. He died due to heart failure shortly after the war and was posthumously awarded with the Righteous Among the Nations title in 1969. See YVA, M.31/1190, Honorary Diploma for Jan Mirek, December 16, 1969, 42).

257. YVA, O.3/2975, Chana Hornung Testimony, October 1966, 4.

258. Apart from Jan Mirek, the title of Righteous Among the Nations was awarded to the following residents of *Kreis* Neumarkt: the Bachul Family of Osielec (YVA, M.31/4718, Materials collected to award the title of Righteous Among the Nations to the Bachul Family), the Jaskółka Family of Bystra (YVA, M.31/148, Materials collected to award the title of Righteous Among the Nations to the Jaskółka Family), the Zawada family and Mieczysław Wójcik of Osielec (YVA, M.31/8840, Materials collected to award the title of Righteous

Among the Nations to the Zawada Family and Mieczysław Wójcik), Helena Frydrych (YVA, M. 31/11258, Materials collected to award the title of Righteous Among the Nations to Helena Frydrych), the Karpiel Family (YVA, M.31/6549, Materials collected to award the title of Righteous Among the Nations to Anna and Józef Karpiel), the Trybus Family of Zakopane (YVA, M.31/6571, Materials collected to award the title of Righteous Among the Nations to Apolonia and Mieczysław Trybus), and Katarzyna Filipek of Tokarnia (YVA, M.31/3879, *Honorary Diploma* for Katarzyna Filipek, October 13, 1988, 11). Except for Jan Mirek, Katarzyna Filipek and the Zawadas, these Righteous Among the Nations extended their help to Jews nonnative to Nowy Targ County, whose faces and names were unknown to the neighbors.

259. YVA, O.3/3226, Frania Tiger Testimony, 35.
260. YVA, M.31/1190, Letter of Chana Windstrauch to Yad Vashem, June 23, 1969, 11.
261. USC, VHA, 21371, Rosalie Gelernter Testimony, Stockton, 2 XI 1996; Lydia Hughes, interview, December 14, 2014, in Boston.
262. I have established the numbers reviewing the ITS database.
263. AŻIH, Office of Vital Records and Statistics, List of persons [residents] registered in Nowy Targ, 1945, 34; List of persons [residents] registered in Jordanów, 1945, 36.
264. Karolina Panz, "Why Did They, Who Had Suffered So Much and Endured, Have to Die?" The Jewish Victims of Armed Violence in Podhale (1945–1947)," *Holocaust Studies and Materials 2017. Journal of the Polish Center for Holocaust Research* (2019): 148–211.
265. AIPN Kr, 110/4239/1, Minutes of the interrogation of Józef Hojoł, 4 IV 1950; 104.
266. AIPN Kr, 06/1/16, Special dispatch of the WUBP in Kraków to the Ministry of Public Security, March 27, 1946, 47–48.
267. Henryk Grüngras of Jordanów was the only one of the registered and survived residents of Kreis Neumarkt, who lived there after the war; he was baptized and got married.

KAROLINA PANZ, PhD, is a sociologist and a member of the Polish Center for Holocaust Research. She works at the Institute of Slavic Studies, Polish Academy of Sciences as the postdoc/coinvestigator in the project "The Kraków Pogrom of 11 August 1945 against the Comparative Background," under the supervision of Dr.hab. Joanna Tokarska-Bakir. Her research interests are Jewish life and the Holocaust in Polish provinces, with special focus on the microhistory of Jews from the Podhale region (southern Poland), where she lives and has Polish-Jewish relatives. Her latest publications include "Powiat nowotarski" [Nowy Targ County], in *DALEJ JEST NOC. Losy Żydów w wybranych powiatach okupowanej* [Night without End: The Fate of Jews in Selected Counties of Occupied Poland], ed. Barbara Engelking and Jan Grabowski (2018); "'The Children Are in a State of True Panic': Postwar Anti-Jewish Violence in Podhale and Its Youngest Victims," *Yad Vashem Studies* (2018); and "Comment échapper à la mort? Le cas des Juifs de la region de Nowy Targ," in *Les Polonais et la Shoah*, ed. Audrey Kichelewski, Judith Lyon-Caen, Jean Charles Szurek, and Annette Wieviorka (2019).

SEVEN

DĘBICA COUNTY

TOMASZ FRYDEL

The setting of this study[1] is Dębica County (*Kreis* Debica), one of twelve counties that comprised the Kraków District of the General Government (GG). It was formed by combining three prewar Polish counties—Dębica, Mielec, and Tarnobrzeg—as well as a small part of Kolbuszowa County in today's Subcarpathian region of southeastern Poland. The county was inhabited by approximately 310,000 inhabitants, about 18,000 (6 percent) of whom were Jews. This mostly agricultural territory with a scattering of small forests would come to encompass 3,083 square kilometers during the German occupation—almost identical in size to the state of Rhode Island in the US. The county contained nine towns: Tarnobrzeg, Rozwadów, Baranów Sandomierski, Mielec, Radomyśl Wielki, Sędziszów, Ropczyce, Dębica, and Pilzno. This translated into a total of 37 communes and 224 villages, which fell under the civilian authority of the *Kreishauptmann* (county governor). Dębica County was among the largest in the district.[2]

THE *JACQUERIES* OF WESTERN GALICIA: POLISH-JEWISH RELATIONS PRIOR TO WORLD WAR II

After World War I, Galician Jews emerged as the most Polonized of all Polish *Ostjuden*.[3] The legacy of Hasidism, a Jewish spiritual revival movement that challenged the authority of rabbinical Judaism, and the period of Habsburg rule over Galicia (1772–1918) did much to determine the distinct character of Galician Jewry in Polish lands.[4] By 1830, the majority of Galician Jews in the postpartition period were Hasidic, with Galicia (next to Bukovina and Congress Poland) as one of the most "Hasidized" regions of the world.[5] Western Galicia,

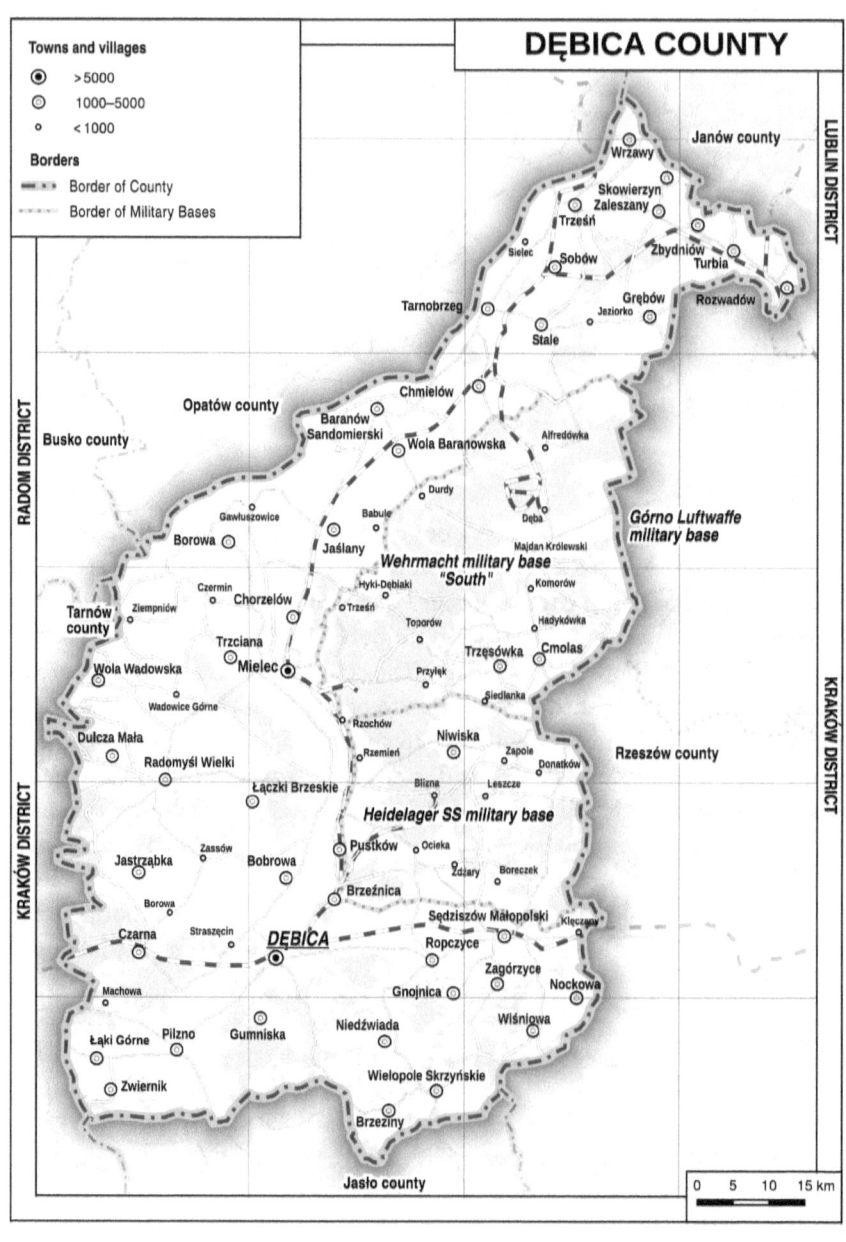

which encompassed the territory of the Dębica region, was influenced primarily by the disciples of Rabbis Elimelekh of Leżajsk, Naphtali Zevi (Horowitz) of Ropczyce, and Menahem Mendel of Rymanów, who quickly established dynastic courts in the region.[6]

The modernization of Galician Jews was delayed by the decision to maintain the Austrian province as an agricultural hinterland, which allowed "premodern Jewish life to continue as nowhere else in Eastern Europe."[7] At the same time, the German-Jewish *Haskalah*, or the Jewish Enlightenment movement, gained substantial numbers of followers considerably earlier in Galicia than in the Russian empire. These confrontations between Hasidism and *Haskalah* lay the foundations for the birth of Jewish nationalism, as well as strivings for Jewish assimilation into German and Polish society. By the interwar period, an inhabitant of a shtetl in the region could observe: "Within one generation, Radomyśl became modern, daring, and rebellious. A complete transformation of values had taken place; as if leaping from the Middle Ages into the enlightened world of rational, practical, historically purposeful concepts."[8]

The state of affairs was more ominous in the Polish province, where the division between town and village had remained strong into the twentieth century. The social and economic tensions that arose from these conditions shaped the specific character of Polish-Jewish relations, especially from the mid-nineteenth century onward. The 1846 Peasant Uprising against serfdom in Western Galicia—described by historians as the "last jacquerie" of Europe—resulted in the slaughter of more than a thousand noblemen and the destruction of approximately five hundred manors; yet no Jews were harmed, as in this period the peasant rebellion was aimed at the *szlachta*, the legally privileged class of landowning nobles. The Dębica and Pilzno regions in particular were affected by this massacre lasting two months.[9]

However, the 1860s marked a sea change in Polish-Jewish relations, in which the peasant-noble conflict was increasingly replaced by a peasant-Jewish conflict. The newly emancipated serfs of 1848 were not as equipped to respond to the challenges of a nascent "rural capitalism" as their Jewish neighbors, whose traditional position as an entrepreneurial middleman minority now became increasingly vulnerable, paving the way for a "sociological collision course" between lower-class Polish Christians and provincial Jews, in the words of historian Keely Stauter-Halsted.[10] In the summer of 1898, these tensions erupted in an unprecedented wave of pogroms across the small towns and villages of Western Galicia. In the Dębica region, Ropczyce and Wielopole Skrzyńskie were most affected by the violence. However, no Jews were reported to have been harmed in these attacks. Unlike the pogroms of 1881 in the Russian empire, the violence was aimed not at Jews themselves but rather at symbols of Jewish economic power—primarily taverns, estates, and distilleries. This struggle of the postemancipation peasant to enter the "rural bourgeoisie" and its attendant economic competition formed the basis of the nationalism of the new political parties, such as the PSL (*Polskie Stronnictwo Ludowe*, Polish Peasant Party), as well as the popular antisemitism of Western Galicia.[11]

A second occasion for the eruption of these tensions occurred in the aftermath of the First World War, from the fall of 1918 to early 1919.[12] During November 1–4, 1918, villagers from the surrounding area began plundering and destroying Jewish property in the town square of Mielec. Similar attacks took place in Radomyśl Wielki, Rozwadów, and Baranów Sandomierski. On November 6, 1918, the region saw the establishment of a short-lived Republic of Tarnobrzeg led by Tomasz Dąbal and the Catholic priest Eugeniusz Okoń, which postulated radical land reform by seizing land from wealthy owners and redistributing it among the poor peasantry. In some parts of the county, rumors circulated that independent Poland would reinstitute serfdom. The riots were often stopped with the help of the army. In some instances, as in Pilzno, the town authorities and a Catholic priest succeeded in stopping the violence and looting in its tracks.[13] Though dozens of stores were plundered and many Jews beaten, no casualties were reported.

The interwar years saw to a continuation of tensions, but these never led to a major antisemitic outburst. Polish and Jewish political life in Galicia was less polarized than in other parts of the country. Many towns had a tradition of power sharing between Polish and Jewish representatives on the local councils. Prior to World War I, the strongest political current was the left wing of the Polish Peasant Party (PSL-Lewica), led by the socialist Jan Stapiński. After the war, support in the region swung to the right wing of the party (PSL-Piast), led by future prime minister Wincenty Witos. Though antisemitic thinking was present in the peasant movement, the influence of the National Democrats was weak in the region.[14] At the same time, the region was home to all Jewish political parties and youth movements characteristic of interwar Poland. In May 1933, Betar, the Revisionist Zionist youth movement, organized a rally in Radomyśl Wielki to protest anti-Jewish discrimination in Germany. On April 2, 1934, the same town hosted a convention of various Zionist groups throughout western Lesser Poland.[15]

Poor economic conditions and the rise of antisemitism in the second half of the 1930s led to a rise in emigration, primarily to France, Belgium, the United States, and Mandatory Palestine. At the same time, as a consequence of the introduction of the Nuremberg Laws in Germany, Austria, and Czech lands, these years also saw an exodus of Jews from these lands to join families in the region.

DĘBICA COUNTY DURING WORLD WAR II

The German Administration

The German army arrived on the bank of the Vistula River in the first week of September 1939. By September 13, all of the towns of the future Dębica County had been captured by the German army, bringing with it immediate violence against local Jews. The *Einsatzgruppen* accompanying the army set fire to synagogues in Mielec, Dębica, Baranów Sandomierski, Pilzno, Ropczyce, and Sędziszów. The brutal murder of some twenty-seven Jews in Mielec—who were rounded up and locked inside the ritual slaughterhouse, which was then set on fire, along with the adjoining synagogue—on the last day of Rosh Hashanah (the Jewish New Year) sent shockwaves throughout the country.[16] These early events set the tone for the rest of the occupation.

In the key period of 1941–1943, the civilian administration of *Kreis* Debica was headed by *Kreishauptmann* Ernst Schlüter.[17] The county was characterized by an unusually strong police and military presence. Two main *Dienstelle* (Gestapo

Figure 7.1. Pages taken from a photo album of a German soldier depicting rituals of humiliation directed at Jewish men forced to sweep the market square: Caption: "The Jewish nest of Radomyśl Wielki. A little work on Saturday (the Sabbath) also does no harm to a Jew." The photos likely date to the beginning of the occupation c. 1939. Photo courtesy of Łukasz Biedka.

Figure 7.2. Top caption: "always nice and clean." Bottom caption: "If [the ground] is not swept, the beard is gone." Photo courtesy of Łukasz Biedka.

outposts) of the Rzeszów branch, under the supervision of Hans Mack, were established in Dębica and Mielec, and somewhat later in Stalowa Wola. In addition to the German gendarmerie posts in the larger towns and *Polnische Polizei* (Polish Police) posts stationed throughout its many communes, the occupation authorities formed auxiliary police forces by recruiting members of the ethnic German community, recast in Nazi ideological terms as *Volksdeutsche*. After the dissolution of the *Volksdeutscher Selbstschutz* in November 1939, its members were subsequently drawn into two formations: the *Sonderdienst* and local *Landwache* or *Dorfwache* units—essentially village police forces. A *Sonderdienst* unit was assigned to the office of the *Kreishauptmann*.

However, what really shifted the scales of German power in the region was the establishment of two enormous military bases within the boundaries of the county: *Truppenübungsplatz Süd* (army base South) with headquarters in Dęba, and SS *Truppenübungsplatz Heidelager*, headquartered in Pustków.[18] Police and military forces in *Truppenübungsplatz Süd* were based in its two main barracks: *Lager* Mielec and *Lager* Dęba. Their main function was to serve as military training centers of the German army. Troops were amassed in the army bases prior to the invasion of the Soviet Union. The Pustków camp was known for the formation and preparation of various German and non-German Waffen SS divisions. After the Allies bombed the launching site of the German V-1 and V-2 rockets at Peenemünde in August of 1943, German planners moved a part of the testing facility to the village of Blizna in the middle of SS Heidelager, which resulted in increased security.

The Volksdeutsche of the Mielec Region

The presence of ethnic Germans was an important feature of *Kreis* Debica. From the outset of the occupation, Nazi planners were ideologically invested in unearthing the alleged cultural influence of Germanic colonization. As miniscule as its population was—numbering some 1,500—the touted *Volksdeutsche* community would come to play a significant role in the region. Out of the German villages that grew out of its Habsburg-era settlements, Czermin (Hohenbach) emerged as the main stronghold of the ethnic German community in the region. Prior to the war, some of its inhabitants were members of the illegal NSDAP and Hitler Youth organization. Many were also members of the DVV (*Deutscher Volksverband in Polen*, German People's Union in Poland), founded in 1924 by members of the ethnic German minority who did not wish to join the minority bloc in the Polish parliament.

In April 1939, the ethnic Germans of Czermin formed an *Ortsgruppe*, or a local branch of the DVV, in the Mielec region, under the leadership of Wilhelm Harlos, which functioned as a genuine "fifth column" organization with a distinct anti-Polish character, mobilized on the eve of World War II.[19] On the night of August 28, 1939, members of this group carried out a terrorist attack by planting a bomb in the Tarnów train station, which left twenty dead and thirty-five wounded. When the Germans invaded Poland in September, members of the *Ortsgruppe* installed radio broadcasting equipment inside the barn of the town mayor, Jakub Hössler, to transmit intelligence to Berlin and the advancing German army; pro-Nazi activists raised the flag of the Third Reich throughout the village to signal their political allegiance, greeting the invading army with bread and flowers.

Under the new Nazi order, the ethnic Germans of the Mielec region were catapulted into positions of power in the local administration. German villages became recruiting grounds for various police and self-defense units. Among the most notorious were Oskar Jeck and Rudolf Zimmermann from Czermin, who would rapidly enter the ranks of the new Gestapo outposts. Both attended the Mielec gymnasium, or academic high school, alongside their Polish and Jewish colleagues. Their intimate knowledge of the local population, languages, and region would be weaponized throughout the war.

Jewish Demographics

According to the sources of the ŻSS (*Żydowska Samopomoc Społeczna*, Jewish Self-Aid) organization produced during the war, approximately 17,719 Jews lived in *Kreis* Debica in 1939.[20] ŻSS sources can also shed some light on the demographic of village Jews dispersed throughout the county, which was not insignificant. According to one document, *Kreis* Debica contained approximately 500 Jewish homesteads.[21] If this figure is multiplied by a conservative family size of four members, it can be assumed that village Jews comprised as many as 2,000 of its approximately 18,000 Jews.[22]

From the very outset of the occupation, the Jewish population would undergo dramatic demographic changes. Precise population figures are therefore notoriously hard to determine. Thus, official German sources gave a figure of approximately 309,700 inhabitants in *Kreis* Debica as of March 1942: 293,000 Poles (95 percent), 15,000 Jews (5 percent), 1,500 Germans (less than 1 percent), and 200 others.[23] A year later, another German source gave a population total of 287,922 inhabitants.[24] In addition, the fluctuations of the Jewish population occurred within broader demographic changes taking place in the county affecting the non-Jewish population, such as the resettlement in March 1940 of approximately 2,000 Poles from the Warthegau, a part of western Poland annexed to the German Reich, to the county and the removal of thousands of villagers from the territory that would encompass the two military bases, which began in 1940. Of those pertaining specifically to the Jewish population, four major changes may be noted.

The first major population displacement took place on October 2, 1939, when the German army expelled the Jews of Tarnobrzeg and Rozwadów across the San River into Soviet territory. In Tarnobrzeg, the Germans drove more than two thousand Jews thirty-five kilometers on foot to the San River, where they were ferried across on boats to Radomyśl nad Sanem.[25] In Rozwadów, the German army rounded up as many as three thousand Jews and forced them across the river, where many ended up in Ulanów. These were de facto the first Jewish deportation actions in *Kreis* Debica. Though German civilian authorities subsequently permitted a few hundred of the expellees to return to Tarnobrzeg and Rozwadów, the effect of these actions was to empty the northern part of *Kreis* Debica of most of its native Jewish population. One should also add here that in the 1939–1940 period, the arrival of the German army itself caused a wave of flight to Soviet-occupied territories among hundreds of Jews, especially men.

The second wave of population movement resulted from the resettlement of Jews from the Reich and other parts of the GG. Jews from other areas of the GG began to be resettled to *Kreis* Debica as early as the spring of 1941. Amid the bigger waves, the establishment of the Krakow ghetto meant the resettlement of 1,788 of its Jews to *Kreis* Debica from March-April 1941.[26] Among others, Jews from the town of Oświęcim (Auschwitz) were resettled in Pilzno and Radomyśl Wielki.[27] These and other Jewish resettlements from various parts of the GG continued into 1942, with a conservative estimate of 3,000 Jews in total.

Third, in the summer-fall of 1941, the Germans removed Jews residing in villages from their properties, though without immediately resettling them to other areas. According to instructions given by the *Kreishauptmann*'s office, Jewish farmers were given one hour to leave their homesteads and the village.[28] In effect, these Jews moved into nearby towns or remained in a state of limbo, with many concentrated around Grębów, Borowa, and Przecław. The Mielec *Aussiedlungsaktion*, or "resettlement action," a Nazi euphemism for violent deportation, of Mielec Jews to the Lublin District on March 9, 1942, marked the final major population removal prior to the liquidation of ghettos in June–July of 1942. On this date, Mielec became the first city in the GG to become *judenrein*, or "cleansed of Jews."

The Jewish Communities of Kreis Debica

According to ŻSS sources, a total of ten *Judenräte* (Jewish Councils) were established in the early months of 1940. In his classic study, the historian Isaiah Trunk noted that in some parts of the GG, the Germans tried to set up "County *Judenräte*," and it is likely that the Dębica Jewish Council functioned in this capacity, which would have placed the other nine Councils under its jurisdiction.[29] In addition, a small five-member *Judenrat* was established in the Pustków *Judenlager* in 1941, whose members also played the role of liaisons between the Dębica and Tarnów *Judenräte*.[30] A miniscule Jewish community of some 130 Jews in the village of Grębów (Tarnobrzeg region) had a short-lived *Judenrat* from the spring of 1941, before the community was resettled to Baranów Sandomierski and Mielec (see table 1).[31]

As in most cases, *Judenrat* members were selected from among the respected prewar Jewish intelligentsia who had not escaped to the Soviet Union. In Dębica, Towje (Tuvia) Zucker was appointed chairman, regarded as "the most honorable Jew who remained in the city, since the head of the community Rabbi Avraham Goldman [had] fled to Russia."[32] Such "appointments" were often accompanied by an atmosphere of intimidation and violence. In Radomyśl Wielki, Jeremiasz Leibowicz, the vice mayor of the city, reluctantly accepted the position of *Judenrat* chairman. In Mielec, the *Landrat* (district administrator) had initially offered the position of chairman to Dr. Joachim Taffler, a respected jurist in the community, but he turned down the offer in the belief that it amounted to a form of collaboration. "Despite the fact that the *Judenrat* appeared to perpetuate the form of Jewish autonomy we had known in the *kehillah* [organized Jewish community], to accept the presidency of an administration that furnished laborers for German firms and forced Jews to wear armbands was a form of collaboration with an occupying power," explained

Figure 7.3. Dębica Jews, likely constructing the barracks of the ghetto in early 1941 after resettlement to a poorer part of town. Archives of the Regional Museum of Dębica.

Taffler to a colleague.[33] Still, Taffler assumed a lower position in the *Judenrat* while Dr. Józef Fink, another respected Mielec lawyer, assumed its leadership.

Ghettos were not immediately set up in most of the locations that contained a *Judenrat*. In early 1941, the Germans established a *Jüdischer Wohnbezirk* (Jewish residential district) in Dębica, or a de facto open ghetto, whose inhabitants could not leave without special permission.[34] Until then, Jews had been free to move about the city, but now the *Kreishauptmann* ordered the 2,200 Jews of Dębica to relocate to a much poorer part of the town, behind the market square. The move caused immediate overpopulation, and special barracks had to be built to accommodate the resettled population.[35] In contrast, German authorities briefly considered creating a ghetto in Mielec, which contained the largest Jewish population in the county, but ultimately abandoned the idea.[36] The Jews of Mielec remained dispersed among the Christian population.

Prior to Operation Reinhard, the Germans appear to have created a closed ghetto only in Tarnobrzeg in July 1941 near the synagogue, which was

Table 7.1 Jewish population of *Kreis* Debica

Population Location	1939	1941	March 1942	June 1942	July 1942	Judenrat Chairman First	Second
Baranów	680	1,150			1,545 ✡L	Mordechaj Gross	—
Dębica	2,900	✡			3,000 OL	Towje Zucker	Józef Taub
Grębów	—				—	Mozes Fortgang	—
Mielec	4,000	4,250	5,200 L		—	Dr. Józef Fink	Izak Kaplan
Pilzno	788	1,240			1,500 OL	Michał Treibicz	Samuel Birnbach
Pustków (camp)	—				1,500	Max Bitkower, Herman Immergluck	—
Radomyśl	1,300				2,456 ✡L	Jeremiasz Leibowicz	Izak Kaplan
Ropczyce	1,200				1,307 ✡L	Arnold Meister	—
Rozwadów	3,000				500 L	Lazar Perlman	Berisz Garfunkel
Tarnobrzeg	2,259	195 O			220 L	Aron Tatenbaum	—
Sędziszów	1,060				1,289 ✡L	Hirsch Hiller	—
Wielopole	532			925 ✡L		Chaim Meller	—
TOTAL	17,719			~14,000–15,000			

Source: Author's reconstruction on the basis of collected documentation.

Key:
O = establishment of closed ghetto
✡ = establishment of open ghetto/Jewish district
L = liquidation of ghetto/Jewish district

surrounded by a barbed-wire fence, with workshops established for the Bergmann company.[37] Otherwise, the majority of formal ghettos were created just prior to the liquidation actions in July. It was probably at this time that the "Jewish residential quarter" of Dębica was surrounded by barbed-wire fence, becoming a closed ghetto.[38] The only other case of a closed ghetto was Pilzno, whose *Judenrat* received an order to move into a *geschlossenes Viertel* (closed quarter), along with some six hundred Jews from surrounding villages, by July 4, 1942.[39] The area appears to have been surrounded by barbed wire and patrolled by Jewish policemen on the inside and the Polish Police and gendarmes along its perimeter.[40] The five open ghettos of Baranów, Radomyśl, Pilzno, Ropczyce, and Wielopole were created one to three weeks prior to the "resettlement actions." Rozwadów could not even speak of a "Jewish district."[41]

MIELEC JEWS: SURVIVAL STRATEGIES PRIOR TO OPERATION REINHARD

Survival through Labor

Prior to the major ghetto clearing operations, the Jewish communities of *Kreis* Debica, like most of Polish society under German occupation, sought self-preservation through accommodation to German demands. This was conditioned from the outset by an unprecedented level of German terror, which only grew in strength over time. Therefore, a modus vivendi with German labor demands, combined with the hope that the tide of the war would gradually turn against the Germans, became the prevalent strategy among the Jews of *Kreis* Debica. The extensive camp complex in the county certainly supported this outlook. However, this would prove to be a double-edged sword when this strategy became ingrained, while German policy toward Jews would take a dramatic turn. One crucial reason why the Jews of Mielec did not give credence to rumors of a resettlement was grounded in this logic: "Rumors spread that all Jews would be evacuated from Mielec. The Jews did not want to believe this, assuming that for as long as they were needed for work, they would be safe."[42]

In fact, the *Judenrat* of Radomyśl Wielki held on to this belief until the bitter end. Its leaders believed that a strategy of labor would convince the Germans to abandon plans to deport the town's Jews. After moving around the region for three months following the Mielec deportation, Dr. Józef Fink, the former chair of the Mielec *Judenrat*, was able to secure a position as secretary of the Radomyśl ŻSS in early June.[43] In his correspondence with the ŻSS Presidium in Krakow, he pointed out, "We possess the largest concentration of Jews within *Kreis* Debica; in particular, we have at our disposal the largest group of displaced persons, around 1,000 people."⁴⁴ By July 1942, the Jewish population of Radomyśl had grown to approximately 2,500 (compared to its prewar population of roughly 1,300). The shtetl had also attracted Jews from other parts of the region due to its relative isolation from German power (Radomyśl was not located near a rail line). The town did not have to contend with the regular presence of the German Police, as only a Polish police station was located there. In addition, the Radomyśl *Arbeitsamt* (Labor Office) and *Judenrat* already had a system in place in which some 500 Jewish laborers were employed on surrounding manors and farms.⁴⁵ The reality of a relatively sleepy Jewish shtetl with a growing pool of potential workers might have given Fink and other *Judenrat* members ideas about turning these favorable circumstances to their advantage.

The last flurry of correspondence found in the ŻSS Radomyśl file points to a desperate attempt to establish a series of workshops in Radomyśl, on the model of Bochnia. Permission to set up a shop was granted by the German authorities of Mielec, but the town needed to secure the necessary capital and work order as soon as possible: "As Radomyśl Wielki is subject to the same *Landkommissar* [district commissioner] as Mielec, they [Fink and Chairman Leibowicz] are especially afraid of resettlement, and are therefore requesting speeding up the order to activate the workshop," reported a delegate from Krakow of a meeting held on Thursday, July 16, 1942.⁴⁶ The plans were cut short three days after the meeting, when the SS carried out its planned *Aktion*.

The Mielec Jewish Elite: German Contacts and the Gray Zone of Protekcja (Privilege)

In the twenty-five months of its existence,⁴⁷ the Mielec *Judenrat*, like all Jewish Councils, had established a series of relationships with surrounding institutions and individuals. For example, the sons of *Judenrat* member Icchak Freiberg—Elimelech and Leo—found work as carpenters with the *Landrat* and private German firms that moved into the area.⁴⁸ Others had established contacts with members of the Gestapo. Many of these contacts would play a role on the eve of the *Aussiedlungsaktion*. However, it was the *Judenrat*'s regular contacts with the *Landkommissar* Alfred Beckert that would prove to be of greatest consequence.⁴⁹

It is not clear whether Fink was forced out of office for refusal to cooperate or requested to step down, but it was Beckert who was instrumental in informing Fink of the true nature of German developments in early March. Thus, on Saturday, March 7, Fink was given permission to leave with his wife, Netti; seventeen-year-old son, Lucjan; and daughter, Alina. Fink also notified his lawyer colleague Mark Verstandig, and the group then relocated to Połaniec (*Kreis*

Radom) to sit out the foreboding developments. It would appear then that only those with contacts among the *Judenrat* or acquaintances in the German administration were privy to the news of an impending resettlement and had an opportunity to try to evade it. The general public was largely left in the dark. As one Mielec Jew observed, "Chairman Fink left town, taking with him his wife and children. He was the only one to get a permit to leave town, because at this time no one was permitted to leave ... The town was left without its shepherd, and we knew then that our fate was sealed."[50]

Fink's absence meant the promotion of two lower-ranking *Judenrat* members: Izak Kapłan to the position of chairman and Reuven Kurz to vice chairman.[51] The second *Judenrat* leadership proved crucial in mobilizing the community to submit a contribution of half a million złoty and other gifts to the Gestapo in exchange for an assurance to forego or stall the resettlement.[52] The false sense of relief of having averted danger persuaded Jews who had previously considered leaving to remain. Those who had left town a day or two prior—like Lieba Berger, her husband, and their two children—returned to Mielec after the new *Judenrat* informed the community that there would be no resettlement.[53]

Thus, all of these contacts were now mobilized. Prior to dispatching Fink, Beckert himself had thrust a bundle of signed, blank travel permits into Fink's briefcase, instructing him "to save anyone he could."[54] Likewise, a certain Horowitz, a sixteen-to-seventeen-year-old refugee from Germany who often did business in the *Landrat*, received a bundle of blank travel permits from Beckert and was told to distribute them to "any Jews trying to escape." Higher social status and knowledge of the German language likely paved the way in these relations. Relationships established with private German firms also came in handy. *Judenrat* member Icchak Freiberg and his family were hidden in the Mielec offices of Bäumer und Lösch, a road construction company, by its chauffeur during the *Aktion*.[55] His son Elimelech Freiberg, in turn, was warned of the resettlement by a friend with ties to the *Landrat* and went into hiding with nearby farmers for three days.[56] Esther Bernstein (née Kurz), tipped off by her brother Reuven Kurz on the *Judenrat*, hid along with her family in the home of their Polish neighbors by the name of Łojczyk. Then, disguised in peasant attire with the help of their Polish servant, they moved to Radomyśl.[57]

The second Mielec *Judenrat* leaders, Kapłan and Kurz, were also rewarded by the Gestapo for their role in helping to secure a contribution from the community by being spared from the resettlement and allowed to move to Radomyśl Wielki. Their subsequent position on the second leadership of the Radomyśl *Judenrat* was announced on the pages of *Gazeta Żydowska*.[58] According to one account, Izak Kapłan was personally escorted with his wife and children from the airplane hangars to Radomyśl Wielki by Gestapo member Rudolf

Figure 7.4. Reuven Kurz, a merchant by trade, member of the Mielec *Judenrat*, then active on the Radomyśl Wielki and Dębica *Judenräte*. Photo taken before the war, courtesy of Cila Drucker.

Zimmermann.[59] The decision to spare Kapłan from the deportation and send him to another shtetl was made by Beckert and the head of the Mielec Gestapo, Hellmut Hensel.[60]

Thus, influence and ties to members of the German administration allowed some members of the Mielec *Judenrat* and their families to avoid deportation. These links would continue to play a role in the evolution of subsequent strategies. Kapłan and Kurz and their families likely benefited from a form of *protekcja*, or privilege, during the subsequent Radomyśl *Aktion* and once again found themselves in leading positions on the Dębica *Judenrat*. In June, the Fink family returned to the county, where, again with Beckert's influence, Dr. Fink was permitted to serve as a delegate of the ŻSS in Radomyśl, as discussed earlier.[61] Fink himself subsequently moved around various ghettos with his family, until he was murdered during the *Aktion* of the Bochnia ghetto in the fall of 1942.[62] Only one member of the Mielec *Judenrat*, Icchak Freiberg, is known to have survived the occupation. However, the significance of their actions lay in the fact that in almost all instances, they bought time and set in motion relationships that helped other family members and acquaintances survive the occupation.[63]

Escape to Congress Poland

The majority of Jews who evaded the Mielec *Aktion* found refuge in Połaniec on the left bank of the Vistula River (Radom District). This study was able to identify forty-six Mielec Jews who fled to Połaniec—twenty-four escaped directly from the Mielec region, while twenty-two returned from the Lublin District after deportation (though not all survived). However, the actual number was likely higher, as the population was large enough for some Połaniec Jews to regard Mielec Jewry as the source of their woes.[64] The situation brought to mind historic echoes of Połaniec as "Congress Poland" and the Lublin District as the czarist "Pale of Settlement."[65] Like Radomyśl, Połaniec was a sleepy shtetl removed from major roads and railway lines. The Połaniec ghetto would not face an *Aktion* until mid-October 1942, giving Mielec Jews a window of some seven months of refuge. Many came into contact with the former *Judenrat* chairman Dr. Fink in the town. The Mielec Jews in Połaniec who had evaded the *Aktion* brought back as many family members as possible from among those deported to the Lublin District. This strategy required the help of a willing Pole to act as an intermediary. For example, Czesław Kubik attempted to bring his Mielec gymnasium professor, Dr. Joel Czortkower, from Włodawa, but he arrived to find him too devastated to return following the murder of his wife. However, three women overheard his conversation and insisted that he take them and their children instead, which he did.⁶⁶ Others were brought directly back to *Kreis* Debica. For example, once in Radomyśl, Reuven Kurz managed to bring back members of his family, including Irene Eber (née Geminder), by paying a Polish woman to make five trips to the Lublin District.⁶⁷

Połaniec thus allowed the Mielec refugees to regroup as families, procure Aryan papers, and make plans for subsequent strategies as the short-lived respite inevitably began to worsen.

OPERATION REINHARD: LIQUIDATION ACTIONS

After all of the above changes, on the eve of Operation Reinhard, the Jewish population of *Kreis* Debica can be estimated at roughly 14,000–15,000. From this figure, the occupation authorities violently expelled 12,000–13,000 Jews from the county in June–July 1942, and others in September–November (see table 2).⁶⁸ The county authorities coordinated the population removal in two stages. First, beginning in late June to mid-July, they drove out Jews from surrounding villages to nearby towns such as Borowa, Przecław, and Wielopole Skrzyńskie. It is at this stage that the Germans began to establish short-lived ghettos in the region. Second, from July 19 to 25, they channeled the Jewish populations of these towns to the Dębica ghetto, where the victims were kept under an open sky, before being placed in cattle cars destined to the Bełżec death camp.

The first tremor of these operations could be felt in the southern part of the county. On June 19, the Jews of Pilzno were informed that they had until July 4 to move into a "closed quarter" of the town.⁶⁹ By July 15, German police forces had driven out 400 Jews from surrounding villages to Pilzno, bringing its population up to approximately 1,500.⁷⁰ Elsewhere, on June 26, the police expelled the Jews of Wielopole Skrzyńskie. The Germans resettled its population of approximately 925 Jews by ordering local farmers to transport them to the Ropczyce ghetto on horse-drawn carts, shooting some 50–56 of the elderly at the Jewish cemetery.⁷¹ According to one account, prior to their departure from Wielopole, a rabbi delivered a speech calling on the faithful "to obey their fate, not resist, because it is an indulgence and a punishment" for the alleged crimes of their ancestors against Jesus Christ.⁷²

On June 30, German authorities established a short-lived ghetto in Baranów Sandomierski. Around mid-July, Radomyśl Wielki began absorbing village Jews from surrounding areas. Subsequent to their dispossession a year before, the Jews who had gathered around the commune of Borowa, perhaps a few hundred, were rounded up by gendarmes and Polish policemen on July 15, 1942.⁷³ They were made to kneel for three hours in the rain, followed by a selection, after which gendarmes executed the sick and the elderly. Many others were shot

Figure 7.5. Painting depicting the murder of approximately 42 elderly Jews of Wielopole Skrzyńskie on June 30, 1942, on the grounds of the Jewish cemetery following a "selection." The artist, Roman Lipa, based the painting on an eyewitness account given by his neighbor and village head of Wielopole, Józef Długosz, depicted to the left of the gendarme. Note the presence of a patrolling Polish Blue policeman. The Hebrew words at the bottom are taken from Psalm 123:3: "Have pity on us because we have suffered more than our share of contempt." Courtesy of Steven Teitelbaum.

during the thirty-kilometer march to Radomyśl Wielki.[74] Similarly, the Jews of Przecław were resettled to Radomyśl Wielki on July 17.[75]

The second stage of resettlements occurred on July 19–25, from the earlier mentioned ghettos to Sędziszów and Dębica. On July 19, some 600 Jews from Rozwadów were rounded up to be taken to Baranów Sandomierski.[76] They were surrounded by the Polish Police and gendarmerie, while a selection took place at a cemetery, where policemen shot between 9 and 20 elderly people.[77] That same day, the Jews of the Tarnobrzeg ghetto, numbering 295 in the fall of 1941, were marched to Baranów. The next day, the German police carried out an *Aktion* in the Baranów ghetto, in the process killing 50–70 Jews deemed "unfit" at the cemetery and dispatching in cattle cars the remaining inhabitants to the Dębica ghetto.[78] Mid-July also saw the creation of a ghetto in Radomyśl Wielki, followed by an *Aktion* on July 19 aimed at a population that numbered 2,456 as of June 1942.[79] There, following a selection, policemen led approximately 400–500 Jews to the Jewish cemetery, the site of their execution and burial; 250 young Jewish men were selected for labor in Pustków; some 250 managed to escape prior to the *Aktion*; and the remaining 1,500 were driven on carts and marched off to the Dębica ghetto.[80]

The next few days saw to the clearing of the Pilzno, Ropczyce, and Sędziszów ghettos in the southern part of *Kreis* Debica. On July 24 the German police liquidated the ghetto of Ropczyce—which numbered 1,338 Jews in May 1942, plus the roughly 900 resettled from Wielopole in June—and transferred its population to Sędziszów, with at least 28 reported killed in the course of the *Aktion*.[81] On the same day, the occupation authorities cleared the Sędziszów ghetto. Its population totaled approximately 1,289 Jews as of June 1942.[82] Thus, together with the Jews of Ropczyce and Wielopole, the number of Jews would have risen to about 3,500.[83] On the day of the *Aktion*, German police forces shot at least 300 elderly Jews and children in the Jewish cemetery,[84] suggesting that the remaining population taken to the Dębica ghetto may have been as high as 2,600.[85] Likewise, the roughly 1,500–1,700 Jews in the Pilzno ghetto were marched to the Dębica ghetto, and at least 17 elderly were murdered on the basis of a list drawn by the *Judenrat* on German orders.[86]

The major deportations from Baranów, Radomyśl, Sędziszów, and Pilzno outlined above were synchronized with the ongoing expulsion of Jews from the Dębica ghetto, which took place from July 21 to 25. The Dębica Gestapo set up a table in the vicinity of Księża Łąka (Priest's Meadow; today, Ogródek Jordanowski) located inside the ghetto, where they carried out selections. By some estimates, German policemen brought between 180 and 600 Jews by truck to a nearby forest near Łysa Góra (Bald Mountain), where they murdered them; several hundred were selected for forced labor in Pustków, Rzeszów (the Messerschmidt factory), and *Flugzeugwerk Mielec* (Heinkel airplane factory).[87] From Dębica, the victims were crammed into cattle cars and delivered to Bełżec in two transports.

After this peak of deadly expulsions, 1,700 Jews are reported to have remained in the Dębica ghetto.[88] The Germans sent a transport of over 2,000 Jews from the Pustków labor camp to Bełżec on September 16, leaving 216 Jewish craftsmen in the camp.[89] On September 1, the *Kreishauptmann* created a new fenced "Jewish district" to formalize the transformation of the Dębica ghetto into an *Arbeitslager* (labor camp) for nearby German firms, such as Offenbeck and Schulz, which began working with a restructured *Judenrat* and a newly established ŻUS (*Żydowski Urząd Samopomocy*, Jewish Assistance Office, in place of the ŻSS), officially employing 600 laborers.[90] A ŻSS report for the month of September reported that a total of 3,461 Jews had been employed in labor camps throughout *Kreis* Debica.[91] The Dębica Gestapo coordinated the last transport of 600–1,000 Jews from Dębica to Bełżec during the second *Aktion* in

Table 7.2 Operation Reinhard liquidation actions in *Kreis* Debica

Location	Prewar population	Date of *Aktion* in 1942	Population prior to *Aktion*
Mielec	4,000	March	5,200
Internal resettlement from small towns and villages to nearby ghettos			
Villages near Pilzno	—	June 19	400–600
Wielopole	532	June 26	925
Borowa	—	July 17	—
Przecław	—	July 17	—
Resettlement from ghettos to town of Dębica: northern part of county			
Rozwadów	3,000	July 19	500
Tarnobrzeg	2,259	July 19	320
Radomyśl	1,300	July 19	2,456
Baranów	680	July 20	1,545
Resettlement from ghettos to town of Dębica: southern part of county			
Ropczyce	1,200	July 23	1,307 + [875 from Wielopole] = 2,182
Sędziszów	1,060	July 24	1,289 + [1,279 from Ropczyce] + [875 from Wielopole] = 3,443
Pilzno	788	July	1,500
Deportations outside of county			
Dębica	2,900	July 21–25	2,000
		Nov. 15	600–1,000
Pustków (camp)	—	Sept. 16	[2,000]
TOTAL	~17,719	—	~18,000

Source: Author's reconstruction on the basis of collected documentation.
Notes:
* The number of Jews deported to the Dębica ghetto in accordance with the population of a given month, minus those murdered during the *Aktion*, as noted in the text.
† The brackets indicate that the population was temporarily deported to the Dębica ghetto, with a final destination of Bełżec.

Selected for labor	Selected for shooting	Percentage	Deported outside of county	Direction
616–636	294	6	4,000	Hangars in Chorzelów; Kreis Lublin
—	—	—		Pilzno ghetto
—	50-56	5–6	[875]*	Ropczyce ghetto
—	—	—		Radomyśl ghetto
—	—	—		Radomyśl ghetto
—	9-12	1.8–2.4	[491]	[Dębica ghetto]†
100	—	—	[220]	Baranów ghetto (in wagons); [Dębica ghetto]
250	400–500	16–20	[1,556]	[Dębica ghetto]
—	20–70	1.3–4.5	[1,525]	[Dębica ghetto]
—	28	1.3	[1,279]	Sędziszów ghetto (1 day)
—	380	11	[909]	[Dębica ghetto]
—	17	1	[1,483]	[Dębica ghetto]
400	240–630	12–31.5%	[1,360]	Bełżec
—	—	—	[600]	Bełżec
—	—	—	[2,000]	Bełżec
~1,400	~1,500–2,200	—	~12,600	

Figures 7.6 and 7.7. Photographs taken by employees of a propaganda department of the *Institut für Deutsche Ostarbeit* (IDO) in Krakow immediately after the Wielopole Skrzyńskie *Aktion*, one of four photographs taken of the village at the time. The description for both reads: "The auctioning of formerly Jewish furniture in Wielopole. *Fot. Propagandamt*, Krakow 1942." Seweryn Udziela, Ethnographic Museum of Kraków, III/40380/F.

November 15.[92] The Germans carried out the final *Aktion* of the Dębica *Arbeitslager* on April 15, 1943.[93]

How Many Escaped? How Many Survived? How Many Died?

The attempt to determine the number of Jews who attempted to escape ghettos or "Jewish residential districts" prior to the "resettlement actions" is fraught with difficulty. The sources often do not provide sufficient information to determine from which ghetto a Jew escaped. In other cases, it is not clear if an individual survived in a camp or by fleeing an *Aktion*. For example, in the case of the Baranów ghetto, whose population was being siphoned off to labor camps in *Truppenübungsplatz Süd*, there are simply too few sources to allow such a reconstruction. In most cases, police searches that immediately followed the *Aktionen* were carried out with such force and speed that only an estimated body count may be produced at best. This is especially the case in the southern part of *Kreis* Debica in the areas around Dębica, Ropczyce, Sędziszów, and Pilzno. Crucial details are now beyond the reach of historians.

Further, the specificity of *Kreis* Debica raises the difficulty with its cohort of as many as two thousand village Jews, who were removed from their homes in the summer of 1941 but were not resettled to a specific location until a year later. It is likely that many of these Jews simply never entered ghettos or left shortly after entering them, which was made easier by the fact that most ghettos in the area were open. For example, Regina Ladner and her family were resettled from the village of Gliny Wielkie in 1941, rounded up in Borowa a year later, and taken to the Radomyśl Wielki ghetto, from which they left the following day and survived the war by moving from village to village.[94]

A few weeks after the end of the war, the Temporary Jewish Committee of Dębica filed a report, in which it was estimated that "approximately 500 people [hid] in bunkers, forests, and on Aryan papers."[95] In some cases, survivors themselves provided estimates of Jews who fled ghettos, as in the case of Chaja Rosenblatt, who wrote that some 250 Jews escaped the Radomyśl Wielki ghetto. In the case of the Pilzno ghetto, Stefan Janusz (aka Dymin), a member of the AK (*Armia Krajowa*, Home Army), made an effort after the war to gather information from Polish witnesses and Jewish survivors. In a testimony deposited at the Jewish Historical Institute, he stated that 65 Jews escaped after the Germans ordered the creation of a ghetto in late June, while 39 escaped the subsequent "resettlement" to Dębica in July.[96] Such numbers provided by witnesses are often inflated, but even impressionistic figures are able to suggest the scale of escape in a particular location.

Table 7.3 Zones of survival

Village	Forest	Town	Unknown (not in camps)	Total
177 (57%)	95 (30%)	27 (9%)	13 (4%)	312 (100%)

Source: Author's reconstruction on the basis of collected documentation.

How many survived? This study has analyzed the fate of a total of 1,257 Jews known to have evaded deportation. Of this number, 312 (25 percent), who managed to survive in the county by hiding, were able to be identified (see table 3), and 945 others (75 percent) lost their lives in the struggle (see table 4). The fragmentary nature of the sources has not allowed recovering the full identity of all victims. In addition, 52 Jews are known to have left the county to hide in another part of the GG, and eight others (mostly women) are known to have opted for work as Polish forced laborers in the Reich, where they lived to see liberation. Further, this study established a minimum threshold of 200 Jews who survived in the labor camps of Dębica County (and subsequent deportations and death marches), though the number is likely significantly higher.

This study has also tabulated the prevalence of German acts of violence toward Poles for the shelter of Jews, as well as individuals awarded by Yad Vashem with the official title of Righteous Among the Nations, that is, non-Jews who risked their lives to save Jews during the Holocaust. In terms of the former, the Germans killed a total of 26 Poles, with 25 Jews murdered alongside their helpers. In terms of the latter, Yad Vashem conferred the honorific of Righteous Among the Nations to a total of 103 individuals, who were active in aiding 118 Jews on the territory of the county.[97]

THE VILLAGE

Village Society and the Judenjagd

In the zone of the village, survival strategies were largely determined by the dynamics surrounding Polish rural society. German authorities had placed great emphasis on capturing Jews who managed to escape the "resettlement actions." Polish historians have labeled this stage the third phase of the Holocaust on Polish lands, characterized primarily by the *Judenjagd* (hunt for Jews).[98] In order to facilitate this process, German authorities instituted a system of village security and surveillance by building on prewar structures such as *samoobrona wiejska* (village self-defense), sometimes referred to as the *Ortschutzwache* in German

Table 7.4 Perpetrators and circumstances of death among fugitive Jews

Perpetrator	Circumstances	Killed	Totals	%
German police*	Own action	12		1%
	Denounced by locals	48	218	5%
	NA	158		17%
German police and Polish police	Own action	9		1%
	Denounced by locals	38	80	4%
	NA	33		3%
Polish police	Own action	9		1%
	Denounced by locals	72	145	8%
	NA	64		7%
Unidentified police forces	—	249		26%
Mixed police and (often) military forces conducting forest manhunts	—	180	429	19%
Polish underground (AK)	—	4		0.4%
Local civilians	—	22		2%
Bandits	—	18	73	2%
Soviet front fighting	—	16		2%
Other (disease, suicide, natural causes, etc.)	—	13		1%
TOTAL		**945**		**100%**

Source: Author's reconstruction on the basis of collected documentation.
* Includes Gestapo, gendarmerie, *Sonderdienst*, *Werkschutz*, *Dorfwache*, and German soldiers on territory of *Truppenübungsplatz Süd* and SS *Truppenübungsplatz Heidelager*.

during the war, whose guard members were often drawn from the ranks of the local OSP (*Ochotnicza Straż Pożarna*, Voluntary Fire Department) and an additional system of *zakładniks* (hostages) and *dziesiętniks* (section leaders), who were responsible for maintaining surveillance over sections of a village on pain of death. In effect, the *Ortschutzwache* became a kind of village militia. The occupation authorities increasingly tightened the screws of this system and broadened its scope with each year of the war. Village heads formed its backbone, and the village guards, hostages, messengers, foresters, gamekeepers, and the like functioned as its nerve endings. The restructuring of village authority and accountability had an impact on the architecture of choices and played an important role in reshaping the social relations of peasant society. This village

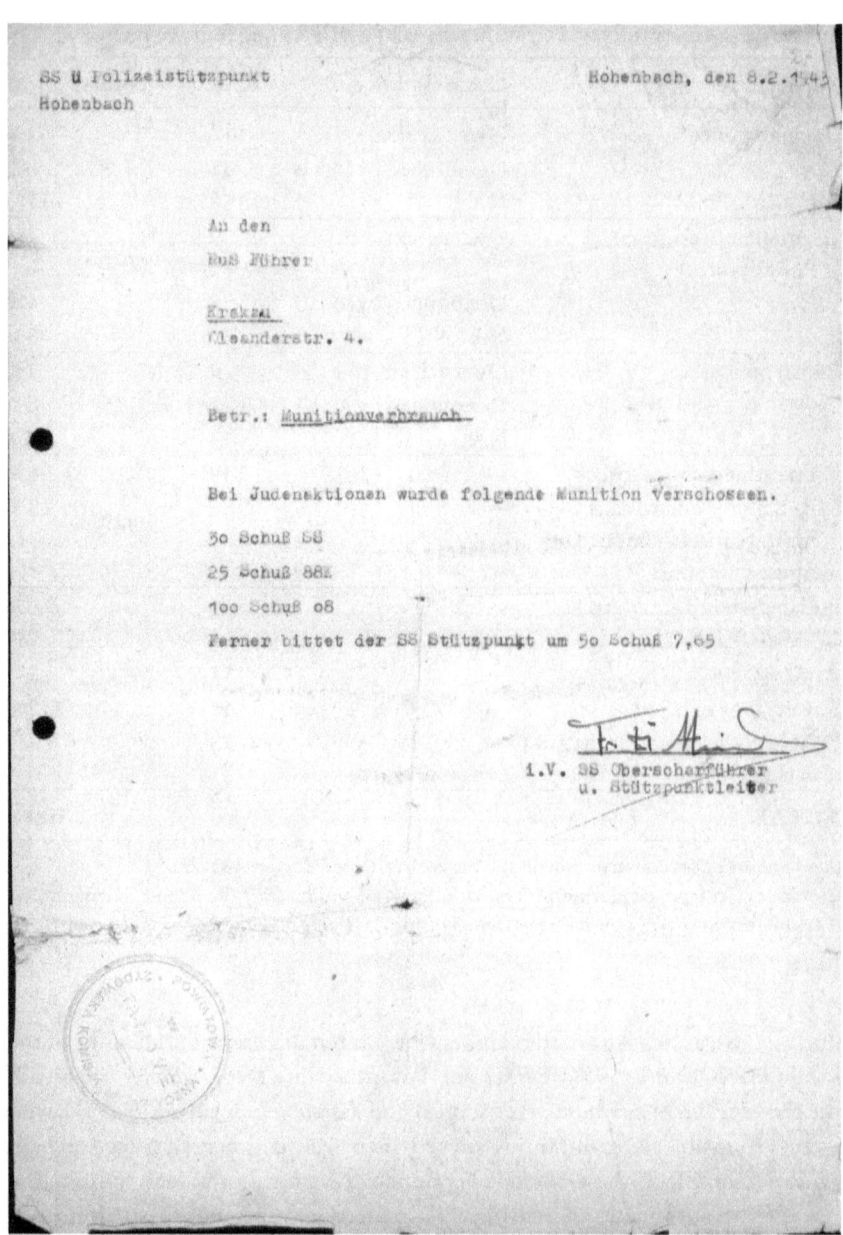

Figure 7.8. Request submitted on February 8, 1943, by the head of the SS *Stützpunkt* (stronghold) in the village of Hohenbach (Czermin) to replenish rounds of ammunition used in recent "Jewish actions." Hohenbach represented the leading *Volksdeutsche* village, which served as a killing site for fugitive Jews captured in the region (AŻIH 279/3).

security system, combined with the threat of collective responsibility, set the stage for a combustible social atmosphere. The aftershock of German state terror against locals for the shelter of Jews, as evidenced by the "pacification" of the village of Podborze in the *Kreis*, could set off a chain reaction of pre-emptive violence against Jews in hiding.[99]

One should not lose sight of the broader context of the occupation, however. While the *Judenjagd* formed a distinct German policy aimed at fugitive Jews, it was accompanied in practice by parallel manhunts for Soviet POWs, Polish laborers, partisans, and others targeted by the authorities. In fact, to take one of these cohorts, the Jewish population of *Kreis* Debica was roughly equal to the seventeen thousand Soviet POWs held in the camps of the county (primarily in Pustków, Majdan Królewski, and Poręby Wojsławskie[100]), whose inmates often escaped and likewise fell prey to the village security apparatus. The importance of these structures and manhunts to Jewish survival strategies is that they played a role in conditioning local attitudes in anticipatory obedience toward fugitives and outsiders more generally. Jewish survival strategies were therefore part of an entangled web of victim groups targeted in different ways. Even if peasant society was negatively predisposed toward Jews on the whole, the participation of peasants in the *Judenjagd* was not as selective as might otherwise seem without taking into account these other targeted groups. Further, local attitudes were shaped by a broader assault on the countryside in the form of various provocation operations and informers, primarily aimed at the resistance movement but also known to target fugitive Jews and to test civilian obedience to German law.[101]

Finally, the *Judenjagd* was all the more effective because the fugitive population seeking shelter in the countryside, with some rare exceptions, was largely left outside of the institutional help of the Polish underground and organizations such as Żegota (the Polish Council to Aid Jews). Established in December 1942, with regional branches set up months later, Żegota was largely an urban phenomenon, one that barely made its presence felt in the Subcarpathian region—and where it did, it was confined to Lwów and Przemyśl and was primarily focused on providing aid to Jews in labor camps.[102] Jewish survival strategies in villages thus took shape in a deeply compromised social landscape, and forms of help offered to Jews were largely bottom-up and individual in nature.

The Fragility of Human Relations in Times of Crisis

The conditions of the village security system set the basic constraints on Jewish survival strategies. These constraints sharpened relative to the growing number of escapes, which peaked on the eve and in the course of the ghetto clearing

Table 7.5 Locations and modes of survival

Village, primarily in one location	Village, in several locations	Wandering between villages	Total number of survivors in villages
84 (47%)	16 (9%)	77 (44%)	177 ([100%])

Source: Author's reconstruction on the basis of collected documentation.

operations. As Leopold Trejbicz noted after the first *Aktion* in Dębica, "The only subject of conversation and the driving force of the remaining handful of Jews was how to save oneself, get out of the ghetto, and escape destruction."[103] Jews who had acquaintances in villages therefore began mobilizing efforts to contact them. In a striking example, so many Jews would be absorbed into the village of Chrząstów near Mielec (numbering some six hundred inhabitants) that for the next two years it would acquire a nickname of the "Jewish ghetto" among Jews.[104]

Indeed, the lion's share of refugees fled into the countryside. According to this study, a total of 312 Jews survived in *Kreis* Debica: 177 (57%) primarily in the vicinity of villages, 95 (30%) in forest bunkers, and 27 (9%) in towns. In terms of the remaining 13 (4%), the documents do not reveal the specific circumstances of shelter, though they did not survive in camps (see table 5).

The degree of one's "Jewish looks" determined whether one could live on the "surface" in the countryside, which would either require the possession of Aryan papers under a false name or concealment from the gaze of the village. In the case of the former, if one had sufficient Aryan looks to pass for a Pole, a cover story was usually concocted: a distant cousin from the city, a widow of a Polish officer killing during the war, and the like. In the second case, "Semitic" features dictated staying indoors during the day and only coming out at night. For many shtetl Jews, the inability to speak Polish without a recognizable "Jewish" accent was likely a deal breaker in this regard.

The small sample of survivors in villages supports the intuition that in these circumstances, a crucial linchpin of survival strategies was the existence of prewar acquaintances, who often served as a link between the shtetl and the village. Yet finding the right acquaintance was key: "When selecting a person to trust and a home to take shelter in, there was no room for error," observed Markus Rohtbart.[105] A poor contact without any investment in the Jews he or she was sheltering was unlikely to ensure long-term survival. In the words of one observer, "People shelter Jews, but when they can no longer do this, instead of

Figure 7.9. Icchak Mechlowicz, a teenager from the village of Przyłęk, incorporated into *Truppenübungsplatz Süd*. Almost the entire Mechlowicz family survived the occupation through a combination of hiding with Poles and working in the camps established on the grounds of the army base. Photo taken shortly after liberation, courtesy of Danielle Wyzgoski.

making things easier for them and helping them to relocate to a different region, they denounce them."[106] However, the other side of the coin in Polish-Jewish relations in rural areas was that close personal contacts were often in short supply. The arc of a long historical process left Jews and Poles, especially peasants, worlds apart. Shtetl Jews in Western Galicia had historically played the role of a classic middle-man minority,[107] which continued to characterize social relations into the early twentieth century. Many shtetl Jews thus found themselves turning to Poles they knew primarily from business dealings: Sometimes these were neighbors, less frequently friends; in most cases, they appear in the sources as *znajomi* (acquaintances). Those who did not have such acquaintances in the countryside—in concrete terms, three thousand Jews resettled from the Reich and other parts of the GG—or who did not establish such contacts previously were forced to turn to strangers for help.

If survival in the countryside largely hinged on non-Jewish acquaintances, village Jews found themselves at an advantage. "Friendship with the Polish citizenry benefited us greatly during this time of great mistrust," noted Markus

Rohtbart. Yet the weakness of individual helpers, even if they were reliable prewar acquaintances, was the unpredictable human element. In a "time of great mistrust," all that is solid in human relations can melt into thin air. Rohtbart reflected on a poor Polish man, Polek, who had consistently received help from Rohtbart's father before the war. During the war, he ran into Polek. "It never occurred to me that I should hide from this man. I believed him to be one of our trustworthy friends. He repaid my family's kindness by turning me in to the mayor of Konty, a village nearby. The war had turned this man into a maniac."[108] Likewise, the teenager Icchak Mechlowicz and his mother, Hannah, often took shelter on the grounds of *Truppenübungsplatz Süd* with prewar Polish acquaintances, Franek and Karolina (Carol) Zielińska. "They never refused us and allowed us to sleep on their hayloft and provided us with food," he wrote.[109] But after a brush with a German patrol searching for Jews, "Carol came into the house, shaking all over. 'For Christ's sake,' she said, 'when are you Jews going to leave us alone?' I completely sympathized with her and told her that I would not try to put her in such jeopardy again," wrote Mechlowicz.[110]

The Perseverance of Social Networks under Occupation

Rohtbart and Mechlowicz were village Jews with many prewar contacts and were able to move around the area in accordance with the changing circumstances. Scholarship on the rescue of Jews by Poles has placed emphasis on the distinction between institutional (organized) help versus individual help and has increasingly shown that the latter was more prevalent.[111] However, less attention has been paid to the various social networks in a time of occupation and genocide,[112] particularly low-level networks, which could grow out of a trusted acquaintance. These were not top-down institutional initiatives coordinated by institutions like Żegota or the underground movement, nor did they arise from lone individuals facing a hostile society—in a number of cases, the individuals involved in helping were respectable members of a community. The cases examined here suggest that networks of helpers constituted an effective survival strategy and show that individual help was not without its own complex structure.

The strength of network-based strategies was their ability to span regions, in which a specific region of shelter represented a single node. Unsurprisingly, a network brought Jews into a county or outside of it. A characteristic of a network was the presence of an *opiekun* (guardian or protector) or family unit coordinating the effort. In a case of a cross-county network, Elżbieta Reibscheid approached her acquaintance Kazimierz Zaczek about helping her escape the Dębica ghetto with her family prior to the first *Aktion*. With the help of a German acquaintance, on the day of the *Aktion*, Zaczek successfully transported

Reibscheid, her mother, and her sister to Kraków (at one point he posed as a German soldier), where he set her up with his acquaintances.[113]

The case of a young Polish couple, Dr. Aleksander and Leokadia Mikołajków, serves as an example of one of the most developed and effective networks in *Kreis* Debica. As a medical doctor, Aleksander headed Dębica's only *kasa chorych* (healthcare fund, or the health insurance system of interwar Poland), with his wife serving as the hygienist. After the establishment of the Dębica ghetto, Aleksander hired thirteen-year-old Ephraim Reich, whose family he knew before the war as members of the healthcare fund, to serve as a messenger between his medical practice and the ghetto.[114] When news spread about the impending *Aktion* in July 1942, Dr. Mikołajków told the boy that he "intended to save his [Reich's] entire family."[115] Indeed, Ephraim managed to pull almost his entire family out of the ghetto (thirteen Jews altogether), who were then sheltered between the Mikołajków' attic, basement, and garage, which neighbored the Gestapo headquarters, for a period of nine months. After the Gestapo seized the garage in the summer of 1943, the Reich family was moved to the property of Józef Kurzyna, where the Mikołajków continued to support them until the arrival of the Red Army.

The help given to the Reich family represented one branch of the network the married couple helped to coordinate. Because both were members of the Polish underground, they could count on support from its local structures, among others a certain Dwornik (aka Ćwik), who was employed in the office of the *Kreishauptmann* and supplied them with *Kennarte* (identification cards) for Jews in hiding. The Dębica branch of the Central Welfare Council (*Rada Główna Opiekuńcza*, RGO), the Polish charity organization, also supported their efforts with food supplies. Further, the couple organized the escape of two brothers, Henryk and Andrzej Wilner, from the Dębica ghetto to Warsaw, where Leokadia's sister brought them into contact with the Polish underground and where both later participated in the Warsaw Uprising.[116] The Mikołajków also helped Dr. Schuldenfrei and family (eleven people in total) to move eighty kilometers away in the Bochnia ghetto, from where they tried to make their way to Hungary, while Leokadia's mother brought Dr. Schuldenfrei's daughter across one hundred kilometers to Opatowa. According to her own account, a total of thirty-two Jews were rescued as a result of this coordinated web of selfless efforts.[117]

Money and Survival

More typically, however, a social network was held together with the help of material reward. A vivid example is the case of Psachje Hönig of Mielec, who by accident came into contact with a prewar business acquaintance, Władysław Dobrowolski, while in Połaniec and asked him to provide shelter for a total of seven family members and acquaintances. Dobrowolski, based in the village of Chrząstów, was a military instructor of the underground Peasant Battalions (*Bataliony Chłopskie*, BCh). Though he does not appear to have been motivated by financial reward and was already involved in helping other Jews, the amount of money invested by Hönig in the effort would allow the network to expand into the Radom District on the left bank of the Vistula River. Hönig's family members were distributed among Dobrowolski's acquaintances on the basis of regular monthly payments in the villages of Chrząstów, Chorzelów, Gawłuszowice, Złotniki, and the outskirts of Połaniec.[118] Hönig even paid five hundred zloty per month for an empty backup shelter. The network had steady volunteers who were willing to shelter Jews, but when Hönig's wife infected one such family with typhus and there were fears of a visit by a health commission, she was moved to another location, where she received medical attention. These moving parts of a network made for a successful survival strategy, though the quality of the help worsened the farther the sheltered were removed from the main "protector"; his wife, Miriam Hönig, and friend Rosenzweig were robbed, beaten, and starved in other locations.

The use of money in a survival strategy had many dimensions. Money as a medium of exchange for goods and services is always as complex as the socioeconomic context in which it operates, all the more so in the amoral economy that emerged under occupation. Mark Verstandig, whose own family was sheltered in a network of paid helpers coordinated by his prewar acquaintance Marcin Walas, a member of the AK in the village of Chrząstów, reflected on his paid helpers, the Walcerz family: "They were a typically pious Catholic family, honorable people with no sympathy for Jews. They allowed us to stay because we paid well and they did not think there was any danger." But he did not regard the condition of material reward as grounds for moral condemnation. "I am not criticizing the Walcerzs—on the contrary, if a greater part of the Polish people had acted in the spirit of this deeply religious family, tens, perhaps hundreds of thousands more Jews could have survived."[119]

A division can be observed between the haves and the have-nots, even among Jews in hiding. Well-to-do businessmen like Hönig could sustain a family and acquaintances across a network of helpers. Most village Jews, however, had little to give, especially once dispossessed in the summer of 1941. Thus, in many cases there were promises to sign over property after the war, as in the case of Regina Ladner from the village of Gliny Wielkie, who motivated a certain Dubiel in this way to find shelter and work for her daughters, Rachela and Szeindla, in the region.[120] Very often, such gestures served as ways of sweetening a deal that

Figure 7.10. Ela Knie after having come out of hiding in the forest ("las") in 1945 (USC, VHA, 12325, interview with Ela Knie-Adlersberg).

was otherwise characterized by daily terror. Jews who did not possess money frequently turned to those gentiles to whom they had previously passed on their belongings, but returning for these always carried with it the risk of denunciation. Others offered help to the farmers sheltering them, typically tailoring services. The proverb of necessity as the mother of invention was something like a conditio sine qua non of Jewish survival during the third phase of the Holocaust. The difficult conditions often generated creative solutions. For example, in the course of hiding in villages and forests, Ela Knie and her husband, David Thaler, learned to produce goods such as soap and moonshine. They peddled these products in the vicinity of their home village of Nagoszyn. Their strategy became so successful that they even began selling their items to farmers on credit.[121] The small profit from these ventures, in turn, allowed them to support other family members sheltered in underground bunkers by local peasants.[122]

Nevertheless, survival strategies based on payment were a double-edged sword: For Jewish "strangers" without acquaintances in the region, money often compelled farmers to open their doors and motivated them to risk their lives, but it also served as a potential basis for robbery, denunciation, and murder—not infrequently by the same people. In addition, the economy of rescue was shaped by a competing system of material reward offered by the Germans for denouncing Jews, such as money, sugar, alcohol, or even the clothes stripped from the murdered. Thus, once allowed to enter the home of a poor peasant woman in Dulcza Mała, Chaja Rosenblatt was haunted by the prospect of a German counteroffer: "The village woman could have turned us over to the Germans, [as] denunciations paid 500 zloty for every Jew."[123]

Money appears to have been most successful when combined with other favorable factors—such as prewar acquaintance or a more intimate connection with those offering shelter—and thus not the sole motive of a survival strategy. In some cases, a host continued to shelter Jews when "the money ran out," because a bond had developed between both parties. For example, Berl Sturm escaped from the Dębica ghetto with his daughter Hania and encountered seventeen-year-old Stefania Job in the village of Łęki Dolne, to whom he promised "compensation" in exchange for taking them in. "I paid her money for a few months," wrote Sturm. "When the money ran out, Stefania did not give up on continued help at all," he added.[124] In fact, Job's determination to save the family grew in subsequent months. More frequently, however, when funding was depleted, an agreement based solely on money was quickly dissolved and a host told the Jews to leave. In some cases, Jewish charges refused to leave. In other scenarios, their hosts refused to let them leave for fear of discovery. Such situations bred a tense atmosphere, which sometimes drove their hosts to take desperate measures.[125]

Conversions in a Time of War

Some Jews believed that conversion to Christianity would benefit their chances of survival. In the Dębica region, a Catholic priest in the village of Nagoszyn, Fr. Józef Fijał, converted five Jews on their own initiative sometime in 1942, two of whom survived.[126] In the village of Sokolniki in the Tarnobrzeg region, a certain Majer Gross and his daughter were brought to the commune hall by the Polish Police, where "Gross then asked for a baptism." The village head brought a priest, who "baptized them, but the next day in the morning [Albert] Alscher shot them."[127] Józef Hercyk (Herzog?) from Tarnów was hiding in the vicinity of Wadowice Dolne. He converted during the occupation and married Maria Stolarz, whom he had previously known.[128] The timing of these decisions suggests that they were made in the belief that as Christians, they would be met with a greater sympathy and desire to help from the Polish Christian community.

Though small in number, the question of converts points to the larger issue of the religious undercurrent of Polish-Jewish relations in the countryside. One is struck by the almost sectarian nature of religious identity in the Polish province, where a space for a secular identity not based in religion was all but nonexistent and religious barriers between Christians and Jews often proved insurmountable. Icchak Mechlowicz, who grew up on the outskirts of Mielec, recalled the marriage of a young Jewish woman to a Catholic Pole prior to the war, which led to the young woman's ostracism in the Jewish community.[129] Although the two families did not live far apart, the Jewish family refused any contact with the neophyte for the next thirty-five years. When the situation under occupation began to worsen, she "sent word to her parents and siblings and offered them a secure shelter from deportation and death, [but] she was not acknowledged and they chose death rather than reconciliation and shelter. 'They perished,' she told us with tears in her eyes."[130] The woman, who remains nameless, survived the war protected by her new family and community.

The fate of the silent cohort of Jewish converts in the shadow of the Holocaust suffers from a general scarcity of sources, as they largely disappear from Jewish accounts due to their ostracism and absorption into the Catholic community.[131] It is therefore impossible to formulate strong conclusions about this cohort; one may note only that prewar converts could count on a greater degree of help from their coreligionists and therefore had greater chances of survival, as well as suggest that more of such "Nuremberg Jews" may have survived without being registered in the historical record.

Jewish Resistance

What role did the Jewish resistance movement play in survival? In the region under investigation, the most active group was the Akiva movement. Aharon (Dolek) Liebeskind, the leader of the Akiva movement in the Krakow ghetto, traveled the region as a delegate of the ŻSS to train Jewish agricultural workers employed on Aryan manors.[132] In reality, however, after taking care of official business, Liebeskind often held clandestine meetings with Jewish youths (mostly affiliated with Akiva), emphasizing the need to create resistance cells.[133] A description of such a visit to Radomyśl Wielki, where he met with a group of youngsters on the outskirts of the town, has been preserved in the sources. Yehuda Laufbahn recalled Liebeskind's words addressed to the group: "We are entering a very difficult period for the Jewish people. Save yourselves, whoever is able. There is no other help than to take up arms, join the partisans, and go into the woods."[134] However, according to Pinchas Reichman, Liebeskind's effort was met with reluctance.[135] Calls for resistance in Radomyśl appear to have been undermined by a belief in labor as the only practical survival strategy, discussed previously. The specifically Hasidic legacy of the region might have also played a role in giving primacy to the spiritual dimension of Jewish survival.[136]

The largest underground formation in the Subcarpathian region to openly accept Jews into its ranks was the GL (*Gwardia Ludowa*, Communist People's Guard), later renamed the AL (*Armia Ludowa*, People's Army) on January 1, 1944. The GL was created by the Polish Workers' Party (*Polska Partia Robotnicza*, PPR) on January 6, 1942. The Rzeszów subregion (aka district Nafta in the terminology of the Communist underground) contained seven GL groups. The first of these—a group led by Lejb Birman—was formed in the fall of 1942 by Jews who had fled the Krakow ghetto, many of them also members of Akiva. Their area of operation was the Dębica region, and most of its new members were recruited from the Rzeszów ghetto, where the PPR had formed a cell. Birman's unit consisted of two groups of Jews who had escaped from the Rzeszów ghetto (the first numbered five people, the second seven). However, the GL units, deprived of support by the local population and poorly armed and trained (only Birman had military training), were easily destroyed by German forces. Birman's group was liquidated by mid-December 1942.[137] The Tarnów subregion practically ceased to exist by July 1943 as a result of a series of pacification actions carried out across the Dębica region, while by August the PPR-GL underground structures of the county were virtually wiped out.[138]

Although most Jewish members of the GL in Dębica County were Jews from the Rzeszów ghetto, the possibility exists that some Jews who escaped from the county's ghettos may have joined its ranks. Unfortunately, the scarcity of sources does not allow the determination of additional details. What remains is fragmentary. AK reports for the Tarnobrzeg region mention a member of the PPR, Mozes Hauser, who was hiding in the villages of Alfredówka, Cygany, and the hamlet of Hermanówka, while expressing the suspicion that he was a functionary of the NKVD.[139] A later counterintelligence report for the same region notes a Communist Party meeting in Kępie Zaleszańskie (Zbydniów commune), which pointed to the presence of two armed Jews (lawyers), a certain Ellenbogan from Zaleszany and Taller from Rozwadów, who allegedly "are switching to this region for agitation purposes."[140]

A small group of armed Jewish fugitives operated in the vicinity of Mokre and Zassów. The group numbered some five members, among them Isak Flam, his brother Bernard (Berek), Bernard's fiancée, and a certain Silberman. At some point, the group then entered the ranks of another unit led by a Russian, which included other Russians, two Jews, and partisans of Hungarian and Czech background.[141] Equally as vague, Jan Błachowicz (aka Kropidło), who played a leading role in the Peasants Battalions in the county, was in contact with a "Jewish resistance unit" in the vicinity of Łączki Brzeskie, though little is known about this unit.[142] However, Błachowicz likely exaggerated the activity of these Jewish partisans in Dębica County. Most likely he came into contact with a "unit" of Jewish fugitives from the Dulecki forest—the largest and only formation of this kind, addressed in a later section. The fragmentary nature of the sources does not permit a more detailed reconstruction of armed Jewish resistance in the county.

Jews and the Polish Underground

In theory, Polish citizens of Jewish background could join the ranks of the official Polish underground under the authority of the Polish government-in-exile in London. In practice, however, local structures often took a different stance.[143] The general reluctance to admit Jews into the Polish underground is confirmed in relation to Dębica County.[144] In 1942, a report from the Rzeszów subregion advised against accepting any national minorities into the ranks of the underground: "Only Poles. And among them only determined and dependable people ... No minority (German, Ukrainian, or Jewish) is allowed to join."[145] From the point of view of fugitive Jews in hiding during the third phase of the Holocaust, this was among the most disastrous decisions of the underground because it further isolated them and undermined their struggle for survival on the Aryan side.

Yet much depended on the leadership of local AK units, whose attitude toward Jews could vary.[146] In a number of cases, fugitive Jews in Dębica County met with support from members of the local underground. For example, in his memoir, Stefan Janusz (aka Dynim), the deputy commander of AK Pilzno, mentioned the existence of an "insurgent group against genocide" in the Jaworze forests, which emerged in 1942 in the aftermath of the Aktion in the Pilzno ghetto.[147] The first group, led by Leon Schneps (Aryan name Leon Gołęczyński), who escaped from the Pilzno ghetto, was comprised of ten fighters and was destroyed by a German expeditionary unit. The second group was made up of eight members, who died fighting against an expeditionary unit at the end of November 1943.[148] Although Janusz operated within the structures of the AK and was himself a witness to many incidents that he described, it is not clear whether the mentioned groups were subordinate to the local AK, although it is known that they received support from its members.[149]

A few months after the Mielec Aktion, Mark Verstandig was recruited by Władysław Jasiński (aka Jędruś), the leader of a local partisan group called Jędrusie, to translate German newspapers for their underground publication *Odwet* (Retaliation). After experiencing a brush with the Polish Police, he turned to the group with a request for membership in the AK, which would increase his chances of survival. After consulting with their superiors, they returned to Verstandig with the news that "the AK did not want Jews."[150] Nonetheless, Jasiński and his group had more independence from the official Polish

Figure 7.11. Lea Haar (née Ostro) with her daughter Lana on October 8, 1942, shortly before going into hiding. Together with three relatives, Lea was murdered by a local AK unit (AK Tuszów Narodowy) in May 1944. The photo was likely taken in the Połaniec ghetto. Lana survived the occupation in the care of a Polish family (USC, VHA, 29550, Interview with Mark Verstandig).

underground and overrode the decision, unofficially accepting Verstandig into their ranks and promising to find him work.

In the case of Verstandig, however, membership in the AK might have worsened his situation and that of his family. It was Verstandig, hiding together with his wife and four other Jews, who represents the only clearly documented case of Jews attacked by a unit of the AK, which resulted in the murder of most of this group in hiding. Verstandig and his family—six Jews in total after the death of his aunt Dwora Verstandig (Ostro) due to malnutrition—paid Szymon Korczak in Chrząstów for hiding them behind a false wall of his barn. On the night of May 30–31, 1944, a nine-member AK unit, led by Antoni Maksoń (aka Sokół), stopped by the home of Korczak, where they beat him and robbed him of 1,800 zloty. Despite Verstandig's proof of membership in the AK in the form of papers issued by Jasiński, they also robbed the Jews but left, only to return shortly after to escort them off the property. Realizing they were being marched toward their execution, Verstandig and his wife, Frieda (who was subsequently wounded), were able to get away, while the four others were shot and their bodies were left in the woods.

The postwar trial determined that the motivation behind the attack was robbery. The order was allegedly issued by the head of the sabotage group, Józef Łącz, but the initiative to kill the Jews was issued on the spot by the partisans themselves, particularly from Antoni Maksoń, after he realized that he had been recognized by Verstandig and decided to cover his trail by getting rid of the entire group. As the historian Elżbieta Rączy summed up, the partisans were primarily afraid of the reaction of the AK district command to the robbery.[151]

The attitude of the AK toward Jews in the region can be summarized as indifferent at best and hostile at worst, and it only turned its attention toward the situation of Jews in so far as it had a direct impact on ethnic Polish society. Any meaningful forms of help toward Jews generally sprang from individual initiatives of members of the underground.

THE FOREST

Twenty-Seven Months in the Dulecki Forest

It was only beyond the zone of the village, in the larger forests of *Kreis* Debica, that survival strategies were able to develop with fewer constraints. The most favorable circumstances were found in the Dulecki forest near the villages of Dulcza Wielka and Dulcza Mała in the commune of Radomyśl Wielki. A critical role was played here by local village Jews, primarily the Amsterdam family. For generations, the Amsterdam and Hollander families of Sephardic origins lived in villages near Szczucin, Mielec, and Radomyśl. Perhaps not without significance, key members of the Amsterdam family came from the villages of Trzciany, Małec, and Wola Mielecka, neighboring the *Volksdeutsche* community of Czermin (Hohenbach), and they knew personally many of their chief antagonists.

Prior to the war, the Amsterdams owned a tavern and were respected by the local community, often donating money to the local Catholic church. Like other Jewish villagers, the extended family was resettled in the summer of 1941 and moved outside of *Kreis* Debica to their homestead in the village of Radwan (*Kreis* Tarnów), where some of them avoided the deportation *Aktion* in Mielec. When in May 1942 the Germans began to force the Jews of that region to the Dąbrowa Tarnowska ghetto, all family members made the move, with the exception of Yochanan, his brother Nisan, and his nephew, who managed to stay behind.[152]

The majority of Jews who found themselves in the Dulecki forest came from the vicinity of Radomyśl Wielki and Dąbrowa Tarnowska. The core group of the Amsterdams spent the initial months moving between villages and hiding in the barns of friendly peasants before a decision was made on September 12, 1942 (Rosh Hashanah—the Jewish New Year) to move into the forest on a more permanent basis. The Amsterdam family also knew the Dulecki forest because they owned a plot of land next to it. A central role was played by Yochanan Amsterdam, who began pulling family members and acquaintances out of the Dąbrowa ghetto and the homes of farmers and into the forest. Others escaped to the forest on their own initiative and found themselves among the group by accident. As a result, the forest was honeycombed with family bunkers. Estimates of Jews hiding in this forest range from 250 to 500, though the lower figure is more probable.

The Jews of the Dulecki forest faced four main challenges: adjusting to the natural environment, evading frequent police searches, procuring food, and later coexisting with roaming bandits. Three main groups emerged among the fugitives. The first of these was under the supervision of members of the Amsterdam family (some forty to sixty Jews), mainly the brothers Yochanan and Abraham, which initially operated as two subgroups.[153] The second group (fifteen to twenty Jews) was led by Fenil Meit; the third was an armed group (fifteen to twenty Jews) under the leadership of Shaya Singer from Radomyśl Wielki, which initially did not accept women. All the Jews organized their lives around two types of family bunkers. The first—embodied by the Amsterdams—could be called an organized bunker system, in which daily life was subject to rigorous supervision by its armed leadership and an almost military system of discipline. In contrast, the second type of bunkers, which could be called unorganized, was likewise based around families and acquaintances but lacked a code of discipline and coordinated leadership. Jews in these family bunkers mostly hid on their own. If one accepts the conservative estimate of approximately 250 Jews hiding in the forest, those living in organized bunkers could have numbered 80–100, while those hiding on their own numbered 100–150. The most information is known about the Amsterdam group, as the majority of survivors came from this group, leaving behind the largest number of sources.

Survival strategies began to evolve and develop rapidly among these groups, especially with the increased rainfall in the fall of 1942. The first challenge, therefore, included adapting to the natural world of the forest (often described as a jungle). The construction of bunkers, suitable for an average of between eight and ten people, was the first step. As a result of frequent search parties, the Amsterdam group developed a dual system of bunker construction: one to live in and another for emergency escape. This was a major strength of the organized bunker system. In terms of the living bunkers, there was a preference for building these in the younger part of the forest, where the trees were lower, as well as locations with coniferous tree growth. For emergency bunkers, they chose the older part of the forest, where trees were generally taller and the field of vision was relatively unobstructed. The reason for this is that when search parties swept through, the area would give the appearance of being empty. The roof of a bunker was generally level with the ground. Dogs heard barking in nearby villages functioned as an alarm system, alerting them that strangers were in the area and a manhunt might be on the horizon. In that case, a group would move to the escape bunker, and a designated person would close the door from the outside and camouflage the entrance before going into hiding elsewhere. Bunkers that were independent of this system, such as that of the Wasserstrum family, did not develop a duel bunker system for emergency situations, which likely contributed to a lower rate of survival.[154]

Every facet of daily existence required some adjustment and adaption. Members of the Amsterdam group recalled that in the warmer months, movement inside the forest was generally restricted to walking in a stream so as not to leave any footprints. The danger of leaving footprints became acute in the winter after snowfall. The solution to this was to pick a night when snow was falling or when the wind was strong enough blow away the footprints. Alternatively, the men in the group built stilts for walking in the snow, which were made to leave marks resembling deer tracks. Communication across distances was done by clicking the tongue three times or other oral sound effects. The principle was to minimize one's visible presence and contact with the outside world.

Responding to the frequent searches and manhunts held the prospect of armed confrontation. The men had gathered guns mostly by purchasing them from local peasants; later, they were acquired in the course of fighting the German and Polish Police. However, a system of discipline had to be developed for how to behave in critical situations. Most of the refugees had never handled a gun during civilian life. Initially, there was no strategy in place during a search when Jews were spotted outside a bunker. Gradually, a utilitarian rule of thumb was adopted in the event of a surprise search party: If someone was spotted near a bunker, that person was to run in a direction away from the bunker and return only after the search was over; he or she was never to run inside a bunker, otherwise the Germans would kill everyone inside. A related problem concerned the presence of children and infants. The sound of children crying during a search could spell the death of all inhabitants of a bunker. Pnina Wassestrum's group applied a strategy of leaving an infant child under a tree while the others spread

Figure 7.12. Painting by Yochanan Amsterdam (living in the Ben Ami moshav in northern Israel) depicting a scene of organized Jewish survival in the Dulecki forest. The painting highlights a division of labor that was characteristic of the group. Two armed men stand guard in the foreground; others wash clothes and prepare food over a fire in the background (USC, VHA, 39822, Interview with Yochanan Amsterdam).

out in the forest.[155] Those from Amsterdam's group may have resorted to more drastic solutions.[156]

Once food began running out, something had to be done about maintaining a regular supply while limiting unnecessary excursions into villages. This meant developing a system for interacting with the outside world. It was decided that people were not allowed to leave the forest individually, but rather only in a designated group assigned for the purpose. The group traveled to trusted Polish providers to purchase food during the night (prewar contacts played an important role). Here, Yochanan Amsterdam showed foresight in forbidding anyone to steal food from peasants' farms. Though an understandable reaction to hunger, as many as 250 Jews regularly taking food from the surrounding population—which was already pressed for food quotas by the Germans—would never make for a good long-term survival strategy. Amsterdam organized a group of youngsters to deliver the food, which was often purchased from farmers eight to ten kilometers away.

Strategies evolved after months of trial and error. The learning curve exhibited by the group led Yochanan Amsterdam to formulate a list of "ten commandments of the forest," which he instructed all individuals under his guidance to follow:

1. You must immediately penetrate into the depth of the forest and have your people take turns in guarding the camp.
2. Fuel for fires should be prepared in the bunker in order to avoid being audible.
3. Dig pits for sanitary purposes lest the odors give you away.
4. Do not wander in the forest during daytime, nor in the villages.
5. Warn the people not to steal from the peasants' fields, because they will be the first to give you away.
6. Dig small, well-camouflaged bunkers for use in case of danger.
7. Do not reveal the location of your hiding place to any of your friends outside the forest.
8. Never use [your] weapon to threaten, only in self-defense.
9. Exercise harsh discipline on your people; talk to them and explain the seriousness of the situation.
10. Keep your people clean; soap is as important as bread. Fortunately, you have plenty of water. Health is most important and should be given special consideration.[157]

Of course, nothing was guaranteed. Robberies often took place, but—according to Yochanan—they were aimed primarily at German villagers, carried out far from the forest shelters, and targeted large estates as opposed to small farmers.[158] However, the accounts of younger members of the group, such as Zvi (Herman) Amsterdam[159] and Israel Klein,[160] suggest that robberies were the rule rather than the exception among some subgroups.

The fourth major challenge was dealing with the presence of bandits, who also used the forest as a shelter from the German and Polish Police. The most infamous group was the so-called *Czarne Sępy* (Black Vultures), led by Wojciech Idzik, Stanisław Kosieniak, and Wojciech Lasota, which had attracted some twenty members in the course of the occupation.[161] Initial contact with the bandits was helpful to the group. In almost all testimonies, survivors state that Idzik, the de facto leader of the group who had a wife and children in the village of Małe, had genuinely tried to help the struggling Jews. According to Yochanan

Amsterdam, it was Idzik who first suggested to Amsterdam in May 1942 that he go to the forest, promising to supply him with weapons and other necessary help. "Just don't let yourself be taken like sheep to the slaughter," he said, later giving him a rifle and two hundred bullets.[162]

Czarne Sępy played an important role in helping neutralize the village security system in the form of foresters and gamekeepers, who were obligated to report all activities to the Germans. Under Idzik's command, they killed two foresters for bringing the police into the forest. Another forester was bribed by the Amsterdam group and received items in exchange for informing the Germans that he saw no signs indicating the presence of Jews. At other times, the forester warned Amsterdam's group to move to the edge of the road, while he guided the Germans into the depths of the forest, claiming that the marks in the snow left by the stilts were in fact deer tracks.[163] Amsterdam's group, probably together with the help of Idzik, robbed the homes of policemen to steal their uniforms. This allowed them to intimidate local farmers by entering their homes posing as policemen, aided by the fact that Yochanan and some of the others spoke German. The Jewish partisans were gradually able to confront German and Polish policemen and disarm them. As a result, Polish policemen were reported to have been afraid of entering the forest alone.[164]

The precarious relationship with the bandits eventually began to backfire, however. In time, some of the bandits began to turn on the easy prey of Jews hiding in the forest. Zvi Amsterdam recalled how Kosieniak once entered a bunker and raped a young girl in front of everyone.[165] In other parts of the forest, the bandits simply murdered those who refused to bend to their will.[166] Further, the outlaws increasingly insisted that Amsterdam's men accompany them to rob local farmers, which ran the risk of a growing perception among the locals of Jews as equivalent with bandits. Eventually, a conflict developed between Idzik and his subordinate Kosieniak, with things taking a dramatic turn for the worse when Kosieniak shot Idzik and Mindel Amsterdam (who married in the forest) in their sleep in the spring of 1943. On December 23, 1943, a young farmer, Stanisław Pietras, murdered Kosieniak and another associate in the village of Wola Wadowska using an axe, effectively ending the reign of terror of *Czarne Sępy* for Jews and Poles alike in the region.

By the fall of 1944, others had joined the main group of forest survivors, now numbering approximately sixty to eighty in all. On November 11, 1944, the last major search had taken place, in which seventeen Jews were captured (as well as ten Poles hiding from labor roundups).[167] The remaining forty-eight Jews in Yochanan Amsterdam's group found themselves in a Catch-22. The Soviet Army had stopped their advance right in front of the eastern side of Dulecki forest; the entire forest now found itself behind the German line. A barbed-wire entanglement and minefield separated the track of land between both armies, leaving Amsterdam's group trapped amid a growing German troop presence and without access to food. The group deliberated between risking starvation and German capture in the forest or running through this no man's land while being fired at by both armies. On November 27, 1944, the forty-eight Jews decided to make a break for the Soviet front, yelling "Hurrah!" while firing at the Germans. In the crossfire and minefield, twelve Jews were killed, but thirty-six made it to the Soviet side. Another ten Jews not affiliated with Amsterdam's group, mostly members of the Wasserstrum family, survived the war in the forest.

THE CAMP

The Labor Camp as Refuge: The Case of Bäumer und Lösch

In late December 1942, a unit of the Peasant Battalions tried to liberate the inmates of the Biesiadka labor camp on the grounds of *Truppenübungsplatz Süd*. Most of the laborers in the camp were Jews. The partisans "opened the gates, encouraging us to leave as quietly and quickly as possible," recalled Markus Rohtbart.[168] However, by all accounts, the majority of inmates did not flee the camp, and of those who did, most returned the following day.[169] As counterintuitive as it may seem today, camps could serve as places of relative shelter. Rohtbart noted, "Unless a prisoner knew the area and had a friend nearby, his chance for survival was greater in the camp itself."[170] In some cases, inmates could exercise a level of control over a camp environment that allowed for a long-term survival strategy.

Most of the camps in *Kreis* Debica were concentrated around its two military complexes. *Truppenübungsplatz Süd* comprised four mixed camps for Poles and Jews (Biesiadka, Bäumer und Lösch, Dęba, and Staszówka/Przyłęk), as well as one labor camp for Jews (*Judenarbeitslager*, or *Julag*) in Huta Komorowska. It was the territory of this Wehrmacht army base that served as an arena for camp-related survival strategies. The SS Heidelager army base, by contrast, held the deadliest camp complex, Pustków, whose grounds contained a forced labor camp (*Zwangsarbeitslager*, ZAL) for Poles, a Julag, and a crematorium. It represented a particular source of terror for the local population. Despite the striking police and military presence on the military bases, a total of thirty-seven Jews are known to have survived on its territory, the overwhelming majority in the more favorable conditions of *Truppenübungsplatz Süd*. A strategy of rotating between camp, village, and forest was developed by some Jews in this area, such as the teenaged Markus Rohtbart and Icchak Mechlowicz. Some of the thirty-seven Jews in this group employed such a strategy, while others simply hid among farmers in villages that had not been resettled or in forest bunkers.

The camp established by Bäumer und Lösch in the Czekaj forest earned the greatest reputation among Jews as a potential refuge.[171] The private German company had originated in Opole and was staffed primarily by German foremen from Silesia, headed by an engineer by the name of Ulbrycht (or Olbrycht), with its main office in the Mielec *Landrat*.[172] The company was responsible for the construction of roads and narrow-gauge railways between different parts of the two military bases, which required a labor force to clear the forest.

Within the camps of *Truppenübungsplatz Süd*, Bäumer und Lösch thus came to play a central role as a potential refuge, especially in the immediate aftermath of the major deportation actions. Its reputation even spread beyond the county. The most vivid example is the case of the Schindler family, who bribed the company's employees in Czchów (where a company branch was located) to transport the five-member family across 120 kilometers in a truck and place them inside the main camp.[173] However, most Jews to enter the camp were from the surrounding area, especially Mielec and Radomyśl Wielki, such as Naftali and Faiga Taffel, who were smuggled out of the Tarnów ghetto in a truck by their brother-in-law.[174] For those Jews who fled the zone of the village, the newfound security of the camp was striking to its new arrivals: "We were finally happy, free, not hidden day and night. No longer dependent on the good or bad disposition of the villagers. At last, an end to dark thoughts."[175]

Bäumer und Lösch also became an arena where the survival strategy applied on the eve of the Mielec *Aussiedlungsaktion* by a small Jewish elite with ties to the *Judenrat* and the German camp administration, mentioned at the outset, resumed and continued to evolve. In the camp, these contacts appear to have evolved into a *protekcja* system, where new inmates entered the camp by means of bribes in exchange for the relative safety of the camp. In this way, Abraham April, who paid to enter the camp, recruited the help of the head engineer in the camp, a certain Podgrzeba, to intervene on behalf of his brother and a friend held under arrest in Przecław and bring them into the camp, though without success.[176]

The presence of *Judenrat* families in the camp was prominent. Recall that the Mielec *Landrat* building was also where certain members of the *Judenrat* and their families were hidden by the company's employees. Leo Freiberg, the son of *Judenrat* member Icchak Freiberg, was already in the camp in the role of commandant when he learned from Ulbrycht of the impending liquidation of the Radomyśl ghetto. When, a day prior to the *Aktion*, a company truck was dispatched to Radomyśl to bring back Jewish workers, Leo Freiberg was permitted to come along in order to warn his parents and acquaintances.[177] Dr. Fink, together with his wife, Netti, and their daughter Alina, left Radomyśl for the Bochnia ghetto prior to the *Aktion*, but their son Lucjan was among the Jews who volunteered for the Bäumer und Lösch camp.[178] Likewise, Izak Kapłan, Reuven Kurz, and some members of the Pustków and Dębica *Judenräte* entered the camp in the fall of 1942.

In June 1943, the Jewish section of the camp was liquidated, and its inmates were transferred to *Flugzeugwerk Mielec*. Out of its 200–250 inmates, 18 are known to have survived both Bäumer und Lösch and *Flugzeugwerk Mielec* and subsequent deportations.

The Labor Camp as a Trap: The Case of Informers

At the same time, the camp became the site of Jewish informers led by Izak Kapłan. Kapłan overtook Leo Freiberg as commandant and collaborated with the Gestapo, leaving a strong mark on Jewish testimonies. As one survivor whose family was directly affected by the actions of these informers recalled,

Figure 7.13. *Left to right*: Pustków *Judenrat* members Herman Immerglück and Max Bitkower with ŻSS delegate Tobiasz Hugon during an inspection visit by the Krakow ŻSS in September 1941.

Figure 7.14. Pustków *Judenrat* members Herman Immerglück (*left*) and Max Bitkower in 1942 (AŻIH, PUS 001; 2619/17).

"They were free to come and go as they pleased, using their freedom not only to betray Jews sheltered by Poles in the vicinity of Mielec, but also to give away anyone who had come into the camp illegally."[179]

Little has been written in a sustained fashion about Jewish informers during the Holocaust in occupied Poland.[180] What we know is piecemeal. Some passing mention of professional Gestapo informers in *Kreis* Debica is found in the sources. For example, from February 1943, the Mielec Gestapo employed a Jewish informer, a twenty-year-old Jewish woman who was given the code name Sophie (Zofia) and tasked with penetrating the Polish resistance movement in the Baranów Sandomierski region under the guidance of Walter Thormeyer, the head of the Mielec Gestapo.[181] However, Kapłan's group did not have its origins in a top-down Gestapo operation but developed from below on the basis of previous survival strategies. Its evolution occurred gradually and involved a number of factors: the activities of the Mielec, Pustków, and Dębica *Judenräte*;

the transformation of the Dębica ghetto into a labor camp; the establishment of the Jewish Assistance Office (ŻUS) in place of the more autonomous Jewish Self-Aid (ŻSS) organization in July 1942; and the emergence of the *Judenjagd* in the post–ghetto liquidation stage of the Holocaust.

As was already mentioned, Kapłan first earned a name for himself with his ascendance, along with Reuven Kurz, to the leadership position of the Mielec *Judenrat*, followed by an active role on the *Judenräte* of Radomyśl and Dębica. The second crucial element of this evolution was the small *Judenrat* of the Pustków *Julag*. The leading positions among its five members were held by Herman Immerglück (a member of the Dębica *Judenrat* and its liaison) and Max Bitkower (liaison with the Tarnów *Judenrat*).[182] These individuals earned a negative reputation among Jewish inmates. When the Jewish camp was liquidated in the summer of 1942, some of its leadership appears to have been spared and transferred to Dębica, where in August 1942 a labor camp was being established in place of the ghetto. Immerglück became its head, Bitkower its secretary, and Kapłan its advisor.[183] At the same time, Immerglück also became the commandant of the Jewish Police.[184] Finally, this period saw the closing down of the ŻSS and its replacement with the ŻUS in coordinating the distribution of aid to Jewish workers.

Kapłan emerged from these circumstances and reshaped institutions as the main liaison between the labor camps of *Kreis* Debica, ŻUS, and the Dębica *Arbeitslager*. As far as is known, he was the only Jew given official permission by the Sipo and SD to travel freely in the county.[185] After the second *Aktion* in the Dębica ghetto in mid-November, which involved close cooperation between the Gestapo and its newly reconstituted Jewish Police, this leadership cadre was transferred to the Bäumer und Lösch camp.

For Kapłan and the others who harnessed themselves to the new post–ghetto liquidation camp reality of the GG, their raison d'être was based on the continued presence of Jewish labor. This may explain the practice of encouraging Jews in hiding to report to nearby camps for labor, reflected in the sources. The known individuals in this group were Kapłan, Immerglück, Bittkower, and Tadek Dortheimer,[186] as well as a certain Fridman. Reuven Kurz; his wife, Faiga; and their daughter Esther eventually made their way into the camp as well.[187] By the spring of 1943, it appears that the operations of the group had become routine: "They were given a separate barrack. On Sunday, Immerglück took roll call. They left in the morning on bicycles and returned at night . . . It later turned out that they rode into the woods where Jews were hiding and denounced them."[188] Some fifteen people are said to have lived in the barrack,[189] which came with benefits: "All of these people had certain privileges in the camp, so they did not have to work on the construction with others."[190]

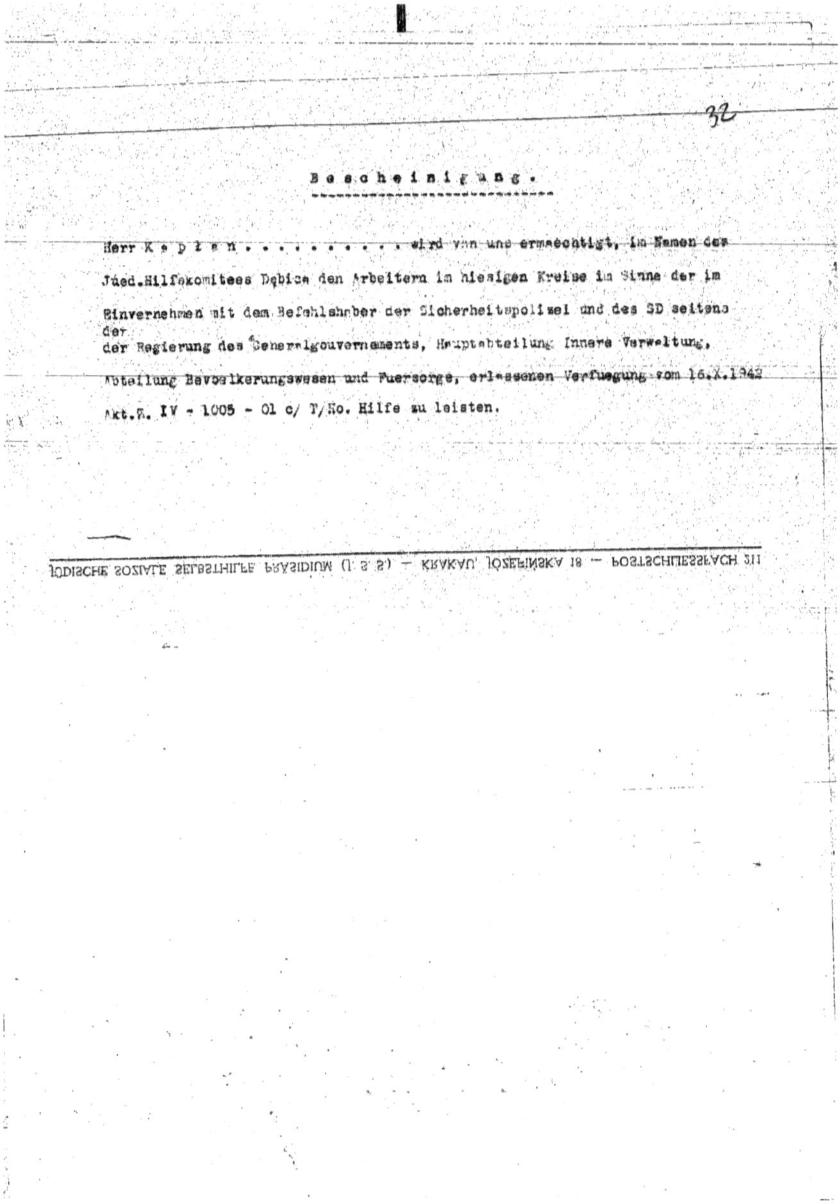

Bescheinigung.

Herr K a p l a n . . . . wird von uns ermaechtigt, im Namen des Jued.Hilfskomitees Debica den Arbeitern im hiesigen Kreise im Sinne der im Einvernehmen mit dem Befehlshaber der Sicherheitspolizei und des SD seitens der Regierung des Generalgouvernements, Hauptabteilung Innere Verwaltung, Abteilung Bevoelkerungswesen und Fuersorge, erlassenen Verfuegung vom 16.X.1942 Akt.R. IV - 1005 - 01 c/ T/No. Hilfe zu leisten.

JÜDISCHE SOZIALE SELBSTHILFE PRÄSIDIUM (J. S. S.) — KRAKAU, JOSEFINSKA 18 — POSTSCHLIESSFACH 311

Figure 7.15. Certificate issued to Izak Kapłan by the Sipo and SD of Dębica on October 16, 1942, as an employee of the Jewish Assistance Office (*Jüdische Unterstützungsstelle für das Generalgouvernement*, JUS), authorizing him to provide assistance to Jewish laborers in *Kreis* Debica, which implied freedom of movement between camps (AŻIH, 211/353, 32).

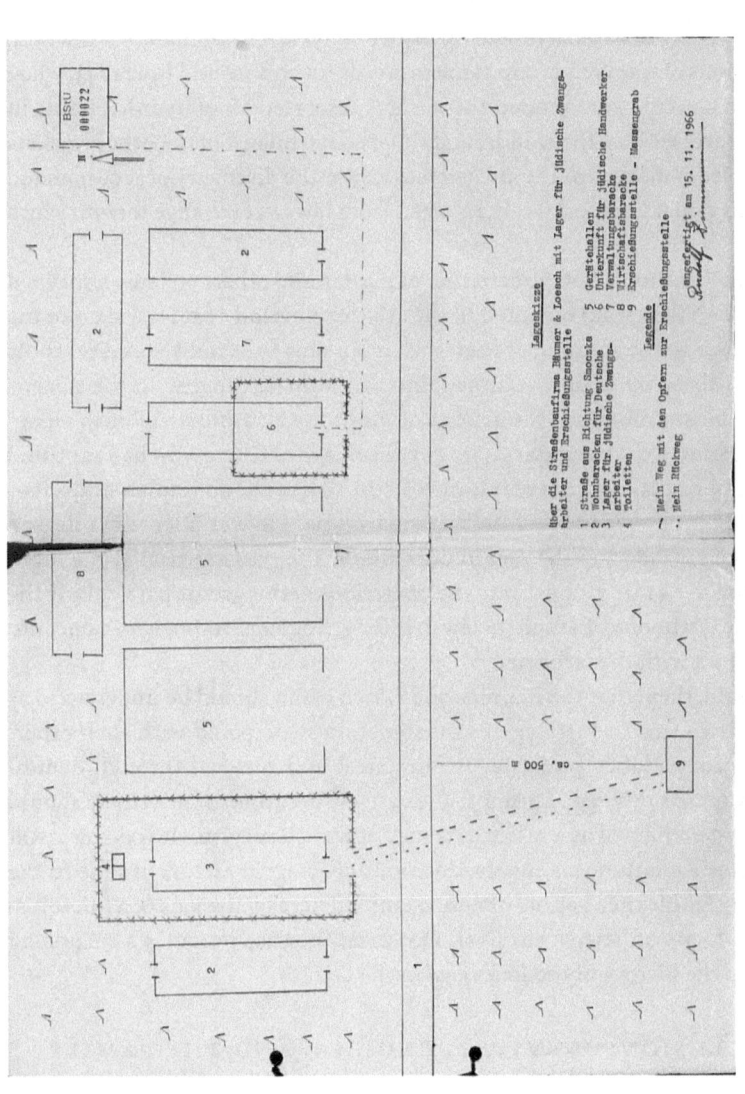

Figure 7.16. Layout of the Bäumer und Lösch camp, as drawn by former member of the Mielec Gestapo Rudolf Zimmermann. The barrack of the informers corresponds to no. 3 on the map; the place of their execution corresponds to no. 9 (Archives of BStU, MfS HA IX / 11 ZUV, no. 35/17, 22).

Precarious as it was, this survival strategy must have given the group a sense of confidence and stability. "We saw the Gestapo arrive, drink together, eat together, and enjoy themselves," recollected a former inmate. Kapłan, a cobbler by training, set up a workshop to make boots for the Gestapo. After three months in the camp, Immerglück brought his wife and son from Krakow, while Kapłan allegedly married a nineteen- or twenty-year-old woman.[191] However, the operations of Kapłan's group came to an abrupt end around June 1943, when the Mielec Gestapo surrounded the barrack, escorted all of its inhabitants in their nightdresses into the woods, and shot them while all of the other workers were away from the camp. The alleged reason was the discovery of accumulated money and valuables, most likely extorted from Jews in exchange for entry into the camp.[192]

What was the impact of the activities of Kapłan and others on Jewish survival in the region? The group operated in the area for a period of at least six months from late 1942 to the summer of 1943. It is impossible to establish precisely how many lives these operations claimed, but an estimate ranging in the dozens would not be ungrounded. The actions of the group also affected Polish villagers. On April 23, 1943, the night guards in the village of Chrząstów had captured a member of Kapłan's group of informers—in all likelihood Kapłan himself—and handed him over to the Mielec gendarmerie. He was allegedly released and was seen wandering the region once more. The postwar trial of the night guards provides a rare glimpse into the operations of this group, particularly the remarkable testimony of a fugitive Jew in hiding, Bogdan Protter, who came into direct contact with the informer.[193]

It appears, then, that the Bäumer und Lösch camp should be understood as the site of two survival strategies that sometimes competed with each other: survival through labor (most Jewish inmates) and survival through denunciation (Kapłan's privileged group). The case of this group of informers should not be overgeneralized as a major category of Jewish survival. It was the result of a complex evolution that involved various contingent factors unique to the county. Its significance has only been magnified here by the lens of a microhistory and a focus on Jewish survival. However, the case provides a surprising footnote in the history of the *Judenjagd* in the GG.

CONCLUSION: SURVIVAL, CHOICES, AND THE FAMILY

The specific course of events in Dębica County introduced elements that were unique relative to other parts of the GG. Because the Germans chose Mielec to be the first town to undergo a "resettlement action"—as a prelude to Operation Reinhard—the cohort of Mielec Jews was forced to confront the new reality sooner than other Jewish communities. A small number of Jews either affiliated with or having contacts in the *Judenrat* and the local German administration were able to gain advance knowledge of the *Aktion* and evade deportation to the Lublin District. A prominent strategy among these fugitives was to take shelter across the Vistula River in the neighboring Radom District, primarily in the Połaniec ghetto, which permitted at least some fifty Jews to regroup as families by bringing back others deported to the Lublin region, before the Połaniec ghetto was itself liquidated in October of 1942.

Once Operation Reinhard was in full swing in the Krakow District, the impending deportation actions gave rise to the major categories of survival strategies from mid-1942 to the end of 1944 in the region. These strategies have been grouped according to three zones of survival—the village, the forest, and the camp—because it was the social and territorial habitus of each arena that shaped its respective strategies. This study is therefore able to vividly show how Jewish survival was at the mercy of geography.

The chapter has analyzed the fate of a total of 1,257 Jews who evaded the killing operations. Of this number, 312 (25 percent) managed to survive in the county by hiding, and 945 (75 percent) died in the struggle. Further, a minimum threshold of 200 Jews survived in the labor camps of Dębica County (and subsequent deportations and death marches), the majority of whom was funneled through *Flugzeugwerk Mielec*. It is important to note that the numbers provided here are not of a final character but only illustrate the scale of the phenomena under investigation, revealing the contours of the major patterns of survival in the Polish province. Today, the full scale of the phenomenon remains beyond the reach of historians.

The post–ghetto liquidation stage of the summer of 1942 appears to have represented a turning of the tide in Polish attitudes and behaviors toward Jews, which is foregrounded by the case of Mielec Jews. Shortly after the Mielec *Aussiedlungsaktion* on March 9, 1942, Mark Verstandig noted that as long as they possessed travel passes, Jews "could move about safely, particularly in any places where the Gestapo were not stationed. It was not yet the 'open season' for Jew-hunting, and Poles had not begun the practice of delivering Jews to the Gestapo."[194] In terms of Jewish survival, the highlighted strategies in this period were shaped by a rapid narrowing of choices. Taken together, the Jews in Bäumer und Lösch and the partisans in the Dulecki forest showcase the full spectrum of the frequently overlooked category of "rescue by Jews" independently of non-Jewish help, as emphasized by historian Havi Dreifuss.[195]

Among the survivors examined in this study, some distinctions emerge between different cohorts, particularly between the Jews of the shtetl (small town) and the *dorf* (the village). Of the 312 survivors examined in this chapter roughly a third of them were identified as inhabitants of villages prior to the war. If the prewar population of village Jews in the county can be estimated at 2,000 (11 percent of the county's Jewish population), a one-third share by this subgroup is not insignificant. The presence of a large proportion of Jewish farmers—a feature unique to the lands of historic Galicia—likely had implications for survival. This demographic has often been overlooked in studies of the Holocaust. Markus Rohtbart expressed an intuition that village Jews were better equipped for survival in camps: "The majority of the people who survived the work camps, I notice in retrospect, had been raised on farms, as I had been. Accustomed to physical labor and a rugged way of life, we were equipped to carry out the most demanding of the tasks required of us."[196] It would not be unreasonable to assume that this also translated to strategies outside of the camp. For village Jews, who had acquaintances in the region, knew the lay of the land, and were accustomed to the challenges of rural life, the decision to remain in the area was likely more intuitive.

The study of Bielsk Podlaski in chapter 1 found that the majority of Jews to have secured long-term shelter did so in villages inhabited by remnants of the petty nobility, whose roots harkened back to the colonization of the region in the fourteenth century. Village Jews stand as a corollary to this observation in the lands of Western Galicia. Among the prominent attributes of survival that this study has flagged are the existence of acquaintances and levels of integration with the non-Jewish surroundings. For shtetl Jews, who continued to occupy the role of the small-town middle-man minority, the spectrum of non-Jewish acquaintances narrowed around former employees and business contacts when seeking help. Village Jews, more integrated with the rural population than the Jews of the shtetl, found themselves at a clear advantage.

The quantitative dimension of this study is able to shed light on many key factors of Jewish survival. Yet the numbers alone do not capture a core dimension. A fundamental force behind the strategic aspects that cut across all class and social differences was the family. In the world of inverted values created under the occupation, the moral dimension of the family formed an invisible thread running through all decisions.

When, on the eve of "resettlement actions," the Germans dangled the prospect of keeping families together, Jewish youth leapt at the opportunity: "The families of workers are to be protected by the Germans and not resettled, so he is ready to work in order to protect himself and us," said Netti Fink of her son Lucjan in the Radomyśl ghetto, as he volunteered to enter the Bäumer und Lösch camp.[197] When, in the midst of uncertainty in the hangars near Mielec, Szaje Altman was given a chance at life among one hundred Jews selected for work in *Flugzeugwerk Mielec*, but a few too many were selected, he decided to rejoin the Jews headed for the unknown: "I volunteered to return, knowing that the fate of the people in the hangars is hopeless, but I wanted to die with family."[198] Likewise, when Czesław Kubik, a young Polish man, traveled to Włodawa to help his old Jewish professor Emil Czortkower and family to escape, he encountered a shattered human being after the shooting of his wife: "I begged the professor again to escape the camp while security was weak. The professor turned down the offer, but he called his daughter Tosia and said, 'Tosia, go with Czesiek, he's like my son.' But Tosia replied, 'Daddy, Mom died, you are going to die, so I will die with you, such is destiny.'"[199]

In other instances, survival was seen as requiring the breaking of family bonds. In the aftermath of the first *Aktion* in the Dębica ghetto, the teenager Irene Geminder became convinced that her family was headed for death: "Father was still unprepared to face the end of the family . . . But in Dębica I ceased to listen to Father's voice. I heard only my own, which clamored for life. My mind was made up: I would leave and I would leave alone. On my own I had a chance, I felt; someone might hide me. On my own I would find a way."[200] The title of her memoir, *The Choice*, is a haunting reminder of the family dilemma at the heart of survival, whose echoes survivors hear to the end of their days.

The Holocaust was a man-made disaster of biblical proportions, but in the GG there was no Noah's ark, only small improvised rafts, most of which were destroyed in the high seas of survival in 1942–1945. Among the drowned and the saved, the individual survivors—in most cases, the sole remaining members of shattered family units—represent the end product of strategies whose core moral and strategic dilemma concerned the family. It was the most taken-for-granted assumption yet the most operative factor. The dilemmas posed by the "choiceless choices" during the Holocaust were not only between life and death but also between life and the family.

NOTES

1. I am grateful for the support of the Claims Conference Saul Kagan Academic Fellowship in Advanced Shoah Studies (Cohort IX) in researching and writing this chapter. Responsibility for content rests solely with me.

2. This work is dedicated to the former inhabitants of the county scattered throughout the world: the late Dr. Irene Eber (Geminder) in Jerusalem (d. 2019), Shaya Feuer (Amsterdam) in Ashkelon, Dr. Edouard Stanisław

Rosenblatt in Paris, the late Regina Goldfinger (Rivka Schenker) in Toronto (d. 2016), and Cila Drucker (Kurz-Bernstein) in Toronto. Conversations about their experiences were of invaluable importance and inspiration.

3. Piotr Wróbel, "The Jews of Galicia under Austrian-Polish Rule, 1867–1918," *Austrian History Yearbook* 25 (1994): 137.

4. For a history of Jews in Galicia prior to 1939, see Michael C. Steinlauf, "Notes on Galician Jews," *Polin: Studies in Polish Jewry* 23 (2010): 421–436.

5. For recent works on Hasidism, see Marcin Wodziński, *Historical Atlas of Hasidism* (Princeton, NJ: Princeton University Press, 2018); David Biale et al., eds., *Hasidism: A New History* (Princeton, NJ: Princeton University Press, 2018).

6. Andrzej Potocki, *Żydzi w Podkarpackiem* (Rzeszów: Libra, 2004), 186.

7. Steinlauf, "Notes on Galician Jews," 425.

8. Baruch Jechiel Wind, "Our Town and Area," in *The Memorial Book of Radomyśl Wielki and Its Surroundings* [in Hebrew], ed. Hilel Harshoshanim and Isaac Turkow-Grudberg (Tel Aviv: Association of Immigrants from Radomishl and Its Surroundings in Israel, 1971), 1158–1159.

9. Marian Morawczyński, *Rzeź 1846 r. Dębica, Pilzno, Tarnów i okolice* (Tarnów: Tarnowskie Towarzystwo Kulturalne, 1992).

10. Keely Stauter-Halsted, "Jews as Middleman Minorities in Rural Poland: Understanding the Galician Pogroms of 1898," in *Antisemitism and its Opponents in Modern Poland*, ed. Robert Blobaum (Ithaca, NY: Cornell University Press, 2005), 42, 44, 51. For a recent monograph on the subject, see Daniel L. Unowsky, *The Plunder: The 1898 Anti-Jewish Violence in Habsburg Galicia* (Palo Alto, CA: Stanford University Press, 2018).

11. Stauter-Halsted, "Jews as Middleman Minorities," 56–59.

12. Konrad Zieliński, "Uwagi na temat pogromów i zajść antysemickich w Galicji jesienią 1918 roku," *Rocznik Mielecki* 10–11 (2007–2008): 119–128.

13. Zieliński, "Uwagi na temat pogromów," 122.

14. Sławomir Mańko, *Polski ruch ludowy wobec Żydów, 1895–1939* (Warsaw: Muzeum Historii Polskiego Ruchu Ludowego, 2010).

15. Stanisław Wanatowicz, "Ludność żydowska w regionie mieleckim do 1939 r.," in *Mielec. Studia i materiały z dziejów miasta i regionu*, vol. 3, ed. Feliks Kiryk (Mielec: Towarzystwo Miłośników Ziemi Mieleckiej im. W. Szafera, 1994), 49.

16. Archiwum Żydowskiego Instytutu Historycznego w Warszawie [Archives of the Jewish Historical Institute in Warsaw (AŻIH)], collection 301, file 1635, Testimony of Dr. Apolinary Frank, 2; Andrzej Krempa, *Zagłada Żydów mieleckich* (Mielec: Muzeum Regionalne w Mielcu, 2013), 44–46.

17. Markus Roth, *Herrenmenschen. Die deutschen Kreishauptleute im besetzten Polen: Karrierewege, Herrschaftspraxis und Nachgeschichte* (Göttingen:

Wallstein, 2009), 501. In 1945, Schlüter committed suicide in his hometown of Rostock.

18. See Tomasz Sudoł, *Poligon Wehrmachtu "Południe." Organizacja, funkcjonowanie obiektu wojskowego, los ludności polskiej i żydowskiej, obozy pracy, zbrodnie niemieckie, opór społeczny i konspiracja* (Rzeszów: IPN, 2009); Stanisław Zabierowski, *Pustków. Hitlerowskie obozy wyniszczenia w służbie poligonu SS* (Rzeszów: Krajowa Agencja Wydawnicza, 1981).

19. Włodzimierz Gąsiewski, *Hohenbach. Kolonia niemiecka Czermina 1783–1944* (Mielec: Agencja Wydawnicza "Promocja," 2013), 55–56.

20. AŻIH, 211/183, Collective lists of responses to a questionnaire regarding the state of hygiene, 1942.

21. AŻIH, 211/696, ŻSS Mielec, Report given by the chairman of the Mielec Judenrat, Dr. Józef Fink, July 7, 1941, 50.

22. It is also possible to derive a less conservative estimate. The files of ŻSS Dębica contain a list of 64 homesteads with a total of 347 Jews. On the basis of this sample, the average family size can be calculated as approximately five Jews per family unit. On this basis, 500 homesteads is roughly equivalent to 2,500 Jews. See AŻIH, 211/348, ŻSS Dębica, list of expropriated Jewish farmers in Mielec County, August 3, 1941, 13–15.

23. Max Freiherr du Prel, ed., *Das General-Gouvernement* (Würzburg: Konrad Triltsch Verlag, 1942), 257.

24. *Amtliches Gemeinde- und Dorfverzeichnis für das Generalgouvernement auf Grund der summarischen Bevölkerungsbestandsaufnahme am 1. März 1943* (Krakow: Burgverlag Krakau, 1943), 19–20.

25. AŻIH, 301/242, Testimony of Ojzasz Kalech, Krakow, 1–3. According to Kalech, the Germans expelled approximately 4,500 Jews from Tarnobrzeg. However, this number is likely exaggerated. According to Tadeusz Zych, the town's prewar population was closer to 2,259. Likewise, Włodzimierz Bonusiak noted that the Jewish population could not have been higher than 2,500. See Tadeusz Zych, *Tarnobrzeg pod okupacją niemiecką 1939–1944* (Tarnobrzeg: Państwowa Wyższa Szkoła Zawodowa im. S. Tarnowskiego, 2008), 51; Włodzimierz Bonusiak, "Tarnobrzeg podczas II wojny światowej," in *Tarnobrzeg. Dzieje miasta 1593–1939*, ed. Feliks Kiryk (Tarnobrzeg: Muzeum Historyczne Miasta Tarnobrzega, 2005), 16–17.

26. AŻIH, 211/344, ŻSS Dębica, Letter to the ŻSS Presidium in Krakow, April 11, 1941, 55. Jews from Krakow were resettled to five locations: Wielopole (250), Sędziszów (226), Radomyśl Wielki (350), Pilzno (112), Ropczyce (240), and Dębica (610).

27. AŻIH, 211/792, ŻSS Pilzno, Letter to the ŻSS Presidium from Michał Treibicz, March 20, 1941, 45; AŻIH, 211/873, ŻSS Radomyśl Wielki, Letter to the ŻSS Presidium from Jeremiasz Leibowicz, March 8, 1941, 26.

28. AŻIH, 211/347, ŻSS Dębica, Letter to the ŻSS Presidium, July 8, 1941, 27. The primary recipients of Jewish properties were to be Polish refugees or resettled Polish farmers, likely from villages encompassed by the army bases.

29. Isaiah Trunk, *Judenrat: The Jewish Councils in Eastern Europe under Nazi Occupation* (New York: MacMillan, 1972), 40.

30. AŻIH, 211/351, ŻSS Dębica, Letter to the ŻSS Presidium, November 9, 1941, 35.

31. AŻIH, 211/430, ŻSS Grębów, Documentation from March 11, 1941–March 5, 1942.

32. Reuven Siedlisker-Sarid, "The Murder of the Jews of Dembitz," translated by Jerrold Landau, in *The Book of Dembitz (Dębica, Poland): Translation of Sefer Dembitz*, ed. Daniel Leibl (New York: JewishGen, 2016), 247.

33. Mark Verstandig, *I Rest My Case* (Evanston, IL: Northwestern University Press, 2002), 107.

34. Siedlisker-Sarid, "Murder of the Jews of Dembitz," 251.

35. Martin Dean, ed., *Encyclopedia of Camps and Ghettos, 1933–1945*, vol. II, *Ghettos in German-Occupied Eastern Europe, Part A* (Bloomington: Indiana University Press, 2012), 498.

36. AŻIH, 301/1029, Testimony of Berta Lichtig, 11.

37. Zych, *Tarnobrzeg pod okupacją niemiecką*, 56–57.

38. Dean, *Encyclopedia of Camps and Ghettos*, 498. The borders of the Dębica ghetto corresponded to Głowacki Street to the north, Kościuszko Street to the east, Żółkiewski (today Żeromski) Street to the south, and between Trzeciego Maja (today Kolejowa) and today's Strumski (then nonexistant) to the west. The main artery of the ghetto was Gancarska Street (Tepper Gesel).

39. AŻIH, 211/794, ŻSS Pilzno, Letter from Leon Kupferblum to the ŻSS Presidium, June 21, 1942, 46; Letter from Kupferblum to the ŻSS Presidium, July 12, 1942, 51.

40. AŻIH, 301/6818, Testimony of Leopold Trejbicz (b. 1927) (Aryan name Władysław Jędrzejowski) and Bronisława Trejbicz (Aryan name Helena Kuśnierz), August 26, 1957, Warsaw, 9.

41. AŻIH, 211/911, ŻSS Rozwadów, Note after a visit to Rozwadów on January 28, 1942, 22.

42. AŻIH 301/2973, Testimony of Szaje Altman (b. 1904), October 17, 1947, Wrocław, 3.

43. AŻIH, 211/875, ŻSS Radomyśl, Letter from Dr. Józef Fink to Dr. Tisch on the ŻSS Presidium, June 11, 1942, 43.

44. AŻIH, 211/875, ŻSS Radomyśl, Letter from Dr. Józef Fink to ŻSS Presidium in Krakow, July 2, 1942, 37.

45. AŻIH, 211/875, ŻSS Radomyśl, Note, May 27/28, 1942, 29. The population was approximately 2,400 at this time.

46. AŻIH, 211/875, ŻSS Radomyśl, Note, Krakow, July 17, 1942, 50.

47. The two-year anniversary of the establishment of the Mielec *Judenrat* was celebrated on the pages of *Gazeta Żydowska* (Jewish Gazette): L.F., "Z miast i miasteczek," *Gazeta Żydowska*, no. 17, February 8, 1942, 2. "L.F." could be Lucjan Fink, Dr. Fink's son.

48. Die Behörde des Bundesbeauftragten für die Stasi-Unterlagen in Berlin [Stasi Records Agency (BStU)], MfS HA IX/11 ZUV, no. 35, file 1, part 2 of 2, Deposition of Izchak Frayberg (Freiberg), January 12, 1964, Petah Tikva, 200–215; Deposition of Elimelech Swi Freiberg, December 14, 1965, Toronto, 206–219; Deposition of Louis Frieberg (Leo Freiberg), December 15, 1965, Toronto, 218–224. The Freibergs altered the spelling of their family name after the war. This chapter preserves the original spelling.

49. References to the *Landrat*, deputy *Landrat* and *Landkommissar* are often interchangeable in the witness testimonies. In most cases, they refer to Alfred Beckert.

50. AŻIH, 301/2973, Testimony of Szaje Altman, 3–4.

51. Both Kapłan and Reuven were permitted to resettle with their families to Radomyśl Wielki, where they were appointed to the positions of Judenrat chairman and vice chairman respectively. See L.F., "Z innych dystryktów," *Gazeta Żydowska*, June 24, 1942, no. 74, 3.

52. AŻIH, 301/1094, Testimony of Markus Streim, Krakow, 2.

53. BStU, MfS HA IX/11 ZUV, no. 35/15, Testimony of Lieba Perlman (née Geldzahler; first married name Berger), November 30, 1965, New York, 25–26.

54. Verstandig, *I Rest My Case*, 133. According to Verstandig, Beckert was a prewar Communist who owed his position to his influential Nazi family. After leaving his post in Mielec, Beckert was killed on January 28–29, 1943, in Staraja Stanitza in the Northern Caucasus.

55. BStU, MfS HA IX/11 ZUV, no. 35/13, Testimony of Izchak Frayberg, 203.

56. BStU, MfS HA IX/11 ZUV, no. 35/13, Testimony of Elimelech Freiberg, 207.

57. USC, VHA, Interview 54138, Cila Drucker (Kurz-Bernstein); Interview with Cila Drucker, Toronto, May 31, 2017, in possession of the author.

58. L.F., "Z innych dystryktów," *Gazeta Żydowska*, no. 74, June 24, 1942.

59. Verstandig, *I Rest My Case*, 142–143. According to another version, "Kapłan and Kurz hid with their families in the *Landrat* after having collected money from the Jews as a ransom." AŻIH, 301/1029, Testimony of Berta Lichtig, 16.

60. BStU, MfS HA IX/11 ZUV, no. 35/14, Deposition of Hellmut Hensel (b. 1910), Bad Segeberg, July 21, 1964, 125. In his interrogation, Hensel recalled the name incorrectly as "Karpler."

61. Fink's frequent visits to the Mielec *Landrat* were mediated by the family's prewar Polish servant, Józefa Luboch. AŻIH, 301/1634, Diary of Józefa Luboch,

given to the Historical Commission of Krakow by Berta Lichtig on June 6, 1946. The diary documents various meetings with Dr. Fink in the region.

62. AŻIH, 301/3443, Testimony of Wolf Guttfreund, Krakow, August 1, 1947, 6; AŻIH, 301/3400, Testimony of Abraham Sternhell, Krakow, August 14, 1947, 2.

63. Kapłan may be an exception here, as according to Verstandig, he allegedly "dispatched his wife and two children to their deaths." Verstandig, *I Rest My Case*, 142.

64. AŻIH, 301/2973, Testimony of Szaje Altman, 9.

65. Verstandig, *I Rest My Case*, 143, 151.

66. Yad Vashem Archives (YVA), M.31, Department of the Righteous Among the Nations, file 4094a, Testimony of Czesław Kubik, Łódź, February 10, 1988, unpaginated file, first page of testimony.

67. Irene Eber, *The Choice: Poland, 1939–1945* (New York: Schocken, 2004), 30.

68. According to the postwar Temporary Jewish Committee of Dębica (TKŻD), twelve thousand Jews were resettled from *Kreis* Debica in late July; AŻIH, 301/794, May 30, 1945, 1. Historian Elżbieta Rączy estimates thirteen thousand; Rączy, *Zagłada Żydów w dystrykcie krakowskim* (Rzeszów: IPN, 2014), 304.

69. AŻIH, 211/794, ŻSS Pilzno, 46.

70. AŻIH, 211/794, ŻSS Pilzno, 52. The *Encyclopedia of Camps and Ghettos* gives a total of 1,500; Dean, *Encyclopedia of Camps and Ghettos*, 551. However, there is some ambiguity in the ŻSS sources. Thus, by May, the population of Pilzno was approximately 1,300. A letter dated July 12, 1942, stated that 600 were "foreign arrivals" (AŻIH, 211/794, ŻSS Pilzno, 51). On July 15, 1942, a document noted that "another 400 people were assigned, so that together there are 1,300 people here in Pilzno" (AŻIH, 211/794, ŻSS Pilzno, 52).

71. AŻIH, 211/183, 10, 27. A population of 925 Jews in Wielopole is listed for May 1942. The number of casualties is taken from the *Encyclopedia*; no deportation figure is provided in the entry. Dean, *Encyclopedia of Camps and Ghettos*, 594. Other sources give a figure of 42 elderly Jews killed following the selection and the date of the massacre as June 30, 1942; see Roman Lipa, "Likwidacja Żydów," *Konteksty. Polska Sztuka Ludowa*, no. 1–2 (2015): 158–159.

72. Lipa, "Likwidacja Żydów," 158.

73. AŻIH, 301/1025, Testimony of Berta Lichtig, 1. Lichtig stated that 1,500 Jews were rounded up in Borowa, which is highly inflated. Lichtig's testimonies should be approached with caution, as she often wrote about events without firsthand knowledge.

74. AŻIH, 301/2280, Testimony of Regina Ladner (b. 1899) (Aryan name Stefania Sieroń), Wałbrzych, April 9, 1947, 1–2; AŻIH, 301/2290, Testimony of Szeindla Ladner (b. 1936) (Aryan name Marysia Sieroń), Wałbrzych, April 10,

1947, 1–2. According to Regina Ladner, the resettlement took place on June 25, 1942.

75. AŻIH, 301/1103, Testimony of Berta Lichtig, 2.

76. AŻIH, 211/183, 11. A population of 600 listed for Rozwadów as of June 1942. The number of those murdered is taken from Rączy, Zagłada Żydów w dystrykcie krakowskim, 300.

77. AŻIH, 301/242, Testimony of Ozjasz Kalech, 3.

78. Rączy, Zagłada Żydów w dystrykcie krakowskim, 301.

79. AŻIH, 211/183, 8.

80. Local historian Jan Ziobroń gives a figure of 500 murdered at the cemetery and 250 selected for Pustków; *Dzieje Gminy Żydowskiej w Radomyślu Wielkim* (Radomyśl Wielki: Jan Ziobroń, 2009), 60; Wolfgang Curilla assumes 400; Curilla, *Der Judenmord in Polen und die Deutsche Ordnungspolizei, 1939–1945* (Paderborn: Ferdinand Schöningh, 2011), 390. Jewish testimonies generally inflate the number to 1,000, as in the case of Fryda Berger (AŻIH, 301/1722, 3).

81. AŻIH, 301/793, Temporary Jewish Committee of Dębica, 1; AŻIH, 211/184, 10.

82. AŻIH, 211/184, 14.

83. AŻIH, 301/5962, Testimony of Michalina Studnicka (née Hollönder) (b. 1916), Warsaw, April 20, 1963, 2. The head of the Dębica Gestapo, Julius Garbler, had executed some 380 Jews in Sędziszów around this time, suggesting that the number may have been closer to 3,000.

84. Rączy, Zagłada Żydów w dystrykcie krakowskim, 301.

85. There is some disagreement among historians regarding the total number of Jews in Sędziszów on the day of liquidation. Rączy gives a figure of 1,000–1,500, while the *Encyclopedia* gives a total of 1,900, 400 shot, and 1,500 deported to Dębica (*Encyclopedia of Camps and Ghettos*, 572). However, if Sędziszów at one point contained the population of three ghettos (Wielopole, Ropczyce, and Sędziszów), the number would appear to be closer to 3,000, with approximately 2,600 deported.

86. Rączy, Zagłada Żydów w dystrykcie krakowskim, 302.

87. Ibid., 303.

88. AŻIH, 301/794, Temporary Jewish Committee of Dębica, 1; AŻIH, 211/352, ŻSS Dębica, Monthly report for August 1–31, 1942, September 22, 1942, 56.

89. Tadeusz Kowalski, *Obozy hitlerowskie w Polsce południowo-wschodniej, 1939–1945* (Warsaw: Książka i Wiedza, 1973), 129.

90. AŻIH, 211/352, ŻSS Dębica, September 2, 1942, 37; Siedlisker-Sarid, "Murder of the Jews of Dembitz," 257.

91. AŻIH, 211/353, October 20, 1942, 20.

92. Fryda Berger gives a date of July 17, 1942, and a figure of 600 (AŻIH, 301/1722, 4); Rączy gives 1,000 (Rączy, Zagłada Żydów w dystrykcie krakowskim,

304). Two different dates recur throughout the sources for the second liquidation action. For example, according to the Dębica Memorial Book, the deportation to Bełżec took place on December 15–16 (Siedlisker-Sarid, "Murder of the Jews of Dembitz," 257), but the Temporary Jewish Committee of Dębica gave a date of November 15 (AŻIH, 301/794, 1, point 7).

93. Rączy, *Zagłada Żydów w dystrykcie krakowskim*, 304.

94. AŻIH, 301/2280, Testimony of Regina Ladner; AŻIH, 301/2290, Testimony of Szeindla Ladner.

95. AŻIH, 301/794, Temporary Jewish Committee of Dębica, May 30, 1945, 1, point 10.

96. AŻIH, 302/202, Memoir of Stefan Janusz, "Z Pilzna na kraj," 1949, 19–20. Janusz noted that the "numbers were provided by the municipal government of Pilzno. Calculations from Samuel Kampf given in 1945"; see AŻIH, 302/202, 20.

97. Due to the limitations of space, all relevant tables that provide the raw data for these numbers, including the names of Jewish survivors and those who were killed or died during the occupation, can be found at https://www.holocaustresearch.pl/index.php?show=567&lang=en. In light of additional data, the numbers have been updated since the Polish-language publication in 2018. Readers are encouraged to contact the author with additional information.

98. Jan Grabowski, *Hunt for the Jews: Betrayal and Murder in German-Occupied Poland* (Bloomington: Indiana University Press, 2013); Christopher R. Browning, "'Judenjagd.' Die Schlußphase der 'Endlösung' in Polen," in *Deutsche, Juden, Völkermord. Der Holocaust als Geschichte und Gegenwart*, ed. Jürgen Matthäus and Klaus-Michael Mallmann (Darmstadt: Wissenschaftliche Buchgesellschaft, 2006), 177–189.

99. Tomasz Frydel, "The *Pazifizierungsaktion* as a Catalyst of Anti-Jewish Violence. A Study in the Social Dynamics of Fear," in *The Holocaust and European Societies: Social Processes and Dynamics*, ed. Andrea Löw and Frank Bajohr (London: Palgrave Macmillan, 2016), 147–166.

100. Kowalski, *Obozy hitlerowskie*, 30–32, 43–49, 61–64, 239–240.

101. For a discussion of "provocation units" in the Krakow District, see: Dawid Golik, "Prowokacja w walce z 'bandami.' Wybrane przykłady niemieckich akcji prowokacyjnych z terenu dystryktu krakowskiego GG," *Prace Historyczne* 144, no. 4 (2017): 691–711.

102. Rączy, *Zagłada Żydów w dystrykcie krakowskim*, 92–94. Regional branches were opened in Krakow (March 1943) and Lwów (May 1943). Among forms of help, in July 1944 the prisoners of the Mielec and Stalowa Wola camps (some 5,000 in total) were given 75,000 zloty in each camp.

103. AŻIH, 301/6818, Testimony of Leopold Trejbicz and Bronisława Trejbicz, 9.

104. Archiwum Instytutu Pamięci Narodowej w Rzeszowie [Archives of the Institute of National Remembrance in Rzeszów (AIPN Rz)], file 353/61, Trial of Jan Miłoś and others, Appellate Court of Krakow (SAK), testimony of Bogdan Protter, main hearing, Mielec, May 3, 1950, 261.

105. Markus Rohtbart, *I Wanted to Live to Tell a Story* (Detroit: M. Rohtbart, 1993), 65.

106. AIPN Rz, 353/53, Trial of village head Wiktor Czekaj of Podleszany, Appellate Court of Krakow, deposition of Michał Fryc, Mielec, April 24, 1949, 150.

107. See Stauter-Halsted, *Jews as Middleman Minorities*, 39–59; Janusz Mucha, "Konflikt, symbioza, izolacja. Stosunki etniczne na polskim Podkarpaciu," *Etnografia Polska* 36, no. 1 (1992): 68–70; Thomas Sowell, "Are Jews Generic?" in *Black Rednecks and White Liberals* (New York: Encounter, 2006), 65–110; Edna Bonacich, "A Theory of Middleman Minorities," *American Sociological Association* 37 (1973): 583–594; Yuri Slezkine, *The Jewish Century* (Princeton, NJ: Princeton University Press, 2008).

108. Rohtbart, *I Wanted to Live to Tell a Story*, 61, 69. The Rohtbarts hailed from the village of Płażówka.

109. From the memoir of Ira Mechlowitz (Icchak Mechlowicz), *I Was Happy When I Was Singing*, prepared by Danielle Wyzgoski (née Gittleman), 55. The memoir is based on an earlier draft written in Yiddish: Icchak Mechlowicz, "Pamiętnik wojenny," May 30, 1946. I am grateful to Danielle Wyzgoski for sharing her grandfather's unpublished memoirs. See also USC, VHA, 13077, Interview with Ira Mechlowitz (b. 1928), 1996 [in English].

110. Mechlowitz, *I Was Happy When I Was Singing*, 61.

111. For the major motifs of rescue in Polish scholarship, see Dariusz Libionka, "Polish Literature on Organized and Individual Help to the Jews (1945–2008)," *Holocaust Studies and Materials* 2 (2010): 11–76.

112. The major exception here is Gunnar S. Paulsson's study of survival on the Aryan side of Warsaw, *Secret City: The Hidden Jews of Warsaw, 1940–1945* (New Haven, CT: Yale University Press, 2002), 26–54. See also Elisabeth Jean Wood, "The Social Processes of Civil War: The Wartime Transformation of Social Networks," *Annual Review of Political Science* 11, no. 1 (2008): 539–561.

113. AŻIH, 301/4118, Testimony of Kazimierz Zaczek, Krakow, undated, 1.

114. USC, VHA, 35580, Interview with Leokadia Mikołajków (b. 1906) from Dębica, 1997 [in Polish].

115. "From among the Righteous Gentiles," in *Book of Dembitz*, 296.

116. USC, VHA, 7142, Interview with Henry Wilner (b. 1923) (Aryan name Henryk Buszek) from Dębica, 1995 [in English]. Home Army pseudonym: Zbyszek.

117. USC, VHA, 35580, Interview with Leokadia Mikołajków. The couple also helped to arrange the shelter of Jewish children in Polish orphanages. Dr. Mikołajków was shot and killed, probably by accident, on the day of the town's liberation by the Red Army, while providing first aid to the wounded during the fighting. See also Zbigniew Szurek, *Rodzina Mikołajkowów (próba biografii). Ofiarność, odwaga, poświęcenie* (Dębica: Grupa Gryf Media, 2013).

118. AŻIH, 301/813, Testimony of Psachje Hönig (b. 1890), undated. Hönig hid without Aryan papers.

119. Verstandig, *I Rest My Case*, 173.

120. AŻIH, 301/2280, Testimony of Regina Ladner, 2–3.

121. USC, VHA, 12325, Interview with Ela Knie-Adlersberg (b. 1919) (Aryan name Ela Kuraba) from Nagoszyn, 1996 [in English].

122. AŻIH, 301/1723, Testimony of Miriam Berger (b. 1935), Krakow, April 20, 1946. Among other family members hiding in the area, the siblings of Ela Knie included Tewel Knie, Fryda Berger (Knie), Chaja Blas (Knie), and their families, hidden in a bunker on the property of Maria Skrzypek in Bobrowa. For a trial related to this family, see AIPN Rz, 353/134, Trial of Jan Czerwiec of Nagoszyn (1949–1952).

123. Chaja Rosenblatt, "Wspomnienia Chai Rosenblatt," in *Szczęście posiadać dom pod ziemią . . . losy kobiet ocalałych z Zagłady w okolicach Dąbrowy Tarnowskiej*, ed. Jan Grabowski (Warsaw: Stowarzyszenie Centrum Badań nad Zagładą Żydów, 2016), 126.

124. AŻIH, 301/4596, Testimony of Berl Sturm (b. 1899) from Dębica, Krakow, July 17, 1946, 2.

125. Anecdotes of direct murder of Jews by locals sometimes reached German authorities. During his time as the head of the Finance Division in the office of the Dębica *Kreishauptmann*, Christoph Führer heard of a farmer hiding Jews: "He is said to have murdered them when they did not want to give him any more money." See Bundesarchiv Ludwigsburg [Federal Archives of Ludwigsburg (BAL)], collection B 162, file 7460, Investigation of policemen Wiśniewski, Urban, and others, deposition of witness Christoph Führer, Kassel, March 6, 1963, 70–71.

126. AIPN, Rz 353/81, Trial of village head Stanisław Biduś and others, vol. II, deposition of Janina Góra (Mantel) (b. 1924) of Nagoszyn, Dębica, September 3, 1947, 44–46; Bochnia, November 21, 1947, 92–93; Deposition of Anna Dykas (Mantel), Bochnia, November 27, 1947, 101–102; Deposition of Fr. Józef Fijał (b. 1908), Tarnów, December 29, 1947, 103–104.

127. AIPN, 353/145, Trial of Jan Skiba, deposition of Stefan Czerepak, 35. Alscher was a prominent gendarme in Tarnobrzeg, later commandant of the Wrzawy *Stützpunkt*. He was executed by Polish partisans in 1943.

128. Adam Kazimierz Musiał, *Lata w ukryciu* (Gliwice: Adam Musiał, 2002), 2:473.

129. Mechlowitz, *I Was Happy When I Was Singing*, 110. "This was a very traumatic and tragic affair at any time in Jewish history . . . It was the most dreadful and tragic thing that could happen to any Jewish family and the family practiced the customary Jewish tradition. Her family sat Shiva for seven days and mourned her 'death,' because to them she shouldn't exist anymore," wrote Mechlowicz.

130. Ibid., 110–111. "The question of her own survival was answered by the fact that her husband and sons were much respected in the village, and they had no enemies among the villagers, so the secret of her once being Jewish was well kept," wrote Mechlowicz. After the war, her home served as a gathering point for Jewish survivors.

131. For a discussion of Jewish converts in the Subcarpathian region, see the case of Faiga/Felicia in the village of Jaśliska and her relations in the Rzeszów ghetto in Rosa Lehmann, *Symbiosis and Ambivalence: Poles and Jews in a Small Galician Town* (New York: Berghahn, 2001).

132. A characteristic report of these activities can be found in AŻIH, ŻSS, 211/1025, Correspondence between the ŻSS Presidium and the ŻSS County Committee in Tarnów, "Note from the travels of Mr. Liebeskind to Tarnów and Pleśna," March 26, 1942, 34–35. I thank Talia Farkash for bringing this to my attention.

133. Jael Peled (Margolin), *Krakow ha-jehudit 1939–1943: amida, machteret, maawak* [Jewish Krakow 1939–1943: Resistance, Underground, Struggle] (Tel Aviv: Ghetto Fighters' House, 1993), 154–155.

134. USC, VHA, 30628, Interview with Yehuda Laufbahn [Iehuda Laufban] (b. 1918), 1997 [in Spanish]. He adds that a handful of young people were inspired by Liebeskind's words and later escaped, including Dora Brutnow and Chaja Rosenblatt. See also Iehuda Laufban, *Y el mundo calló . . . La Shoa, desgarradora realidad* (Argentina: B. Jinich, 1997), 82–85.

135. Pinchas Reichman, "Life in Camp," in *Radomyśl Wielki Yizkor Book*, xlvi. "By stressing the seriousness of the situation, he [Liebeskind] tried to talk them into joining the ranks of the underground. But the Germans acted according to a prearranged plan; soon an order was issued saying that families willing to volunteer men to labor camps would be allowed to stay in their homes. Thus the town was soon drained of its best youthful elements. They volunteered for labor camps thinking that their families were secure; Dolek Liebeskind's plan was never taken into consideration," wrote Reichman.

136. Baruch Friedman-Bleicher reflected on his parting with his father, a student of Zans (Sącz) Hasidism, as he boarded a truck to Pustków prior to the *Aktion* in Radomyśl: "He could have brought me a machine gun, but he brought *Tefillin* [phylacteries]." See USC, VHA, 28924, Interview with Baruch Friedman-Bleicher, 1997 [in German].

137. Mariusz Krzysztofiński, *Komuniści na Rzeszowszczyźnie 1918–1944/1945* (Rzeszów: IPN, 2010), 188–193. The Rzeszów-Tarnów District consisted of three subregions: Tarnów, Rzeszów, and Jasło.

138. Ibid., 211–212. Birman's unit moved into a barn for the night in the village of Poręby Nienadowskie, where they were denounced by the village head and murdered by a German expeditionary unit. In reprisal, GL "Iskra" executed the village head.

139. "Report by Jawor regarding Communists on the territory of the AK region," June 24, 1943, pt. 10, in Tadeusz Zych, ed., *Archiwum Jawora. Dokumenty obwodu Armii Krajowej Tarnobrzeg* (Tarnobrzeg: Wydawnictwo Samorządowe, 1994), 36–37.

140. "Counter-intelligence report of February 1944," Dział III "K," in Zych, ed., *Archiwum Jawora*, 80.

141. USC, VHA, 50581, Interview with Isak Flam (b. 1918) from Mokre, 2000 [in English].

142. AIPN Rz, 363/5, Trial of village head Jan Skrzypek, main hearing, deposition of Jan Błachowicz, Mielec, April 25, 1951, 160.

143. For more on the limited access of Jews into the ranks of the Polish underground, see Dariusz Libionka, "ZWZ-AK i Delegatura Rządu RP wobec eksterminacji Żydów polskich," in *Polacy i Żydzi pod okupacją niemiecką 1939–1945. Studia i materiały*, ed. Andrzej Żbikowski (Warsaw: IPN, 2006), 107–113. Cf. Joshua D. Zimmerman, *The Polish Underground and the Jews, 1939–1945* (New York: Cambridge University Press, 2017), 258–261. Zimmerman argues that attitudes against allowing Jews into the underground increased under the leadership of Gen. Bór-Komorowski from July to August 1943.

144. Dębica County encompassed two Home Army inspectorates of the Rzeszów Subregion: Inspectorate Rzeszów (for the districts of Rzeszów, Dębica, and Kolbuszowa) and Inspectorate Mielec (for the districts of Mielec, Tarnobrzeg, and Nisko). See Grzegorz Ostasz, *Podziemna armia. Podokręg AK Rzeszów* (Rzeszów: IPN, 2010), 35–46, 57–67.

145. AAN, 1637/XI-45, AK Rzeszów Subregion and Inspectorate, "The main principles of underground work," Antek, undated, 9.

146. In the words of AK member Józef Rzepka (aka Znicz) given after the war, "Home Army authorities did not issue any order on this matter that would order me to offer decisive help to the Jews. This matter was addressed within the scope of each outpost." Cited in Elżbieta Rączy, "Stosunki polsko-żydowskie w latach drugiej wojny światowej na Rzeszowszczyźnie," in *Polacy i Żydzi pod okupacją niemiecką*, 932, appendix, no. 12, deposition of Józef Rzepka. From May 1943, Rzepka was the first adjutant of AK Inspectorate Rzeszów; from April, he was the deputy commander of the northern region of AK District Rzeszów.

147. AŻIH, 302/202, Memoir of Stefan Janusz, 2–3. Schneps kept the name Gołęczyński after the war.

148. Ibid., 4. Only the names of four members of the second group are given: Mozes Tanenbaum, Sara Kampf, Amalia Kampf, and Rivka Kampf. They were armed with two machine guns, five grenades, and a handgun.

149. Ibid., 2. According to Gołęczyński, these groups were supported by Józef Ryba, a member of the AK in Jaworze Dolne, who was arrested by the Germans for sheltering Jews and subjected to torture but refused to denounce anyone. See Elżbieta Rączy, *Pomoc Polaków dla ludności żydowskiej na Rzeszowszczyźnie w latach 1939–1945* (Rzeszów: IPN, 2008), 85.

150. Verstandig, *I Rest My Case*, 168–169.

151. See also: Elżbieta Rączy, "Negatywne postawy Polaków wobec Żydów w powiece mieleckim w latach okupacji niemieckiej," *Rocznik Mielecki* 12–13 (2009–2010): 141. For more on this incident, see AIPN Rz, 107/1208, Trial of Michał Maksoń and others; AIPN Rz, 358/113, Investigation of Antoni Chłopek; USC, VHA, 29550, Interview with Mark (Marek) Verstandig (b. 1912) from Mielec, 1997 [in English]; Verstandig, *I Rest My Case*, 182–186.

152. USC, VHA, 39822, Interview with Yochanan (Janek) Amsterdam from Małec (b. 1921), 1998 [in Hebrew]. All translations of oral testimonies in Hebrew were by Omer Shamir. Most of the information concerning the experience of the Amsterdams in the Dulecki forest is based on Yochanan's account. Other relevant interviews include USC, VHA, 23374, Interview with Rose (Shoshana) Hollander (Leser) (b. 1923) from Krakow, 1996 [in English]; USC, VHA, 531, Interview with Mina (Minka) Fried (Pinkas) (b. 1914) from Wola Wadowska, 1995 [in English].

153. The core of the Amsterdam family was comprised of the following: father Jehuda; sons Yochanan (Janek), Abraham (Romek), Menachem (Moniek), and Nisan; daughters Mindel (Minka), Golda (Genia), and Dobcia; children of Menachem, Zvi (Herman) and Chawa (Genia).

154. USC, VHA, 46584, Interview with Pnina (Pesia) Levenberg (Wasserstrum) (b. 1935) from Dębica, 1998 [in Hebrew]. For more on the Wasserstrum family, see AŻIH, 301/3866, Account of Dawid Wasserstrum (b. 1933) from Dębica, Krakow, undated. The Wasserstrum family also had relatives in the village of Dulcza Wielka.

155. USC, VHA, 46584, Interview with Pnina Levenberg. The baby, Lea Shefets (b. 1942), survived the occupation.

156. Yeshayahu Feuer (Amsterdam) (b. 1932/33) from the village of Wola Wadowska recalled incidents of infants being suffocated in order to protect the whole group. Interview with Yeshayahu Feuer, Ashkelon, summer 2015, in possession of the author.

157. Yochanan Amsterdam, "Life in the Forests," *Radomyśl Wielki Yizkor Book*, xlv.

158. Amsterdam, "Life in the Forests," xlv. "When one of my people wrecked a potato patch, I went over at once that very night and paid the damages and

more, just so the owner would keep quiet. I promised that it would never happen again," wrote Amsterdam.

159. Testimony of Herman Amsterdam, in Maria Hochberg-Mariańska, ed., *The Children Accuse* (London: Vallentine Mitchell, 1996), 147–148. He wrote of the group led by his father Abraham (Romek): "At night he [Abraham] would go with some others to the village to buy food, and when the money ran out he went stealing. For as long as it was possible, we stole potatoes, beetroot, cabbage, and so on from the fields, and when that stopped, Father stole from farms." This is a translation of AŻIH, 301/881, Testimony of Herman (Zvi) Amsterdam (b. 1930) from the village of Trzciana.

160. Israel Klein, *Mi-palit le-chaluc* [From Refugee to Pioneer], privately published, n.d., 23, translated from Hebrew by Anna Kawałko. Klein wrote, "We would surround a homestead armed with the guns ... We laid the farmers under their beds, a few of us stood guard over them armed so that they would not move, while the others filled bags with food that we found in the house, sometimes also clothing." Klein (b. 1926) was from Radomyśl.

161. For more on the Black Vultures, see Adam Kazimierz Musiał, *Krwawe upiory. Dzieje powiatu Dąbrowa Tarnowska w okresie okupacji hitlerowskiej* (Tarnów: Oficyna Wydawnicza KARAT, 1993), 70–145.

162. Amsterdam, "Life in the Forests," xlv.

163. USC, VHA, 39822, Interview with Yochanan Amsterdam.

164. AŻIH, 301/1145, Testimony of Helena Aussenberg (Bernkopf) (b. 1914), Krakow, October 15, 1945, 7.

165. Zvi Amsterdam, *27 hodashim ba-yaar dolche* [27 Months in the Dulecki Forest], privately published, 1992, translated from Hebrew by Anna Kawałko.

166. AŻIH, 301/3215, Testimony of Helena Aussenberg, Krakow, June 1, 1947, 7.

167. Rosenblatt, "Wspomnienia Chai Rosenblatt," 138–142.

168. Rohtbart, *I Wanted to Live to Tell a Story*, 65.

169. Weronika Wilbik-Jagusztynowa, *Bataliony Chłopskie na Rzeszowszczyźnie. Dokumenty, relacje, wspomnienia* (Warszawa: Wydawnictwo Ministerstwa Obrony Narodowej, 1973), 91; Mirosław Surdej, *Oddział partyzancki Wojciecha Lisa, 1941–1948* (Rzeszów: IPN, 2009), 29; Alina Fitowa, *Bataliony Chłopskie w Małopolsce 1939–1945. Działalność organizacyjna, polityczna i zbrojna* (Warsaw: Państowe Wydawnictwo Naukowe, 1984), 104; Krempa, *Zagłada Żydów mieleckich*, 159.

170. Rohtbart, *I Wanted to Live to Tell a Story*, 65. For a discussion of camps as safe havens, see Martin Dean, "Strategies for Jewish Survival in Ghettos and Forced Labor Camps," in *Holocaust Resistance in Europe and America: New Aspects and Dilemmas*, ed. Victoria Khiterer and Abigail S. Gruber (Newcastle upon Tyne: Cambridge Scholars, 2017), 38–49.

171. Krempa, *Zagłada Żydów mieleckich*, 146–153. There is disagreement among historians about the number of camps set up by this company and their precise locations. Krempa argues convincingly for a single camp in the Czekaj forest, away from surrounding villages, most of which were depopulated for the army base, which gave rise to different camp names among inmates and locals.

172. BStU, MfS HA IX/11 ZUV, no. 35/14, Deposition of David Kuppermann, New York, December 14, 1965, 225–226; BStU, MfS HA IX/11 ZUV, no. 35/13, Deposition of Izchak Frayberg, 203–204. Kuppermann stated that the head engineer in the camp itself was Pogrzeba (Podgrzeba). According to Frayberg, Ulbrycht was a cousin of Governor Hans Frank.

173. USC, VHA, 12246, Interview with Max Schindler from Wytrzyszczka, 1996 [in English]. Schindler stated that some one hundred Jews entered the camp in this way.

174. USC, VHA, 14987, Interview with Nathan (Naftali) Taffel from Radomyśl Wielki, 1996 [in English]. In Bäumer und Lösch, they rejoined their older siblings, who had entered the camp prior to the *Aktion* in Radomyśl.

175. Rosenblatt, "Wspomnienia Chai Rosenblatt," 129.

176. BStU, MfS HA IX/11 ZUV, 35/13, Testimony of Abraham April from Przecław, New York, December 6, 1965, 31.

177. BStU, MfS HA IX/11 ZUV, no. 35/13, Testimony of Louis Frieberg, 219. Some forty Jews from Radomyśl were brought to the camp in the truck. Frieberg noted that he owed his life to Ulbrycht, for which he never had a chance to thank him after the war.

178. AŻIH, 301/1634, Diary of Józefa Luboch, typescript, 21. Lucjan Fink (b. 1925) later rejoined the family in the Bochnia ghetto. After the war, he moved to Israel and adopted the name Arie Fink.

179. Eber, *The Choice*, 130.

180. For the most recent work on the subject, see Alicja Jarkowska-Natkaniec, *Wymuszona współpraca czy zdrada? Wokół przypadków kolaboracji Żydów w okupowanym Krakowie* (Krakow: Universitas, 2018).

181. Krempa, *Zagłada Żydów mieleckich*, 20–23.

182. AŻIH, 211/351, ŻSS Dębica, November 9, 1941, 35.

183. Siedlisker-Sarid, "Murder of the Jews of Dembitz," 258.

184. USC, VHA, 9980, Interview with Izaak Sturm (b. 1926) from Dębica, 1995 [in English].

185. AŻIH, 211/353, ŻSS Dębica, Bescheinigung, issued on October 16, 1942, 32.

186. Dortheimer was a *kapo* in the Pustków camp. In postwar lists of collaborators compiled by the Central Committee of Polish Jews (CKŻP), his name sometimes appears as Tadek "Bortheimer." AŻIH, 313/152, CKŻP, Special Courts, "List of Jews who collaborated with the Germans," 53, 67.

187. Eber, *The Choice*, 129–130.

188. AŻIH, 301/3503, Testimony of Jakub Grynblum from Sandomierz, Łódź, November 13, 1947, 1. Berta Lichtig suggested that they traveled as far west as the Staszów region (forty kilometers away) across the Vistula River, which is likely an exaggeration. AŻIH, 301/1027, Testimony of Berta Lichtig, 1.

189. BStU, MfS HA IX/11 ZUV, no. 35/13, Deposition of Abraham April, 30.

190. BAL, B 162/28387, Case files of Hellmut Hensel and others, deposition of Zoltan March, New York, December 1, 1965, 339.

191. BStU, MfS HA IX/11 ZUV, no. 35/13, Deposition of Abraham April, 30.

192. AŻIH, 301/3503, Testimony of Jakub Grynblum, 2.

193. AIPN Rz, 353/61, Deposition of Bogdan Protter, 258–261.

194. Verstandig, *I Rest My Case*, 148.

195. Havi Dreifuss, *Changing Perspectives on Polish-Jewish Relations during the Holocaust* (Jerusalem: Yad Vashem, 2012), 80–81.

196. Rohtbart, *I Wanted to Live to Tell a Story*, 80.

197. AŻIH, 301/1634, Diary of Józefa Luboch, typescript, 21.

198. AŻIH, 301/2973, Testimony of Szaje Altman, 5.

199. YVA, M.31, 4094a, Testimony of Czesław Kubik, 1.

200. Eber, *The Choice*, 46–47.

TOMASZ FRYDEL received his PhD in history at the University of Toronto. He is a fellow of the Fondation pour la Mémoire de la Shoah (FMS) in Paris. His research has appeared in several edited volumes, including *Microhistories of the Holocaust* (Berghahn, 2017) and *Perpetrators and Perpetration of Mass Violence: Action, Motivations and Dynamics* (Routledge, 2018). In 2019–2020, he was a fellow at the Jack, Joseph and Morton Mandel Center for Advanced Holocaust Studies in the US Holocaust Memorial Museum and served as a lecturer at Stockton University.

EIGHT

BOCHNIA COUNTY

DAGMARA SWAŁTEK-NIEWIŃSKA

BOCHNIA COUNTY BEFORE THE WAR

This article describes the attempts by Jews to survive the extermination in Bochnia County, which included the towns of Bochnia and Niepołomice, as well as the communes of Bochnia, Bogucice, Lipnica Murowana, Łapanów, Niegowić, Niepołomice, Rzezawa, Trzciana, Uście Solne, and Nowy Wiśnicz.

Like other texts in this publication, this article is based on sources such as administrative documents, court files, testimonies and memoirs, and the documentation regarding the granting of the title of Righteous Among the Nations. Databases containing information about Holocaust victims and survivors proved useful too.[1] Among the sources characteristic of this county are the underground Jewish periodical *Hechaluc Halochem*,[2] initially published in Kraków and then in Bochnia and Nowy Wiśnicz; Irena Glück's occupation-period journal, written until the August 1942 extermination action; and Justyna Dränger's memoir produced in the cell of the women's ward of the Montelupich prison in the spring of 1943, which contains information about her stay in the Nowy Wiśnicz area. The information acquired from archival sources was supplemented with publications by local historians.[3]

Bochnia County was an agricultural area dominated by small farms no larger than 4.9 acres.[4] The northern part of the country is a plain, whereas the southern part is mountainous (the Beskid Wyspowy Mountains). Forests covered a significant portion of the county's territory, including the approximately 27,000-acre Niepołomice Forest northwest of Bochnia.[5] The salt mine in Bochnia, which employed a few hundred people, and the rare private factories only slightly improved the local population's economic situation.

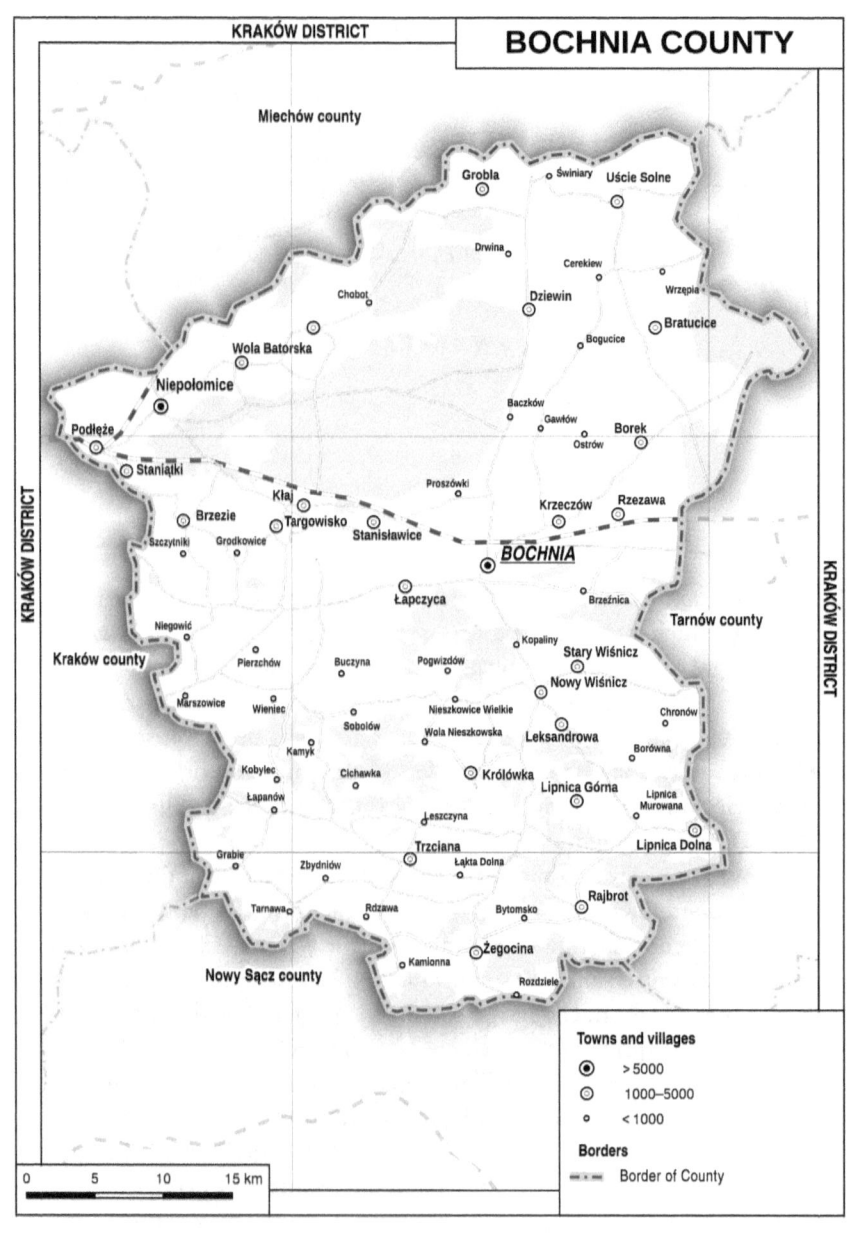

In 1931, the county had 5,656 Jewish inhabitants, or some 5 percent of the population.⁶ Most of them lived in three main centers, Bochnia, Niepołomice, and Nowy Wiśnicz, where they made up half of the population. Nowy Wiśnicz, which in the eighteenth century belonged to the Lubomirski magnate family, became an important Hasidic center. Rabbi Szlomo Halberstam (1847–1906) lived and was active there in the late nineteenth century. In 1881, he set up a yeshiva, which moved to Bobowa eleven years later.⁷ During the interwar period, Halberstam's supporters ran their prayer houses in both Bochnia and Nowy Wiśnicz. Not terribly affluent, the Jewish community of Nowy Wiśnicz supported itself through craftsmanship, petty trade, and farming.⁸ The situation looked similar in other, smaller localities in the county.

The Bochnia Jewish community was slightly different. Before the war, the number of its members exceeded three thousand. Economically diverse, it included a group of well-to-do Jewish entrepreneurs. The Eksteins ran the brick yard, which in the late 1920s had thirty employees; Samuel Silberring owned the Secesja printing house, which employed fifteen people; the Szancers ran a soap manufacture and a mill; and the Greiwers owned a large store.⁹

JEWS IN THE COUNTY FROM THE OUTBREAK OF THE WAR UNTIL DEPORTATION

In early September 1939, some of the Jews from Bochnia County, particularly men, decided to flee to the east. In the chaos of the first days of September, there were instances of local inhabitants breaking into the houses and stores abandoned by the refugees.¹⁰

Having seized Bochnia on September 7, 1939, the Germans immediately began to oppress the local Jews.¹¹ Two weeks after they entered the county, they set the synagogue and the bathhouse in Niepołomice ablaze, forcing a local Jew to participate in the devastation.¹² In Bochnia, as early as the fall of 1939, German soldiers and clerks expelled the wealthier Jews from the tenements in the market square area and ordered them to move into the old Jewish quarter, where they were forced to find accommodation in the rundown and congested buildings.

The period following the end of the military operations and the establishment of the civil occupation administration was relatively peaceful. The area of prewar Bochnia County was incorporated into a larger unit, Kraków County (*Kreishauptmanschaft Krakau-Land*), while Bochnia became the seat of the *Landkomisariat*, that is, a branch of the *Kreishauptmanschaft*, which covered prewar Bochnia County.¹³

The first mass execution in the county took place on December 18, 1939, in retaliation for an attack on and the killing of two German policemen in Bochnia.

Figure 8.1. Identification card of Moses Grünbaum, who worked for Jewish Social Self-Help organization. He was a member of the Niepołomice Jewish Council. During the action, he was selected to work. He was a prisoner of several camps. He was one of the few Jews of Niepołomice who survived. Jewish Historical Institute.

In addition to the murder of the two perpetrators, fifty more people were arrested and executed at Uzbornia. Among the victims were three Jews: Salomon Schonfeld, Maks Faber, and Jankel Rosenzweig.[14]

As in the rest of occupied Poland, Jews in Bochnia County were subject to regulations that gradually limited their rights: the marking of Jewish stores, armbands, limitation of freedom of movement, and more. Approved by the German authorities at the end of 1939 and the beginning of 1940, *Judenräte* (Jewish Councils) operated in larger localities inhabited by Jews. The *Judenrat* in Bochnia was headed by Samuel Freudenheim, a veteran of the First World War and captain of the Austro-Hungarian Army, who during the interwar period owned a large storehouse of Okocim Beer in Bochnia. The *Judenräte* in Niepołomice and Nowy Wiśnicz were chaired by trader Chaim Mames, a relative of a prewar member of the town council, and Abraham Friedman, respectively.

During the winter of 1939–1940, the German authorities resettled some two hundred Jews from the former Poznań Province to Bochnia.[15] The financial situation of those resettled from the territories incorporated into the Reich was dire, as they had been brutally cut off from their work and sources of income. The local branches of the ŻSS (Żydowska *Samopomoc Społeczna,* Jewish Social Self-Help), an organization supervised by the German authorities responsible for the Jewish population's welfare in the General Government (GG), made an effort to provide aid for the newcomers. In July 1940, the Niepołomice Judenrat wrote the following to the ŻSS Presidium: "The military operations have left the local indigenous Jewish population completely devastated and devoid of clothing, with 80 percent of the indigenous population without any means to buy anything whatsoever. Moreover, in the local community there are 140 Jewish families deported from the Reich who arrived here literally in their only shirt due to the immediacy with which they were forced to leave their homes."[16]

In 1940 and 1941, more groups of Jews gradually arrived in the localities in the county: deportees from Kraków, people who voluntarily left the GG capital shortly before the establishment of the ghetto in March 1941, and refugees from eastern Lesser Poland, which was under Soviet occupation. In Niepołomice, the number of Jews increased fivefold.

March 1941 saw the establishment of a Jewish residential quarter (ghetto) in Bochnia, initially of an open character.[17] Beginning in June, Bochnia ghetto residents could not leave the quarter without permission, but at that time they were still not separated in any way from the rest of the town. Following the county governor's decision of April 7, 1941, Jewish inhabitants of the county were resettled from the countryside to larger centers.[18] Aside from Bochnia, in the localities where Jews were still allowed to live, they were assigned quarters with an open character, which meant that the Jews were allowed to move about the given locality. Although the Jewish population was not completely separated from the gentile one, it was as early as October 15 that year that capital punishment was introduced in the GG for Jews leaving their place of residence without a suitable permit. According to Irena Glück's diary written in Niepołomice, in 1941 she moved relatively freely about the town and the surrounding area and even went for walks to the nearby Niepołomice forest, but during the subsequent months this became increasingly dangerous. In April 1942, she wrote that the boy who used to wander from village to village trying to sell just about anything for food was found shot dead in the forest.[19]

One of the most important factors determining the Jews' lot was forced labor. Apart from laboring in workshops and performing various kinds of manual labor to meet the ongoing German demands, Jewish workers from Bochnia County were assigned by the Bochnia *Arbeitsamt* (Employment Office) to work on external work details, to which they commuted daily, or once every couple of weeks. For instance, in May 1942, 225 men from Niepołomice were working outside the town, mostly in the Kraków Kabel factory, in ammunition warehouses in Kłaj (Bochnia County, near the Niepołomice forest), and in the Hobag company. Four men were deported to a labor camp in Pustków.[20] Bochnia Jews were deported to work in the Kraków Bonarka brickyard or at the military airfield in Czyżyny. They labored for companies managed by the Germans or, in the cases of Kłaj and Czyżyny, directly for the Wehrmacht. Niepołomice Jews were employed mostly in felling in the Niepołomice forest or in land drainage on the Vistula River.

The year 1942 saw the opening of three Kraków *Judenlager* (labor camps for Jews, *Julag*)—*Julag* I in Płaszów, *Julag* II in Prokocim, and *Julag* III in Bieżanów.[21] Unlike the workplaces supervised by the civilian or military authorities, the *Julags* were subordinated to *Der SS-und Polizeiführer im Distrikt Krakau* (the Kraków District SS and Police Leader). Their forced laborers worked mostly on extending the railway and roads from Kraków to the east. Due to the imposed work pace, the laborers toiled round the clock in two shifts. Most laborers working in the Kraków Julags were men.

The first deportation campaign in Kraków commenced on May 31, 1942, and continued until June 8. Over seven thousand Jews were deported to the death camp in Bełżec, and several hundred were murdered in the ghetto. A significant percentage of the victims had no permanent employment.[22] After these events, it was generally thought in Bochnia County that employment gave protection from deportation. Unemployed ghetto residents were willing to offer bribes for official employment in the Bochnia Städtische Werkstätten [municipal workshops].[23] Aside from working in labor camps and municipal workshops, other jobs thought to guarantee safety were those in the Judenrat, ŻSS, or OD (*Ordnungstdienst*, Order Service, Jewish police); that OD was headed by Bochnia attorney Szymon Rosen, ŻSS branch director Estera Rosen's husband. Jewish police stations were located also in Niepołomice and Nowy Wiśnicz. Menachem Mendel Selinger, a Bochnia ghetto survivor, explained after the war that he had joined the OD for safety: "As late as August 16, 1941 [it should be 1942], several days before the campaign, I too joined the OD. I did that because I had no *Einsatz*[24] and everybody could sense the approaching resettlement of Jews, which was imagined as deportation to some distant locality to work. I paid three *Judenrat* members to join the OD."[25]

It remains unknown exactly when Bochnia earned a reputation of a town relatively safe for Jews, who began to stream into the county from various parts of occupied Poland even before the deportation campaigns in the district. One of these Jewish refugees was Zila Rennert, who had lived with her family in Lvov since September 1939. With the situation in Lvov becoming increasingly dangerous and unbearable, in early 1942 her family decided to risk a dangerous train journey and change their place of residence. Looking for a safe place was one of the strategies that preceded the deportation period. "Encouraged by letters from our friends who lived in Bochnia, where, as they claimed, the anti-Jewish repressions were less severe, we decided to join them," wrote Rennert in her memoir.[26]

DEPORTATIONS

The German police authorities operating in the county consisted of the Criminal Police (Kripo), which had its station at Oracka Street 4 in Bochnia. Its chiefs in chronological order were Willy Keblitz (1939–1940), Wilhelm Schömburg (1941–1943), and Walter Weinhold (1944).[27] Other Kripo employees included Johann Konarski, Alfred Paciej,[28] Eugeniusz Wróbel,[29] and Franciszek Puchała. The Kripo chiefs were German, while the rank-and-file employees were either German or Polish. Beginning in 1940, Bochnia had a gendarmerie station on Biała Street,[30] headed by Wilhelm Liebmann. During the postwar investigation regarding the operation of the Bochnia gendarmerie, fifteen names of occupation-period gendarmes were mentioned, but in the Holocaust context the witnesses most often indicated Robert Bogusch, Beck, Göbel, Franck, and Edmund Schindler.[31] Göbel commanded the guards who watched over the Bochnia ghetto throughout its existence. According to the occupation period law, all of the Bochnia gendarmes were German, though some of them came from Silesia or from the prewar Poznań Province, so they spoke Polish fluently.[32] Polish Blue police stations were located in Bochnia, Niepołomice, Nowy Wiśnicz, Lipnica Murowana, Trzciana, Zabierzów Bocheński, Łapanów, Podłęże, Rzezawa, Bogucice, Niegowić, and Uście Solne. The Blue policemen were Poles or *Volksdeutsche*. Many of them were prewar Polish policemen; some had served in the county prior to 1939, while others had been transferred from other parts of the county.

Saturday August 22, 1942, was designated by *Der SS-und Polizeiführer im Distrikt Krakau* and announced by *Kreishauptmann* Schaar as the day when Jews from smaller localities (Lipnica Murowana, Targowisko, Trzciana, Rzezawa, Uście Solne, Łapanów, Bogucice, Zabierzów, and Nowy Wiśnicz) and the Bochnia commune were to report to the ghetto in Bochnia, with the exception of Jews from Niepołomice, who were to move to Wieliczka, which was closer. The objective of the concentration was not revealed. The Jews concentrated in the Bochnia ghetto learned about the upcoming campaign several days in advance. According to testimonies, some of them still thought at that time that its objective was resettlement to Ukraine, where labor was in demand.[33]

Table 8.1 The Course of the Extermination Actions in the County

Date	Event description
1942: First action in Bochania	
Monday, August 17	Bochnia *Judenrat* receives a letter from the country governor informing about plans to resettle Jews from the nearby localities to Bochnia,
Thursday, August 20	County Office notifies the *Judenrat* in Nowy Wiśnicz about the upcoming resettlement,
Friday, August 21	Jews begin to be assembled in the Bochnia barracks,
Saturday, August 22	— Resettlement from Lipnica Murowana, Targowisko, Trzciana, Rzezawa, Uście Solne, Łapanów, Bogucice, Zabierzów, and Nowy Wiśnicz to the square outside the barracks in Bochnia.
	— Resettlement from Niepołomice to Wieliczka.
	— Police and SS forces from Kraków arrive in Bochnia.
	— In the evening, a poster is displayed in Bochnia calling on all of its Jewish inhabitants to report to the barracks the following morning.
Sunday, August 23	— 7:00 a.m.: Jews from Bochnia to report to the barracks.
	— Executions of those who failed to report to the barracks.
Monday, August 24	Bochnia Jews continue to be assembled in the barracks
Tuesday, August 25	— Early morning: Baudienst workers dig graves in Baczków.
	— 9:00 a.m.: executions of Jewish children and elderly in Baczków.
	— Train transport leaves from Bochnia to Bełżec.
Thursday, August 20,	— Execution of Jews from Wieliczka and Niepołomice at Kozie Górki.
	— Train leaves from Wieliczka to Bełżec.
Monday, August 31	Poster in Bochnia calls on the Jews to reregister at the German police station in Bochnia.

1942: Second Action in Bochnia

7 November 1942, Saturday	OD surrounds the railway station.
10 November 1942, Tuesday	Police forces arrive from Kraków.
11 November 1942, Wednesday	— Action commences at dawn.
	— Train leaves from Bochnia to Bełżec.

1943: Third Action in Bochnia

Wednesday, September 1	Police forces from Kraków arrive in Bochnia.
Thursday, September 2	— 4:30 a.m.: Police forces surround the ghetto.
	— The Jews are called to the roll call square in ghetto A.
	— Gathering in ghetto B, executions of the old and sick.
	— 8:00 a.m.: 80 policemen enter the ghetto and begin to search the buildings.
	— Selection.
	— Two trains leave at 2:00 p.m. One goes west to Auschwitz and the other goes east to Szebnie.
	— 6:00 p.m.: SS forces leave the ghetto.
	— At night, SS surrounds the ghetto from the outside.
Friday, September 3	— From 7:00 a.m. until the afternoon: searches of houses and sewers, executions.
	— Collection of corpses.
	— SS leaves the ghetto.
	— At night, Polish policemen guard the ghetto fence
Saturday, September 4	Collection and cremation of bodies at Solna Góra in Bochnia.
The following days	Searches in the ghetto, executions of the captured Jews.

Sources: AŻIH, testimonies; *Hechaluc Halochem*; *Wiadomości Bocheńskie*, no. 3 (2015).

Figure 8.2. Location in Bochnia where Jews were gathered during actions and where selection was conducted. Ghetto Fighters House.

People's reactions to the news about the upcoming deportation and the choices they made before the deportations determined their later fate and survival odds. During the final days of August 1942, *Kreishauptmannschaft Krakau-Land* and *Landkomisariat* Bochnia became *Judenrein*, "free of Jews," with the exception of the ghetto in Bochnia, which existed for a year after the August action.

Permanent inhabitants of Bochnia expected that the resettlement would first affect the Jews from Nowy Wiśnicz, Łapanów, Lipnica, and other localities, who had flocked into the ghetto until August 22, with their number estimated at three thousand. The vast majority of the adult Jews already living in the ghetto had proof of employment, which was erroneously regarded as a guarantee of exemption from the deportation. On August 22, SS forces from Kraków arrived in Bochnia along with the German gendarmerie, the *Sonderdienst* (auxiliary formations made mostly of local Germans), and Polish policemen from other areas of the Kraków District. They were commanded by *Hauptscharführer* SS Wilhelm Kunde; the clerk for Jewish affairs coworking with the Commander of Security Police and SD in Kraków, *Hauptscharführer* SS Hermann Heinrich, who worked in Kraków; and Bochnia Kripo Chief Wilhelm Schömburg. That evening, posters were displayed calling on all Bochnia Jews who did not have freshly stamped work permits to report the next day at 7:00 a.m. to the old barracks by the railway station, where Jews from other localities were also

Table 8.2 Number of victims of the actions in the county

Action in the county	Number of victims	Comments
First action: August 22–28, 1942	2,600–3,000	Deported from Bochnia to Bełżec
	500	Executed in Baczków
	n/a	Executed in Bochnia
	9	Executed in Niedary/Uście Solne
	15	Rzezawa, execution of the Jews going from Brzesko to Bochnia
	Up to 2,400	Jews from Niepołomice deported to Bełżec from Wieliczka
	66 or more	Jews from Niepołomice executed at Kozie Górki (the total number of victims was 700, but only some of them were from Niepołomice)
	n/a	A group of Jews deported from Wieliczka to Płaszów and other labor camps
Second action: November 9–11, 1942	200–500	Deported to Bełżec
	100	Deported to Płaszów
	21	Jewish prisoners from Nowy Wiśnicz executed
	70	Executed in Bochnia
	14	Patients of a hospital executed in Bochnia
Liquidation of the Jewish subcamp in Kłaj, June 1943	300	Deported to Płaszów
Third action: September 2–4, 1943	3,000	Deported to Auschwitz
	1,000–1,200	Deported to Szebnie
	200	Found in bunkers in Bochnia executed
	60–70	Murdered at Solna Góra in Bochnia

Total number of victims
Deported in transports: 9,300–10,500
Murdered on the spot: 1,000

Sources: AIPN, GK 163/8, Questionnaires about mass executions and graves; *Hechaluc Halochem*; Kuwałek, *Obóz zagłady w Bełżcu*; Rączy, *Zagłada Żydów w dystrykcie krakowskim*; YVA, Testimonies; AŻIH, Testimonies.

assembled. On August 23, German police began searching the ghetto for people hiding without the stamps; most of those found were executed on the spot. The search continued for a few days. Witnesses talk about dozens of corpses. The exact number of victims of the August action in the county and the subsequent actions in Bochnia remains unknown. Table 4 presents figures based on the available sources:

According to the ŻSS's final data for the summer of 1942, the number of Jews living in the town of Bochnia was approximately 5,000. Along with the Jews brought from other parts of the county, including Nowy Wiśnicz, immediately before the action their number increased to 8,000.[34] Three thousand of them were deported to Bełżec,[35] some 500 people were executed in Baczków,[36] 700–800 obtained the work stamps and were allowed to remain in the ghetto,[37] and 800–1,000 hid in bunkers.[38] It remains unknown how many people were shot dead in Bochnia. There is no data regarding nearly 3,000 people, but it is possible that the initial estimated number of the Jews assembled in Bochnia (8,000) is exaggerated. After the action, in the fall of 1942, the town of Bochnia had 2,000–3,000 Jewish residents.[39]

A full list of the victims executed in Baczków and at Kozie Górki does not exist, but it is possible to reconstruct the course of the executions on the basis of Polish testimonies. Workers from the *Baudienst* (Construction Service) assisted at both executions. Young unemployed Polish men were forced to work for the *Baudeinst*. They were recruited for a few months' service according to their year of birth, and in Bochnia County they performed land drainage, forestry, and road works. Prior to the August action, by order of the German authorities, groups of these young men dug pits in two places in the Niepołomice forest—near Baczków (several kilometers from Bochnia) and close to Niepołomice (Kozie Gorki). The digging of graves in Baczków commenced at dawn on the day of execution. After the war, one of the former *Baudienst* workers estimated that the graves prepared could hold four thousand bodies in total, which might have been a precaution in case of difficulties with organizing a transport to Bełżec.[40]

The execution in Baczków commenced on the morning of August 25. That was when the *Baudienst* workers learned that they would assist at the execution and were made drunk by the Germans. In the Bochnia ghetto, the *Baudienst* workers loaded onto trucks those who could not climb inside or refused to do so on their own.[41] After reaching the execution site, the *Baudienst* workers deprived the Jews of all their possessions, stripped them naked, and arranged them in rows by the edge of the pits. The victims were executed by gendarmes and functionaries of other German police formations, supervised by an unidentified man in a black SS uniform. The execution in Baczków was conducted by the

German police forces, who were at some point assisted by Polish policemen.[42] The execution was witnessed by individuals who happened to be working in the area or were curious enough to go have a look. The last escape attempts were made during the transport to the execution site. This is how the course of the events was described by Maria Gąsiorek, a mother of a *Baudienst* worker: "I saw Jewish women faint and fall out of the truck; I saw the Jews jump out by the lodge in Baczków; those who fell out and those who jumped out were hit with clubs by the Germans and the *Baudienst* workers, who were there to help the Germans, and then they were thrown back into the truck."[43]

Shortly after the action in the Bochnia ghetto, posters were displayed calling on the remaining Jews to reregister. The workshops were reopened. However, this peaceful period did not last long. During the second action, on November 10–11, 1942, a few hundred Jews were murdered, and two to five hundred Jews were deported to Bełżec. The estimates of the number of the victims of that action are based on postwar testimonies, though witnesses provided different figures.

The two main groups of victims of the second action were the Jews who worked in agricultural work details outside the ghetto[44] and the prisoners transported from the prison in Nowy Wiśnicz. Quite a lot is known about the latter group because there are two slightly different surviving lists of 152 names from that transport. These were people who had been sentenced to several years in prison for various criminal offences; for example, theft, illegal trade, illegal animal slaughter, or desertion from work.[45] Twenty-one of them were executed in the court building in Bochnia, while the rest were deported to Bełżec. Aside the prisoners from Nowy Wiśnicz, some seventy other Jews from Bochnia and neighboring localities were executed on the spot.

Shortly after the second action in Bochnia, posters were displayed regarding the Jews' right to stay in the Kraków District. As per the ordinance issued by the *Höhere SS-und Polizeiführer* (HSSPF, Higher SS and Police Leader), from then on Jews could live only in Kraków, Bochnia, Tarnów, Przemyśl, or Rzeszów,[46] where restghettos were established following the deportation actions.[47] In the fall of 1942, the ghetto in Bochnia, which had been semiopen, was surrounded with a wooden fence and also partly with barbed wire.

The fate of those who survived the August and November actions depended on the decisions they then made, the most important of which was whether to stay in the Bochnia ghetto (the only remaining ghetto in the county) or seek rescue in the countryside. In the fall and winter of 1942, the Bochnia ghetto received another influx of Jews, who moved into the houses and apartments vacated by the deportees. In the spring of 1943, the number of Jews reached the level from before the first deportation—approximately four thousand people.

Table 8.3 Number of Jews in Bochnia County (excluding those in hiding)

Main Jewish centers	Prewar	July 1942	March 1943	August 1943
Bochnia	3,150*	5,069†	4,025‡	5,000§
Nowy Wiśnicz	1,200‖	3,268#	—	—
Niepołomice	480**	2,500††	—	—
Lipnica Murowana	n/a	100‡‡ (1940)	—	—
Łapanów	n/a	120	—	—
Labor camp in Kłaj	—	100	300§§	—
TOTAL	5,656‖‖	11,157	4,325	5,000

* AN Kr, 29/206/165, Wybory do rady miejskiej [Elections to the town council].

† AŻIH, 211/241, Sprawozdanie delegatury ŻSS w Bochni za miesiąc lipiec [Report of the Bochnia ŻSS branch for July], August 5, 1942, 35.

‡ AN Kr Bochnia, 30/1/938, Bestandsaufnahme der Bevölkerung im Genergouvernement am 1. März 1943, Stadt Bochnia [Census data for the town of Bochnia], March 18, 1943.

§ AŻIH, 136, Varia z okresu okupacji [Occupation-period miscellanea], Sprawozdanie z działalności KŻ Kraków za okres lipiec i sierpień 1943 r. [Report on the operation of the Jewish Committee in Kraków for the months of July and August 1943], Kraków, September 17, 1943, 3.

‖ AŻIH, 211/1106, Ankieta delegatury ŻSS w Wiśniczu Nowym [Questionnaire of the Nowy Wiśnicz ŻSS branch], August 4, 1942, 47.

Ibid., 48.

** AŻIH, 211/721, Notatka z listu z Niepołomic z dnia 18/XII 1940 [Note from a letter from Niepołomice dated December 18, 1940], 33.

†† AŻIH, 211/726, Sprawozdanie delegatury ŻSS w Niepołomicach za miesiąc lipiec [Report of the Niepołomice ŻSS branch for July], August 2, 1942, 44.

‡‡ *Gazeta Żydowska*, Kraków, vol. 34 (1940).

§§ AN Kr Bochnia, 30/1/938, Bestandsaufnahme der Bevölkerung im Genergouvernement am 1. März 1943, Stadt Bochnia [Census data for the town of Bochnia], March 18, 1943.

‖‖ The numbers in the column do not add up because the prewar data for smaller towns and villages are not complete. The total number of 5,656 comes from the census of 1931.

After the liquidation of the Kraków ghetto in March 1943, Bochnia, Tarnów, Przemyśl, and Rzeszów were the last towns in the district where Jews were still allowed to live. In January 1943, the ghetto in Bochnia was transformed by the Germans into a *Zwangsarbeitslager* (forced labor camp), divided into part A for workers and part B for individuals who did not work. The position of the camp director was given to SS officer Franz Josef Müller, whom some of the ghetto residents remembered as a relatively calm or even "cultured" man. It was only during the liquidation of the ghetto that Müller proved as merciless as other men holding similar positions. Nonetheless, until September 1943 life in Bochnia was more peaceful than in, for instance, nearby Tarnów. The other German holding a high position in Bochnia was Kripo commander Wilhelm Schömburg, who according to witnesses was interested predominantly in making a profit out of the Bochnia Jews.

Ordinary Jews could not officially contact German officers, as the law decreed that all matters had to be settled through the agency of the *Judenrat*. Nonetheless, according to many testimonies, such contacts were indeed established. The composition of the *Judenrat* had changed since the first action, as some of the clerks had been deported to Bełżec, among them, the first chairman of the *Judenrat*, Samuel Freudenheim, who had been considered a decent, honest man, though not particularly resourceful and devastated by the situation. The authorities appointed Symcha Weiss his successor. The new chairman, along with OD Commander Szymon Rosen and his wife, Estera, set the tone for the Council's activity.

According to the available information, no local OD man died during the first or the second action in Bochnia. Marian Rotkopf who served as a Jewish policeman, summed this up as follows: "An OD man was more likely than other Jews to save himself and his family ... When I returned to Bochnia in 1945, I concluded that many of the OD men were alive, more than twelve."[48]

The last official German data regarding the number of Jews in Bochnia are dated March 18, 1943, and they were collected on the occasion of the census in the GG. At that time, the ghetto had 4,235 Jewish residents, who lived in 586 apartments. There were 2,035 women and 2,200 men. According to the census, a few children under the age of ten had remained in the ghetto, 167 boys and 64 girls.[49]

The main difference between the third action in the Bochnia ghetto, which took place during September 2–4, 1943, and the two earlier ones was that there were no signals prior to the deportation. According to testimonies, the Jews learned about this last action when police forces commanded by SS-Sturmbannführer Wilhelm Haase surrounded the ghetto. They were more numerous then in two previous actions. There was no Polish police involvement inside of the ghetto. Menachem M. Selinger suspected, that the authorities were concerned that Bochnia ghetto might take up an example of Warsaw and were afraid of Jewish armed resistance.[50] He mentioned presence of not only German SS, but also unidentified Ukrainian and Latvian forces. As a result of the action, most of the remaining Jews were deported to Auschwitz or Szebnie, or murdered in Bochnia.

In the chronologically closest issue of *Hechaluc Halochem*, published on September 10, 1943, the number of Jews before the deportation was estimated at 4,000,[51] whereas according to Elżbieta Rączy, their number was 4,500–5,000.[52] Owing to a report filed by Żegota (the Polish Council to Aid Jews), the number of Jews who took shelter or left the ghetto shortly before the last action is known. According to police lists, after summing up the deported, executed, and those allowed to stay to clear the area, there were still over 500 missing Jews who had been listed. This indicates that more than 10 percent of the 4,000–5,000 residents of the Bochnia ghetto took shelter or fled.[53] Most of them were captured during the next several weeks after the liquidation action. The witnesses remember several hundred people who were captured and killed in Bochnia during or shortly after the final liquidation action, but these data are divergent and imprecise.

Approximately 250 people were ordered by the authorities to remain in the ghetto to clear the ghetto area. This group included predominantly *Judenrat* members and OD functionaries, or individuals associated with them. In October 1943, most of these Jews were deported to Szebnie.[54] The last Jews clearing the ghetto remained in Bochnia until February 1944.

EFFECTIVENESS OF SURVIVAL ATTEMPTS IN THE COUNTY

Based on all available materials, presented is a table demonstrating information about the Jews who survived the occupation. It concerns those who were staying in the county during the August 1942 action or later (as mentioned earlier, the influx of Jews to that area continued until the summer of 1943). Some of them had lived in the county since before the war, while others were resettled from Kraków or chose to move there during the first years of the occupation. These are probably not all of the Jewish survivors, because even though every available source was consulted, it is possible that there are still new ones to be found. Some of the survivors left no trace in the files or testimonies.

The categories in the table indicate the main ways in which some of the Jews from Bochnia County managed to survive the occupation. Of the 395 survivors, 87 survived in the county, 134 survived by fleeing across the Slovakian border, and 23 survived outside the county. Summing up these three figures, 244 people survived because they had decided to flee or take shelter.

One of the objectives of this study is an attempt to determine which of the survival strategies were effective and to what extent, so it is of utmost importance to calculate the exact number of the Jews who fled from the ghettos.

Table 8.4 Survivors of Bochnia County

Survivors	Survival in the county	Escape abroad	Outside the county in the GG	Forced labor camp outside the county	Other or no data
395	87	134	23	118	33

Source: Data based on author's research.

Table 8.5 Murders committed on Jews who left the ghetto, tried to hide, or to leave the county*

Number of victims	German gendarmerie†	Gendarmerie assisted by Polish police or as a result of information provided by them	Blue policemen‡	Local underground	Local civilians	Other causes of death§	Unexplained circumstances
297‖	88	37	32	7	13	4	116

* Numbers represent victims. Executions during actions in ghettos are not included.
† An independent action conducted by the gendarmerie or one resulting from information provided by the locals.
‡ An independent action conducted by the Polish police or one resulting from information provided by the locals.
§ This figure includes two Jews in hiding who died of natural causes, as well as two suicides.
‖ Only data from sources in which at least some personal data allowing identification of the victim was included.

The only reliable surviving data on this topic is with regard to the third action in Bochnia. The information about the five hundred escapees mentioned in the Żegota report came from police data, to which the Polish Underground State might have had access through the agency of, for instance, Franciszek Puchała—a Kripo from Bochnia and at the same time a member of the AK (*Armia Krajowa*, Home Army). After the war, Puchała testified that he had access to lists of Bochnia Jews. Much less is known about the escapes during the 1942 action in the county. Consequently, the estimate had to be based on the number of escapees included in witness testimonies, which vary significantly. Based on this premise, the total number of Jews who sought rescue from the first action to the end of the occupation may be estimated at no fewer than one thousand.

Table 8.5 illustrates information on those who murdered Jews attempting to leave the ghetto, escape, or hide in the county.

According to postwar estimates made by a judge of the municipal court in Bochnia, some 18,000 Jews in total had gone through the Bochnia ghetto.[55] This large number probably included all of the temporary residents and the Jews who left the county before the first action. When one adds 2,500 refugees from Niepołomice, the total number exceeds 20,000.

There are several reasons why it is impossible to present exact quantitative data on the rescue attempts made by Jews from the Bochnia County during and after the actions. First of all, the vast majority of these attempts facilitated temporary survival, but not survival until the end of the occupation. Take for example those who were in hiding during the first action but returned to the ghetto after its end: most of them lost their lives during the following actions. Another reason why this picture is incomplete is the scarcity of sources regarding those who died. Many of the victims remain anonymous, and some witness testimonies provide only an estimated number of the executed or deported. Moreover, the Bochnia ghetto functioned for a relatively long time, and even after its liquidation, the town remained a stage in escapes to Slovakia. Consequently, during the said period there was a noticeable and steady influx of Jews from other counties, which makes it difficult to distinguish between local victims and those for whom the county constituted just a fragment of the planned route.

Having outlined the numerical data, elements of the survival strategies will now be presented, divided into several types, and discussed in separate subchapters: attempts to avoid deportation made during the actions, procurement of foreign documents and attempts at legal departure, escape across the Slovakian border, deportation to a labor camp, underground activity, and hiding in the county.

RESCUE ATTEMPTS MADE DURING THE ACTIONS

The first element indispensable to survival was finding shelter or fleeing during the extermination actions. Because the first deportation plans were known several days in advance, the Jews from smaller localities were forced to make a difficult decision—they could either report for deportation as per official orders or risk their lives and not appear in the designated place. Refusal to report for deportation was key to later survival. People resettled to Bochnia from smaller localities on August 22, 1942, were highly unlikely to be permitted to remain because they could not find employment in the ghetto. Almost all of them were deported in the first transport to the death camp in Bełżec on August 25 or murdered on the same day during a mass execution in Baczków.

Others tried to prepare hideouts in the ghetto in advance. Some of the most frequently mentioned places included attics and basements. Building various hideouts required careful preparations; among those created after the first action campaign were a number that had been built for weeks. At the same time, attics and basements were the most frequently searched parts of houses, so for a hideout to be effective, it had to be well thought out. There were different reasons why people hiding in bunkers were discovered. Sometimes the policemen guessed on the basis of the house's construction that there was some hidden space inside. Before an action, an unauthorized person might have learned about the construction of the hideout. There were also instances of the Jews leaving their bunkers too early, thinking that it was already safe. Edmund Schönberg is the author of a very interesting testimony about the construction of bunkers in the town. He prepared several, and after the war he described them and drew detailed illustrations.

During the action, it was announced that those who left their hideouts would not be harmed. Later, however, the buildings were to be searched and the Jews discovered there executed on the spot. Consequently, many people left their shelters voluntarily and reported for deportation, particularly during the first action, when the lot of those deported from Bochnia was still uncertain. At this time, people might have chosen deportation over certain death if their hideout had been discovered.

The groups looking for Jews in hiding consisted of several people: policemen, and often a person hired to force open the door. A local Jewish armorer, who lost his closest family during the first action, was one of the individuals who performed that function under duress during the third liquidation action in September 1943, when he was forced by the Germans to open thirty to forty bunkers.[56] At the same time remaining members of OD were ordered to search

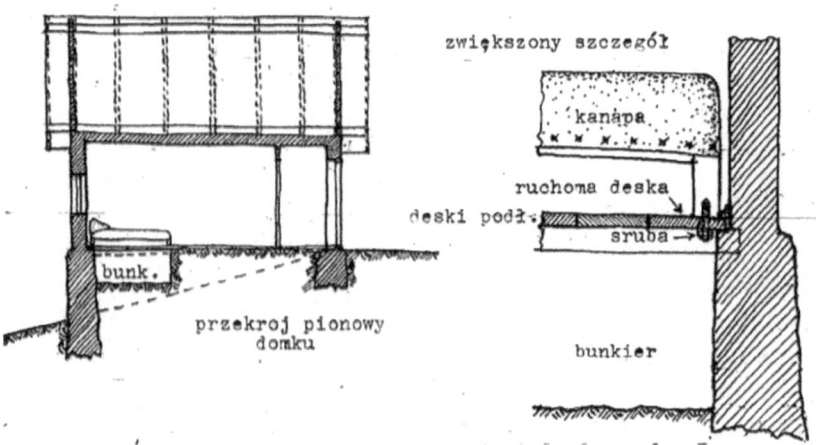

Figure 8.3. Blueprint explaining how bunkers were constructed. It was drawn after the war by survivor Edmund Schönberg as an addition to the detailed description of hideouts used in Bochnia. Some members of his family survived two actions hiding in a bunker. They were murdered in 1943. Jewish Historical Institute.

for Jews hiding in bunkers and they were effective in this task, because of good knowledge of the area. After the war some of them were accused of collaboration with the Germans and put on trial in the Polish court[57].

One method for avoiding deportation often mentioned in the testimonies was fleeing from the county, mostly to Kraków. Upon news of the approaching action, some Jews decided to seek help among gentiles utside the ghetto. Contacts between the Bochnia Jews and the Polish population remained relatively frequent until August 1942. A small number of Poles still officially lived in the ghetto, which had not been fenced in yet. Janina Kowalik, a Polish woman who had been the Hersztajn family's babysitter from before the war, decided not to part with her employers' children despite the anti-Jewish persecutions. After six months spent in Lvov, she returned with the three children to Kraków, and in March 1941 they moved to Bochnia. They lived for some time in the local ghetto, but the youngest child remained in Kraków. Kowalik then moved into a house on the Aryan side, with the older children staying in the Bochnia ghetto with their parents. Kowalik supported herself by selling things she transported every day to Kraków, which she also used as an occasion to transfer messages between Kraków and Bochnia. During the first action in Bochnia, she hid the children in her rented apartment, but her landlady threw them out after the deportation began. Consequently, Janina left for Kraków, first with the boy. The next day she returned for the girl, who had spent the entire night hiding in a toilet, and she took her to Kraków too. After the first action, the children returned to Bochnia. During the second one, the family was in Kraków, that time having left in advance.[58]

Survivor testimonies and files of the postwar trials under the Decree of August 31, 1944 (the so-called August Decree, concerning the punishment of Fascist-Nazi criminals, those guilty of murders and mistreatment of civilians and prisoners of war, and traitors of the Polish nation) give us an idea about the attempts made to find shelter outside Bochnia during the deportation campaigns. Jews from villages and small towns sometimes turned for help to their Polish neighbors. Because they lived in small localities, they knew one another very well. The most frequent reaction was refusal motivated by fear for one's life, as anyone caught helping Jews was punishable by death. In Bochnia, posters were displayed informing, for instance, that "any Pole who, in any form, through his actions jeopardizes or hampers the deportation campaign or supports such activity shall be executed. Any Pole who takes in or shelters a Jew during or after the deportation, or aids such efforts, shall be executed." Reflecting on the motivations of the neighbors who refused to help the Jews, one must not ignore the fear of punishment. One should bear in mind that the German authorities threatened death also to those who took in Jewish property for safekeeping or appropriated it, but that did not discourage some of the local population from looting. The next point in the said announcement read, "Any unauthorized Pole who enters the home of a deported Jew shall be executed as a looter."[59] This means that both people providing aid to the Jews and looters of their homes were risking their lives. According to survivor testimonies, the Jewish property was looted quickly and on a large scale, which suggests that there was no shortage of those willing to take the risk to make a profit on the property abandoned by the victims.

Some of the Jews decided to wait without any help in the nearby woods until the end of the deportation. August nights in Poland are sufficiently warm for one to survive outdoors, and the weather in 1942 was fine. Passivity was not the worst reaction as some of the peasants, together with the Blue police or independently, joined in the search for the Jews in hiding in order to rob them and then hand them over to the authorities. This is how Markus Halpern, who lived in Chrostowa, Niegowić commune, remembered the deportation period:

> On August 22, 1942, we were to report to Bochnia due to the planned action. We had a long discussion about what to do. Mommy wanted to flee, but grandpa did not and he stayed. We fled into the forest: mommy, my brother, my sisters, two aunts, two cousins, grandma, and I. We stayed in

the woods for three days until Tuesday afternoon, August 25. In the forest, we were robbed by peasants who wanted to hand us over to the police. Several days later, having nowhere to buy food and no money for it, we went at night to a peasant we knew, who had our field, house, and cattle. He refused to give us anything. We barely managed to beg some milk out of him. We slept in a field that whole time. We hid in bushes in our village, but we were discovered by peasants who were looking for us. They took us to the village leader, and from there we were sent to Bochnia.

The Halperns were brought to the ghetto on August 25, 1942; that is, on the day of the transport to Bełżec. They were sent to the railway station right away, but they missed the train: "When we reached the square outside the station, the train had already pulled away. The people were waving at us. One of the Gestapo functionaries became furious; he hopped onto our horse-drawn wagon, and we drove along the ghetto streets. We were afraid that he would shoot us, but he took us to prison."[60]

The Polish police and civilians eager to look for Jews posed a mortal danger to the escapees. One these collaborators was tried after the war on suspicion of participation in the capture of an anonymous Jew who tried to flee Bochnia during the first action. A woman who lived nearby gave the following testimony:

> When I was at my grandma's on Proszowska Street ... I noticed two Polish policemen chasing a Jew across the fields by the house ... and the policemen were crying: "Catch that running Jew!" I remember that Tabor, who lived on Proszowska Street, was watching the chase. Hearing the policemen's calls to catch the Jew, Tabor ran after him and caught up with him in the fields, where the Jew collapsed, but I do not know what happened later. I could not bear to look at the policemen. All I know is that that Jew was taken away by the policemen to Bochnia, but I cannot say what happened to him. Let me add that Tabor chased that Jew for as far as one hundred meters into the fields to catch him, while the policemen stopped [running] and walked slowly in the direction of the running Jew because they knew that Tobor would capture him.[61]

After the deportation period in August 1942, the Jews who tried to hide and were captured met one of two fates. If they were apprehended by the locals and escorted to the village leader, they were either escorted or transported to the Bochnia ghetto. But if the Polish police or the German gendarmerie were called, the captured Jews were executed in a nearby forest, field, or cemetery. This is how Antoni Łucki described one of these executions: "In late August 1942, Doctor Izajasz Fragner, a sixty-year-old attorney from Nowy Wiśnicz, was escorted to Lipnica (Bochnia County) with his wife and her sister, Maria Wieselman

[Wiedelman]. They had been captured in a hideout where they had been staying for several days. After two to three days spent in jail, they were executed by the 'Blue' police with participation of one German. The execution took place on the edge of the new Catholic cemetery in Lipnica, which was also where the victims were buried."[62] It remains unknown who denounced the hiding Fragners to the gendarmerie. After the war, the District Court's Public Prosecutor's Office launched an investigation, with Izajasz's prospective daughter-in-law as the main suspect because there was a rumor that she appropriated the Fragners' property. The case was eventually discontinued because the testimonies collected indicated that the suspect was innocent.[63]

A unique event that took place in Wiśnicz became engraved in the memory of the Polish witnesses of the Jews in hiding. In August 1942, an eighteen-month-old infant of the Pinkes family from Nowy Wiśnicz was taken in by the Gicalas—a childless married couple from the neighboring Stary Wiśnicz. The infant boy's parents decided to take refuge elsewhere. The child was sheltered for two days, but then, under the influence of the Gicala's' neighbors and family, Wojciech Gicala decided to seek the local village leader's advice as to what to do with the child. This is where the witness testimonies differ. The village leader claimed after the war that he had advised Gicala to take in the child, but under the pressure exerted by others, Gicala decided to carry the child to the Polish police station in Nowy Wiśnicz. By contrast, Gicala's wife claimed that he had been ordered to do so by village leader Stanisław Banaś. At the station, Polish policeman Ignacy Szmańda refused to believe that the child had been abandoned, and he demanded that Gicala show him the money that, in his opinion, the child's parents had paid Gicala to take care of the boy. Despite interrogation and beating, Gicala insisted that the child had been abandoned. The policeman apparently lost his patience; gendarme Franck was brought from Bochnia to Nowy Wiśnicz, where he executed both the child and Gicala. He also shot dead seven other Jews captured during the deportation by the Polish Police or local inhabitants, who had been detained in the local jail. Their surnames remain unknown.[64] This is the only known instance of a Pole executed after voluntarily escorting the Jew he was hiding to a police station. Gicala's case was used by German propaganda as an example of capital punishment meted out to rescuers. On August 31, 1942, the Municipal Office in Nowy Wiśnicz sent the following circular to the village leaders: "Today, Gicala, a Stary Wiśnicz inhabitant, was executed for sheltering a Jewish child. Making this known, I warn all inhabitants of the commune that those who either shelter Jews or help them hide shall be executed. Let the above be known to the Gromada inhabitants in the manner practiced there."[65]

The rescue attempts during the third action in Bochnia were similar to those made during the two earlier ones, but with two differences. First of all, there was no longer any town in that Jews were allowed to stay or to where they could try to escape. Second, following the liquidation of the ghetto, the Jews became unable to leave their hideouts and legalize their stay in Bochnia.

SURVIVAL STRATEGIES DURING THE EXISTENCE OF THE RESTGHETTO IN BOCHNIA

Some Jews stayed in hiding outside only during the actions, after which they returned to the Bochnia ghetto.[66] The Blue policemen and the OD men who watched the fence focused on those leaving the ghetto. The Jews hiding in forests and villages in the county in 1942 and 1943 continued to stream into the ghetto until as late as the summer of 1943 because they were running out of money to pay those helping them, and they faced a constant threat of denunciation and death by the gendarmes or policemen. Some Jews hid in forests and lived in the ghetto intermittently.

After the extermination action conducted in the county in August 1942, the survivors in the Bochnia ghetto tried to protect themselves in various ways. One such method was obtaining documents proving that one was a citizen of a different country, or at least getting an entry visa. Jews in possession of foreign documents were allowed to live outside the ghetto and freely move about the town. A Jew applying for foreign citizen status had to present documents to Kripo Chief Schömburg. Foreign documents could be obtained in three ways. The first was to present one's actual passport or other documents proving one's eligibility. The second was buying falsified documents.[67] Some Jews falsified documents on their own; that was the method Henryk Schönker's father used to fabricate a photocopy of documents for himself and his family, basing them on his relative's actual documents.[68] The third method was to add somebody as a family member to an existing document, which required assuming a different (though still Jewish) identity.

Obtaining foreign documents had obvious advantages, but it was also dangerous. Jews living outside the ghetto were closely watched by the police, also on suspicion of possessing a certain wealth, which was often true as visas or falsified documents were affordable mostly to wealthier Jews. On August 26, 1943, the public prosecutor's office of the underground Court Martial indicted Blue policeman Alfons Malinowski, the chief of the Polish police in Trzciana, who served as the Bochnia ghetto guard. Among the various charges regarding his actions to the detriment of Poles was also the following: "While on duty at the Bochnia ghetto guard post, he walked outside Bochnia, forcing foreign Jews to give up their jewelry under threat of being shot."[69]

In the spring of 1943, rumors started circulating the Bochnia ghetto regarding the exchange of prisoners of war between Germany and the Allies. Interestingly, an analogous situation, studied by Agnieszka Haska, occurred in Warsaw.[70] Following the announcement of that possibility, over two hundred people reported voluntarily to the police. They were then arrested and transported to the Montelupich prison in Kraków. Some of them were deported to Bergen-Belsen, where a group survived until liberation, while the rest were deported to the Płaszów camp, where save for a handful, they were murdered.

Among Bochnia Holocaust survivors, there is a relatively large group of people who, in 1943, went south across the Slovakian border and then farther on to Hungary. Fleeing across the border to Slovakia was not an entirely new idea, as already during the first year of the war, Poles and Jews used that route to leave occupied Poland. The process of smuggling people across the border was complicated and required the cooperation of at least a few people on both sides of the border. Analyzing the Slovakian organizations' documents, Robert Rozett concluded that during 1943–1944, between 1,100 and 2,000 Jews went from occupied Poland to Hungary.[71]

The situation of Slovakian Jews in 1943 enabled them to cooperate to help not only the Slovakian Jews deported to the GG but also Polish Jews who sought refuge. The smuggling across the border and ensuring the safety of the refugees in Slovakia was coordinated predominantly by members of various Zionist organisations, the Slovakian "Working Group," and the Jewish communities in localities by the border, such as Kežmarok or Bardejov.[72]

To leave Bochnia County and the GG, one had to first reach the Slovakian border. That could be done in two ways: obtaining falsified documents, leaving the ghetto, and going by train to a locality near the border; one route led from Bochnia through Tarnów to Piwniczna, and the other led from Bochnia to Kraków and farther on to the Podhale region—or hiring a specially prepared truck with a driver who had a permit to use it. Such vehicles had a double bottom, underneath which several people could hide in a horizontal position. After placing the second bottom on top, the whole installation was then covered with merchandise—vegetables, furniture, brooms, or coal. Such a manner of transport gave a chance to those who could not travel by train, for instance, due to their so-called "bad" appearance, which meant physical features attributed by gentiles to Jews.

Escapes abroad were a complicated and pricy method because the escapees had to pay their guides. They also required long preparations, some of which did not end well. After crossing the border, most of the escapees decided to continue their journey in the direction of Hungary, a country safer for Jews in 1943, with only a small number of the escapees remaining in Slovakia. The first Jews escaping from Bochnia through Slovakia reached Hungary in March 1943. According to Rozett's findings, 80–90 percent of the over two hundred Jews who escaped from the GG and reached Slovakia by June 1943 had arrived from Bochnia. According to the Slovakian Working Group's data, until November 1943 approximately seven hundred Jews from occupied Poland arrived in Hungary via Slovakia, with an additional two hundred remaining in Slovakia.[73] The last escapes from Bochnia I know about took place in October–November 1943. Those escapees had survived the third action and knew that that was the last moment to try to flee.[74] Escapes from the General Government continued to be organized until the spring of 1944, but Bochnia ceased to be their center—after the liquidation of the ghetto, there was no reason for the escapees to pass through there.

Only a small group of the richest and well-connected Jews could escape to Slovakia. Some of them maintained contact with the German authorities, predominantly with corrupt Kripo chief Schömburg or at least knew people who had direct access to him. Among the influential people from Bochnia ghetto who went to Slovakia and then farther on to Hungary were Bełz Rebbe Aron Rokeach, his brother Mordechaj Rokeach, and several members of the Halberstam family;[75] OD functionaries Salomon Greiwer, Moniek Greiwer, Marian Rotkopf, and Menachem Mendel Selinger, influential *machers* Salomon Weininger and Eliezer Landau.[76]

SURVIVAL IN CAMPS

Though this article's subject matter is limited to Bochnia County, it must be emphasized that people deported to labor camps constituted a relatively large percentage of the local ghetto survivors. Of course, the Jews deported to the Bełżec death camp during the first or the second action did not survive. By contrast, the lives of Jews deported to the Szebnie labor camp and from there to Auschwitz or Płaszów and more distant camps took a different course. Documents and testimonies relate the fate of 118 Jews deported from Bochnia to Szebnie, Płaszów, Auschwitz, and Bergen-Belsen, who survived until liberation in various camps. One can wonder to what extent their survival was an effect of a well-thought-out strategy, factors such as young age, fitness, a stroke of luck, or chance. According to the testimonies, even after the first action, during which a lot of potentially valuable workers were murdered, Bochnia residents were convinced that those able to work were more likely to survive.

Figure 8.4. Photograph of Maniek and Henryk Wiener taken in Nowy Wiśnicz. Maniek had connections with the Jewish resistance. He was arrested in Bochnia in March of 1943 and murdered in Płaszów in April. Henryk (Izrael) Wiener was also taken to Płaszów and then sent to Brünnlitz. He survived until liberation. USHMM.

Underground Activity

A group of Jewish youth from prewar Zionist Youth organizations, mostly Akiva, chose a different strategy.[77] Many activists of that organization stayed in the county during different periods, among them Szymon Dränger and Gusta Dawidsohn-Dränger. Farming courses and the concurrent formation of the local *Halutz* movement's structures were centered on the manor in Kopaliny (halfway between Bochnia and Nowy Wiśnicz), where, beginning with the spring of 1942, the Jewish youth, officially and in cooperation with the ŻSS, performed farm and forest works. One of the organizers of this initiative was Józef

Wulf, future historian of the Holocaust. Most of the Akiva movement members fled from Bochnia County to Kraków before the August 1942 extermination action. Some of them returned in early 1943, when the structures of the Jewish resistance movement were being infiltrated by the German Police following the attack on Germans in the Cyganeria café in Kraków.[78] Most of the fighters who came to Bochnia took shelter in a bunker in the local ghetto. In mid-March 1943, the location of the hideout was revealed, with the ten or eleven people hiding inside transported by the police to Kraków.[79]

When the organization members were arrested in Bochnia, Gusta Dränger, detained in the Kraków prison, was writing a memoir. The text was composed between January and April 1943 in two copies. The author wrote on paper available to her, for instance from food parcels. Stored by the female prisoners, the memoir survived, was published in 1946 by the *Wojewódzka Żydowska Komisja Historyczna* (Provincial Jewish Historical Commission in Kraków). Dränger described the beginning of the underground activity of the Jewish youth in Kraków and the first, unsuccessful, attempts at partisan activity in 1942. She also devoted much space to an analysis of motifs and stances of people from her milieu.[80]

On April 29, 1943, Szymon and Gusta Dränger escaped from prison and returned to Bochnia County.[81] At that time, the underground group's operation was limited to Nowy Wiśnicz and several other localities in the area. It organized mutual support and self-defense of the Jews hiding in that area. They were aided by Elżbieta Kalita and her daughter Maria.[82] Szymon Dränger was staying at Klimek's near Nowy Wiśnicz; the house became a local center of activity for the young people recruited from Akiva. While in hiding, Dränger spent whole days typing.[83] He copied, for instance, leaflets that were scattered in villages. More important, however, he worked on the *Hechaluc Halochem* periodical, where he presented the views of the *Halutz* youth and plans for future action, informed about current events, and described his stay in and escape from the Montelupich prison. The periodical also contained practical advice, such as a detailed instruction manual for building a dugout, together with instructions about the location selection, construction, camouflage, and necessary equipment. The article ended with a recommendation regarding weapons: "In every dugout there should be at least one firearm. The best choice is an automatic handgun with sufficient ammunition. If somebody denounces you and you cannot flee, make them pay dearly for your life and [that of] your loved ones."[84] Unfortunately, that advice was very difficult to follow. In all of the testimonies regarding that period, information was found regarding only two firearms in possession of the Jews hiding after the Bochnia ghetto's liquidation, one being a broken revolver without ammunition, which was used as a deterrent.

Figure 8.5. Hilel Wodzisławski (1918–1943) wearing the Polish Army reserve uniform. The photograph was taken before the war. Ghetto Fighters House.

One of the most moving articles, entitled "Współczesne marraństwo" (Modern Murranos) and printed in the September 3, 1943, issue, is a description of the situation of Jews in hiding:

> Those who have had direct contact with the lot of the modern Marrano; those who have seen him isolated from the world in the mountains and woods, forced to rely on his own resourcefulness and cunning, at the mercy of the sun, rain, gale, frost, and a peasant who could denounce him for a loaf of bread; those who have seen him registered under an assumed name and devoid of a place where he could take a deep breath, he who constantly trembles in fear of recognition; those who meet him forcing his way in an antisemitic milieu not through just rights but through lies; finally, those who have seen him fall into the hands of the police, still trying to fight back despite his wrecked nerves—these people must come to admire the man who can fight like that for his life. There is indeed a great deal of nameless heroism in all of those who, unnoticed by anyone, carry on their silent struggle and in spite of it leave this world silently, defeated by human hatred.[85]

In the same September issue, at the moment of the Bochnia ghetto's liquidation, the periodical published an address to the peasants calling on them to show their solidarity against the common enemy and warning those who denounced Jews to the authorities of the consequences of their actions. The last known issue of *Hechaluc Halochem* is dated October 22, 1943.

Józef Wulf's wife Janina and their son Dawid was hiding in Nowy Wiśnicz area. Firstly, at the home of a teacher Elżbieta Kalita, later in the bar he run by Michał Łuczyński, which before the war belonged to Hilel Wodzisławski's family.[86] Located in a walled-off section of the ice chamber, the hideout also served as a meeting place for the Jews associated with the Akiva movement.[87] Wodzisławski aka Antek, was the coordinator and informal leader of the Jews hiding in the Nowy Wiśnicz area. He was aware of the location of the bunkers and stayed in contact with a number of people, including Poles he knew from before the war. Among them was Andrzej Ludwikowski, an AK member and Polish policeman who had worked at the local police station since before the war. Ludwikowski warned those in hiding about upcoming danger. In 1943, he deserted the police and went into hiding too.[88] Wodzisławski was also familiar with the local peasants, who before the war frequented the bar run by his family.

According to the testimony of Margot Dränger, who was hiding in the same area, on October 8, 1943, on the eve of Yom Kippur, Wodzisławski and his brother Johanan, two Kauper brothers, and Szymon Dränger decided to take revenge on the Polish family that had denounced two Jewish women in order to steal their property.[89] The farmer's son attacked Hilel Wodzisławski with an axe, wounding him seriously, and then fled. Wodzisławski spent the final days of his life in the bunker, where he died on October 12, 1943. Gusta and Szymon Dränger were arrested again in November 1943 and transported to the Kraków Gestapo's headquarters on Pomorska Street, from where they were taken to the prison on Montelupich Street to be executed.[90][91]

Hiding in the County

From the first action in Bochnia in late August 1942 to the third one in early September 1943, the lot of Jews in Bochnia County differed depending on whether they decided to hide in the countryside or live in the ghetto. After the final liquidation action, only a handful of people remained in Bochnia with an order to clear the ghetto area. The rest had to flee and try to hide. For some of them, this was something new; others had been hiding nonstop since August 1942. For the latter, the only change occasioned by the ghetto's liquidation was that there was no longer any alternative to living in an attic or a dugout. Following the third action, the Jews had had only two options: hide or die. Fleeing across the border required a great organizational and financial effort that lay beyond the reach of most Jews from the county. I found information about eighty-seven people who survived the occupation in the county until January 1945.

The mechanisms of pursuing and killing Jews after the end of the deportation actions in a different part of the Kraków District were described by Jan Grabowski in his book *Hunt for the Jews: Betrayal and Murder in German-Occupied Poland*.[92] This research on Bochnia County indicates that the "hunt for Jews" in that area looked similar in many respects. The following pages shall focus predominantly on the effective survival strategies, as owing to survivor testimonies, they are what is most known. It must be assumed, however, that a great deal of the information about denunciations and executions was not included in the documents as the victims died, and it was in the interest of not only the perpetrators but also the witnesses to keep that a secret.

The Poles' stance toward Jews in hiding changed with time, becoming increasingly unfavorable. Today, it is difficult to say whether the progressively hostile attitude toward the Jews resulted from growing fear, the influence of the propaganda, or perhaps mostly due to the fact that those in hiding were running out of money to pay for help. This is how Margot Dränger described that situation:

> On that entire wooded terrain, stretching near Bochnia, Niepołomice, Wiśnicz Nowy, Łomna, and other settlements, the Polish peasants were sheltering Jews. Prior to the outbreak of World War II, these peasants had maintained close personal relationships with the local Jews, who were their neighbors. They knew each other well and often did business together. That was why during the German occupation, they often provided hiding places to the Jews with no ulterior motive, often risking their own lives. However, as the war dragged on, many of them changed their attitude. They revealed the location of the Jewish hideouts, denouncing the Jews for a kilogram of sugar; they belonged to the Home Army and often murdered the Jews to obtain their money.[93]

Though fear of German repressions was undoubtedly one of the reasons, it certainly cannot explain the phenomenon. The sources accessed inform about capital punishment meted out to two Poles from Bochnia County for hiding Jews: Michał Łuczyński and Stanisław Kluba.[94] A third man whose death might have resulted from helping Jews was Stanisław Engel, who falsified documents in Niepołomice for Poles and Jews in hiding. As a result of exposure, Engel was arrested and died in Auschwitz.[95] A report filed by the KWC (*Komitet Walki*

Cywilnej, Committee for Civil Resistance) also mentions an anonymous peasant from Niepołomice who had been shot by the Polish policemen for having harbored a Jew.[96]

The death sentence was introduced for helping Jews, but the same punishment could be meted out for radio possession, the illegal slaughter of a pig, underground activity, and many other "misdemeanors." According to the calculations made by ZBoWiD (*Związek Bojowników o Wolność i Demokrację*, the Society of Fighters for Freedom and Democracy), a total of 493 Poles from Bochnia County were killed by the Germans (including individuals who died in camps and as a result of military operations).[97]

Polish and Jewish testimonies from that period, as well as trial files, inform about the lot of Jews hiding in that countryside in 1943 and 1944. Some of these stories are moving or terrifying, while in other cases only shreds of information have survived. For instance, *Kronika miasta Niepołomic*, written by local researchers Anna and Antoni Siwek, contains the following entry: "The tragedy of the Jews continued, as during 1943–1944 the Jews hiding in the woods or captured on roads or in villages were occasionally executed. That was how old Niepołomice confectioner Lewi Windstrauch, who ran a cake shop in the market square, died. That was also how mostly very young Jews died after falling into the hands of the Germans or—and this unfortunately has to be admitted—the 'Blue' police."[98]

The significant role played by the Polish police in the capture and murder of the Jews is repeatedly mentioned in occupation-period and postwar sources. The underground *Małopolska Agencja Prasowa* (a press agency) published a short note: "Search for Jews. On the initiative of 'Blue' policemen Ignaszak and Buczyk, in the village of Podłęże between Niepołomice and Wieliczka, the Germans organized a major hunt for Jews, during which about a dozen people in hiding were arrested, including a few Poles."[99] Several weeks later, one could also read about the continuation of the policemen's activity: "In the locality of Igołomia [on the opposite bank of the River Vistula], the 'Blue' police arrested a group of Jews in hiding, but as they did not want to execute them, they escorted them to the police in Niepołomice, where the execution was conducted by policemen Ignaczak, Buczek, and Kuczek."[100] A more detailed description of a different execution can be found in the files of an investigation conducted after the war against the Niepołomice Blue policemen. That time, the casualties included Poles—young men hiding in order to avoid deportation to forced labor. A fragment of a witness testimony regarding the death of Szmul Metzendorf reads:

One day in early October 1942 at midday, I was digging potatoes with women. After a moment... we suddenly heard shots about one kilometer away. After a short while, we noticed a man running down a field path whom... I identified as Szmul Metzendorf, a Jew from Zabierzów. He was running about fifty steps away from us. As he drew near, I noticed that that that running man was being pursued down the same field path by Adolf Mierzwa, a 'Blue' policeman from the Zabierzów police station, who was cycling with a rifle on his back. At some point, police officer Mierzwa jumped off the bike, threw it to the side, and began to pursue the running Jew on foot. After we walked several steps, the tired Jew stopped, and then police officer Mierzwa ran up to him, grabbed him by the collar, kicked him from behind, and ordered him to run. When the Jew Metzendorf started running away, police officer Mierzwa fired thrice at him from his rifle, instantly killing Szmul Metzendorf, who collapsed onto the ground.[101]

It remains unknown where Szmul Metzendorf had been staying since the deportation, and under what circumstances he was discovered.

The policeman best known for his criminal activity in the county was the Polish police chief from Niepołomice, Jan Ratajczak. He acted to the detriment of not only the Jews but also Poles. The postwar People's Militia Chief wrote about him, "He was a ruthless tormentor of Poles, and it seems that there are no Niepołomice inhabitants whom he had not harassed."[102] During the occupation, Ratajczak had been sentenced to death by an underground court. An unsuccessful execution attempt was made on October 1, 1944. With a gunshot wound in the head, Ratajczak was hospitalized in Bochnia. After the war he was sentenced again, on August 23, 1948, this time by the Regional Court in Kraków. According to witness testimonies, Ratajczak and his subordinates killed at least a few Jews and transferred more to the German gendarmerie. One of the victims of that group of Niepołomice policemen was the seven-year-old daughter of Józef Peiper, who had been sheltered by a local peasant in Grobla near Niepołomice. As a result of a denunciation, she was captured by Ratajczak, who escorted her to the station and then executed her in a forest. Realizing her dire situation, the girl begged him before her death "not to grab or shoot her."[103]

The extensive testimonies given by witnesses and defenders present the usual course of the arrests and executions of the Jews in hiding. First, the night watch, neighbors, or a helper denounced the Jews to the Polish police.[104] The policemen then escorted the given person to a secluded place to execute them personally, or more often they brought gendarmes over to that end. After the execution, the perpetrators ordered a local inhabitant to bury the bodies. Some of the murders were witnessed by Poles, which proves that the perpetrators were not trying to keep their killing of Jews a secret.

Most executions were conducted by German gendarmes, about a dozen of whom were stationed in the area of interest. The gendarmerie station was located in Bochnia, from where the gendarmes patrolled the area and also set out to conduct executions after they had been informed by the Blue police about captured Jews.[105] During the final years of the occupation, individual gendarmes were assigned to supervise and work in local Blue police stations, which at that time were called *Stützpunkte*.[106] Additional information was found concerning the lot of 297 Jews murdered in the county outside the three extermination actions. The actual number of the Jewish victims is larger, as at least 350 people killed by gendarmes at the Jewish cemetery in Bochnia were excluded. The key witness of these executions was the gravedigger Henryk Groblicki, who did not know the identity of most of the victims. This figure includes the Jews murdered during the actions, as well as the newcomers captured while traveling under false papers on the Kraków-Tarnów train.[107]

More is known about the survivors. Though every story of hiding is unique, based on the testimonies regarding Bochnia County, one can come to a few more general conclusions. The experiences shared by many of the Jews in hiding are wandering, walking on foot, and frequently changing the place of refuge, though often over only short distances.[108] Moreover, all of the Jews who did not have Aryan papers and survived in the county until the end of the occupation used help intentionally provided by Poles and other Jews. Without such help, survival was impossible, as those in hiding needed food and drink, a place to sleep, clothing, medicine, and news about what was happening.

Many of the Poles who decided to help the Jews did not limit themselves to aiding just one person or even one family. Bochnia County rescuers formed very loose and informal, though distinct, networks of people engaged in supporting those in hiding. Sixty-one of them have been recognized by Yad Vashem as Righteous Among the Nations. Some of them helped the Jews escape or provided emergency assistance during an action. Forty-one of the Bochnia County Righteous provided long-term support in the area by sheltering the Jews in their own homes or delivering food to those hiding in bunkers over a long period of time. Not all of the rescuers have been recognized, with their total number difficult to estimate. Based on the testimonies, it may be concluded that including the Righteous, over a hundred people were actively engaged in rescue efforts in the county. It is impossible to give a clear answer to the question as to what factors made one decide to provide help to the Jews in hiding. Obviously, one needed courage, decency, and readiness to break the occupation-period law.

An analysis of the available elements of the biographies of the several dozen Righteous and other rescuers failed to reveal any regularities regarding their background or social class. Most of them were peasants, but this is unsurprising, as Bochnia County was largely rural. They ranged from wealthy farmers to the landless poor; among them were people who were barely literate and a respected teacher from Bochnia (Stanisław Fischer).[109] Jews in Bochnia County were assisted by judge and AK member Jan Wyrwicz,[110] two Nowy Wiśnicz prison employees, and also several professional smugglers. The rescuers' motivations differed. Some of them were driven by religious considerations. Others decided to help having financial gain in mind. Many simply wished to help somebody they knew, or they were convinced on account of their sense of morality that it was "the right thing to do."

The story of the Fruchthändler family consisting of parents, four brothers, and a sister presents various survival strategies and reactions of local inhabitants. Instead of going to Bochnia ghetto hiding on idle land, in fields, and in stables, the Fruchthändlers managed to stay in the countryside until February 1944. They avoided capture until Władysław N. from Kłaj brought the Blue police to the abandoned house in which they had recently found shelter. The father was captured and taken to Bochnia, where for some time he performed manual labor for the Germans, after which he disappeared without a trace. One of the sons was shot by a Blue policeman while attempting escape. From then on, the remaining five members of the family went into hiding in Kłaj in a barn close to the post office and the Kazimierz and Rozalia Czubaks' house. Post office clerk Tomasz Wąsik, who was in the know, gave them bread and enabled them to exchange letters with acquaintances in Płaszów camp. Informed by the neighbors, the Polish police again tracked down the Jewish family and conducted a search on December 27, 1944. The three brothers managed to escape owing to their own quick reaction and Czubak's courage, who despite beating did not reveal the actual location of the hideout (he confessed to helping Jews but said they were hiding elsewhere). Knowing that he could no longer help the Fruchthändlers directly, Czubak sent the remaining male members of the family to his friend, Franciszek Włodarczyk, where they survived until liberation. At that time, the mother and daughter were staying in a neighboring village, sheltered by Mrs. Czubak's sister. Another Jew hiding at the Czubaks' was twelve-year-old Józef Nabel, whom the Czubaks' ten-year-old daughter hid in a telephone booth at the post office during a search conducted by the Blue police.[111]

In Bochnia County, there were also instances of Jewish families sheltered continuously in one place until the end of the occupation. The Kępa family lived in Podgrabie near Niepołomice, in a small hamlet located in the immediate vicinity of the Vistula River's embankment. Andrzej Kępa was a raftsman on the Vistula. In 1940, the Heisler family arrived from Kraków and moved in with Kępa's neighbor Franciszek Siwek. Upon his request after the August 1942 extermination action, the Kępas took in the Heislers, who were joined by Zofia Heisler, whom Siwek had escorted out of the Kraków ghetto. Initially living in the attic, the Heislers then moved into a bunker next to the house, prepared by Mr. Kępa. They lived there until January 1945, and after the liberation they stayed in Niepołomice for one more year. "My family and I provided help to the Heislers altruistically, guided by the dictates of our religion. I am a scholar of the Holy Writ, and following our religion's commandments I was obliged to aid our neighbors, because I thought that I too had a right to expect such assistance from others," explained Andrzej Kępa after the war.[112] Some of the rescuers provided aid to their prewar friends. That was the case with Dolek Steiner, who, after his escape from the Płaszów camp, returned to his hometown of Zabierzów Bocheński, where he hid in the stable of his neighbor, Jan Szczęśniak. The two men shared an interest in horse breeding. Though at first the landlord agreed to shelter his Jewish neighbor for only a week, eventually Dolek stayed with the Szczęśniaks until the end of the occupation.[113]

Bearing in mind the rescuers' great courage and dedication, it should be stressed that they constituted a small group. The aggregate statistics of victims in Bochnia County indicate that most of the Jews who were looking for assistance found none or received it only temporarily, which led to their death. Those who managed to find permanent shelter with the Poles were in a relatively good situation. Those who were frequently forced to change their place of stay, constantly risking death due to a denunciation or a chance encounter with the police, were in the worst position.

Witness testimonies tell of several groups of Jews who tried to survive on their own in dugouts in the county. That strategy was unsuccessful, as the individuals in hiding occasionally had to leave their shelter to stock up on food. Thus, they risked being seen and denounced to the police or the gendarmerie. One execution of dugout dwellers took place in 1943 in Żegocina. A group of gendarmes and Blue policemen commanded by gendarme Bogusch arrived in the village. The local village leader received an order to bury the execution victims. His testimony includes a description of the dugout: "Together with the people I collected I went to that place, deep in the forest, about 1,500 meters from the road that cut through that forest. There I found a kind of a small dugout, that is, a deep shelter dug in the ground, covered with fir branches, where Jews dwelling in that dugout had been hiding. I also noticed clothes taken out from that damaged dugout, straw from the beds, and some quantity of the carbide which the Jews had used to light their dugout. Inside the dugout lay corpses of seven adult Jews."[114]

The last executions conducted by the Germans in Bochnia County took place on January 1, 1945, when gendarmes Bogusch and Beck shot several people in the Bochnia cemetery.

Living on Aryan Papers in Bochnia County

Another group of Jews tried to survive in Bochnia County pretending to be non-Jewish Poles or Ukrainians. There were two ways of assuming a false identity: as a reaction to an emergency, or as a long-term strategy.

Assuming an Aryan identity for a specific occasion was a necessity for those Jews who had to leave the ghetto, for instance, by fleeing to a different town during an action. Very few Jews were authorized to travel to other towns. Permanent passes to move along a specific route were given to certain OD members and ŻSS employees inspecting the ghetto. Other Jews could travel on the basis of one-off passes or illegally obtained false documents, or in an even riskier way—without a pass.

The Jews who assumed false identity for months or even years were in a different situation. The research for this article resulted in information concerning nineteen people who survived in the county in that way. One of them was Sarna (Julia) Janicka, who left the Bochnia ghetto with her young child in the summer of 1943. She went to the village of Borek, where she moved in with a poor widow. Janicka posed as a Ukrainian whose fiancé had been taken away by the Soviets. She had an ally in the village, Władysław Ryncarz, who knew her true origin, helped her from afar, and gave her instructions. Following Ryncarz's advice, Janicka moved into an abandoned house in the same village. She had met Ryncarz through her husband Roman, who in 1942 was a PPR (*Polska Partia Robotnicza*, Polish Workers' Party) messenger between the party and the *Halutz* youth. In 1943, Janicka moved to the Bochnia area. Together with several other Jews, her husband wished to join the BCh (*Bataliony Chłopskie*, Peasant Battalions), about which he contacted the regional commander of the organization, Władysław Ryncarz (aka Dąb, Orzeł). His offer was rejected, but Ryncarz tried to aid them on his own by providing false documents to Janicka and helping her husband hide in the countryside.[115] In mid-1944, German soldiers, who had arrived from Romania, were assigned accommodation in the house in which Janicka was staying. The men lived there until almost the end of the occupation.[116]

Another group of Jews hiding in Bochnia County were children taken in by Polish families. That was the case with Rosa Berll from Bochnia, who was entrusted to Franciszek and Genowefa Świątek. The Świąteks adopted Berll and introduced her to their neighbors as their female relative's daughter. The child's carers treated her like their own daughter. After the war, Berll learned about her origin. She lived with her foster family until the age of twenty-one. As an adult, Berll left for Israel and then the United States.[117] Other children were not so lucky. For instance, Maria Straucher, born in 1938, survived the war living with a Polish couple who abused her: they called her names; hit, kicked, and starved her; and poured freezing water on her.[118] A few girls, among them Nina Leiman, hid on false papers in a dormitory run by the Felician sisters in the Benedictine nuns' cloister in Staniątki. In December 1944, the nuns moved back to Kraków by order of the Germans.[119]

Michał Zellner from Wieliczka, who stayed in the county after the deportations, mentioned an unsuccessful attempt to survive by assuming a Polish identity. The people who sheltered Zellner told him multiple stories about people in hiding. One such individual was a Jewish woman who lived in the village as a Polish woman, went to church and confession, and even sang religious songs beautifully. She was denounced by her landlady, who was purportedly jealous of her husband's perceived interest in her. Even though the Polish police deemed that the Jewish woman's documents genuine, she was thrown out of the house only to be raped by local men. After some time, the Blue policemen asked the gendarmerie to investigate the matter more thoroughly. The gendarmes beat the woman up, transported her to Bochnia, and found out not only that she was Jewish but also that she was keeping in contact with her husband, who was staying in Tarnów on false papers. That led to the couple's death. Purportedly, every Saturday a meeting at the village leader's place was organized to discuss the ordinances that prohibited taking "strange" people into the village, on account of the fact that numerous Jews were hiding using false documents.[120]

POLISH UNDERGROUND DETACHMENTS' ATTITUDE TOWARD THE JEWS IN HIDING

According to testimonies of several people hiding in the county, not only the German and Polish Police, but also Polish underground detachments posed an immediate danger. Bochnia County was an area of the operation of detachments of different provenance.

Though numerous, the BCh and the People's Security Watch (*Ludowa Straż Bezpieczeństwa*, LSB), composed of supporters of the farmer's movement, rarely appeared in the Jews' testimonies. The surviving occupation-period documentation does not permit a more precise determination of the local LSB and BCh attitude toward the Jews. It did not let Jews into its ranks, though some individual members did help Jews of their own accord. At the end of 1943 and in 1944, some members of BCh and LSB joined the AK.

SN (*Stronnictwo Narodowe*, National Party) forces operated mostly within NOW (*Narodowa Organizacja Wojskowa*, the National Military Organization). NOW partially merged with the AK in the fall of 1943. In November that year, there were mass arrests that weakened the organization.[121] One NOW member was Władysław Węgrzyn aka Poniatowski from Wieniec, a subordinate of Gustaw Rachwalski aka Pogrom. After the merger with the AK, Węgrzyn was promoted to platoon leader.[122] Earlier, in September 1942, he agreed to help two Jewish women he knew: Genia Raber and Sabina Blaufeder. Then with participation of other inhabitants of the village, he handed them over to the Blue police. The women were shot dead by gendarme Franck.[123] There is no evidence in the files that when Węgrzyn denounced the Jewish women, he was acting with the knowledge or by the order of his underground superiors. In 1944, the county was in the area of operation of the NSZ (*Narodowe Siły Zbrojne*, National Armed Forces). The scarce surviving archival materials of Bochnia County NSZ contain almost no references to Jews. The blacklist published by the local cell, which contained surnames of informers, included the name of post office employee Tomasz Wąsik, mentioned earlier. He was condemned for "sheltering Jews and refusing to help the [Poles] evacuated from Warsaw."[124]

The AK constituted the largest military organization in the county. Beginning with July 1943, the local AK was led by Julian Więcek aka Topola. June 1944 brought the most famous operation of the local underground. Commanded by Józef Wieciech aka Tamarow, an AK detachment, launched an attack on a prison in Nowy Wiśnicz, freeing some 120 Polish political prisoners, including members of underground detachments. The prisoners dispersed in the area, hiding in forests as well as in the homes of AK soldiers and supporters. According to the memoir of Julian Wieciech, Tamarow's brother, none of the released men was captured by the Germans, which shows that Poles were very successful in hiding in the area.[125]

Manhunts conducted by large groups of SS detachments (German and also Ukrainian) and the gendarmerie brought over from other places were an element of the anti-partisan policy. One such roundup took place in Lipnica Murowana on October 29, 1944, when two AK members were killed and another nine were arrested and deported to Auschwitz. Although houses in the locality were searched and looted, there is no information about the Germans finding any Jews on that occasion.[126] According to some testimonies, the Jews who had survived in the Nowy Wiśnicz area until mid-1944 were afraid of partisans almost as much as the Germans. Margot Dränger painted a very negative picture of the AK detachments' behavior toward the Jews:

"Partisan AK groups were running rampant in the woods. These groups were on the lookout for Jews. It was often in the Polish peasant's interest to reveal the location of a Jewish bunker. It sometimes happened that a peasant murdered somebody to rob them and was afraid of revenge by the victim's relatives. Here in these woods, everybody knew one another from before the war, and the peasant knew to expect revenge after the war... Sometimes the peasant denounced his neighbor, also a peasant, who was sheltering a Jew, and in return he received a kilogram of sugar."[127]

In the fall of 1944, a group of Polish partisans came to Władysław Wyrwa's house, where Margot Dränger was hiding, looking for Jews. Finding nobody there, they went to a nearby bunker, where a group of Jews was taking refuge. Among them were Hela Hanin and her husband, Fela; Fred Schneider; Johanan Wodzisławski, Hilel's brother; and three unidentified Jews. The partisans killed the residents of that dugout, who before death tried to defend themselves—they shot dead one of the approximately twenty attackers and wounded another. Hela Hanin was the only one to survive.

After the war, the public prosecutor's office launched an investigation regarding the activity of Józef Wieciech (mentioned earlier), who was suspected of participation in the attack on the Jewish hideout. That matter was revealed as a secondary thread, because the public prosecutor's office was interested mostly in the firearms that might have been in the suspect's possession and his purported anti-communist activity. During the occupation, Wieciech was the commander of the AK post, which operated in the Lipnica Murowana commune. He testified that the bunker near Wyrwa's house was attacked by a group of Polish partisans composed of former prisoners from Nowy Wiśnicz, who had been informed about the Jewish bunker by a local man. The partisans opened machine-gun fire at the bunker and threw in a grenade (here the testimonies differ), killing the Jews inside. Aside from the bodies, Yiddish documents were found in the bunker.[128] Wieciech, who did not participate in that attack, claimed not only that he had not acted against the Jews but also that he had helped a few. That version of events was confirmed by his brother in arms, Jan Szymański. According to their testimonies, the attack on the Jewish bunker resulted from the detachment's members' insubordination.

Faced with the danger posed by the partisans and ordinary bandits who pretended to be partisans running rampant in the county, the Jews tried to arm themselves to offer resistance in case of need. Because they had almost no access to firearms, they endeavored to have at least clubs or axes at hand.[129]

According to the testimonies of Jews who survived in the county, a relatively large number of Jews in hiding were murdered in the fall and winter of 1944. The most dangerous period was the one immediately following the third action in the fall of 1943, when roundups and searches were organized by the German police. The second most dangerous period was late 1944. It may be surmised that the large number of murders of Jews prior to 1944 resulted from several factors, none of which can be deemed decisive. The Jews who hid in bunkers and forests during the warmer periods were forced to look for food and shelter in Polish homes. During the winter, it was also possible to follow their footprints in the snow to the hideouts. Polish refugees after the Warsaw Uprising streamed into the county, and the local population was more eager to help them than the Jews. In addition, an increasing number of partisan detachments were active in the area, some of which were loosely connected with the AK structures, along with detachments of a bandit character. Another important factor was the issues connected with the attitude toward the Jews—some of them were running out of money and could no longer pay for help. Still others had possessions that could be easily looted by those trying to make a profit at the expense of the helpless. The fear of leaving witnesses of denunciations and looting might have also been of certain importance.

THE SITUATION AFTER THE WAR

The Red Army seized Bochnia County in mid-January 1945. The fiercest fighting between the Soviet troops and the retreating Germans went on in the southern part of the county. Local partisan detachments also participated in the struggle against the Germans. Jews from the county began leaving their hideouts. Similarly, survivors of the German camps started coming back during the subsequent weeks and months.

On March 7, 1945, Bochnia had thirty Jewish inhabitants. Even though before the war they owned houses or apartments, some ten weeks after Bochnia's liberation by Soviet troops, most of the Jews were homeless because their homes had been destroyed or were occupied by other people. The returning local Jews assembled in the house of Arje Schancer, who made it available to them.[130] Another thirty Jews were living in the neighboring villages. Fearing for their own safety, however, they wished to move to Bochnia. The town's mayor, Ferdynand Kozłowski, tried to prevent this by demanding special settlement permits from the Jews.[131]

The Jews who returned to the villages or left their hideouts felt that they were still in danger. The level of postwar anti-Jewish violence in Bochnia County was not as high as in the neighboring Miechów County or in Podhale, but the problem did exist. The Jews feared mostly bandits and pro-independence detachments. Samuel Landwirth, who came from Bochnia County and after the war lived in Kraków, was among the victims of the postwar violence in Bochnia.

On June 6, 1945, he set out for the market in Łapanów and was shot dead on the way.[132] Samuel Reiss was murdered the same day in nearby Łąkta Dolna.[133] The perpetrators remained unknown.

Owing to a detailed investigation, the murder about which most is known is the one committed on August 17, 1945, by members of detachments commanded by Aleksander Wilowski ("Tur"), which operated in Bochnia County. In this case, Józef Weinstock, son of a local butcher and Mauthausen survivor, was murdered in Czchów in the neighboring Brzesko County.[134]

Jews were not the only victims of the postwar violence in the county. According to the UB (*Urząd Bezpieczeństwa*, Security Office), during 1945–1960 a total of 121 people died at the hands of the "reactionary underground" in Bochnia County, including 49 civilians, 46 UB or People's Militia functionaries or soldiers, and 20 members of the PPR.[135] Some of the perpetrators of the violence partially reflected in the previously stated figures were Soviet soldiers stationed in the county, as well as UB and MO functionaries.

The attitude of the county inhabitants to the Jews who were returning from or leaving their hideouts can be gauged from a memo on the county convention of the PSL (*Polskie Stronnictwo Ludowe*, Polish People's Party) held in Bochnia on August 19, 1945, to which Jan Tomasz Gross referred in his book *Fear: Anti-Semitism in Poland After Auschwitz*. According to the memo's author, one of the speakers motioned for expulsion from Poland not only of Germans but also Jews, and he claimed that Hitler should be thanked for the destroying the Jews. At least some of those assembled approved of that opinion, though Chairman Władysław Ryncarz voiced his protest and deprived the speaker of the right to continue his speech.[136]

Jews living in Bochnia had to face antisemitism even though there had been no Germans in the county since January 20, 1945. However, their Polish collaborators, who had participated in the persecution of Jews, remained. Former Blue policeman Czesław Budziński remained in Bochnia after the war. His case was handled by a postwar court after his neighbour reported that he had boasted "venting [in the ghetto] on that motherf***er Struma, who refused to leave the basement during the roundup ... [by] hitting him on the head with a rifle butt."[137] Six months later, the witness withdrew his testimony saying that even though he had heard from OD man Gutter that Struma had been killed by the witness' neighbor, that man had two neighbors who were Blue policemen.[138] In 1949, the other one was already dead.[139]

According to the data collected after the war by the CKŻP (*Centralny Komitet Żydów w Polsce*, Central Committee of Polish Jews) in 1945 and 1946, at least 136 and 28 Jews registered in Bochnia and Niepołomice, respectively.[140] Among them were Jews who had been in the county until its liberation (19); Jews who returned from German camps (37), Hungary or Slovakia (7), and the USSR (10); and one Jewish woman who had been captured in a roundup and deported to Germany to perform forced labor, which she survived posing as a Christian Pole. Ten people who registered in Bochnia or Niepołomice had been hidden outside the county during the occupation. I have no data regarding the remaining 80 people or the information coming from various sources about their place of residence until 1945 is contradictory. Almost all of them left Bochnia before the end of the 1940s.

NOTES

1. The database of the International Tracking Service (ITS); Yad Vashem databases: Central Database of Shoah Victims' Names and the Database of the Righteous Among the Nations; Archive of the Jewish Historical Institute (Żydowski *Instytut Historyczny*, ŻIH): database of the names of people mentioned in the files of the Central Commission of Polish Jews (*Centralny Komitet Żydów w Polsce*, CKŻP). I am grateful to Agnieszka Haska and Aleksandra Bańkowska for their help in my query.

2. *Hechaluc Halochem* [Pioneer in Combat], periodical of the Military Organization of Halutz Jewish Youth (*Bojowa Organizacja Żydowska Młodzieży Chalucowej*). The surviving copies are stored in the Yad Vashem Archives, Stanisław Fischer Museum in Bochnia, and in the collection of the Bochnia Inhabitants and Bochnia Region Enthusiasts Association. I am grateful to Stanisław Kobiela and Stanisław Mróz for making these documents available to me.

3. These include *Kronika miasta Niepołomic* by Anna and Antoni Siwek, published in Niepołomice in 1989, and the *Wiadomości Bocheńskie* periodical, published by the Bochnia Inhabitants Association. In 2015, a special issue of that periodical devoted to the Jewish Memory Route in Bochnia was published. Particulary important introduction to the history of the Bochnia ghetto was an online publication written by Issachar Zelinkovsky *Ghetto Bochnia. On the trail of the family I never knew*, record11.com (accessed December 5, 2021).

4. Józef Hampel and Jerzy Zawistowski, "Stosunki gospodarcze i administracyjne w latach 1919–1939," in *Bochnia. Dzieje miasta i regionu*, ed. Feliks Kiryk and Zygmunt Ruta (Kraków: Urząd Miejski Miasta Bochnia, 1980), 351–352. In 1939, the smallest farms constituted 63.3 percent of all farms in the county.

5. Tadeusz Ziętara, "Środowisko geograficzne," in *Bochnia. Dzieje miasta i regionu*, 25.

6. Edward Szturm de Sztrem, ed. *Drugi powszechny spis ludności z dn. 9.XII 1931 r. Mieszkania i gospodarstwa domowe. Województwo Krakowskie bez mista Krakowa*, (Warszawa, kom. red. Głównego Urzędu Statystycznego 1938), 80.

7. Piotr S. Szlezynger, "The Jewish Quarter in Nowy Wiśnicz," *Scripta Judaica Cracoviensa* 9 (2011): 27. The history of the Halberstam dynasty was discussed in more detail in Adam Bartosz, *Galicyjskim szlakiem chasydów sądecko-bobowskich* (Kraków: Austeria Klezmerhojs, 2015), 92–121, and in the same book in the two chapters by Iwona Zawidzka, devoted to Bochnia and Nowy Wiśnicz, respectively, 377–397.

8. Piotr S. Szlezynger, Iwona Zawidzka, Żydowski *Wiśnicz: najnowsze badania dotyczące żydowskiej społeczności* (Kraków: self-published, 2016), 27–65.

9. Hampel and Zawistowski, "Stosunki gospodarcze i administracyjne" 360.

10. See for instance Archiwum Narodowe w Krakowie [National Archive in Kraków], Regional Court in Kraków, 29/1988/2074, Akta w sprawie Juliana Palonka i tow [Files regarding Julian Palonek and others], Protokół ustnego zawiadomienia o przestępstwie [Record of an oral notification of a crime], January 18, 1940, no pagination.

11. Muzeum w Bochni [Museum in Bochnia] (hereafter MB), H/3491, Relacja Stanisława Fischera [Testimony of Stanisław Fischer], 11.

12. AŻIH, Relacje Żydów Ocalałych z Zagłady [Testimonies of Jewish Holocaust survivors], 301/1332, Relacja Mojżesza Grünbauma [Testimony of Mojżesz Grünbaum].

13. Elżbieta Rączy, *Zagłada Żydów w dystrykcie krakowskim w latach 1939–1945* (Rzeszów: IPN, 2014), 30; Jacek Chrobaczyński and Jerzy Gołębiowski, "Polityka okupanta wobec ludności," in *Bochnia*, 434. In this text, I use the word *county* (*powiat*) to denote the area of the former Bochnia County, though I wish to stress that during the occupation Bochnia County did not exist as a separate territorial unit.

14. Instytut Pamięci Narodowej Oddziałowa Komisja Ścigania Zbrodni przeciwko Narodowi Polskiemu w Krakowie [Kraków Branch of the Institute of National Remembrance—the Commission for the Prosecution of Crimes against the Polish Nation] (hereafter IPN OK Kr), Ds. 32/68, Akta w sprawie Otto Wächtera, Namentliches Verzeichnis [Files of the case of Otto Wächter, List of names], December 18, 1939, 6.

15. Archiwum Żydowskiego Instytutu Historycznego [Archive of the Jewish Historical Institute] (hereafter AŻIH), 313/105, CKŻP Sąd Społeczny [CKŻP, Social Court], Akta w sprawie Mariana Rotkopfa i Szymona Rosena [Files of the case of Marian Rotkopf and Szymon Rosen], Zeznanie Menachema M. Selingera [Testimony of Menachem M. Selinger], June 18, 1947, 42.

16. AŻIH, 211/721, Judenrat w Niepołomicach do Prezydium ŻSS w Krakowie [Letter by the Niepołomice Judenrat to the ŻSS Presidium in Kraków], July 25, 1940, 2.

17. Muzeum Historyczne Miasta Krakowa [Historical Museum of the City of Kraków] (hereafter MHMK), Collection of Posters, Obwieszczenie o

utworzeniu żydowskiej dzielnicy mieszkaniowej w Bochni [Announcement of the establishment of the Jewish residential quarter in Bochnia], March 14, 1941.

18. Archiwum Narodowe w Krakowie Oddział w Bochni [Bochnia Branch of the National Archive in Kraków] (hereafter AN Kr Bochnia), 30/22/20, Gmina Nowy Wiśnicz [Nowy Wiśnicz Commune], Zawiadomienie skierowane do Menasche Lipskiera [Notification addressed to Menasche Lipskier], 1069.

19. AŻIH, Pamiętniki Żydów Ocalałych z Zagłady [Memoirs of Jewish Holocaust survivors], 302/270, Dzienniczek Ireny Glück [Journal of Irena Glück], entry of April 16, 1942.

20. AŻIH, 211/725, Delegatura ŻSS w Niepołomicach do Komitetu Opiekuńczego Powiatowego ŻSS w Krakowie [Letter from the Niepołomice ŻSS to the ŻSS County Welfare Committee in Kraków], May 8, 1942, 4.

21. The scholars differ as to the exact dates of the *Julags'* establishment. According to Ryszard Kotarba, *Julag* I began to operate in the spring of 1942, *Julag* II in June 1942, and *Julag* III at the turn of October–November 1942. Ryszar Kotarba, *Niemiecki obóz w Płaszowie 1942–1945* (Warsaw–Kraków: IPN), 51–52; Podhorizer-Sandel, "O zagładzie Żydów w dystrykcie krakowskim," Biuletyn ŻIH, no. 2 (1959): 105.

22. Aleksander Biberstein, *Zagłada Żydów w Krakowie* (Kraków: Wydawnictwo Literackie, 1986), 62–65.

23. Dagmara Swałtek-Niewińska, "Salomon Greiwer i Warsztaty Miejskie w Bochni," Zagłada Żydów. Studia i Materiały 12 (2016): 253.

24. Here: a proof of employment.

25. AŻIH, 313/105, Testimony of Menachem M. Selinger, June 18, 1947, 42.

26. Zila Rennert, *Trzy wagony bydlęce. Od pierwszej do drugiej wojny światowej—podróż przez Europę Środkową lat 1914–1946*, translated by Magdalena Rodak (Warsaw: ŻIH, 2016), 222.

27. Chrobaczyński and Gołębiowski, "Polityka okupanta," 435.

28. IPN OK Kr, S 23/04/Zn, Akta prokuratora w sprawie zbrodniczej działalności żandarmerii w Bochni [Public prosecutor's files regarding the criminal activity of the gendarmerie in Bochnia], Sprawozdanie z 21 VIII 1966 r. [Report of August 21, 1966], 5.

29. Ibid., 303.

30. IPN OK Kr, S 23/04/Zn, Zeznanie Jerzego Freudenheima z 27 X 1966 r. [Testimony of Jerzy Freudenheim, October 27, 1966], 17.

31. IPN OK Kr, S 23/04/Zn, vol. 1, Sprawozdanie dotyczące zbrodni żandarmerii w Bochni [Report on the gendarmerie crimes in Bochnia], August 17, 1966, 4a.

32. The two gendarmes mentioned the most often in the context of the murders committed on Jews came from Katowice (Rudolf or Leon Beck, a butcher by occupation, *Volksdeutsch*) and Bielsko (Robert Bogusch, a prewar footwear salesman and also *Volksdeutsch*).

33. According to Robert Kuwałek, in the summer of 1942, few Jews from the localities near Kraków were aware where the Kraków Jews had been deported to in June that year. In Kraków there were rumors about Bełżec, but they were still relatively vague (Robert Kuwałek, *Obóz zagłady w Bełżcu* [Lublin: Państwowe Muzeum na Majdanku, 2010], 190–191).

34. AŻIH, 301/1700, Testimony of Henryk Mondheit, undated; AŻIH, 301/1636, Testimony of Henryk Czapnicki, undated.

35. AŻIH, 301/1144, Testimony of Cyla Renert [Zila Rennert], undated; AŻIH, 301/4459, Testimony of Henryk Mondheit, November 29, 1949.

36. IPN OK Kr, S 23/04/Zn, Pismo Okręgowej Komisji Badania Zbrodni Hitlerowskich w Krakowie [Letter from the Kraków Branch of the Commission for Investigation of Nazi Crimes], August 21, 1955, 1966.

37. AŻIH, 301/1700, Testimony of Henryk Mondheit; AŻIH, 301/3813, Testimony of Józef Weinstock, August 24, 1948.

38. AŻIH, 301/2392, Testimony of Salomon Greiwer, undated; AŻIH, 301/3813, Testimony of Józef Weinstock.

39. AŻIH, 301/3288, Testimony of Leon Epsztajn, February 8, 1948.

40. AIPN, GK 163/8, Zbiór ankiet sądów grodzkich dotyczących miejsc i faktów zbrodni hitlerowskich [Collection of the municipal court's questionnaires regarding the location and facts of the Nazi crimes], Kwestionariusze o egzekucjach masowych i grobach masowych [Questionnaires regarding mass executions and graves] (hereafter ASG), Protokół przesłuchania świadka Wojciecha Synowca [Record of the interrogation of witness Wojciech Synowiec], September 25, 1945, 25.

41. For more about Baudienst's participation in executions in other localities in the Kraków District, see Jan Grabowski, *Hunt for the Jews: Betrayal and Murder in German-Occupied Poland* (Indiana University Press, 2013), 121–129; Refusal to render work for *Baudienst* could result in a severe punishment; desertion could end in deportation to a concentration camp or execution.

42. Alojzy Świerkot aka Ryś, the commander of the "Odwet"' BCh detachment, which operated in Żegocina, wrote the following in the July 15, 1943, entry in that detachment's chronicle: "'Reckoning' with the Bogucice 'Blue' police commander for his vile acts to the detriment of the Polish population; helping liquidate Jews in a forest near Baczków; collected: 1 rifle, 20 pieces of ammunition, 1 pistol, 2 bikes, 2 uniforms, and 2 pairs of boots. The commander was punished: 30 lashings, the other policemen was not punished." http://archiwum.zegocina.pl/historia/tekstyzrodlowe/tekstzrodlowy18.htm (accesed December 12, 2021).

43. IPN OK Kr, S 23/04/Zn, Zapisek urzędowy rozpytania Gąsiorek Marii [Official record of the interrogation of Maria Gąsiorek], June 18, 1969, 153.

44. AŻIH, 301/5321, Testimony of Anna Steinberg, undated.

45. AIPN, GK 109/19, Akta Niemieckiego Ciężkiego Więzienia w Nowym Wiśniczu [Files of the high-security German prison in Nowy Wiśnicz], Listy żydowskich więźniów z 10 XI 1942 r. [November 10, 1942 lists of Jewish prisoners], 52–55; Lista z 31 VIII 1942 r. [list of August 31, 1942], 38–51.

46. Rozporządzenie Friedricha Wilhelma Krügera, wyższego dowódcy SS i policji w GG [Ordinance issued by Friedrich Wilhelm Krüger, *Höhere SS-und Polizeiführer* in the General Government], November 10, 1942, cited in Robert Kuwałek, *Obóz zagłady w Bełżcu* (Lublin: Państwowe Muzeum na Majdanku, 2010), 117.

47. Dariusz Libionka, *Zagłada Żydów w Generalnym Gubernatorstwie* (Lublin: Państwowe Muzeum na Majdanku, 2017), 185.

48. AŻIH, 313/105, Akta w sprawie Mariana Rotkopfa i Szymona Rosena [Files regarding the case of Marian Rotkopf and Szymon Rosen], Zeznanie Mariana Rotkopfa [Testimony of Marian Rotkopf], March 12, 1949, 160.

49. AN Kr Bochnia, 30/1/938, Bestandsaufnahme der Bevölkerung im Genergouvernement am 1. März 1943, Stadt Bochnia [Census data for the town of Bochnia], March 18, 1943.

50. Selinger M. M. *Wir Sind so Weit*, vol 1, 75.

51. *Hechaluc Halochem*, vol. 33, September 10, 1943.

52. Rączy, *Zagłada Żydów w dystrykcie krakowskim*, 286.

53. AŻIH, 136, Varia z okresu okupacji [Occupation-period miscellanea], Sprawozdanie z działalności KŻ Kraków za okres lipiec i sierpień 1943 r. [Report on the operation of the Żegota Committee in Kraków for the months of July and August 1943], Kraków, September 17, 1943, 13.

54. AŻIH, 301/137, Testimony of Zygmunt Goldszmit, undated.

55. AN Kr, 439/1062, Sąd Apelacyjny w Krakowie [Appellate Court in Kraków], Kierownik Sądu Grodzkiego w Bochni Stefan Zapała do prezesa Sądu Apelacyjnego w Krakowie [Letter from the Municipal Court manager in Bochnia, Stefan Zapała, to the President of the Appellate Court in Kraków], October 10, 1945.

56. AIPN Kr, 502/725, Akta Sądu Okręgowego w Krakowie w sprawie karnej Samuela Frischa [Files of the Regional Court in Kraków regarding the penal case of Samuel Frisch], Zeznanie świadka Karola Grossa [Testimony of witness Karol Gross], August 26, 1946, 102.

57. IPN Kr 502/725, Wyrok Sądu Okręgowego w Krakowie [Judgment of the Regional Court in Kraków], February 27, 1947, 169–171; IPN Kr 502/1091 Akta sądu Okręgowego w Krakowie w sprawie karnej Szymona Rosena [Files of the Regional Court in Kraków regarding the penal case of Szymon Rosen], Protokół rozprawy głównej [Record of the main hearing], March 17, 1948, 553–772.

58. YVA, O.3/2551, Testimony of Janina Kowalik, March 01, 1963. In 1943, Janina Kowalik helped organize the escape of the Hersztajn siblings—Celina, Dawid, and Natan—via Slovakia to Hungary, where the three of them survived until liberation.

59. MHMK, Obwieszczenie kreishauptmanna Schaara z 22 VIII 1942 r [Announcement of *Kreishauptmann* Schaar, August 22, 1942].

60. AŻIH, 301/1142, Testimony of Markus Halpern, undated.

61. AN Kr, 439/1273, Akta w sprawie karnej Jana Tabora [Files of the criminal case of Jan Tabor], Protokół przesłuchania świadka Krystyny Kicy [Record of the interrogation of witness Krystyna Kica], 51. Another witness, Jan Nowak, gave a similar account in his testimony submitted to the AŻIH (301/4318). Tabor was sentenced to fifteen years' imprisonment, but in 1952 the Supreme Court changed that sentence to seven years. In 2003, the Regional Court in Kraków dismissed the petition for invalidating the judgment.

62. AŻIH, 301/1790, Testimony of Antoni Łucki, undated.

63. AIPN Kr, 502/3569, Akta Prokuratury Sądu Okręgowego w Krakowie w sprawie Olgi Kupiec [Files of the Public Prosecutor's Office of the Regional Court in Kraków regarding the case of Olga Kupiec], Protokół przesłuchania podejrzanej Olgi Kupiec [Record of the interrogation of suspect Olga Kupiec], September 2, 1948.

64. IPN OK Kr, S 23/04/Zn, Zeznanie Anny Gicala [Testimony of Anna Gicala], May 25, 1975, vol. 2, 381; Zeznanie Edwarda Bachuli z 16 II 1967 r. [Testimony of Edward Bachula, February 16, 1967], vol. 1, 66.

65. AN Kr Bochnia 30/22/24, Gmina Nowy Wiśnicz [Nowy Wiśnicz Commune], Okólnik z 31 VIII 1942 r [Circular letter of August 31, 1942], 53.

66. USC, VHA, 9558, Interview with Nathan Krieger, December 4, 1995.

67. The complex subject matter of producing fake documents for Jews from Kraków and the area who were in hiding was sketched by Bartosz Heksel in his article "Krakowska Rada Pomocy Żydom," which was published in Bartosz Heksel and Katarzyna Kocik, Żegota: ukryta pomoc (Kraków: Muzuem Historyczne Miasta Krakowa 2017), 197–208.

68. Henryk Schönker, *Dotknięcie anioła* (Warszawa: Ośrodek Karta–Dom Spotkań z Historią 2011), 205.

69. AIPN Kr, 010/7074, Akt oskarżenia Sądu Specjalnego [Indictment prepared by the Special Court], Szerszeń, August 26, 1943, 3. The surviving files do not say what happened to that case.

70. Agnieszka Haska, *"Jestem Żydem, chcę wejść." Hotel Polski w Warszawie, 1943* (Warsaw: Centrum Badań nad Zagładą Żydów i Wydawnictwo IFiS PAN, 2006), 55–100.

71. Robert Rozett, "From Poland to Hungary: Rescue Attempts 1943–1944," *Yad Vashem Studies* 24 (1994): 191–192. Devoted to the help provided by Slovakian Jews to Polish Jews, Rozett's article shows the organized help structures,

the operation methods, and the financial costs connected with escapes to Slovakia and further to Hungary.

72. Ibid., 182. For more about the situation of Jews in Slovakia, see Gila Fatran, "The Struggle for Jewish Survival during the Holocaust," in *The Tragedy of the Jews of Slovakia, 1938–1945: Slovakia and "The Final Solution of the Jewish Question"* (Oświęcim: Auschwitz-Birkenau State Museum and Banska Bystrica: Museum of the Slovak National Uprising, 2002), 141–161.

73. Rozett, *From Poland to Hungary*, 185–186.

74. AŻIH, 301/4226, Testimony of Holländer-Wierzbik, July 25, 1946.

75. The topic of the efforts of the Orthodox community in Hungary and Slovakia to provide help to Polish Jews has been studied by Esther Farbstein. In her publications, she used precious documents previously unknown to historians. Esther Farbstein, *Hidden in the Heights. Orthodox Jewry in Hungary during the Holocaust* (Jerusalem: Mossad Harav Kook, 2014), 151-282; *Hidden in Thunder. Perspectives on Faith, Halachah and Leadership during the Holocaust* (Jerusalem: Mossad Harav Kook, 2007), 67–145.

76. Both Salomon Weininger and Eliezer Landau were accused by some survivors of collaboration with the Nazis. Their role was ambiguous, as they indeed were in contact wth the German authorities, but there are testimonies confirming their efforts to use their position to help other Jews (Alicja Jarkowska-Natkaniec, *Wymuszona współpraca czy zdrada? Wokół przypadków kolaboracji Żydów w okupowanym Krakowie* [Kraków: Universitas 2018], 304–316, 343–350). Especially Eliezer Landau is praised for his role is organizing the escape of Rebbe of Belz and his brother Rebbe of Bilgoraj from Bochnia ghetto (Yosef Israel, *Rescuing the Rebbe of Belz. Belzer Chassidus—History, Rescue, Rebirth* (Brooklyn, NY: Mesorah Publications, 2005, 257–287).

77. More details about Akiva in Kraków can be faound in book by Katarzyna Zimmerer, *Kronika zamordowanego świata. Żydzi w Krakowie w czasie okupacji niemieckiej* (Kraków: Wydawnictwo Literackie, 2017), 396–407.

78. On December 22, Jewish fighters conducted a successful attack on the Cyganeria café in Kraków, which at that time admitted only German customers. Several customers of the locale were killed, and about a dozen were injured. After the attack, the group was liquidated, with its leader, Adolf Liebeskind ("Dolek"), executed and many members arrested.

79. AŻIH, 301/2314, Testimony of Dawid Wulf, December 31, 1946; AŻIH, 301/1928, Testimony of Maurycy Perlman, undated; Menachem M. Selinger, *Wir sind so Weit… The Story of a Jewish Family in Nazi Europe. Memories and Thoughts 1939–1945*, ed. Tanja Beilin, translated by Robert Burns (Milano: Il Faggio 2020), vol. 2, 460–462.

80. Gusta Dawidsohn-Draengerowa, *Pamiętnik Justyny* (Kraków, Wojewódzka Żydowska Komisja Historyczna 1946), 25. The English edition of the book was published as *Justina's Narrative*, ed. Eli Pfefferkorn and David H.

Hirsch, translated by Roslyn Hirsch (Amherst: The University of Massachusetts Press 1996).

81. Szymon Dränger was a prisoner in infamous Montelupi prison in Krakow, and Gusta was imprisoned in a women's ward called Helclów. When the Jewish fighters in Krakow learned that a group of prisoners was going to be taken to Plaszow, they organized their escape. Szymon was rescued from the transport to the camp, Gusta escaped the same day. Their escape was described in the testimony of Kalman Hammer, Ghetto Fighters House, 5021, September 14, 1943.

82. AŻIH, Central Jewish Historical Commission of the CKŻP, 303/XX/536, Zaświadczenie o udzielonej pomocy [Certificate confirming the provision of help], December 19, 1946, 29.

83. YVA, O3/3284, Testimony of Johanan Kalfus, September 1, 1967.

84. *Hechaluc Halochem,* vol. 32, September 3, 1943.

85. Ibid.

86. In most publications, the family name is written Wodzisławski. In prewar archival files from Nowy Wiśnicz, the family name was Wojdzisławski.

87. AŻIH, 301/2314, Testimony of Dawid Wulf.

88. According to the Kraków *Księga pamięci,* Hilel Wodzisławski used the name Antek Ludwikowski. *Memorial Journal in Honor of Perished Jews from Kraków 1939–1945* (Jamaica, NY: New Kraków Friendship Society, 1965), 38.

89. YVA, O.3/1683, Testimony of Margot Dränger, September 1, 1960. A slightly different version of the events is presented in the chapter of the Kraków *Księga pamięci,* published in 1967 and devoted to the resistance movement in Kraków, written by Moshe Singer (*Memorial Journal in Honor of Jews from Kraków,* 33). According to this version, Hilel and his companions went to avenge the Jewish child killed by the locals.

90. AŻIH, 301/2423,Testimony of Wanda Lewicka, undated.

91. *Hechaluc Halochem,* vol. 38, October 15, 1943.

92. Jan Grabowski, *Hunt fot the Jews. Betrayal and Murder in German-Occupied Poland* (Bloomington: Indiana University Press 2013), 48–62.

93. YVA, O.3/1686, Testimony of Margot Dränger.

94. IPN OK Kr, S 24/04/N, Protokół przesłuchania świadka Emila Kluby [Record of the interrogation of witness Emil Kluba], March 2, 1971, 306.

95. Anna Siwek and Antoni Siwek, *Kronika miasta Niepołomic 1000–1945,* 45.

96. Archiwum Akt Nowych, Armia Krajowa [Home Army], 1326/203/VIII-2, Miesięczny raport sytuacyjny [Monthly report], November 30, 1943, 9, 10. I would like to thank Tomasz Frydel for drawing my attention to this document.

97. Chrobaczyński and Gołębiowski, *Polityka okupanta,* 442.

98. Siwek and Siwek, *Kronika miasta Niepołomic,* 42.

99. *Małopolska Agencja Prasowa,* April 30, 1943.

100. *Małopolska Agencja Prasowa,* June 4, 1943.

101. AIPN, GK 164/6036, Akta w sprawie Andrzejewskiego Antoniego, Mierzwy Adolfa i Ratajczaka [Files of the case of Antoni Andrzejewski, Adolf Mierzwa, and Jan Ratajczak], Zeznanie Edwarda Burkota z 16 III 1946 r. [Testimony of Edward Burkot, March 16, 1946], 11.

102. AN Kr, 1989/6857, Akta w sprawie karnej Ratajczaka i tow. [Files of the penal case of Ratajczak et. al.], Pismo komendanta MO w Niepołomicach J. Wajlera do Prokuratury Sądu Specjalnego w Krakowie [Letter from the Niepołomice People's Militia Commander, J. Wajler, to the Public Prosecutor's Office of the Special Court in Kraków], March 2, 1946, 1.

103. AN Kr, 1989/6857, Zeznanie Antoniego Sikory [Testimony of Antoni Sikora], March 4, 1947, 131.

104. In some cases, the village leader (*sołtys*) acted as the middleman between the denouncer and the police, but in Niepołomice the incriminating information was provided directly to the Polish Police station.

105. Gendarmes from Wieliczka also operated in the Niepołomice area.

106. IPN OK Kr, S 23/04/Zn, Protokół przesłuchania świadka Michała Plewy z 21 IV 1970 r. [Record of the interrogation of witness Michał Plewa on April 21, 1970], 228.

107. AN Kr, 29/691/UW II 1008, Urząd Wojewódzki Krakowski [Kraków Province Office], Starostwo Powiatowe Bocheńskie do Urzędu Wojewódzkiego Krakowskiego [Letter from the Bochnia County Governor Office to the Kraków Province Office], May 26, 1948.

108. Wandering was a shared experience of a significant percentage of Jews hiding in the countryside, Barbara Engelking, *"Jest taki piękny słoneczny dzień..." Losy Żydów szukających ratunku na wsi polskiej 1942–1945* (Warsaw: Stowarzyszenie Centrum Badań nad Zagładą Żydów, 2011), 55–75; English edition, *Such a Beautiful Sunny Day... Jews Seeking Refuge in the Polish Countryside, 1942–1945* (Jerusalem: Yad Vashem, 2016).

109. YVA, M.31/9952, Righteous Among the Nations, File of Stanisław Fischer.

110. YVA, M.31/12420, Righteous Among the Nations, File of Jan Wyrwicz.

111. AŻIH, 301/4645, Testimony of Józef Fruchthändler, undated.

112. YVA, M.31/5427, Righteous Among the Nations, File of the Kępa family.

113. AŻIH, 349/24/1965, Dział Dokumentacji Odznaczeń Yad Vashem w ŻIH [Department of Documentation of Yad Vashem Righteous Among the Nations in ŻIH], Testimony of Janina Włosak, née Szczęśniak, October 4, 1993.

114. IPN OK Kr, S 23/04/N, Testimony of Andrzej Gomułka], May 5, 1975, 362.

115. Irena Powell, *The Daughter Who Sold Her Mother: A Biographical Memoir* (Bloomington, 2016), Kindle edition.

116. AŻIH, 301/5393, Testimony of Stefan Janicki, July 4, 1952; USC, VHA, 19429, Interview with Roman Janicki, August 28, 1996. Roman and Stefan

Janicki are the same person; the man used various pseudonyms during the occupation. His birth name was Abraham Pinkas.

117. YVA, M.31/6404, Files of Franciszka and Genowefa Świątek.

118. AŻIH, 301/3292, Testimony of Maria Straucher, December 2, 1947.

119. Interview with Janina Ecker, née Leiman, recorded in 2013 within the framework of the Ocalić od Zapomnienia [Saving from Oblivion] program, conducted by the Historical Museum of the City of Kraków. The interview is available online at http://ocalicpamiec.mhk.pl/portfolio/janina-ecker/. Nina stayed in the cloister from 1943. The children sheltered by the Felician sisters were not included among the number of the Jews who survived in the county because they left that area before the end of the occupation.

120. AŻIH, 301/2393, Testimony of Michał Zellner, February 7, 1947.

121. Fitowa, *Ruch oporu* in *Bochnia. Dzieje miasta i regionu*, 451.

122. AN Kr, 29/439/1485, Akta Władysława Węgrzyna [Files of Władysław Węgrzyn], Zeznanie Władysława Węgrzyna [Testimony of Władysław Węgrzyn], Bochnia County Public Security Office, April 11, 1950, no pagination.

123. See my article, "Dla płaszcza, walizki i jabłka." In a postwar trial, Władysław Węgrzyn was sentenced to life imprisonment, but the sentence was then commuted to fifteen years.

124. AIPN Kr, 075/85, Sprawa obiektowa dot. Byłych członków Narodowych Sił Zbrojnych z terenu powiatu bocheńskiego [Case of former members of National Armed Forces in Bochnia County], Raport P. [Report by P.], November 11, 1944, 199.

125. Julian Wieciech, *Wróciłem* (Kraków: Zamkor, 2004), 35.

126. Ibid.

127. YVA, O.3/1683, Testimony of Margot Dränger.

128. AIPN Kr, 111/2482, Akta w sprawie Józefa Wieciecha [Files of the case of Józef Wieciech], Protokół przesłuchania Wieciecha Józefa przez Wojskową Prokuraturę Rejonową w Krakowie [Record of the interrogation of Józef Wieciech by the District Military Prosecutor's Office in Kraków], February 14, 1950.

129. YVA, O.3/1683, Testimony of Margot Dränger.

130. USC, VHA, 9558, Interview with Nathan Krieger.

131. AN Kr, 29/691/UW II 1073, Protokół spisany przez Uszera Weinfelda, wiceprezesa komitetu żydowskiego w Bochni [Report written by Uszer Weinfeld, Deputy Chairman of the Jewish Comittee in Bochnia], March 7, 1945, no pagination.

132. AIPN Kr, 0125/211, vol. 2, Komenda Wojewódzka Milicji Obywatelskiej w Krakowie [People's Militia Province Headquarters in Kraków], Pismo z powiatowej komendy w Bochni [Letter from country Headquarters in Bochnia], June 11, 1945, 18. The name of the victim in the report is incorrect.

133. AIPN Kr, 041/42, vol. 4, Wykaz zamordowanych przez bandy reakcyjnego podziemia w latach 1945–1946 [List of the victims of the reactionary underground bands during 1945–1946], October 5, 1964, 17.

134. AIPN Kr, 110/4638, Akta w sprawie przeciwko: Fryderyk Satoła [Files of the case against Fryderyk Satoła], Protokół przesłuchania świadka Szymona Platnera [Record of the interrogation of witness Szymon Platner], January 20, 1951, 157. Julian Kwiek wrote about that case in his article "Zabójstwa ludności żydowskiej w Krakowskiem w latach 1945–1947. Fakty i mity," *Kwartalnik Historii Żydów* 4 (2013): 681–682. Mentioned earlier in this text, Józef Weinstock from Chrzanów, who survived the Bochnia ghetto, is a different person.

135. AIPN Kr, 041/42, vol. 4, Wykaz zamordowanych przez bandy reakcyjnego podziemia w latach 1945–1946 [List of the victims of the reactionary underground bands during 1945–1946], October 5, 1964, 2.

136. AN Kr, 29/691/UW II 914, Sprawozdanie z powiatu bocheńskiego [Report from Bochnia County, August 21, 1945], cited in Jan Tomasz Gross, *Strach. Antysemityzm w Polsce tuż po wojnie. Historia moralnej zapaści* (Kraków: Znak, 2008), 284; English edition, *Fear: Anti-Semitism in Poland After Auschwitz* (New York: Random House Trade Paperbacks, 2007). During the occupation, Władysław Ryncarz was the regional commander of the Peasants' Battalions, and he helped the three-person Janicki family survive. Powell, *The Daughter Who Sold Her Mother*.

137. AN Kr, 439/1197, Akta w sprawie karnej Budzieńskiego Czesława [Files of the criminal case of Czesław Budzieński, Protokół przesłuchania Krzywdy Jana [Record of the interrogation of Jan Krzywda], January 21, 1949, 107.

138. Ibid., Zeznanie świadka Jana Krzywdy w czasie rozprawy 15 IX 1949 r. [Testimony of witness Jan Krzywda during the hearing of September 15, 1949], 127.

139. Ibid., Zeznanie świadka Jana Łuczaka w czasie rozprawy 15 IX 1949 r. [Testimony of witness Jan Łuczak during the hearing of September 15, 1949], 126. Budziński was found guilty by the court and sentenced to prison, but it should be underlined that based on existing files, his guilt was not proven without reasonable doubt.

140. AŻIH, CKŻP, Wydział Ewidencji i Statystyki [Registration and Statistics Department], 303/V/425, Centralna kartoteka Żydów w Polsce [Central Records of Polish Jews].

DAGMARA SWAŁTEK-NIEWIŃSKA is a graduate of Jagiellonian University (MA in Cultural Studies). She is a PhD candidate in the Graduate School of Social Research of the Polish Academy of Sciences and a member of the Polish Centre for Holocaust Research. Her dissertation explores Social Networks and Strategies of Survival of Jews in Krakow County, 1939–1945. She is author of several articles on the Holocaust, including "'*Gospodarowanie' żydowskimi meblami w Krakowie w latach 1939-1945. Działalność Möbelbeschaffungsamt* (Möbelbeschaffungsamt and the disposal of Jewish furniture in Krakow 1939–1945)," in *Klucze i Kasa. O mieniu żydowskim w Polsce pod okupacją niemiecką i we wczesnych latach powojennych 1939–1950*, ed. J. Grabowski and D. Libionka (Warsaw, 2014); and "*Salomon Greiwer i warsztaty miejskie w Bochni* (Salomon Greiwer and the Municipal Workshops in Bochnia)" in *Zagłada Żydów. Studia i Materiały* (12) 2016.

INDEX

Italic numerals indicate illustrations.

A. H. from Szczebrzeszyn, 85
Abkowicz, Dina, 148, 169n136
Abkowicz, Nechama, 148, 169n136
Abramowicz, Chaim, 14
Adam, Karl, 62
Adameczek from Charlejów, 203
Adameczek, Barbara, 221
Adameczek, Marianna (Blima Kurchant), 200–203, 221
Adameczek, Marianna, 221
Adamiuk, Józef, 45n88
Adamów, xxx, 191, 200; Adamów labor camp, 180
Adler (née Lustrin), Rywka, 103n60
Ajchel, Wincenty, 122, 127, 128
Ajzenberg, Dora, 203, 221
Ajzensztat from Bielsk Podlaski, 14
Albert from Stuttgart, 45n85
Alberti, Michael, 332n32
Aleksandrów, 55, 56, 61
Alfredówka, 384
Alperin, Welwel (Welw), 46n114, 47n117
Alscher, Albert, 382

Altenloh, Wilhelm, 18
Altman, Herszek, 106n117
Altman, Salomon, 278n55, 287n131
Altman, Szaje, 403
Altstock, Maurycy, 280n79, 286n125, 291n156, 291n165, 293n171
Alyskevych. Mykolai, 243
Amsterdam family, 387
Amsterdam group, 388–390, 392, 393
Amsterdam, Abraham (Romek), 388, 415n153), 416n159
Amsterdam, Dobcia, 415n153
Amsterdam, Golda (Genia), 415n153
Amsterdam, Jehuda, 415n153
Amsterdam, Menachem (Moniek), 415n153
Amsterdam, Mindel (Minka), 392, 415n153
Amsterdam, Nisan, 388, 415n153
Amsterdam, Yochanan (Janek), 388, 390–392, 415n152, 415n153
Amsterdam, Zvi (Herman), 391, 392, 416n159
Andrzejewski, Józef, 302

Ansel, Werner, 62
Antoniak from Złoczów, 240
Applefield, David, *312*
April, Abraham, 394
Ashenberg, Ela, 83
Atamanow Michał (Umer Achmołła Atamanow), 91, 106n118
Auerbach, Fajwel, 262
Augustin, Hans, 62
Augustów, 12; Augustów, POW camp, 42n42
Auschwitz/Auschwitz-Birkenau death camp, xxxivn22, 14, 16, 18, 19, 20, 49n144, 109, 147, 320, 328, 345–346n249, 427, 429, 433, 444, 449, 457
Aust, Julius, 282n97
Austria, 352
Awigdor, butcher from Łuków, 179

Babia Góra, 300
Babice, 55, 61
Bachner, Leokadia, 293n171
Bachul family, 346n258
Baciki Średnie, 29
Baczki, xvi
Baczków, 426, 429–431, 464n42
Bagno, 83
Bakanow, Aleksiej, 275n36
Bala from Rabka, 343n213
Balkans, 166n75
Banaś, Stanisław, 441
Bandera, Stepan, 274n30
Bandyk, Anna, 346n249
Bańkowska, Aleksandra, 52n180
Baranów. *See* Baranów Sandomierski
Baranów Sandomierski, 349, 352, 357, 359, 396; Baranów Sandomierski ghetto, 360, 365–371
Barda, Ryszard, 64
Bardejov, 443

Barglik, Maria, 345n249
Barglik, Stefan, 345n249
Barn, Leibish, 179, 180
Bartosiak, Halina, 182
Bartoszewski, Konrad, "Wir," 87, 105n105, 105n106
Bartov, Omer, 291n162
Baśladyński, Władysław, 292n165
Baum, Ilena, 275n36, 286n126, 290n150
Bavaria, 113
Baziak, Eugeniusz
Bąk, Jan, 138
Becher, Aba, 82
Beck, Nioniek, 313, 345n249
Beck, Rudolf (or Leon), 425, 455, 463n32
Beckert, Alfred, 361, 362, 364, 407n54
Bejman, Rózia (later Shoshana Golan), 82
Bekerman, Mendel, 14
Belarussian Soviet Socialist Republic, 92, 39n9
Belgium, 352
Bełz, 56, 444
Bełżec death camp, 62, 65, 69, 70, 71, 72, 84, 89, 177, 249, 250, 251, 253, 268, 282n91, 306, 307, 309, 311, 365, 367, 368, 369, 410n92, 424, 426, 427, 429, 430, 431, 433, 437, 440, 444, 464n33
Bełżek, Władysław, 101n43
Ben Ami moshav, *390*
Berendt, Grzegorz, xix
Berenstein, Tatiana, 177, 227n11, 280n75, 287n131
Bergen-Belsen concentration camp, 443, 444
Berger family, 412n122
Berger (née Knie), Fryda, 409n80, 409n92, 412n122
Berger (Perlman, née Geldzahler), Lieba, 362

INDEX 475

Berger, Miriam, 412n122
Bergholz, Max, 166n75
Berlin, 78, 244, 355
Berll, Rosa, 455, 456
Berman (Bergman), Herman, 286n131
Bernstein (née Kurz), Esther, 362
Beskid Wyspowy Mountains, 419
Bessarabia, 60
Bezirk Białystok. See Białystok
Biale, David, 404n5
Białka, 338n111
Białobrzegi commune, 176
Białostocki, Józef, 27
Białowieża, 31; Białowieża commune, 9; Białowieża Forestry (*Puszcza Białowieska*), 9
Biały Dunajec, 346n249
Biały Kamień commune, 235, 239
Biały, Majer, 47n124
Białystok, 9–11, 34, 37, 65; *Bezirk Białystok* (Białystok District), xiii, xiv, xvi, xx, 9, 10, 18, 31; Białystok ghetto, 14, 16, 19; Białystok oblast, 5; Białystok POW camp, 42n42; Białystok region, 6, 8, 12, 16; Białystok, voivodeship, xiii
Biderman (née Prengler), Helen, 179, 183, 187, 228n26
Biderman, Max, 229n38
Biderman, Szachna, 182
Biedka, Łukasz, 353, 354
Bielany, 224
Bielawska (Bielawski), Menucha, 133, 160
Bielawska, Paula, *120*
Bielawska, Sara Frajda, *120*
Bielawski family, 119, *120*, 129
Bielawski Moshe, 160
Bielawski, Szraga Fajwel (Shraga Feivel) 119, *120*, 121, 128, 129, 132, 133, 143, 157, 159, 160, 161, 166n82

Bielecki, Blue policeman, 150
Bieliński, Antoni, 130, 135
Bielsk. *See* Bielsk Podlaski
Bielsk County. *See* Bielsk Podlaski County
Bielsk Podlaski County (*Kreishauptmannschaft Bielsk Podlaski*), xiv–xxvii, xxi, xxvi, xxxvin36, xxxvin37, xxxvin39, xxxvin40, xxxviin41, 1–53; Bielsk Podlaski district, 11; Bielsk, prewar county, xii, xxxiiin15, 4, 5
Bielsk Podlaski, viii, xiv, xxx, 3, 5, 7, 8, 10, 12, 13, 14, *19*, 19, 29, 31, 35–37, 44n64, 45n85, 45n86, 402; Bielsk Podlaski camp (*Straff-Lager*), 47n124, 47n126; Bielsk Podlaski ghetto, 14, 15, 18–21, 43n60
Bielsko, 463n32
Biesiadka labor camp, 393
Bieżanów labor camp (*Julag* I), 424
Biłgoraj County (*Kreishauptmannschaft Biłgoraj*), xv, xvi, xix, xxi, xxvi, xxxiiin15, xxxvin35–37, xxxvin40, xxxviin41, 54–108, 177; Biłgoraj, prewar county, xii, xiii
Biłgoraj, xiv, 55, 56, 58, 60–64, 67–72, 74, 75, 78, 79, 80, 83, 92, 93, 100n36, 100n37, 166n74, 335n79
Biługa, Jan, 163n30
Bin, Szymon, 64
Birger, Mr., 202
Birk family, 75
Birk, Chana, 75
Birk, Dora, 78
Birman, Lejb, 384, 414n138
Birnbach, Samuel, 359
Biszcza, 55, 61
Biszewo, 24
Bitkower, Max, 359, *395*, *396*, 397
Black Sea region, 21
Black, Peter, 100n37, 107n122

Blas family, 412n122
Blas (née Knie), Chaja, 412n122
Blauder, Chaim, 329
Blaufeder, Sabina, 457
Blicharz, Jan, 101n43
Blizna, 354
Blustein, Arie (Icie?), 37, 51n171
Błachowicz Jan, "Kropidło," 384
Błaszczak, Edward, "Grom," 105n105
Błaszczuk family, 29
Bobowa, 421
Bobrowa, 412n122
Bochnia County (*Kreishauptmannschaft Bochnia*), xiii, xv, xxi, xxv, xxvi, xxxvin35, xxxvin40, xxxviin41, 419–472; Bochnia commune, 419; Bochnia, prewar county, xii, xxxiiin15
Bochnia, 361, 419, 421, 422, 423, 425–429, 431, 432, 433, 438, 439, 441, 444, 445, 449, 451, 452, 453, 455, 459–461; Bochnia labor camp, 432; Bochnia ghetto, 317, 319, 364, 379, 417n178, 423, 430, 431, 433, 434, 436, 437, 440, 442, 443, 446, 448, 455, 467n76, 471n134
Boćki, 14, 18; Boćki commune, 26
Boćkowski, Daniel, 39n9, 39n10
Bogucice, 425, 426; Bogucice commune, 419
Bogusch, gendarme, 454, 455
Bogusch, Robert, 425, 463n32
Bogusze, POW camp, 42n42
Bojmie, 117
Bojmie, 169n139
Bołotny, Mieczysław, 76
Bomze, Alte, 275n36
Bonusiak, Włodzimierz, 405n25
Boraks, Gustaw, 139
Borek, 455
Borensztajn, Jankel, 224

Borensztejn, Estera, 201
Borowa, 357, 365, 368, 371
Borowiec, 91
Bortatycze, 63
Borwicz, Michał, xxxvn31
Borze, 115
Böttcher, Herbert, 307
Bór-Komorowski, Tadeusz, 414n143
Branew, 83, 85
Brańsk, xxi, xxxiiin13, 8, 12, 14, 18, 24, 25, 27, 29, 33, 34, 37, 44n64, 44n74, 46n114–47n117; Brańsk commune, 24, 26, 29, 29; Brańsk ghetto, 19–21, 28, 29; Brańsk vicinity, 29, 32, 34, 36
Brańsk-Kolonia, 48n129
Brański, Szymszon, 45n88
Brejtbard, Towi, 49n143
Brenner, gendarme, 116
Brenner, Srul, 47n115
Breskin from Prużana, 16
Breslau, 319
Brest oblast, 5
Brik, Szmul, 83
Brix, Friedrich, 9
Brody county, 243
Brody, 244, 245
Broide, Jose, 47n117
Brook, David, 175
Browning, Christopher R., x, xiv, 101n45, 181, 192
Brukier from Siemiatycze, 37
Brünnlitz, 445
Brutnow, Dora, 413n134
Bryk, Lejba, 93
Bryk, Leon, 83
Bryk, Natan, 83, 84, 105n94
Bryk, Nusym, 93
Bryk, Rywka, 83–85
Brynkus, Cyryl, 345n249
Brzesko, 429; Brzesko County, 460
Brzesko Nowe, 166n74

Brześć, 178, 52n172
Brześć County, 9; Brześć, prewar county, xiii. *See also* Polesie voivodeship
Brzeziński, Chaim, 32
Brzeżany county, 249
Brzozów, 138
Brzyska Wola, 78
Buczacz (Tarnopol voivodeship), 291n162
Buczyk, Blue policeman, 450
Budziński, Czesław, 460, 471n139
Budziska, 116
Bug River, 115, 178
Bühler, Josef, xxxiiin18
Bukovina, 349
Bukowa River, 63
Bukowa, 63
Buksenbaum-Brik, Chana, 83
Bünau, Heinrich von, 10
Bürger Josef, 186, 190, 192
Bursztein, Symcha, 27, 42n44, 47n124
Bystra, 346n258
Bystre, 26

Cachro, Helena, 346n249
Cajzel family, 291n165
Cajzel, Abraham, 291n165
Calais, 301
Carynnyk, Marko, 275n34
Celiny, 223; Celiny commune, 176, 224
Chabówka, 309, 311, 320
Chajkin from Prużana, 16
Chajt, Icek, 23–24
Charin, Dr. 48n130
Charin, Julian, 30
Charlejów, 200, 202, 203
Chawal, Naftali, 45n88
Chazan, Róża, 26
Chazan, Rubin (Ruben), 26, 39n13
Chazen, Sheldon (Szaja), 39n13

Chełm, 184, 187
Chlipała, Michał, 333n37
Chmiel, Aniela, 81, 82
Chmiel, Janina, 82
Chodakiewicz, Marek Jan, 52n173
Chojewo, 48n128
Chomelańczuk, Stanisław, 168n124
Chomiec, 256
Chomontowski, Wacław, 149, 150
Choroszcz, POW camp, 42n42
Chorzelów, 380; Chorzelów hangars, 369
Chowaniak, Karol, 346n249
Chowaniak, Stanisław, 346n249
Chowaniak, Tekla, 346n249
Chrostowa, 439
Chrzanów, 471n134
Chrząstów, 376, 380, 386, 400
Chwalko, Józef, 34
Chyc family, 324
Chyżyny, 186
Cichosz, Zygmunt, 225
Ciechanowiec, 8, 14, 19, 39n13, 43n63, 47n125; Ciechanowiec commune, 26; Ciechanowiec ghetto, 18
Ciechanów ghetto, 20; Ciechanów vicinity, 13
Cieplice, 55, 61
Cracow District. *See* Kraków District
Cukier, Józef, 324, 325
Cukierman, Salomon "Salk," 179
Curilla, Wolfgang, 165n65, 409n80
Cwajman sisters, 103n60
Cygany, 384
Cymerman, Mosze, 83
Cymerman, Ryszard, 164n30
Cymlich, Israel, 131
Cyranko family, 161
Cyranko, Motel, 160, 161
Czapek, Grzegorz, 26
Czapek, Konstancja, 26

Czapla, Tomasz, xxxiin13
Czarkowski, Bolesław, 34
Czarkowski, Kazimierz, 128
Czarny Dunajec, 301, 329, 335n73, 344n230; Czarny Dunajec labor camp, 311, 319–321
Czarnystok, 82
Czartoryski, Stanisław, 314
Czchów, 394, 460
Czech lands, 352
Czechy Zabłotne, 24
Czekaj forest, Bäumer und Lösch labor camp, 394, 395, 397, 399, 400, 402, 417n171, 417n174
Czermin (Hohenbach), 355, 374, 387
Czerwiec, Jan, 412n122
Czerwony, Erwin, 282n97
Częstochowa, xxxiin16, 72
Czorsztyn, 321, 337n110, 338n117, 345n240
Czortkower, Emil, 403
Czortkower, Joel, 364
Czortkower, Tosia, 403
Czortków county, 249
Czubak, Kazimierz, 453
Czubak, Rozalia, 453
Czubaszek, Krzysztof, xxxiin13, 173, 179, 182, 184, 188, 228n22, 229n50, 230n81
Czubaszek, Stanisław, 224
Czubernat, Tadeusz, 311
Czyżew, 14, 18
Czyżyny, 424

Danilczuk family, 29, 48n128
Danilczuk, Antoni, 48n128
Danilczuk, Apolonia, 48n128
Datner, Szymon, xx, xxi
Dattner, Roman, 334n56
Dawidowicz, Abram, 45n88
Dawidowicz, Genia, 102n60
Dawidowicz, Rywka, 78

Dawidsohn-Dränger, Gusta, 445, 446, 448, 468n81
Dąbal, Tomasz, 352
Dąbie commune, 176
Dąbrowa Tarnowska County, vii, xxxvn33
Dąbrowa Tarnowska, 166n74, 335n79; Dąbrowa Tarnowska ghetto, 387; Dąbrowa Tarnowska vicinity, 388
Dean, Martin, xxxvin38, 165m59, 276n52, 416n170
Dewitz, Victor von, 295, 298, 299, 302, 334n65
Dęba labor camp, 354, 393
Dębica County (*Kreishauptmannschaft Debica*), xv, xxi, xxiii, xxv, xxvi, xxxiiin15, xxxvin36, xxxvin37, xxxvin40, xxxviin41, 349–418; Dębica area, 371; Dębica, prewar county, xii, xiii, 349; Dębica region, 351, 382, 384
Dębica, xxxiin13, 349, 354, 357, 359, 363, 368, 371, 379; Dębica ghetto, 358, 360, 364–367, 369, 376, 378, 379, 382, 396, 397, 403, 405n22, 406n38, 409n85; Dębica labor camp, 371, 397
Dęblin, 175, 178; Dęblin labor camp, 187
Dębno, 337n110, 338n117
Diestelhorst, *Oberleutnant*, 116
Dietz, Dieter, 181, 192, 229n38
Dinerman, Herszel, 49n143
Distrikt Galizien. *See* Galicia District
Distrikt Warschau. *See* Warsaw District
Długi Kąt, 69
Długopolski, Władysław, 345n249
Długosz, Józef, 366
Dminin labor camp, 180, 228n30
Dmowski, Roman, 162n6
Dobrogowski family, 29
Dobrogowski, Konstanty, 29, 47n125
Dobrogowski, Stanisław, 29
Dobroszycki, Lucjan, xxxvn31
Dobrowolski, Władysław, 380

Doliński, Fiszka, 29, 47n122
Doliński, Lejbka, 29, 47n122
Doliński, Lejzer, 5
Domański, peasant, 222
Dominiak, Józef, 154, 164n30
Dortheimer, Tadek, 397, 417n186
Dortmund, 100n36
Downiłowicz, Mrs., 320
Dränger, Gusta. *See* Dawidsohn-Dränger, Gusta
Dränger, Justyna, 419
Dränger, Margot, 448, 449, 457, 458, 468n89
Dränger, Szymon, 445, 446, 448, 468n81
Dreifuss, Havi, 401
Drexler, Hans (or Franz), 244
Drogicka, Estera, 31
Drohiczyn, xxi, 15, 18, 23, 25, 37, 52n173; Drohiczyn ghetto, 20, 21; Drohiczyn vicinity, 32, 36
Drohiczyn-Kolonia, 26
Drohojowska, Anna, 337n110, 345n240
Drucker (Kurz-Bernstein), Cila, 363, 403n2
Druzgała, Jan, 342n194
Dubiel, 380
Dudziak family, 82
Dukler family, 308
Dukler, Leon, 308, 338n111
Dula, Stanisław, 127
Dulcza Mała, 382, 387
Dulcza Wielka, 387
Dulecki forest, 385, 387, 388, *390*, 392, 401
Dwornik, "Ćwik," 379
Dyle, 63
Dym, Mendel, 89
Dymbort (née Guterman), Freda, 102n59
Dzianiński, Stanisław, 342n183
Dzianisz, 341n183

Dzieciątek, 123
Dziecinne-Kolonia, 41n36
Dzików Stary, 55, 61
Dzioboń family, 324
Dzioboń, Bronisława, 324, 325

East Mazovia, 3
East Prussia, xiii, 9, 10
Eastern Borderlands (*Kresy*), xx, 39n11, 59
Eastern Europe, x, 60, 351 Europe
Eastern Galicia, 235, 237, 260, 266, 288n138, 288n139, 291n161
Eber (née Geminder), Irene, 365, 403n2
Eberhardt, Piotr, xxxvn31
Ecker (née Leiman), Janina, 470n119
Ehrlich, Ludwik, 73
Eichmann, Peter, 334n63, 102n57
Eisenmann, Mojżesz, 318
Ekstein family, 421
Elbaum, Sonia (later Irena Burstin), 83
Elberg, Jakow, 14
Elgas, Stanisław, 127
Elimelekh of Leżajsk, Rabbi, 351
Ellenbogan from Zaleszany, 384
Elman, Józef, 49n142
Elman, Szmul, 49n143
Engel, David, 52n180
Engel, Stanisław, 449
Engelking, Barbara, 3, 53, 469n108
Engels, Erich, 252, 284n110
Engländer family, 301
Engländer, Józef, 300, 329
Epstein, Szlomo, 14
Erlich, Aaron, 193
Essen, 100n36
Estrach, Joël, 183
Eupen, Theodor van, 117
Europe, 56, 238, 351; Europe, prewar, vii. *See also* Eastern Europe

Faber, Maks, 422
Fabrykant (aka Faberka), 102n54
Fabrykant, Ignacy, 73
Faiga/Felicia from Jaśliska, 413n131
Fajl, Szloma, 72
Falkowski, *schutzman*, 48n129
Falsberg, Jan, 286n125
Farber, Wolf, 26
Farbiarz, Lusia, 143, 144
Farbstein, Esther, 467n75
Fatran, Gila, 467n72
Fefer, Estera, 91, 93, 105n100, 107n121
Feit, Baruch, 329
Felczer, Rita, 319
Feldman, Benjamin, 25
Feldman, Ester Amir, 46n101
Feldman, Liba, 25
Feldman, Mira, 228n26
Fenster, Lilian, 182, 201
Feuer (Amsterdam), Yeshayahu, 415n156
Feuer, Shaya, 403n2
Figiel, Tadeusz, 164n30
Figler, Tomasz, 123, 165n54
Fijał, Józef, 382
Filipek, Katarzyna, 345n249, 347n258
Filipiak from Rabka, 343n213
Finder, Gabriel N., 292n166
Fink family, 364
Fink, Alina, 361, 395
Fink, Józef, 358, 359, 361, 362, 364, 394, 407n61
Fink, Lucjan (Arie), 361, 395, 402, 417n178
Fink, Netti, 361, 395, 402
Finkelstein sisters, 233n126
Finkelstein, 224
Finkelsztejn family, 26, 46n114
Fischel, *Landrat*, 179
Fischer, Fritz, 194
Fischer, Ludwig, 130
Fischer, Marta, 308
Fischer, Stanisław, 453
Fishman, Sevek, 122
Fiszbajn, Moszko Farel, 182
Fiszgop, Estera, 28
Fittkau family, 31
Fladell (Fledel), Henryk, 78
Flam, Bernard (Berek), 384
Flam, Isak, 384
Fluchtlander, Lejzor, 101n43
Flug from Józefów Biłgorajski, 76
Folwarki commune, 235
Fortgang, Mozes, 359
Fragner family, 441
Fragner, Izajasz, 440, 441
Frajberg, Perla, 78, 83
Frajda, Irena Krawczyk's mother, 201
Frampol, 55, 56, 58, 61, 66, 68, 69, 71, 72, 75, 78, 8–85, 88; Frampol vicinity, 81
France, x, 301, 352; France, German-occupied zone, x; France, Vichy, x
Franck (Francke), gendarme, 425, 441, 457
Frank, Hans, 306, 344n223, 417n172
Freiberg (Frieberg), Elimelech, 361, 362, 407n48
Freiberg (Frieberg), Icchak (later Izchak Frayberg), 361, 362, 364, 394, 407n48, 417n172
Freiberg (Frieberg), Leo (Louis), 361, 394, 395, 407n48, 417n177
Frejdkies, Kalman, 14
Frelas family, 82, 103n60
Freudenheim, Samuel, 422, 433
Freudenthal, Carl, 186
Fridman, 397
Fried (Pinkas), Mina (Minka), 415n152
Friedländer, Saul, 227n10
Friedman, Abraham, 422
Friedman, Sylvia, 177, 224, 225
Friedman-Bleicher, Baruch, 413n136
Friedrich, Gustav, 116
Fruchthändler family, 453

INDEX   481

Fruchtlender, Lejzor, 93
Frydel Tomasz, 349, 418
Frydman, Abraham, 49n143
Frydman, Józef, 144, 145
Frydman, Józik, 49n143
Frydrych, Helena, 347n258
Fueg-Lobenstein, gendarmerie deputy commander, 244
Führer, Christoph, 412n125
Fuks, Beniamin, 25
Fuks, Cipora, 25
Furer, Mordka, 64
Furman, Abraham, 313, 318, 339n151
Furman, Abraham (b. 1898), 339n151
Furman, Ms., 222

G., Kazimierz, 146
Gacek, Maria, 316, 341n177
Gaeber, Bernard, 280n79, 291n158
Gajówka, 148
Gajst, Israel, 72
Galant, Jakow, 14
Galicia, xxxvin34, 65, 349, 351, 352, 402, 404n4; Galicia District, xiii, xiv, xxxiiin18, 243, 244, 246, 249, 256, 284n110, 289n145, 303, 335n78; *See also* Eastern Galicia; Western Galicia
Galler, Józef, 330
Gałek, Feliks, 41n34
Gałki, 150, 152
Garbler, Julius, 409n83
Garfunkel, Berisz, 359
Gawłuszowice, 380
Gąsiorek, Maria, 431
Gelbart, Dionizy (Edward Gadomski), 73
Geminder, Irene, 403
General Government (*Generalgouvernement*, GG), xiii, xiv, xviii, xx, 10, 12, 59, 60, 62, 64, 65, 111, 130, 148, 177, 243, 247, 301, 303, 322, 323, 349, 356, 357, 372, 377, 400, 403, 423, 433, 443, 444
Germany, postwar xi
Germany. *See* Reich
GG. *See* General Government
Gicala couple, 441
Gicala, Wojciech, 441
Gil (Giler?), gendarme, 121
Giler, gendarme, 116
Gilewicz, Dr., 240
Ginzburg, Carlo, xxxiin3
Gittleman, Danielle, 377
Gliniska, 63
Glinka (née Gołąbecki), Anna, 48n129
Gliny Wielkie, 371, 380
Globocnik, Odilo, 65, 177
Glück, Irena, 419, 423
Glücksman family, 308
Glücskman, Eda, 308
Glücskman, Georg, 308
Glücskman, Lusia, 308
Glücskman, Saul, 308
Głowacki, Albin, 272n18
Gnatowski, Michał, 49n147, 272n18
Göbel, gendarme, 425
Gold, Franciszek, 302
Goldberg from Prużana, 16
Goldberg, Jehoszua, 28
Goldberg, Kadisz, 49n144, 49n145
Goldenberg family, 290n150
Goldenberg, Marek, 290n150
Goldfinger family, 297
Goldfinger, Chana, 297, 299
Goldfinger, Regina (Rivka Schenker), 403n2
Goldgraber, Abram, 106n117
Goldgraber, Dawid, 106n116, 106n117
Goldman, Avraham, 357
Goldman, Izaak, 335n80
Goldwasser, Dwora, 27
Goldwasser, Kalman, 27
Goldwasser, Szlomo, 27, 52n173

Golik, Dawid, 333n38, 334n63, 334n66, 335n71, 335n73, 410n101
Gollert, Friedrich, xxxiiin18
Gołąbki commune, 176
Gołogóry, 253, 263; Gołogóry commune, 235, 239, 244
Gołoś, Edward, 138
Goniowski, Jan, 289n145
Gonta, Mikołaj, 41n33, 41n36
Goraj, 55, 56, 61, 68, 71, 83, 84
Gorajec, 65, 88, 89, 106n116
Gorce Mountains, 318
Göring, Hermann, 9
Gorlice, County, x
Gorzoch, 164n30
Góra Kalwaria, 56
Góra, Moszek, 126, 127
Górski, Wiktor, 292n165
Grabowska, Henryka, 121
Grabowski, Jan, xxxivn24, 109, 102n59, 171n179, 172, 287n135, 449, 464n41
Grabowski, peasant, 224
Grabski, August, 39n11
Grajewer from Bielsk Podlaski, 14
Grajewo, 12, 42n42
Gramss, Ernst, 112, 113, 114, 116, 137, 138, 155
Grand Duchy of Lithuania, 111
Grassgrün, Dawid, 300, 329
Grądzki, Czesław, 112
Greiwer family, 421
Greiwer, Moniek, 444
Greiwer, Salomon, 444
Grębków, 115, 117, 145, 150, 152, 169n139; Grębków area, 155
Grębów, 357, 359
Grinbaum, 200
Grobla, 451
Groblicki, Henryk, 452
Grochal, Piotr, 151, 153, 154
Grodzicka, Rojzke, 26

Grodzicki family, 26
Grodzicki, Mosze, 26
Grodzicki, Szlomo, 26
Grodziński, Icchak, 28, 29
Grodzisk, 15, 18; 24; Grodzisk commune, 26
Gross, Jan Tomasz, viii, 460, 471n134
Gross, Majer, 382
Gross, Mordechaj, 359
Grójec area, 155
Gruda brothers, 32
Gruda family, 23, 37
Gruda, Chaim, 26
Gruda, David, 52n173
Gruda, Fiszel, 15
Gruda, Gdal, 52n173
Gruda, Kiwa, 38, 52n173
Gruda, Leja, 26
Gruda, Lejzor, 26
Gruda, Szloma, 52n173
Grudziądz, Czesław, 123, 165n54
Grudziądz, Lutek, 165n54
Grum, Jan, 82
Grum, Katarzyna, 82
Grünbaum, Moses, 422
Grüngras, Henryk, 317, 347n267
Grünspan, Salomon, 301
Gryciuk, Franciszek, 175
Grynblum, Jakub, 418n188
Grynszpan, Inka, 31
Grywałd, 337n110, 338n117
Grzimek, Josef, 286n131
Gułów commune, 176
Gurszyn, Mrs., 152
Gutman from Węgrów, 146
Gutter, ODman, 460

Haar (née Ostro), Lea, 386
Haar, Lana, 386
Haase, Wilhelm, 433
Hajek, Karolina, 263

INDEX

Hajnówka, 31
Hajnówka, 41n34; Hajnówka POW camp, 42n42
Halberstam family, 444
Halberstam, Rabbi, 421
Halbersztat, Shmuel, 125
Halperin, Rabbi, 42n45
Halpern family, 440
Halpern, Efraim, 280n79Efraim, 287n131, 288n141
Halpern, Markus, 439
Hamfing, Abraham, 78
Hammer, Kalman, 468n81
Hanaczów, 289n145
Handelsman, Gierszon, 224
Hanin, Fela, 458
Hanin, Hela, 458
Hanowski, Herszel, 49n143
"Hans," gendarme, 122
Harklowa, 311
Harlos, Wilhelm, 355
Hartmann, Friedrich, 116
Haska, Agnieszka, 443
Hassenberg, Thomas, 282n97
Hauser, Mozes, 384
Hedwiżyn, 63
Heinrich, Hermann, 428
Heisler family, 454
Heisler, Zofia, 454
Heksel, Bartosz, 466n67
Heller, Aron, 186, 190
Henryk Olesiak, "Storm," 153, 154
Hensel, Hellmut, 364
Herc, Edward, 99n15
Hercyk (Herzog?), Józef, 382
Hermanówka, 384
Herrmann, Willi, 282n97
Hersz, Ruwen, 130, 131
Hersztajn family, 438
Hersztajn, Celina, 465n58
Hersztajn, Dawid, 466n58

Hersztajn, Natan, 466n58
Herz, Ludwik, 330
Hilberg, Raul, 291n162
Hilberg, Raul, xiv
Hiller, Hirsch, 359
Himmler, Heinrrich, 20, 31, 40n17, 354, 359
Hirsekorn, Gestapo interpreter, 117
Hirszberg, Nisen, 200
Hitler, Adolf, 9, 179, 332n32, 460
Hochman, Juliusz, 343n209
Hodyszew, 34
Höfle, Hermann, 65
Hollander family, 387
Hollander (Leser), Rose (Shoshana), 415n152
Hołda, Michał, 310
Hönig family, 380
Hönig, Miriam, 380
Hönig, Psachje, 379, 380
Honigman Szmul's wife, 83
Honigman, Szmul
Hoppe, Colonel, 334n66
Hoppe, gendarme, 116
Hornung, Chana, 320, 325, 328
Horowitz from Germany, 362
Hössler, Jakub, 355
Hot (née Nestelbaum), Bella, 83
Hreczanik, Abraham, 245
Hrubieszów county, 60; Hrubieszów, 100n37
Hryciuk, Grzegorz, 283n101, 283n105, 291n161
Huberman-Iwan, Ryszka, 201
Hübscher, gendarme, 116
Hucisko Oleskie, 263
Huf, Dina, 83
Hugon, Tobiasz, 395
Hungary, xxx, 297, 301, 379, 443, 444, 461, 466n58, 466n71, 467n75
Huta Komorowska labor camp, 393

Huta Krzeszowska, 55, 61, 73
Huta Pieniacka, 262
Huta Werchobuzka, 262
Hwozdulowicz from Rabka, 316, 341n175
Hyć brothers, 24

Idzik, Wojciech, 391, 392
Ignaszak, Blue policeman, 450
Igołomia, 450
Immerglück, Herman, 359, 395, 396, 397, 400
Israel, *390*
Israel, Yosef, 467n76
Iwanek, Blue policeman, 150, 152, 169n144
Iwaszczuk from Węgrów, 144
Izbica, 65
Izbica, Michał, 125
Izraelit, Lejzer, 49n143

Jaczew, 115
Jakier from Złoczów, 252
Jaktorów labor camp, 256
Jakubiak, Irena, 202
Jakubik, Zbigniew, 99n15
Jakubowska, Walentyna, 29
Jakubowski couple, 29
Jakusze commune, 176
Jamiński, Tomasz, 67, 100n42
Jamsin, Alter, 14
Janicka, Sarna (Julia), 455
Janicki family, 471n134
Janicki, Roman (Stefan; né Abraham Pinkas), 455, 469n116, 471n136
"Jankiel Berko Josel," 88
Janower, Hillel, 64
Janowicz, Icchak, 16, 20
Janowska-Ciońćka, Anna, *304, 305*
Janów Forest (*Lasy Janowskie*), 55, 84
Janów labor camp, 256
Janusz, Aleksandra, 150–152

Janusz, Stefan, "Dymin," 371, 385, 410n96, 414n147
Jarczew commune, 176
Jarkowska-Natkaniec, Alicja, 417n180, 467n76
Jarnice, 119
Jarosz, (Tolek?), 164n30
Jarząbek from Jadów, 138
Jarzębowska, Agnieszka, 52n180
Jasiński, 165n54
Jasiński, Władysław, "Jędruś," 385, 387
Jasiorówka, 160
Jaskółka family, 346n258
Jasło, 336n94
Jastrzębska-Szydłowska, Zuzanna, 48n131
Jastrzębski, Roman, 30
Jaworski family, 263
Jaworze forests, 385
Jeck, Oskar, 355
Jelechowice, 252
Jęczmień couple, 144, 145
Jęczmień, Mosze (Mojżesz), 44n74
Job, Stefania, 382
Jojne brothers, 190
Jordan, Gerhard von, 244
Jordanów, 297, 299, 309, 310, 313, 316, 317, 326, 329, 334n66, 341n180, 342n194, 344n230, 346n249, 348n267; Jordanów commune, 295; Jordanów region, 342n193
Josiel from Oleksin, 29
Josiel's family, 29
Józefów. *See* Józefów Biłgorajski
Józefów Biłgorajski, 56, 60, 61, 66, 64, 67, 68, 71, 75, 76, 83, 85, 88, 99n15,
Józefów forest, 89
Jurczuk, Antoni, 52n173
Jurczuk, Stefania, 28, 37
Juryczkowski, Jan, 72
Jużelewski, Adolf, 31

INDEX

K., Ignacy, 146
Kacenberg, Lejb, 75
Kaczyński, Walek (Walenty), 78
Kagan, Chaja, 27
Kahan, Herszek, 75
Kajanka, 26
Kajanka-Kolonia, 25
Kajetanówka, 82
Kajzer, Mrs., 152
Kalata, Helena, 325
Kalata, Józef, 325
Kalata, Marianna, 325
Kalata, Zofia, 325
Kalb, Benzion, 300, 301
Kalech, Ozjasz, 405n25
Kalecka, Cyla, 30
Kalinka, 247
Kalinowska, Akulina, 24
Kalinowski, Janek, 165n54
Kalisz, 60
Kalisz, Michał, x
Kalita, Elżbieta, 446, 448
Kalita, Maria, 446
Kałuszyn, 126, 152; Kałuszyn ghetto, 130
Kamecki, Stanisław, 224
Kamerman (Holler), Bluma, 85
Kamieniec Litewski, 15, 19
Kamieniecka, Dr, 50n155
Kamień, Mojżesz (Mieczysław), 38
Kampf, Amalia, 415n148
Kampf, Rivka, 415n148
Kampf, Samuel, 410n96
Kampf, Sara, 415n148
Kandzia, Josef, 302, 315
Kapelan, Bolesław, 291n156
Kapłan, Izak, 359, 362, 364, 395–, 398, 400, 407n51, 407n59, 408n63
Karaś, Stanisław, 310
Karbowski, Maniek, 119
Karczew labor camp, 124
Karpiel family, 347n258
Karpiel, Anna, 347n258

Karpiel, Józef, 347n258
Karpikacz, Leibl, 180
Karsten, Uwe, 116
Katowice, 463n32
Katz, Anshel, 200, 224
Katz (née Fuchs), Cipora, 46n101
Katz, Lejbke, 5
Katzmann, Friedrich, 246
Kauper brothers, 448
Kawęczynek, 85
Kawiński, Kazimierz, 41n36
Kazakhstan, 239
Kazimieruk, Antoni, 29, 47n124
Kazimieruk, Antoni's wife, 29
Kąty, 78, 83, 84
Keblitz, Willy, 425
Keller, Aleksandra, 302
Kening (aka Twerski), Pola, 83
Keselbrener, Herszel, 193
Keselbrener, Jakow, 193
Kestenbaum, Jehuda, 320
Kestenbaum, Nachman, 83
Kežmarok, 443
Kędra, Jan, "Błyskawica", "Jaskółka," 87, 88
Kępa family, 453, 454
Kępa, Andrzej, 453, Andrzej, 454
Kępie Zaleszańskie, 384
Kica, Krystyna, 466n61
Kielce, xxxiiin16
Kiełbasin, POW camp, 42n42
Kieżmark, 300, 329
Kindeusz, Jan, 45n89
Kinrus, Wanda, 76
Kisielewski, Edward, 288n143
Kisłowicz, Aron, 81
Kiss Henryk, 334n66
Kitaj-Drobner (Drobnerowa), Helena, 242, 245, 264, 279n64, 291n157, 291n158
Kleeberg, Franciszek, 178
Klein, chief of gendarmerie in Bielsk, 10

Klein, Hans, 186
Klein, Israel, 391, 416n160
Kleinbaum, Mosze, 5
Kleinberg, Alicja, 302, 303, 305, 306
Kleinberg, Antonina, 304
Kleinberg, Ewa, 305
Kleinberg, Ewa, 306
Kleinberg, Hania, 305, 306
Kleinberg, Wilhelm, 304, 305, 306
Kleiner, Dawid, 106n117
Kleiner (née Fink), Ita, 106n117
Kleiner, Stanisław, 73
Klejnik, 24
Klejniki, 45n85
Klejnot, Moszek, 45, 45n89
Klemensów, 63
Klemp, Stefan, 100n36
Kleszczele, 15, 18, 27; Kleszczele commune, 27; Kleszczele ghetto, 15, 21
Klimek, 446
Klin-Połosy, 44n85
Klinicka, Maria, 28
Klinicki family, 27
Klinicki, Zygmunt, 46n114
Kluba, Stanisław, 449
Klukowski, Zygmunt, 57, 58, 63, 64, 65, 66, 67, 86, 90, 96, 97n5
Klymiv, Ivan, "Lehenda," 274n30
Kłaj, 453; Kłaj labor camp, 424, 429, 432
Kłajpeda, 31
Kłos fmily, 28
Knap, Aleksandra, 78
Knell, F., 257
Knie (Knie-Adlersberg), Ela, 381, 412n122
Knie, Tewel, 412n122
Knobler, Natan, 320
Koch, Erich, 9, 40n23
Kock, 173, 176, 178, 185, 191, 196; Kock ghetto, 180, 184, 185, 187, 194
Kocudza, 55, 61
Koczery, 50n155

Koczery-Kolonia, 29
Kögel, Erwin, 299
Kögel, gendarme, 116
Kohn, Rózia, 291n157
Kolb, Roman, 64
Kolbuszowa, prewar county, 349
Kołodziejczyk family, 73
Kołomyja, 65; Kołomyja county, 249
Kołtów commune, 235
Komodzianka, 83
Konarski, Johann, 425
Koniarska, Ewelina, 158
Koniarski, Andrzej, 158
Königsberg (Królewiec), 10, 180
Konin County, 60
Koniuszek, Helena, 50n
Konty, 378
Kopaliny, 445
Kopciowski, Adam, 231n231
Korczak, peasant, 157
Korczak, Szymon, 386
Korfes, Otto, 241
Korytnica, 115
Korzeniowska, Mrs., 343n211
Korzeniówka, 27
Kosieniak, 392
Kosieniak, Stanisław, 391
Kosiński from Koczery-Kolonia, 29
Kosmala, Józef, 163n30
Kosower, Chawcia, 37
Kosower, Meir, 37
Kosower, Rachela, 37
Kosów Lacki ghetto, 130, 165n58
Koszak, gamekeeper, 24
Kotarba, Ryszard, 463n21
Kotler, Alina, 27
Kotler, Borys, 27
Kotler, Eugenia, 27
Kovpak, Sydir, 89
Kowalczyk, Marianna, 144
Kowalik, Janina, 438, 439, 465n58
Kozak, Leja, 45n88

Kozak, Liba, 45n88
Kozak, Rubin, 45n88
Kozak, Stefan, 346n249
Kozaki labor camp, 248, 252
Kozie Górki, 426, 429, 430
Kozłowski, Ferdynand, 459
Krakowski, Shmuel, xx, xxi, xxxvn29, xxxvn31, xxxvin34
Kraków County (*Kreishauptmanschaft Krakau-Land*), 421, 471
Kraków District, xiii, xiv, xxxiiin18, 65, 295, 310, 336n94, 349, 401, 410n101, 428, 431, 449
Kraków, xii, 10, 62, 182, 267, 299, 300, 304, 304, 305, 307, 309, 316, 334n61, 337n111, 340n161, 346n249, 360, 361, 370, 379, 400, 410n102, 419, 423, 424, 426, 427, 431, 434, 438, 439, 443, 446, 448, 451, 454, 456, 459, 464n33, 466n67, 467n77, 467n78, 468n81; Kraków ghetto, 317, 319, 326, 356, 384, 432
Krasne commune, 235
Krasnobród, 65
Krasusy commune, 176
Kraśnik, 65, 177
Kraus, Leon, 329
Krawczyk, Irena, 201, 202
Krawiec, Izrael, 32
Kreda family, 130, 161
Kreda from Węgrów, 131, 132, 133
Kreda, Isaac, 161
Kreis Garwolin, 186
Kreis Radzyń, 173
Kreishauptmannschaft Zloczow. See Złoczów County
Krempa, Andrzej, xxxiiin13, 417n171
Krężel, Jan, 344n222, 346n249
Krościenko, xvi, 301, 309, 335n80, 338n117, 344n230
Krośnica, 338n117, 344n222, 345n249
Król family, 324

Królewiec. *See* Königsberg
Królik, Władysław, 150–153, 169n144, 170n170
Krüger, Friedrich Wilhelm, 178, 191
Krüger, Hans, 334n56
Kruhów, 260
Kruszewski from Siemiatycze, 20
Krynica, 332n28
Krynka, 224
Krynki-Sobole, 26
Kryńska, Mrs. from Krynki-Sobole, 26
Kryński family, 26
"Krysia," Jewish nurse, 87
Krzeptowski, Wacław, 322, 324, 325, 344n223
Krzeszów, 55, 56, 61, 62, 64, 68, 69, 71, 72, 83, 92
Krzówka, 202
Krzywda, 200
Krzyże, 31
Księżopole-Budki, 135
Księżpol, 55, 61
Kubik, Czesław, 364, Czesław, 403
Kucyk, Arie, 139
Kuczek, Blue policeman, 450
Kulesza, Franciszek, 67, 101n43
Kulesza, partisan, 154
Kuncewicz, Tadeusz, "Podkowa," 88, 89, 106n109
Kunde, Wilhelm, 428
Kunreich, Artur, 336n80
Kupczyk, Józef, 5
Kuper, Jankiel, 146
Kuperhand (née Grodzicka), Miriam, 26
Kuperhand, Szloma, 37
Kuppermann, David, 417n172
Kurabiak, Blue policeman, 136
Kuraś, Józef "Ogień," 329
Kurchant family, 202, 203
Kurchant. *See* Adameczek, Marianna, 221

Kurek family, 30
Kuriański, Władysław, 164n30
Kurkowski, Czesław, 145
Kurnig, gendarme, 116
Kurpiel, Jakub, 345n240
Kuryłówka, 55, 61
Kurz family, 365
Kurz, Esther, 397
Kurz, Faiga, 397
Kurz, Reuven, 362–365, 395, 397, 407n51, 407n59
Kurzyna, Józef, 379
Kusze, 76
Kuś, Bronisław, 308
Kuwałek, Robert, 429, 464n33
Kwaśniowska, Mrs., 320
Kwiatek, Chaim, 123, 165n54
Kwiatkowa, Chaim's mother, 123
Kwiek, Julian, 471n134

L., Czesław, 167n99
Lacher, Sara, 103n60
Lackie Wielkie labor camp, 246, 248, 250, 251, 252, 255
Ladner family, 371
Ladner, Rachela, 380
Ladner, Regina, 371, 380
Ladner, Szeindla, 380
Lambor, Walter, 282n97
Lampe, Franz, 10, 43n60
Landau, Eliezer, 444, 467n76
Landsberg, Dziuniek, 245
Landwirth, Samuel, 459
Lange, Stanisław, 164n30
Langer family, 324
Langner, gendarme, 116
Lanzmann, Claude, 201
Lasota, Wojciech, 391
Latawiec, Andrzej, 335n72
Laufbahn, Yehuda (Laufban Jehuda), 383, 413n134

Lehmann, Rosa, 413n131
Lehrman, Chaim, 190
Leibl, son of Józef, 180
Leibowicz, 361
Leibowicz, Jeremiasz, 357, 359
Leiman, Nina, 456
Lejzerzon, Moszko, 182
Lenc Henryk, 287n131, 293n171
Lender, Hersz Lejzor, 186, 190
Lerman, Pinkas, 160
Lesser Poland (Małopolska), 301, 352, 423
Lessing, Theodor, 232n115
Leszczyński family, 26, 46n101
Leszczyński, Bolesław, 25, 26
Levenberg (Wasserstrum), Pnina (Pesia), 415n154
Levi, Giovanni, ix
Lew family, 45n86
Lew, Benjamin, 51n170
Lew, Benia, 37
Lew, Golda, 45n86
Lewicki family, 285n125
Lewin, Abraham, 164n34
Leżajsk, 78
Liberman, Salomon, 291n157
Libionka, Dariusz, xxxivn24, 57, 170n169, 411n111, 414n143
Lichaj, Stanisław, 346n249
Lichtenstein, Szmuel, 181
Lichtig, Berta, 407n59, 418n188
Liebermann family, 338n112, 341n179
Liebermann-Józefowicz, Berta, 338n112, 341n179
Liebeskind, Aharon (Dolek), 383, 413n132, 413n135
Liebmann, Wilhelm, 425
Lindenberger, Lonek, 329
Liniarski, Władysław, "Mścisław," 6, 35
Lipa, Roman, 366, 408n71
Lipiny Dolne, 62, 83

Lipiny Górne, 62
Lipińska, Barbara, 179, 228n28
Lipniak, 223
Lipnica. *See* Lipnica Murowana
Lipnica Murowana, 425, 426, 428, 432, 440, 441, 457, 458; Lipnica Murowana commune, 419
Lipowce, 244
Lipsk labor camp, 328
Lipski, Renia, 121
Lishko, camp commandant, 180
Lithuanian Soviet Socialist Republic, 92
Liw, 120
Löwner, Erich, 62
Lubartów, 65, 177, 184, 187
Lublin District, xiii, xxxiiin18, 60, 65, 67, 90, 100n37, 177, 178, 357, 364, 365, 369, 401; Lublin Province, 55 Lublin region, 91, 100n36
Lublin, 65, 79, 92, 134, 178, 199, 221; Lublin ghetto, 177
Luboch, Józefa, 407n59, 417n178
Lubomirski magnate family, 421
Ludwig, N., SS officer, 244
Ludwigsburg, 194
Ludwikowski, Andrzej, 448
Lumerman, Irving, 86, 201, 105n100
Lustrin, Lea, 103n60
Lwów (Lvov, now Lviv), 65, 73, 178, 247, 252, 256, 284n110, 292n169, 301, 313, 375, 410n102, 424, 425, 438; Lvov area, 265

Łada, 83
Łapanów, 425, 426, 428, 432, 460, Łapanów commune, 419
Łapiguz labor camp, 180
Łaskarzew, 189
Łaszyński, village elder, 123, 165n54
Łazy, 48n128

Łącz, Józef, 387
Łączki Brzeskie, 384
Łąkta Dolna, 460
Łempice-Kolonia, 47n125
Łęki Dolne, 382
Łętownia, 316, 317, 326, 345n249
Łochów, xvi, 111, 113, 115, 116, 117, 136, 149, 169n139; Łochów County, 160
Łojczyk family, 362
Łomna, 449
Łomża County, 8; Łomża, prewar county, 4
Łomża, 12
Łonie, 244
Łopianka, 149, 150
Łódź, xii, 60, 161, 202; Łódź ghetto, 140
Łucki, Antoni, 440
Łuczak, Czesław, xxxvn31
Łuczak, Jan, 471n139
Łuczyński, Michał, 448, 449
Łukasiuk, Władysław, "Młot," 52n173
Łukaszkiewicz, Zdzisław, 42n41
Łukowa, 55, 61, 66, 67, 68, 88
Łuków County (*Kreishauptmannschaft Lukow*), xv, xxi, xxiii, xxx, xxxviin35–37, 173–233; Łuków, prewar county, xii, xiii
Łuków, xvi, xxx, xxxiiin13, xxxiiin15, 173–181, 184, 188, 189, 192, 200, 203, 221–226, 228n26; Łuków commune, 176; Łuków ghetto, 182, 183, 185, 190–192, 194, 199, 201
Łyda, Franciszek, 83
Łysa Góra (Bald Mountain), 367
Łysobyki commune, 176

Machcewicz, Paweł, 40n22
Maciejowice, 189
Mack, Hans, 354
Madajczyk, Czesław, xxxiiin18
Magunia, Waldemar, 9

Majblum, Zygmunt, 244, 246, 252
Majdan Królewski labor camp, 375
Majdan Niepryski, 78
Majdanek death camp, 19, 177, 178
Majecki, Henryk, 16
Majewski, Stanisław, 64
Majster, Łajbel, 49n144
Maków. *See* Maków Podhalański
Maków Podhalański, 300, 301, 307, 308, 309, 311, 313, 314, 317, 319, 335n73, 335n80, 337n111, 340n161; Maków Podhalański commune, 295; Maków Podhalański region, 342n193
Maksoń, Antoni, "Sokół," 386, 387
Malcanów woods, 226
Malcanów, 190, 191, 192
Maler, Szmul (Szmuel), 83, 104n84
Malinowski, Alfons, 442
Maliński family, 148, 169n136
Malsfey, Hans, 302, 322, 335n78
Małe, 391
Małec, 387
Małek family, 83
Małkinia, 109, 118, 129, 134, 135, 136, 154
Małopolska. *See* Lesser Poland
Mames, Chaim, 422
Mandatory Palestine, 352, 52n172
Mandelbaum, Rachel, 166n82
Mandelbrat, Szlomo, 15
Maniowy, 321, 329, 337n110, 338n117
Mann, Hans, 244, 276n51
Männich, Walter, 335n71
Marbach, 320
Marek, Karolina, 346n249
Marfiak, Edward, 309
Markiel, Tadeusz, xxxivn24
Markiewicz family, 27
Markiewicz, Jerzy, 89
Markowa vicinity, xxxivn24
Markowizna, 48n128
Markowski, Artur, 39n11

Markowski, Jan, 224
Markowski, Stefan, 222
Marmur, Chaim, 21, 44n78
Maryański, Walery, 274n30
Masovia region, 111
Matusiak, Lucjan, 149, 150
Matyga, Józef, 345n249
Mauthausen, 460
Mayer, Szlojme, 285n125
Mazgaj, Andrzej, 320
Maziły, 69
Mazur, Franciszka, 337n110
Mazurek, Felicja, 83
Mazurek, Mikołaj, "Dąb," 260, 288n143
Mazurkiewicz, Krystyna, 73
Mechlowicz, Hannah, 378
Mechlowicz, Icchak
Mechlowicz, Icchak (Ira Mechlowitz), 377, 378, 383, 393, 411n109, 413n129, 43n130
Mehltreter, Sebastian, 300, 301
Meister, Arnold, 359
Meit; Fenil, 388
Melchior, Małgorzata, 232n108
Mellar, Paul, 282n97
Meller, Chaim, 359
Menahem Mendel of Rymanów, Rabbi, 351
Mendelson, Jankiel, 160
Menden, 73
Merec from Kusze, 76
Met brothers, 88
Met, Abram, 106n117
Met, Chaskiel, 106n117
Met, Icek, 106n117
Met, Jankiel, 89
Met, Josef, 106n117
Metzendorf, Szmul, 450, 451
Meyer family, 286n126
Meyer, Josef, 262

INDEX 491

Mędykowski, Witold, 40n22
Mężyńska, Estera, 30
Miechów, 166n74, 336n94
Miechów County, 459
Miedzna, 115, 117, 134, 169n139; Miedzna commune, 137, 139
Mielec prewar county, 349; Mielec region, 355, 364; Mielec vicinity, 396
Mielec, xxxiiin13, 349, 352, 354, 357–365, 376, 379, 383, 385, 387, 394, 397, 400, 401, 403, 407n47, 407n54, 410n102; Mielec ghetto, 394
Mielnik, 15, 18
Mierzwa, Adolf, 451
Mięc Hieronim, "Korsarz," 105n105
Międzyleś, 137, 138, 139
Międzyrzec. *See* Międzyrzec Podlaski
Międzyrzec Podlaski, 177, 178, 180, 186
Międzyrzecki, Romek, 130, 131, 135
Miklasze, 41n33
Mikołajków, Aleksander, 379, 412n117
Mikołajków, Leokadia, 379, 412n117
Mikulska-Renk, Danuta, 78, 79, 80
Mikulski family, 83
Mikulski, Jan, 78, 79, 80, 81, 83
Milejczyce, 15, 18
Miller (née Wiener), Ester, 83
Miller, Harry (Hersz Meier), 119
Miller, Leon (Lonek), 83
Minder, Zofia, 306
Mińsk Mazowiecki, 150, 155; Mińsk Mazowiecki ghetto, 118
Mirek family, 328
Mirek, Jan, 317, 326, 328, 329, 346n256, 346n258
Miśkiewicz, Nikodem, 27
Mitulin, 288n143
Mława, 181
Mokre, 384
Monkiewicz, Waldemar, 16, 45n85, 47n126, 50n155

Monsher Ben (né Berko Monczar), 43n63, 43–44n64
Moosburg POW camp, 113
Mordy labor camp, 124
Morer, Israel, 32
Morgenstern, Jakub Mendel, 113
Morgenstern, Józef, 184
Morgenstern, Menachem Mendel, 184
Morgensztern, Mordko, 182
Morza, Helena, 27
Moscow, 34
Moskal, Grzegorz, 334n58, 334n61
Mosze, Rachela, 102n60
Motek from Węgrów, 146
Motyka, Grzegorz, 288n138, 288n139
Możdżeń, Stefania, 345n249
Mrozik, Stanisław, 64
Mrozy labor camp, 124, 126
Müller, Franz Josef, 432, 433
Müller, Hermann, 244, 250, 251, 282n97
Müller, *Schupo*, 116, 120, 122
Musial, Bogdan, 99n12, 100n37
Musiał, Adam Kazimierz, 416n161
Muzykant, Dawid, 11
Myszka, Michał, "Jawor," 88

N., Władysław from Kłaj, 453
Nabel, Józef, 453
Nagoszyn, 381, 382
Naphtali Zevi (Horowitz) of Ropczyce, Rabbi, 351
Naprawa, 308, 313, 318, 338n112, 342n194
Narew, 15, 18, 31
Nasielsk, 179, 184
Nasielski, Szepsel, 183
Naumiuk, Włodzimierz, 45n85
Nazarewicz, Józef, 41n31
Nejman, Czesław, 146
Netherlands, x

Netzer (Tiger), Frania, 306, 313, 316, 328, 329, 346n253
Netzer, Gustaw, 305, 306
Netzer, Jetti, 316, 328
Neumann, Anton, 186
Neumann, *Landrat*, 132
Nicolaus, Kurt, 116
Niedary/Uście Solne, 429
Niedzielko, Romuald, 103n73, 288n139
Niedźwiecki, Tadeusz, "Sten," 88
Niegowić, 425l Niegowić commune, 419, 439
Niepołomice forest (*Puszcza Niepołomicka*o, 424, 430
Niepołomice, 419, 421–426, 429, 432, 436, 449–451, 453, 460, 461, 469n105; Niepołomice commune, 419
Nosel, Wolf, 224
Nowakowski, Marian, 163n30
Nowelska, Barbara, 190
Nowicki, Antoni, *11, 17*
Nowodworski, Dawid, 164n34
Nowogródek region, 12
Nowomińsk
Nowy Lipowiec, 88
Nowy Sącz County, 332n28
Nowy Targ County (*Kreishauptmannschaft Neumarkt*), xv, xvi, xvii, xxi, xxv, xxvi, xxxiiin15, xxxvin35–37, xxxvin40, xxxviin41, 295–348; Nowy Targ, prewar county, xii, xiii
Nowy Targ, 295, 297–300, 302, 303, 306, 307, 309–313, 315, 316, 319, 325, 328–330, 335n72, 335n73, 335n78, 337n110, 341n177, 344n230, 345n249; Nowy Targ commune, 295; Nowy Targ jail, 307, 318, 320, 324, 325, 342n191; Nowy Targ labor camp, 311, 320, 321

Nowy Wiśnicz, 419, 421, 422, 424–426, 428, 429, 430, 432, 440, 441, 445, 446, 449, 453; Nowy Wiśnicz area, 448 area, 457; Nowy Wiśnicz commune, 419; Nowy Wiśnicz prison, 431, 457, 458
Nurzec, 15

Oberländer, Sabina, 313
Ochman, Chaskiel, 181
Ochotnica, xvi, 311, 313, 338n117, 339n151
Odessa, 97n5, 247
Okoń, Eugeniusz, 352
Okulicki, Leopold, 35
Okulus, Władysław, 120, 121, 122, 123, 125
Olecko, 40n26
Oleksiak, 170n155
Oleksin, 29, 45n89
Oleksin-Kolonia, 22, 26
Olender, Szmuel Lejb, 64
Olendzki, Jankiel, 24
Olesko, 235, 239, 243, 244, 245; Olesko ghetto, 248, 250; Olesko labor camp, 248, 252, 256, 282n91
Olędzki (Olendzki) family, 29, 47n123
Olsztyn, 10
Opasiak-Piasecka, Małgorzata Maria, 183, 229n50
Opatowa, 379
Opoczno, 166n74
Opole, 394
Oppenheimer, Józef, 330
Oprisnik, gendarme, 116
Orańczyce, 20, 49n144
Orla, xxi, 15, 18, 41n36, 42n45; Orla ghetto, 21
Orlinski, Many, 201
Orzeszówka, 139
Osielec, 340n156, 346n258

Oskard, Estera, 45n88
Oskard, Moszko, 45n88, 45n89
Oskard, Sara, 45n88
Ossówno, 115
Ostasz, Grzegorz, 414n144
Ostrowiec Świętokrzyski, 335n79
Ostrów Mazowiecka, 114; Ostrów Mazowiecka, penal camp, 124, 178
Osuchy, 87, 88, 89
Oświęcim, 356
Ożydów, 271n11; Ożydów commune, 235

Pace-Kolonia, 29
Paciej, Alfred, 425
Paczos, Mieczysław (or Stanisław), 74, 102n59
Pankiewicz, Andrzej, 287n131
Panz, Karolina, 295, 333n47, 347
Para, Stanisław, 346n249
Parczew, 177, 178, 185, 186
Paris, 418
Parysów, 189
Paster, Laura, 304
Paszkow, Władek, 81
Paszkowska, Olga, 28
Patoki, 24
Patzwahl, Eitel Friedrich, 241
Paulssonn Gunnar S., 411n112
Pawlik, Ignacy, 290n155
Pawliszczyn, Michał, 275n36
Peiper, Józef, 451
Pela, 136
Peller, Helena, 316
Peller, Maria, 341n175
Perkowski, Józef, 34
Perlman, Lazar, 359
Perlmutter, Majer (Martin), 262, 286n126, 287n131, 293n171
Persak, Krzysztof, 40n22
Pierkowski, 160

Pietia (grandpa), partisan, 107n121
Pietras, Stanisław, 392
Pietrasze, 19
Pietsch, Rudolf, 116
Pigul, Staszek, 165n54
Pikielny, Dr. 179
Pilichowski, Czesław, xxxvn31
Pilzno, 349, 352, 356, 359, 365, 368, 385, 408n70; Pilzno area, 351, 371; Pilzno ghetto, 360, 367, 368, 369, 371, 385
Pinkes family, 441
Pinkus, Irena Krawczyk's father, 201
Pistreich, Salomon, 328
Pitek, Zofia, 341n175
Piwniczna, 332n28, 443
Piwowarek, Aleksander, 86
Platner, Szymon, 471n134
Pleśna, 413n132
Ploug, Frida, 200
Płaszów labor camp (*Julag* I), 321, 328, 345n249, 424, 429, 443, 444, 445, 453, 454, 468n81
Płuhów commune, 235; Płuhów labor camp, 248, 252, 255
Pobikry, 14, 19, 24, 30, 43n63
Pobocz, 247
Podborze, 375
Podgórniak, Edward, 164n30
Podgrabie, 453
Podgrzeba, 394
Podhale region, xvi, 295, 297, 298, 300, 307, 313, 318, 322, 323, 325, 329, 443, 459
Podhorce commune, 235
Podhorizer-Sandel, Erna, 463n21
Podlasie region, 3, 4, 111
Podłęże, 425, 450
Podwilk, 345n249
Podwołoczyska, 247
Pogorzelski, Stanisław, 139, 168n113
Pogrzeba (Podgrzeba), 417n172

Pohl, Dieter, 274n30, 276n51, 284n110
Pola from Zawoja, 308
Polak, Jan, 314
Polakiewicz, Simcha, 168n124
Polakowski, 91
Polakowski, Bolesław, "Wiarus," 88
Poland, xi, 6, 21, 59, 111, 112, 142, 195, 355, 439; Poland, eastern, 238; Poland, occupied, x, xii, xx, 13, 147, 166n74, 177, 422, 424, 443, 444; Poland, postwar, 38, 92, 161, 293n172; prewar, xiii, 4, 5, 56, 176, 379; southeastern, 55, 349; Soviet-occupied territories viii, 4–6, 113, 178, 186, 238, 239, 272, 356, 357, 423; territories incorporated into Reich, xx, 60, 113, 166n74, 332n32, 356, 423; western, 115
Polek, 378
Polesie, voivodeship, xiii, 9
Poletely-Kolonia, 29
Połaniec, 361, 365, 380; Połaniec ghetto, 364, 386, 401
Popielów, 158
Popławski family, 26, 48n127, 50n154
Popławski, Stanisław, 29
Popławy-Kolonia, 47n122, 48n130, 50n154
Poręby Nienadowskie, 414n138
Poręby Wojsławskie labor camp, 375
Porytowe Wzgórze, 89
Postek, Kazimierz, 123, 165n54
Potok Górny, 55, 61, 82
Potok, 83
Potsdam, 116
Poważe, 222
Powell, Irena, 471n134
Poznań Province, 423, 425; Poznań region (Wielkopolska), 186
Poznań, 190
Półtorak, Kazimierz, 45n89

Prawda commune, 176
Prażmowski, Władysław, 170n156
Prekerowa, Teresa, xxxvn31
Prengler brothers, 175
Prengler, Abram, 182
Prengler, Hershel, 179
Prengler, Shlomo, 178
Prokocim, 338n112; Prokocim labor camp (*Julag* I), 424
Pross, Wilhelm, 116
Prostyń, 115; Prostyń commune, 137
Protter, Bogdan, 400
Prusin, Alexander V., 292n166
Prussia, 31
Prużana County, 9; Prużana, prewar county, xiii
Prużana, xxxivn22, 9, 13, 15, 16, 17, 31, 32, 49n144; Prużana ghetto, 17, 20, 32, 45n87
Prybut, Arie, 37
Prybut, Joel, 45n88
Przecław, 357, 365, 366, 368, 394
Przemyśl, 247, 336n94, 375, 431, 432
Przemyślany, 244, 245; Przemyślany commune, 244; Przemyślany county, 243, 289n145
Przepiórka, Efraim, 119
Przepiórka, Gitl, 144
Przewołoczna, 271n11
Przeździak, Bolesław, 224
Przybyszewski, Józef, 34, 50n156
Przyłęk, 377
Ptak, Mosze, 144, 145
Ptaszek, Franciszek, 339n151
Ptaszek, Ita, 26
Ptaszek, Wolf, 26
Puchalski family, 26
Puchała, Franciszek, 425, 436
Puławski, Adam, 289n145
Puławy, 100n37

Pustków labor camp, 354, 357, 359, 366, 367, 368, 375, 393, 396, 397, 409n80, 413n136, 417n186, 424
Putkowska, Władysława, 140

Raber, Genia, 457
Rabka, 298, 301–307, 311, 313, 315, 316, 317, 319, 322, 326, 328, 329, 334n56, 334n66, 335n72, 341n175, 343n213, 344n230; Rabka labor camp, 320, 321
Rachwalski, Gustaw, "Pogrom," 457
Radecznica, 55, 61, 65, 66, 84
Radkoś, Stanisław, 320
Radom District, xiii, xxxiiin16, xxxiiin18, 364, 380, 401
Radom, xxxiiin16, 65, 178, 335n79
Radomyśl nad Sanem, 356
Radomyśl. *See* Radomyśl Wielki
Radomyśl Wielki, xxxiiin13, 349, 351, 352, 353, 356, 357, 359, 362, 363, 365, 383, 407n51, 413n136, 416n160, 417n174; Radomyśl Wielki commune, 387; Radomyśl Wielki ghetto, 360, 364–369, 371, 394, 397, 402; Radomyśl Wielki vicinity, 388
Radoryż commune, 176
Radowski, Gisela., 343n211
Radowski, John, 343n211
Radwan, 387
Radzymin area, 138
Radzyń Podlaski County, xiii, 177, 178, 186
Radzyń. *See* Radzyń Podlaski
Radzyń Podlaski, 177, 181, 184, 186, 190
Raebel, Paul, 282n97
Rajewski, Aleksy, 88
Rajs, Romuald, "Bury," 35, 36
Rajzman, Samuel, 138, 139, 161
Rapta, Michał, 334n58, 334n61
Rastenburg (Kętrzyn), 31

Ratajczak, Jan, 451
Ratułów, 341n183
Ratyński family, 145–147
Ratyński, Wiktor, 145–147
Rawicki, Misza, 49n143
Rączy, Elżbieta, x, 387, 408n68, 409n85, 409n92, 410n102, 414n146, 415n149, 429, 434
Rdzawka, 316
Rechelzon, Mulka, 47n116
Reckman, Richard, 180, 181, 192
Reduta, 41n36
Reibscheid family, 379
Reibscheid, Elżbieta, 378, 379
Reich family, 379
Reich, 8, 59, 69, 73, 74, 183, 276n52, 277n52, 352, 356, 362, 443, 461; Reich, forced labor, xxiv, xxv, 89, 90, 95, 168n124, 259, 264, 372; resettlement, 377
Reich, Ephraim, 379
Reich, Wilhelm, 329
Reichman, Pinchas, 383, 413n135
Reiss, Samuel, 460
Rembertów ghetto, 130
Remizowce commune, 235
Renner, Ulrich, 10
Rennert, Zila, 424, 425
Republic of Tarnobrzeg. *See* Tarnobrzeg
Reznik, Abraham, 15
Reznik, Łazarz, 15
Rhode Island, 349
Riegelhaupt, Jeno, 320
Ringelblum, Emanuel, 73, 150, 152
Rogińska, Janina, 144, 145
Rogińska, Joanna, 144, 145, 169n131
Rogoźnica labor camp, 180
Roguszewska, Stanisława, 160
Rohtbart, Markus, 376, 378, 393, 402

Rokeach, Aron, Rebbe, 444
Rokeach, Mordechaj, 444
Romania, 228n28, 455
Romaniuk, Zbigniew, xxxiin13, 44n74
Romanówka, 23, 24
Ropczyce, 349, 351, 359, 365; Ropczyce area, 371; Ropczyce ghetto, 360, 367, 368, 369, 409n85
Rosen, Estera, 424, 433
Rosen, Szymon, 424, 433
Rosenbaum, Wilhelm, 301, 302, 303, 304, 308, 311, 313, 322, 334n56, 334n58
Rosenblatt, Chaja, 371, 382, 413n134
Rosenblatt, Edouard Stanisław, 403n2
Rosencwajg, Izrael, 16
Rosenthal, Rubin, 13
Rosenzweig, 380
Rosenzweig, Jankel, 422
Rosse, Lejb, 45n88
Rostek, Stanisław, 147
Rotbart, Nehama, 117
Rotensztejn, Jankiel, 45n88
Rotfeld, Adam Daniel, 292n169
Rothowa, Zehawa, 286n126, 291n157
Rotkopf, Marian, 433, 444
Rottman, Izrael, 81
Rottman, Mojsze, 81
Roynik, Ester, 324
Rozen, Pesza, 45n88
Rozen, Samuel, 275n36
Rozenbaum (Rozenbojm), Bencjon, 78, 83
Rozenbaum (Rozenbojm), Chaim, 78, 83
Rozenberg family, 144, 145
Rozenberg, Fiszel, 182
Rozenblum, Mal, 183
Rozenfeld, Szloma, 182
Rozenman, Abram, 232n117
Rozett, Robert, 443, 444, 466n71

Roztocze region, 84
Rozwadów, 349, 352, 356, 359, 360, 366; Rozwadów ghetto, 368
Rubanek, Henryk, 73, 102n57
Rubin family, 152, 153
Rubin, shoemaker, 152
Rubinstein, Dina, 125
Rubinstein, Henry (Hersz), 186, 189
Ruchna, 115
Ruder, Mendel, 279n64, 286n126, 287n131, 290n150, 291n156, 291n157
Rudka, 18, 47n123, 47n125
Russia. See Soviet Union
Russian empire, 351
Ruszkowska, Marianna, 158
Ruszkowski, Andrzej, 158
Ryba, Józef, 415n149
Rybnik, Abraham, 49n143
Rychlik, Mrs., peasant, 326
Ryczkowski, Jan, 45n89
Ryczywół, Berl, 223
Ryncarz, Władysław, "Dąb," "Orzeł," 455, 460, 471n134
Rzepka, Józef, "Znicz," 414n146
Rzeszów, 256, 336n94, 354, 431, 432; Rzeszów ghetto, 384, 413n131; Rzeszów labor camp, 367; Rzeszów subregion, 384, 385, 414n144
Rzezawa, 425, 426, 429; Rzezawa commune, 419

Sachnowska, Kamila, xxxvn29
Sadowne, 115, 117, 123, 136, 148, 169n139
Safran, Hillel, 256
Saj, Edward, 83, 84, 105n94
Saj, Paweł, 83
Saki, 27
Sałachna, peasant, 326
San River, 356
Sandkühler, Thomas, 276n52

Sapirstein (née Feldman), Szoszana, 46n101
"Sarenka," owner of bar, 31
Sasów, 235, 236, 239, 243–245, 251, 253, 256, 267, 282n91; Sasów ghetto, 248, 250; Sasów (Sasów-Chomiec) labor camp, 248, 252, 287n131
Satoła, Fryderyk, 471n134
Sauerstrom family, 308
Sauerstrom, Adolf, 308, 338n111
Schaar, *Kreishauptmann*, 425
Schancer, Arje, 459
Scherner, Julian, 307, 310
Schindler family, 394
Schindler, Edmund, 425
Schindler, Max, 417n173
Schindler, Oskar, 330
Schlüter, Ernst, 353, 405n17
Schmidt, gendarme, 116, 155
Schneider, Fred, 458
Schneider, Jakub, *298*
Schneider, Joel, *298*
Schnepf-Kołacz, Zuzanna, 81, 158
Schneps (Gołęczyński), Leon, 385, 414n147, 415n149
Schoeder, 163n30
Schömburg, Wilhelm, 425, 428, 433, 442, 444
Schönberg, Edmund, 437, *438*
Schöne, Edmund, 240, 273n25
Schonfeld, Salomon, 422
Schöngarth, Eberhard, 334n61
Schönker, Henryk, 442
Schöps, Chaim, 287n131
Schotz, 252
Schröder, Friedrich, 116, 117
Schröder, *Obersturmführer* SS, 10
Schuldenfrei family, 379
Schultz, *Oberleutnant*, 31
Schulz, Friedrich, 112

Schwach, Hubert, 282n97
Schwager, Mojżesz, 248
Schwartz, gendarmerie commander, 244
Schwede, 43n60
Schweitzer, Gestapo driver, 116
Second Polish Republic. *See* Poland
Segal, Beryl, 49n143
Segal, Lolek, 49n143
Sehmisch, Richard Arno, 334n54
Selinger, Izaak, 343n209
Selinger, Menachem Mendel, 424, 433, 444
Serock, 179, 184
Serokomla, 196, 202, 203, 224, 232n117; Serokomla commune, 176
Sędziszów, 349, 359; Sędziszów area, 371; Sędziszów ghetto, 366, 367, 368, 369, 409n83, 409n85
Shapiro siblings, 105n98
Shapiro, Drejzl. *See* Zylbercweig Drejzl
Shapiro, Morris (Mordka), 83, 85
Siberia, 239
Siedlarczyk, Wojciech, 345n249
Siedlce, 118, 136, 150, 176, 178, 202; Siedlce area, 148; Siedlce ghetto, 118, 130
Siedliska, 223
Siedlisker-Sarid, Reuven, 410n92
Siek family, 78, 83
Siek, Magdalena, 52n180
Sielicki family, 31
Siemaszko, Ewa, 288n139
Siemiatycze, xxi, 8, 9, *11*, 16, *17*, 20, 23, 24, 25, 27, 30, 31, 37; Siemiatycze commune, 27; Siemiatycze ghetto, 15, 18, 20, 21, 26; Siemiatycze vicinity, 32, 36
Sienkiewicze-Kolonia, 29

Sieradzka, Eugenia, 83
Sierpińska (Ślepińska?) from Tarnogród, 103n60
Sikorski, Franciszek, 290n155
Silberman, Bernard Flam's fiancée, 384
Silberring family, 308
Silberring, Samuel, 421
Silesia region, 161, 394
Singer family, 306
Singer, Emanuel, 319
Singer, Józef, 335n78
Singer, Maria, 335n78
Singer, Moshe, 468n89
Singer, Shaya, 388
Sinołęka, 115
Siring, Jan, 64
Sitarz, Janina (Ducherka), 81
Sitkiewicz, Stanisław, 189
Siwek, Anna, 450
Siwek, Antoni, 450
Siwek, Franciszek, 454
Skanecki, Blue policeman, 136
Skarżyński from Saki, 27
Skibińska Alina, xxxivn24, 55, 39n11, 108
Skibińska, Alina
Składkowski, Felicjan Sławoj, 111
Skórce, 24
Skrzypek, Maria, 412n122
Skrzypkowski brothers, 29
Skrzypkowski family, 30
Skrzypkowski, Maciej, 29, 30
Skrzypkowski, Zygmunt, 30
Skrzyszew commune, 176
Skupie, 136
Skupień Florek, Andrzej, 342n186
Skwarzawa commune, 235
Slodzian, Pinchas, 181
Slodzian, Szachna, 181
Slovak Republic. *See Slovakia*
Slovakia, xxx, 177, 182, 194, 297, 298, 301, 329, 346n249, 434, 436, 443, 444, 461, 466n58, 466n71, 467n72, 467n75
Sławiński, a peasant, 224
Słochowski, Lipa, 14
Smarklice, 52n173
Smilovic, Annette
Smoliński family, 263
Smoluch, Hersz, 32
Smoter Grzeszkiewicz Regina, xxxiiin13
Sobczak family, 83
Sobczak, Stanisław, 81Stanisław, 83
Sobibór death camp, 65, 89, 177
Sobolew, 189; Sobolew ghetto, 130
Sobolewski family, 27
Sobolewski, Anastazja, 31
Sobolewski, Paweł, 47n115
Sobolewski, Walerian, 31
Socha Ireneusz, xxxiiin13
Sochy, 90
Sokolniki, 382
Sokolow-Wengrow Kreishauptmannschaft. *See* Węgrów County
Sokołów. *See* Sokołów Podlaski
Sokołów Podlaski County, 156, 162n1; Sokołów Podlaski area, 155
Sokołów Podlaski, 112, 116, 117, 118, 119, 124, 125, 134, 135, 149, 153–156, 164m30
Sokołówka commune, 235, 239
Sokołówka, 261; Sokołówka ghetto, 248
Solna Góra, 427
Solska Forest (*Puszcza Solska*), 55, 61, 84, 85, 91
Sołomach family, 27
Sosnowy, Jan, 83
Sosnowy, Stefania, 83
Soviet Union, vii, xiii, xix, xxix, 4, 8, 12, 92, 161, 171n185, 183, 190, 195, 267, 276n52, 293n173, 328, 329, 354, 461
Sól, 55, 61

Spector, Shmuel, xix
Sperling family, 31
Spytkowice, 345n249
Stachuń (née Hajek), Bronisława, 290n155
Stalowa Wola, 354, 410n102
Staniątki, 456
Stanin commune, 176, 191
Stanin labor camp, 180, 228n31
Stanisławów, 65
Stankowski, Albert, xxxiiin20, xxxvn31
Stanner, Leopold, 311
Stańczyk family, 75, 103n69
Stańczyk, Stanisław, 83
Stańczyk, Wiktoria, 83
Stapiński, Jan, 352
Stara Wieś, 82
Starachowice, labor camp, x
Staraja Stanitza (Northern Caucasus), 407n54
Starawieś, 115
Stare Bystre, 341n183
Starkopf family, 148
Starkopf, Adam (alias Adam Błudowski), 136, 148
Stary Wiśnicz, 441
Staszek, 165n54
Staszów, 418n188
Staszówka/Przyłęk camp, 393
Statkiewicz, Antoni, 41n36
Stauter-Halsted, Keely, 351
Stein, Jehuda, 333n42
Steiner, Dolek, 454
Steinlauf, Michael C., 404n4
Steinwurzel, Henek, 245
Sterdyń forests, 156
Sterdyń, 160
Sterlicht family, 345n249
Stetsko, Yaroslav, 243
Stoch family, 324
Stoch, Antonina, 324, 325

Stoczek. *See respectively* Stoczek Łukowski; Stoczek Węgrowski
Stoczek Łukowski, 173, 176, 184, 185, 189, 190; Stoczek Łukowski ghetto, 186, 194
Stoczek Węgrowski, 115, 117, 123, 147, 169n139; Stoczek Węgrowski commune, 147, 148; Stoczek Węgrowski ghetto, 119, 141, 142, 113
Stolarz, Maria, 382
Storch family, 341n183
Storch, Eugeniusz, 341n183
Storch, Rachela, 341n183
Storch, Rozalia, 341n183
Storch, Wiktor, 341n183
Strassler family, 257, 258
Strassler, Szymon, 279n64, 286n131
Straucher, Maria, 456
Strawczyński, Oskar, 138
Strawczyński, Zygmunt, 138
Struma, 460
Struve, Kai, 275n34
Stryj, 334n65
Studnicka (née Hollönder), Michalina, 409n83
Studnik, Meir, 28
Sturm, Berl, 382
Sturm, Hania, 382
Stutthof concentration camp, 29, 47n125
Subcarpathian region, xxxivn24, 349, 375, 384, 413n131
Suchodolski, Franciszek, 160
Suchowolce, 29
Suchpol commune, 9
Sukiennik, David, 123
Sułów, 82
Susiec, 69, 100n36
Süsskind, Salomon, 301, 321
Suwałki, 12, 40n26, 179, 184, 228n26
Swałtek-Niewińska, Dagmara, 419, 470n123, 471

Sylbersztejn, Abram Chaim, 180
Szabes, Hersz (Hershl Shabbes), 32, 49n149
Szachner, Ojzasz, 326
Szadkowski, Marian Ryszard, 287n131
Szaflarski, Wojciech, 325
Szaflary, 325, 345n249
Szafraniec, Andrzej, 302
Szancer family, 421
Szapiro, Fajwel, 26, 48n127, 50n154
Szapiro, Lejbl, 26, 48n127, 50n154
Szarajówka, 90
Szatensztajn, Ezechiel, 113
Szatkowski, Wojciech, 344n223
Szczawnica, 298, 301, 307, 334n66
Szczebrzeszyn, xxxiiin13, 55, 56, 58, 60, 61, 64–68, 71, 72, 76, 82, 84, 86, 88, 89, 92, 96, 97n5, 166n74
Szczęśniak family, 454
Szczęśniak, Jan, 454
Szczucin, 387
Szczygielski, Pinie, 45n88
Szebnie labor camp, 427, 429, 434, 444
Szefer, Andrzej, 286n131
Szemberg, Tołpa, 158
Szendzielarz, Zygmunt, "Łupaszko", 35
Szereszów commune, 9
Szklaruk, Włodzimierz, 47n124
Szlajcher, Chaim Mordechaj, 105n107
Szlajcher, Israel, 86, 105n100
Szlembark, 337n110, 338n117
Szmańda, Ignacy, 441
Szmuel, Goldwassers' cousisn, 27
Szmurły, 29, 47n123
Sznajder, Jakow, 14
Szoszkes Welw, 32
Szpaki, 36
Szprung, Szloma, 82
Szprung, Szmul, 82
Szpyt, Florian, 290n155
Sztainberg, Szmil, 183
Sztajnberg family, 83

Sztajnberg, Abram, 83
Sztejman, Mrs., 37
Sztemer, Icie, 82
Sztern, Mosze, 14
Szurek, Jean-Charles, 173, 221, 233
Szurek, Zbigniew, 412n117
Szwab "Kucikowa," Stanisława (Perel Langer), 323, 324
Szwab family, 324
Szwab, Bolek, 324
Szwab, Jacek, 324
Szwarzberg, Batszeba, 31
Szydłowski, *Colonel*, 48n131
Szymański, Jan, 458

Ś., Władysław, 292n165
Śliwowo-Kolonia, 24
Ślomka family, 84
Śmigły-Rydz, Edward, 179, 228n28
Świątek, Franciszek, 455
Świątek, Genowefa, 455
Świątek, Michalina, 189
Świder, Eugeniusz, 223
Świerkot, Alojzy, "Ryś," 464n42
Świrydy, 28

Tabak, Sara, 45n88
Tabor, Jan, 440, 466n61
Tadra, Ewa, 83
Tadra, Jan, 83
Taffel, Faiga, 394
Taffel, Naftali (Nathan), 394, 417n174
Taffler, Joachim, 357, 358
Tajwlowa and her family, 75
Talczyn, 185
Taller from Rozwadów, 384
Tanenbaum, Mozes, 415n148
Targowisko, 425, 426
Tarnobrzeg prewar county, 349; Tarnobrzeg region, 357, 382, 384
Tarnobrzeg, 349, 352, 356, 359, 405n25; Tarnobrzeg ghetto, 358, 366, 368

Tarnogród, 55, 56, 60, 61, 65, 68, 69, 74, 92; Tarnogród ghetto, 64
Tarnopol, 244, 247, 250, 260, 282n97
Tarnopol oblast, 272n19; Tarnopol, voivodeship, 235
Tarnów, 336n94, 357, 382, 413n132, 431, 432, 433, 443, 452; Tarnów ghetto, 394, 397
Tatenbaum, Aron, 359
Tatra Mountains, 333n48
Taub, Józef, 359
Taykhman, Jakov, 275n36
Tchórzewski, Eugeniusz, 106n109
Tchórzewski, Jerzy, 124
Tedsen, Karl, 116
Teichman, Mojżesz, 286n125
Teitelbaum, Steven, 366
Tennenbaum, Samuel, 279n64
Tereszpol, 55, 61
Thaler, David, 381
Third Reich, *See* Reich
Thormeyer, Walter, 396
Tiger, Frania. *See* Netzer Frania
Tłuszcz, 118
Toczyska, 190
Tokarnia, 345n249, 347n258
Tomana, Jan, 342n194
Tomaszów Lubelski, 58, 65, 99n15
Tomaszów Lubelski county, 60
Topaczewska, Zisl, 37
Topczewo, 48n130
Topólcza, 73
Torczyner, Leon, 284n112, 286n126, 287n131
Toronto, 418
Trapp, Wilhelm, 185
Traum, Rubin, 316
Trawniki, 107n122
Treblinka death camp (II), xvi, 14, 15, 16, 18, 19, 65, 89, 109, 118, 119, 121, 123, 125, 126, 129, 131, 134, 135, 136, 137, 138, 139, 141, 142, 150, 153, 154, 155, 156, 162n1, 167n99, 177, 178, 185, 189, 190, 192, 193, 195, 201, 224
Treblinka labor camp (I), 117, 134, 155, 156, 162n1
Treblinka, village, 162n1
Treibicz, Michał, 359
Trejbicz, Leopold, 376
Tripf, Zelig, 103n60
Trunk, Isaiah, 230n80, 357
Trybowski, Czesław, 342n183
Trybus Family, 347n258
Trybus, Apolonia, 347n258
Trybus, Mieczysław, 347n258
Trzciana, 425, 426, 442; Trzciana commune, 419
Trzciany, 387
Trzebieszów, 191, 192; Trzebieszów commune, 176
Trzeszczotka, 45n85
Trześniower, Mr., 344n213
Tsanava, Lavrentiy, 39n9
Tubenthal, Walter, 10, Walter, 40n26
Tuchowicz, 191
Tupta, Wojciech, 334n58, 334n61
Tur family, 30, 48n130
Tur, Paweł, 24
Tur, Wacław, 48n130
Turchowicz commune, 176
Turkevych, Stepan, 243
Turkowice, 62
Turkowski, Romuald, 175
Tuszów Narodowy, 386
Tykocki, Josel, 50n155
Tykoćkin, Mojsze, 14
Tylicz, 332n28
Tylmanowa, 338n117, 339n151
Tyrpa, Franciszek, 310
Tyszowce, 63

Udziela, Seweryn, 370
Ufir, Jan, 345n249
Ukraine, 21

Ukrainian Soviet Socialist Republic, 92, 293n172
Ulan commune, 176, 191; Ulan labor camp, 180
Ulanów, 356
Ulbrycht (or Olbrycht), 394, 417n172
Ulreich, Anna, 271n15
Union of Soviet Socialist Republics. *See* Soviet Union
Uniów, 292n169
United States, 79, 190, 195, 201, 349, 352, 456
Urban, policeman, 412n125
Uri, son of Liezer (Leibman Ashkenazy), 111
Urman, Feliks, 74, 78, 83
USSR. *See* Soviet Union
Usznia, 291n165
Uście Solne, 425, 426; Uście Solne commune, 419
Uzbornia, 422

Vershigora, Pyotr, 89
Verstandig (Ostro), Dwora, 386
Verstandig family, 386
Verstandig, Frieda, 387
Verstandig, Mark, 361, 380, 385–387, 401
Vienna, 244
Vistula River, 353, 364, 380, 401, 407n54, 407n59, 408n63, 424, 450, 453, 454
Vogelgesang, Pelagia, 143
Völker, *Ordensjunker*, 112
Vugman, Leonid, 293n171

Wadowice, 340n161
Wadowice Dolne vicinity, 382
Wagner (Abraham), Helena (Hencia), 73
Wagner couple, 328

Wagner, Eleonora, 313, 326, 328, 329, 346n253
Wagner, Hencia (later Helen Abraham), 103n60
Wajnberg (née Goldberg), Basia, *80*
Wajnberg, Mosze, *80*
Wajnberg, Rywka (later Rita Goldshmid), *80*
Wajnberg, Rywka, 83
Wajnsztok (née Rottman), Tema, 81
Wajnsztok, Tema, 75
Wajnsztok, Tema, 82
Wajntraub, 180
Wajntraub, Mosze Aron, 179, 186
Wakslicht (née Gidbert), Estera, 79
Wakslicht, Cudyk, 79
Wakslicht, Miriam (Małka, Maria; later Lila Stern), 79, 83
Waksmund, 338n117
Waksszul, Efraim, 64
Walas, Marcin, 380
Walcerz family, 380
Walczak, Antoni, 224
Walczak, Feliks, 224
Wanatowicz, Stanisław, xxxiiin13
Wander, Chaim, 280n79, 286n125
Wander, Samuel, 287n131
Warenhaupt, Chaim, 319
Warenhaupt, Emanuel, 300, 319
Wargacz, Godel, 83
Warka, 56
Warsaw District, xiii, xxxiiin18, 134, 177, 178
Warsaw, vii, xii, 31, 65, 118, 134, 150, 152, 156, 158, 161, 179, 181, 187, 189, 335n79, 379, 443, 457; Warsaw ghetto, 118, 130, 131, 134, 135, 148, 182, 183, 185, 186, 433
Warszawski, Chaim Hirsz, 52n172
Warszawski, Jehoszua (Szaja), 52n172

Warszawski, Symcha, 37
Warthegau (Wartheland), 181, 299, 300, 332n32, 356
Warzok, Friedrich, 246, 247, 251, 254, 279n71
Waser, Mina, 26, 48n127
Waserman, Zelman, 27
Wasowski family, 102n55
Wasowski, Jerzy, 73
Wasowski, Józef, 73
Wasserman, Necha, 83
Wasserstrum family, 389, 393, 415n154
Wasserstrum, Dawid, 415n154
Wassestrum, Pnina, 389
Waterszulaza, Galia, 49n143
Waterszulaza, Josel, 49n143
Wąsik, Tomasz, 453, 457
Weber, Rudolf, 116
Weigler, Herman, 280n79, 282n91
Weiner (Weiman?), Bunim, 15
Weinhold, Walter, 425
Weininger, Salomon, 444, 467n76
Weinstein, Eddie, 135
Weinstein, Sonia, 26, 48n127
Weinstock, Józef, 460, 471n134
Weis, Gisha, 286n126
Weiser, Piotr, xxxiin20, xxxvn31
Weiss, Susan, 187
Weiss, Symcha, 433
Weissmann, Robert Philipp, 301, 302, 303, 307, 309, 311, 322, 333n50
Weistuch, Rubin, 103n60
Wela (surname unclear), 82
Wendt, Otto, 244, 276n52, 278n55
Werbkowice, 62
Wereszczyński, Jan, 222
Wermut, Boruch, 75, 93
Western Belorussia, 5
Western Galicia, 349, 351, 352, 377, 402
Western Ukraine, 239

Westrajch, Abraham, 83
Westrajch, Elza (Elżbieta), 83
Westrajch, Maria, 83
Węgierski, Jerzy, 288n143, 290n155
Węgrów County (*Kreishauptmannschaft Sokolow-Wengrow*), xiii, xix, xv, xvi, xxi, xxvi, xxxvin36, xxxvin37, xxxviin41, 109–172; Węgrów area, 142, 148, 153, 155, 157; Węgrów prewar county, xii, xiii
Węgrów, xiv, xix, xvii, 109, 111, 112, 113, 115, 116, 117, 119, 120, 123, 125, 126, 127, 129, 133, 135, 139, 140, 143, 144, 145, 148, 149, 150, 154, 155, 156, 157, 158, 159, 161, 164n30, 169n139; Węgrów ghetto, 114, 117–119, 124, 131–133, 141, 142, 165n58, 166n74
Węgrzyn, Władysław, "Poniatowski," 457, 470n123
Wichalak, Blue policeman, 136
Wicher, Józefa, 346n249
Wicyń (now Smerekiwka), 261, 288n143
Wiecheć, Klemens, 346n249
Wiecheć, Piotr, 346n249
Wiecheć, Regina, 346n249
Wieciech, Józef, "Tamarow," 457, 458
Wieciech, Julian, 457
Wieczorek, Stanisław, 233n132
Wieliczka, 306, 425, 426, 429, 450, 456, 469n105
Wielopole. *See* Wielopole Skrzyńskie
Wielopole Skrzyńskie, 351, 359, 360, 365, 366, 367, 368, 370, 408n71, 409n85
Wiener, Efraim, 14
Wiener, Henryk (Izrael), 445
Wiener, Maniek, 445
Wiener, Sura, 83
Wieniec, 457

Wieselman (Wiedelman), Maria, 440
Więcek, Julian, "Topola," 457
Wilczek, Stanisław, 224
Wildfeuer family, 345n249
Wildfeuer, Edgar, 337n110
Wildfeuer, Miriam, 344n222
Willhaus, Gustav, 247
Wilner, Andrzej, 379
Wilner, Henryk, 379
Wilno region, 12, 35
Wilowski, Aleksander, "Tur," 460
Windstrauch family, 329, 341n180
Windstrauch, Chana, 316, 317, 328, 341n180, 342n188
Windstrauch, Izaak (Iziek), 299, 328, 341n180
Windstrauch, Lewi, 450
Winiarczykowa Góra, 76
Winiarski, Wilhelm, "Czarny Kruk," 318 342n194
Winkler, Horst, 282n97
Winnica, 52n172
Winterfeld, Hennig von, 184
Wiprawnik, Szaja, 31
Wischnitzer, Izak, 279n64
Wisznia, Abraham, 193
Wiszrubski family, 31
Wiszrubski, Adela, 30
Wiszrubski, Emilia, 31
Wiszrubski, Eugenia, 30
Wiszrubski, Regina, 30
Wiśniewski, policeman, 412n125
Witecki, Edward, 122
Witkowski, Czesław, 102n59
Witos, Wincenty, 352
Witów, 323, 324
Włocławek, 60
Włodarczyk, Franciszek, 453
Włodawa, 364, 403
Wnuk, Rafał, 88, 92, 106n109
Wöbke, Karl, 251
Wodziński, Marcin, 404n5
Wodzisławski family, 448
Wodzisławski, Hilel (Antek), 447, 448, 458, 468n88, 468n89
Wodzisławski, Johanan, 448, 458
Woińska, Janina, 50n154
Wojciechowski, Marian, 308
Wojcieszków, 191, 201; Wojcieszków commune, 176, 223
Wola Duża, 78, 79, 83
Wola Kisielska, 190
Wola Mielecka, 387
Wola Różaniecka, 55, 61
Wola Wadowska, 392, 415n156
Wolant, Izrael, 181
Wolant, Majer, 181
Wolbrom, 319
Wolfson, Józef, 5
Wolson, Rachela, 37
Wołoszyn, Jan, 83, 105n98
Wołoszyn, Rozalia, 105n98, 83
Wołoszyn, Tekla, 85, 105n98
Wołyń, xix
Wood, Elisabeth Jean, 411n112
Wójcik, Mieczysław, 340n156, 346n258
Wójcik, Władysław, 120, 121
Wójtowicz, Florian, "Listek," 88
Wólka Wyganowska, 36
Wraubek, Józef, 300, 302, 333n37, 334n63, 335n72
Wrobel, Eta, 183, 199, 200, 228n34, 229n38
Wrotnów, 137–139
Wróbel, Chaim, 47n115
Wróbel, Eugeniusz, 425
Wrzosek, Franciszek, 145, 146
Wulf, Dawid, 448
Wulf, Janina, 448
Wulf, Józef, 446, 448

Wyklick, E., 257
Wyrwa, Władysław, 458
Wyrwicz, Jan, 453
Wysokie Litewskie, 15, 16, 19, 30
Wysokie Mazowieckie county, prewar, 4
Wyszków, 115, 117, 169n139; Wyszków area, 155; Wyszków commune, 145

Zabierzów. *See* Zabierzów Bocheński
Zabierzów Bocheński, 425, 426, 451, 454
Zaczek, Kazimierz, 378
Zajęczniki-Kolonia, 23
Zakopane, 298, 299, 301, 302, 303, 307, 309, 317, 329, 330, 334n56, 334n66, 335n72, 335n73, 347n258; Zakopane commune, 295; Zakopane labor camp, 311, 320, 321
Zalc, Mosze, 83
Zalc, Mosze's sister, 83
Zaleszany, 36
Zalewski, Karol, 23, 30
Zambrów, POW camp, 42n42
Zamość, 63, 65, 65, 78, 92, 177; Zamość county, 60, 62; Zamość region, xxxiiin13, 58, 60, 66, 89, 88, 90
Zamoyski family, 56
Zamoyski, Jan, 73
Zanie, 36
Zapalec, Anna, 235, 293, 294
Zarce (?), 180
Zaremba, Mendel, 182
Zarwanica, 243
Zassów, 384
Zaśko (née Nieśpiał), Maria, 83
Zaśko, Stanisław, 83
Zawada family, 340n156, 346n258
Zawoja, 308, 309, 313, 340n163, 346n249

Zazule forests, 263
Zazule, 252, 256
Ząb, 324
Zbydniów commune, 384
Zellner, Michał, 456
Zelman, Mordechaj, 113
Zero, Lejzor, 58
Zgórznica, 190
Zielińska, Karolina (Carol), 378
Zieliński, Franek, 378
Zikmund, Otto, 244
Zimmerer, Katarzyna, 467n77
Zimmerman, Joshua D., 414n143
Zimmermann, 334n63
Zimmermann, Erhardt, 301
Zimmermann, Rudolf, 355, 364, 399
Zimnacha, Blue policeman, 136
Zimny, Szlomo, 14
Ziobroń, Jan, xxxiiin13, 409n80
Ziomaki, 145, 147
Złoczów (today Zolochiv in Ukraine), viii, xxvi, 235–238, 240–247, 253, 256, 256, 257, 258, 259, 261–265, 267, 269, 274n30, 275n34, 283n105, 284n110, 293n172; Złoczów commune, 235; Złoczów ghetto, 246, 248–254; Złoczów labor camp, 248, 254–256
Złoczów County (*Kreishauptmannschaft Zloczow*), xiv, xv, xvii, xxi, xxiii, xxvi, xxvi, xxvii, xxxvin35–37, xxxvin39, xxxviin41, 234–294; Złoczów, prewar county, xii, xxxiiin15, 243; Złoczów region, 239
Złotki, 26, 137
Złotkowski family, 26
Złotniki, 380
Zollman, Eleonora, 340n156
Zollman, Leopold, 340n156
Zucker, Towje (Tuvia), 357, 359
Zuckerkandel from Złoczów, 250

Zukerkandl family, 236
Zwierzyniec, 55, 56, 60, 61, 65, 68, 69, 83, 88; Zwierzyniec ghetto, 64
Zych, Tadeusz, 405n25
Zylbercweig (née Shapiro), Drejzl, 83, 85

Źrebce, 82

Żale, 30
Żbikowski, Andrzej, 40n22, 52n180
Żegocina, 454, 464n42
Żelechów, 189
Żemiński, Stanisław, 184, 192, 229n57
Żółtak, Szyja, 26
Żuchowski, Marian, 41n35
Żyto, Józef, 182
Żywica, Judel, 131

www.ingramcontent.com/pod-product-compliance
Lightning Source LLC
Chambersburg PA
CBHW021413300426
44114CB00010B/483